COAC CER

NATIONAL S ERICA

mp
MASTERS PRESS

NTC/Contemporary Publishing Group

...Data

...ciation of America.

...r—Coaching—United States.   I. National Soccer
Coaches Association of America.
GV943.8.C62   1996
796.334'07'7—dc20

96-33571
CIP

Published by Masters Press
A division of NTC/Contemporary Publishing Group, Inc.
4255 West Touhy Avenue, Lincolnwood (Chicago), Illinois 60712-1975 U.S.A.
Copyright © 1996 by NSCAA
Printed in the United States of America
International Standard Book Number: 1-57028-094-0

00 01 02 03 04 05 RCP 22 21 20 19 18 17 16 15 14 13 12 11 10 9 8 7 6 5

TABLE OF CONTENTS

PREFACE

· ·

One of life's lessons is to "never, ever volunteer!"

Unfortunately this writer is a slow learner and when asked by the NSCAA Board of Directors to compile a book on soccer coaching I found myself unable to resist the call to serve with the result that last January of 1996 found one beginning a publication journey that would conclude in late September. It was quickly agreed by all concerned that the best approach for a soccer coaching book would be one that highlighted the best articles that have appeared in *Soccer Journal*, the offical publication of NSCAA.

The process was actually "kick-started" (note the verbiage — this being soccer!) in 1989 when Joe Bean, men's soccer coach at Wheaton College (IL) and myself, began research for a book detailing the history of the National Soccer Coaches Association of America. Our target was to have it ready in time for the 50th Anniversary of the founding of the organization in 1991. As events would unfold we did have a segment completed by the Atlanta Convention of 1991— but it would take until 1993 for the book to be completed.

The process of examining the history of the NSCAA involved rereading past copies of *Soccer Journal*. Thus when the process of culling material for the book *Coaching Soccer* commenced there was prior research to call upon.

As for the history of *Soccer Journal* those who will examine the chapter in this book titled "Our Beginnings..." will find that subject covered as part of the overall yearly review of NSCAA historical benchmarks. The original publication was named *Newsletter* and served to both bond the founding members of NSCAA as well as an educational instrument that would offer articles to improve soccer coaching in this country.

Since its debut in 1941, those two objectives have remained constant for the magazine. A number of editors served the publication initially including Larry Briggs, Earle Waters and Dick Schmelzer. In 1953 Schmelzer turned the editorship over to Don Yonker and the gentleman coach from Philadelphia would mind the store for the next 27 years. Coincidently, 1953 also saw the name of the publication changed to *Soccer Journal*.

For most of its life and until 1980, the magazine was a quarterly publication. When the NSCAA Board of Directors indicated to editor Yonker that it wanted to increase the number of issues published he retired from the position and in the process indicated that he thought that there was someone who could fill his shoes. You guessed it — the guy who can't keep from taking on one too many projects!

Along the way editor Yonker grappled with trying to meet budgets by solicitation of advertising and thank goodness that soccer persons such as George St. Amond, Max Doss, Hyde Shoes, Bob Green and many others helped support the magazine through placement of display adverts.

Also important, obviously, were the professional efforts of many soccer coaches over the years who contributed their energies and creativity in formulating articles for publication in the magazine. Amazingly the articles that you will find in *Coaching Soccer* have been written without stipends paid and reflect well on the authors' professionalism. The intention by those concerned was that the coaching of the sport might be improved through a sharing of coaching ideas.

As the process of evaluation of articles for *Coaching Soccer* began, the editor was able to call on true soccer professionals in every case to contribute their valuative expertise. The following individuals were invaluable in fine-tuning the many articles that I had examined and placed in the various chapter headings: Joe Bean and Jack Huckel (History); Jack Detchon (Soccer Theory); Joe Bean and Ron Ost (Soccer Coaching Philosophy); Jeff Tipping (Teaching Soccer Technique); Joe Machnik (Goalkeeping); Jeff Vennell and Alan Maher (the Tactics chapter); Dr. Don Kirkendall (Physical Preparation); Mel Lorback (Psychology of Coaching); Don Woog and Ron Quinn (Youth Soccer); and Jay Engeln (Indoor Soccer) and Doug Williamson (Team Management). Restarts was a chapter coordinated by the author, while I must credit the women coaches and NSCAA Board of Directors for insisting on a chapter on Coaching Women's Soccer. That too, became my domain.

But while private "thank yous" have been expressed to the aforementioned chapter editors, I would like to publicly extend my appreciation to them on behalf of the soccer coaching community for help in bringing this book to culmination.

Finally, the book would not have been possible without the authors taking the time to initially put their ideas in print. So to all our authors — thanks for extending yourselves!

While there may have been an idea of the type of book on soccer coaching we would seek to publish, what we arrived at is a book that we feel has value at almost every level of soccer coching involvement. We think that it can be a good resource book for any soccer coach trying to become everything that a good coach has to be — teacher, counselor, role model, person who can inspire, and a variety of other roles.

Primarily we hope that this book reflects well on the many persons who have helped *Soccer Journal* play a role in the improvement of soccer coaching and subsequently the play of the game in the United States.

Tim Schum
Binghamton University
Binghamton, NY

● ●

ABOUT THE EDITOR

Tim Schum is a Professor of Physcial Education at Binghamton University (NY) and currently serves as Associate Director of Recreation at the school. He coached the men's team at Binghamton for 29 years, retiring in 1992 with 259-125-43 record. The Colonials were selected to post-season play for 16 of the seasons including eight NCAA appearances and eight ECAC selections. The team won two ECAC titles (1972 and 1976) and captured six State University of New York Athletic Conference titles during his tenure.

His service to soccer includes initiation of the Vestal Youth Soccer Association and the area-wide Broome County Soccer Association in his community. BCSA affiliated itself with the United States Youth Soccer

Association and Schum was active as an ODP coach during the 1970s and early 1980s.

He would serve the National Soccer Coaches Association as its president in 1982-83, and alongside that role has edited its publication, *Soccer Journal*, since 1980.

He was accorded the NSCAA/NISOA Merit Award in 1987 and both the Bill Jeffrey Award and the NSCAA Honor Award in 1994 for service to the game of soccer. He is also a member of his high school (Wilson HS, Spencerport, NY) and college (University of Rochester) Halls of Fame.

He currently serves as a member of the NSCAA Coaching Academy staff where he enjoys the opportunity to share his soccer experience with coaches.

ACKNOWLEDGMENTS

This book is dedicated to those who have influenced my life in soccer:

- My father, Harold "Chick" Schum who served as my soccer coach through my schoolboy years at Spencerport High School in the suburban Rochester NY area and my many friends who took (and gave) some over the boot shots to one's ankles;

- To Leo Bernabei who introduced me to the club soccer scene in Rochester, NY where we were able to view soccer played at a high technical level;

- To the many players at Brockport State who inspired a young player by their well-organized approach to the game under one of the U.S. coaching giants at the time—coach Hunter Parker;

- To my coach at the University of Rochester, Lyle Brown, who improved my technique and provided an important role model for my own initial efforts when I began to coach;

- To Gordon Allen (West Irondequoit High School) and David Henderson (then Harpur College, now Binghamton University) for hiring a young coach and mentoring him through his formative coaching years;

- To Al Miller at Hartwick College for spending time pointing me to more creative forms of coaching and also for introducing me to the USSF Coaching Schools;

- To Dettmar Cramer, the great German coach, who is perhaps the finest teacher of any subject matter that it has been my privilege to study with;

- To Walt Chyzowhych for sharing his expertise with all of us and for carrying on the mission of improved soccer education for American coaches;

- To Don Yonker for his professional example to all we young coaches and for having the confidence to turn over "his baby" to a journalistic neophyte;

- To the many, many soccer friends who have challenged me to improve my coaching knowledge including all those members of the NSCAA Board of Directors who have supported me in my efforts with *Soccer Journal*;

- To Peter Gooding and Jeff Tipping for appointing me to the NSCAA Academy staff where I feel that things have come full cycle — I can give back to coaches what so many have given me;

- Finally, thanks to all the great young men at Binghamton University whom it was my pleasure to coach over nearly 30 years. Not many persons can say they enjoyed every working day — but I did and have and it was "the boys" who made it so much fun!

The book is also dedicated to those who have influenced by personal life including:

- My mother Anne and father Harold for supporting me both in sports and education;

- My wives Ann and Jane for their aid in encouraging me to spend time on the game;

- My children (Chris, Carrie and Jennie) for letting soccer play a dominant role in their young lives and Ann's children (Ingrid, Dolfo, Andres, Astrid and Christina) for their support over the years.

Finally thanks to Dr. Joel Thirer at Binghamton University for providing both fiscal and other forms of support in allowing this book to reach fruition as well as the office staff of Michele Swartz, our student helper Julie Gayle and my Binghamton University staff for their untold hours of support in this project. Now we can return to business as normal!

• •

CREDITS:

Proofreaders: Pat Brady and Bryan Banschbach
Diagrams: Scott Stadler and Deborah Delk
Cover design: Suzanne Lincoln
Cover photos: Brett Whitesell, Tony Quinn & Perry McIntyre

CONTRIBUTORS

Bob Alego was assistant strength coach at UCLA when he wrote for the magazine. Currently he is the head trainer for the Oakland Athletics Baseball team.

Robert Baptista coaches at both Roberts Wesleyan College (NY) and at Wheaton College (IL). He was the 1975 recipient of the NSCAA Honor Award.

Stuart Barbour has coached at the secondary level in Canada including coaching the boys and girls team at Cairine Wilson Secondary School in Ottawa.

Bob Barry is the soccer coach at Iolani School in Hawaii. He is a frequent instructor at goalkeeper camps in the U.S. He serves NSCAA as state director for Hawaii.

Joe Bean has been both President of NSCAA and accorded its Honor Award. He is the long-time coach at Wheaton College (IL) following stints at the University of Bridgeport and Quinnipiac College. He has chaired the joint NSCAA/ISAA Ethics Committee for many years.

Cal Botterill is an Associate Professor at the University of Winnipeg in Canada. He teaches sport psychology, mental skills and growth and development there.

Dr. Steve Boutcher is a senior lecturer in the Department of Human Movement at the University of Wollongong in Wollongong, Australia. His writing appeared in the Sports Psychology Training Bulletin.

Peter Broadly is the men's coach at Catawba University (NC). A native of England, he first coached at UNC-Greensboro as an assistant to Mike Parker. He also is active as a state coach for the North Carolina YSA.

Doug Burke coached over 30 years at Houghton College (NY) where his teams were noted for their fair and winning play. His team captured the National Christian College Athletic Association championship.

Ruth Callard has been active in promoting women's sports including service as editor of The Women's Soccer Foundation's publication, *Network*. She was serving as president of the WSG Board of Directors at the time of publication of *Coaching Soccer*.

Dr. David Carr is currently chairman of the Sports Studies Program at Ohio University. His article for *SJ* was written while he was completing his doctorate

at Virginia Tech where he served for four years as assistant men's soccer coach.

Andy Caruso has been active as a businessman (Kwik Goal, Ltd.) and as a youth soccer coach and author.

Clive Charles enjoyed a long professional playing career in England before coming to this country where he played in the NASL before entering coaching at the University of Portland. His Division I men's and women's teams are among the nation's most competitive units. He is also currently assistant coach with the U.S. National Men's Team.

Gene Chyzowych is one of the nation's winningest coaches in a career centered at Maplewood (NJ) High School. He is a one-time coach of the U.S. National Team and operates the nation's longest operating soccer camp.

Bobby Clark is the former National Team goalkeeper for Scotland. Following a long professional career in Great Britain, he moved to the U.S. where he enjoyed a successful coaching career at Dartmouth College. He recently served as the National Team coach for New Zealand and is now men's coach at Stanford.

Pat Croce is president of Sports Physical Therapists, Inc. in Wayne, PA. The article cited "Coaching Soccer" originally appeared in the *Physical Therapy Forum*, V. VIII, #39.

Dr. Simon Davies is director of sport psychology and men's soccer coach at Albion College (MI).

Klaas deBoer was 1985 COY while handling the indoor reins of the Canton Invaders of the American Indoor Soccer Association. He was NSCAA COY while coaching collegiately at Cleveland State University and also served as an assistant in the NASL (Detroit Express and Los Angeles Aztecs) and the MISL (Detroit Lightning).

Jack Detchon is currently the men's soccer coach at Kenyon College (OH). He is a native of England where he was involved in soccer as an FA Staff coach for many years. He serves as a member of the NSCAA Academy staff.

Karl Dewazien is a U.S. Soccer A licensed coach and has taken coaching courses in Germany, the Netherlands and attended FIFA International Youth Academies. He has authored a series of books that comprise the FUNdamental soccer series, including some that have been translated into Spanish. He is a frequent featured speaker and clinician in this country.

Tony DiCicco has served as the National Team goalkeeper coach for both the U.S. men's and women's teams. Most recently he was appointed coach of the U.S. National Women's team. He also operates his own goalkeeper academy.

Bob Dikranian was a US Soccer staff coach for many years and his work at Southern Connecticut State University including directing the team to the 1987 NCAA Division II title.

Chris Dimitriou established the women's soccer team at Binghamton University, taking it to post-season play in its sixth season of play in 1990. In 1991 he became assistant men's coach at Binghamton under Tim Schum and in 1993 was appointed head coach. That year he directed the team to the ECAC title and in 1994 took the school to its ninth NCAA Division III appearance.

Jim DiNobile is the men's coach at Eckerd College in St. Petersburg, FL.

Anson Dorrance is the most successful coach in women's soccer with his North Carolina Tarheels capturing all contested NCAA Division I championships since 1982 — except two. He also led the U.S. Women's National Team to the first FIFA World Championship in China in 1991.

Dr. Edward Etzel is a licensed psychologist at West Virginia University where he works as an outreach psychologist for the Department of Intercollegiate Athletics.

Walter Ersing coached for many years at Ohio State University and is currently Professor Emeritus from that institution. He has been active as a soccer official in Ohio since leaving coaching.

Dr. Debra Feltz is an associate professor of physical education in the School of Health Education, Counseling Psychology, and Human Performance at Michigan State University. She also is a staff member in the Institute for the Study of Youth Sports and edits that group's newsletter, "Spotlight." She also conducts workships for youth coaches.

Dr. Tom Fleck is currently the director of coaching for the Florida State Youth Soccer Association. He has coached collegiately (Lehigh University), been an administrator in the game at both the professional (NASL) and national youth (USYSA) levels, and an NSCAA Academy and US Soccer staff coach. He is past president of the NCAA (1984-85).

Dr. Ian Franks formerly coached the Canadian Olympic soccer team from 1980-1983. He was Director of the Center for Sports Analysis at the University of British Columbia in Vancouver at the time of his writings for the magazine.

Bob Gansler led the U.S. National Team to the World Cup in 1990 and also was the Director of Coaching for US Soccer during his coaching tenure. He is currently coaching at the professional level.

Allen Gary at the time of his submission to *SJ* was coaching high school soccer in Alabama. He had received his doctorate in physics from the University of Georgia and was both a USSF licensed coach and a NISOA referee.

Dan Gaspar has been a leader in teaching goalkeepers. Included in his resume is a stint in Portugal where he instructed the national team goalies of that country. He is currently owner of the Star Goalkeeper's Camp.

Dr. Alan Goldberg has both written and conducted clinic sessions for the NSCAA at its annual conventions. He is the owner of the company Competitive Advantage located in Gardner, MA.

Ric Granryd was the assistant soccer coach at California State University, Chico.

Dr. Colleen Hacker was the women's coach at Pacific Lutheran University for many years, leading the team to NAIA championships in 1988, 1989 and 1991. The latter two years also found NSCAA COY for her work. She is a NSCAA Academy staff coach where she often lectures on sport psychology.

Charles Hardy is a professor in the Department of Sport Science and Physical Education at Georgia Southern University. He formerly edited *The Sport Psychology Training Bulletin*. He currently edits *Performance Edge —The Letter of Performance Psychology*.

Paul Hartman was the Director of Athletics at the University of Wisconsin, Stevens Point.

George Herrick is one of the nation's most successful high school coaches at Vestal (NY) High School. He holds the US Soccer "A" License.

Frans Hoek formerly was the keeper for Ajax in Holland and has served the national team program in that country as goalkeeper coach. He frequently has lectured and served on goalkeeper camp staffs in the U.S.

Richard Howard has both played for and been on the national team coaching staff of Canada. He also played goalkeeper professionally in the NASL.

Bobby Howe was a professional player in England before coming to the U.S. to play in the NASL. He has been active in youth coaching work in the Seattle area, including service as director of coaching for the Washington State Youth Soccer Association. He is currently the US Soccer coordinator of coaching.

Jack Huckel is the men's soccer coach at Skidmore College (NY). He currently serves as assistant historian for the NSCAA.

Norm Jackson has coached for many years in California and was California Youth Soccer Association South director of coaching when authoring his contribution to this book.

Gordon Jago has coached professionally both in England and the U.S. His U.S. stints included Tampa Bay Rowdies (NASL) and most recently the Dallas Sidekicks of the CISL.

Dave Keck was the coach at Westerville South High School and President of the Ohio Scholastic Coaches Association in the 1970s.

Dr. Donald Kirkendall was affiliated with the Cleveland Clinic for many years and later taught at Illinois State. He is currently with the Duke University Medical Center in the Physical Therapy Department. He is a former soccer player who was an Olympic trialist in 1974.

Loren Kline was the coach at the University of Delaware for many years.

Manuel Lagos was coaching at the University of Minnesota at the time of his article and was the coach at St. Paul Academy during the 1970s.

Chris Lantz was a graduate student at West Virginia University and an assistant editor of the *Sport Psychology Training Bulletin* at the time of his publication in *SJ*.

Jim Lennox is the coach at Hartwick College (NY). His teams are perennial NCAA Division I contenders with the 1977 team capturing the national title. He is NSCAA Academy Director of Coaching *emeritus*.

Dr. Jack Levine is a pediatrician living and coaching youth soccer in Great Neck, NY. He originally wrote the article cited for *Kickoff*, the publication of the Long Island Junior Soccer Association.

Timo Liekoski has coached at the college and professional levels of coaching since the 1970s. His posts have included Hartwick College as well as stops in the NASL (Dallas, Edmonton and Houston), MISL (Cleveland), and AISL (Canton). He was assistant U.S. national team coach during World Cup '94.

Hal Liske wrote his story on coaching ethics for referees for the May, 1989 issue of *Soccer California*.

Dr. Mel Lorback led West Chester State University to the 1961 NCAA soccer title. He was professor in the Physical Education Department at the school where he lectured in sport psychology.

Joe Luxbacher has been coaching at the University of Pittsburgh for many years following a professional playing career in this country. He has authored two books on soccer and holds a doctorate in athletic administration.

Joe Machnik pioneered goalkeeper training camps in the U.S. He has been involved in every aspect of soccer in the U.S., as a college coach, professional and national team coach, and collegiate and professional referee. He has also authored books on goalkeeping.

Alan Maher follows Dutch soccer methodology closely and has contributed many articles to various U.S. publications on that subject. He is also the author of two books on soccer, *The Complete Soccer Handbook* and *Attacking Soccer with the Neutral Player*.

Dr. Chris Malone is on the faculty at State University of New York at Cortland where he coached the women's team to the NCAA Division III finals twice, winning the national title in 1992.

Lynn Berling-Manuel serves as the Publisher and Editor-in-Chief for *Soccer America*, the weekly publication for soccer in the U.S. She also has written and lectured extensively on soccer marketing.

Frank Marra wrote his article on reminders for coaches as they interact with the media for the August, 1989 issue of *Referee* magazine.

Dr. Jay Martin has achieved the best winning percentage of any collegiate coach while directing the fortunes of the Ohio Wesleyan University men's team. He is also the Director of Athletics at OWU and served as NSCAA president in 1996.

Tom Martin has enjoyed a successful coaching career at both Davis & Elkins University (WV) as well as at his current assignment, James Madison University (VA).

Robert Mastruzzi was Superintendent of Schools for the Borough of Manhattan.

Ron McEachen has successfully coached at both Middlebury College (VT) and the University of Vermont. He has lectured at NSCAA Conventions and been a member of the NSCAA Academy Staff. Most recently he is the assistant coach for the New England Revolution (MLS).

Dr. Gary Miller is an associate professor in the Department of Educational Psychology at the University of South Carolina.

Jay Miller built the Division II program at the University of Tampa into one of the nation's most competitive, with the team capturing the NCAA title in 1981. He is currently a US Soccer Regional Coach and assists with various National Team programs.

Mark Newman has been an American coach interested in goalkeeping and served for a time as the goalkeeper coach under coach Bruce Arena at Virginia.

Dave Nicholas is one of the nation's most successful secondary school coaches at Lincoln HS in Portland,

OR. He has served as a U.S. Soccer staff coach during his career.

Frank Olszewski is the men's coach at Towson (MD) State University. He graduated from Johns Hopkins University where he majored in psychology.

Marianne Oren is an editorial assistant at the Youth Sports Institute at Michigan State University. She also is working part-time as a licensed professional counselor in the Lansing, Michigan area.

David Partridge was a faculty member at the University of British Columbia at the time of his submission to the magazine.

James Prunier has been involved in youth soccer in New Jersey for many years and edited the popular *Science Tactic Quizzes* for the NSCAA.

Ron Quinn has coached on the high school level (Moravian Academy, PA), at the college level (men's coach at Allentown College, PA and women's coach at Xavier University, OH), and been a member of both the NSCAA Academy Staff and U.S. Soccer coaching staff. He is the author of a book on youth coaching *The Peak Performance: Soccer Games for Player Development*.

Matt Robinson is currently teaching in the sports managment program at Allentown College (PA). He worked for a time as a sports reporter in York (PA).

Tom Rowney has worked extensively in youth soccer in this country and is currently the women's coach at Oregon State University.

Andy Roxburgh has contributed to the soccer education of coaches in the U.S. through lectures and clinics and various NSCAA meetings. He is a one-time Scotland National Coach and is currently an FIFA Staff Coach.

Michael Russo has been selected four times as the NSCAA's NCAA Division III Men's Coach of the Year while coaching at Williams College. He led the team to the NCAA Division III championship in 1995.

Sigi Schmid has coached at UCLA since 1980, leading the Bruins to the NCAA Division I title in 1985. He was an assistant coach for the U.S. World Cup team in '94. Schmid is a US Soccer staff coach and a noted lecturer and clinician in the sport.

Tim Schum has edited *Soccer Journal* since 1980 and served as NSCAA President in 1982-83. He was accorded both the NSCAA Honor and the Bill Jeffrey Awards in 1994. He coached Binghamton University (NY) for nearly 30 years.

Vern Seefeldt served as director of the Youth Sports Institute at Michigan State University. The article first appeared in the winter, 1985 issue of *Spotlight*, the YSI official publication.

Jape Shattuck has contributed to U.S. soccer as both a coach and coaching educator. He served on the staff at Hartwick College and led Harvard to NCAA play while head coach in Cambridge. His instructional videotapes, through his company, International Tactics, Ltd., featured footage that aided in improving both individual and team tactical play.

David Smart has played a role in developing championship goalkeepers for the men's team at Southern Connecticut State University. He also directs the Performance Goalkeeper School.

Jan Smisek was the first U.S. women's coach to achieve the US Soccer "A" coaching license. She currently coaches at The Evergreen State College (WA).

Dave Simeone has been active as a staff coach or director of coaching for the Florida, North and South Texas and N.Ohio Youth Soccer Associations. He has also served for several years as the youth representative on the NSCAA Board of Directors.

Malcolm Simon has written two books on soccer and coached collegiately at the New Jersey Institute of Technology for many years.

Rodney Spears has coached high school soccer in Houston for many years and is the past president of the Texas Association of Soccer Coaches.

Jeff Sturges is co-author with Dan Gaspar of the book *Goalkeeping—The Ball Stops Here*. He is a former three-time All-Vermont goalkeeper while performing at Middlebury College.

Jeff Tipping is the NSCAA Director of Coaching. He captained the Hartwick College team that captured the 1977 NCAA Division I championship and has built Muhlenberg College men's team into one of the top Division III programs.

Tom Turner played and later coached for several years at Cleveland State. Most recently he has been involved with youth coaching in Ohio.

Cor Van Der Meer has been very active in youth soccer in Washington State and writes extensively for the Washington YSA newsletter.

Frans Von Balkom was coaching the Busch Soccer Club teams in St. Louis at the time of his writings. He coached in Europe prior to coming to the U.S. and was coaching professionally in Japan in 1996.

Hubert Vogelsinger has coached at both the collegiate and professional levels in this country and operated an extensive camp program that bears his name for many years. He has presented clinics throughout the country and also written a book on soccer as additional accomplishments.

Alan Wade has served the NSCAA as both a clinician and through articles in *Soccer Journal* over a long period of time. He was a professor of physical eductation at Loughborough University in England for part of his career, later serving the English FA as its Director of Coaching for many years.

Susan Walter was a second year graduate student in sport psychology at Michigan State University at time she wrote *Working Effectively with Parents*. Her interest in athletics is two-pronged. First is to enhance the quality of sport for youth and secondarily to work with athletes in terms of their personal development.

Dan Woog lives in Westport, CT and has been connected with soccer both as a coach and writer for most of his adult life. Each month he edits "The Youth Soccer Letter" for *Soccer America*. His coaching has included stints at his *alma mater* Staples High School and at the youth Level in Westport.

Mike Worcik was the head strength coach at Syracuse University at the time he wrote for the magazine. He has moved to the professional ranks with his most recent stop as strength coach for the Dallas Cowboys.

Marvin Zuidema has been the men's coach at Calvin College (MI) for many years. He has also been active on the NCAA Soccer Committee and the joint NSCAA/ISAA Ethics Committees.

Our Beginnings:

A Brief History of Soccer and the NSCAA

• •

> ### Inside
> ### Shot
> **A Short Eurocentric History of Soccer**
> *Jack Huckel*
>
> **The Formation of the National Soccer Coaches Association of America**
> *Joseph Bean and Tim Schum*

This chapter will present an overview of the history of soccer beginning with its origins in Europe and its import to the United States. Jack Huckel, men's soccer coach at Skidmore College (NY), offers a chronological assessment of the sport from what he terms "pre-history" through the sport's more recent success on these shores, namely the staging of U.S. World Cup '94.

Unfortunately there is, at present, no definitive history of the sport that has been yet chronicled by U.S. Soccer, the nation's FIFA-sanctioned affiliate. So much of soccer's legacy resides in archives and writings of individuals such as the late U.S. Soccer historian, Sam Foulds. Soccer can be thankful for the relatively recent establishment of the National Soccer Hall of Fame in Oneonta, New York for it appears that that organization will, in time, be able to examine various memorabilia and offer a comprehensive record of the development of the sport from the early 1900s to the present.

In the meantime, as this book focuses on coaching articles that have appeared in the National Soccer Coaches Association of America's magazine, Soccer Journal, *this chapter will seek to recapture for the reader the progress and contributions of NSCAA to the progress of the sport in this country.*

It will do so in two ways.

Yearly summaries as contained in the book "The First 50 Years, The History of the National Soccer Coaches Association of America," have been reproduced with the permission of the authors of that work, Joe Bean and Tim Schum. They offer those interested in the sport's history in this country a timeline that details its progress in terms of individual coaches who worked for its inclusion in the athletic programs of various U.S. colleges and secondary schools. As we chart the growth of NSCAA we will also see the impact of various events outside the school settings.

From its origins in 1941 to the present, NSCAA has been a major contributor to the advancement of soccer in terms of its twin concern for enhanced soccer instruction and, secondarily, for promotion of the game.

⚽

A Short Eurocentric History of Soccer
Jack Huckel

Pre-History to World War I

The sport we call soccer is known throughout most of the world as simply football. Its origins lie somewhere in pre-history; as a competition that pitted villagers in early England, as a game that substituted for war in Aztec civilization, or as a Native American game called "pasuckquakkohowog", there are many avenues of development to the game. As with most games, its popularity waxed and waned throughout its pre-organization years.

For the "Right Honourable Game Football", though, death came officially when the Court Circular printed "...our painful duty to report the death...which melancholy event took place in the Court of Queen's Bench on Wednesday, Nov. 14th, 1860. The deceased Gentleman was, we are informed, a native of Ashbourn, Derbyshire, at which place he was born in the Year of Grace, 217..." The case was brought by "...certain of the powers that be determined that this harmless old custom should be done away with..." The 'powers that be' won in local court and on appeal. Perhaps it was this event that brought the game from the street to the park. The sport begins, however, with the codification of its laws and this is recorded in history.

In 1863 thirteen men representing football clubs from England and Scotland met to formally organize the game. The group did not agree on a single set of laws; some wished to continue the use of hands and advocated carrying the ball, while others were deter-

Immigration to the U.S. kept soccer alive as this 1920s photo of a game in New York City attests. Social/ethnic teams organized around soccer. (The photo is courtesy of the John Albok collection which is housed in the National Soccer Hall of Fame in Oneonta, NY.)

mined to make football a game which relied predominantly on the feet, thereby severely restricting body contact and eliminating the use of hands altogether. No accommodation was found and the two camps split. One founded Rugby Union Football and the other established the Football Association (FA). The FA was quick to provide the first Laws of Association Football in 1863 and the sport of soccer began.

In 1862 the Oneidas of Boston formed the first football/soccer club in the Americas. Garrett Smith Miller brought the provisional rules of association football to the States and formed the game around them. The Oneidas played throughout the 1860's, going undefeated from its forming until 1865. In the United States, though, the controversy about which rules to play by was still evident. When Princeton visited Rutgers on November 6, 1869 for a "football" match (the game gridiron football claims as its first), the competition was much closer to what today we would call soccer. The return match, played a week later in Princeton, was a different variant, as each game was played according to the rules of the home team.

The Football Association, meanwhile, followed its founding by organizing a competition among the various clubs in England. The FA announced a single elimination or knockout competition, the FA Cup, in 1871, with entries solicited for the first tournament which was to begin in the following year. The Wanderers of London won the first FA Cup by defeating the Royal

Engineers of London. The FA Cup continues to be an important competition that is open to all English teams, amateur or professional. In addition the clubs themselves joined together to form league competition in 1889. League and Cup competitions sprang up, first within the confines of the United Kingdom, then expanded throughout Europe and the many countries that were tied to England through colonization, trade, or political hegemony.

By the rebirth of the Olympic Program in 1896, virtually all of the European nations had football playing clubs, as did most of South American countries. England had already begun to send representative teams to play matches in Europe and the sport gained in popularity. The 1896 Olympics in Athens did not include football/soccer as a medal sport, but a demonstration match was played. The 1904 Olympics in St. Louis, Missouri, introduced soccer as an official Olympic sport, Canada won the gold medal even though only three teams (none from Europe) took part in the competition. A full tournament was organized for the 1908 London Olympic Games, and the team representing Great Britain won the first of two successive gold medals.

The growth and internationalization of soccer, and the admission of the sport into the Olympic family led to an international conference in Paris on May 21, 1904. Representatives from France, Belgium, Holland, Denmark, Sweden, Switzerland, and Spain culminated several years of discussions by founding FIFA, the Fédération Internationale de Football Association. Notably absent from this group were the English, who acknowledged the formation, but little else. The FA had formed the International Football Association Board (whose membership comprised England, Scotland, Wales and Ireland) to govern the Laws of the game and it saw in FIFA a challenge to English pre-eminence in the game. England had also been stung by the Olympic Committee decision that it would be represented by a single Great Britain team. The FA was concerned that FIFA would also declare that there would be one team from Great Britain, rather than separate teams for each of the home countries. By 1906 agreement between the FA and FIFA had been reached. An expanded International Board with FIFA representation would remain the sole law making body and each of the countries that made up Great Britain would be a separate member of FIFA, allowing each to compete individually in any tournament FIFA organized. Over the course of history, FIFA and the FA have fought many battles, with FA having withdrawn from the international organization in 1919 due to residual political tensions from World War I, re-entering three years later, and, again, in 1928 after disagreements over opening FIFA competitions to all players, amateur and professional.

WORLD WAR I TO WORLD WAR II

The FA was formed by "gentlemen" of England who envisioned football being played by gentlemen. As clubs formed and prestige began to be attached to success in various competitions, both cup and league, "gentlemen" decided to employ the best soccer players in order to gain the accolades that came with winning. Most early club owners owned factories or other businesses and employed players as workers in them, with the expectation that a part of job security was contingent upon soccer success. On the continent, "class" was less important and professionalism advanced rapidly, with many clubs explicitly employing young men to play the game. When FIFA began planning for its first international tournament and made the decision that professionals could represent a nation in competition, England, Scotland, Wales, and Ireland left the fold and did not rejoin until after World War II. These defections saddened the soccer world, but they did not halt the organization of the first World Cup in 1930. Because Uruguay had won the 1928 Olympic Tournament, FIFA awarded the first national team tournament to that country.

During the early 1900's European immigration to the United States meant a solidification for the sport of soccer. The game was introduced into every major population center. Hotbeds of soccer ran from Boston through Fall River, Massachusetts, to New York and Philadelphia, where the American Soccer League was the pre-eminent competition. St. Louis and Chicago were also hotbeds of soccer and had very competitive leagues. Most teams were semi-professional; the players were paid a modest game day wage for playing. Some teams, like Bethlehem Steel and the Ben Millers, were company teams, while others, such as the Philadelphia Ukrainians and the New York Hispano were organized by ethnic clubs. European club teams visited the U.S. regularly and the matches were enthralling and hotly contested. The United States of America Football Association (which went through several alphabet soup changes on its way to becoming today's U.S. Soccer, an amalgam of leagues and competing organizing councils) was accepted into FIFA membership in 1913. Thus began international recognition of soccer in the United States.

The United States Soccer Football Association entered a team in the first World Cup competition. Its players were predominately from the ASL teams or the St. Louis area. The team had a very successful tournament, defeating Belgium and Paraguay by identical 3-0 scores in the first round games, before a rugged Argentinean squad advanced to the final by defeating the U.S. 6 - 1 in the semi-final. World Cup competition continued with Italy winning in 1934 at home and in France in 1938. Italy eliminated the U.S. in the preliminary round of 1934 World Cup and, in 1938, the U.S. chose not to compete.

THE 1950'S

World War II forced a halt to virtually all international sporting activities. Still, soccer was played in the military and the game remained alive. All sport saw an explosion of activity in the post war years. Whether it was to help push the horrors of war behind, or to recapture the joy of activity, the leagues throughout Europe quickly resumed play, as did the leagues in the United States. FIFA organized the first post World War II World Cup for 1950 and Brazil, the host country, built the largest stadium in existence, Maracanã, with a capacity of 200,000. England made its first appearance in the World Cup and, surprisingly, returned home after the first round.

England was grouped with Chile, Spain and the United States for the qualifying round. In the first group matches, England defeated Chile handily 2-0, while the U.S. lost to Spain 3-1 on two late goals. The second round of group matches saw the U.S. (coached by U.S. coaching legend Bill Jeffrey) face England in Belo Horizonte. As Harry Keough of the U.S. team noted, "If we had played them 10 times, they would have beaten us nine times, but this was the other day." The U.S. won 1-0 on a headed goal by Joe Gaetjens, a veteran of the New York Cosmopolitan League. Many soccer historians consider this to be the greatest upset in World Cup history. In the final group games, both the U.S. and England completed their participation with losses. For the U.S. the upset was an opportunity. For England, the founder of the game, it precipi-

Bill Jeffrey is a U.S. coaching legend and led the U.S. team to its historic victory over England in the 1950 World Cup.

tated a decline in international prestige. For host Brazil, the heavy favorites to win their first tournament, it was a joyless final when Uruguay won its second championship 2-1 in Maracaña.

The 50's brought soccer to the top of Europe's sporting calendar. Great teams and great individuals emerged from across the continent and the game's appeal brought larger crowds and, therefore, larger stadiums. The first great team of this era was the Magic Magyars, the national team of Hungary. The Magic Magyars strolled through the 1952 Olympics in Helsinki with a composite scoreline of 20-2 and easily won the gold medal. In 1953 the team of Ferenc Puskas and Nandor Hidegkuti visited London's venerable Wembley Stadium, the home ground for England's national side, to meet the founders of the game. England, who had never lost at home to a non-British side, was comprehensively savaged in a 6-3 rout.

Hungary entered the 1954 World Cup as prohibitive favorites and kicked off the final against West Germany with supreme confidence, after drubbing the Germans 8-3 in an earlier group match. Between 1950 and 1956 this Hungarian team would lose only one match in 48, but the one loss would come in its most important match, the World Cup Final. The Germans countered the Hungarian strategy, fought hard, and the confidence the Hungarians brought to the match worked against them. The Magic Magyars, for the only

time in their great era, failed to score when they had to and West Germany finished the day as World Champions, 3-2.

Hungary was the best team in Europe during the first half of the 50's, a team for the ages. They brought a new style to the game, reversing the "W" formation, with a spearhead center forward and two wing players, into an "M" formation, with two attacking forwards, supported by a deep-lying center forward.

At this same time, a European Federation (UEFA) and an African Federation were formed to provide international competition on a regional scale. In Africa, an African Nations Cup tournament was organized, while in Europe a host of competitions were created. The first one was the European Champions Cup, where the winner of each member country's top league earned entry into a knockout tournament. UEFA also organized the Fairs Cup (now the UEFA Cup), and a European Nations Cup, a quadrennial national team tournament opposite the World Cup calendar.

THE 1960'S

The European Cup has evolved into the most prestigious club championship in the world, although each regional confederation of FIFA now organizes a similar tournament. Reál Madrid, with Puskas and Sandor Kocsis of the Hungarian National Team, Alfredo DiStefano from Argentina, as well as many other international talents, won the first five European Champions Cup competitions. The 1960 final, the last of Real's championships, was played at Glasgow's Hampden Park in front of 135,000 enthralled fans, and has been accorded the accolade as the greatest club match of all time. The match paired a determined Eintract Frankfort side against, perhaps, the greatest club side in history. While the Germans scored first, DiStefano (twice) and Puskas replied for Real. The first half ended 3-1, and the game was just warming up! In the second half, Real burst forward from the beginning and the show of skill and attacking power was on. Real scored two goals in the first 15 minutes to lead 5-1. Eintract continued its contribution to this great game by scoring two more goals before Real replied with two more goals: the final score 7 - 3. The match was everything that could have been envisioned when the idea of international club competition was first discussed.

Real Madrid was not the only exciting team in the last half of the 50's. No national team had won a World Cup away from its own continent until 1958. Brazil not only brought to Sweden, the World Cup host, and to the attention of the world, a new idea in formation, exceptional individual ball skills; it also brought a 17-year old named Edson Arantes do Nascimento-Pele. Brazil, unspectacularly, worked its way through the group matches and into the

Soccer legend Pele first gained world-wide attention in 1958. He would later receive
the NSCAA Honorary All-America Award in 1990. (photo by Perry McIntyre, Jr.)

quarterfinals, where Pele scored the winner in a 1-0 victory over a tenacious Welsh side. It was during the semifinal against France that Pele leapt to the world's attention with a hat trick. He followed with two goals in the Final, a 5-2 victory against the home team, to secure his reputation as the brightest young talent in world soccer.

THE 1960's

The early 60's saw no team galvanize in the way either Real Madrid or Brazil had done in previous few years. Brazil, without an injured Pele, won a second consecutive World Cup in Chile in 1962, and new club teams rose in Europe, with Benfica of Portugal winning two European Cups, and the two Milan teams, AC and Inter, winning the other three, before Real reappeared for another European Champions Cup win in 1966.

As both national and club competition received more interest, so the participants began to take the games more seriously. The prize and prestige for winning became more important as these competitions gained popularity and financial success, consequently team play became more defensive and more brutal. The Italians brought a system called "catenaccio" to the European Cup, and other teams played defense more cynically, eliminating the skill of the opponent through tough tackling. There was a fear that ruthless

defenders and the evolving tactics of team defense would obliterate the skill of the game. This trend was evident in the 1962 World Cup and in the European club competitions.

During the 1966 World Cup, when some nations focused on stopping opponents by any means necessary, the effects of defensive soccer were readily evident, and those effects were seen by even more people than usual as world wide television coverage came to the World Cup for the first time. Top players Pele and Eusebio of Portugal were repeatedly fouled. Pele was injured badly enough that he was forced to miss Brazil's final group match and he left saying he would never again play in the World Cup. While this World Cup may well have contained more cynical play than any previous tournament, it also provided a thrilling final between the hosts England and West Germany.

That match, played at Wembley Stadium, was a classic contest and the most controversial in World Cup history. The first half ended with the score tied at 1-1, and, when Peters scored to put England ahead 2-1, and the game moved into its final moments, it looked as if England had finally claimed the prize its heritage in soccer would say it deserved. West Germany was given a free kick outside the penalty area in the final moments. The Germans poured into the area. The ball was played in and Wolfgang Weber put the

World Cup final into its first extra time period in history by sliding in at the far post and side footing the ball past a diving England goalkeeper, Gordon Banks. The first period of extra time brought the controversy as England forward Geoff Hurst spun on a cross and crashed the ball off the underside of the crossbar. The ball bounced to the ground and spun out of the goalmouth. All England rose with arms upraised to signal a goal. As the Germans played the ball away from the goal, the referee consulted the linesman, and the goal was given. Was it in? Did it fully cross the goal line? Film evidence remains inconclusive and the argument continues whenever this game is remembered. In the second extra time period Hurst sealed Germany's fate and became the first and only player to score three goals in a final. England captain Bobby Moore accepted the Jules Rimet Cup as World Champions. Finally the country that had introduced the game to the world, was now World Champion.

The last half of the decade leading into the 1970 World Cup staged in Mexico saw many teams from many nations rise to the top of the heap. Celtic of Scotland, Manchester United of England, AC Milan of Italy, Feyenoord and Ajax of Holland shared the European Champions Cup; Borussia Dortmund and Bayern Munich of West Germany, AC Milan, Slovan Bratislava of Czechoslovakia, and Manchester City of England shared the European Winners Cup: only in the UEFA cup was there any sort of dominance as four different English teams won the competition in five years. The newest competitors in Europe were the Eastern European countries entering the fray with more and more success. Hungary and Bulgaria contested the final of the 1968 Olympic games with the Hungarians recalling the success of the Magic Magyars with a 2-1 triumph.

In the United States, full time professional soccer came on the scene. In 1967 two leagues made their appearance, the United Soccer Association (USA) and National Professional Soccer League (NPSL). The USA brought teams from the European leagues to compete representing American cities. The league winner in 1967 was the Los Angeles Wolves, who, in reality, were the Wolverhampton Wanderers of the English First Division. The NPSL was not a recognized league by the U.S. Soccer Federation, so finding the players to staff teams was difficult, but not impossible. The next year the two leagues joined to form the North American Soccer League (NASL) and dropped the concept of importing full teams from outside the country. The teams in the league came and went in those years, but full time professional soccer was on the ground dribbling, running, defending and shooting, even if it was to small crowds.

THE 1970'S

By 1970 the skill of Brazil had advanced beyond "the win at all costs" defensive play of many teams.

Pele returned to the international scene and the World Cup, played at high altitude in Mexico and at midday to allow prime time television viewing in Europe, was the most open since 1958. Brazil met defending champion England in a group match and won 1-0, with both teams advancing to the quarter final round. Four former champions advanced to the semi-finals: Uruguay, Italy, Brazil, and West Germany, with Brazil and Italy advancing to the final. In front of 110,000 fans, Brazil electrified the throng with remarkable individual skills and finishing power, blitzing the Italians 4-1. Brazil, with its third World Cup championship, took home the Jules Rimet Cup permanently and showed the world that skill could triumph over defensive tactics.

The early 70's saw the emergence of Ajax Amsterdam and Bayern Munich of West Germany as the top club teams. Each won three European Cups in a row and provided the nucleus for their respective national teams. Johann Cruyff of Holland and Franz Beckenbauer of West Germany were the leading players. Ajax club and Holland national coach Rinus Michels brought "Total Football" to the lexicon, along with the nicknames of "Clockwork Orange", in recognition of the Dutch team's orange jerseys and the "Dutch Whirl." Ajax's final Champions Cup win came in 1973 and the run-up included a quarter final victory over Bayern. For the next three years Bayern Munich raised the Champions Cup as top club in Europe.

West Germany hosted the 1974 World Cup and the final was played in Munich between Holland and West Germany. Before the Germans had touched the ball, the Dutch had strung together 14 passes from the kickoff, Bertie Vogts had fouled Cruyff in the penalty area, and Johann Neeskens had put Holland ahead 1-0. The Germans, staggered but resolute in their play, got a goal back on a Paul Breitner penalty kick and scored a second before half on a typical Gerd Müller accurate, if not powerful, finish of a cross into the penalty area. The second half witnessed Dutch possession and attacking flair against German organization and grit. The Dutch could not do what Brazil did in 1970, and the day finished with Beckenbauer holding the new World Champions Trophy aloft.

Beckenbauer brought a new dimension to the game that would influence how future defenders would play. Against England in 1966 and Italy in 1970 he had played as a wing halfback. For 1974 he was installed at the new "libero" position, given a role to cover in defense and to go forward to create attacking opportunities for his team. His marvelous technical ability, field vision and tactical sense brought more new ideas to soccer and, while defending was still important, defenders for Holland and for West Germany were also expected to be part of the offensive play.

The whole team game has been the predominant pattern on all levels since 1974. Clearly, players had to become better athletically to be able to accomplish this new strategy of all players moving into the attack and all players fulfilling defensive responsibilities. While systems have evolved since this date, and not every nation can fill each position with the talent needed, virtually every winning team in club and international competition has been one where every player fulfills an attacking and defending role.

Argentina hosted and won the 1978 World Cup with a flowing style reminiscent of the 1974 Dutch team. In the final Argentina defeated a strong Dutch team that lacked only the inspiration and improvisation of Johann Cruyff. Holland did bring another ingredient to the game in 1978, scoring long range goals, as twice in the tournament, they scored important goals from 40+ yards. In the final, such a long range effort kept them in the match, but in extra time, the running of the Argentineans, spurred on by a roaring home crowd showering the field with confetti, produced a winning goal scored by Mario Kempes.

The NASL was reaching its zenith in the late 70's. The big name was the New York Cosmos, who started out playing in a ragged New York City stadium on Randall's Island, under the Triborough Bridge, then moved to Giants Stadium in suburban New Jersey. The Cosmos raised the stakes in American professional soccer by signing Giorgio Chinaglia of Italy, Vadislav Bogicevic of Yugoslavia and Franz Beckenbauer of West Germany, and by drawing a retired Pele to the United States to bring the league to its greatest heights. The Cosmos drew crowds of 77,000+ for matches with opponent teams that included Bobby Moore from the 1966 England team, Gerd Müller of the 1974 West German winners, and Johann Cruyff of Holland.

In Europe the ascendancy of Liverpool of the English League had begun. Liverpool played a marvelous flowing passing game, much different from the more traditional robust, long passing style of most English League teams. For much of organized competitive soccer history, soccer had been a game of players, with few coaches or managers recognized as a key ingredient in the success of a team. But Liverpool put the names Bill Shankley and Bob Paisley on the front page, along with players like Kevin Keegan and Kenny Dalglish. Teams also found it much more difficult to repeat as champions. Freedom for the players meant higher wages and the opportunity to move from one club to another. The European Community Agreement opened the Common Market countries to the transfer of players from one country to another. The Borussia Mönchengladbach team Liverpool defeated in the 1977 European Champions Cup Final and 1978 semi-final featured Alan Simonsen from Denmark as the leading scorer.

Johann Cruyff was a soccer legend who found a home in the NASL. He played for both Los Angeles (above) and the Washington franchises. (photo by Milt Crossen)

THE 1980's

The World Cup moved to Spain in 1982 and expanded from the traditional 16 team tournament that had been planned from the earliest days of the competition to a 24 team tournament. It was a recognition that as more countries were joining FIFA, more countries were developing quality players for the highest level of the game. It was also a function of internal FIFA politics, as Joao Havelange of Brazil was elected president on a promise to open more places in the World Cup to the African, Asian, and CONCACAF (the Federation for North and Central America and the Caribbean) Federations. Traditionalists believed that the expansion was a mistake and that not enough teams were prepared to provide attractive matches to the traditional powers, such as Italy, Germany, and Brazil, in world soccer. The conservatives were right in some cases, but very wrong in others. In first round matches Poland defeated Peru easily 5-1, yet Camaroon played an exciting 1-1 tie with Italy; in Group B Algeria stunned West Germany 2-1; Group C saw El Salvador buried by Hungary 10-1: and in Group E Northern Ireland, featuring 17 year old Norman Whiteside, the new youngest player to compete in the Cup, defeated host Spain 1-0. The new teams added excitement to the tournament and gave the early games more color than had been in evidence before. Of the added teams, though, only Northern Ireland proceeded into the second round of sixteen teams.

While the final had the elements of an exciting event, matching Italy and West Germany, it was the semi-final between the German team and France that became the classic game of this World Cup. The two teams played a cautious first 90 minutes and entered the two 15 minute extra time periods tied at 1-1. The first extra period saw France score twice to take a 3-1 lead and surely the match was over. But the resolute Germans scored one and entered the second overtime a goal behind. With time winding down, Klaus Fischer executed an overhead kick to draw Germany level. In the end the first World Cup game to be determined by penalty kicks entered the history books with the Germans going on to the final.

The 1982 World Cup saw an exquisitely talented Brazil eliminated by their own naive play as well as the talents of an opportunistic Paolo Rossi as Italy won a second round match 3-2. Defensive play, individually and tactically, was catching up to the offensive play that had characterized the game in the past few years. The Brazilians learned a lesson that would take them more than a decade to apply successfully. Refereeing that allowed harsh defensive play was also a concern as the young and highly gifted Diego Maradona was made ineffective by tight marking, tough tackling, and a series of fouls. Maradona was not yet ready to meet the harsh demands of the international scene; but FIFA wanted the brilliance of players like Maradona to be exhibited and it worked through the International Board and the Referees Commission to open the game up over the next ten years so players with attacking flair could not be hounded into submission by physical defending that would go unpunished.

The United States television network ABC broadcast the 1982 World Cup Final in its entirety and soccer in the U.S. was on the upswing. Youth play was growing by leaps and bounds. The attractiveness of the all movement game, freedom from the coaching ills that marked Little League baseball, the physical concerns others rose about Pop Warner football, and the ability to put a player in uniform for a pittance, brought out kids, parents, and, even, grandparents to see boys and girls kick the soccer ball.

Unfortunately, on the professional level, the same could not be said. The zenith for the NASL had occurred in the late 70's when the New York Cosmos had its team of illustrious international stars. Crowds fell away as these great internationals retired. Many teams were unable to match the free spending ways of the Cosmos or went bankrupt trying. The exciting games and big crowds just seemed to melt away, as did the NASL.

In Europe, the problem was not financial, but physical, as "hooliganism" reared its ugly visage. The 1975 European Champions Cup between Liverpool of England and Juventus of Italy barely made it onto the field. Prior to the game followers of the two teams rioted in the stands and 39 fans died. This was not the first instance of fan violence, but it was the most vicious to date. As a result English club teams, for it was Liverpool "fanatics" that attacked the Italians, were banned from European competition for five years. Initiatives to ban the England team from the 1986 World Cup were considered but did not materialize.

In the midst of all this sorrow, there came once again, a player of rare talent to lead his team to the pinnacle of success. Diego Maradona made his first impact in the World Youth Championships of 1977. His skill, vision, quickness, and scoring ability had led the Argentine youth squad to the championship. Left off the 1978 team by manager Cesar Menotti because he felt Maradona was not mature enough, Maradona arrived at the 1982 World Cup as the leader of Argentina's campaign to repeat. For Maradona, 1982 was the height of frustration. He was seemingly fouled at every turn. The challenge of the physical abuse, combined with his immaturity and petulant personality, led him to end the tournament under a red card after a foul in Argentina's match against Brazil.

Perhaps because less was expected of him in 1986 when the World Cup moved to Mexico, he rose to legendary heights. As the leader of an Argentine team dominated by active midfielders, he was the most active, dribbling through opponent defenses, creating passing opportunities through great movement when he didn't have the ball, but mostly through an ability to open the opponent's defense with deftly weighted, unerringly accurate passes. Argentina marched through the World Cup, tying Italy in the first round, then progressing inexorably to a grand final against West Germany.

Along the way Maradona scored world class goals against Italy, against England in the quarterfinals, and two against Belgium in the semifinal. West Germany, now managed by Beckenbauer, willed its way into the final, scoring just enough to progress, defeating Mexico in penalties in the quarterfinals, and France again, in the semifinals, though this time in regulation. The Germans were, once again, a strong team, but they lacked the player to bring inspiration to the contest, and it was inspiration that finished the West German squad on the day. With the score 2-2 and less than 10 minutes remaining, Maradona controlled the ball in the midfield, somehow twisted and turned past two tightly marking defenders, then split the defense with an inch

Tab Ramos of the U.S. sets to cross the ball in a first round match versus Czechoslovakia in 1990 World Cup play in Italy. Despite high expectations by U.S. fans, the Czechs prevailed by a 5-1 score.

perfect pass to send Jorge Burrachaga alone on goal and Argentina to its second World Championship.

IN THE UNITED STATES

In the United States the demise of the NASL and the continued growth of youth soccer lured a new group of investors to begin yet another professional league: the Western Soccer League on the west coast, and the American Soccer League along the east coast. The two separate entities had moderate success as large regional leagues and collaborated for a national championship, with the Western League and American League winners meeting in a single winner take all match. As happened with the NASL, though, some owners saw the chance to form a national league and pushed this idea through at the next meeting between the two leagues. Owners of the clubs formed The American Professional Soccer League (APSL) with Western and Eastern Divisions. Teams that had lost small amounts of money or had made small profits were swamped with the bills to travel across the country. On the field the teams were competitive and brought a level of play above the college game and, perhaps, at the second division level in Europe, but it was a disaster in the box office. The number of teams rapidly declined in four years from 24 to five, and another opportunity for professional soccer in the U.S. continued, but on a greatly reduced basis in isolated pockets, teams coming and going from year to year

and prospects for success as a major league seemingly nil.

At the international level, though, the U.S. was finally finding some success. After being in the World Cup wilderness since 1950, the U.S. went to Trinidad and Tobago needing a win to qualify for the 1990 World Cup in Italy. FIFA had awarded the U.S. the right to host the 1994 World Cup and failure to qualify for Italy would be a major embarrassment for both. Many FIFA members complained about having the 1994 World Cup in a country where soccer was a minor and unappreciated sport. The U.S. prevailed on the day as Paul Caligiuri's left footed half volley from 30 yards somehow found the right corner of the net. Forty years after the defeat of England in the 1950 World Cup, arguably the greatest upset in World Cup history, the U.S. finally returned to the Finals.

While the party in anticipation of play in Italy was joyous, the reception was not. Czechoslovakia soundly defeated the U.S. 5-1 in the first match. Against Italy the U.S. held on for dear life, losing 1-0, and met Austria in the final group match, losing 2-1. While the team had not been successful on the field in terms of results, they had gained some respect for the hard working attitude of the players. They had been embarrassed by the loss to the Czechs and had produced much better efforts in the final two matches. Several of the players were approached by European club

Michele Akers (10) has helped propel women's soccer to the sports pages of this country leading the U.S. women's team to triumphs at the World Championship in China (1991) as well as the first Olympic soccer title in 1996.

(photo by Perry McIntyre, Jr.)

teams to sign professional contracts and the experience they would gain in playing full-time professional soccer would be important for the U.S. National Team in the future.

THE 1990's

One of the major attractions of youth soccer in the United States had been its coeducational nature. Boys and girls played the game together in younger age groups and, as the girls matured, teams, leagues, then high school teams, and, finally, college teams were formed for female players. The U.S. was the major force behind international women's soccer and the U.S. Soccer Federation brought the idea of a Women's World Championship to FIFA. In 1991 China hosted the first edition of this international tournament. The U.S. team, composed of solid defending players and outstanding attacking players like Michelle Akers, Carin Jennings, April Heinrichs, Christine Lilly, and Mia Hamm slammed goal after goal on their march to

immortality as the first to win the FIFA Women's World Championship.

During this time Francisco Marcos organized a regional league, the Southwest Independent Soccer League. It was the small league, small expenses, part-time player concept that many believed could form a basis for a future full-time national soccer league. Between the late 80's and 1994 the league grew from these modest beginnings to an interconnecting group of leagues, the United States Inter-regional Soccer Leagues, with 80+ teams, split into a professional division, an amateur division, and a women's division. Teams played on a regional basis, with some cross-over league play, but always on a limited regionalized concept to keep expenses small. The league set team budgetary guidelines and the league-winning teams gathered together at a central site for a long weekend of matches to determine the USISL champion.

As the world began looking toward the 1994 World Cup, English club teams returned to the continent, but it was the Dutch club Ajax, with a flowing style reminiscent of Holland of the 70's that had risen as the top team and style to copy. In the U.S. preparation for the World Cup brought renewed interest for a national league of international quality. As a part of the bidding process for the awarding of the World Cup, the U.S. Soccer Federation had stated its goal of having a true national league in place by 1994. While much discussion and planning had transpired, the league was not playing in 1994. The Federation, now name changed to U.S. Soccer, stated its desire to focus the needed energies on organizing the "...best World Cup in history." according to U.S. Soccer President Alan Rothenberg.

The world converged on the United States for the last 24-team World Cup, as France will host a 32-team tournament in 1998. Rothenberg's comments proved accurate: there was greater attendance, greater excitement and a historic final, if only for negative reasons. The 1994 Champion Brazil won in penalty kicks after 120 minutes of scoreless soccer in front of 104,000 fans at the Rose Bowl in Pasadena, CA. Games were staged all across the States, from Boston, New York, and Washington in the northeast, Orlando in the south, Dallas, Detroit, and, Chicago in the midwest, to San Francisco and Los Angeles in the west. Crowds were of historic proportions and play was as open and free flowing as any World Cup since 1970. The "light-weights" such as the US, South Korea, and Saudi Arabia again added extra dimension to the competition, with South Korea's match against defending champion Germany in the first round a standout. The South Koreans were superbly conditioned for the heat of Dallas and Germany was fortunate to escape a 3-2 victor as the final 15 minutes saw an effervescent Korean team running at a tiring German side. Germany was lucky to escape embarrassment, and later were

Romario proved to be the offensive spark Brazil needed as it claimed the 1994 World Cup which was played in the U.S. to record-breaking crowds. (photo by Perry McIntrye, Jr.)

knocked out by a Bulgarian squad ably and excitedly directed by Georgi Hagi.

The history of this great game keeps evolving as great teams and players rise and fall. The world game, and the game in the US, have many precious moments. In the States, a visit to Oneonta, New York and the National Soccer Hall of Fame, to whom this author is indebted for research support, is a grand walk through the many great days of American soccer.

At the end of day, as the English say, it is the great game of soccer that creates it own history. Albert Camus, the noted existential philosopher and writer has written: "I quickly learned that the ball never came to you where you expected it. This helped me in life... For, after many years in which the world has afforded me many experiences, what I most surely know in the long run about morality and the obligations of men, I owe to sport, I learned it with R.U.A.[the University of Algiers soccer team]. That in short, is why R.U.A. cannot die. Let us preserve it. Let us preserve this great and good image of our youth. It will keep watch over yours, as well." *France Football*, 1957

REFERENCES

America's Soccer Heritage: A History of the Game, Sam Foulds and Paul Harris, Soccer for Americans, 1979

Soccer! The Game and The World Cup, Elio Trifari and Charles Miers, Editors, Rizzoli International Publications/La Gazzetta dello Sport, 1994

The Complete Book of Soccer/Professional Hockey, Gene Brown, Editor, Arno Press, New York, 1980

1976, First Edition, *The Complete Handbook of Soccer*, Zander Hollander, Editor, Signet Books, New York, 1976

1977 Edition, *The Complete Handbook of Soccer*, Zander Hollander, Editor, Signet Books, New York, 1977

1978 Edition, *The Complete Handbook of Soccer*, Zander Hollander, Editor, Signet Books, New York, 1978

1980 Season, *The Complete Handbook of Soccer*, Zander Hollander, Editor, Signet Books, New York, 1980

The Encyclopedia of World Soccer, Richard Henshaw, New Republic Books, 1979

The Faber Book of Soccer, Ian Hamilton, editor, Faber and Faber, 1992

The Simplest Game: The Intelligent American's Guide to the World of Soccer, Paul Gardner, Little, Brown, and Company, 1976

The Sunday Times History of The World Cup, Brian Glanville, Times Newspapers Limited, 1973

World Cup España '82, Franz Beckenbauer, Transtel Publishing, Inc., 1982

⚽

THE FORMATION OF THE NATIONAL SOCCER COACHES ASSOCIATION OF AMERICA
Joseph Bean and Tim Schum

The National Coaches Association of America was conceived by a small band of college coaches who were concerned that their interests were not being met by the existent Intercollegiate Soccer Football Association. That largely Eastern-based group met annually for the purpose of recognizing the outstanding collegiate team of that particular year. The coaches also discussed rule changes as well as a general exchange of ideas. It was during the January, 1941 ICSFA meeting that the idea of forming the National Soccer Coaches Association of America was conceived.

Documented accounts indicate that the founding coaches present included: John Brock, Springfield (MA) College; Howard DeNike, East Stroudburg (PA) State Teachers College; Walter McCloud, Trinity College (CT); Tom Taylor, United States Naval Academy; Richard Schmelzer, Rensselaer Polytechnic Institute (NY); Walter Leeman, Yale University; William Benner, West Chester State Teachers College (PA); Earle Waters, West Chester State Teachers College (PA); Tom Dent, Dartmouth College; Robert Dunn, Swarthmore College and Bill Jeffrey, Penn State University.

The first annual meeting of the NSCAA took place at the Pennsylvania Hotel in New York City in 1942.

These men agreed the following objectives would guide NSCAA:
• encourage the development of the sport of soccer in the secondary schools, colleges, and universities;
• develop mechanisms to better publicize the sport;
• organize clinics to better teach the sport;
• evaluate current teaching methods and improve them to make for better teaching of the sport;
• seek to enroll more soccer coaches in the NSCAA to better achieve the above goals.

These goals have been the focal point of preceding generations of soccer coaches. Many new programs were instituted to enhance each objective. Along the way, internal changes took place to further advance the cause. As an example, after 25 years without an executive director, one was appointed on a part-time basis in 1970. This was Bob DiGrazia from the University of California-Berkeley. Bob continued in this role until 1981, when Dr. John McKeon undertook the responsibilities. John, in turn, was succeeded by current full-time executive director, Jim Sheldon, in January of 1993.

These three men, along with all the past presidents and officers have provided the energy and leadership to assure the NSCAA's steady growth. From the 1941 membership of less than 100 the NSCAA has expanded to a membership of over 11,000 by 1996.

Part of the lure to coaches for NSCAA membership have been the programs that have been introduced over the years that have appeal to coaches:

• The establishment of a membership committee in 1941, under chairman Walter E. McCloud;
• *"The Newsletter"* published in 1941, editor Larry Briggs, University of Massachusetts
• First Oscar Award presented in 1944, John D. Brock, first recipient;
• Oscar Award renamed Honor Award in 1949, first recipient Bill Jeffrey;
• All-American program introduced in 1949, Dr. Fred Hollaway established the selection guidelines;
• Florida Soccer Forum held in 1952, forerunner of NSCAA Coaching Academy;
• Film Library established in 1953 with Glenn Warner, the initiator;
• *Soccer Journal* replaces *"The Newsletter"* with Don Yonker the editor;
• First "marketing" venture, 1957 - Wheaties Sports Federation gives $1,000 annually to NSCAA for eight years to promote its All-America team;
• Dual Honor Awards presented for first time in 1957 with Earle Waters and Allison Marsh the recipients;
• Soccer Camp phenomena begins in 1961;
• First NSCAA conventions held outside New York City with the 1972 meeting in St. Louis;
• Sportcraft Coach-of-the-Year program established in 1973;
• First major marketing agreement signed in 1978 with Dr. Pepper the All America sponsor;

- Film library transferred in 1978 to Modern Talking Picture;
- *Soccer Journal* changes editors and format in 1980 with Tim Schum replacing Don Yonker as editor;
- Film Library replaced with affiliation with a video-tape library system;
- New NSCAA Constitution in force in 1980 with Bob Nye first set to serve as the first two term president;
- Membership doubles in decade - 1,100 in 1970 to over 2,300 in 1980 and triples to over 9,000 in 1990;
- National Advisory Board established in 1980;
- National Coaching Academy established in 1984.

All of these events have helped to establish the NSCAA as the premier coaching fraternity in the world. No other sport can equal in number of members or programs sponsored by NSCAA since its 1941 origins. The future is only limited by the imagination and zeal of our current and future NSCAA leadership.

NSCAA HISTORICAL HIGHLIGHTS

Following are notes taken from the book *The First 50 Years, 1941-1991, The History of the National Soccer Coaches Association of America* on the 50 year history of the National Soccer Coaches Association of America as written by Joe Bean and Tim Schum.

The notes serve as benchmarks in terms of the personalities and activities of the NSCAA over its half century of service to soccer. They also mark trends in the game in this country over that same period of time.

1941 - A Year to Remember

NSCAA originates at post-Intercollegiate Soccer Football Association meeting of ten coaches at Harvard Club in New York on January 13, 1941...Tom Dent of Dartmouth College credited with original suggestion of forming a coaches association...John Brock of Springfield College elected first president...four of the original ten charter members are living including Don Baker (Ursinus); Charles Scott (Pennsylvania); John Squires (Connecticut); and Howard DeNike (East Stroudsburg State)...167 members joined NSCAA in 1941 paying $1 dues...13 working committees were formed in 1941...Richard Schmelzer headed the All-America committee...June 7, 1941 marked the first issue of the NSCAA in-house publication, *The Newsletter*. It was 14 pages and published at the University of Massachusetts under the editorship of Larry Briggs...indoor soccer being played at Madison Square Garden...

1941-50

Development and Vision

1942 - Earle "Muddy" Waters elected president of NSCAA and serves the only three year term in association annals...he and other NSCAA member coaches serve in Navy and teach soccer as part of the physical

Larry Briggs edited the first Newsletter for the NSCAA while the soccer coach at UMass.

training in the V5 Program. Among their subjects is Gerald Ford!...Commander Tom Hamilton (later to be athletic director and football coach at the U.S. Naval Academy), first recipient of the Oscar Award (fore-runner of the NSCAA Honor Award) for his support of soccer in the V5 training program...total association income for year was $65.50 - expenses totaled $49.88...there were 102 members, not all were paying members!...*Newsletter*, edited by Larry Briggs, mailed to all members...

1943 - Thomas Taylor, coach at the U.S. Naval Academy, named Oscar Award winner. He worked closely with Navy V5 program...first NSCAA constitution written by T. Fred Holloway, soccer coach at SUNY Cortland...annual meeting continued in New York City...

1944 - Waters concludes third term as NSCAA president...John T. Brock selected as Oscar Award winner...NSCAA clinic at the William Penn Charter School in Philadelphia attracts 500 people...

1945 - Richard Schmelzer, coach at RPI (NY), elected third president of NSCAA...all soccer coaches serving in the armed forces are collectively honored as the Oscar Award winners...Lydia Lindgren of Baldwin (NY) first acknowledged women's coach, leading Bridgehampton (NY) boys to the area soccer title...

1946 - Robert Dunn, Swarthmore College, is elected NSCAA president...Richard Schmelzer becomes editor of *The Newsletter* with Larry Briggs publisher...Dr. G Randolph Manning, president of USSFA, named winner of the Oscar Award. Only USSF president to receive the award...NSCAA agrees to annually publish a list of acceptable referees in *The Newsletter*...first questionnaire on rule changes appears in *The Newsletter* authored by Howard DeNike...

1947 - Scottish-born Douglas Stewart, coach at Penn, who edited the *Soccer Guide* for 27 years, named Oscar winner...Larry Briggs elected NSCAA president...Don Yonker coaches Philadelphia schoolboys in their annual fall match with New York City counterparts...

1948 - Bill Jeffrey, coach at Penn State and chief clinician for the NSCAA, elected president of the group...James Walder of Philadelphia, becomes the first of two referees selected to receive the Oscar Award...Fred Holloway system for selection of players to the NSCAA All-America teams is introduced...a list of acceptable referees is published in *The Newsletter* with ratings including such items as "partially doubted", "times not wanted" as well as a list of schools "blackballing" an official!...

1949 - John Wood of Oak Park (IL) High School becomes the first high school coach to serve as president of NSCAA. He later became coach of the U.S. Olympic team in Helsinki...dues were raised to $2...the "Oscar Award" is renamed the Honor Award with Bill Jeffrey the first recipient of the "new" award...the first advertisement appears in *The Newsletter*; Doss Soccer Supply Company advertisement ($90) covers the entire cost of the February issue (three yearly issues) - $78.62!...

1950 - Pat O'Connor (Carnegie Institute of Technology) elected president... Bill Jeffrey coaches U.S. team to historic 1-0 upset of England in World Cup in Brazil...membership is less than 300...George Ritchie of Wethersfield High School (CT) becomes the first high school coach to receive the Honor Award. George organized, coached and officiated soccer in new England...a visual aids library instituted by NSCAA under the leadership of Glenn Warner (U.S. Naval Academy)...soccer officials hold their annual meeting in conjunction with NSCAA for the first time...Hugh Barron of Springfield (MA) heads the new secondary schools committee of NSCAA and first reports of activity for that group. *The Newsletter*...balance in treasury is $150...

1951 - 1960

Growth and Innovation

1951 - Two Ivy League coaches honored, with Bruce Munro (Harvard) elected president and Tom Dent

Glenn Warner of Navy was both the President of NSCAA and recipient of its Honor Award in 1953

(Dartmouth) named Honor Award winner...Hyde Shoes places first full page advertisement in *The Newsletter*...

1952 - T. Fred Holloway is elected president of NSCAA...coaches gather in Sarasota, Florida for the first NSCAA-sponsored "Soccer Forum" under the leadership of Glenn Warner...Larry Briggs winner of the Honor Award...membership announced as 261...

1953 - Glenn Warner becomes the only person to both serve as president of NSCAA and receive the Honor Award in the same year...Richard Schmelzer resigns as editor of *The Newsletter* to take over as editor of *Soccer Guide* with Don Yonker (Drexel) to serve as new editor of the NSCAA publication...dues raised to $4 for college coaches; $2 for secondary school coaches. (a $1 membership for college students was also instituted)...Midwest Soccer League plays a season without the offside rule...Matt Busby of Manchester United visits U.S. for series of coaching clinics..

1954 - Carlton Reilly (Brooklyn College) serves as NSCAA president...E.Paul Patton, USSF administrator from Pennsylvania, selected as Honor Award winner...Cliff Stevenson's Oberlin team on 32-game win streak...Newsletter 'keymen' serve as unofficial editorial board for publication...NSCAA institutes requirement that membership by coach needed in or-

The first NCAA Soccer Tournament was staged in 1959. Here soccer officials George Moll and Harry Rodgers (striped shirts) pose with (from left) Charlie Scott (Penn), Don Minnegan (Towson State), Doyle Royal (Maryland), LaRue Frain (President-West Chester University), Mel Lorback (West Chester), Bob Dunn (Swarthmore), Mickey Cochrane (Johns Hopkins) and Ray Kraft (NCAA Rules). Game matched Maryland and West Chester with the latter winning 1-0.

(photo courtesy of Bowling Green State University Office of Public Relations)

der for selection of player for the NSCAA All-American team...Temple University named mythical champions of college soccer...Glenn Warner and Irv Schmid (Springfield) give coaching clinics to armed forces stationed in Europe...100 youth soccer teams playing in St. Louis under direction of Bob Guelker of the CYC...first article on coaching ethics written for *The Newsletter* by Eric DeGroat...

1955 - DeGroat becomes NSCAA president...John Wood is the Honor Award winner...six regional college teams serve as basis for NSCAA All-American team...films from the NSCAA library priced at $1 or $2 (if over 100 miles from director Chris Chachis at Orange County Community College {NY})...NSCAA and ISAA agree to jointly sponsor clinics which will cover both coaching and officiating...Max Doss of Soccer Sport Supply publishes first soccer equipment catalog...

1956 - Charles Scott elected president and Richard Schmelzer receives the NSCAA Honor Award...the number of youth soccer players in Baltimore grew four times between 1954-56 while St. Louis now fielding 219 youth teams...FIFA experimenting with kicking from touch in Finland...SUNY-Brockport and Penn State crowned mythical collegiate champions...for the first time certificates are awarded to all players selected

to the NSCAA all-regional teams in the All-American selection process...

1957 - John Eiler (East Stroudsburg) elected as NSCAA president and establishes the first ethics committee...first marketing agreement is signed by NSCAA with the Wheaties Sport Foundation funding the NSCAA All-America Team; agreement remains in effect until 1965...NSCAA still meeting in New York City with Statler Hotel the site as first joint winners of the Honor Award are announced. Allison W. "Eli" Marsh (Amherst College) and Earle "Muddy" Waters are the selections... Waters selects new title for NSCAA publication with *The Newsletter* now becoming *Soccer Journal*...Waters retires form West Chester and Mel Lorback named as his replacement...Trinity College (CT) selected as top collegiate team...

1958 - Huntley Parker, Jr. (SUNY-Brockport) elected president of NSCAA. He and John Eiler are the only coaches to serve terms as presidents of both NSCAA and ISAA...work underway to establish All-American teams for both the junior college and secondary schools levels of play...Florida Forum revived in St. Petersburg...T. Fred Holloway named to receive the Honor Award... Richard Schmelzer resigns as editor of *Soccer Guide*; committee functions to edit publication thereafter... Ted Chambers is the new coach at Howard University... Tom Fleck (West Chester) and Cliff McCrath (Wheaton) are members of the collegiate All-America team...NSCAA has 278 members on rolls...semi-circular penalty kicks are used in NCAA play...5400 youth playing in St. Louis...

1959 - Don Yonker NSCAA president as membership hits 500 mark... Robert Dunn named Honor Award winner...St. Louis under Bob Guelker wins the inaugural NCAA Soccer Tournament while the first NAIA tourney is staged at Slippery Rock under leadership of Jim Egli, Pratt Institute the winner...issues of foreign players and amateurism dominate collegiate soccer...

1960 - Dr. John Squires NSCAA president sees need for more clinics and films and better coaching for youth soccer...Isadore "Doe" Yavits (Ithaca College) receives Honor Award in poem form from Mickey Cochrane... NSCAA meetings in NYC hold two session at same hour for the first time... waterproof English Surridge ball makes U.S. debut...Paul Sanderson (Suffield Academy), head of secondary schools committee, signs up 50 new high school members... membership falls to 419...balance in treasury is $3,390...

1961-1970

Change and Challenge

1961 – Heinz Lenz assumes NSCAA presidency...registration fee for the annual meeting at New York's Manhattan Hotel is $1...Carlton Reilly named Honor Award winner, cited as "Dean of New York City Coaches"...International Soccer League in NYC makes debut under Bill Cox who supports NSCAA secondary schools committee's work...Max Doss supplies NSCAA emblem patches to all All-American players, including first junior college selections...first junior college post-season tournament held at Orange CCC (NY)...*Soccer Journal* publishes first summer edition, now four issues each year... West Chester wins NCAA title over St. Louis...Mal Simon of Newark Engineering (NJ) writes articles on spring training for collegiate teams

1962 - Marvin Allen (North Carolina) named NSCAA president...Joe Guennel who was instrumental in the growth of soccer in the midwest, selected as Honor Award winner...in addition to the NSCAA patch, All-America players receive a gift of a pair of Hyde soccer shoes...Don Yonker founds the first soccer camp in this country, the International Soccer Camp in Honesdale (PA)... Tom Dent passes away...summer issue of *Soccer Journal* focuses on secondary schools news...Mickey Cochrane (Johns Hopkins) begins to compile collegiate records, the first being longest win skeins...new NCAA College Division Tournament debuts with Denison College (OH) the first champion...

1963 - James Reed (Princeton) serves as NSCAA president...John Kalloch (MA) named Honor Award recipient for work as both a coach and official...Max

Doss and Soccer Sport Supply become the first company to exhibit at the annual New York City meeting...Joe Machnik (LIU) selected to the collegiate All-America team as is Bill Vieth (St. Louis). Bill's son, Tim, will become a high school All-America player in 1988!...Joe Guennel heading youth soccer movement in Colorado...

1964 - M.W. "Chic" Jacobus of Kingswood School (CT) becomes the fourth high school coach elected NSCAA president...the annual meeting attracts 225 coaches; membership estimated at 700...Don Yonker is the Honor Award winner...the National Intercollegiate Soccer Officials Association of America formed...Joe Morrone, secretary-treasurer of the new organization, edits the group's newsletter...over 350 secondary school coaches have joined NSCAA since 1959...the throw-in from touch returns to collegiate soccer...

1965 - Irv Schmid (Springfield College) serves as president of NSCAA and group hires a part-time executive director in Gordon Anziano who is located in Springfield (MA)...John Eiler named winner of Honor Award...NSCAA job placement service initiated...Ted Chambers retires from coaching at Howard University...Gene and Walt Chyzowych open All-America Soccer Camp...the University of Buenos Aires pays playing visit to U.S. and plays several matches on east coast area...

1966 - Alden "Whitey" Burnham (Darthmouth) becomes the fourth Ivy League coach to serve as NSCAA president...Bill Jeffrey passes away at annual meeting in New York City...founding member Charles Scott receives the Honor Award...seven summer soccer camps in operation...two professional leagues begin play in US, the National Professional Soccer League and the North American Soccer League...Pele makes U.S. playing debut with Santos in New York City...West Germany-England World Cup finale draws outstanding television ratings...James Walder receives first NISOA Honor Award...

1967 - James Bly (Duke) dies while serving as NSCAA president, is succeeded by Stu Parry (Akron) who fulfills the Bly term and also for 1968...Irv Schmid, mentor to over 100 coaches while at Springfield College, is the Honor Award winner...Harry Rodgers appointed NCAA rules interpreter...28 films available from NSCAA film library...Walter Winterbottom of English FA featured speaker at annual NSCAA meeting...NSCAA membership reported near 2000 mark...Joe Morrone travels to Poland and writes article on Polish goalkeeper training for *Soccer Journal*...

1968 - President Parry reports that membership has dropped to about 900...Huntley Parker, Jr. named Honor Award winner...Colin Robson of England writes on grid training for *Soccer Journal*...Peter Green, Ltd. advertising in magazine for first time...first NJSCAA-sponsored championship won by Florissant

NSCAA stalwarts shown in NSCAA archive photo. From left, Bill Jeffery, Charles Scott, Harry Rodgers, and James Walder. Rodgers and Scott are the only officials to receive the NSCAA Honor Award and, combined, officiated over 100 years of soccer.

CC (MO)...Phil Woosnam and the Atlanta Chiefs (NASL) conduct 443 clinics...Joe Morrone at Middlebury takes team on whirlwind, 16-game tour of seven European countries, including Russia...

1969 - Mickey Cochrane becomes NSCAA president...NSCAA memorabilia to be housed at Haverford College...honorary memberships to be awarded any 20-year member...secretary-treasurer office to be divided per constitutional change...collegiate soccer 100 years old...Bob DiGrazia serving as NSCAA executive secretary...membership now 1200...Marvin Hassell of the English FA offers first USSFA coaching courses in San Diego and St. Louis...

1970 - Mel Schmid (Trenton State, NJ) elected NSCAA president...Harry Rodgers becomes the second referee to receive the NSCAA Honor Award...Lincoln Phillips helping unretired Ted Chambers at Howard University...Wisconsin-Green Bay televises its game with the Air Force Academy...NSCAA executive board includes representatives from the secondary schools and junior colleges...World Cup from Mexico shown on closed circuit basis at New York's Madison Square Garden...

1971-80

Marketing Vision and Constitutional Change

1971 - Frank Nelson of Nyack High School (NY) becomes NSCAA president...Donald Minnegan of Towson State (MD) selected for the NSCAA Honor Award...Jimmy Reed retires after 40 years of coaching at Princeton...NSCAA dues increased to $10...first NSCAA Junior College All-America team announced...Dick Schmelzer retires from RPI...Ted

Chambers takes Howard to the NCAA soccer title...Bill Brew of Quinnipiac heads first NSCAA ethics committee...ISFSA and NSCAA each contribute $1000 to underwrite establishment of USSF coaching schools...

1972 - Warren Swanson, Mitchell Junior College (CT), becomes youngest NSCAA president at age 36. He also will be the only junior college coach to hold the position...St. Louis becomes the first city other than New York to host a NSCAA convention...John McKeon and Al Miller arrange charter flight for east coast members for $72 - round trip!...NSCAA film library expands to west coast...first NSCAA information booklet printed as aid to membership...first Secondary Schools All-America team selected...Jimmy Reed selected as Honor Award winner...Carlton Reilly passes away...*Soccer America* debuts...Colonel William Anders of the Apollo 8 Mission receives the first NSCAA Honorary All-America Award...first ISAA Senior Bowl played in Orlando with Wayne Sunderland organizing the game...reprints of articles from the English soccer publication Football Academy appear in *Soccer Journal*...ISFA weekly ratings of collegiate teams underway...collegiate games now played in halves.

1973 - Dr. John McKeon (East Stroudsburg) serves as NSCAA President...Dr. John Squires presented the Honor Award. General William Westmoreland receives the Honorary All-America Award... Sportcraft, Ltd. becomes sponsor of the NSCAA Coach of the Year program and Bob Guelker of SIU Edwardsville is the first COY winner. Bob leads team to first NCAA

College Division Tournament title...Bob Robinson appointed NSCAA treasurer...Wayne Sunderland selected as first recipient of ISAA Bill Jeffery Award for college soccer...T. Fred Holloway retires from coaching...Al Miller leads Philadelphia Atoms to NASL title in team's first season...Dettmar Cramer conducts USSF coaching schools...first National Christian College Athletic Association Tournament held at Messiah College (PA)...Quincy College and coach Jack MacKenzie travel to Brazil on playing tour...

1974 - Mel Lorback (West Chester State) is NSCAA president...annual meeting held in Boston...Alden "Whitey" Burnham is the Honor Award winner...Dave Ross (Suffolk CC (NY)) is the first NSCAA/Sportcraft junior college COY while Ron Gilbert is the first NSCAA/Sportcraft secondary schools COY...*Soccer World* and *Soccer Monthly* magazines make debut in U.S. ... Partners of the Americas soccer exchange program with Brazil in full swing...Frank Longo and Tony Schinto lead group of midwest schoolboys on playing tour in Brazil...SUNY-Brockport wins the first NCAA Division III title...out-of-season play by New Jersey schoolboys restricted by state edict...overtime periods added to collegiate play...

1975 - Sam Porch (Glassboro State (Rowan College), NJ) serves as NSCAA president and has establishment of a coaching code of ethics as a principal objective of his term of office...Bob Baptisa (Wheaton College) selected to receive the Honor Award...annual convention held in Chicago...Fred Parker hired as attorney for NSCAA to ensure due process in matters dealing with ethical conduct of coaches...Pele joins the New York Cosmos...Ted Chambers concludes 50 years of coaching and teaching at Howard University...Dettmar Cramer leaves U.S. National Team coaching position...Don Yonker learns German to better translate coaching articles from the German magazine *Kicker*...

1976 - Dr. Fred Taube (SUNY-Cortland) is the NSCAA president...convention held in Philadelphia as that city and the U.S. celebrated the bicentennial...'Chic' Jacobus cited with NSCAA Honor Award...Joe Machnik conducts the first goalkeeping camp... "Coaching to Win" published by Don Yonker and Alex Weide...experimental regular season game using soccer-lacrosse-hockey rules is played between Western Maryland and Washington College (MD)...Glenn Warner retires at Navy as does Marvin Allen at North Carolina...NSCAA Constitution revised with USSF granted a seat on its governing board...

1977 - Terry Jackson (Weslyan University (CT)) ascends to the NSCAA presidency as annual convention is held in San Francisco...Bob Guelker selected to receive the Honor Award... Don Yonker retires from coaching at Drexel.. NSCCA clinic features England's

Sir Alf Ramsey...Stan Startzell is the new director of soccer for Special Olympics, Inc...ISFAA name change to ISAA...

1978 - Joe Bean (Wheaton College) serves as president with marketing matters and constitutional revision as the primary focus of his team...Dr. Pepper signed to sponsor All-America program...the film library transferred to commercial firm, Modern Talking Pictures (IL)...Mickey Cochrane receives the Honor Award in Boston...both Mickey and John Eiler (East Stroudsburg) retire from coaching...NASL Marketing's Richard Luppi designs new NSCAA logo...first "Letter to the Editor" section appears in *Soccer Journal*...first Dallas Cup is contested...first Ivy League title for women won by Brown University...

1979-Miller Bugliari (Pingry School, NJ) becomes the last president to serve a one year term of office...convention held in Atlanta...Ted Chambers of Howard University presented the Honor Award...new NSCAA Constitution ratified and lengthens terms of office while expanding the Board of Directors...30- and 40- year membership pins are awarded at Philadelphia convention...joint NSCAA-ISAA effort underway to write the coaching code of ethics...3455 secondary schools playing soccer, a 51% increase since 1970...Joe Palone retires at Army while soccer field at Brown is dedicated to Cliff Stevenson...NSCAA membership approaching 2000...

1981-90

Providing a Base For the 21st Century

1980 - Tim Schum named editor of *Soccer Journal*, replacing Don Yonker who retires after 27 years as head of the magazine. New monthly format announced...Yonker is the featured speaker at luncheon before play of the 75th Harvard-Haverford soccer match in Philadelphia in September. Harvard-Haverford is recognized as the first intercollegiate soccer match...Partners of the Americas soccer exchange program is disbanded...Donald Baker, long-time coach at Ursinus College and one of the founding members of NSCAA, presented with the Honor Award...Bob Nye, college of Wooster coach, operating under the new NSCAA Constitution, becomes the first two-term President since Earle Waters...John McKeon replaces Bob DiGrazia as the NCSAA executive director...membership dues now $25 with 2300 members on rolls...separate Honor Award and All-America Banquets held for the first time in association annals...Philadelphia convention sets attendance records...Oneonta (NY) begins work to establish a Soccer Hall of Fame under direction of Albert Colone...January issue of *SJ* also serve as convention guide for Houston meeting. It includes first four color advertising in NSCAA history with full page adverts by W.H. Brine and Champion Products gracing the magazine...San Francisco wins the NCAA Division I title...Rocco Montano named NISOA Honor Award

Long-time Journal editor Don Yonker (center) is shown receiving a plaque with the cover of the first issue he edited depicted on the cover at the 1984 NSCAA Convention in Philadelphia. Wife Doris is on the left while current editor Tim Schum is on the right. (photo by Thomas Costello)

winner...1980 presents the first year of Metropolitan Life's sponsorship of the Coach of the Year Program and also the first year for Dr. Pepper as sponsor of the All-America Award program.

1981 - The United States Youth Soccer Association and NCSAA agree to jointly sponsor a series of youth coaching clinics in each of the eight new NSCAA regional areas in 1981. Joe Morrone will chair the program...Joe appears on the cover of SJ along with son Joe, Jr, winner of the 1981 Herman Award for outstanding collegiate play...and NSCAA now operating with 19 member national Advisory Board with eight officers; eight regional representatives and three at large representatives...the first color cover for SJ features members of the First Girls' Secondary Schools All-America team; a Girls' College All-American team is also selected for the first time ...NSCAA charges first time members a fee of $15 with dues thereafter at $25 a year...Max Doss of Soccer Sport Supply honored in Houston for his long-time support of NSCAA...Larry King named NISOA Honor Award winner...the NSCAA All-America team structure is expanded to honor male collegiate players at the Division I, II, III and NAIA levels of play for the first time...Walt Chyzowych serving as head clinician for NSCAA after resigning as U.S. National Coach...NSCAA membership booklet now sponsored by Sportcraft, Ltd...first complete NSCAA treasurer's report published in March issue of SJ. Overall income is $99,653.45, leaving balance of $3,544!...Charles Matlack is named winner of the NSCAA Honor Award following retirement from coaching at Earlham

College (IN)...NISOA holds first summer training camp for its officials at Elizabethtown College (PA)...NSCAA becomes incorporated in Pennsylvania as a non-profit organization...Peter Gooding, Region I rep, conducts regional convention in December for New England area...first NSCAA election ballot is carried in *SJ*...

1982 - McDonald's takes over the sponsorship of the NSCAA All-America program from Dr. Pepper and the program is expanded to include a Youth All-America team of 26 players on the boy's team and 18 players on the girl's team. It is expected that 280 players will be honored by 1983...Bill Thomsen and members of the Canadian Soccer Association staff fill in at the last minute at the Chicago Convention...Tim Schum serving as both editor of *Soccer Journal* and President of NSCAA. He states that NSCAA membership goal is 3000 by the end of 1983...50 exhibitors display their wares in Chicago...NSCAA working with the YMCA organization to stage coaching clinics for that organization's youth soccer program. Nearly 275,000 youngsters playing in YMCA-sponsored programs...the NCAA will sponsor a women's championship for the first time in 1982...Joe Barriskill, longtime USSF stalwart, passes away...Nels Dahlquist receives the NISOA Honor Award in his native Chicago...Walt Chyzowych named recipient of the ISAA Bill Jeffrey Award...NSCAA operating budget passes the $100,000 mark for the first time...NSCAA/ISAA Ethics Committee under chairman Dr. Greg Myers completes and publishes its Code of Ethics for coaches...Whitey Burnham resigns as chairman of the

Walter Chyzowych was head clinician for the NSCAA
during his long association with the game in this country.
He was the recipient of the Bill Jeffrey Award for
contributions to U.S. collegiate soccer.

NSCAA Collegiate All-America Committee follow-ing 12 years of service. He is succeeded by Terry Jackson...new NSCAA Awards Committees to moni-tor the All-America program and the Coach of the Year program now involve over 60 members...58 coaches now honored by Metropolitan Life as part of its Coach of the Year sponsorship program...agreement signed with U.S. Army to sponsor weekend clinics throughout the U.S. at key bases as well as honor high school MVPs in their schools. A high school all-star game will also be sponsored by the Army in conjunc-tion with NSCAA...Harry Keough resigns as coach at St. Louis. Harry is honored as the recipient of the NSCAA Honor Award in Orlando...

1983 - NSCAA convention staged in Orlando and the first outdoor clinic sessions in NSCAA history are held. 60 companies exhibit in Orlando. First coaches tournament held at convention...600 youth coaches now members of NSCAA as membership climbs over the 3000 mark...Chris Chacis, long-time NSCAA worker at the junior college level, passes away...NSCAA and Ryan's International announce

discount on NSCAA soccer clothing...Dennis Long, President of Anheuser-Busch, named winner of rein-stituted NSCAA Honorary All-America Award in Orlando...NSCAA/Metropolitan Life COY program expands to honor coaches of women's teams at colle-giate and secondary school levels of play...NSCAA members Bill Shellenberger, Walter Bahr, Steve Negoesco and Ray Buss celebrate 300th coaching victories...U.S. Army stages 10 nationwide spring and fall clinics for NSCAA...photos of high school cham-pionship teams are published in *SJ*...USSF offers new two-week National License for coaches...NSCAA of-fers interested members a chance to attend the NISOA Camp in Elizabethtown (PA) as a means of improv-ing communication between coaches and officials...*Kick*, a monthly magazine published by NASL Marketing, makes nationwide debut... McDonald's pulls out of All-America team sponsor-ship with NSCAA retaining role...a NSCAA commit-tee to design a residential and non-residential coach-ing program meets in April in Chicago and includes Peter Gooding, Jerry Yeagley, Jim Lennox and Bob Gansler. It names the curriculum the "NSCAA Acad-emy Program" and it is approved by the NSCAA National Advisory Board in June. Jim Lennox (Hartwick College) is named the Director of Coach-ing for the NSCAA Academy Program...Metropolitan Life to expand its NSCAA COY program by honor-ing a junior college women's team coach...a youth coach representative will be elected to the NSCAA BOD for 1984...NSCAA agrees to co-sponsor a new award with NISOA. It will be named the NSCAA/ NISOA Merit award...U.S. gears up to host 1984 Olympic soccer at four sites...a "Medical Aspects of Soccer" pre-convention conference is added to 1984 NSCAA Convention agenda in Philadelphia...over 1500 NSCAA coaches present NSCAA/Army MVP Awards to high school seniors throughout the country...sponsorship of men's collegiate soccer teams climbs from 434 to 532.

1984 - Bob DiGrazia named 43rd NSCAA Honor Award winner at annual convention in Philadelphia...former *SJ* editor Don Yonker honored for his 28 years of service with presentation of plaque at Honors Award Banquet...1000 coaches register for meeting with 500 more estimated to have come to the meeting for the All-America Banquet. 550 coaches use pre-registration process...80 exhibitors show soccer wares and area 'sells out' for the first time!...the NSCAA Academy Program is approved at the annual NSCAA Business Meeting...membership climbs to 3200...Clay Berling, publisher of *Soccer America*, is named winner of the NSCAA Honorary All-America Award...the first winner of the NSCAA/NISOA Eth-ics Committee Award is Joe Bean of Wheaton College...Dr. Thomas Fleck becomes the 40th NSCAA President...first NSCAA/U.S. Army National High

School Match debuts at West Point in late June. 2500 fans watch two teams battle to 3-3 tie...2200 MVP Awards made by U.S. Army to high school players. Nearly 3000 coaches attended 10 NSCAA/Army Soccer Clinics program...NSCAA/Met Life Secondary Schools All-America program expands from 33 to 55 players on both the boy's and girl's teams...NSCAA budget over the $200,000 mark...winner of the Bill Jeffrey Award are Owen and Pat Wright for their efforts on behalf of the ISAA Rating Board...Olympic soccer competition in U.S. sees 1.4 million fans flocking to the games, a new record. Soccer outdraws all other sports in terms of attendance...first NSCAA Parent-Coach Certificate Program offered by Ron Quinn and Curt Lauber in Red Hill (PA)...the NSCAA Film Library is disbanded...NSCAA invited to send representative to the High School Federation Rules Committee for the first time...

1985 - NSCAA and U.S. Army kick off third year of weekend clinics program...Duke, Santa Clara University, C.W. Post (NY) and Washington University (MO) hosted residential Academy programs this year...NSCAA Convention in Washington attracts 1025 registrants. 260 attended a Thursday Medical Symposium. 72 companies displayed in the exhibit area. 1050 attended the Honors Award Banquet with Julie Menendez cited as the Honor Award winner. The All-America luncheon honors 175 NSCAA selections with Eunice Kennedy Shriver present to receive the NSCAA Honorary All-America Award. Bill Shellenberger and Tony Shinto are acknowledged as the selections for the NISOA/NSCAA Merit Award...the NASL closes shop in February...NSCAA income climbs over $250,000 mark with 3700 members on books...Irv Schmid retires after 36 years of coaching at Springfield (MA) College with Mickey Cochrane also hanging up his whistle at Bowling Green State University (OH) after 30 years of coaching soccer and lacrosse...former NSCAA Honor Award winners Richard Schmelzer and M.W. "Chic" Jacobus both pass away...in second NSCAA/Army Soccer Classic at West Point, Dan Donigan of East named game MVP as the East wins 3-2 in a match that attracts 5,000 spectators...New Balance Athletic Shoe signs to sponsor the NSCAA All-America program...NSCAA ends agreement with NASL Marketing and elects to form a Marketing Committee to oversee such agreements...issues of *SJ* now 60 pages on a regular basis...final tally shows over 4000 players and coaches attending NSCAA/Army Clinics programs.

1986 - St. Louis Convention well-attended with 925 coaches at the meetings. 71 firms exhibit in St. Louis, setting a new record for booths, 94...Cliff McCrath wins 300th game, Seattle Pacific wins NCAA Division II title and Cliff is selected as NSCAA Honor Award Winner...Bill Jeffrey Award is presented to Dr. Raymond Bernabei of NISOA for his work at upgrad-

Walter Bahr shown during his Penn State coaching days, was a dynamic force both as a player and coach in this country. He received the NSCAA Honor Award in 1987.

ing collegiate officiating in this country while NISOA presents its Honor Award to Mario Donnangelo. NSCAA/NISOA Merit Awards presented to Gene Davis (PA) and Alan King (MA)...Joe Morrone takes over as 41st NSCAA President...tally on NSCAA/Army Soccer Clinics program estimates 4000 coaches and players attending seven sessions in 1985 with seven more planned for 1986....adidas and NSCAA sign discount equipment purchase agreement...NSCAA/New Balance All-America team selections now total 343 players...Oneonta Soccer Hall of Fame raises $500,000 to purchase land for future site development...NSCAA membership climbs to 4200...Bob Guelker dies suddenly in St. Louis...overall seven NSCAA/Army Clinic programs attached a total of 5700 players and coaches to the ten spring and fall offerings...three officials are mandated under new NCAA playing rules...NSCAA residential Academy Programs set for five sites...Paul Sanderson, who led the drive to enroll secondary school coaches with NSCAA, passes away at age 56 in Vermont...the NSCAA/Army Soccer Classic is dropped due to cutbacks in Army recruitment...NSCAA coordinates with the Soccer Industry Council of America on a project which enables coaches to share fund-raising ideas...W.H. Brine continues to sponsor convention indoor soccer tournament for coaches with Boston University the site for the 1987 tourney...Challenge Soccer is again the sponsor for the NSCAA membership program.

1987 - Annual NSCAA Convention held in Boston...Walter Bahr is selected to receive the '86 Honor Award at the meeting...78 exhibitors are on hand as are 1345 registered coaches, a new record... 225 out of a possible 373 NSCAA/New Balance All-America players were in Beantown to accept their awards...President Joe Morrone completes organizational flow chart...Academy residential courses attract 153 coaches in 1986 while non-residential courses enroll 360 coaches...NSCAA membership is 4800 while income for 1986 showed $432,000 taken into association coffers...NSCAA contracts with Trace Video to offer members discounts on video tape purchases...Harry Rodgers reports that he is in his 61st year of soccer officiating...ISAA announces sponsorship of men's and women's Academic All-America Teams...USSF announces it will bid for the 1994 World Cup...Terry Jackson and Ray Buss are recipients of the NSCAA/NISOA Merit Awards...Vince Forst is named winner of the NISOA Honor Award...Bruce Munro passes away at age 71. He was president of NSCAA in 1951...Also passing away were USSF administrator Kurt Lamm and adidas founder, Horst Dassler...153 coaches attend NSCAA Residential Academy summer courses...Steve Negoesco of San Francisco University achieves 400th coaching victory...

1988 - For the first time in 30 years, double winners are announced for the NSCAA Honor Award. John McKeon and Jimmy Mills are so honored at the Washington Convention before an Honors Award Banquet crowd of 1500 persons...a new record 1600 members would register for the meeting and 220 All-America players would assemble for the NSCAA Luncheon...the exhibit area sold out for the second straight year with 116 booths displayed...the Academy residential courses awarded 196 diplomas while 551 coaches participated in the non-residential courses offered by NSCAA...the Board of Directors add a fifth at-large position for women...William Holleman takes office as the 42nd President of NSCAA with membership now at the 5300 mark...NSCAA budget is over $450,000 mark in income...USSF is awarded the World Cup for 1994!...a special topics clinic was staged in Rochester (NY) in May with Jeff Tipping, Anson Dorrance and Doug May the clinicians. 143 coaches attend the weekend clinic...Dorrance becomes the first coach to win both NSCAA/Met Life Coach of Year

Awards for men and women as he is voted Division I men's COY for his work with the North Carolina team...Walter Bahr retires as coach at Penn State...Walt Ersing named winner of Ohio Collegiate Soccer Association's first Honor Award...winner of the Bill Jeffrey Award is Indian's Jerry Yeagley...Eddie Clements receives the NISOA Honor Award while Bill Holleman and Tim Schum receive the NSCAA/NISOA Merit Award...NSCAA reduces membership fee for youth coaches to $15...NSCAA and Gatorade begin fall rating poll for high school boy's teams. Shenendohowa (NY) High School is declared the mythical champion at season's end. Chairman of the effort is Gene Chyzowych of Columbia HS (NJ)...NSCAA/Met Life Women's Division I & II All-America team selected for first time while NSCAA/Met Life Coach of the Year program adds male private/parochial selection to process...

1989 - NSCAA membership now over 6200 mark with an 800-telephone number installed to facilitate NSCAA business...Philadelphia meeting utilizes three hotels and registers over 1500 members...the exhibit area sells out with 68 companies in attendance...over 1850 persons at banquet recognize 47th Honor Award winner Joe Bean of Wheaton College...850 persons gather to honor 210 NSCAA/Met Life All-America performers in Philadelphia...USS.F. President Werner Fricker is honored as the seventh NSCAA Honorary All-America selection for his work in attracting World Cup '94 to the United States...NISOA honors Norman Lord (VA) with its Honor Award for his extensive service to officiating...Fred Schmalz of Evansville receives the Bill Jeffrey Award while the NSCAA/NISOA Merit Award recipients are Ray Cieplik (CT) and Ebbie Dunn (MO)...Al Laverson finishes 41st season as assistant at Drexel...Bill Shellenberger ends 34 years of coaching at Lynchburg College (VA)...Bob Robinson, founder of the Pennsylvania SCA in 1972, is honored by the group with presentation of its Honor Award...286 coaches attended the NSCAA Academy residential courses while 430 coaches enroll in non-residential Academy offers...NSCAA treasurer reports $493,000 in income for 1988...USSF selects Willie Roy and Jerry Yeagley to the Soccer Hall of Fame...Mike Berticelli named NSCAA Director of Coaching, succeeding Jim Lennox in the post...*Soccer International*, a new soccer monthly, makes its U.S. debut...

THE THEORY OF SOCCER

· ·

This chapter will critically examine what soccer coaches should understand in terms of separating the game into its basic principles.

As one views a match what makes for effective soccer and effective soccer players? Author Alan Wade will help us to understand what coaches and spectators alike should look at when trying to discern good soccer from bad.

Obviously the game of soccer is about changes in style, modifications in player roles and transformations in strategy. Coach Wade discusses those developments in the game.

Ian Franks offers a statistical analysis of the game based on his work at determining what is effective soccer from a more objective viewpoint.

Franks' ideas are debated by Wade in the final writing offered in this segment of the book.

In summary, this chapter will set the stage for other works in the book that will help coaches transform the theory into reality by offering the correct methodology needed in order that more productive soccer be the result of the practices undertaken by their teams.

⚽

EFFECTIVE SOCCER IN THEORY AND IN PRACTICE
Alan Wade

HISTORICAL PERSPECTIVE

When football broke from rugby during the late 1800's the former offered a sport based on foot skills while the latter combined both "kicking and hacking both ball and opponent." In England, in 1962-63, player contracts became "open" (players were no longer restricted in terms of monetary compensation); as the more money the club made the more found its way into their paychecks. Clubs, managers, and players had only one thought — to win — at all cost if necessary!

Suddenly, soccer underwent tremendous metamorphosis. It returned to its roots, in many ways. Violence prevailed, both ball and player suffered painfully. This focus had its cost - the diminution of skill in the game. Abetted by the huge increase of football on television, creative, clever play assumed a downward spiral. All over the British Isles, young players were forming playing habits based on what they viewed on the teleview. Pictures are worth a thousand words! In this case the pictures promoted not skill and subtlety but cynical violence.

English football has never really recovered. Even the 1966 World Cup triumph, thought to be proof positive that all was well with the game, failed to limit the damage. The frantic soccer espoused by soccer statisticians (and camp followers) post 1982, only exacerbated England's problems, terminally almost!

WHAT IS SKILLFUL SOCCER?

Skillful soccer players are those who, individually or together, exhibit the predominant use of technical and tactical cleverness and composure in their play. Consequently their play demonstrates precision and accuracy in its execution.

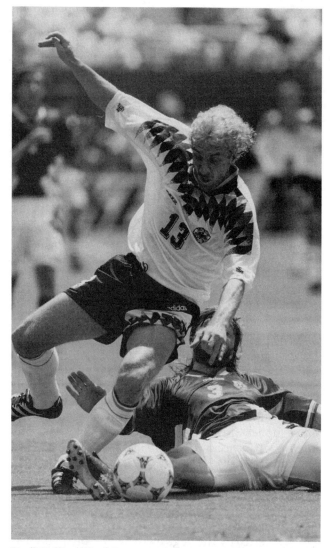

Rudi Voller (13) of Germany demonstrates balance while trying to evade skillful tackle of Bulgaria's Trifon Ivanov (3) in 1994 World Cup play. Cleverness and timing are examples of highly-developed skillful play. (photo by Tony Quinn).

WHAT IS EFFECTIVE SOCCER?

Effective soccer adopts such methods and attitudes as may be necessary to achieve the required result. Play is functionalized by limiting the technical and tactical options available to players.

WHAT IS POOR SOCCER?

Unskillful soccer, on the other hand, has a predominate use of the game elements of power, speed and athleticism rather than technical and tactical expertise.

"CAUSE AND EFFECT" OF POORLY DEVELOPED SOCCER

The following are important reasons for a nation's poorly developed soccer.

Cause 1— The decrease in amount of time devoted to voluntary soccer play by players 5-12 years of age. The effect is to reduce the levels of technical compe-tence and assuredness among this age group. As they mature, technical disability and limitations affect those with whom they play, thus further eroding skill.

Cause 2 — Lack of effective soccer teachers to com-pensate for the dimmunization of "soccer play based" technical skills. An affective teacher is one who can relate a technique to its place in the game. Soccer technique, when placed in realistic, controlled prac-tice situations, enables players to transform tech-nique into skill. An ineffective teacher of soccer skips the development of skill and instead forces young players into functional team play based on factors other than soccer skill. Soccer skill is shown when techniques are used with correct judgement and per-ception.

Cause 3 — The vast increase in the number of teams and the length of the seasons played for players be-tween 8-10 years of age. Teams are organized and managed (but not coached or taught) by untrained, unsuitable adults. Players learn to play to win when they should be learning how to play. Young players need nurturing such that they develop confidence in themselves shown by increased assuredness in individual and collective play. Instead the focus is on the manager or coach many of whom need soc-cer more than soccer needs them!

Cause 4 — Conflict of interests between junior school teams and competitions, themselves often organized by unsuitable teachers, and those in Cause 3. The effect is to coerce the best players into playing pres-surized soccer, i.e., playing effective and functional soccer when they should still be involved with ex-perimental, developmental soccer.

Cause 5 — The significant deterioration in technical skill at the top levels of play. The effects are many. One is an increased athleticism in professional foot-ball. A second is increased negative functionalism in play. There is a "stop good players from playing" mentality at work here. Coaches assign limited and negative functional roles to players, i.e., "Mark that player out of the match!" Or worse still, "Take the player out!"

There is a significant tactical use of player groups to stop opponents from playing creatively forward and through midfield. In England most playmakers are 36 years or older. They know how to make space and time. Younger players have been indoctrinated into giving opponents neither time nor space and conse-quently never have time or space themselves.

Skillful players are risk takers; they have to be. Fi-nally, cheating in the game increases in direct propor-tion to win at all cost attitudes. Skill takes a back seat to intimidation and to physical confrontation. In-creased severity of fouling is a direct result of this nar-row focus for the professional game.

SERIOUS SOCCER

Serious soccer, and by implication, serious coaching, has always been more of an illusion than a reality in English soccer. The qualities of those "preferred" for coaching positions in the professional game, or wherever talented players are involved, are more of the "old comrades" variety than those gained through rigorous study, qualification and serious application. Compare this with most European countries, not least Germany, easily the world's most consistent and successful soccer nation. Germans are great analyzers of problems. German soccer, top to bottom, has coaches who understand correct application of soccer methodology. Their motto: "Great players deserve great coaches!"

COMPARISONS BETWEEN "QUALITY SOCCER'" VERSUS "POOR SOCCER"

- Ball is kept mostly on the ground in quality soccer. Ball is usually in the air in poor soccer;
- Ball is controlled instantly and passed accurately in good soccer, but struck first time with minimal concern for the consequences in poor soccer;
- Shots are frequent, powerful and accurate as against wild and optimistic shots in a poor game;
- Shots come from skillfully created opportunities in good soccer as opposed to those resulting from rebounds or defensive errors in poor play;
- Players can create space and time in good play whereas in poor play no one can or tries to space (and time);
- There is a perceived consistent pattern to a good team's play as against the aimlessness and fanatic effort of a poor soccer team;
- Quality soccer has positive positional play of a high order while poor play results predictably ineffective player movement or none at all;
- Attackers can exploit their skills in quality soccer while poor games see intimidation or hard fouling used to destroy skill of opponents;
- Defenders both mark and cover for each other creating good interception and counter-attacking opportunities in quality soccer. Tackles and interceptions are quick, crisp and fair in execution. Poor teams take opponents late in the tackle with the execution crude and unfair. Poor teams lack the imagination or courage to counter-attack positively.

Quality soccer involves variable tactical options. Tactical options, absolutely vital in top soccer, are limited by the technical expertise of the individual players. Technical expertise must be directed into the skill combinations involving one or more cooperating players and eventually into skillful team play of the highest order. Without technical "class" a team may play functional perhaps, to some extent, effective soccer, but it can rarely play genuinely skillful soccer.

Teams strategies based on power, speed, ultra-directness, pressure and limited tactical (and therefore technical) commitments may have some success through shock. When their effort wavers or fails and shock wears off, they have nothing to fall back on. The physical output of pressure teams is always limited. Skillful teams, lacking success, can always fall back on increased effort if necessary.

England has practiced self-delusion for too long. The enormous and sophisticated edifice of schoolboy soccer in England is run exclusively by teachers. It fosters the impression that involvement of teachers means that schoolboy players are well taught. Even 50 years ago a tiny minority of teachers were competent to teach soccer or bothered to teach it in any meaningful way. Significantly fewer are competent to do so today, if for no other reason than the final proportion of the teaching profession has been severely reduced in the last two decades. Players, in desperate need of technical help, are in the hands of people at all levels in the game who are not competent and cannot meet their needs.

WHAT IS NEEDED TO PRODUCE EFFECTIVE, SKILLFUL SOCCER?

Over a period of years I came to identify the key principles of play. Subject to slight modification and adaption coaches everywhere should and can accept these as the "bedrock" of the game. Failure to recognize and acknowledge principles creates serious developmental obstacles. There can be no sound foundation for taking the game forward, no reference points by which progress may be assessed. Without acceptable principles of play at different developmental levels, direction will go "every which way" and ultimately... "nowhere."

Following is an outline of what I consider to be the four basic areas of understanding that all coaches should apply in their coaching:

1. Possession.

Possession of the ball is everything in the game; in attack and defense. It is one thing to know that ball possession is everything, but quite another to understand it and the logical implication arising out of it. Possession allows a team to:

- Determine in what parts of the field the match will be played;
- Control the pace of the game;
- Enable players to control the space available in different phases of play;

> # Skillful players are risk-takers, they have to be

• Affect the movements of certain opponents, at times most of them (i.e., if you have the ball, they have to chase it. If not, possession is used to create "man-up" situations);

• Control substantially the physiological (and psychological) demands made upon its players (i.e., tired players will breakdown in all phases of their activity more readily than skillful teams who collectively conserve their energy).

The more a team concedes possession to opponents, the greater the probability of opponents winning. Putting possession of the ball at risk frequently and unnecessarily must be a sure way of losing rather than winning matches, unless the difference in class and quality between the two teams is so great that the situation justifies a desperate gamble. The most certain way of defending is keep possession. Without the ball, opponents cannot attack. They may hustle and pressure, but opponents are almost helpless until they get, or are given, the ball. A winning team may have possession taken away, but it should rarely put possession at risk other than at a time and place of its own choosing.

If the principle of POSSESSION is accepted then it has inescapable implications for individual techniques, for team tactics and for practice and training.

2. Position

Control possession and a team controls position. Possession enables a team to play the game where it wishes. The more the game is played in the opponent's half of the field and nearer their own goal, the greater the probability of achieving profitable shooting positions and less the probability that the other team will threaten the other goal.

3. Surprise

Sometimes referred to as deception, surprise is that of individual and group tactical variability. Surprise is fundamental: applicable to both attack and defense. In attack, individual players and tactical groups, faced with a well organized and disciplined defense, inevitably will have to try something different in order to penetrate. Sudden challenges of direction of play or changes of pace, well supported and applied with individual and group tactical skills, will disrupt even the best organized defense. In defense, individual players and tactical groups, when faced with problem players or problem methods, use surprise to disrupt opponents' confidence and composure. A high pressure team may change to low pressure defense, and vice versa, forcing a rethink by opponents. Creating high pressure defensive 2 v. 1 situations against selected opponents on an unpredictable basis is another "surprise" defensive adjustment that may prove profitable.

4. Depth in Attack and Defense

For every action in soccer there is an opposite reaction. To solve the soccer puzzle one has to understand that... not merely to know it.

The opposite of penetration is containment.

A player in attack wants to make a fast and direct line for goal when dribbling when in his attacking third of the field. Opposing defender(s) will seek to slow him down and "jockey" him wide away from the goal. The defenders must keep the player in front of them at all times.

The opposite of dispersion is compression.

Attackers will try to keep play on as wide an attacking front as possible; space and time are needed for thoughtful decision-making. Defenders try to compress play into smaller areas of the field to limit free ball play.

The opposite of mobility is balance.

Switching the direction of play and creating frequent and surprising positional interchange makes play unpredictable. By refusing to allow defensive relationships to be disturbed a team retains good balance against any attacking thrust or changes in the point of attack.

Deception is common to both attack and defense in principle. A deceptive individual player may defeat an individual defender but a team collectively will be organized to cope with much of the surprise generated by an opponent.

If coaches and players place a high value on quality soccer then it is up to the coach to create the environment for relevant teaching and coaching. Both coaches and players must agree (and understand) that it is the basic principles of play that must be the foundation of mutual confidence. Whether coaching and practice are collective, technical or tactical or combinations thereof, principles must be the basis for the onset of any teaching process and therefore, change.

In the learning and improvement process there is a logical progression from percept to precept to concept.

THE EVOLVING GAME OF SOCCER
Alan Wade

Competition. In the advanced soccer world the amount of serious competition is increasing. Losing or drawing a match is increasingly unacceptable. Factors influencing this attitude include finance (money), the demands of television sponsorship, player costs, and generally increasingly antagonistic attitude to failure by the public.

Player skills and capacities. Diminution of intensive and long daily commitments to free soccer play by youngsters 5 to 13 years of age has led to signifi-

U.S. Olympic Gold Medal team member Mia Hamm (9) demonstrates close ball skill as she settles ball out of the air while under the pressure of a Japanese defender in an international match played in Washington, DC. Hamm's skill development is among the best in the world due to her long hours spent training with the ball. (photo by Brett Whitesell)

cant drops in individual technical levels and ranges. Restrictions on physically demanding natural play of all kinds, birth to 15 years, has resulted in a less hardy generation of young players.

Practice and training. The replacement of free play and self-imposed practice with organized full team competitions has resulted in limited technicians being required to conform to strict tactical organization. Win-oriented competition has replaced casual, self development play. The diminished hardiness of players has been compensated for by the institution of controlled and demanding training regimes from early ages.

Expressionist, tactically cunning players have almost disappeared, replaced with more and more "made" players of highly functional all-round capabilities.

Third World players retain significantly higher levels and incomparably greater ranges of technical skills. These skills have been acquired experimentally or by imitation of senior players still allowed to exercise self-choice in solving game problems.

The last because as yet they haven't had to learn any better (worse?).

IDENTIFYING NEEDS
- In terms of the game's trends and tendencies: Can we identify precisely what our needs are?
- Can we quantify the extent to which we are meeting them/not meeting them if possible?
- What are the obstacles to meeting those needs?

PLAYER DEVELOPMENT
- To what extent, if any, are there breeding grounds for "natural" players?
- Can we identify those breeding grounds?
- Can those breeding grounds be extended and/or expanded? Can we "seed" new breeding grounds?
- If the availability of nurtured players greatly exceeds that of "naturals" how can we be sure that they achieve optimum levels of development?
- To what extent is senior playing style an important influence in young player development? Is it changeable?
- What are realistic expectations for a national playing style?

ORGANIZATIONAL REQUIREMENTS
- Could identifiable organizational needs be met? If not, why not?
- Could national, regional, district and local objectives be agreed on and achieved?
- What are the vital resource needs without which development has little or no chance?
- If appropriate and relevant progress ladders are not in place, how might they be constructed?
- What are the absolutely basic soccer requirements by which all soccer player development programs might be developed and evaluated?
- What should effective players in different areas of operation be able to do?

WHAT IS THE PROFILE OF AN EXCEPTIONAL PLAYER?

Backs
- Moving towards "own" goal, control the ball and turn to interpass out of trouble or kick clear;
- Volleying a pass or clearance over the shoulder;
- Intercept a pass clearly or change that move into a tackle;
- Pass accurately "down the line," long and short;
- Interpass "outside to in" safely and deceptively;
- Understand the principles and the practice of marking, tracking and covering;
- Compete to head the ball from positions to the side of or from behind determined opponents.

Central Strikers
- Facing own goal, with a feint, control and turn to shoot, or pass or run the ball;
- Facing own goal, control in the air and turn or lay off a back pass;
- Facing own goal, lay off a back ball first touch;

Questions which an experienced soccer scout would ask when looking over a prospective professional player would include:

1. Does he play the game skillfully?
   - Does he have good touch and tight control when receiving and when "on the ball"?
   - Can he make time and space for himself when pressured by opponents?
   - Does he have deceptive techniques or is he an "obvious" player?
   - Can he get himself out of difficulties using individual skill to do so?
2. Does he command the game?
   - Does he play for himself or does he play for others?
   - Can he cause opponents problems when he doesn't have the ball?
   - Can he free himself from tight marking and can he free other players?
   - Does he react to play as it develops or is he usually a move or two ahead?
   - Is he a short- or a long-sighted player?
3. What are his physical capabilities?
   - Is he an easy and fluent mover?
   - Does he have good agility?
   - Has he got good change of pace or outstanding pace?
   - Can he turn on high levels of sustained work rate if he needs to?
   - Does he use athletic ability or does he depend on it?
   - Is he a strong player in 1 v. 1 situations?
4. What sort of competitor is he?
   - Does he set out to impose his will on opponents?
   - Does he react to intimidation?
   - How does he react to cheating?
   - Does he have physical courage? Can he take it and give it?
   - Does he have the mental toughness to see him through situations which are going against him?
   - When his team is losing or has lost, it he still a winner?

- Give and take simple short wall passes in the air or on the ground;
- Control and shoot, two touches maximum, and hit the target;
- Whenever receiving the ball, be able to shield it from challenge effectively;
- Understand the requirements of the penetration and how to lose markers;
- Know how to "work" opponents to gain the advantage in heading for goal.

Wide Strikers

- Cross the ball on the run, from the goal line areas, a distance of about 50 meters, to hit the important target areas;
- With the latest change of kicking action, cut back the ball along the ground over 30 meters, plus or minus;
- Turn back and with the "inside" foot deliver a 50-meter pass accurately;
- Shoot on the run with both inside and outside feet;
- Run at and past opponents (dribble) with the use of one trick and one option;
- Set up and deliver simple wall passes;
- Collect the ball in the air or on the ground with one touch and take it into effective crossing or shooting positions;
- Understand the need for optimum width and its effect on space availability for other players and the effectiveness of positional interchange.

Midfield Players

These players are the best all-round players of the game and should be able to meet most of the requirements for backs and strikers.

- Receive, control and run with the ball while shielding it effectively;
- Lay off first time passes backwards and to the side with accuracy and touch;
- Good control in the air with an ability to two touch pass for shot, pass, volley or half volley;
- Shooting with accuracy and power, from 25 meters, plus or minus;
- Deceptive and accurate ground passing through small gaps over 25 meters, plus or minus;
- Accurate long passing, 50 meters or so;
- Ability to intercept passes, to anticipate;
- Understanding forward defensive responsibilities and appreciation of counter-attacking possibilities;
- Know how to time the moves to defeat opponents in the air with flicks and direct headed strikes when they have significant height and jumping advantages.

PLAYING STYLE

Finally, where playing style is a developmental possibility and we have to depend on "made" (nurtured) players, the following are key factors:

- Players should understand the advantages of controlled possession in all phases of play; attack, defense and transition situations. To achieve controlled possession, players should be able to set up interpassing sequences where no recipient is played into difficulty;

- Players should know how, when and where to establish starting positions for moving attacking possessions forward (penetration);
- All players should be aware of immediate counter-attacking possibilities and the positions from which it will involve worthwhile risk of possession. They should be able to assess very quickly the range of ball needed and their capability for achieving it with good control and accuracy. They should at the same time be able to assess the availability of supporting players to ensure exploitation of the counter move. Finally, they should be able to assess the risk value to the team of a quick counter-attack.

The Relationship Between The Characteristics Defined And The Requirements Of A Player In International Competition

Modern strategical and tactical considerations require modern players to be highly competent, all-round players. Literally, they should be able to function effectively in all "phases" of play. High class soccer has reacted to the pressures induced by high (unreasonable?) levels of expectation by following a trend towards low risk, high predictability of play. Play which is predictable and involves minimal risk has to be highly organized, and organization is best achieved with a majority (all?) of players who have few deficiencies and high levels of general competence.

Those responsible for molding very young players cannot see that to produce the genius which, say, Pele represents it is necessary to inspire those players to experiment freely. They must be encouraged to find out what they can do. They should be taught what they can't do; they'll find out soon enough. The greater the expectations for team success, the greater the limitations placed upon players - at all levels in the game.

CRITERIA FOR JUDGING THE QUALITY OF A SOCCER MATCH

- The ball is always on the ground or always in the air?
- The ball is controlled and passed accurately or hit first time?
- Shots at goal are frequent and accurate or rare and opportunistic?
- Shots come from skillfully created openings or on ricochets and errors?
- Players vary play by passing and dribbling or always pass, never dribble?
- Players have space in which to play or have no time to make space?
- Play has a clear pattern and purpose or is patternless and aimless?
- Play involves frequent interchanges of position or players appear in same areas throughout the match?
- Attackers can work to use their skills or are usually fouled?

- Defenders mark and cover quickly intercept and tackle fairly?

ANALYSIS OF ASSOCIATION FOOTBALL*
Dr. Ian Franks

The term analysis has been used freely in many fields and disciplines. Therefore, the area upon which I shall focus my discussion will be carefully and specifically defined. Quantitative analysis gained from all levels of Association Football will form the basis of this paper. I shall examine the findings taken from research that have measured several aspects of team play. These could include information about passes, possession turnovers, shots, crosses, etc... In nearly all cases this type of team analysis has been concerned with events surrounding the path of the ball. The methods by which these data have been collected have varied from a simple "tick" or "cross" in the appropriate column, to a complex notation system that has to be decoded after the game. Recently, several computer systems have been developed that can store, display, and analyze a series of coordinates received from touch sensitive digitization tablets. It is crucial, however, to realize that the central concern is not computer-aided analysis but the quantitative recording of key factors that are responsible for successful performance in the sport of Association Football.

Analysis of a sporting situation usually infers that there is some inherent organization and predictability within the situation. Also there is an implicit assumption that the events that are being analyzed are not all completely random. If these assumptions were false, then one should expect that anything and everything is possible. However, it does appear that the game of soccer has a certain amount of organization, and the events follow one another in a fairly predictable and sequentially dependent manner. What is it then that determines this organization and structure of competition? It appears that the rules of the system determine, to some extent, the constraints within which meaningful activity can take place. The rules of competition also lay out quite succinctly the objectives of the system.

It has previously been argued that a simple two state model can describe the game of soccer. Possession of the ball becomes the critical feature of this structure. That is not to say "keeping ball possession" is important, but by using possession as a critical component of analysis all other events can be included and accounted for. During any game either one of the two teams has possession of the ball. The objective of the team with possession is to score goals and the opposing team's objective is, therefore, to prevent the team with possession from scoring goals. Tactics and strategy are devoted to fulfilling these objectives.

On average, each team has possession of the ball on approximately 200 occasions, and since the objective of the game is to score goals then these 200 possessions could hypothetically translate into 200 goals per team. The scoring of 200 goals is not common in a soccer game. In fact, it has been found that successful teams (league champions) usually only average between two and three goals per game. Therefore, 99% of all team possessions are lost to the opposing team without a goal being scored. What happens, then, to these other 197 team possessions? A detailed analysis of these lost possessions may help in understanding what the structure of the game was and also allows a meaningful description of the game to be made.

Let us examine these lost possessions. Each possession is lost in a particular area of the field and each loss can be attributed to a particular action. For example, a goal results in a loss of possession. That is, the opposing team takes possession for a "kick off." Also, most shots at goal result in a possession loss. On the other hand, a possession loss could occur in and around one's own goal area, e.g. a pass that is intercepted by the opposing team. It would appear, therefore, that some qualitative judgments regarding the type of lost possession is needed. Decisions about what is an acceptable lost possession can be made given that we refer back to the objectives of the game (i.e., scoring goals).

It is obvious that goals can only be scored from certain areas. The physical size of a soccer field prohibits players from scoring goals from within their own half of the field and up to 40 meters outside the opponent's goal. Goals have been scored from other areas but they account for an extremely small percentage of the total number of goals scored. The task for all players is to move the ball into an area of the field from which a shot can be taken. Team possessions that are lost in areas from which shots could have been taken would satisfy a large part of the final objective. Getting the ball into these areas can be considered as a sub-objective for individual players and teams to attain. If possession of the ball is continuously lost in these shooting areas and shooting opportunities do not arise, the problem for the coach is less formidable than if ball possession was lost in areas other than this shooting area. Priorities for possession loss can be identified as: first, goals; second, shots; third, shooting opportunities; and fourth, attacking third of field. Possession losses that occur in the defending third of the field are dangerous and should be examined carefully in any post game analysis. This will be discussed in detail later.

HOW ARE GOALS SCORED?

Goals are a result of shots taken, and for every 10 shots taken one goal is scored. This shot-goal ratio has been reliably found at all levels of competition for the past 35 years. Given this fact, teams wishing to score two goals per game should strive to lose at least 20 possessions shooting at goal. Also, in theory therefore, if a team were to increase the number of shots at goal there would be a higher probability of scoring more goals and hence winning more games.

The results of team analysis suggest that most goals are scored from within a certain shooting angle that extends from the goalposts to the corners of the penalty box, and radiates outward approximately 35 yards. Attacking players who find themselves in these positions should be made aware of this fact and encouraged to take every opportunity to shoot. Given that a shooting opportunity is not available, the player's next priority should be to dribble. It has been found that dribbling into congested areas around the penalty area yields free kicks or opens up shooting opportunities, or frees other marked attacking players. The final option should be to pass, which may seem counter to many traditional views. However, passing in this shooting area has been shown to be the least productive action in terms of creating shooting opportunities and hence producing goals.

The major priority is, therefore, to take all shooting opportunities that are presented to the player within the shooting angle. And it should be remembered that not all shots will be "on goal." Some will be wide, others high, and some blocked or deflected by players. However, with the exception of high shots, shooting at goal, either "on" or "off target" will produce situations from which other shots may arise. One fundamental problem in coaching players in the technique of shooting is to ensure that players keep their shots below the goal height (8 feet). Nothing can result from a shot that is too high, but many events can lead from shots that are too wide. In practice situations the priority ordering is: first, take shooting opportunities; second, technique of shooting, low shots; third, technique of shooting, on target shots; finally, other players being ready inside the penalty area for unexpected results from the shots. These practice situations should also vary in such aspects of play as the angle of the approaching ball, the distance away from the goal, the number of players in and around the ball and the way in which the shooting opportunity arose.

It was thought, after reviewing a considerable number of past games, that the approach play that led to goals was not significantly different than the approach play that led to shots that did not result in goals. Goals were thought to occur randomly from a population of shots. However, there has been some recent data from the 1986 World Cup analysis that may alter our views on this matter. Over the past 35 years, analysis has been conducted on many thousands of goals in first-class competitions, including recent World, European and South American championships. The predominant finding that has surfaced from nearly all analyses is that over 80% of goals are scored from team play that involves four passes or less. This would indicate that goals are scored from team play that is direct and fast in nature. The recent analyses of the 1986 World Cup found that goals arise from team play that is even more direct than the team play that produces a shot that is not a goal. That is goals come from fewer consecutive passes than do shots that are not goals.

This finding, that goals are not scored from many intricate passing moves, has been the center of a recent controversy in England. It has led certain teams to adopt a very direct style of play that has been relatively successful in terms of overall results. Many misinterpretations exist, both of the findings from analysis and of the reasons why these teams, with the direct style of play, are successful. In order to dispel most of this misunderstanding it is important to know, first, what the results of the analysis are, and second, what implication do these results have in terms of preferred playing styles.

WHAT LEADS TO THE SCORING OF GOALS?

First and foremost, it does seem that direct play leads to goals being scored. This is not a new finding. Experienced coaches will remember that in the early 1960s a major principle of team play was termed "penetration," which was defined as bypassing as many defensive players with the ball as possible. It was extremely important that passes were made, runs with the ball were made, and shots were taken that went behind and between defenders. Penetrative play often involves a long forward pass and it has been found that long forward passes into space behind defenders are a major contributor to goals being scored. The important factor here seems to be that not only are long passes made behind defenders but that several

I t does appear that the game of soccer has a certain amount of organization, and the events follow one another in a fairly predictable and sequentially dependent manner.

cooperating team members are in positions to ideally receive the ball, or are in positions that will allow them to challenge for the ball. Having several players who are specifically deployed in attacking positions, and having the ball played into the opponent's third of the field would require that the rearmost players (the ones who are making these long passes) move forward and keep the team "compact." That is, keep the ten outfield players playing in an area that spans, at most, one half of the field. The reason for maintaining compactness as a team unit is that data from team analysis have shown that if opposing teams win possession in their own defending third of the field, there is a higher probability of them losing that possession in their own half of the field if opposing players can apply defensive pressure (in numbers) in the immediate vicinity of the ball. In addition, compact team play leads to good supporting play and an improved percentage of completed passes.

Given that a team would play long passes behind the opposing team's defenders and all team members strive to keep play compact, then the game will be played at a fairly fast pace. This would require a high level of fitness from all team members. Teams that choose to play this direct style of soccer and are fit tend to score a large proportion of their goals in the final 20 minutes of play. This style of play would dictate certain other qualities that were required of the team apart from fitness. For example, all members of the team would have to be able to defend as an individual and as a team unit. Moreover all team members would be required to involve themselves in physical challenges for the ball. Also certain players (fullbacks and midfield) would have to be technically proficient at playing a high lofted pass accurately in excess of 40 yards, and midfield players would have to be skilled at predicting where the defensive clearance (or "knock down") would be played in order to challenge for the ball in the middle third of the field. It is this middle third area that sees more action than any other part of the field. Therefore, players working in this area should be extremely fit, both physically and mentally. Front players should be fast and able to create space and arrive in that space at the correct time. For it is these players who must strive to fully utilize long penetrating passes. One other personal quality that would appear to be essential, especially for players who play in and around the opponent's penalty area, is that of courage. Players who will go into areas of physical danger are few and so this quality must be nurtured in all our players.

As can be seen, the simple statement of "direct play" brings with it many other essential features, the above being only a small sample. Therefore, for a coach to read into the descriptive statements of analysis concerning how goals are scored, the fact that long high balls should be kicked into the opponent's goal area

Here a Colombian player unleashes a bent ball around the Danish wall in a soccer international played in Miami. The importance of set plays in terms of team preparation cannot be underestimated by the coach. (photo by Perry McIntyre, Jr.)

and chased by one or two players will produce unsuccessful performance and also give a false impression of the benefits of direct play. A complete understanding of all the ramifications of this style of play, including the selection of players, must be thought through carefully and with the facts of analysis available to guide the thinking process.

THE IMPORTANCE OF SET PLAYS

A large percentage of all goals arise from set plays (corners, free kicks and throw-ins). The usual figure that has been put forward is approximately 40% of all goals originate from set plays. This figure is somewhat high and does not represent the actual amount in the 1982 World Cup Final. Approximately 30% of goals came from set plays in this competition. However, this figure is still a considerable proportion of the total number of goals and as such should be given equivalent priority when preparing a team for competition.

Corners are an excellent source of goals and teams that "draw" corners by having flank players dribble on the outside of defending fullbacks increase their chances of gaining corners, hence they improve their chances of scoring goals from corners. Inswinging corners played to the front half of the goal seem to be the most profitable. However teams should deploy attackers in three key areas of the goal in anticipation of this corner, at least two players in the front half of the goal, one player just outside the far goalpost, and at least one player moving into an area near the penalty

spot. In addition, two players should position themselves in anticipation of the ball being cleared to the edge of the penalty area.

It is critical to choose players who have special talents for these particular roles. For example, aggressive players who will attack the ball should be stationed at the near post, and players who are accurate at shooting "first time, on-the-volley" should be placed just outside the penalty area. The one key element in all corner kicks is the quality of the kick itself. Players who are designated to take the kick should practice regularly and achieve over 80% success every practice.

Directness is the common factor that underlies most successful free kicks. Free kicks in the shooting area that was defined earlier are excellent shooting opportunities and should be taken. Players who can hit a still ball and impart "spin" or "swerve" should practice frequently from many different positions outside the penalty area and also with a defensive "wall of players" between the ball and the goal. Free kicks that are wide of the penalty area in the attacking third of the field should be crossed into the penalty area so that the cross goes behind the defenders and also eliminates the goalkeeper. (I will say more about this when I discuss data gained from analysis on "crosses.') Free kicks that are not in the attacking third of the field should be looked upon as opportunities to move the ball as quickly as possible into the attacking third of the field, given the fact that the opposing team cannot pressure the ball.

The throw-in has received little attention as a potential goal-scoring play, but the facts are that opposing defenders do not "mark" or "track down" players from throw-ins and this has been the cause of many goals. Also, goals originate from long throw-ins that are delivered toward the near post and headed back into the goal area. If sufficient attackers are placed inside the goal area, this tactic appears to produce strikes at goal and also goals. The benefit of this play is that no attacking players can be offside from this direct throw. It would seem that there would be great rewards for players who practice long throws from all positions along the touchline, since this is also an opportunity to move the ball, without defensive pressure, into the opponent's third of the field and hence into a potential shooting area.

ANALYSIS OF CROSSES

There is an increasing trend toward the scoring of goals from crosses. However, although over 25% of all goals originate from a ball that is crossed into the penalty area, the cross-goal ratio is only 27:1. At first glance this appears to be an extremely inefficient means of scoring goals since the shot-goal ratio is only 10:1. This problem was analyzed in detail with some very interesting findings. First, although the cross-goal ratio was 27:1, the 11 crosses that were contacted by an attacker" goal ratio was only 8:1 and of these the "crosses that lead to strikes" goal ratio was 5:1. It would seem that if you can have an attacker contact the cross, and this contact leads to a strike on goal, your probability of scoring is twice what it would have been given another type of shot. Also, there should be close scrutiny paid to the quality of crosses since many teams make crosses that are not contacted by attackers. That is, too many poor quality crosses are being delivered. Two other findings that this crossing analysis produced were that nearly all the crosses that resulted in goals in the 1986 World Cup were played behind the defenders and also eliminated any chance of the goalkeeper making contact with the ball. In addition, the cross does not necessarily have to be played in the air for it to be successful. Many of the goals in this World Cup competition that came from crosses were scored with the feet and not the head.

The conclusions that may be drawn from this analysis would point to the fact that crosses are a key factor in successful performance. However. because of the large number of unsuccessful crosses it would seem that coaching methods have not been stressing the key elements that make a cross dangerous. First, crossing opportunities should be taken given that there is an opportunity to play the ball behind defenders. Second, when the opportunity arises, front players must be ready and in a position to move behind defenders in order to contact the cross (too often front players are initially poorly positioned). Third, the cross should be delivered so that it goes behind the defenders and eliminates the goalkeeper. Usually a good mark for the crosser is play the ball along the top of the "six-yard box." The ball can be delivered in the air or along the ground. Finally, the front player must move to contact the ball and, preferably, take a shot.

> A large percentage of all goals arise from set plays (corners, free kicks and throw-ins). The usual figure that has been put forward is approximately 40% of all goals originate from set plays.

DEFENDING

The results of team analysis that are concerned with regaining possession provide possibly the most conclusive evidence in favor of tight defensive pressure. If possession of the ball is regained in the opponent's third of the field, the chances of a shot at goal resulting are approximately 65%. If possession is regained in the middle third of the field, then the chances of that subsequent team possession resulting in a shot on goal are reduced to 25%. Whereas, if possession is regained in your own team's third of the field, the chances of scoring have been reduced to only 10%. Also when possession is won in the opponent's third of the field in "free play" (not from a set play), the chances of scoring goals approach this same 65% figure. Two implications would seem to be obvious from this data. First, do not increase the probability of losing possession in your own half of the field. Making short passes and square passes, in and around your own penalty area, increases the probability of a loss in possession. Second, the team's first defensive priority should be to regain possession in the opponent's third of the field.

FRAMEWORK FOR ANALYSIS

Given it is understood how goals are scored and conceded, and given that a team should play in a style that maximizes the probability of scoring and preventing goals, then what type of data should be collected during competition?

LOST POSSESSIONS

As previously mentioned, the basis for this analysis is ball possession. So it is imperative that we know:
• How many possessions did the teams have?
• Where were they lost? (defending, middle or attacking thirds of the field)
• Were they lost in "free play" or during a "set play"?

Recommendation 1

Lose as many possessions in the attacking third of the field as possible and reduce (to zero if possible) the number of possessions lost in "free play" in one's own defending third of the field. Winning teams have been recorded as losing over 60% of all possessions in the attacking third of the field. The emphasis changes from who has possession of the ball to where the ball is in relation to the goal and the attacking team members.

REGAINED POSSESSIONS

The converse of losing possession is gaining possession and information should be gathered on:
• Where did we win possession of the ball?
• Was possession won in "free play" or during a "set play?"

Recommendation 2

Win possession of the ball early. Organize the defensive structure of the team so that possession is regained in the attacking third of the field. When possession is won, attack directly and quickly in an attempt to produce a strike at goal.

SHOTS AND SHOOTING OPPORTUNITIES

From my earlier hypothetical model it was suggested that all possessions should be lost in the act of shooting at goal. Information regarding shooting is therefore critical.
• Was there an opportunity to shoot?
• How many of these opportunities were taken?
• Where was the shot taken from?
• What was the result of the shot? [On target (goal or saved), Off target (high, wide, high and wide), blocked.]

Recommendation 3

All shooting opportunities should be taken from within the shooting angle. Shots should be preferably on target, but definitely not high.

CROSSES AND CROSSING OPPORTUNITIES

If the ball is outside the shooting angle, there is an opportunity to cross the ball into the penalty area. The following questions relate to crosses.
• How many crossing opportunities were there?
• How many crosses were taken?
• Of these crosses, how many were contacted first by an attacker?
• Where did the cross go to? (Behind or in front of defenders)
• Did the cross eliminate the goalkeeper?
• What was the result of the cross?

Recommendation 4

Take the opportunity to cross. The quality of the cross is crucial. It must be played behind defenders and eliminate the keeper. There must be at least one attacking player in the penalty area who will run behind the defenders in order to make first contact with the cross.

SET PLAYS

Information regarding details of set plays is of vital importance. Details regarding the following should be gathered.
• Throw-ins.
• Corners.
• Free Kicks.

Categories of cause, position, execution (planned or not), and results of set plays are essential features of this analysis.

Recommendation 5

On all set plays in every area of the field each player must understand his/her role and what the expected outcome of the set play may be. This understanding can only come from practice. All set plays must be practiced in a realistic setting.

TECHNICAL DEMANDS OF PERFORMANCE

The techniques that are required by players to operate within a team that plays in a direct manner are no different than the techniques demanded of all players. The priorities placed upon each of these techniques, however, may be vastly different. The first and most important technique is that of receiving the ball. Players must be able to bring the ball under control from all possible positions, especially balls that arrive at head or chest height. Allied to this, players must understand under what conditions they should bring the ball under control with their first touch, and under what conditions they should play the ball away the first time. These building blocks of technical expertise for all players must also be a priority for developing young players. Practice sessions should be designed that allow players the opportunity to experience many and varied receptions in many and varied realistic playing environments. This practice should enable the player to provide himself/herself with time. This time should be spent in looking forward and selecting the next appropriate technique (shot, dribble or pass).

The next crucial technique, especially for developing young players, is that of dribbling and running with the ball. Although dribbling should only be confined to the attacking third of the field, all players should have the ability to take on opposing players in one v. one situations. With more experienced players, it must be stressed that there are certain areas in which dribbling yields the best returns. Also, running with the ball forward through areas of "no opposing pressure" is a critical technical component of any team that wishes to advance ball possession into the attacking third of the field. Along with these techniques, the coach should stress to the players understanding of when to run with the ball, when to dribble past opponents and when to shoot or pass.

Over the past thirty years, short (less than 20 yards) passing has received more attention than any other technique. Whereas this technique is important (especially for young players) in order to understand the principles of good supporting play, its importance has been considerably overexaggerated by the misconception that top class teams utilize this technique most frequently in the scoring of goals. International teams do make many short consecutive passes. However, these are usually to no avail. For example, the chances of a team scoring a goal from a possession that has included more than seven consecutive passes is well below 1%. Although teams make many consecutive passes, the manner in which they score goals is very different and very direct. What this overconcern with keeping ball possession using many passes has done is to move the emphasis away from teaching players how to, when to, and where to play long (greater than 30 yards) accurate passes. It is interesting to note than when teams are running out of time (five or 10 minutes left in the game) and need to score goals in a closely-contested game, the number of long forward passes increases dramatically. The technique of long passing should be stressed with all players. This includes clearance by goalkeepers. Goals that arise as a result of long goalkeeper kicks are increasing in number. Goalkeepers can, with practice, deliver the ball into the attacking third of the field, and with the correct arrangement of players, this ball possession can ultimately result in a shooting opportunity. One caution to coaches of players younger than 12 years of age - the necessary musculature to deliver a 30 yard pass in the air is not fully developed in these prepubescent players and, there-fore, reduced objectives should be given to these players and more priority should be given to the other techniques.

Shooting and crossing are considered to be the primary source of goals and, as such, should be given high priority in every coaching practice. The usual methods used in teaching these two techniques have not taken into account the need for players to transfer learning from the practice session to the game. This is because events unfold in time and certain events precede others in a game. This feature of sequential dependency is not clearly understood by many coaches. Having players realize that there is an "opportunity to..." is essential. From a player's perspective, the game is a series of opportunities to produce a given technique. There are opportunities to play the ball forward, there are opportunities to cross the ball, opportunities to shoot, opportunities to tackle, and these opportunities can be taken or not. The first objective is to create the opportunity and having done so, players must recognize the opportunity and take it. If the opportunity is not taken, then nothing can be said about the technique. Only when the opportunity to produce the technique is taken can the coach assess the quality of that technique. If players are made aware of how the coach sees the game in terms of opportunities, then the players can fulfill the objectives given by the coach.

> The coach should stress to the players understanding of when to run with the ball, when to dribble past opponents and when to shoot or pass.

The area of play that has received the least attention with all players, young and old alike, is that of defending as an individual. All members of the team should practice individual defending as they would any attacking skill. Without the correct defensive skills, players will always be a liability to the team for that portion of play when their team does not have possession of the ball. Only after individuals know and can execute the technique of defending is it possible for the coach to address the components intrinsic to defending as a team unit.

THE KEY TO SUCCESSFUL COACHING

Whereas the previous suggestions and recommendations have dealt with the key factors of successful performance for players, this final section addresses the key to successful coaching performance. A large portion of coaching entails the detection and correction of errorful performance (detection and reinforcement of accurate performance is also included). In order to detect and analyze performance in a continuous team game such as soccer, it is essential that some record of performance, other than subjective opinions gained from casual observation, be obtained. Several studies have been conducted that have tested the accuracy of observations by coaches during continuous team games. The basic finding in all these studies has been that coaches are extremely errorful in their analyses of the competitions being observed. This is not only true for novice coaches but is also true for coaches of international calibre. In certain circumstances they perform no better than chance. There are many reasons why we should not be surprised at this finding. Human memory is extremely fallible and is easily biased by personal expectations. The logical solution to the problem is to make a recording of the critical events during a competition. This can be done using a pencil and paper checklist, a sophisticated computer-aided recording system, a tape recording of observations or a videotape of the entire game. Each of these methods provides a memory aid for the coach, but perhaps the most useful for coaches and players is the use of videotape as a data recording device. All coaches who have struggled with recalling the memory of events when talking to players about performance errors or when planning the next practice should consider the powerful educational medium of the videotape. Consider the situation where the coach can show players particular game events and make salient points about strategy, tactics or techniques. Then the players go out and practice in realistic situations, these practice environments having been derived from watching the competition. While these players are practicing, a videotape is being compiled of their practice. The players then end the practice by comparing the practice performance (on video) with the previously recorded competition performance. With the advent of relatively inexpensive portable video technology this scenario is within the reach of most coaches. It only requires a concerted administrative effort on behalf of a few individuals.

The problem for coaches is to determine what aspect of the videotaped game is most crucial, since only one or two points should be addressed per practice. Showing the entire videotaped game to players may actually retard performance because of information overload. Information on the key factors of a successful performance will not only give a good quantitative description of the performance, but will also guide

the coach in choosing the key elements that have to be addressed in practice and edited from the competition tape.

This brief summary of results gained from analysis is the foundation for new performance criteria. Coaching by analysis (or "by the facts") is relatively easy in concept for the players to understand but requires a great deal of logical thinking from the coach. Understanding what analysis to complete directs the observations of the coach and allows for the development of priorities in performance and, hence, practice. If the coach can relate these priorities to the players, then the expectations of both coach and player are known. The player has realistic, objective goals for performance and can use the facts gained from analysis to match against these goals. The feedback process for coach and player is now a tangible item that can be viewed (videotape) and quantified (analysis).

* Acknowledgements for research funds relevant to this paper go to Sport Canada, the Coaching Association of Canada and the Canadian Soccer Association

REFERENCES

Alderson, G.H., Brackenridge, C.H. "Match Analysis", paper written as a result of a seminar on Match Analysis, 18-19th April, 1985. Pub: National Coaching Foundation, Leeds.

Bedingfield, W, Marchiori, G.. Gervais, P. "Game strategy: Film and Computer Analysis" in N. Wood (Ed.). Coaching Science Update, 23-24, 1982.

Brooke, J.D., Knowles, J.E. "A Movement Analysis of Player Behavior in Soccer Match Performance", a paper presented at the British Proceedings for the Conference in Sports Psychology, Salford. 1980.

Franks, I.M., Goodman, D., Miller, G. "Analysis of Performance: Quantitative or Qualitative," S.P.O.R.T.S., March, 1983.

Franks, I.M., Goodman, D. "A Hierarchical Approach to Performance Analysis," S.P.O.R.T.S., June 1984.

Franks, I.M., Goodman, D. "A Systematic Approach to Analyzing Sports Performance," J. of Sports Sciences. 4, 49-59, 1986.

Franks, I.M., Goodman, D. "Computer Assisted Technical Analysis of Sport," Coaching Review, May/June, 1986.

Franks, I.M., Sinclair, G.D., Thomson, W, Goodman, D. "Analysis of the Coaching Process," S.P.O.R.T.S., Jan.,1986.

Franks, I.M., Wilson, G.E.. Goodman, D. "Analyzing a Team Sport with the Aid of Computers," Can. J. of Sports Science, 12, 120-125, 1987.

Franks, I.M., Patterson. G., Goodman, D. "The Real Time Analysis of Sport: An Overview," Can. J. of Applied Sports Science, II (1), 55-57, 1986.

Franks, I.M., Miller, G. "Technical Analysis of Association Football Games: World Cup (1982)," Center for Sports Analysis, U.B.C.. 1983.

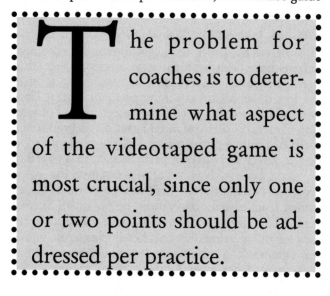

The problem for coaches is to determine what aspect of the videotaped game is most crucial, since only one or two points should be addressed per practice.

MacDonald, N. "Avoiding the Pitfalls in Player Selection," *Coaching Science Update*. 41-5. 1984.

Mayhew. S.R., Wenger, H.A. "Time Motion Analysis of Professional Soccer," *J. of Human Movement Studies*, Vol. 11, pp. 49-52, 1985.

Pollard, R. "Soccer Performance and Its Application to Shots at Goal," Sports Stat. Special, Dept. of Research Hanuman Vyayam Prasarak Mandal, Vol. 4, No. 2, April 1986.

Pollard, R. "Soccer Performance Analysis and the Quantitative Comparison of Playing Styles," Unpublished Manuscript, 1983.

Purdy, J.G. "Computers in Sports: From Football Play Analysis to the Olympic Games," in Ladnay, S. and Machol, R. (Eds.) *Optimal Studies in Sports*, Amsterdam, North Holland, 196-205, 1977.

Reep, C., Benjamin, B. "Skill and Chance in Association Football," *J. of Royal Statistical Study*, 581-585, 1968.

Reep, C. Pollard, R., Benjamin, B. "Skill and Chance in Ball Games", *J. of Royal Statistical Study*, 134, 623-629, 1971.

Reilly, T., Thomas, V. "A Motion Analysis of Work Rate in Different Positional Roles in Professional Football Match Play," *J. of Human Movement Studies*, Vol. 2, pp. 87-97, 1986.

Thomson, B. "Anatomy of Season," *S.P.O.R.T.S.*, Nov. 1985.

Van Gool, D., Van Gerven, D., Boutmans, J. "Telemetred Heart Rate Recorded During a Soccer Game," a paper presented at the Conference on Microcomputers in Sport, Liverpool U., 1983.

STATISTICAL ANALYSIS OF SOCCER
Alan Wade

BACKGROUND

The background of the application of statistical techniques in England begins in 1946-47 and includes the eleven seasons until 1956-57 and the Munich air disaster when the heart of the Manchester United team perished. Manchester United won the League three times, were second four times and won the FA Cup once. Wolverhampton Wanderers won the League once and were second two times and won the FA Cup once. These clubs were labeled by the press as the "White Knight" and "Black Knight". Manchester United's philosophy was to obtain the very best players, at all levels, put them on the field and let them play with freedom of expression.

I have chosen to present a critique of Ian Franks's paper because the implications of his conclusions are important to soccer in North America and they may be seriously misleading, even dangerously so.

Wolves' philosophy was to recruit good young schoolboy players and bring them up in "The Wolves' Way", highly-trained, superbly disciplined and playing percentage soccer.

Manchester United had a very "laid back" approach to practice and training. Whenever players felt the inclination to work hard, they were advised to lie down until the feeling went away.

Wolves applied themselves totally to preparation, especially to the physical conditioning aspect of it. The prospect of preseason training positively frightened some players and caused English captain Billy Wright, a 100-plus match international, into an early retirement! This was the beginning of the "nurture or nature" controversy in English soccer.

Method, organization and overwhelming physical commitment versus imaginative action options, fluid tactics and composed, elegant effortless soccer - those were the opposing sides of the "soccer street!"

Wolves were the first English club to use work study methods and statistical analysis to justify their choice of playing style, of suitable players, of the appropriate strategies and tactics and finally the development of training regimes towards those ends.

I confess that I am a supporter of work study.

I also welcome the analysis of statistical information arising out of work study...but not by statisticians! They may indicate trends and probabilities. They are not facts.

I have chosen to present a critique of Ian Franks's paper because the implications of his conclusions are important to soccer in North America and they may be seriously misleading, even dangerously so.

Some are based upon a far from complete understanding of soccer, in its various forms, and the interdependence of each upon the others. Some comments are highly speculative even from a statistical point of view. All however are delivered with the authority and weight of a distinguished academic and a highly competent coach in what is a very new field of study. Many coaches in the USA, particularly those with collegiate and physical education backgrounds, are likely to be intrigued by Ian Franks's work and by his conclusions. And so they should be. But the logic of many of his extrapolations is seriously flawed from a soccer standpoint. I hope to show you how.

I shall try to deal with the paper in two ways: First from the perceptive of a player and coach; the second from the statistical and analytical point of view. Implicit in Ian's paper, in my view, are a number of unwarranted assumptions. The first is the assumption that success in soccer must/should be quantified and that by implication, soccer success is measured exclusively on a win-lose basis. On a win-lose continuum, perhaps, but on a strict win-lose basis — never.

STAGES OF PLAYER DEVELOPMENT

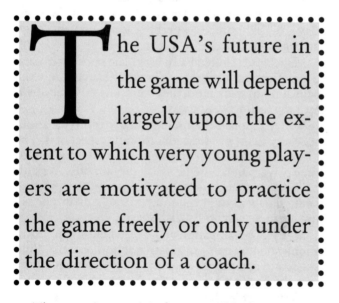

The USA's future in the game will depend largely upon the extent to which very young players are motivated to practice the game freely or only under the direction of a coach.

There are in my view four, possibly five, stages of development through which a soccer player may pass. I emphasize "may". First he plays soccer, in its crudest form, not as a cooperative activity but as an ego trip in which personal possession and clever manipulation of the ball is the source of extrinsic and, quite soon, intrinsic satisfaction approval. This stage, in developed soccer countries, may start as early as the first attempts to walk, say from two-six years of age.

The second stage embraces the years from approximately seven-11 years of age and includes the important change from entirely egocentric motivation to the beginnings of voluntary, cooperative play. To a limited extent, the player begins to appreciate reward and recognition from successful interplay with at least one other player. In team play he still tends to cooperate

more with his "friends" than with other members of the team and therefore his team identification is selective and still largely ego-centered. Intrinsic motivation and satisfaction is becoming well established and powerful.

The third stage includes the onset of puberty, begins at about 12 years and goes until about 15 years old. At this stage most players are very result conscious in so far as the result reflects creditably or otherwise on the players and his "gang" (the team or most of them). He is more interested in his team winning as long as he is recognized as having played well by his peers. Self esteem, self-respect, personal achievement, status and recognition all are at work at this time.

The next and fourth stage, from 15 years of age onwards for most players, is highly team (gang or social group) orientated. An increasing number of players seek and gain satisfaction (recognition) from personal actualization of their contribution to the collective endeavor.

The team's achievement is more important than the individual's for most players and all are prepared to go along with this criterion, especially if there is a strongly influential "cabal" within the team which says so.

An interesting aside, one of the crucial factors in managing a team is for the coach to be fully informed about the workings of powerful cliques within a team and, where possible, to actually control them without appearing to do so. Self esteem is highly developed, changing in some to self accomplishment, personal development, etc.

This fourth level is the level at which the great majority of players remain for the rest of their playing lives.

A few progress to a fifth level which is that involving the highest level of play.. serious "pro" soccer if you like; levels of play at which the ends determine the means to a significant extent.

In my view, it is only at levels four (to some extent) and five (almost wholly) that any implication that soccer success is exclusively measured on a win-lose basis has any validity.

Levels one to four exist in the main for the participatory pleasure of the players. Depending upon the bias of such early influences to which they might have been subjected, they will place total, great, some or not much importance upon winning and the game played will be none the worse for that. Those early influences will decide where upon the "play to win" versus "play for play's sake" continuum the greater part of the USA's future in the game will be established. That will depend largely upon the extent to which very young players are motivated to practice the game freely or only under the direction of a coach. And levels one through four do not exist for the exclusive benefit of level five. Many people in professional soccer, certainly in England, think they do... or at least should!

FRANK'S ANALYSIS

Mr. Frank's paper goes on to assert that "The quantitative recording of key factors is responsible for successful performance in the sport of Association Football. "What about players? There is little, if any, validity for that assertion, in my view. It may be Ian Franks's opinion, and he is entitled to state it - but not as a matter of fact.

Assuming that analysis has any validity for performance enhancement at the highest levels of play where, undoubtedly, results matter, we need to examine very closely certain other assumptions which are made to justify various implications and conclusions.

POSSESSION SOCCER

The first of these is the statement that... "The objective of the team with possession is to score goals and the opposing team's objective is, therefore, to prevent the team with possession from scoring goals..."

Sounds reasonable enough? Well, within my personal experience, many teams, given certain conditions in a match, do not use possession to score goals. I have known many to begin a game intent upon preventing their opponents from playing, at all costs almost, and only prepared to accept goals if presented on a plate. Total "no-risk" soccer in fact was their aim. This may be deplored as an extreme of negative thinking but it may represent a realistic strategy based upon a team's perceived deficiencies in the light of an opposing team's overwhelming superior resources.

Ball possession can be used to kill time or to move play into areas from which, even if possession is lost, it will be of little advantage to the side regaining it.

Possession of the ball can be used offensively or defensively. It is also commonplace to find a team without possession, and losing heavily perhaps, gambling upon regaining possession even at the risk of their opponents scoring. In other words, regaining possession is more important than preventing goals.

There would be little point in defending to prevent another goal from being scored during the last ten minutes of a championship match when losing 2-0!

STRATEGY AND TACTICS —INTERTWINED

Those of you who have read my book on Soccer Strategies will now begin to realize why I wrote it and why it is important for coaches to think through the implications of different strategies and their concomitant tactics, not the least of which is the choice of an appropriate playing style. Tactics and strategies may (or may not) be employed to achieve the purposes set down in Ian Franks's paper.

There is no doubt, of course, that the greater the incidence of risks taken near to one's own penalty area, the greater the probability that one will be punished.

The nearer to the opposing penalty area, the greater the justification for risks if goals are to be scored. Having said that, there will be times and occasions which justify a player choosing to make a high risk play in and near to his own penalty area. A valid soccer conclusion would be that the more often he chooses a high risk option, the more his opponents may encourage him to do so in order eventually to catch him at it. Divorce courts are witness to this strategy at work in domestic situations!

When closer to the opposing penalty area, of course, the greater the justification for taking risks if goals are to be scored. And if, having moved the ball successfully into the "high probability" scoring zone at the other end of the pitch, directly or indirectly, my team failed to achieve a shot on target, significantly more often than not, I would have to examine the qualities of play and of players!

The extent to which my players would be asked to step up the incidence of shots to this number or that should be determined exclusively by the limits of their shooting skills and the coach's ability to produce effective practices for their improvement.

SHOT: GOAL RATIO EXAMINED

In the section devoted to an analysis of the circumstances governing the scoring of goals, I have to take issue with Dr. Franks's paper on statistical grounds. Reference is made to a 35-year period from which goal scoring statistics reveal a shot goal ratio of 10:1. Upon this basis the paper recommends that.. "teams wishing to score two goals per game should strive to lose at least 20 possessions shooting at goal..."

That's not quite the way I would have put it - but allowing for journalistic license, any shot:goal ratio established over a 35-year period can have little relevance to your team or mine. Teams are made up of specific players—with all their individual assets and liabilities. Ian Franks hedges his bet by saying that "IN THEORY" if a team increases its number of shots, its successful shots should increase...presumably pro rata?

"In theory" is about right.

That sort of conclusion drawn from, to say the least, rather spurious evidence led one of Britain's most successful and, in America, best known "coaches" to the conclusion that: "There are lies, damned lies and statistics." — Winston Churchill, Chief Coach, The United Kingdom, 1941, The Battle of Britain.

As a matter of conjecture, what exactly constitutes a shot at goal to a statistician? Are we certain that all the shots at goal referred to in the 35-year period were judged by identical criteria? If I propel the ball towards my opponents' goal at a velocity of one foot per second is that considered a shot? If the ball ricochets into the goal off my left ear...or off some other improbable part of my anatomy...is that a shot?

Clearly in different situations, with different players, a team's strategy and its complementary tactics for scoring will change. It may pay certain teams to settle for significantly fewer shots delivered more accurately and with greater deception and power. It seems to me that over a long period, valid statistics for this, last and next season are lost in a mass of largely irrelevant data but nonetheless sustaining the magical shot goal ratio of 10:1.

It is one thing to make a quantitative assessment. It is quite another matter to have qualitative factors that are of infinitely greater importance.

PASSES AND GOAL PRODUCTION

The statistical evidence presented goes on to state that eight out of 10 goals are scored from interplay involving four passes or fewer; to which most coaches might say "so what?" Currently in English professional soccer, four successive passes would be a occasion for celebration amongst those few of us who place a high value on acute perception and upon accuracy of execution. English professional teams are not noticeably better at scoring goals than foreign teams. In fact, when exposed to the free back system in international matches, they are significantly less so.

Of course four passes or fewer are likely to produce goals. Counterattack exploits the probability that, having played under some stress to defend and having gained possession, some players, especially backs, tend to relax and are shocked into semi-paralysis should their opponents quickly regain possession and counterattack.

Any team losing concentration, whatever the cause, will be exposed by incisive interpassing.

Statistically one could argue, I suppose, that team A should deliberately give the ball to team B when near to team B's penalty area so that team A might shock team B by regaining possession to counterattack with fewer than four passes and thereby play more effectively! That argument is at least as logical, statistically as some of those put forward in Ian's paper.

And in case you are under the impression that such controversy as exists in England involves on one hand a significant number of teams devoted to subtle, multipassing moves in attack, you should disabuse yourselves of any such fanciful notions. Any such teams are in modest minority... more's the pity for English soccer.

SCORING FROM SET PLAYS

There is no disputing that a significantly high proportion of goals ARE scored from set plays... corner kicks, free kicks, throw-ins... close to, but outside the penalty area. That may be as much a criticism of teams' lack of skill, subtlety and motion and ambition in attack as commendation for those teams' organization at set plays.

Good soccer coaching at the top level involves the development, through practice, of a number of action options to meet most foreseeable situations while allowing players the license to choose for themselves how, when and where those options will be employed. If teams can't control affairs at set plays where they enjoy unopposed possession of the ball, the freedom (within the laws) to take up whatever positions they choose, and, not least, to decide when the action will commence one must question the need for coaching and practice of any kind.

When set play statistics were first presented to me by a former physical education student they included penalty kicks at a time when foul play attained unprecedented heights in the English First Division. Attackers were encouraged to "earn" penalties or direct free kicks near to the penalty area by dribbling the ball and inviting fouls. So the straight forward statistic showing that three (3) out of 10 goals are scored from set plays is not surprising. But how many set plays have to be completed to "guarantee" one goal?

CROSSING PASSES

When analyzing the use of passes made from wide positions into the penalty area, Ian Franks indulges in statistical sleight of hand of no little dexterity. First he says that the 'cross pass': goal ratio is "only 27:1." Well, any team working its way into positions to deliver that number of decent crosses into the penalty area and earning no more than one goal for twenty-seven attempts has got to ask questions about the crosses or the players. My own scrutiny would be directed at the former. The analysis goes on to show that only eight out of 27 crosses tend to be contacted by attackers and 19 wasted. From that stage on the conclusions concerning early crosses are, to be kind, a bit "iffy".

Maybe the poor statistical significance of early crosses... and early crosses have reached almost epidemic proportions in England... shows that few players know and few coaches remember where from and how the most effective crosses are, and always have been, delivered. That area has always been as near to the goal line as possible.

From the goal line and using his natural, i.e., his outside foot, the delivering player can, with almost

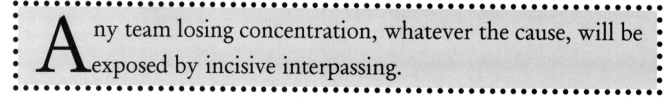

Any team losing concentration, whatever the cause, will be exposed by incisive interpassing.

no discernible alteration of his kicking action, play passes into a relatively large segment of the penalty area. Secondly, while he is reaching the crossing position, defenders will be running back to seal off likely target areas and to mark the target attackers. It is a fact of soccer life that most defenders in these situations over-recover and are exposed by crosses pulled back and away from goal. The defenders are running in one direction and the ball is travelling in the other. The early cross behind back defenders and out of the goalkeeper's reach, along the front of the goal area, is a very difficult skill with almost no margin for error, hence the low success rate. Success depends on attackers beating opponents to the ball and as with all crosses, high or low, front post or back post or wherever, I will wager that more goals will be scored by attackers feinting to move behind defender, before moving in front of them to contact the cross, than by seeking the ball behind defenders. Frankly the accuracy demand, which can be so greatly magnified by moisture on the ball or by less than perfect ground conditions or by wind, makes it necessary for the early cross to be used with much greater discretion.

Interestingly, the early cross, which was first used to any significant extent in England by West Ham, was developed to defeat the increasing tendency, at the time, to double up against wingers to prevent the getting to the goal line to cross the ball. West Ham used the tactic to open up better opportunities for goal line crosses. Now we find crossing from his goal line a poor second option for the attacker!

RECOMMENDATIONS

I shall now move on to the recommendations which Ian Franks makes in the section headed "Framework for Analysis".

I take no issue with the majority of them.

As I have already said, ideally every attacking move should lead to a shot at goal. In modern soccer, at the top levels, the vast majority do not. In basketball it is almost unthinkable for a team gaining possession to fail to get in a shot; the only question, it seems to me, is whether the team has the individual and collective skills to shoot from inside or outside positions. Individual and collective basketball skills are produced by long practice with and without the direction of a first class coach. So what's so different about the problems faced by a soccer team? Any team willing to play and practice possession-to-shoot soccer will become better at it. Having said that, you don't have to know much about the game to play percentage soccer.. or factory football as I would refer to it in England. Maybe that's an attractive option for would-be "coach puppeteers" who seek to win by manipulation.

The end product will not be a pretty sight and for players it will mean the complete emasculation of individual talent and initiative.

> **A**ny team working its way into positions to deliver that number of decent crosses into the penalty area and earning no more than one goal for twenty-seven attempts has got to ask questions about the crosses.

In his "Framework for Analysis", Franks makes another assertion which is, in my opinion, open to debate... "the converse of losing possession is gaining it.. " Let's look at the various recommendations in detail.

Recommendation 1

The converse of losing possession is not "gaining it", as Ian Franks claims, but "keeping it". I don't wish to argue about semantics, but the difference is an important one. The most skillful way of playing the game, the surest and the safest way, is by keeping possession of the ball until the objective of keeping it has been achieved. As I have already said, that objective can vary from team to team, from game to game and even during a game.

To many of the questions which Ian Franks feels should be asked by coaches I would at least add the supplementary question "why"? It may be impossible to answer statistically but it is likely to provide a coach with much greater insight into team and player performance and add a qualitative element to the answers. Statisticians aren't concerned with qualitative answers, of course, but coaches most definitely are... or should be!

Recommendation 2

Certainly do what you can to win the ball back early WITHIN THE CAPABILITIES OF YOUR PLAYERS. If you have relatively frail but highly skillful strikers it is of little use expecting them to produce stern, confrontative effort in defense. Players lacking speed have to defend differently from those who are faster. Strategies and tactics are constrained by the players at a coach's disposal, not by rules of play.

Recommendations 3 and 4

The recommendations here go too far. It simply is not possible to play the game as it should be played on a "thou shalt" basis. There are certain areas into which and from crosses MAY be played to advantage. One of these, in certain conditions, is from behind defenders into space in front of the goal area. But that is only one option, NOT THE ONLY option. And players don't HAVE to cross the ball in order to penetrate the penalty area. They can interpass or dribble, especially when close to what many coaches will identify as weakly-defended zones, those towards the outfield corners of the penalty area.

Obsessional concern with crosses is counter-productive. The obvious, done all the time, is self-defeating and contrary to the principles of sound tactical play in which deception is the key element.

Clever players use the probability of a cross to set up an alternative option and vice versa. The area in front of the six yard box ISN'T the only worthwhile target space.

TECHNICAL DEMANDS ON PERFORMANCE

One of the consequences of playing high-pressure, direct, purely functional soccer is that the style of play significantly influences the tactical and the technical content of the game. In my view, any style of play has a significant and predictable effect on tactics and technique. The more extreme the style, the greater the effect, which is why I emphasize the importance of decisions about style in my book.

It is easy to say that the ultra-direct style requires the same techniques as any other style, but the fact is that it causes a number of skills quickly to disappear from players' repertoires, eroded through atrophy.. in other words, through lack of use.

Urgency, for example, in playing the ball behind defenders means that, under any sort of pressure, players tend to hit the ball first time and often hopefully. They lose whatever touch they had in bringing the ball under control and the skill of selling a dummy to trick an opponent disappears. Finding players with these skills in English First Division soccer is almost an impossibility, hence the serious problems faced by England in international competition.

All the responsibility for control is pushed onto the pass receivers who, because above all they have to be very athletic, lack high quality control and manipulative techniques.

Considerations involving good and bad passing angles; delivering passes with correct weight; developing deceptive foot, body or eye movements before passing; even the skill of giving good ground passes all tend to atrophy and disappear. As for selling dummies and then running the ball, precious few players in England are capable of or willing to run the ball positively, confident that teammates will show space to support their runs and pull opponents off the dribbling line.

The implications of adopting ultra-direct methods are that hardworking players become more valuable

> Trying to persuade functional, factory footballers to play with more skill is an entirely different kettle of fish and well nigh impossible in the short and medium term.

than those with skill and skillful players modify their skills to become hard workers. Where does that leave the game?

Given the need, a coach can always persuade and train skillful players to play with more effort. They may not like it but they CAN do it. Trying to persuade functional, factory footballers to play with more skill is an entirely different kettle of fish and well nigh impossible in the short and medium term.

So what do you do when a hardworking team begins to play badly? Ask them to work harder?

TRANSFER OF TRAINING

Towards the end of this section on technical demands, Ian Franks makes a strange comment. He refers quite properly to the crucial importance, in coaching, of understanding the principles behind the effective transfer of training from practice situations to match play. In my judgement, and probably Ian's, far too many practice situations are designed to meet the organizational needs of the coach rather than the skill improvement needs of the players. The higher you go in English soccer, the truer that statement will be. Ian Franks goes on to refer to the need for coaches to understand how events in soccer.. unfold in time and certain events precede and succeed others in the game". He says that "sequential dependency," as this is called, isn't clearly understood by coaches and he's quite right. The strange thing is that it is their failure to apply (understand?) sequential dependency principles that has always brought me into disagreement with statisticians!

The tactics, skills and techniques can only be studied and analyzed within the context of play, including all those factors, extrinsic and intrinsic, which affect it.

THE KEY TO SUCCESSFUL COACHING

I wish that I could find it. The more I know the more there seems to be to learn!

There is no doubt, of course, that used sensitively and with discretion, video does offer positive feedback possibilities of a most valuable kind. Visual proof is almost proof positive... almost but not totally. Telling a player, for example that when receiving the ball, predictably he turns right and moves onto his right foot is one thing, showing him doing it is quite another. There are many players who take unkindly to criticism, real or implied, justified or not, constructive or destructive. Video used to prove the coach right... even if he is... and the player wrong is a tempting but dangerous use of the facility.

So where does all this lead us?

Statistical analysis is a fine tool but a poor master. In my view it has been used by some coaches and statisticians to justify certain attitudes to the game which they sought to adopt before they chose to analyze it. Too often analysis has been selective and, in certain cases, biased, which meant that conclusions drawn have been to some extent flawed. Nevertheless the establishment of basic facts is necessary and coaches do have fallible memories. Be careful. Make sure that the questions you want answered CAN be answered by statistical study and that YOU interpret the statistician's work in soccer terms. Statistics is about probabilities and trends, not about certainties. And if your statistician can't produce the information you require, get another statistician, not a different way of playing!

Soccer, played well, is a simple game played at its best by far from similar people. It allows for enormous intellectual and perceptual motor ability and its possibilities for technical and tactical versatility and virtuosity are limitless unless we allow it to be reduced to movement to numbers, to a kind of sequence dancing in fact.

You have the choice: think carefully before you choose. The future of the greatest game in the world may depend upon it.

Chapter 3

DEVELOPING A SOCCER COACHING PHILSOPHY

Inside Shot

The series of articles included in this chapter seek to provide coaches at all levels of play with crucial understandings as they develop or examine their philosophy of coaching.

All professions are founded on basic underlying principles of conduct. Ethics related to coaching is given thorough coverage here with the most recent NSCAA Code of Ethics produced as a guide for all readers.

As the coach is generally considered a role model for those in his/her soccer community, the expectations inherent in that position is also examined by various authors. What are the responsibilities of one who would be called "Coach?" What is the proper representation that a person should portray as a coach?

How to win and how to lose are both important appreciations that all coaches must learn and professionally dealing with these emotions is very important to the overall success that a coach will achieve in his/her career.

Finally, the attitude of the coach is noted as being essential in terms of its short term and long range implications on the development of their players. Acquiring the right coaching perspective towards such matters as the rules of the game and officials as well as total player development are among the topics addressed in this segment of the book.

Such sentiments as "Nice people do not finish last, nice people finish best" (Doug Burke) and "There is no greater satisfaction in life than realizing that you have made a significant contribution to a young person's life" (Paul Hartman) epitomize the central themes of this chapter.

OUR ETHICAL RESPONSIBILITIES TO COLLEAGUES
Joe Bean

I want to address four statements that are a part of the NSCAA Code of Ethics that could be overlooked by some coaches. It may be helpful to all of us who are in the midst of our soccer schedules to remember our ethical responsibilities toward our fellow coaches.

First, in Article V, #5, it states, "Coaches should avoid references to unethical recruitment and possible violations by their peers." I feel that it is our duty and responsibility to confront a fellow coach personally and give him information regarding possible violations in recruitment, eligibility or other matters prior to the season. If the season has started, it could still be mentioned and corrections be made. Don't wait until the season is over and the coach and his team are selected to play in a postseason tournament. If you have personally confronted your peer before tournament selection and corrections have not been made, then you have the right and responsibility to report it to the proper authorities, i.e., his athletic director or the NCAA Selection Committee.

Secondly, in Article VII, #2, we find that..."the use of videotape or motion picture equipment to scout an opponent's regularly scheduled game is prohibited." I believe this should also include practice or exhibition games as well. We all might be surprised at the number of "friends" that may be taking family video tapes during a game that eventually find their way to the coach's video recorder. This is something we must guard against to be fair to our coaching colleagues.

Thirdly, in Article VII, #4, the statement reads, "When discussing the advantages of his organization, the coach has an obligation to be truthful and forthright. He must refrain from making derogatory statements about another coach or organization." It is best to say nothing if you have nothing good to say. That is probably the best and most ethical approach to take. If you are aware of wrongdoings, again, you have the responsibility of confronting that coach about the issue on a personal basis.

Fourth, in Article VIII, #4, we find, "It shall be considered unethical for a coach to have any verbal dissent during the game with an opposing coach or bench." Don't hang out the wash to dry in public view! Besides being untimely, remarks made during the heat of battle are often taken out of context by the recipient. Calm down, readjust your tie and offer to buy your opponent a cup of coffee and discuss your differences. The price of the cup of coffee could prove to be one of your best investments.

In summary, one of the most ethical and gentlemanly examples of responsibility of a coach toward another was demonstrated by Page Cotton, the coach at DePauw University (IN) in their first game of 1988 against my team, Wheaton College. Page and I conferred over the phone on several matters two days prior to the game. In the course of the conversation he voluntarily told me that one of his starters from last year would have to sit out the game against Wheaton because he had been redcarded in the last playoff game in 1987. I didn't know that. The only monitoring system available presently is a coach's conscience and ethical standards. Page Cotton is an example of what is

involved in "Our Ethical Responsibilities to Colleagues." I hope all of us will pursue this line of reasoning in all of our decisions as it relates to our fellow coaches.

ETHICS AND SPORTSMANSHIP: AN NSCAA PARTNERSHIP
Joe Bean

One of the objectives of the founding fathers of the NSCAA was "to encourage the development of soccer in the schools of the nation." This objective was part and parcel of an underlying principle that the development of soccer would enhance ethical behavior and sportsmanlike conduct along the way.

In the early 1960's the Ethics Committee, chaired by Don Minnegan of Towson State (MD) endeavored to cope with two basic problems that hindered the development of soccer. One was the lack of consistent and firm action by the then Intercollegiate Soccer/Football Association in dealing with player eligibility and alleged professionalism. It was a problem because each organization had its separate ethics committee and acted independently. This resulted in a two-pronged approach which sent mixed messages to all the coaches. As a solution the NSCAA and the renamed Intercollegiate Soccer Association of America merged forces in the early 80s to support one Ethics Committee, embodied by a separate Code of Ethics.

With this change, the Ethics Committee was mandated to carry out the Code of Ethics through proper education and communication to the entire membership. It has endeavored to do this first under the chairmanship of Greg Myers of the U.S. Naval Academy, and since 1990 under my chairmanship.

The other glaring problem, and most difficult one to communicate, is the lack of understanding of many coaches that ethical behavior and sportsmanship go hand in hand.

In 1962, Don Yonker, then editor of *Soccer Journal*, lamented on the need for coaches to avoid "rough-house tactics" and "the hard-nose approach" and teach more technical and tactical approaches to the playing of the game. He later called in the Ethics Committee to act, stating, "We submit it's time that coaches rated the play of each other for sportsmanship, and let the committee attend games with a tape recorder and record some of the verbal nonsense rampant at the games—with the idea of playing back the worst of the taped at the annual meeting! His last admonition was "to identify the teams who employ these cheap, unsporting gimmicks, and avoid scheduling them—like they would avoid the plague."

Another long standing stalwart of the NSCAA and a past-president, Richard Schmelzer, also made a strong statement regarding the role of ethics in coaching. He made the statement after reading a copy of the revised Code of Ethics that Greg Myer's committee had worked out. In part he said, "We all know that a soccer coach should be a good boy scout and be noble, kind, considerate, fair, etc. But what we should know is how much competitiveness is allowable and what is not, when one becomes a stinker by taking advantage of rules, etc...." He further stated; "Coaches get jobs according to their win and loss records, so winning is an important part of their job security. Young coaches especially, need guidance as to what is frowned on and what is allowed." He concluded by saying, "No mere statement of ethics can turn people into such sterling characters as I have indicated, but it can help coaches try to set examples of conduct for their players. We have all seen players and coaches who were magnanimous in defeat and bent over backwards to give opponents their due. That's one of the charms of non-bigtime sport. Such sportsmanship is an old soccer tradition, and I hope that American commercialism won't spoil it..."

Some of the above ideas might be harsh and would be viable to implement in any sanctioning of coaches. However, the concepts of integrity through sportsmanship and ethical behavior through a common bond of fraternalism is most noteworthy. Ethical behavior and sportsmanship should be partners.

CODE OF ETHICS

One of the ongoing aspects of work for the NSCAA has been to impress on its members expected standards of conduct that soccer coaches at all levels of coaching are expected to adhere to.

Following is the most recent work of the NSCAA Ethics Committee.

Coaching associations may wish to have this reproduced in hopes of aiding coaches as they develop their coaching philosophy. This code, while focusing on soccer in an educational setting, contains some fundamental information that serves as a good reference point for coaches at all levels of play.

● ●

NATIONAL SOCCER COACHES ASSOCIATION OF
AMERICA CODE OF ETHICS AND CONDUCT

Preamble

The following ethical standards and code of conduct outline a philosophy that is paramount to the game of soccer and must be emphasized in combination with skill development and style of play. Soccer is a sport which belongs to the players. It is a game which offers physical challenges, emotional satisfaction and lifelong values and experiences for those who play.

Within this context, coaches should prioritize the welfare of their players and dedicate themselves to upholding the highest standards of professional conduct and competence. Sportsmanship and ethical values highlighting respect, fairness, civility, honesty, integrity and accountability are a foundation for the sport. Men and women who enter the soccer coaching profession either on a professional or volunteer basis should advocate these standards and supplement the NSCAA's ethical framework with their own moral conduct and behavior. In this way, coaches preserve the stability of the soccer community and promote a positive reputation for the coaching profession.

Coaches' ethical behavior is demonstrated in relationships with the athletes, colleagues, officials, parents, administrators, clients and communities. Coaches are ambassadors for the sport of soccer, their programs, clubs, association and/or institutions. They are role models and must understand the tremendous influence their words and actions have on the players who comprise their teams. For this reason, coaches should consider their primary responsibility the continuance of moral values and ethical conduct which advance the spirit of the game and adhere to established rules.

Article One: Responsibilities to Players

1. The importance of winning must never supersede the players' safety and welfare. Winning should be the result of preparation and discipline with considerable emphasis placed on the highest societal ideals and character traits. These values are not sacrificed for prestige or personal gain.

2. Requirements for participation on a soccer team must not impede a player's opportunity for achieving academic success. The student athlete's education must be of foremost concern.

3. Coaches must adhere to the rules of the game. They must not seek unfair advantage by teaching deliberate unsportsmanlike behavior or accepting illegal gains over an opponent.

4. The demands coaches place on their players must be consistent with the guidelines consistent with the guidelines established by respective governing bodies, conferences, institutions and/or associations overseeing athletic competition.

5. The diagnosis and treatment of injuries is a medical problem and coaches must defer to the proper medical personnel without interference. Coaches must follow the directives of appropriate medical authorities.

6. Coaches must not promote the use of anabolic agents or stimulants for the purpose of gaining athletic advantage. Medications and drugs are prescribed and authorized only by physicians.

7. Coaches must take an active role in the prevention and treatment of drug, alcohol and tobacco abuse.

8. Coaches must never knowingly jeopardize the eligibility and participation of a student-athlete.

Article Two: Responsibilities to the Institution

1. Coaches must promote the educational goals and missions of their institutions and behave in such a manner that the principles, integrity and dignity of their instutions are not compromised.

2. Coaches must not ask faculty members or teachers to give inappropriate considerations or exceptions for athletes.

3. Coaches must not interfere with the duties or jurisdiction of other institutional departments such as admissions, compliance and the various academic disciplines.

4. Coaches must assure their programs are being conducted and promoted ethically an also be aware of any institutional activities which may affect their programs' performance and reputation.

5. Student records and transcripts are considered strictly confidential and must be used only for official purposes (i.e. NCAA Clearing House).

6. Coaches must adhere to institutional policies regarding athletic program funding and personal remunerations received for related professional activities and endorsements.

7. Coaches must discuss problems with their athletic directors in a professional manner and then support institutional decisions concerning policies, rules and regulations relating to soccer.

8. Coaches must immediately notify their athletic directors or respective administrators of any situation that violates governing body, conference, club, league or institutional rules.

Article Three: Rules of the Game

1. Coaches must thoroughly acquaint themselves with the rules of soccer. They are also responsible for assuring their players understand the intent and application of the rules.

2. Coaches must adhere to the letter and spirit of the game's rules and not circumvent the rules to gain an advantage.

3. Coaches are responsible for their players' actions on the field. Unsportmanlike tactics (i.e. the intent to injure opposing players), illegal substitutions, taunting, deliberate faking of injuries and "professional fouls" are considered unethical.

4. Fair play must be encouraged and emphasized within the training sessions and competitions.

Article Four: Officials

1. Impartial, competent officials are essential for the success of any competition. Coaches must not criticize officials publicly or privately and must follow institutional, conference or organizational rules dealing with comments on officiating.

2. Coaches, institutions and leagues must support their local and national soccer officials' associations.

3. Coaches should attend as many officials' rules meetings as possible. Coaches are also encouraged to invite officials to discuss rules interpretations with their teams.

4. The following points outline game day conduct: a) treat officials with respect; b) if possible, provide officials with a private room, away from opposing teams; c) if criticism is going to be leveled against officials, complaints must be made in writing to the appropriate organizations or local boards responsible for officiating assignments; d) coaches and teams must not address the referee before, during or after the game in a demeaning way; and e) coaches must not incite players or spectators against referees.

5. Coaches must never use slow motion video replay equipment in public to check a controversial decision made by an official. It is unethical to show critical calls to sportswriters, sports announcers, team members, alumni and/or the public with the intent of labeling an official incompetent. Any use of the media to castigate officials is unacceptable.

Article Five: Public Relations and the Media

1. In many situations, the game of soccer requires significant explanation to the media. Public relations becomes part of the job description for many coaches. Members of the news media and sports information community must be treated with respect, courtesy and honesty.

2. Coaches must not make derogatory or misleading comments to the media about officials, opposing teams and coaches, spectators, parents or other institutions.

3. Coaches have a responsibility to educate their players concerning proper conduct for media interviews.

4. Coaches must not use the media or a public forum to reveal unethical recruiting practices or rules violations by opposing teams and colleagues. Such matters need to be addressed administratively.

5. Coaches must respect the policies and prodedures established by their sports information departments, conferences or leagues concerning relations with the media. Policies which are established must give all members of the media equal access to designated officials or participants. Coaches must assure that all commitments made by players or staff regarding media interviews or photograph sessions are honored.

6. Coaches must not be associated with professional games, nor should coaches ever be present where gambling on sports teams is permitted and encouraged.

7. Statements reflecting soccer's role within the educational process are encouraged and benefit the game.

Article Six: Recruiting

1. Coaches must strictly adhere to all institutional, conference, state and national governing body rules pertaining to recruiting.

2. It is unethical to recruit a player from another team or four-year institution. When a student-athlete voluntarily seeks a transfer, coaches must follow established guidelines.

3. When promoting and describing their institutions or programs, coaches have an obligation to be honest and forthright. At the same time, they must refrain from making derogatory statements about other colleagues or institutions.

4. Coaches must not make false promises to prospective student-athletes.

5. Coaches must refrain from using non-institutional coaching responsibilities (i.e. ODP or club coaching affiliations) to enhance their programs' recruiting process.

6. High school coaches must adhere to appropriate conference and state regulations. Recruiting at this level is discouraged and considered unethical.

Article Seven: Other Responsibilities

1. Coaches must avoid any conduct which is construed as physically or verbally abusive.

2. Coaches must avoid verbal dissent during a game with an opposing coach or bench.

3. Coaches of host teams are expected to meet with opposing coaches prior to a game and assure that the visiting teams' needs are met.

4. Coaches must carry out all obligations concerning employment contracts unless they are released from these commitments through mutual agreement. If a coach is considering interruptions or termination of service, he/she must give appropriate notice.

5. Coaches must honor all professional relationships with colleagues, associations, the media, officials and the public. Conflicts of interest and exploitation of these relationships must be avoided.

6. Coaches must perform their duties on the basis of careful preparation, ensuring their instruction is current and accurate. Coaches must continually seek new opportunities for professional development and education. Coaches must remain current on health, safety and training developments relevant to the sport of soccer. Coaches are encouraged to seek advice from peers and colleagues whenever such consultation is in the best interest of the student-athletes.

7. Relationships and communication with player agents must be in accordance with the law and governing body rules and regulations.

8. Coaches must not receive compensation from professional teams for talent scouting or player negotiation.

9. A coach must not solicit or engage in sexual relations with any minor on his/her team. Specific sexual harrassment issues are addressed by the respective institutions, associations, clubs or leagues.

10. The use of video tape or motion picture equipment to scout an opponent's regularly scheduled game is prohibited.

11. It is unethical under any circumstances to scout a team, by any means whatsoever, except in regularly scheduled games.

12. A coach's behavior and values must bring credit to his/her program, institution and the sport of soccer.

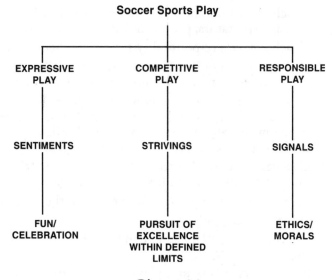

Diagram 3-1

Soccer, Ethics and Education
Marvin A. Zuidema

Those of us who have been coaching soccer for many years sometimes look ahead and wonder where sports in America are headed. With our specific interest we wonder what direction our interscholastic, intercollegiate and youth soccer sports programs will take. Almost every week we read a new article that centers on corruption and violence in sports. The *NCAA Newsletter*, the *Chronicle of Education, Soccer America*, as well as our local newspapers and weekly magazines, feature reports that center on the ethics of sports in America. With the World Cup coming to the United States in 1994, we will also begin to see the ugly side of international sport raise its head. Soccer will now have publicized its drug tests, contractual disagreements, citizenship issues, player violence, crowd rowdiness, ticket scandals and other unsavory news.

When soccer began in the United States as schoolboy competition in the 1940s, the sport had a freshness that many of us have learned to appreciate. Competition may have lacked adroitness—but it was wholesome. The rules of the game came almost by gentlemen's agreement. "Who you play" was often a matter of finding someone to play rather than a matter of playing someone to improve your power rating. Officials were friends, not enemies! And the good feeling of victory was tempered with thankfulness for being able to participate while the agony of defeat was valued as learning experience.

The rapid growth of soccer in America, whether it be interscholastic or intercollegiate play, youth sport activity, or World Cup competition, is interesting to watch.

In this article, I would like to address what I consider to be the essential elements of sport participation with the hope and prayer that playing soccer may remain a wholesome and wonderful experience. It is my thesis that a proper philosophy of sports participation is filled with questions of ethics and education.

Celebration

Diagram 3-1 presents what I believe to be three root elements of sports play regardless of the competition level. The first element is celebration. Game and practice participation should be filled with the sentiment of fun! "I play soccer" should mean "soccer is a kick!" Play is thus an attitude, a state of being, rather than a sportive activity. And soccer indeed is a fun sport! The thrill of a well-hit ball, a perfect trap, a beautifully-driven header or free kick, a diving save, a well-executed fake or tackle, and the "goal" are things of beauty. Only soccer players truly know the art and beauty of soccer.

Soccer may have had a slow impact in this country because most of us, as youth, did not experience the art of soccer when we were young. The 80s have revealed that once players truly understand the game, they can indeed communicate to others the nuances that make the sport what it is to millions around the world. Soccer is simple, yet complex. The game involves simple skills, but technical ability when refined into skill, does not come easily as players well understand. Soccer is simple in its rules (except perhaps for the offside rule), but the rules are not easily learned. Yes, it is true that the sport really hasn't gained acceptance as a big spectator sport in the United States, but this lack of appreciation may be largely due to the fact that participation, not spectatorism, gives most soccer players their identity with the sport.

Or as so many have stated—soccer is a game to be played, not watched. And American sport needs participants! We need vigorous, active children and adults, not wallflowers and couch potatoes. And while soccer seems to lack any tactics to the uninitiated, the heart of the game is creative two and three-player combinations. I urge all of us to let soccer remain what it is: a simple game filled with vigorous, active and expressive fun.

Let's protect soccer play from the evils of dishonesty, violence, money, greed, personal glory, and institutional empire-building which so easily rob the sport of its simplistic beauty and expressive nature. All this means that we may have to concentrate on keeping youth and school sports fun, and we must guard against the professionalization of the game. This may mean that youth and school sport organizations must pay attention to training coaches and officials from a play perspective rather than worrying about select teams and game uniforms. It also could mean that school and college sports must regulate recruiting, and possibly even limit scholarships. It may mean that we must evaluate the ethics of scholarship services which solicit paid advertisements promoting the sale of even amateur players to the highest bidder. Finally, it may mean that our national goal to have a competitive World Cup soccer team must not interfere with the play of the thousands of youth, prep school and collegiate players who simply enjoy the game, and who don't need rules and regulations that might help the national game, but rob kids of the right to play, (i.e., the NCAA limited substitution rule).

COMPETITION

A second root element is competition. Soccer is a team game involving two groups that wish to engage in competitive play. But what is competition? There are many answers to this question, and how you answer has ethical and moral overtones. Should we agree not to compete, but to love? The world would probably be a better place to live in if we could all agree to such a way of life. But such a view of competition suggests that competition is morally bad. I submit that competition is really not bad or good in itself, but it is the "use" we make of competition that gives competitive play moral overtones. Competition can easily become a duel, a bitter struggle between two teams each trying to "kill" the other. The net effect of such competition is an overzealous battle for supremacy which often ends in anger and hate. And sports play is supposed to be fun! How much better a game where two teams play to the best of their abilities, and even though one team wins, all players shake hands after the game and honestly say "great game!"

Others would suggest that the heart of competition lies in goal-setting and prize-seeking. This is surely part of competition. But we should all remember the temporal nature of victories, trophies and awards. Compete to win, but don't let winning become an obsession. Championships and awards are great but they don't have eternal significance nor do they mean as much as doing your best within the spirit of the rules.

I submit that a wholesome view of competition is to strive for excellence within agreed-upon limits and within established boundaries. Intensity of effort is essential in sports play. Competition should motivate players to pursue excellence! Yet, the search for excellence must have boundaries with limits. Such questions as number of players on a team, amount of practice time, recruitment policies, number of coaches, bench and field behavior, playing the rules or playing by the rules, and coaching ethics fall within these boundaries.

Soccer at the collegiate level has always been an enjoyable pursuit of excellence, because we usually

> Soccer at the collegiate level has always been an enjoyable pursuit of excellence, because we usually have been able to agree on the boundaries for the pursuit of excellence.

have been able to agree on the boundaries for the pursuit of excellence. At issue today in the collegiate and prep ranks is the question of how education and sports are to be blended. The years of formal education quickly pass and are best spent at schools and colleges which work hard at presenting and instilling the knowledge, skills and attitudes which are offered through academics rather than promoting soccer as a way of life. I believe education and athletics are compatible! But we must stand firm on the principle that athletic participation must not distract from the educational process but rather add to value-filled education. Athletics can be education, but we must teach values in our athletic programs. It is important to remember that either positive or negative values are taught or caught in all athletic play because competition demands the totality of being. Values come from the what, why and how of play. I trust that all of us can testify that the sport of soccer is an ideal game for merging challenging, intense play with values education.

FAIR PLAY

The third root element of sports play is responsible actions involving fair play. Research has failed to determine whether sport can build character or whether athletes with certain values are attracted to certain sports mores. Yet we know that sports play tests ethical values. Courage, tenacity, resourcefulness, giving and fairness all are tested in sports play because, despite the ardent drive to win, players and coaches are asked to stick to the rules. Gamesmanship is as big a part of soccer play as competition and fun! I deplore, and I trust you do also, the sport norms that honor only winners, condone violence, encourage a hate for opponents, accept dishonesty, glorify coaches and players who intimidate others, and allow athletes to live and play as they please. I respect and uphold personal character that honors and reflects perseverance, self-control, integrity, stewardship, service, cooperation, respect for opponents and officials, and social and game justice.

Share, Care and Play Fair is an excellent slogan to govern responsible play.

I would like to conclude by asking some questions. You will probably discover that your answers demand ethical decisions, but also that your answers determine to a large extent the real values in your sports play.

1. Do you feel good about your involvement in soccer?
2. Can you play fair even without an official to interpret play?
3. Do you respect officials?
4. Do you respect your opponents?
5. Can you win without conceit?
6. Can you lose without ill will?
7. Do you respect your teammates? Coaches? Managers?
8. Do you thank God for your talents?
9. Do you work up to your ability level?
10. Do you keep fit?
11. Can you control your emotions?
12. Can you accept honor with humility?
13. Can you play the game joyfully?
14. Does sportive play cause you to serve self or serve others?
15. Do you take justice into your own hands or use proper avenues?
16. Are you getting the most out of your education?
17. Are you playing the game or are you using the game?

Everyone desires that your soccer play remain expressive, competitive, and responsible. Soccer is a great sport when played intensely, expressively and responsibly. Enjoy the great game of soccer.

SOCCER COACHES AS MODELS
Doug Burke

Soccer coaches are, or should be, concerned with ethics. Otherwise, why has the NSCAA and ISAA established an Ethics Committee? The primary purpose of the Ethics Committee has been to review reports of soccer matches which have experienced unusual numbers of yellow and red cards.

At present, the NSCAA/ISAA Ethics Committee is trying to develop a better understanding of proper behavior for soccer coaches. As we witness a breakdown of ethics in every walk of life today, it should be a noble goal for soccer coaches to offer a high level of ethical conduct to the public. Soccer coaches have the opportunity to lead the way for the entire coaching fraternity as good models in their approach to officials, opponents, recruiting, and winning.

ETHICS DEFINED

There are many definitions of the word "ethics." The dictionary gives several:

1. The discipline dealing with what is good (virtue) and bad (vice)
2. A set of moral principles or values
3. The study of right or wrong
4. A system of accepted professional conduct of behavior
5. The seat of ethics is in our hearts, not in our minds.

Another way to look at ethical behavior is to ask ourselves "How do we wish to be treated day by day?" "How do we want our players to be treated?" Treat others as we wish to be treated. Follow the "Golden Rule."

The message then of the NSCAA/ISAA Ethics Committee is that ethical behavior is important to the game of soccer. To establish and practice proper ethics is the responsibility of each coach. The coach should have ethical guidelines as to how the soccer program will operate.

Basically, ethics is a "people problem." Ethical people will behave in the proper manner. Unethical people will behave in unethical ways. It is therefore important that we all be coaches of high moral character. Coaches should surround themselves with quality people. This includes assistants, athletes, interested alumni and others. With quality people most problems of acceptable conduct will be solved.

An example of a "people problem" was witnessed recently by our women's soccer coach. As she left the field following a game, she heard the opposing coach giving explicit instructions to her team on how to grab an opponent's uniform without being caught by the official. Coaches who teach holding, encroachment, and how to hack a good striker are teaching young people that anything goes as long as you do not get caught.

ETHICS AND SOCIETY

Ethics is also a problem of our society. The news media makes it very clear that our society has a serious problem with ethics. This past spring ABC Television's Peter Jennings explored ethical problems in business, politics, sports, and religion. The title of the program was "Lying, Cheating, Stealing." The bottom line of the program was that indeed unethical behavior permeates every area of our society.

The news media kept up this reporting throughout the summer with stories of ethical dilemmas faced by Oklahoma football, Kentucky basketball and baseball's Pete Rose. Those of us who are in soccer

W**e need coaches, athletes, and officials who have the commitment to do what is right no matter what the cost.**

know too well the unpleasant incidents involving soccer during the past year. In the fall of 1988 the NSCAA/ISAA Committee received reports of a number of games where the behavior of players and coaches were detrimental to the game. We trust that in the future coaches will take control of themselves and their players and that all reports will be complimentary.

ETHICS AND WINNING

At the root of the ethical problems in our society is the drive to get head, to be first, to win. Winning in sports has become an all-consuming affair. We have come to believe that winning is the entire objective of any game and the coach and athlete should do whatever is necessary to win.

Winning is a noble goal. However, as coaches and athletes, we should pursue that goal in a noble way. This means that we play by the spirit of the laws of the game and that we show respect to persons such as officials, spectators, opponents, and teammates.

Americans have made losing unacceptable. The pursuit of winning is an unhealthy endeavor in many soccer programs. The Minnesota Vikings have played in four NFL Super Bowls yet they have been labeled losers.

If you pursue the goal of winning within the spirit of the rules, you are a winner and not a loser. That is to say you practice and play at or near your potential. We need coaches, athletes, and officials who have the commitment to do what is right no matter what the cost. Another way of putting it: "Nice people do not finish last, nice people finish best!"

Most of our coaches and athletes are people of high ethical conduct. These individuals are models to imitate. When coaches' and players' actions are detrimental to the game of soccer they should be sanctioned by the appropriate body.

American society has been greatly influenced by Judeo-Christian morality. These ethics provided guidelines for individual and corporate behavior. Religious principles were taught by the church, home, and school.

Modern society has seen a breakdown in these institutions, which has eroded their influence on people. This places the coach in a crucial role as a leader on the soccer field. The attitude the coach brings to the game will have an impact on the athletes. The soccer coach can be a significant educator in teaching ethical

concepts. Athletes look to the coach to model or signal the behavior expected or permitted.

SOCCER AS A TRAINING GROUND

Soccer is an excellent training ground for life. The soccer field is a fertile place for the discovery and development of moral and spiritual values. The impressions made on the athlete on the field of competition are deeper and longer-lasting than those impressions from the classroom.

The competitive environment of the soccer field is loaded with adjustment problems in which ethical standards and behavior patterns are involved. These situations are real and not merely verbal concepts. The soccer player has many opportunities to act in an ethical way in the course of a contest.

Soccer coaches, commit yourselves, your players, and your programs to high standards of ethical conduct. Pursue the noble goal of winning in a noble way. Then you will bring honor to the great game of soccer.

COACHING 101
Dr. Paul E. Hartman

It takes time to be a successful coach. Just as an athlete needs to learn the fundamental skills and mature into an experienced player, the coach needs to go through a learning period. While experience is being acquired, there are guidelines to follow that will lead to a successful coaching career. These guidelines center around hard work, the development of a sound philosophy, thorough organization, and integrity.

A young coach must realize that he or she is in a profession which is different than most other vocations. A sacrifice must be made in terms of one's time. Dedication to a particular sport requires 100 percent effort. This effort starts early in the morning and often goes well into the night. A person must work at coaching because of the very nature of the competitive environment. Proper administration of the entire program takes time and is essential to success. The elimination of mistakes in game situations requires many hours of preparation, practice, and evaluation.

This also means that the coach's family must have a great deal of understanding. There will be many times when you cannot make it home for dinner or are gone for an entire evening or weekend. A coach cannot simply get away from responsibilities inherent in planning, recruiting, counseling and sharing with both the team and the community.

For the young, hard-working coach, developing a sound philosophy is essential. The philosophy of any individual does not evolve quickly and changes throughout a person's career. However, guidelines are needed and, therefore, it is necessary to formulate sound concepts from the outset so that both the students and coaches involved in the program and the program itself are kept on track toward one purpose.

The manner in which you deal with students is extremely important. Sport is an educational experience for young people. The years of competitive participation are a time of rapid growth. At times problems and situations arise with which you must deal. A sound philosophy will guide you both on and off the field and often eliminate potential problems while helping you solve those which arise. Discipline is essential, but there must also be flexibility and understanding. The sport must be fun for the participants, but they must also realize that objectives are not obtained unless they are willing to join with the coaching staff in giving 100 percent. Let the players and coaches help you formulate your philosophy. This will put your thoughts into proper perspective and you will gain support from those who are working with you. Keep in mind that each player is an individual. Although there must be general rules for the entire team, all players will not react in the same way or as expected.

It is often wise to explain your philosophy to the entire team so that they will accept one another for what they are and thus develop cohesiveness through understanding. In essence, you are developing a philosophy of life and thus your methods must stand the test of time.

Your coaching philosophy is equally important and must be based on sound principles. It must cover all rudiments of the game. You must stand behind your

convictions. If you have faith in what you are teaching, then that confidence will be conveyed to your players. Each coach has a somewhat different philosophy and yet many are successful. The key, therefore, is in the execution of that philosophy.

The key to execution is organization. A well-organized coach is a successful coach. Organization implies thorough planning and thorough preparation for all phases of the game. Practices are well-organized, game plans are set based on the strengths and weaknesses of both teams involved, players and coaches know what is expected of them both during the season and in the off season. In general there is no confusion as to what needs to be done or how it will be done. Care needs to be taken, however, not to overdo. Many times, young coaches tend to get bogged down with details and complicated strategy which is unnecessary and confusing. Organization can be sound, yet simple. It is better to do a few things well than a number of things poorly. Assignments should be made clear and every aspect covered. It is wise for young coaches to develop a checklist. Where possible, authority and responsibility should be delegated, but this must be preceded by organized staff meetings. Try not to spend time on the non-essential aspects of the game. Know what you must do and channel all your energies to accomplishing those objectives.

The integrity of today's coach is extremely important. Coaches should be honest with their players and with their sport, able to confront players face to face and tell them what they are doing wrong and how to improve. You must be able to explain to young players why they are not starting or why they are being dropped from the team.

Coaches should be fair in their judgment and ethical in all aspects of the game. If these rules are not followed, there will be a breakdown in morale; dissention will develop and you will not have the respect of either your players or your fellow coaches. Those who take unfair advantage of others sometimes win, but eventually are the big losers. Coaches must remember that they are role models for the young people who play for them. Set a good example and you will have respect. If you work hard, are well organized, and honest, the players will follow such leadership.

Young coaches should remember that coaching is the highest level of teaching. A young player learns much more by working several hours a day every day of the week for a period of years than can be conveyed in a few hours a week in the classroom for one semester. You will have a profound influence on the lives of many individuals. If former players thank you, drop in to say "hello" or write a note to you now and then, you have done a good job.

A young coach always needs to be aware of his public. It is not just the young people you will be working with, but parents, school officials, the press,

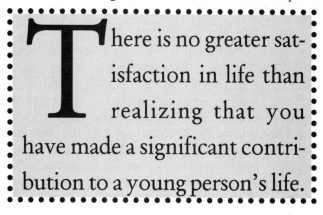

There is no greater satisfaction in life than realizing that you have made a significant contribution to a young person's life.

alumni, and people in the community. Therefore, be careful what you say. Do not criticize your players in public, but be liberal with your praise. Promote your program, let people know what you are doing and what you need from them in order to meet your objectives. Get to know the parents, the press, the people in the community. Be enthusiastic about your work and support will come your way.

Coaches who work within an educational program should remember that academics come first. A coach who plays down education or advocates missing classes will not be successful. By working within and promoting the system, you will receive many benefits. Schools and colleges are proud of their athletic teams. It is a privilege to be associated with athletics and this privilege should not be abused.

Coaching is not for all people and you may not have the talent to be a successful coach. You should perhaps evaluate where you are going in life after you have tried coaching for a few years. If coaching is not for you, look for another job. If coaching is in your blood, and you reap a sense of excitement and enjoyment from working with young people, then stay with it. There is no greater satisfaction in life than realizing that you have made a significant contribution to a young person's life.

Their success is your reward.

Spirit Of Sportsmanship
Robert Baptista

Is sportsmanship worth it even if it means giving up a hard-earned victory?

I had to answer this question some years ago after my Wheaton College soccer team had defeated our arch rivals from Lake Forest College, 1-0, in a game which should have clinched the conference championship for us.

Although Lake Forest was playing without their injured leading scorer and All-American candidate, they had a tough veteran team which always seemed to play its best against us. The action was fast and furious but late in the first half we capitalized on a Forester mistake and scored a goal. Our homecoming crowd went wild.

The battle continued throughout the second half but our defense was equal to the challenge. When the final horn sounded, spectators swarmed onto the field to join us in celebrating the thrilling victory. It was a long time before the team finally gathered in the locker room for our post-game prayer.

Most of the players had dressed and departed when my captain and goalkeeper took me aside. "Coach, I think they scored a goal and the game really should've been a tie."

I listened in disbelief as he described an unbelievable combination of circumstances.

I remembered that early in the second half Lake Forest had attacked and just missed a shot on goal at the far end of the field. "It didn't miss, Coach", my goalie insisted. "It actually went in."

He explained that as the shot was taken he had lunged toward the goalpost but the ball had eluded his outstretched fingers. He'd hit the ground hard and upon regaining his feet found the ball was several yards behind the net. Instinctively, he'd retrieved it and put it back into play.

Then he began to wonder. How could the ball have missed the goal? No matter how far he stretched he couldn't reach the goalpost and the ball had just grazed his fingertips. As the action moved up the field he'd examined the goal net and there it was — a hole just large enough to let the ball slip through. They had scored!

How could a goal go undetected? He remembered that as the Lake Forest player had taken the shot he was upended by a defender and both players had gone sprawling in front of the goal. Apparently someone had momentarily blocked the referee's view at the critical moment and no one else was in position to see what actually happened.

When our goalie realized the situation it was too late to stop play and try to explain. Any attempt to award a goal to our unpopular opponents would not have been understood. So he'd finished the game but his conscience and sense of fair play wouldn't allow him to keep the secret to himself.

I still wasn't convinced. So I returned to the field and found that there was indeed a hole in the corner of the net. But my goalie's story needed further confirmation. Although spectators were prohibited from standing directly behind the goal during play, there was one local fan who always managed to spend considerable time there. A phone call to him confirmed my fears. Yes, the ball had gone through the hole and the other team had really scored.

I was not sure what our next step should be. There was no provision to overturn a referee's decision after the game but we were responsible for a defect in equipment which had cost our opponents a tie or possibly a victory. I phoned the referee for advice and he suggested we "forget it." It wasn't quite that simple.

By Monday we had made our decision. Team members agreed we would offer to call the game a tie and replay it if necessary to decide the conference championship. The decision wasn't easy. No one was jumping for joy about the prospect of giving up a hard-earned victory. It was simply a matter of what was

Winning is important but honoring the basic principles of life is far more significant.

fundamentally right. Led by our goalkeeper, the team concluded that by taking the proposed action we had more to gain than to lose. It was a matter of principle and no one fell into the trap of trying to spiritualize the decision.

Lake Forest officials were dumbfounded when I phoned, but accepted our offer with obvious appreciation. It probably did more to cement good relations between the schools than any other event in our history.

The repercussions went beyond anything we had anticipated. At a chapel service on campus an explanation of our action brought thunderous applause from the student body. The media got wind of things and the story appeared in newspapers across the country. Many people made the observation that there really seemed to be a difference at a Christian college.

Perhaps the most gratifying result was the reaction of the Lake Forest coach. Some weeks later he told me he was convinced his team had scored a goal. Unknown to me, he had also gone back to the field and confirmed the hole in the net. "I knew there was nothing I could do about it, so I decided to keep the information to myself."

He was convinced we would learn about the undetected goal and wondered what we would do. "Through the years I've heard about the philosophy of your school and your people, and I questioned if being Christian would make any difference if confronted with a decision like this. I'm impressed that your actions really support your words."

EPILOGUE

The game was replayed with the conference championship at stake. This time Lake Forest was at full strength. In pregame warmups our goalkeeper dislocated his shoulder in a freak accident and was unable to play. However, our team rallied around our inexperienced goalie and completely dominated play to win 3-0. It's tempting to attribute our victory to divine intervention on behalf of the "good guys" but God's blessings would have been no less real had we lost. Winning is important but honoring the basic principles of life is far more significant.

PROCESS OR PRODUCT? A CHALLENGING AND PROVOCATIVE CHOICE FOR THE COACH
Dr. Walter F. Ersing

Much has been written in recent years on violent play and intentional fouling in soccer. Several factors contributing to violence in the game have been identified, analyzed and discussed in soccer literature.

Generally recognized among the influencing factors are the attitude of coaches, permissive referees, and player indifference to rules. A final contributing factor is the glacial-like decision making by national and international rules legislative bodies that could construct and implement preventive and corrective measures on game violence.

Though the seriousness of increased violent play and intentional fouling needs to be addressed in general, a discussion of one contributing factor— the attitude of the coach—seems even more urgent. This urgency became even more evident as a result of two experiences of mine. One involved a comment from a coach who offered an opinion that the coaches' collective philosophy should prevail in determining the nature, amount and severity of questionable physical contact and intentional fouling that would be permitted in a game. The other experience that convinced me was when I was a spectator at an NCAA regional playoff game in which play was brutal and violent throughout. No one in a leadership position made a significant effort to bring the game back to one resembling soccer. The severity of play was so disturbing to a select number of coaches at the game that it became the major topic of discussion on the floor at a regional coaches meeting held a day later at the tournament site.

What is clear from these two experiences, and literature in general, is that one of the most significant factors (many will argue the ultimate source) in controlling the behavior of players on the field and thus the quality of the sport of soccer, is the coach. It can be said that the coach's role, particularly at the youth, high school and college levels, is crucial in making significant impact not only on the players' behavior in the game, but also on his or her behavior in general. It is this one particular factor— the role of the coach— that I will attempt to address through a discussion of two coaching styles.

It is evident as one views players' actions in a game, a pattern of behavior emerges relative to their use of inappropriate physical contact, including intentional fouling actions. This pattern of team player behavior relates directly to the style demonstrated by their coach both in the game and in his/her daily coaching role. By measuring a team's pattern of player behavior and that of the coach as well, one can see emerging two distinct styles or schools of coaching. One coaching style/school can be identified with characteristics that tend to be "process" focused while the other is "product" oriented.

THE PROCESS AND PRODUCT STYLES OF COACHING

Through observation, a coach is noted as either a "product" coach or a "process" coach or is on a continuum moving toward one style of coaching or the other. In some instances, however, a coach may be attempting to move away from one school and toward another because of external negative or positive forces (i.e., parents, school administration, alumni).

"Process" Coaching Style

The prevailing philosophy governing this style of coaching places greater value on the appropriateness of how one accomplishes a task rather than the end product that results from doing the task. The individual player and his/her contribution to the team become the primary focus. This style tends to emphasize the positive qualitative nature of how one goes about doing things rather than the quantitative nature resulting from the doing. More specifically in this approach, the coach:

- Has winning as a goal, but how one accomplishes it—process—is given greater value;
- Emphasizes legal individual and group tactics in teaching game strategy;
- Makes an effort both in theory and practice to control and discourage use of illegitimate individual tactics;
- Recognizes the need for the enforcement of the rules relative to profanity, encroachment on restarts, delay tactics, and dissent and corrects such unsporting actions in daily practices;
- Accepts the enforcement (although disappointed that his/her player did not act in a more disciplined manner) of the rules pertaining to profanity, encroachment, delay tactics, dissent and restarts;
- Recognizes and accepts game stoppages for rule enforcement purposes, regardless of the type of foul, as part of the "game's flow;"
- Generally has the coaching staff primarily focus on player performance. Only approaches officials at halftime and in an appropriate manner to discuss a concern or receive an explanation of a specific rules interpretation;
- Does not attempt to influence how the game is called by the official. Prepares his/her players to adapt themselves as to the various styles of officiating they might expect;

- Recognizes the variation of performance of officials as part of the game. Does not engage in gamesmanship and uses established procedures to either express a concern or to show appreciation for the role of officials in the development of the sport;
- Focuses on developing self-discipline throughout the team (both coaching staff and players). This means not allowing styles of officiating or opponent's poor standards of conduct to interfere with this objective;
- Views his/her coaching responsibility as an educational opportunity in which positive teaching and learning can take place. The individual and his/her contribution to the team becomes the focus rather than the game outcome;
- Demonstrates through his/her own behavior and that of his/her staff and players that winning is a commendable goal but achieving it in a noble way is of even greater importance.

The "Product" Coaching Style/School

The primary attitude of this style places the emphasis on outcome with minimal attention to the appropriateness on how one goes about obtaining that objective. In this style the individual is secondary; the achievement of certain outcomes is primary. The game experience is part of a means to an end. It is not used appropriately to shape and make positive changes in individual behavior.

In the "product" approach, the coach:

- Focuses primarily on game results;
- Implements tactics both within and outside of game rules to achieve the goal of winning;
- Encourages and/or coaches illegitimate group and deceptive individual tactics (i.e., intentional techniques of holding, encroachment options, off the ball fouls etc.). Rarely discusses legitimate alternatives;
- Disregards the rules relative to profanity, encroachment, delay tactics, dissent and restarts. Feels cards for such offenses are unnecessary and irrelevant and interfere with the flow of the game;
- Shows impatience and becomes vocally abrasive in games where such rules are enforced;
- Is a proponent of "letting them play" except for obvious and/or serious fouls. Essentially believes in "no harm, no foul" criteria in whistling fouls;
- Reacts to an official's call he/she disagrees with through abusive public expression. Tends to defend his/her players when they are reprimanded by officials. Minimally addresses own players when they seem to be getting out of control;
- Encourages both the coaching staff and players to attempt to influence how the game is called by the officials. Feels he/she has the right to engage in gamesmanship during and after the game. Utilizes another member of the coaching staff to carry out such intimidation;

Coach Mike Berticelli of Notre Dame talks to his Irish team at halftime. How a team plays in relation to a series of ethical measures is the mark of established coaches such as Berticelli and others. (photo by Perry McIntyre, Jr.)

- Uses the argument of game flow and "let them play" to mask disdain for rule enforcement in general;
- Views his/her coaching responsibilities as primarily directed toward winning. Fails to recognize the teaching and learning potential inherent in the coaching environment.

It is the author's hope that the discussion of the perceptions of two styles of coaching offers coaches an opportunity to reflect upon their own philosophy of coaching and to analyze their own positions.

In the final analysis, however, the individual coach must ultimately answer the question as to which coaching philosophy—the "process" or the "product"—is truly theirs or whether they are moving on a continuum toward the implementation of one style. Paramount to answering this question will be the feedback you receive and the natural respect accorded you by members of your coaching profession, players and officials.

Striving for excellence in all dimensions of life—personal and professional—is a worthy and challenging goal. If we attempt to implement the values of truth, honesty and individual dignity within our family, in the classroom and on the field with one's team, we will have achieved great things.

Because the coach holds a position of leadership involving young people, the everyday challenge becomes one of striving for and making progress toward life's highest ideals and values. The coaching profession can benefit from individuals who believe and practice such lofty, professional ethics.

A recent study that examined commitment to continued participation in sports among almost 2,000 youth provides some valuable evidence as to the impact of the coach on sport involvement (Lebo, 1992). Of all the factors measured, the role of having positive coach support had the strongest relationship to sport enjoyment and continuance. Of interest was the fact that winning was the lowest or weakest factor in maintaining youth sport involvement. Further, the study indicated that young athletes find enjoyment in sports for all the idealistic reasons that one hopes to instill in youth.

The attitude of the coach toward rules, decency and fair play cannot be ignored. The struggle to adhere to the intent and spirit of the rules of play will involve important, consistent choices by each coach. It is evident the role of the coach is a critical variable that will determine whether fair play dominates soccer matches in this country.

REFERENCE

Lebo, Harlan (1992) "It's How You Play the Game" *Discovery, UCLA Magazine*, Summer, 1992, P. 13.

ON THE RESPONSIBILITY OF THE COACH
Robert Mastruzzi

High schools throughout our nation have the awesome responsibility of preparing youngsters to enter the adult world, either as college students or as part of the work force. Appropriate preparation requires not

THE FIVE BASIC TYPES OF COACHES

Norm Jackson

The Hard-Nosed Coach
- believes strongly in discipline
- rigid about schedules
- very well organized
- enforces rules
- uses threats to motivate
- does not get personally close to players
- teams usually well-organized
- good team spirit when things are going well

Negative points: Dissension and unnecessary tension occur when things are not going well because of coach's inability to handle sensitive players.

The Nice-Guy Coach
- players want to play for him
- uses positive means to motivate his team
- often experiments
- his teams are relaxed and cohesive

Negative points: Characterized as weak because he cannot handle players who take advantage of him.

The Intense, Driven Coach
- constantly worried and pushes himself
- spends hours on preparations
- considers setbacks as personal affronts
- his demands might be unrealistic and his team might burn itself out before the season ends or before crucial games.

Negative points: Intense involvement often leads to emotional displays, which tend to embarrass the players, the team or organization.

The Easy-Going Coach
- does not take things seriously
- gives the impression that everything is under control
- he puts little pressure on the team
- players do not complain
- players feel relaxed and free to question and often benefit from uninhibited discussions.

Negative points: Too casual about training and produces a team that is not fit. The coach also produces a team than often panics when under pressure.

The Business-Like Coach
- uses sharp logic and intellect to resolve problems and outguess the opponents

Negative points: Lacks compassion. He is unable to motivate his team emotionally and has little rapport with players who need his support and attention.

All the above traits can be found in different combinations in each coach. There is no single coaching style that can be held as perfect. Elements of each style can find a place in handling particular situations or players. If a coach pays attention to details; is realistic in setting goals; is knowledgeable about soccer and applied psychology; is sensitive to players' needs; can be strict when necessary; has leadership ability and possesses self-confidence and above all, can teach and motivate then that person may become a successful coach.

only the teaching of skills, but also the development of positive attitudes and ideals. The school endeavors to accomplish these objectives in many ways, including a variety of extracurricular activities, the most far-reaching of which is interscholastic athletics.

As a former coach, teacher, supervisor, principal, and now, superintendent, I can fully appreciate the significant and wholesome impact the sports program has on high school students.

The athletic coach enjoys a special relationship with the youngsters placed in his or her charge, an association that many parallel to the one that exists between parent and child. It is not an uncommon view that the coach is the most influential adult with whom a youngster may come in contact while in high school.

The greatest contact I have maintained through the years is with the young men I coached many years ago. I have seen this phenomenon repeated with others, never failing to be amazed at the closeness of the friendship and the presence of mutual admiration.

The influence that the coach exerts over the athlete, especially in high school, carries with it incredible responsibility, for too often the course of a lifetime is directed during these formative years.

OBLIGATIONS OF COACH

What, then, are the substantive characteristics and traits that the coaches seek to develop? What are their moral and professional obligations to youngsters?

Preparation for competition. Anyone who has been involved with athletics, including the spectator, knows that physical fitness and success for a competitor means possessing strength, stamina, and endurance that must be beyond the ordinary. Similarly, it is vital that the player be taught the skills that are necessary for good performance.

However, it is equally important, if not more so, for the participant to be prepared emotionally for competition. It is no wonder that the word "upset" is so familiar in the athlete vocabulary. So often, a team or individual rises to the occasion and rides a tide of emotion to defeat an opponent that is clearly superior. The degree to which youngsters are prepared physically, psychologically, and with adequate skills, is in direct proportion to the quality of the coach. The confidence that he or she instills in players is an intangible that is vital to success.

Winning spirit, pride and tradition. Athletes must be convinced that they are the best. There is no way participants can enter into competition without feeling that they can win. The coach who contributes to the development of such attitudes is also enhancing the individual's self-image and sense of worth because there is a feeling of being the best.

Pride and tradition are qualities that are natural outgrowths of interscholastic competition, especially when a coach is capable of fostering spirit and camaraderie among teammates.

Though mention is made of the winning spirit, it is important to note that character and pride are developed in both victory and defeat. Although it is true that the nature of competition requires a winning attitude and stresses the importance of winning, it is crucial for the athlete to learn how to win and lose graciously and with dignity.

Tenacity and perseverance. Nothing in life comes easy. This adage is particularly true in any competitive experience. In order to achieve goals and objectives, one must work hard and persevere. The athlete who views preparation as a part-time experience is destined to be a loser.

The student-athlete makes a commitment that requires countless hours of practice, drill, and routine while maintaining satisfactory academic standing. Dedication to the task and allegiance to teammates are attitudes that responsible coaches instill in their charges, along with the courage to face challenges that arise as a result.

Ethics. One of the major outcomes of participation in athletics is the development of sound moral fiber. The athlete learns to judge others by virtue of ability and character, not hearsay and innuendo. Nowhere are the ideals of brotherhood reinforced and the evils of prejudice destroyed more than on the athletic field. Respect for one another is earned through deed and action, which is the way it should be, and self-respect evolves in the same way.

The coach advocates that winning is a primary objective, but it must be achieved fairly and with integrity. The athlete must learn to play hard, but within the framework of rules. The fact is that in sports the rule book is akin to the Bible.

Relationships with others. Teamwork, sportsmanship, fair play, are words that originated in sports but are now part of the vernacular because of their descriptive nature. Interestingly, they are words of positive connotation that are used to illustrate desirable qualities and wholesome interpersonal relationships.

A team cannot be successful without the closest kind of cooperation among individuals. Of even greater significance is the fact that the tremendous emphasis on effective interaction helps to develop leadership and followership, qualities that are essential to the composition of a winning team. There are those who set direction and others who must follow the lead.

Another phrase frequently heard in sports is "team of destiny." It appears that some teams are truly destined to win, but the fact of the matter is that fate has little to do with the result The underdog who achieves the miracle of victory is always characterized by inspiration, desire, and an unwillingness to accept anything less than success. The great upset does not occur by chance, but rather as a result of unbelievable effort inspired by a magnificent coach.

Advisor and counselor. The intimate relationship that exists between players and a coach allows him to advise and counsel in an extraordinary way. There are no doubt countless former athletes whose lives were affected dramatically because of the influence of their coaches.

The coach is a direct liaison with colleges for many athletes, not only to promote scholarships, but very often simply to arrange for admission. Many individuals are leading more productive and enjoyable lives than they might have because they were effectively guided by a caring and concerned coach.

One need only look at the durability of the coach-athlete relationship, which often lasts a lifetime, to understand the impact that the mentor has on the student.

Throughout my professional career, I have been addressed by students as "Mr. Mastruzzi," except by the kids who played for me. They called me "Coach," a term that signifies respect, admiration and a great deal of affection. I would have been disappointed had they referred to me in any other way.

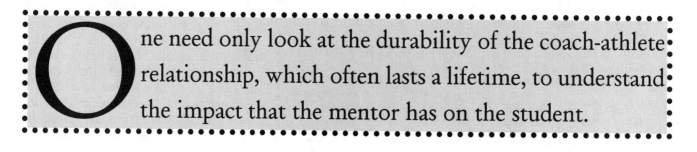

One need only look at the durability of the coach-athlete relationship, which often lasts a lifetime, to understand the impact that the mentor has on the student.

Today, far too many young people are attempting to seek identity in environments that are lacking in adult role models. The sense of belonging that comes from team involvement is especially important when societal values are under attack, social institutions, including the family, do not exert the influence they did years ago, and peer pressure can be overwhelming.

There is considerable transference of the stabilizing values that result from participation in athletics. Coaches, therefore, assume a tremendous responsibility as they direct and lead youngsters, for they are in reality preparing them for life, not merely for a game. I would hope that all wear the mantle with dignity and integrity.

THE OTHER ASPECTS OF COACHING
Dave Keck

Two years ago our local American Soccer League franchise folded and a number of the players remained in Columbus and continued to promote youth soccer in the area. One of them commented last summer on why he was doing this. He replied, in effect, that the coaching of young players was woefully weak, and that he was trying to help remedy that.

I believe that training better soccer players is less than half of our job. To be sure, I have been a coach who has attended innumerable clinics to gain whatever edge I could over opponents. I also still strive to have that "one year" when everything goes right and a real winner is produced. But I rather suspect that I am most like most high school coaches in the country.

Very few of my players will play in a top-rate college program. We don't challenge for the league championship very often. There probably won't be too many professional players coming out of our program. This, I think, is true of most teams. So what of all the other players? What do we offer them? Are we going to spend a good amount of time on the most important aspects of coaching any sport?

Because we should not leave concepts such as sportsmanship, responsibility, concern for others, self discipline and a genuine knowledge and appreciation for the game to chance. We coaches must stress this aspect of coaching as well as planning for any games or teaching tactics or techniques.

Coaches have a unique opportunity in high school and youth soccer. We are told that soccer is the sport of the future. It is inexpensive, fun, and great exercise.

Every player is the "quarterback" when he has the ball. We therefore have a unique opportunity and obligation to use soccer as a means to an end, not just an end to itself.

One of the most frustrating things is watching little league soccer in local communities after having given a clinic for new and experienced coaches. Everyone accepts ideas about sportsmanship, fun in playing, etc., in the gymnasium during the clinic. These are often forgotten as a team goes for the championship or plays what the coach perceives as the big rival.

In clinics I try to emphasize that these principles must be exemplified by the actions of a coach or parent. Youngsters easily sense hypocrisy. For example, is it worth sacrificing the high school soccer career of players by locking them into a goalkeeping position in little league because they happen to be your best goalkeeper and you might lose without him? I have seen many good little league goalkeepers get burned out before they even get to high school. They have little chance of excelling in the field because they never played there.

A couple of years ago, I was coaching a not-so-select seventh and eighth grade team. There were two players on that team that help illustrate a point. One player was very heavy and had always been played you guessed it — fullback. I asked him about his soccer experience, and he replied, "I'm a fullback," not, "I'm a soccer player!" I played him at every position on the field, mostly midfield. He couldn't play for long stretches, and he didn't come out for the high school team due to his lack of fitness. But during that season he was able to play several positions, have fun, and for the first time in his playing career, scored a goal.

The other player had been somewhat of a star on every team he had played. He always played forward. He was a scorer. "I'm a wing," he said. One game he played wing fullback for our team and a goal was scored because he failed to give proper support. We lost the game as a result. But that young player learned and likely will not forget the concept of support. He is more ready to play total soccer well and not just a "wing."

It seems so trite to say, but how often do we as little league coaches and parents fall into the "little league baseball" syndrome? Do we talk sportsmanship, then yell at the official to impress the parents or kids? It's much easier to explain that we are "sticking up for the players," but much better if we concentrate on soccer and help the kids do things that they and you as a coach can do something about. We can help improve officiating with work behind the scenes before the season ever starts.

It seems to me that a little league experience should provide adequate experiences for the recreational as well as the gifted or select player, while at the same

INTEGRITY: THE ESSENTIAL INGREDIENT
Hal Liske

Safety...Equality...Enjoyment...These are three principles of most sports: safety for the players during the play, equality in the decisions of the officials on matters in question, and enjoyment during the game for all players, officials and spectators. Soccer has one additional facet that separates it from most other sports, the notion of "gentlemanly conduct." Gentlemanly conduct is that behavior which is expected of the player during a match. This conduct is not violent or harsh. It is principled and, above all, fair. We, as referees, are called upon to decide whether soccer play is fair. We are charged with the responsibility of keeping the game within the boundaries of this spirit. It is our responsibility to ensure that games do not fall into disrepute.

This responsibility is a far greater one than is expected of officials of other sports. It calls for decisions to be made using the Laws as a guide as well as a notion of fairness. It is essential that referees have the highest ethical standards.

In a recent referee clinic, Mr. Harry Baldwin presented a lesson on ethics. He presented the five principles of ethical power for officials.

1. **Purpose.** I see myself as being an ethically sound person. I let my conscience be my guide. No matter what happens, I am always able to face the mirror, look myself straight in the eye, and feel good about myself.

2. **Pride.** I feel good about myself. I don't need the acceptance of other people to feel important. A balanced self-esteem keeps my ego and my desire from influencing my decisions.

3. **Patience.** I believe that things will eventually work well. I don't need everything to happen right now. I am at peace with what comes my way.

4. **Persistence.** I stick to my purpose, especially when it seems inconvenient to do so! My behavior is consistent with my intentions. As Churchill said, "Never! Never! Never! Never! Give up!"

5. **Perspective.** I take time to enter each day quietly in a mood of reflection. This helps me get myself focused and allows me to listen to my inner self and see things more clearly.

In these principles, we can find several things which will help us on the field as referees. First and foremost, we must see ourselves as ethically sound. We must know within ourselves that the decisions that we make on the field are based solely on the circumstances. We must be able to make decisions without the need for approval from the players. The natural confidence from knowing that things will turn out for the best is very evident and is an essential part of the successful referee.

time offering examples of sportsmanship, an understanding of the game, practice at tactics and skills and a concern for one another.

It is for these reasons that in our programs, at whatever level, we not only teach how to play soccer (hopefully right), but also how to do everything associated with the game right. All of our players must know about and help with cleaning the field before a game, help secure the nets properly, as well as line the field and take care of equipment. Many of these players will become coaches some day. Some are already. After all, how many of us coaching in high school were actually outstanding players in either high school or college?

I think that sometimes we subtly send false messages to our players. We do not get across what coaching objectives should be emphasized. In many of our leagues, for example, do we always select the coach who wins the championship as the "coach of the year"? There is no question that striving to win is a great and worthwhile goal. Those who achieve the pinnacle of success should be recognized. But don't we all know someone almost every year who takes poor talent and turns it into respectability? Or comes closer to getting the maximum out of his or her players than even the championship coach did? Wouldn't we send a clear message to our players by selecting that coach once in a while? How many of us have grade requirements that are higher than those of the school or of the state athletic association? We always say that grades come first, but do they really when it comes to action?

Do we allow the officials to take care of the game when our players are too physical, particularly if we are benefitting from it? It seems to me that it is the coach's responsibility to enforce certain positive behavior on the field by his own players. As coaches, we control what the players want the most — playing time. Shouldn't that be used to ensure high standards of total performance by our players?

We would all like to turn out better American players. We would all like to win championships, have all-state players and have that great team. Very few of us do. Yet we can all use soccer as a unique example of sportsmanship, whatever the setting. We often forget in our zeal that we are teachers first.

Luke 12:48 says, "Every one to whom much is given, of him will much be required; and of him to whom men commit much they will demand more."We have been given great responsibilities as coaches to work with young people. There is much talent among coaches waiting to be tapped beyond just soccer knowledge. Let's turn out great soccer players, yes, but let's also turn out great young men and women.

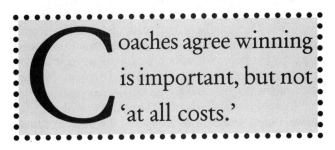

THE BIG 'W' IN PERSPECTIVE:
Tim Schum

A very interesting letter arrived recently from Coach Dave Morris of Damascus (MD) High School. Coach Morris noted a trend in *Soccer Journal* articles suggesting "that coaches sit down and shut up while reminding us of the minimal importance of winning. While it is clear that many youth (and high school and college, etc.) coaches behave atrociously, one suspects that these members of our profession are not capable of reading the articles in question."

Dave continues: "Furthermore it is the pursuit of excellence, and winning is an important measure of this, it defines all the benefits of athletics. By striving to reach new heights, by setting challenges, specific goals (i.e, winning), we are able to grow as people and as athletes.

"The fact that certain people are unable to balance this feedback with other important considerations is tragic, but should not necessarily shape the flow of ideas in our profession. The teams I have been associated with have always made every effort to win. It is only through this effort that we are able to hold ourselves accountable and benefit from the experience (whether we win or lose).

"With this in mind, I would like to express my hope that more of *Soccer Journal* will be dedicated to the sharing of ideas that can help us reach our goals on the field. This is by far the best forum for the discussion of ideas by the foremost minds of our profession. I learned as much about soccer in the four days of the NSCAA convention as I did in 15 years of playing at the club level......"

Coach Morris concluded with: "How about helping the rank and file become better teachers and ambassadors for our sport? Let us see how our most successful peers motivate players and teach the game. How do successful coaches encourage players to reach their potential? How do they promote soccer in their communities? Don't tell us to sit silently, help us decide what to say. Don't remind us winning isn't important, show us positive ways to help our teams reach their goals. Nobody likes to be preached to, but most people welcome constructive advice. Bring it on!"

All of us certainly appreciate constructive criticism and perhaps as Dave indicates, "we are preaching to those who aren't listening in the first place." The perceived editorial inclination of *Soccer Journal* has probably been evolutionary in nature. Perhaps those types of reminders on coaching conduct relate to the fact that, as an organization, NSCAA is dedicated to the promotion of the sport by setting ethical standards of behavior for the soccer coaching profession. By publishing such editorial material, the magazine is helping to achieve that organizational objective.

It is this corner's, and I know the NSCAA's, attitude, that far too many coaches of soccer at various levels place the end result of a victory as the foremost objective of their job. They disregard cumulative skill development of the players, invoke tactics that are either rudimentary or unimaginative in nature and disregard the psychological impact of the "winning at all costs" attitude on the players' emotional development.

Perhaps the emphasis on "sitting down and shutting up" needs comment. The real "emphasis" here is that if coaches are the "cheerleader type" they will be very good at cheerleading, but not offer too much in the coaching analysis phase of their coaching assignments. (Those who attended the early USSF coaching courses run by Dettmar Cramer will recognize a play on words here. Cramer, at the time, criticized American coaches who would run their soccer players laps around the field as training great lap runners, but surely not training great soccer players.)

Coaches (and here I confess to running towards the cheerleader type in my own early coaching experience) must recognize that players expect an objective analysis of the various phases of the soccer that are exhibited in the game. Granted, videotape is a great aid here, but players need to have confidence that their coaches can present a clear, accurate analysis of each match, either during timed breaks in the action or following the match.

When questioned, one coach shared with me his estimate of his college coach's ability through an incident that occurred at halftime of a game. Seems the team had not comported itself very well and at the break the coach gave his team a tongue-lashing that concluded with the statement that the players, through their poor play, "were taking food out of my kids' mouths."

"Hell," said the interviewee, "all I and my teammates wanted to know was how were we going to change things in the second half to play better and win the game."

The NSCAA Academy program, at every level, discusses a proper coaching philosophy and never does it discourage the objective of a coach training his play-

> Coaches agree winning is important, but not 'at all costs.'

ers and team to strive for victory. The danger is the "winning at all costs" philosophy and as noted on many occasions, the failure of the team to play constructive, entertaining soccer. In a larger sense, the coach and his/her team are ambassadors for the sport, not only at their local and regional level, but on a national level as well. Winning is only half the battle in turning the American Sports fan on to soccer.

Many times the Academy staff coaches tell the candidates that "the game is the great teacher" for it will indicate to you and your team if things are going well as well as identify those aspects of the game that need shoring up in future team training sessions.

We are certain that by his commitment to his team Dave Morris has demonstrated his concern for the "W." Through his/her practice preparations and at matches, every coach also indicates to his/her charges the desire for the "W." A continued NSCAA objective will be to emphasize the proper balance in the pursuit of that goal.

⚽

Player Violence and the Coach
Dr. Joe Luxbacher

Violence in sport has gained widespread media attention in recent years. Hardly a day goes by without some mention of a bench-clearing brawl, a stick swinging incident or a beanball war. While these episodes are not limited to a single sport, it seems that soccer has been particularly susceptible to outbursts of aggression. The millions of fans who viewed the 1982 World Cup matches found the games characterized by a great deal of violent play, with the most publicized incident being the vicious fouls committed by Argentine star Diego Maradona against a Brazilian opponent. Although increased media coverage gives the impression that the problem is a recent one, in actuality numerous episodes of sports violence have been documented throughout the history of athletic competition.

Traditionally such behavior has been generally accepted by players, coaches and fans as "part of the game." It has even been argued that sport serves an important mental health function by providing a socially acceptable outlet for the venting of aggressive impulses. Many believe that athletes actually benefit from "letting off steam" during competition. As a result, violent behavior which is not tolerated in a non-sport environment is often accepted within the confines of the playing field.

The great emphasis placed upon winning has also served to legitimize various types of illegal tactics, with the professional foul now commonplace in the sport of soccer. A professional foul is one that is intentionally enacted at a time when it actually benefits the team committing the infraction. For example, a defending player may choose to trip an opponent in a non-critical area of the field, rather than allow the individual to penetrate the defense for a strike on goal. In highly competitive sport, where a team's won/lost record is the sole measure of success, such behavior is generally regarded as a "good penalty". Quotes from prominent sport figures attest to that fact. Jack Charlton, a former English international player known for his rough style, confessed: "You do what is necessary in the circumstances. If I were playing in an international and saw someone getting away with the ball and I could not catch him, I would flatten him. Jupp Kapellmann, a former German national team player and player for Bayern Munich, echoes Charlton's philosophy when he summed up the situation in the Bundesliga, "We do not much differ from animals. We carry out our struggle for existence with all means. Each one must try to execute the other one."

These comments speak for themselves, and reflect the overriding philosophy of play at high levels of competition. Violent behavior is not limited to professional sports, however, having become quite prevalent at the collegiate and high school levels. As a result school officials, coaches, and administrators of athletic programs have begun to give considerable attention to finding effective means of dealing with the problem.

Sports Aggression

One of the major hurdles facing investigators has been defining what actually constitutes sport violence or, as it is commonly referred to, sport aggression. Numerous definitions have been coined over the years, most depending upon the personal perspective of the writer or researcher. The result has been added confusion to an already confusing concept. Anyone who has participated in competitive athletics, whether be it as coach or player, would agree that one must be aggressive to perform effectively. In that context aggressiveness encompasses such qualities as commitment, hustle, determination, and enthusiasm; behaviors that may be more appropriately labeled as assertive. It is imperative that players exhibit such behavior in order to achieve athletic success. Usually, when coaches exhort their athletes to be aggressive, they are actually encouraging them to be more assertive in their actions. They are not implying that players should deliberately attempt to inflict harm on opponents, although incidental injury may sometimes occur due to the nature of the sport. For instance, a soccer coach may instruct his players to tackle hard in order to win the ball. A hard, clean tackle could inadvertently result in injury to an opponent, although that was not the intent.

Aggression, or violence, is behavior predicated upon an intent to harm the opponent. Two basic types have been identified with regard to athletic competition. Reactive (hostile) aggression has as its driving purpose injury to another individual. It is spontaneous behavior, usually triggered by emotional anger, with the individual lashing out in an attempt to inflict pain on an adversary. Instrumental aggression, on the other hand, is premeditated action. Although the purpose is still to inflict injury, the primary aim of the behavior is to achieve a reward other than that of injury itself. For instance, a goalkeeper may intentionally collide with an opposing forward when playing a high cross, hoping to dissuade the opponent from challenging him for the ball. The ultimate benefits derived from instrumental aggression include intimidation of opponents, popularity among peers, and personal success.

A fine line exists between actions considered to be assertive and those considered to be aggressive. In terms of actual behavior, both reactive and instrumental aggression involve the intent to injure, while assertive behavior does not. A casual observer will have a difficult time differentiating between aggressiveness and assertiveness, since only the athlete really knows the intent behind his action. For the purpose of discussion I will consider aggression and violence as synonymous, implying behavior used for the specific purpose of injuring or intimidating an opponent.

AGGRESSION THEORIES

Numerous theories, some specific while others general, have been offered as an explanations as to why players commit acts of violence against opponents. These can be grouped into three general categories: instinct theories, frustration-aggression theories, and social learning theories.

Instinct theories are premised on the belief that humans possess an innate aggressive drive that gradually accumulates and must be periodically expressed. Sports are considered to be an ideal outlet for the release of these aggressive urges, and as a result this explanation of aggressive behavior has generated much support from sports enthusiasts. Research findings, however, do not support the basic premises of the instinct theories. Evidence does not support the contention that humans possess an innate aggressive drive.

Frustration-aggression theories propose that aggression originates from an individual's frustration at efforts to achieve a specific goal. Sport is considered a primary source of the frustrations confronting athletes. Although these theories have some merit, it is quite clear that the frustration does not always lead to aggressive responses. Frustrated athletes may instead experience depression, anxiety, or embarrassment. Even if they do become angry, the potential for aggression must be present. Athletes in non-contact sports, such as swimming or tennis, may become frustrated and angry, yet the nature of those sports prohibit the expression of aggressive behavior toward an opponent. Contact sports such as soccer, hockey, and basketball provide ample opportunity to vent one's frustrations on the nearest animate object— an opponent.

> A fine line exists between actions considered to be assertive and those considered to be agressive.

Social learning theories focus on patterns of behavior that individuals learn in coping with their environment. From this perspective, aggression is viewed as a learned behavior, not an instinctual or frustration-produced drive. Learning theorists do not rule out that aggressive behavior may have its origins in individual predisposition, but propose that violence in sport is best explained as players exhibiting behavior that they consider appropriate under the circumstances. Sports such as soccer, where much emphasis is placed upon toughness and aggressiveness, provide an ideal environment for the learning of aggression. If the aggression proves successful, or if the player perceives that his coach and peers support such behavior, then it is likely that the behavior will be repeated in similar situations in the future. Research findings generally support the position that social learning theories provide the best explanation for much of the violence pervading modern sport.

According to learning theory, the potential exists for behavior to be altered or changed, providing optimism that the incidence of violence in sport may be lessened. The athletic coach, as a result of the many hours shared with players, is in a favorable position to influence the behavior of his or her athletes in game competition.

COACH/PLAYER RELATIONSHIP

I recently completed an investigative study which looked at the potential influence of the coach on player attitudes and subsequent behavior. Players who participated in the research were assessed for measures on four factors thought to affect the likelihood of sport aggression. The factors considered included reactive and instrumental aggression. moral view of sport, and professionalization of attitude. Moral view of sport was defined as the player's notion of acceptable or non-acceptable behavior in game competition. An individual's professionalization of attitude provided a measure of what he considered most important in playing a game: winning, playing well, or playing fairly.

As attitudes become more professionalized a greater emphasis is placed upon winning. Measures for each of the factors were related to the individual's perception of how much emphasis his coach placed upon "winning at all costs." In this manner it was possible to determine whether the player's perception of the values espoused by his coach was significantly related to the player's own professed attitude concerning competition.

Three hundred and twenty-one high school soccer players (males) were surveyed. The subjects, whose ages ranged from 14-18 years, comprised 16 teams. Based upon previous research findings, it was predicted that the players' perceptions of the values and attitudes espoused by their coaches would influence the players' own attitudes regarding sport and competition. Results were interpreted to provide additional support for that contention. In general, players who perceived their coach to highly value a "win at all costs" philosophy expressed significantly greater levels of reactive aggression, were more willing to use illegal tactics during competition (lower moral view), and professed a more professionalized attitude, when compared with players who perceived their coach as placing little value on "winning at all costs." These findings lead to speculation that perceptions of the coach influenced the players' own attitudes toward the factors under investigation, variables believed to affect the likelihood of violence in sport. One must realize that the study, conducted in the natural setting, lacked the rigorous controls which are readily available in the laboratory. In addition, the influence of parents, peers, fans, and the media was not considered. All of those socializing influences, in theory, may contribute in determining an athlete's tendency to aggress. Regardless, findings generated in the study suggest that the coach exerted subtle influence on the attitudes of players under his charge. This relationship is quite understandable, since players realize that they must meet the coach's expectations if they are to win a spot on the team.

Various situational factors, many of which can be manipulated by the coach, seem to be related to an increased incidence of sport violence. For example, previous research findings suggest that an athlete's perception of his opponent may influence the individual's behavior. If the opponent is viewed in a negative light, as an enemy to be despised, then the probability increases that violence may be directed toward that person. It is common knowledge that many coaches believe that in creating a negative impression of opponents the motivation for victory will be enhanced. Such is not the case. Athletes can and should be motivated through positive means, structured around an objective evaluation of the opponent's strengths and weaknesses, rather than by mere emotional arousal.

PREPARATION IMPORTANCE

Athletes should be thoroughly prepared for the tactics, temperament, and general behavior typically exhibited by their opponents. Research has demonstrated that certain behavior which routinely occurs, although technically illegal, is more or less accepted by players and does not evoke retaliatory aggression. Examples might be tripping in soccer or holding in ice hockey. Unexpected behavior, however, whether legal or illegal, oftentimes produces aggressive responses from the victim. Findings also suggest that, if a player perceives the opponent's aggressive actions to be intentional, then that individual is more prone to retaliate than if he or she felt the aggression to be accidental. This connection between perception of intent and the corresponding response provides cause for the coach to ensure that his or her team members are thoroughly aware of the opponent's style of play. Specific preparation for the upcoming opponents will help players in successfully adjusting to the varied situations which may occur.

The outcome of a soccer game, as well as the gap between the winning and losing score, have been found to influence the frequency of violent behavior in the match. Volkamer (1972), in a study of German soccer teams in more than 1800 games, found that more aggressive penalties occurred as the point differential became greater. Less aggressive play was evidenced when the scores were extremely close, possibly due to the players' reluctance to commit a foul which would decrease the team's chances for success. Volkamer also found that losing teams committed more fouls than winners, and that teams playing at home committed fewer fouls than did visiting teams. He attributed this to the unfamiliar surroundings and hostile fans confronting the visiting sides. Although Volkamer's findings raise interesting speculation, one must consider that using the foul count as a measure of aggression may be misleading. While many fouls undoubtedly occur due to intentional violence, some may occur inadvertently due to overzealous play or even physical ineptness.

CONCLUSION

It appears that soccer, and contact sports in general, are structurally conducive to aggression and violence. The nature of the game, with athletes performing at high speeds and displaying great intensity within a confined space, makes it highly unlikely that violence will ever be entirely purged from soccer. Even so, coaches are in a position to ensure that the incidence of violence can be held to a minimum. Coaches must be aware of situations and circumstances which promote violent behavior. In addition, they must not underestimate their influence as a role model. If players perceive their coach as condoning aggression and violence as a means of achieving success, then it is probable that players will exhibit such behavior. Assuredly there are other avenues through which the problem of sport violence can be addressed. However, the athletic coach provides a focal point through which efforts can be channeled. As coaches we must realize and accept this responsibility.

Ateyo, D. *Violence in sports*. New York: Van Nostrand Reinhold Company, 1978.

Bandura, A., and Walters, R. Social learning and personality development. New York: Holt, Reinhart and Winston, 1963.

Berkowitz, L. *Aggression: A social psychological analysis*. New York: McGraw Hill, 1962.

Cox, R.H. *Sport psychology*. Dubuque: Wm. C. Brown Publishers, 1985.

Cratty, B. *Social psychology in athletics*. Englewood Cliffs: Prentice Hall, Inc., 1981.

Cratty B. *Pschology in contemporary sport* (2nd Ed.). Englewood Cliffs: Prentice Hall, Inc., 1983.

Dollard, J., Doob, L., Miller, N., Mower, O., and Sears, R. *Frustration and aggression*. New Haven: Yale University Press, 1939.

Heinial, K. *Junior football players as cross-national interpreters of the moral concepts of sport*. Department of Sociology and Planning for Physical Culture, Research Report No. 4. Finland: University of Juvaskyula.

Lorenz, K. *On Aggression*. New York: Bantan Books, 1963.

Smith, M. *Violence and sport*. Toronto: Butterworth & Co., 1983.

Volkamer, N. *Investigations into the aggressiveness in competitive social systems*. Sportwissenschaff, l, 33-64, 1972.

Wankle, L.M. "An examination of illegal aggression in intercollegiate hockey." In: I.D. Williams & L.M. Wankle (Eds.), *Proceedings of the Fourth Canadian Psychomotor Learning and Sport Psychology Symposium*. Waterloo, Ontario: University of Waterloo, 1972.

ON REFEREEING: TO OFFICIATE THE MATCH OR GUIDE THE GAME?
Hubert Vogelsinger

We begin talking about referees by not talking about refereeing.

We start instead with a couple of simple premises: that soccer, like all sports, is creative physical expression and that creative physical expression is a type of art.

It is a short step from there to the reasonable position that sport, and therefore soccer, is an art form, essentially not much different from violin or ballet. Except for one little thing. No one punches Jascha Heifetz in the face while he plays his violin. No one chops Nureyev's ankles during the dance.

We decry violence in general but consider it a particular outrage when violence, or even a minor distraction, is permitted to intrude on the sacrosanct area of artistic expression.

But on the field, court or rink it is different. Violence seems to be becoming an art in itself with some sports selling themselves with their rowdiness. Thus do we get "The Broad Street Bullies","The Doomsday Defense", and so forth. But I think most reasonable people will agree that even if violence is a short term attraction it is a long term threat. And it is particularly threatening to soccer.

As a new sport in the United States, one whose direction and style is not yet firmly set, we are often tempted to imitate the more established sports in using violence as a selling point. Right now soccer happens to be growing like Jack's beanstalk. Great. But wild growth is not direction. And our position on the conduct of the emerging American game is one that will determine if the beanstalk is to grow straight up the stake or sprawl all over the yard in a big, uncontrolled mess. Here, at this decisive juncture in the development of American soccer, is where we should begin talking about referees and their responsibility to the game.

You know, superficially, what you should expect from the ref. You've heard it all before. He must be mentally alert, physically fit, decisive and have a thorough knowledge of the rules of the game. But these are minimum requirements. They are obvious and I won't dwell upon them.

Higher Laws. There are, as Thoreau once said, higher laws and principles than the ones printed on paper and commonly adhered to. Rule enforcement and on-the-spot decisions may be the referee's job. But his duty, his higher obligation to the game, is to apply those laws so that the game develops normally, naturally, safely and attractively. To do this, I think the truly outstanding referee will try to concentrate on three things:

1. **Skill without Fear.** First, he will create an atmosphere in which players feel free to express their art without fear. Soccer is a skillful game. That is its beauty. But in order for skill to prevail there must be no unnecessary physical contact.

But, likewise, there must be an appreciation for defensive art, too. There is nothing wrong with a good, hard tackle as long as physical contact is not used to compensate for lack of skill. So when I charge the referee with creating an atmosphere of freedom of expression I mean not only that the skillful dribblers feel free to employ their art without worrying about being stuffed under the turf. But I mean also that a skilled defender must not play in fear of a good, clean shoulder charge or a tackle being penalized because it registered an "eight" on the Richter scale.

2. **The Spirit of the Laws.** Secondly, the better referee will go about his/her work not with a myopic and slavish adherence to the letter of the law—though he must be consistent—but with compassion and understanding for emotions of coaches and players.

There are hopes, dreams and ambitions at play on the soccer field, The outstanding referee will understand this. Don't get me wrong. I believe in the mailed fist. I know the referee's authority must be shown and felt. But I think there is a place for the velvet glove, too.

The game isn't played by wind-up dolls. It is played by boys and girls whose long, arduous hours of preparation are fired by the excitement of the moment. A firm but understanding referee can sometimes do more good with a stern look or word - especially in the early stages of a match - than with a yellow card or ejection.

I've often thought that when youngsters are left to their own devices their game proceeds reasonably well under a curious system of self-policing. Oh, they'll yell and argue a little but the game manages to get played. However, bring in a referee and all of a sudden you get two games - soccer and beat-the-ref. So there are times when low visibility and dignified aloofness will enhance the referee's authority and stature every bit as much as the harshest of penalties or a shouting match with player or coach.

I don't say you should tolerate deliberate or dangerous infractions or endure on-running vilification by a coach or player. I ask only for "judgment calls" to involve true judgment, that is, justice tempered by some allowance for the pressures of the moment.

3. **Guide the Match and the Game.** Finally, the referee will remember that his work affects not just a match but the game. Soccer will be what you allow it to be, and on this score I must speak a mildly critical word.

I think some American referees have a difficult time sensing the flow of the game and encouraging the artful, rather than physical, facets of the game to develop. I've seen some matches that look more like tackle football or rugby because the bigger, rougher boys had more leeway than the smaller, skillful ones.

The referee who allows this type of match not only abdicates his responsibility to protect the well be-

ing of all the players but he does a disservice to the game by allowing violence to impinge on art. This is the fist in Heifetz' face. This is the kick in Nureyev's ankles. And this could be a malignancy in soccer's development.

I've said before that the emerging American soccer style will be a tough, skillful one. That will be a part of its beauty and character. But physical does not mean unskillful and tough does not mean violent.

There is in this country an insidious pull in the direction of violence. If soccer is to avoid falling under its sway, if the game's art is to be preserved, then we need the firm and understanding guidance of far-sighted referees who see their jobs as directing not a soccer game but the game of soccer.

⚽

BE CAREFUL: YOU ARE BEING WATCHED
J. Malcolm Simon

"...picked up 39 technical fouls last year, third straight league-leading total."

"Coach ... engaged in a brief shoving match with his counterpart .... They weren't fooling either!"

"...was fined $1000 and suspended for the remainder of the season for his physical assault on a referee...

"Keen competitive spirit runs deep in the American psyche. Losing gracefully is an acquired characteristic. It never took with Coach..."

It is generally agreed, that among the key responsibilities of an athletic coach are teaching ability, tactical understanding, organizational ability, and the ability to demonstrate skills. However, I put it to you that nothing is as important as the responsibility a coach has of setting a strong positive example of behavior for his athletes. Westcott states that coaches cannot avoid being conspicuous models for a variety of personal and social behaviors. This responsibility cannot be overemphasized. Because of the nature of athletics, coaches are constantly setting examples of behavior for their athletes in areas such as personal health and health habits, fitness and activity habits, sportsmanship, discrimination, honesty, and fairness.

The coach cannot meet his responsibility with a "Do as I say, not as I do" philosophy. It has been demonstrated that a coach's behavioral example has a stronger influence that his verbal recommendations. Thus, the coach who tells his players to play hard and clean, yet ignores "dirty" play is, in essence, condoning and encouraging such unethical conduct. Likewise, the coach who constantly berates officials should not expect better behavior from his players irregardless of anything he might have told them.

It has been boasted that participation in athletics has a positive influence in molding desirable social attitudes such as fair play, desirable reactions to winning and losing, understanding the worthiness of peers and team cooperation for a common goal. However, these desirable attitudes do not develop "happenstance". The fostering of desirable social, psychological and emotional growth cannot be guaranteed by athletic participation. It is just as possible to develop undesirable characteristics such as cheating to win rather than playing by the rules, crying over losing and gloating about winning.

The coach's model is the key to whether athletes develop desirable or undesirable values. Our athletes need to identify with coaches of high calibre and not with those who demonstrate unethical behavior. We must be constantly aware of our influence over our players. We must set the proper example, not exemplify the coaches who make the types of news we see printed on sports pages today. Coaches have unique opportunities to influence athletes in a wholesome way. We must remain cognizant of our roles as leaders or we will miss these wonderful opportunities.

FOOTNOTES

1. Westcott, Wayne I,. "Physical Educators and Coaches as Models of Behavior" *Journal of Physical Education and Recreation*. March, 1979, p. 31.

2. Sidentop, D. *Developing Teaching Skills in Physical Education*. Boston: Houghton-Mifflin Company 1976.

3. Bryan, J. and Walbeck, N. "Preaching and Practicing Generosity: Children's Actions and Reactions." *Child Development*. 1970, pp. 329-353.

CODE OF CONDUCT FOR THE SOCCER SPECTATOR
Allen Gary

1. As spectators, we will refrain from booing or yelling at officials at any time during a game because we are aware of the following:

- Such behavior on our part sets a poor example of sportsmanship;
- Such behavior reflects negatively on our community, our team, our players, and ourselves;
- Most youth soccer officials have had limited experience and formal training and do the best job they can given these limitations;
- Most soccer officials make correct calls even though we sometimes see the incident otherwise;

- If officials do make incorrect calls during a game, the following circumstances usually apply:
  - √ The number of poor calls usually balances out for both teams;
  - √ No one is perfect;
  - √ The officials don't have the same observation point afforded spectators sitting in the bleachers;
  - √ As occasional incorrect call seldom effects the outcome of the game;
  - √ There are more effective channels for correcting poor officiating than verbal abuse during the contest;
  - √ We don't really know how difficult it is to officiate a soccer game until we've run on the pitch in an official's boots;

2. During a game we will refrain from yelling at players on either team because we are aware of the following:

- They are young people, not soccer professionals, who, due to limited playing experience and great enthusiasm, may make mistakes;
- Encouragement and praise should made in public; constructive criticism is best made in private;
- The coach is the best equipped to analyze and correct deficiencies in soccer skills. Our attempts to be helpful in this respect may only confuse the players;
- The golden rule applies. Treat other players with the courtesy, respect, and consideration which we want other supporters to show our own players.

3. At soccer games, we will refrain from being argumentative or using abusive languages toward supporters of the players on the opposing team because we are aware of the following:

- We are being judged by others on our actions and words. We will always strive to insure that the results of this judgment is a verdict of *sportsmanship*;
- We will conduct ourselves in such a courteous and restrained manner that if called upon to do so, we could line up in front of the bleachers after the game and shake hands with each supporter of the opposing team in the same way the players are expected to do after each contest.

4. If our team loses, we will demonstrate our ability to cope with the loss in both deed and word, because we are aware of the following:

- In athletics, as in other aspects of life, it is not always possible to win no matter how supreme the effort;
- When victory eludes us, we must learn to accept it as graciously as we do our triumphs;
- It may be just possible that a loss is due to the fact that the opposing team played the game better than our team.

- Our players should learn from our reactions to a loss that:
  - √ We feel they played their best, which just wasn't good enough on this particular day;
  - √ They should hold their heads up high; there is no shame attached to honest effort — win or lose;
  - √ There is always something to learn from a loss.
  - √ There is nothing gained from brooding; players should be encouraged to put the game behind them and look forward to the next opportunity to play;
  - √ Seeking scapegoats, such as 'biased officials', 'poor turf', or 'poor performance' by one or two teammates is not a mature or healthy reaction to the loss. Such a crutch prevents acceptance of reality.

5. Whether away from or at the field, our words and actions should convey a philosophy of athletics which includes:

- The real purpose of soccer competition is to have *fun*, to be able to participate to improve skills, to learn sportsmanship, to develop a sense of responsibility and self-discipline, to develop a group loyalty and comradeship, to learn to compete within established rules, to accept decisions of authorized officials, to seek interpretation or change through proper channels, and to develop sound minds and bodies.

TEACHING SOCCER TECHNIQUE:

THE BUILDING BLOCKS OF THE GAME

• •

"Without technique, there are no tactics" is a soccer axiom that few in soccer would dispute. Put another way, a team can't function collectively unless every player is able to properly pass and receive the ball, as well as dribble, head, shoot and tackle the ball with a reasonable degree of effectiveness.

This chapter will share with readers information about the techniques of the game. The initial series of articles will analyze technique in terms of dissecting it into its component parts. The second set of articles will offer progressive practice sessions for coaches to utilize as they train players in specific techniques. Some of the sessions are the collective thoughts of the NSCAA Academy staff and are structured to proceed in the fundamental, match-related and match-conditioned format that is part of the advised NSCAA Academy coaching methodology.

Obviously if players in this country were practicing with the ball on their own in a consistent manner coaches would be moving immediately to small group and team tactics in their practices. But thus far our players do not indulge in "sandlot" or "street soccer." As a result there is a need for coaches to be able to analyze technique and then understand the incremental approach with which that technique can be transformed into skill — skill being the ability to utilize the technique under game conditions.

⚽

DEVELOPING TECHNIQUE

PASSING

NSCAA Staff Members: Ron Ost, Karen Stanley, Tim Schum and Jeff Vennell

As with all technique that is taught at the NSCAA Academy level, a session on passing will begin at the fundamental level, proceed to the game-related stage and finish with a match (5 v. 5 with keepers).

Passing ability must be developed in each and every practice session to some degree. The coach must recognize that the two main considerations in achieving a high level of passing skill are the direction (accuracy) and speed (sometimes referred to as the "weight") of the pass. These two aspects of passing must also be intertwined with good communication between the passer and the receiver of the ball.

Coaching passing is somewhat laborious. It demands repetition and the coach can seek to bring diversity to his/her practices by using different methodologies to achieve passing skill in the team. Numerous exercises can be applied in the team setting to upgrade the team's passing ability including: possession games; conditioned games (limited touches); grid work; small-sided games; shadow play.

It might be noted that passing practices are in reality receiving practices with the opposite emphasis.

WARMUPS

1. In 2s, checking and passing with the emphasis on the receiver checking to the ball at an angle. Player X2 dribbles the ball; X2 observes X1 and when X2 looks up to play the ball, X1 checks back at an angle;

• X2 plays ball to close foot (foot closest to passer) and X1, upon reception, plays the ball back to X2;

• X2 plays ball to further foot (foot furthest from passer) and X1, upon reception, controls ball and turns with it. (Diagram 4-1)

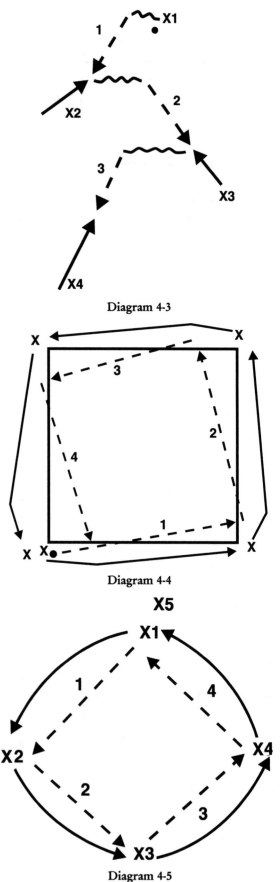

Diagram 4-3

Diagram 4-4

Diagram 4-5

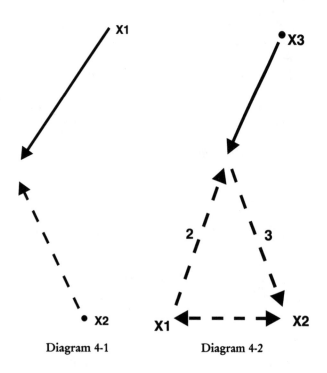

Diagram 4-1   Diagram 4-2

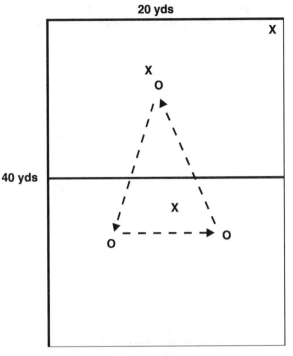

20 yds

40 yds

Diagram 4-6

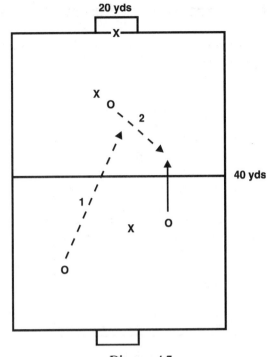

20 yds

40 yds

Diagram 4-7

The coaching emphases in this exercise include:
• Weight and accuracy of the pass;
• Checking run made when passer's head is up;
• Checking run made at an angle.

2. In 3s, while X1 and X2 interpass, X3 looks for one or the other to look up and then checks back at an angle to receive the ball and then plays it back to the person not playing them the pass. Repeat adding which foot want ball played to, etc. (Diagram 4-2)

3. In an open area, in 3s and 4s, each player with a number. Pass to each other in sequential order, #1 to #2, etc. Each time player receiving ball must control, dribble and look up to find his next receiver who must check at angle, etc. (Diagram 4-3)

The coaching emphases should include:
• Angled passes (if runs are angled, passes are angled);
• Angled checking runs;
• Get ready in terms of selection of pass by looking at the next player before the ball gets to you.

4. In 5s, against the clock. 20 x 30 grid. Clocked time. Players pass across corner to next player and follows pass. Continue sequence until everyone resumes their starting position. Lowest total elapsed time is goal for each group. (Diagram 4-4)

The coaching emphases should include:
• Pass to teammate's front foot (play to space);
• Receive ball across body;
• Use one-touch restriction if possible;
• check position of receiver as ball is getting to you.

5. In 6s, pass and follow pass. Open-ended in terms of space. (Diagram 4-5)

The coaching emphases should include:
• Pass at angle;
• Receive ball across body;
• Pass to the lead foot (play to space);
• Move from two-touch to a one-touch restriction;
• Look at the next target before ball arrives.

6. Possession game to teach third-man passing. 40 x 20 yard grid divided into two halves. 2 v. 1 in one half and 1 v. 1 in other. The two in 2 v. 1 must keep possession while using their teammate in 1 v. 1 for third-man combination. If opponents get ball, they become 3 v. 2 by activating the idle player and the other team drops off a man. (Diagram 4-6)

MATCH-RELATED

7. Same game as #6 above but teams go to goal by carrying ball over halfway line or passing over it and going to goal. Always have 2 v. 1 advantage. Play restricted passing (two-touch, etc.). (Diagram 4-7)

7a. 2 v. 2 in 20 x 40 yard grid. Attempt to pass to a target player who can move along endline. Team that "scores" maintains possession and goes the other direction. Can add a support player on each sideline to make exercise easier. (Diagram 4-7a)

TEACHING ANGLED PASSING

8. Field 60 yards long by 45 yards wide (3-15 yard wide zones). Goals at the end of each zone. Play 2 v. 2 in each zone (6 v. 6 in total). (Diagram 4-8)

• Players must stay on zones;

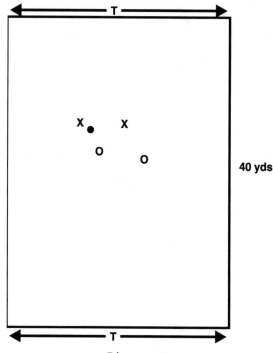

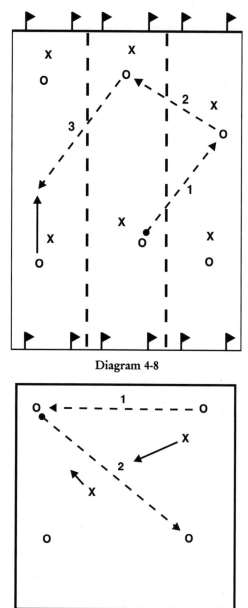

Diagram 4-7a

Diagram 4-8

Diagram 4-9

• Ball cannot be passed to player in same zone.
  Game demands only angled passes.

9. Same as #8, but players can go into other zones, but ball cannot be passed to a player in the same zone.

10. Same as #8 and #9, but remove zones, leaving but two goals on endlines of field.

TEACHING PENETRATING PASSES

Remembering the soccer motto "The best pass you can make is the longest pass you can make and still keep possession," the following exercises are designed to emphasize the penetrating pass.

11. 4 v. 2 in a 20 x 20 yard area. Keep possession until you can split the two defenders with a through ball. Emphasis on one-touch and two-touch passing to create the through ball. Also work on various forms of deception (i.e., faking to receive ball and letting it run to opposite foot, etc.) prior to passing the ball. (Diagram 4-9)

12. 2 v. 2 in 30 x 20 yard rectangle. The emphasis is on playing the ball forward immediately. (Diagram 4-10)

• The players can only score by first playing the ball to one of two targets at the side of their goal;

• They can receive a vertical 1-2 off the target or;

• The target can play to a third man for a shot on goal;

• Targets are limited to one-touch passing.

13. 5 v. 3 to line. 10 players in 50 x 30 yard grid. Five attackers attempt to maintain possession versus three defenders and try to play through ball for

teammate to control and dribble under control over goalline. (Diagram 4-11)

• Teams exchange roles following a goal with two spare players joining the exercise and two X players going off.

• Play ball sideways if no forward pass available.

MATCH-CONDITION

14. 5 v. 5 to two endline goals in 50 x 30 yard area. Both teams have both endline (one for each team) and sideline players (one for each sideline) to use for additional support. (Diagram 4-12)

• Players score goal with combination play off end targets and must dribble over line for score;

• Players can relieve pressure by using a sideline support pass.

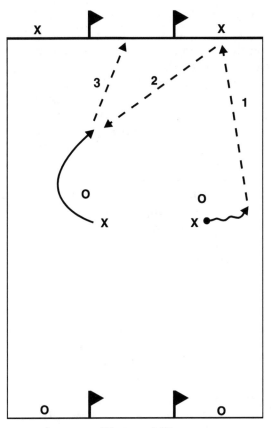

Diagram 4-10

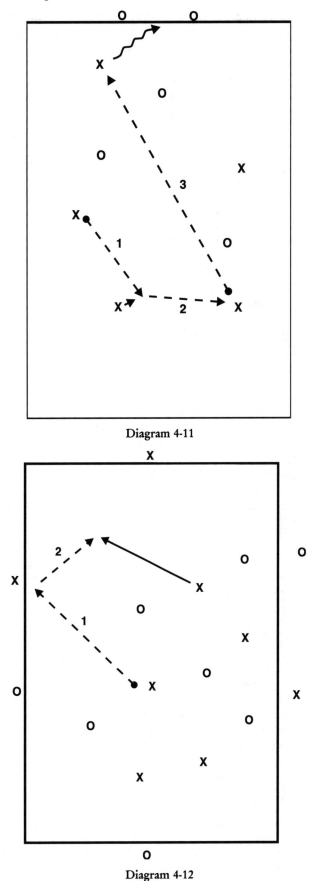

Diagram 4-11

- Emphasis on making penetrating pass and role of third man in support of pass.
15. 5 v. 5 with keepers would conclude the activity with no restrictions.

⚽

IMPROVING YOUR OFFENSE: THE IMPORTANCE OF THE FIRST-TIME PASS
Tom Rowney

In the past few years, the ideas of Wiel Coerver have had a significant impact on the content of practice sessions and coaching clinics throughout the United States. Coerver's developmental approach focuses on producing players who are able to maintain individual possession of the ball with poise and balance. Although teaching techniques that allow players to be comfortable in possession are an important part of the development of skillful soccer players, individual possession may be a facet of the game that has been overemphasized recently. Where overemphasis on individual possession occurs the long-term result will be to produce players who dwell on the ball too long, fail to observe penetrating passing opportu-

Diagram 4-12

nities, and consequently allow disorganized defenses vital time to reorganize. To counter these problems we need to think about improving the ability of players to play the first-time pass and to combine with teammates to produce skillful one-touch soccer.

THE IMPORTANCE OF ONE-TOUCH SOCCER

One-touch soccer refers to the playing of several, often consecutive, first-time passes among teammates. The ability to play skillful one-touch soccer takes on greater importance as players reach the high school, college, and professional levels. At these levels players are usually well coached in defensive tactics and are less susceptible to being beaten by individual possession skills. Defenses are, therefore, much more difficult to break down. One-touch play can be devastating to even the most well-organized of defenses for three major reasons:

- Play becomes unpredictable for defenders because the point of attack constantly changes. Defenders therefore, have to make more decisions about whether to mark space or mark an opponent.

- The speed which the ball can be played into forward positions not only makes the recovery of beaten defenders more difficult but forces goal-side defenders to make covering/marking decisions much more quickly. When defenders are required to make such decisions at greater speed and with greater frequency, defensive errors are more likely to occur.

- Teams that become competent at first-time passing also tend to be more effective in transition from defense to offense. For example, interceptions or clearances are less likely to be made "high, wide, and handsome" and are more likely to be made to teammates.

ELEMENTS OF ONE TOUCH SOCCER

Skillful one-touch passing is dependent on a player's vision, the technical ability to make a variety of passes, and his understanding of each situation. Good supporting runs and communication from teammates are also vital elements.

1. Vision

Although players can show vision in defensive situations, when most coaches speak of great vision they are usually referring to an offensive skill. In this sense, vision refers to a player's ability to observe the movements of the ball, opponents, and teammates, and to exploit, with maximum effect, openings in opposing defenses.

To be successful with the first-time pass it is essential that players be constantly aware of the position of teammates and opponents. In addition, they must anticipate possible passing opportunities, particularly penetrating ones, even though they may not be involved in the immediate play. As the pass arrives, the individual player should already have made a decision as to the direction of his/her first-time pass.

2. Technical Ability

Excellent vision without the technical ability to exploit that vision is redundant. To play quality first time passes one needs the technical ability to pass the ball with the head, chest and both feet. Moreover, first-time passes (as with all passes) should be accurate, well-timed, correctly-paced, and played, if possible, with disguise. Although playing the first-time ball makes it difficult to alter the timing of the pass, subtle alterations are possible by allowing the ball to "run across" the player before the pass is made. This may also serve to improve passing angles and allow teammates more time to make supporting runs.

Finally, quality first-time passes are dependent on a player's ability to be aware of, and quickly adjust his body position and to play the ball first-time while unbalanced.

3. Understanding

In this context, understanding refers to a player's ability to decide between appropriate and inappropriate situations in which to play the first-time pass. Although there are no hard and fast rules on this subject there are some general guidelines.

The first-time pass is generally appropriate:

- When the receiving player is under pressure from an oncoming opponent or surrounded by several opponents. In such situations it is likely that supporting teammates will be unmarked or marked less tightly.

- When the receiving player is marked tightly and facing his/her own goal. Although most coaches suggest that players in this situation should "play the way you're facing," good one-touch players are also able to pass to teammates situated on their blind side.

- When a penetrating forward pass is possible. Players should be encouraged at all times to look for penetrating forward runs from teammates.

The first-time pass is generally not appropriate:

- When supporting runs by teammates have not been made. Obviously, without support it is more sensible to keep possession of the ball until support is available.

- When the player has space in front of him in which to control and run with the ball. Players who have the opportunity to run with the ball into forward space should be encouraged to do so since such runs draw defenders towards the ball and create vital space in other areas of the field.

- When the pass is too difficult or there is a high probability that it will be intercepted. The key coaching phrase here is not to try and "force the play."

- When receiving ground passes on a poor playing surface. This makes it difficult to produce a con-

Diagram 4-13

trolled first-time contact. In such situations the player should control the ball if the space is available.

4. Supporting Runs

To play effective one-touch soccer it is crucial that players make early supporting runs as a teammate is receiving the ball. Supporting runs are commonly thought of as movements of teammates behind the player with the ball. However, it is more realistic to regard any run that creates a passing opportunity for the player in possession as a good supporting run. Early supporting runs allow the passing player time to observe such runs and to choose the appropriate passing response. He is also given extra time to concentrate on making a technically correct pass.

5. Communication

Communication is, of course, an important aspect in all facets of team play. In one-touch soccer, early and clear calls both from the passing and supporting players are vital to success.

PRACTICING ONE-TOUCH SOCCER

The technical and tactical aspects of first-time passing should be introduced to young players as early as possible though the timing will depend on the technical ability and tactical awareness of the individual team. However, as a general guideline, players should begin practicing one-touch soccer on a regular basis at around age twelve.

Initially, some one-touch practices may prove to be rather difficult for younger players. However, the practices can easily be tailored to the ability level of the individual group. For example, the practice area can be increased, or the number of players conditioned to one-touch reduced, to provide a more optimally challenging practice. Once the various aspects have been introduced it is important that one-touch play be practiced regularly so that players develop the ability to play first-time passes at speed and under pressure.

1. Initial Grid Practices

A. In Diagram 4-13 there is a 4 v. 1 situation in a 10 x 10 yard grid. The emphasis is on practicing passing the ball with the inside, instep, and outside of both feet.

A one-touch condition can be placed on any or all of the four passing players depending on the ability of the group. The practice should continue for two-three minutes before changing the defender.

B. In Diagram 4-14 the practice is developed into a 20 x 20 yard grid and a 4 v. 2 situation. Emphasis is now placed on coordinated one-touch passing and early movement to provide support. Each player in turn, and eventually all four players, should be restricted to one-touch.

Passing players should particularly look for the pass that penetrates between both defenders, the "window pass". The difficulty of the practice can be in-

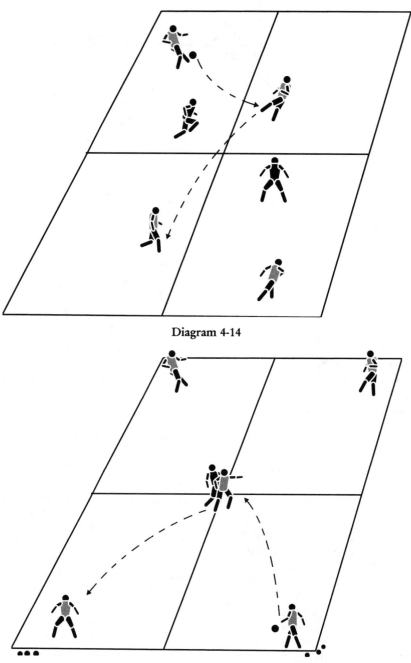

Diagram 4-14

Diagram 4-15

creased by reducing the size of the grid to 20 yards by 10 yards.

C. The previous practices have focused on first-time passes played along the ground. The practice in Diagram 4-15 is a 1 v. 1 situation in a 20 x 20 yard grid with emphasis on producing first-time passes with the head, chest and volley techniques.

The coach or the middle player should nominate one of the four server/receivers to throw towards his teammate in the center of the grid. The middle player must then play a first-time pass to the corner players on his blind side as well as those facing him. This prac-

tice can be done with or without the defending player, but if opposition is introduced the defending player should not position himself between the server and passing player.

2. Functional Practice

Successful one-touch play brings about the greatest rewards in the offensive half of the field. It is therefore important that forward and midfield players receive repeated practice in this area. The following practice progression is designed to focus on first-time passing for forward players. The emphasis is on "taking the pace off" long passes to produce accurate "lay-offs"

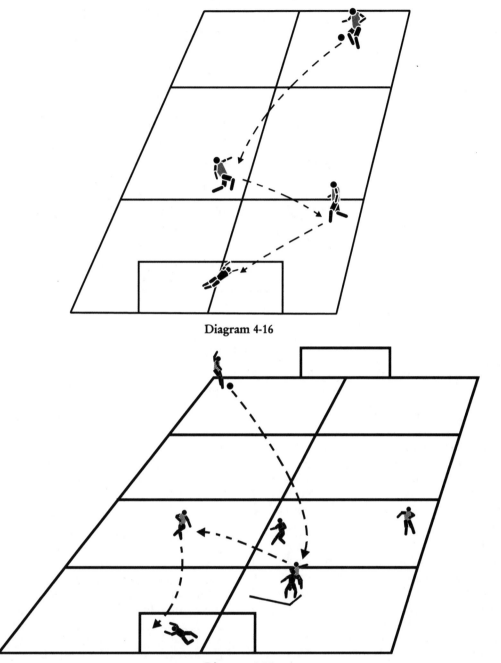

Diagram 4-16

Diagram 4-17

and using coordinated one-touch play with supporting players to create shooting opportunities. The initial practice Diagram 4-16 takes place in a 20 x 40 yard grid area with three players and a goalkeeper.

The serving player plays a variety of ground and air passes to one of the two players positioned approximately 25 yards from the server. The receiving player must play a first-time pass with the correct pace and direction to his partner who should attempt to shoot first-time if possible.

This practice can be developed by introducing another forward and two defenders, thus creating a 3 v. 2 situation. (Diagram 4-17)

The attacking players should use checking and "showing" runs to create space to receive the initial pass. After the receiving player has played a first-time pass, the attacking team must combine, using one-touch play where appropriate, to produce a shot on goal. Defenders should be conditioned to start in a goal-side marking position until after the initial pass. The final progression in this practice takes place in a 40 x 60 yard area (Diagram 4-18) and is essentially a 6 v. 6 situation (plus two goalkeepers).

The two forward and two defending players on each team are restricted to their respective halves of the field. Defenders are further conditioned to mark

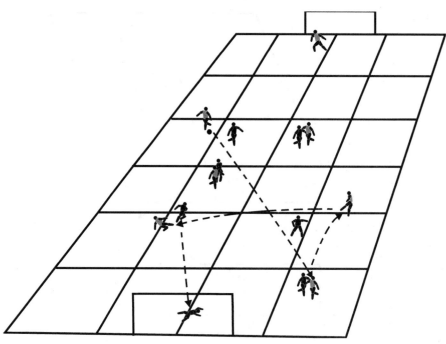

Diagram 4-18

goalside. The two midfield players on each team are allowed to move freely between each half to provide support for their respective forward players. The practice is started with one of the defenders being allowed to pass to a forward teammate in the other half of the field. The receiving forward must play a first-time pass to his forward partner or to his supporting midfield players. The players then combine to create a shooting opportunity. For more advanced players the grid area can be reduced or another midfield player can be added to each team.

3. Small-Sided Games

Concentrated one-touch practice can be achieved in 6 v. 6 or 7 v. 7 games under a variety of conditions. For example, rather than have all players restricted to one-touch, the coach might select only three players per team to play under a one-touch condition. A new one-touch group can be chosen every five minutes. In small-sided games, however, players will often focus all their attention on playing short passes along the ground. Thus, little practice is achieved in the receiving and passing of lofted balls. A more realistic practice can be achieved by conditioning players to play every third or fourth pass in the air or by starting each sequence of play with a lofted pass from the goalkeeper or a defender. In the latter case, the defender should be allowed to start the practice without the challenge of opponents.

4. 11 v. 11 Practice

Eleven-a-side practices should initially be isolated in the defending, middle or attacking thirds of the field. This will allow players to concentrate on the appropriateness of one-touch soccer in relation to the area in which play takes place. At this stage players should focus on when to play, and when not to play, the first-time pass. It is therefore inadvisable to place a continuous one-touch condition during the 11 v. 11 practice. Rather, players should be conditioned to one-touch in certain situations, e.g. when tightly marked from behind and with one's back to the opponents' goal. The session should end with a full-field game and the players free from all conditions.

MOTIVATING PLAYERS TO ONE-TOUCH

One-touch soccer is, in essence, the purest form of coordinated and unselfish team play. Consequently, players who have above-average or outstanding individual possession or dribbling skills may initially be reluctant to incorporate one-touch techniques into their game. In such circumstances it is imperative that the coach emphasize that players who cannot, or will not play the first-time pass, severely reduce the effectiveness of the team as a whole. Players might be reminded that even the great "individuals" understand the importance of the first-time pass. Maradona's pass to set up Burrachaga for the winning goal in the '86 World Cup Final is a perfect example. In reviewing one of the '86 World Cup highlight films it was found that of the 57 goals scored from dynamic situations, 23 were the immediate result of the first-time pass. The coaching implications are clear: it is important that we work to develop players who are composed in possession and have the latitude to demonstrate individual possession and dribbling skills. However, it is equally important that we combine such skills with the ability to pass with vision, speed, accuracy and penetration. Regular practice at first-time passing should establish a strong foundation for such a melding of skills.

⚽

RECEIVING: THE FIRST TOUCH IS THE MOST IMPORTANT

Ron McEachen, Tim Schum and Jeff Vennell
NSCAA Academy staff members

In arranging practices that focus on receiving the ball, coaches should generally divide the first part of the session into two parts: the first will focus on receiving balls on the ground; the second will concentrate on receiving balls in the air.

The coaching points covered in each of the sessions will build on each other but the major emphasis will be on "preparing the ball" so that it is as close as necessary depending on the situation (degree of pressure the receivers find themselves under). Another definition might indicate that the technical receptions of the ball need to be as efficient and quick as possible in order that continued possession can be tactically maintained by one's team. In discussing the reception of balls from the air, particular emphasis should be placed on players' choices in terms of which body surface is used to receive the ball. The progression of this technical session will proceed from a fundamental to a match-related to match-condition phases.

In the case of the fundamental exercises, they have been labeled B for beginning level players, I for intermediate players and A for advanced players. In some cases they are applicable to more than one group of players. Obviously, by using restrictions, coaches can gear exercises to reach any level of players (i.e., more space for an exercise allows more time for players to react to a situation).

FUNDAMENTAL PHASE

Ground Passes

I. 5s in 20 x 20 yard grid, one ball (use cones) (B level)

A. Pass right to start exercise and follow pass. Review fundamentals of reception including:

- Receive ball across body with farthest foot (right foot in case of first phase of this exercise);
- Look at next target before the ball gets to you so that you already know how to position body or where you are going to pass the ball. Take a mental picture of the situation;
- Receive the ball with your toe pointed upward and the ankle locked to increase the surface area hitting ball;

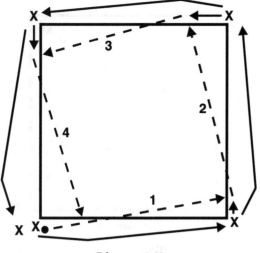

Diagram 4-19

- Do not stop the ball, keep it within close range to draw the defender, then move it away from him/her toward the next target;
- Under pressure, look to play the ball away from the pressure with a long first touch—use feints or false cues as appropriate in this situation;
- Make eye contact with next receiver so that he/she knows when to begin the run and then strike ball so that the receiver can receive it in stride;
- Keep hips open to target for efficiency of passing movement and to allow for maximum passing options.

B. Pass to left as second phase of activity.

C. Can conduct drill with more players (up to 12) and race against the clock with drill concluded when the ball returns to the first passer of the ball. If two groups, have competition. (Diagram 4-19)

II. 5-6 in 20 x 20 yard grid, two balls (B level)

A. Two outside players on the grid play balls to a player in the grid who then controls and prepares the ball so that it can be played out to one of players without a ball on the perimeter of the grid. Review fundamentals including:

- All of points covered in I;
- Eye contact by receiver with passer as checks to receive the ball;
- Practice turning quickly with ball;
- Emphasize timing of run to ball (eye contact with passer);

B. Change on one-minute intervals.

C. Add a defender (using either frontal pressure or pressure from behind) and do the following:

- Prepare ball away from defender;
- Use deception to beat defender;
- Use outside and top of foot for deception. (Diagram 4-20)

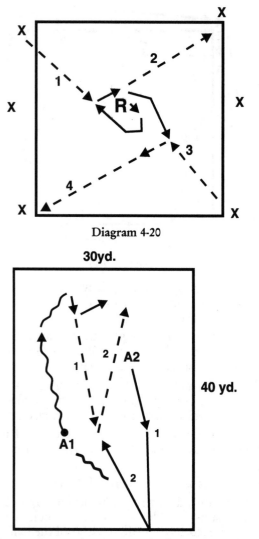

Diagram 4-20

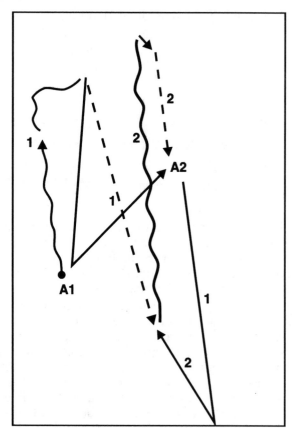

Diagram 4-22: Only "A" group shown; "B" and "C" twosomes would be operative at same time

Diagram 4-21: Only "A" group is shown; "B" and "C" twosomes would be playing at same time.

III. Three teams of two players each (six total) in 30 x 40 yard grid. (I level)

A. Working in 2s (three teams of two players, As, Bs, Cs), dribbler controls ball and waits for his/her receiver to run to farthest line in grid. The receiver then checks to receive the ball with the front foot, two-touch for control, play back to his/her partner. Repeat the process. After one minute, change roles. Review fundamentals including (Diagram 4-21):

• All points covered in II;

• Find place in crowded grid to receive the ball;

• Checking run to ball must be at match speed.

B. Instead of playing the ball back, the receiver accepts the ball with the foot open to the same side as that which the ball arrives and turns in (Diagram 4-22) that direction (i.e., ball played to the left side of the body, turn to the left) and sprint-dribbles to farthest line in the grid and plays it to checking receiver who waits until dribbler has

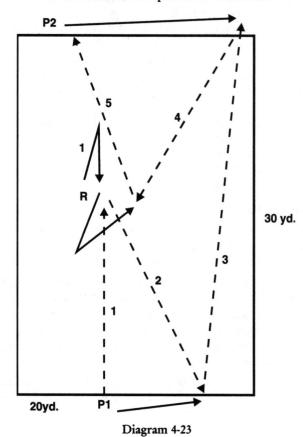

Diagram 4-23

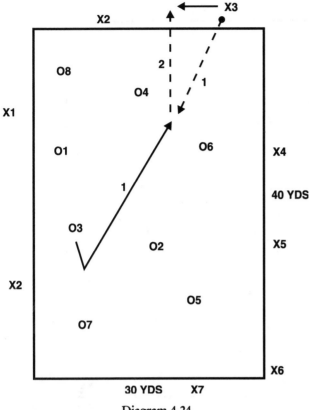

Diagram 4-24

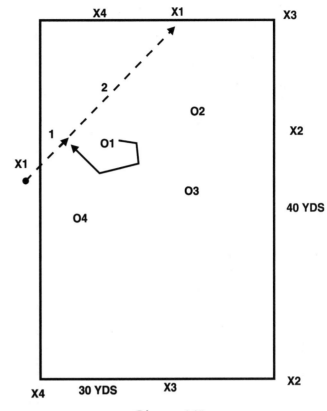

Diagram 4-25

turned and faces him/her before the checking run is made (a reversal of roles from A.); one minute.

Review fundamentals including:

• All points covered in III;

• Observe ability of receiver to coordinate with dribbler;

IV. Three teams of two players in 20 x 30 grid. (I level)

A. The receiver initiates pass with run to ball, controls ball, returns it at angle to passer, moves away as ball is played to opposite corner. Upon control by third player, receiver checks to ball and repeats control and angled passback; one minute, change roles.

B. All return passes two-touches by receiver.

C. Various surfaces of foot used on first touch.

D. One-touch receptions.

E. Add defender. (Diagram 4-23)

V. 16 players in a 40 x 30 yard grid. (I-A levels)

A. X1 is linked with O1, X2 with O2, etc., each player outside grid with a ball. Play is continuous between each pair of players with O1 checking away and working on timing as checks back to receive ball. Exchange roles.

B. Xs pass to any Os who check for the ball, reverse roles. (Diagram 4-24 & 4-25)

VI. 12 players, four groups of three players. (A level)

A. Player in grid receives ball, takes a mental picture and identifies the position of the third member of the group and moves body so that he/she is in a good position to repass the ball to the third member.

B. Add two to four defenders. If defenders win ball, replace player who gave up the ball. One minute maximum for defenders.

AIR BALLS

VII. Warmup, two groups of three players (B level)

A. Passer using throw-in technique throws ball to a receiver who controls and dribbles by the tossing player who rushes forward to apply pressure. Both players continue to the end of the line they are moving toward with dribbler leaving ball for the next tosser. (Diagram 4-26)

VIII. Dutch warmup, team exercise (B-I-A levels)

A. Half the group with balls, half without. Player with ball tosses to another player for designated receptions (i.e., chest receptions). Receive five tosses from one player, change players and receive five more from that player, etc.

B. Add to A by having first player to receive five balls from four different players the winner.

C. Add to A by having receivers control balls from as many different players as possible in 90 seconds. It is understood that players rotate from being passers to receivers.

IX. Three in grids, several balls with each server. (Diagram 4-27)

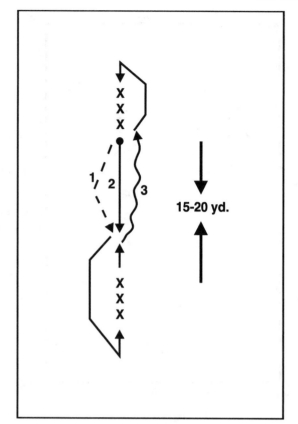

Diagram 4-26

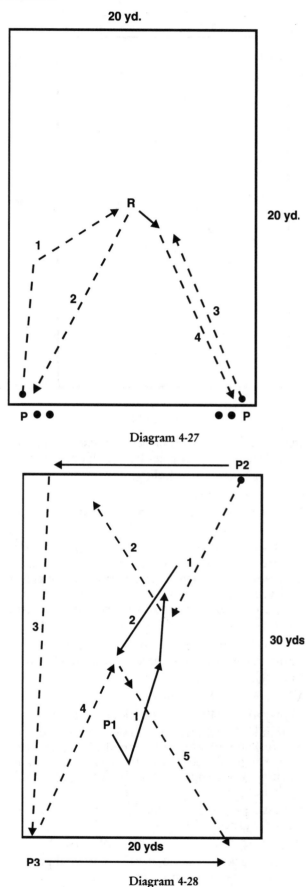

Diagram 4-27

A. Two players serve balls from hands, from volley kick, from surface (advanced players) to checking player. Services below knees, above knees, to chest areas. Server plays to receiver, receiver prepares return ball to passer, faces second server and repeats. One minute and rotate roles. Review fundamentals including:

• Get in line of flight with ball;

• Decide upon flight of ball which body part to use for control;

• Present body part to the ball;

• Relax body part at impact if ball is to be collected;

• Move ball from the landing area;

• Win the ball early, don't wait for it.

B. Control and play ball out of air to self and then to third player.

C. Sprint to far line of grid and check back to ball at speed and prepare return.

D. Add services from various angles, left and right, use two servers.

E. Add a defender.

X. 3-4 in open field, one ball.

A. Receiver checks (P1) to ball, plays back at angle to initial passer (P2). P2 now plays a long (30-40-yard) air ball to P3. While ball is in flight, P1 checks away

Diagram 4-28

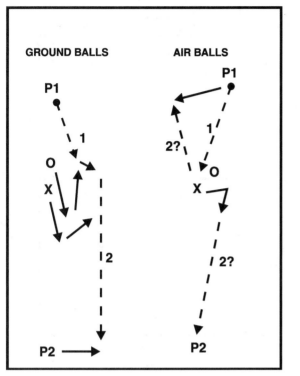

Diagram 4-29

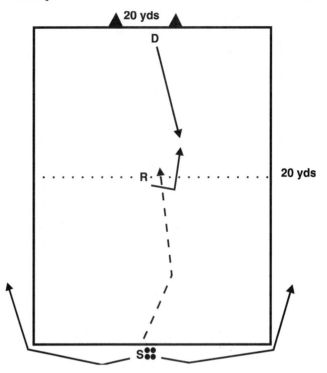

Diagram 4-30

and upon reception and preparation by P3 checks to him/her and the whole process repeats itself. (Diagram 4-28)

Review fundamentals:

• All covered but with emphasis on receptions/support of longer passes, timing of checking runs.

B. Add defender to checking player.

C. Add fourth player, P4 behind P3 and once pass is made, player follows pass each time. P1 receives, lays ball to P2, takes P2 place; P2 plays long ball to P3 who supports him/her at angle, runs to middle and receives pass from P3; lays ball off to P3 who plays long pass to P1 and runs to support, etc.

XI. Four players, defensive pressure. (Diagram 4-29)

A. P1 plays ground pass to checking receiver O and under the pressure of defender X, the receiver turns ball and plays to P2. X now becomes the receiver, etc.

B. P1 plays air ball over top of O to X who depending on degree of control, can play to either P1 or P2. If to P2, then O receives the next air ball.

XII. 3s in grids, server plays ball in air to receiver who turns and takes on defender to goal. Use cones for goals.

A. Defender moves initially on the first touch by the receiver. Play 1 v. 1 and upon completion of play, repeat. One minute and rotate roles. Review fundamentals:

• All covered in VI and VII;

• Ability to control ball out of air with change of direction;

• Prepare the ball away from the defender (spin turn technique can be used here);

B. Defender moves on the flight of ball. (Diagram 4-30)

MATCH-RELATED

XIII. 4 v. 2 in 20 x 30 yard grid

Review fundamentals including:

• Keep hips open to all support players;

• Emphasis on good reception and positioning to keep maximum passing angles open;

• Four play for possession with two-touch restriction. Emphasis on splitting two defenders with a through ball;

• All points covered in other exercises;

• Use of first touch in preparing the ball for the next pass;

• Use of feints, ball runs to deceive defenders, buying time for easy possession. (Diagram 4-31)

XIV. 6 v. 6 to two goals

A. Unlimited touches. Play 4 v. 2 in each half. Field is 60 x 40 yards with no one allowed over halfway line. Four attackers vs. two defenders in each half. Defending team marks 2 v. 2 in other half with two others retreating into goal until possession is regained at which time it can play 4 v. 2 until ball is played to its strikers in other half (2 v. 2 again!). Use restric-

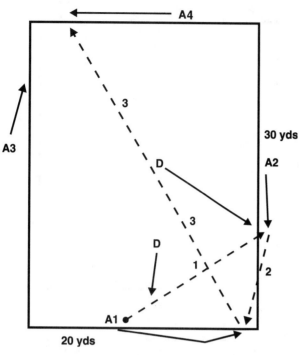

Diagram 4-31

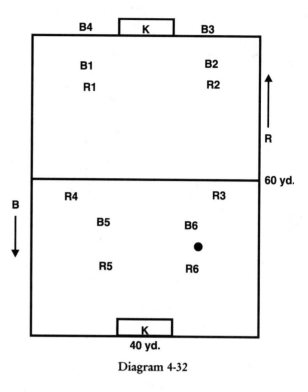

Diagram 4-32

tions in match (touches, etc.,) if objectives are not being achieved.) Review fundamentals:

- When in possession, be composed;
- Use first touch to:
  √ relieve pressure, angle of touch, distance of touch (i.e., can beat defender with a good first touch);
  √ attack non-pressurizing defender;
  √ set up a pass or shot;
  √ keep possession.
- Control made easier by good body position for reception. (Diagram 4-32)

MATCH-CONDITION

The session should end with a 6 v. 6 in a 60 x 40 yard wide field. While there has been some designation as to the level of expertise demanded by the fundamental exercises discussed in this practice session, the match-related exercises and the concluding match can be conditioned in various ways by the coach in order to achieve certain objectives dependent upon the ability level of the players being instructed.

Conditions that can be imposed include:

- Number of touches (two-three touches generally; one-touch for expert players);
- Long, narrow field for more vertical passing;
- Wider field encourages wing play;
- Channels on the touch lines of the field encourage crossing/heading play;
- Four goals would encourage mobility of play by the participants.

DRIBBLING: DODGING WITH A SOCCER BALL

Jack Detchon, Tim Schum, Jeff Tipping and Jeff Vennell*

Dribbling: **A vital technique for young players to develop, a crucial component of any team's attack, and a technique that is worthy of a specific training session.**

Most coaches would agree that that inclusive statement accurately describes the technique of dribbling. How to transfer technique into skill is the crucial coaching question. What follows is a compilation of thoughts by NSCAA Academy coaches on that subject.

With an effective training session, a coach can make a difference with the individual players as well as the team. Through training, the player can improve his or her individual skills and improve his or her tactical decision-making skills. As these physical and mental skills develop, the team will evolve into a more dangerous and intelligent attacking force.

This article will offer a logical progression of a training session devoted to dribbling. Ideas offered by mem-

* Ed. Note; Matt Robinson compiled the thoughts of NSCAA Academy coaches Jack Detchon, Tim Schum, Jeff Tipping and Jeff Vennell for this article.

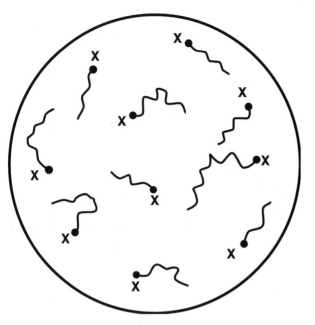

Diagram 4-33

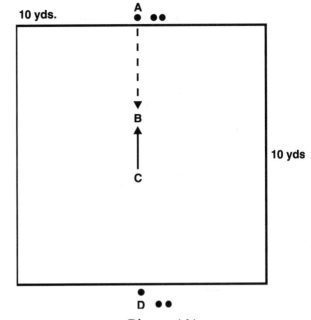

Diagram 4-34

bers of the NSCAA National Coaching Staff are incorporated in the article, and the training session follows the progression that is emphasized in the NSCAA Coaching Academies. The training session focuses on the three types of dribbling-possession, speed and attacking—and will move from the warmup to fundamental phase, then to the tactical stage, to match-related conditions and finally to match-condition stage. Although this particular training session incorporates the three types of dribbling into one session, coach Jeff Vennell notes that each individual type of dribbling can be the object of a training session. If a coach senses the need to make the session specific to a type of dribble, he should be comfortable in doing so.

WARMUP

Organization: Designate an appropriate area on the field. The size of the space may range from the field's center circle to the penalty area to a half field. The size depends on the number of players and their skill level. The better the skill the smaller the space. (Diagram 4-33)

In executing the warmup, the players dribble about the area following the commands of the coach. The commands may consist of dribbling with various surfaces of the feet, dribbling for tight control, to individual offensive moves, to changing direction with speed. If a coach or team is familiar with particular moves, (e.g. Coerver moves) they can be demonstrated and practiced during this time. It might be a good idea to have players individually demonstrate such maneuvers or individual moves you have noted they excel in. In this way you help in the development of their self-confidence and the honing of their leadership skills.

The intensity of the work should increase throughout the duration of the warmup, and even though it is

a warmup, the coach should stress the importance of proper feinting, and the explosion after the feint is executed. Also vision is being improved as the players must keep their heads up in order both to avoid collisions with other players and to find open space.

This warmup is economical in nature in that it is a mild cardiovascular workout while the player is becoming acclimated to the major emphasis of the training session.

FUNDAMENTAL/TACTICAL TRAINING

The training session focuses on shielding, speed dribbling, and attacking with the dribble. With each type of dribbling, the coach can utilize a fundamental stage where there is no pressure, and gradually introduce pressure to make the exercise more tactical in nature.

SHIELDING

Organization: 10 x 10 yard grid with four players to a grid.

To begin this part of the session, player A plays the ball to player B. B shields the ball from player C for five seconds. C then receives a ball from player D and then will shield from player B. The defensive pressure should intensify each time, but the defender should not steal the ball. This restriction is imposed in order to give players a chance to be successful in perfecting their shielding skill. The players in the middle will switch after five trials each. (Diagram 4-34)

More pressure is added at the next stage. Players should match up for a one-minute game of keepaway in the grid. There are no goals, for the focus of the drill is possession by shielding. By rotating players through this several times, the coach can increase the intensity of the defender each time. At first the defender may be restricted from stealing the ball, but

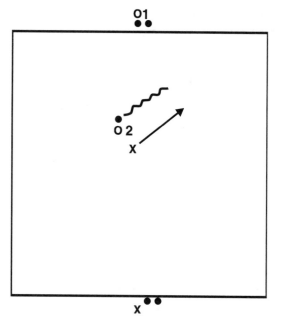

Diagram 4-35a

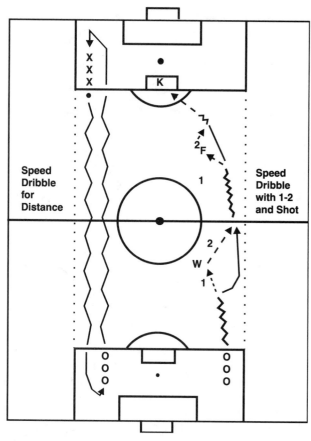

Diagram 4-36

the intensity should be increased to the point it is an all-out game of keepaway. The players on the side have balls that can be put into play, so that the players in the middle work the whole minute. When the minute is up, two players from the side rotate into the grid for their minute's practice. Perhaps of importance is the matchups in the grids. By carefully selecting which players are opposing each other, the coach can assure that equal 1 v. 1 competitions are taking place in each work area. (Diagram 4-35a)

Another stage of shielding development is to have 1 v. 1 games in the same grid size take place to one goal. In Diagram 4-35a we have O1 playing the ball to O2 with X defending. O2 will seek to penetrate but practice shielding while doing so. If the ball were lost by O2, another ball is served with a time limit of 60 seconds to the exercise. Later X would be allowed to counter-attack to the opposing goal line.

The coach can use this part of the session to cover the major teaching points regarding shielding. These important fundamentals include:

• Keeping the body between the ball and the defender;

• Playing the ball with the farthest foot from the defender;

• Keeping the body at a right angle to the defender so that the player does not have his back completely closed to opportunities in front of him;

• Legally using the arm to make space, and

• Moving either laterally or away from the defender.

The objective is to keep possession as long as possible, and wait for the defender to make the mistake of overcommitting. If this occurs, the player can move to an open space and resume the shielding. Along with the technical training, players will also develop a tactical awareness of when to move to open space with

the ball. All field players should participate in this training for players in every position are placed in the situation of shielding. Finally, the one-minute grid work is very economical in that it is great fitness training for the players.

SPEED DRIBBLING

Organization: 45 x 90 yard area, two large goals. Players in lines at the end of the area. Coaches may want to shorten the length for younger players. (Diagram 4-36)

The players will speed dribble the length of the area. Emphasis should be placed on the player keeping the toe pointed down, using the instep, or laces, to strike the ball; playing the ball long on the first touch and increasing the number of touches on the ball and keeping the ball closer to the body as the player gets close to goal or to an opponent. The speed dribble then can be incorporated with shooting, executing a wall pass, and then crossing the ball.

A defender then will be introduced. At first the defender will be passive. This will enable the attacking player to focus on keeping the ball closer to the body and increasing the number of touches as the defender and attacker are about to meet. It is effective to have the defender move towards the attacker to make the situation more game-like. Rarely in a game does an attacking player dribble toward a stationary defender. After a few

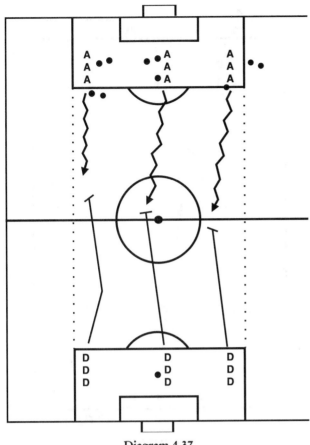

Diagram 4-37

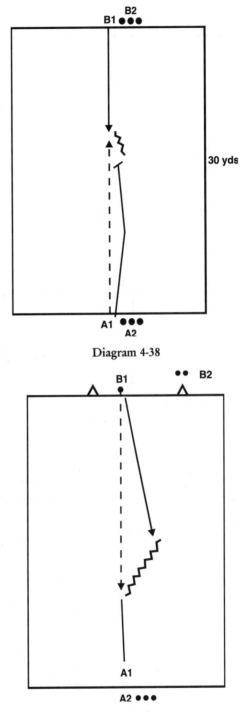

Diagram 4-38

Diagram 4-39

repetitions, the restrictions are taken off the defender and the attacker must attack with the speed dribble and work to get past the defender. The coach should encourage the player to look for the opportunity to play the ball behind the defender and explode past the defender and to be first to the ball. Once in that space, the attacker should cut off any opportunity for a recovery run by the defender by cutting in front of the defender, If the defender wins the ball, he or she attacks to the opposite endline. (Diagram 4-37)

This is excellent functional training for outside backs and midfielders who must attack the flanks regularly, and an excellent conditioner for all field players as they work on this segment of dribbling.

ATTACKING WITH THE BALL

Organization: 20 x 30 yard grid, four players to a grid.

Attacking with the ball is the opportunity for the player to utilize offensive moves he or she has developed. In this exercise, the attacking player will receive the ball from the defender at the other end of the grid and look to attack to the opposing endline. After each exchange, the roles of the players in the grid are reversed. (Diagram 4-38)

Again, the intensity of the defense will move from passive to full as more repetitions are completed. There can be restrictions on play by the defense, e.g., cannot move until the attacker has first touched the ball or later, move once the pass to the attacker is on its way.

The two players outside the grid can retrieve balls, and will be rotated in by the coach. After rotating players, the exercise progresses to the dribbler attacking toward a small goal and if the defender wins the ball, he/she attacks the endline. (Diagram 4-39)

Finally, two goals are set up and both players will attack the small goals. Again, two players with balls can insure that the drill continues for the duration of

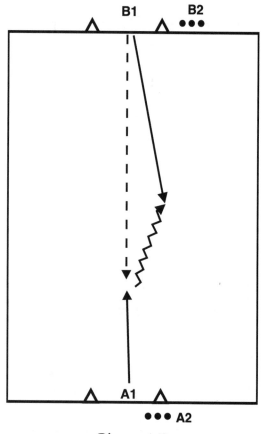

Diagram 4-40

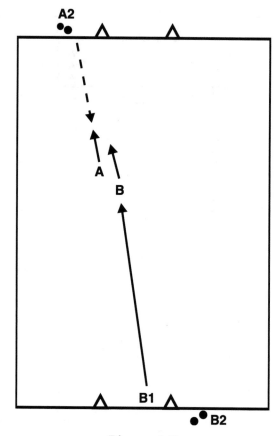

Diagram 4-41

time selected by the coach. Coaches need to remember that dribbling is largely an anaerobic exercise and to ensure quality the right dosage of time needs to be determined (i.e., a minute for high school players, more for mature players, less for youth players). This will assure that a quality effort is given each time. (Diagram 4-40)

The drill also can incorporate the shielding aspect of dribbling by having an outside player playing the ball to the attacker, and the attacker shielding until the opportunity presents itself to turn and attack the goal. (Diagram 4-41)

This exercise offers opportunity for a coach to emphasize the technical skills of attacking with the ball. The player should be encouraged to attack the front foot of the defender, for it is with the back foot a defender will tackle. Again the player should be encouraged to look for the opportunity to play the ball behind the defender, and explode past the defender into the open space, and cut off any opportunity for a recovery run by the defender by cutting in front of the defender. It should also be emphasized that a change of speed and direction is vital in a successful attack with the ball.

GAME RELATED

Organization: Field 44 x 90 yards with clear markings of the thirds of the field, fourteen field players,

two goalkeepers and two servers. Two players from each team in the middle third. Three defenders in each third opposed by two attackers. (Diagram 4-42)

Balls are played from the servers at the end of the field and also by the coach at midfield.

The player is presented the opportunity to utilize the three techniques of dribbling in a tactical situation. In this exercise, the concept of dribbling in different parts of the field is emphasized.

• In the back third, a player should dribble sparingly, and play the ball simply. A dribbling mistake in the back third may prove costly in the form of an uncontested counterattack goal. The players in exercise should use their 3 v. 2 advantage to pass the ball to or through midfield to teammates.

• In the middle third, the player may need to buy time by possessing and shielding the ball before playing it forward into the front third, or the player may attack from the middle third to the front third with the dribble.

• In the front third, the player should be encouraged to attack the defender with the dribble and to take chances. A coach may insert a rule that states the front player, once receiving the ball, must attack the defender with the dribble.

In short, the tactical decisions being made by the back players are much different than those being made

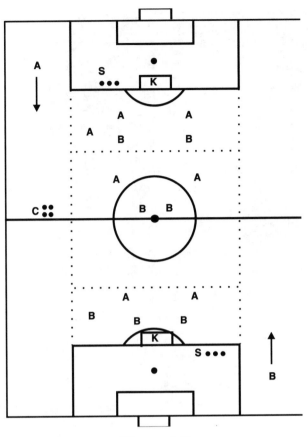

Diagram 4-42

by the front players. The back players *must* be cautious if they must dribble, while the front players should be encouraged to be daring and creative in order to enhance the number of opportunities to score.

The progression of the exercise entails the players at first being restricted to their respective thirds. The ball may only move through the thirds by a pass. The coach then lifts the restriction and players are permitted to move into other thirds to support, or they may make penetrating attacks with the ball into other thirds.

GAME CONDITION

Organization: The same field size as game-related stage, but eliminate the thirds of the field markings. In the game condition stage, the coach lifts the restrictions from the game-related stage. The servers from the end become sweepers. Even though the markers of the thirds are gone, players must realize which third they are in and make the proper tactical decision.

CONCLUSION

Dribbling, without question, is one of the vital skills of the game. Coaches should devote time to the skill so that the players are proficient technically and tactically in the skill. As stated earlier, dribbling itself is worthy of a specific training session, and a coach may even feel compelled to focus specifically on one aspect

of dribbling if needed. This decision should, as always, be based upon the needs of a particular team.

DRIBBLING
Frans Van Balkom*

INTRODUCTION

In the eyes of opponents, successful dribblers are very unpredictable and are masters of the art of feinting. A player who tries to take on (dribble) opponents each time he has possession of the ball becomes predictable, will frequently lose the ball, and exposes himself to injury. Successful dribbling actions are enhanced by the support and behavior of the dribbler's teammates. A player in ball possession must have various tactical options when in ball possession, because if opponents know that his only option and aim is to dribble, their defensive task becomes much easier.

It is also helpful when a team is able to play the ball around. Good support, near and off the ball, helps a great deal in setting up players to make good dribbling runs. A sudden action of a dribbler catches defenders sometimes not prepared and by switching and changing ball sides frequently, the opponent's defense will be stretched and becomes unbalanced and chances for successful dribbling occurs.

Dribblers who can create openings against tight-packed, high-pressuring defenses are vitally important in today's modern game.

DRIBBLING MOVES

There are a great number of dribbling moves, some very simple, others complex. When using them, they are combined with other skills such as feinting, shielding etc. To dribble successfully, speed and timing are important. A player may learn up to 40 different moves, but will usually rely on special/favorite moves when under real pressure. One of the most acclaimed dribblers ever, Sir Stanley Matthews, was known for using only one special move. He varied that move a good deal. The move was named after him and is known as the Matthews Move! By allowing players to practice moves regularly, their timing and feeling for when and how to use the move improved. To become a successful dribbler, continuous practice and repetition of the moves is very important. Everyone can learn all the moves. Some learn faster than others, usually because of better coordination. But, not everyone can be equally successful when using the moves. Personality, character, inborn physical attributes like

---

* *See Methodology segment of this chapter for implementation of these techniques*

Mia Hamm of North Carolina uses body swerve to beat Duke's Missy Durham (15) in ACC women's action.
(photo by Tony Quinn)

power and speed, and other factors play a big role in how successful a player will be as a dribbler.

A coach must know and understand each player's ability regarding dribbling. A good team is a combination of various types of players, each playing a big part in the building of a successful team, and the coach must be aware of their strong and weak points in order to get the best possible results.

Move #1 Push Left, Sprint Right

Dribble ball with right foot towards oncoming player. Push ball with instep of right foot past left side of opponent (to dribbler's right), and sprint past his right side to collect ball behind him.

Move #2 Scissor

There are a number of scissor moves. The Single Scissors, Behind, Over, and Around the ball are some. One of the most effective is the one around the ball and is as follows: Dribble the ball with the right foot towards opponent's right side. Step with right foot from the inside, around ball (the right foot passes between the ball and the left leg, goes around the front of the ball and is planted to the right side of the ball). Place right foot down and play ball with outside of left foot past opponent's right side. Especially effective when close to opponent as ball is shielded from the opponent.

Move #3 Double Scissors

Dribble ball with right foot. Take small step with right foot toward the right, over and past ball. Take a big step with left foot to left, past the ball then play ball with outside of the right foot past opponent's left side and accelerate. Acceleration and body feints are important in all moves.

Move #4 Matthews Move

Start this move with a dead ball. Place left foot next to ball and lean to left. Lift right foot off the ground and push the ball slightly inside (toward the left) with the inside of the right foot. Then push off with left foot and play ball with outside of right foot to right past opponent's left and sprint past him to collect ball.

Move #5 Circle Around Ball

Dribble with right instep. Then circle with right foot from outside (right foot moves to the right, comes back across the front of the ball and back toward the body) around ball, play ball again with instep or outside of right foot and accelerate.

Move #6 Cap Under Body

Dribble with right foot. Cap ball with instep of right foot back and towards left foot. Then play ball with inside of left foot past right side of opponent and accelerate.

Move #7 Swivel

Dribble with right foot, feint, cap with right foot and drop right shoulder. Then cap ball with left foot back and across body to right side and play ball with inside of right foot to right side past opponent's left side and accelerate.

Move #8 Pulling The V

Dribble ball with right foot at an angle toward opponent's right side, forcing him to step to his right. Then pull ball with sole of right foot back towards you, pivot on left foot and play ball with inside of right foot to right at an angle past defender's left side and accelerate.

Move #9 Outside Inside

Start move at slow pace. Play ball with right foot alternating with inside outside. Right foot is kept off the ground and short forward hops are made on the left foot. Ball is played with inside of foot on outside (of the ball) and with outside of foot on inside (of the ball). After about 10 ball touches, suddenly push ball outward, or cap ball inward, and push off with left foot accelerating sideways and forward (on angle), beating opponent on right or left side.

Move #10 Roll Off

Dribble ball with right foot, step with sole of right foot on top of the ball and roll ball outward. Then push the ball with the inside of the right foot across the body to the left. Put right foot down and play ball with outside of left foot to left past defender's right side and accelerate.

⚽

SHIELDING
Frans van Balkom*

INTRODUCTION

In modern soccer, the game is dictated by defensive tactics. The game has changed over the last 35 years considerably. From the all-out attacking game, history has shown that the introduction of the WM System brought a better balance between the attack and the defensive aspects of play. The popularity of the Brazilian 4-4-2 system of play brought even more defense to a game highlighted by increased midfield play. Now, we find coaches talking about an even tighter marking system of play defined as the 4-5-1.

Thus we find today's attacking players matching up against very fit, tight-marking, compactly-organized defenders who apply tremendous pressure in their attempts to win the ball. This relentless pressure in the opponent's half of the field makes it very difficult to hold onto the ball or even make a safe pass to a teammate. For that reason (pressure) it becomes vitally important to become proficient at shielding the ball and to develop the ability to play the ball free when

* see Methodology section for implementation of shielding into practice activities

under pressure. When it is not possible to directly play the ball due to tight-marking defenders, the ability to shield the ball and/or play the ball free will allow your team to maintain possession.

DEFINITIONS

Shielding is the use of a number of special ball-shielding skills which allows you to effectively use your body to maintain possession when under pressure from an opponent.

Playing the ball free requires a number of specifically developed skills, including shielding and feinting, which allows the player in possession to create space to play (pass) the ball, or to move away from an opponent. In tight situations, playing the ball free presents a much lower risk factor than when trying to dribble past opponents.

FUNDAMENTALS

Fundamentals which help a player to successfully receive the ball under pressure and to create more time in preparation to shielding or playing the ball free are:

• Good basic ball control (trapping) skills;
• Moving into free space before receiving the ball;
• Proper timing of when to come off the marking defender before receiving a pass;
• Good understanding between the player passing the ball and the player receiving the ball;
• Pace and accuracy of the pass.
• Observation of the surroundings (field of play) before receiving the ball;
• If possible, the pass should be made to the unmarked side of the receiver;
• Feinting before receiving the pass.

SHIELDING AND PLAYING THE BALL FREE MOVES

1. Outside of the Foot Shield-Dribble the ball with the outside of the right foot and keep the ball close. Change the dribbling foot every five yards by pushing the ball across the body with the inside of the dribbling foot and begin dribbling with the outside of the left foot Another way to shield the ball by changing the dribbling foot is as follows:

Dribble the ball with the outside of the right foot, touching the ball every time the right foot comes forward then touching it every five steps. To change the dribbling foot, step sideways to the right with the right foot (as if to go that way). Since the step to the right didn't involve touching the ball, it (the ball) is now in position to be dribbled forward with the outside of the left foot. Change the dribbling foot about every five steps.

Important Points

• Keep the ball close to the feet;
• Don't see the ball only (good peripheral vision will allow the ball handler to see the ball and the sur-

rounding area). Young players should be taught early not to look directly at the top of the ball;

- Start at a slow pace without pressure from an opponent;
- Next, to create a little pressure, give each player a ball and have them practice dribbling (as above) in a confined area. Add more pressure when the skill is mastered at a high pace;

2. V Move – Using the instep of the left foot, dribble the ball forward at an angle toward the right. Keep the toes of the dribbling foot pointed down. Pull the ball back towards the body with the sole of the left foot, pivot to the left on the right foot and play the ball on a forward angle to the left with the inside of the left foot. Repeat the move every five yards and alternate the starting foot.

Important Points

- The V Move is very well suited to play the ball free when under pressure;
- After the completion of the V Move, it is very important that the players sprint away for three-four yards.

3. Roll Back Turn Dribble the ball forward with the right foot. Reach out and pull the ball back with the sole of the right foot. Pivot and turn on the left foot. Plant the right foot and play the ball forward in the opposite direction with the instep of the left.

Important Points

- When the ball is rolled back with the sole of the right foot don't stop it near or under the body or let it roll backwards;
- Turn quickly, plant the right foot and move off;
- It can be used for shielding and playing the ball free.

4. Pull the Ball Behind the Standing Leg Dribble the ball with the instep of the right foot. Use the sole of the right foot to pull the ball straight back. Don't plant the right foot. As the ball rolls past the standing left leg, use the inside of the right foot to push the ball behind the left leg toward the left. Plant the right foot and play the ball to the left with the outside of the left foot.

Important Points

- Reach out to the ball with the right sole when starting the move;
- Practice the move and alternate the starting foot in order to be able to go right or left with the ball;
- Once the move is mastered, insist that it be performed at high speed and that the player must accelerate in the new direction.

5. Step-over the Ball Dribble with the right foot. Imagine an opponent coming to you on an angle from your left side. Step sideways (from right to left), with the right foot passing over the top of the ball. Simultaneously plant and pivot (to the right) on the

right foot and play the ball in the opposite direction with the inside of the left foot.

Important Points

- When the opponent challenges you from an angle on your left side, the Step-over the Ball with the right foot should be across the top of the ball (from left to right) and it should be a long step towards the opponent. This long step will put your body between the opponent and the ball and allow you to shield it;
- If the challenge comes from a player who has moved up alongside of you (coming from behind), the right foot should step straight forward (to the front) over the ball. Then pivot, turn and go in the opposite direction;

6. Tap Outside Foot Dribble forward with the right foot. From well behind the ball, take a long step (with the right leg) straight forward and over the top of the ball. During this long step, rotate the right leg to the right so that the outside of the right foot is directly in the path of the ball when the foot hits the ground. Play the ball back in the opposite direction with the outside of the right foot and pivot on it at the same time. Now play the ball with the inside of the left foot as you move off with the ball.

Important Points

- Stretch out with the right leg from well behind the ball, and bring the right foot straight over the top of the ball;
- As the right foot is passing over the ball, rotate the right leg (to the right);
- As the outside of the right foot is coming down in front of the ball, the outside of the foot actually touches the ball before the foot hits the ground;
- When learning this move, use a slowly rolling ball.
- Lack of hip flexibility will be a problem in the beginning, but proper practice and execution will help overcome the hip problem.

7. Inside Turn Dribble forward at a slight angle, touching the ball with the inside of the right foot each time that the foot comes forward. Roll the ball (from the top) with the sole of the right toe back towards the body. At the same time, pivot and turn on the left foot and play the ball in the opposite direction with the inside of the left foot. Dribble five yards and repeat the move starting with the left foot.

Important Points

- In the beginning, practice the pivot and turn without the ball. Later use a dead ball and then a slowly moving ball;
- Reach out with the sole of the toe to pull the ball back and turn quickly to shield the ball;
- Once the move is mastered, perform/execute at a higher pace and add realistic pressure;

Here we see demonstrated correct shielding technique by a Virginia player in a match versus the University of Connecticut. Note ball is on foot furthest from the defender.

(photo by Brett Whitesell)

- Practice the move with both feet;
- The same move can be performed without the step over the ball and is useful when changing direction when not under tight pressure.

8. Pull Across the Body and Step Over Dribble with the instep of the right foot. Reach out with the front part of the sole (beneath the toes) of the right foot and roll the ball across the front of the body towards the left side. The right foot, immediately after rolling the ball to the left, steps straight forward. This step forward presents the body as a shield to an opponent coming toward the ball. The ball is then played to the left with the outside of the left foot. Repeat the move with the left foot.

Important Points
- To begin practicing this move, use a dead ball which is slightly in front of you (18 inches);
- Practice the first part of the move by itself. Roll the ball across the body with the sole of the right foot. With the same (right) foot, step straight forward after rolling the ball to the left. Just to emphasize the action, you may want to continue walking forward a few steps as the ball rolls to the left behind you;
- Practice the complete move starting with a dead ball;
- Later use a ball moving slowly forward.

FINAL POINTS

All shielding moves should be mastered by the time a player has reached 14 years of age. These shielding moves should be mastered in addition to all other ball skills. Without a solid foundation in and proficiency of the basic skills, it is impossible for a player to develop. Without basic skills, tactical coaching is a waste of time because tactics can only be implemented if players have a command of basic skills.

Playing good tactical soccer means using ball skills wisely and in the interests of the team. A team deficient in good ball skills cannot have good individual, group or team tactics.

⚽

TACKLING TAKES BOTH: PROPER TECHNICAL SKILLS AND GOOD TACTICAL DECISIONS
Jeff Tipping and Jack Detchon*

When defending is discussed it is often in the context of the team. Yes, the defensive system employed by a coach, whether it be man-to-man or zonal, is important, but what is as important and often overlooked is the individual technical and tactical defensive abilities of the individual players.

All coaches want players who are aggressive defensively, but if this aggressiveness is not tempered with sound technical skills and tactical decisions, the aggressiveness can lead to breakdowns in the defending. Common individual mistakes include a player's speed of approach, containing, players not tackling at the proper moment, or a player reverting to slide tackling in the open field as a first resort rather than a last resort.

Following is a practice session that addresses the individual skills of tackling, closing down, and containing from the front and back as well as exercises that incorporate these skills into a team's defense.

WARMUP EXERCISE

Organization: Two players to a ball on either the endline or sideline. The warmup will serve two purposes: preparing the player both mentally and physi-

* as reported by Matt Robinson

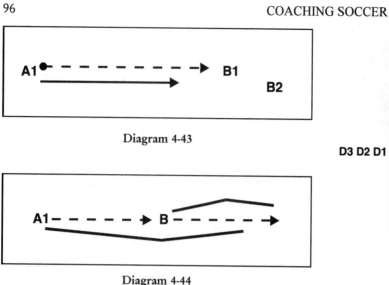

Diagram 4-43

Diagram 4-44

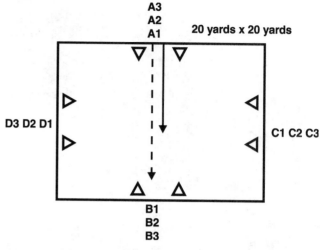

Diagram 4-45a

cally for the session. The player will be introduced to tackling, closing down, and containing while also getting his body prepared to the physical demands of the session.

To begin the warmup, player A1 passes to player B1 and closes down on player B. Player B dribbles at A who backpedals, keeping the ball and player B in front until they get back to the line. Then the players switch roles. Several pairs of players may be executing the same exercise at the same time. (Diagram 4-43)

Player B should not be concerned in beating player A with a penetrating dribble at this point. The attacker is helping with the defensive warmup. Although it is still the warmup, the coach should stress to the defender the importance of moving quickly after playing the ball, but slowing down as he or she gets closer to player B. Young players especially have the tendency to overrun the defensive player. In the second stage of the warmup, player A plays the ball between player B's legs. As player B chases the ball down, player A closes down and prevents player B from turning. (Diagram 4-44)

Again, even though a warmup, the coach should stress the importance to player A of keeping about an arm's length distance between himself and player B.

In the final stage of the warmup the two players will work on block and poke tackling. Each player will stand about a foot from the ball. On the coach's command, both players will plant their left foot and follow through with their right foot to execute a block tackle. A second exercise is to reverse the feet.

Next, the players will be on angle to the ball. On command they will use the toe of the front foot to knock the ball past the other player.

FUNDAMENTAL STAGE

Organization: Four cone goals, set on each side of a 20 x 20 yard grid. Four lines. (Diagram 4-45a).

In stage one of the fundamental stage, player A1 passes to B1 and closes down from the front. B1 now attempts to beat A1 with the dribble and go to goal. When either a tackle is executed or a goal is scored, player C1 plays to D1. At the conclusion of the drill players A and B switch as do players in lines C and D.

A key coaching point should be the importance of the defender closing down quickly but slowing the approach as she or he nears the attacker. The defender should begin with long strides to cover long distance, but as he or she nears the opponent, small steps should be employed to slow down and to be ready to defend. The defender wants to transform the attacker into a ball watcher. When an attacker's head is looking down at the ball, he cannot see teammates who may be open or who have potentially better scoring opportunities. When slowed and in a position to pressure the attacker, the defender should adopt a sideways stance. This is done for several reasons.

First, for proper block tackling one foot must be planted for the follow-through foot to make contact on the middle of the ball. With one foot in front of the other, the plant foot is set. The motion needed includes starting with a low center of gravity and following through with the other foot. If the feet are set side by side, it would take two motions, first planting the foot and then following through, to execute the block tackle.

Second, the player is in proper position to execute a poke tackle. The defender can use the toe of the front foot to knock the ball from the attacker. If the defender attempts the poke, he/she must be able to recover if the poke is unsuccessful.

Third, if the defender is beaten, he/she needs only to turn 90 degrees rather than 180 degrees to make a recovery run.

Finally, the defender can channel the attacker to a second defender or towards the sidelines, which in es-

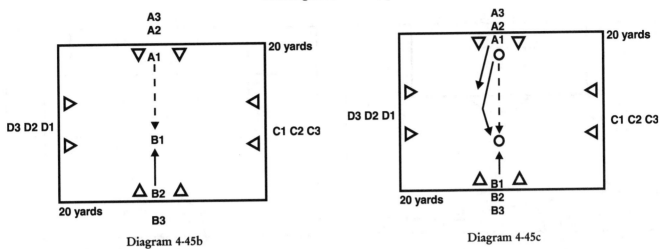

Diagram 4-45b   Diagram 4-45c

sence is a defender in itself. This makes the attacker predictable in regard to the direction he/she is moving.

The main object is delaying. In a game situation, if the defender on the ball is able to delay the attack, it allows teammates to apply pressure to the attacker from the rear and also allows teammates to organize a collective defensive effort behind the defender on the ball.

Another important coaching point at this stage is the decision when to tackle. The player should be within one step of reaching the ball, and should tackle the instant the attacker last touches the ball. Even with good tackling technique, a poor decision on when to tackle can lead to a team breakdown.

The second stage involves A1 playing the ball to B1. B2 follows B1 and must prevent B1 from turning and scoring (Diagram 4-45b). After play is finished with either a goal by B1 or a tackle by B2, A1 moves to the B line, B1 moves to the A line and B2 becomes B1 and will play the ball to A2 who will come to meet the ball and be challenged by A3. The C and D lines follow the same progression.

An important coaching point here is the necessity of the defender keeping the attacker's back to the goal and his/her head looking down at the ball. When an attacker's back is to the goal, his/her view and options are limited to the back view. When his/her head is down, he/she cannot utilize other forward, more penetrating and dangerous options.

A defender should prevent the attacker from turning, and wait for the attacker to make the mistake. The defender should keep an arm's length so if the attacker turns, the defender is in a position to block tackle. By being too close, the defender runs the risk of fouling or overcommitting and allowing the attacker to move into open space with the dribble or to flick the ball behind and penetrate.

Stage three calls for a 1 v. 2 situation. The tactics of individual defending now are combined with the con-

cept of cover and balance. A1 passes the ball to B1 and A1 and A2 go to defend (Diagram 4-45c). A1 is the first defender, but A2 should be in a support position with proper angle and distance. The angle should be 45 degrees on the side A1 is channeling the attacker. This position is taken so that A2 can be in position to tackle or close down if A1 is beaten. By being too close, A2 could be beaten at the same time as A1. If too far, A2 might not be able to make up the ground necessary to tackle or close down the dribbler.

The fourth and final stage calls for a 2 v. 2 situation. Again, balance and cover are emphasized. In this case, A2 is still in a support position, but he/she also must be concerned with a second attacker, B2. If B1 does play the ball to B2, A2 must close down to become the first defender, while A1 adjusts and gets into a support position with proper angle and distance while still focusing on B1, who is now without the ball. After the A-B teams conclude their exercise, the C-D groups play. This gives each group a chance to reorganize and creates a good playing rhythm.

FOCUS STAGE

Organization: Full field split into two halves. Four sets of five-yard goals (here use the flat, platter-like goals). Eight players in each half of the field, each with one ball. (Diagram 4-46)

In this functional training game, each player has the primary responsibility of defending his/her own goal and player, but also should be concerned with providing cover for teammates.

Important coaching points in this stage again include the necessity of applying pressure on the ball and the importance of being in a position both in angle and in distance to assist a fellow defender if he/she is beaten by the attacker. The defender on the ball should apply pressure so the attacker is a ball watcher, and the other defenders should still be conscious of his/her player and goal, but also assisting in providing cover.

An easy way to emphasize the concept is referring to it as "squeezing centrally behind the ball." If the

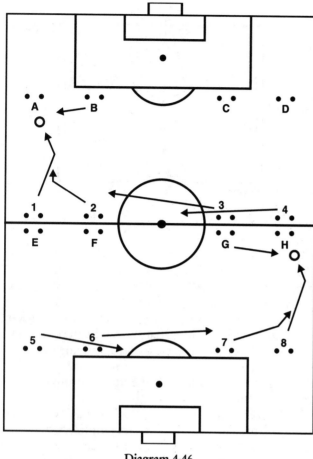

Diagram 4-46

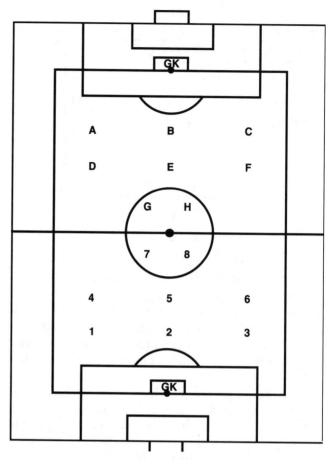

Diagram 4-47

attacker is beaten, he/she should always have a backup, a covering player in position to step up. If the ball is on the opposite side of the field, a defender can afford to move centrally behind his/her teammates. If the ball is played long across, the defender has time to adjust and step up to apply pressure on the ball while teammates make adjustments to squeeze centrally behind him/her.

In Diagram 4-46 we see how, when play begins with player A, these types of collective defending strategies are invoked.

TECHNICAL/TACTICAL TRAINING SESSION

Organization: Move goals to penalty spot to have field 96 x 60 yards.

Eight field players a side in a 3-3-2 alignment plus a goalkeeper. (Diagram 4-47)

The technical and tactical skills presented in the earlier stages of the workout are now incorporated into match-like conditions.

The object of the game is for a team to chip the ball to the opposing goalkeeper. A point is awarded if this is executed. The defensive team must apply pressure on the ball at all times to prevent an attacker from having the time to lift the ball towards goal or change field. All principles of tackling, closing down and cover and balance are incorporated in the exercise.

This stage offers an opportunity for a coach to address players' tendencies to slide tackle. A slide tackle should be a last resort. With a slide tackle, the player is committing their whole body. A slide tackle should only be used if the defender knows he/she has the needed cover or the play is near a sideline or endline. If neither is the case and the attacker beats the tackle, he/she can attack without pressure. A slide tackle, though effective, should not be used in every tackling situation. It must be used with discretion.

MATCH CONDITIONS

Goals are moved back to the endline and a full scrimmage is conducted with no restrictions. Defensive principles are still emphasized in the scrimmage. Play should be stopped if a teachable moment occurs. Since the theme of the session is defense, if an individual defensive lapse occurs, the coach should address it, and not write it off as a good play on the part of the tackler.

CONCLUSION

Individuals make up the collective defensive effort. An individual breakdown can and in most cases will lead to a collective team breakdown. Some coaches may have the tendency to focus on offensive concepts and neglect the defense. This will catch up with the team in the long run.

Ample practice time should be spent on proper technical skills and tactical decisions as regards tackling. Good, hard and clean block tackles are key to strong collective defending. Proper technique along with good judgement in regard to when to tackle will make a team a strong defensive unit. The time spent on tackling will be worthwhile, for in the end it will be the team that benefits.

Roy Wegerle executes a defensive header in US Cup '95 action at Foxboro as Nigeria's Iroha closes in. U.S. won 3-2 on the way to the US Cup '95 title. (photo by Tony Quinn)

HEADING

Ron Ost, Tim Schum, Karen Stanley and Jeff Vennell -NSCAA Academy Staff Members

As with all technique that is taught at the NSCAA Academy level, a session on heading will begin at the fundamental level, proceed to the game-related stage and finish with a match (5 v. 5 with keepers).

WARMUP

1. Each player with ball emphasis on striking the ball at the hairline. Players self head ball back to hands as jog across field and back. Stop at each line (sideline to sideline) and stretch.

2. Pairs with one ball. Moving across width of field, player running backwards tosses ball to oncoming player who alternates heading to tosser's feet, then his/her hands.

3. Pairs with one ball. Tosser on end of grid (15-20 yards long), header attacks ball for either defensive or attacking headers as moves forwards or backwards to play ball.

4. Players with ball each, head juggling to self; add movement to a line and back while working in pairs. Make relay race, have to return to starting point if lose control of ball.

5. Pairs juggling. Have hit ball twice and pass to teammate; 3x, 4x, 5x and work numbers back to one-touch.

FUNDAMENTAL STAGE

1. Pairs. Hold ball head height and head it out of hands (don't toss it). Forces player to hit through the ball.

2. Pairs, lying on stomach. Use upper back and neck to head for power. Chin starts tucked down and then as ball is headed, extends forward.

3. Pairs, sitting position with hands and feet on the ground and hips lifted off ground. As tosser throws ball, header pushes his/her hips forward, and as they head the ball, drive hips back for power.

4. Sitting position in 2s. Emphasis on arching back, "chin in, chin forward" head posture as meet ball tossed by teammate (no backspin on the ball indicates proper "striking" technique with the head).

• Watch that header doesn't drop chin and hit ball with top of head;

• Strikes ball at full thrust; meets the ball "out front" of body or in front of vertical axis of the body;

• Strike ball on its top half (offensive heading) and head "down."

5. Kneeling position with hyperextended hips in 2s. Emphasis on striking "through the ball" with head and upper body to impart power to ball. Also have follow through such that header lands on his/her hands when finished.

• Double groups and have two kneeling players self toss and try to play ball under hands of a second

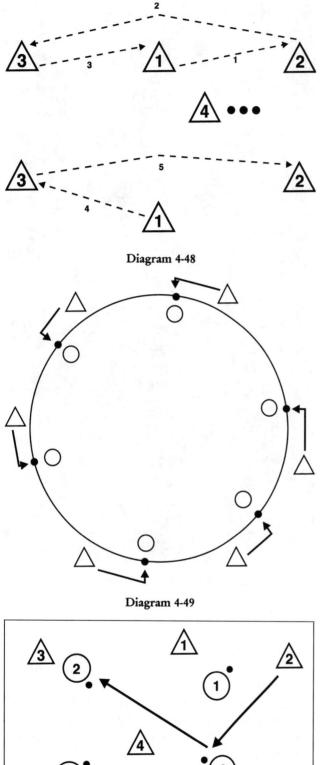

Diagram 4-48

Diagram 4-49

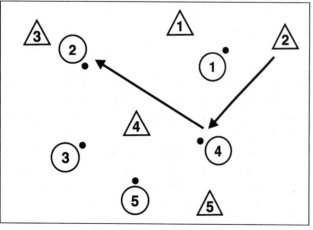

Diagram 4-50

player five yards distance away. Others have extra balls and retrieve. One minute games.

6. Standing position in 2s. Emphasis on hips and legs (staggered positioning of legs) in striking the ball. Watch total coordinated effort of body in heading. Introduce defensive heading with emphasis on striking bottom half of the ball for height.

• Short, short, long game. In 4s (extra player with balls), start with player in middle (X1) self-tossing to self and short ball out second player (X2) who then heads long ball to X3. X3 plays ball in to a pivoted X1 who plays short ball back to X3 who serves long ball to X2, etc. Watch where surface of the ball is struck. (Diagram 4-48)

7. Groups of 3 with a player in middle, player redirects hand served balls to one of the open players. Emphasis on varied serves such that heading player adjusts body position to head the ball "in front" of them and, as much as possible, faces with his/her upper body toward the intended target player.

8. Jumping for headers

A. 12 players, six form circle and hold ball with two hands at head height for six players to run at and jump and head in clockwise, counterclockwise fashion. Rotate players' roles.

• Watch for takeoff on foot closest to the ball;

• As approach the ball from side must try to turn such that upper body is square to ball;

• Watch that arch and head thrust is per earlier instruction. (Diagram 4-49)

B. 3s, tosser, stationary player, header (fourth player with extra balls)

• Header performs headers over stationary player with two-footed takeoff from standing start;

• Header performs headers over stationary player with short run up and one-footed takeoff;

• Have stationary player continuous jumping to distract header;

• Have headers try to strike balls offensively and defensively;

Have headers try to strike balls to the server who moves to one side after tossing the ball to the header.

One ball per two players. Player performs three headers (offensive, defensive, choice) with a player with a ball; players then move to another player with a ball. Alternate players with and without the balls. Next round — slide left, jump and head; slide right, jump and head; dive and head.

• Can time (one minute?) and tally greatest number by each team;

• Can require a certain number of headers by each individual and lapsed time for team; (see Diagram 4-50 with Δ2 moving to take a ball from an O4, then moving to another player O2)

10. Moving triangle. Δ2 tosses ball to moving Δ1 who heads to feet of Δ3. (Diagram 4-51) Change and have head to hands of either the server or third

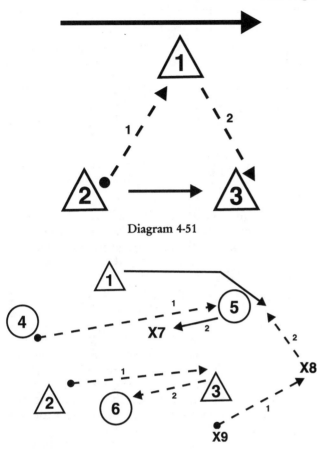

Diagram 4-51

Diagram 4-52

Diagram 4-53a

Diagram 4-53b

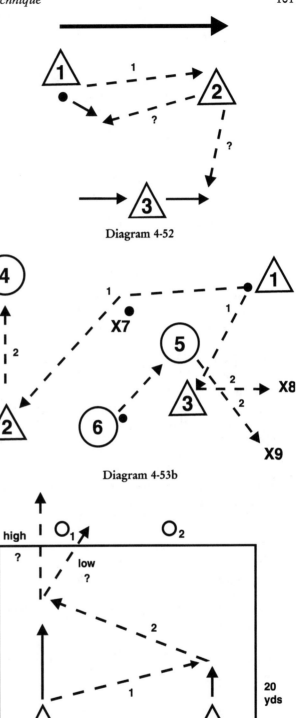

Diagram 4-54

player. (Diagram 4-52) Change and have punt ball out of hands to players rather than toss ball.

11. Three groups of three triangles, each with a ball in a large area. Balls must always be tossed to a teammate but upon toss header may play ball to an open target of any triangular group. Repeat as triangles move freely about. Try with punts from hand; try with balls played from ground. (Diagrams 4-53a & 4-53b)

12. 2 v. 2 in 10 x 20 yard grid. Two players must stand on their endline acting as goalkeepers to defend their goal (the 10 yard line). The other two players head the ball back and try to score by heading it over the endline. The ball starts with a toss, but then must be headed back and forth only. If the ball drops, the two who were heading retreat to defend their goal line. The other two players pick up the ball where it dropped and attack by heading back and forth. If the keepers catch the ball they start the tossing, heading action, etc. Score by heading the ball over keepers (defensive heading) or by playing ball below head height (attacking heading). (Diagram 4-54)

MATCH-RELATED ACTIVITY

1. Defensive Heading

A. 4s, three servers with balls play to defender who, depending on angle of service, etc., heads balls with

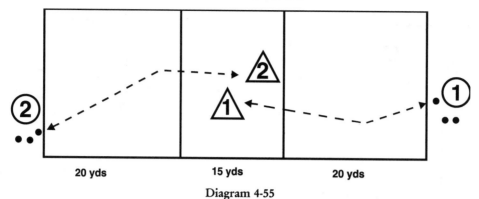

20 yds   **15 yds**   **20 yds**

Diagram 4-55

following principles in mind:
- Leave late to attack ball;
- Use one-footed takeoff from run;
- Must jump first;
- Head through bottom of ball;
- Clear ball high, wide and long.

To conclude put a defender on header (1 v. 1).

B. 4s, servers and headers. 02 plays over Δ1 to Δ2 who heads back to O2; O1 plays to Δ2 over Δ1 who heads back to O1. Repeat. (Diagram 4-55)

2. Offensive Heading

A. 2 v. 2, 15 X 20 yard grid. When on attack create 2 v. 1 as nearest player to goal (O1) drops back over endline. Server tosses to open attacker Δ2 for header downward to endline. (Diagram 4-56)

B. 2 v. 2 + 1 on both sides of a two-sided goal with ball volleyed or chipped with feet to other side of goal. Can designate offensive or defensive team or rule that team controlling the ball adds free player to create a 3 v. 2. No keeper at first, add keeper later. (Diagram 4-57)

3. Offensive & Defensive Heading

A. Large circle (e.g., six on the outside with balls with 1 v. 1 in the middle). Begin with reduced pressure, designating the header and whether want to head offensively or defensively from tosses.

- Progress to full pressure;
- Progress to 1 v. 1 with winner heading ball back to tosser;
- 1 v. 1 with toss from another player.

B. Play corner kicks to 2 v. 2 in penalty area. Keeper cannot go outside his/her goal area. Designate offensive and defensive teams or team winning the ball is the offensive team. Play for clearance or header on goal. Alternate the side of the services. (Diagram 4-58)

C. 2 v. 1 with runs to far and near post and services from both sides of field (and at various angles) to open attacker. (Diagram 4-59) Make 2 v. 2 to goal with services.

4. Play restricted games

A. 5 v. 5 in 50 x 60 yard area, with goals, keepers.

Teams can only advance the ball by a throw-head-catch regime. No more than two steps after catching the ball. Only headers can score goals. Defenders challenge on all headers and can intercept balls headed by the other team to a teammate.

B. 2 v. 2 in 44 (wide) x 50 yard area. Three teams of four players, play two-three minutes matches. Two large goals plus two two-sided or staked goals placed at the midpoint of the touchlines. Four players alternate serving in sequential order from either endline. Point for either header on goal or shot resulting from heading pass to shooter who scores with feet. Two points for goal scored directly from header or defensive header that goes through one of the two wide midfield goals. Attacking team has two touches after reception of service. Keepers provided by one of the teams with two others chasing down balls over endline. Teams alternate playing, defending goals and providing servers. Keep points for a team's total ability to shoot on goal, score on goal with header, play to targets with headers or clear balls with head into side goals. (Diagram 4-60)

C. Channel Game — 4 v. 4 + keepers on 44 x 50 yard field; balls in each goal. Servers in channels are neutral players playing with team that plays ball to them. Servers are unopposed and seek to serve accurate balls for headers on goal. Defenders seek to play ball wide with headers. (Diagram 4-61) Take servers out and if an attacking player with the ball can escape to the channel they have free run to cross the ball.

D. 4 goals, 2 on each endline, 5 v. 5 plus keepers, 60 x 60 yard area. Attackers seek to put players to each goal, keeper defends both goals. (Diagram 4-62)

5. Play unrestricted games — 8 v. 8 on 75 x 84 yard field. Award points for every successful offensive header or defensive header. Double points for headed goals.

CONCLUSION

Obviously, coaches must tailor these exercises to the ability level of the players they are dealing with. Restrictions must be imposed in come cases to allow for success in dealing with headers from either the attacking or defensive side of the ball.

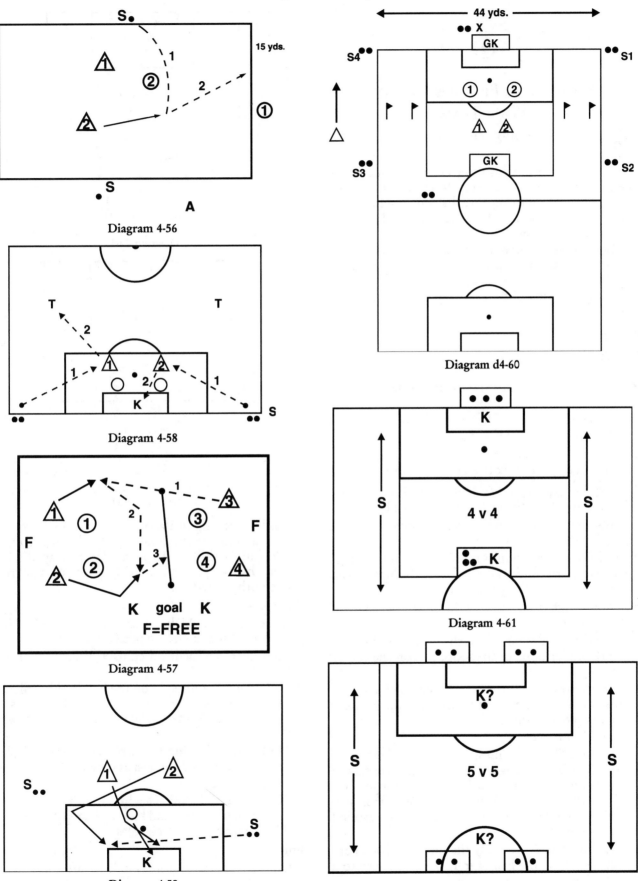

Diagram 4-56

Diagram d4-60

Diagram 4-58

Diagram 4-57

Diagram 4-61

Diagram 4-59

Diagram 4-62

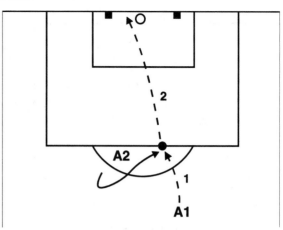

A Shooting Progression for Your Team
George Herrick

Soccer is a fast-moving game and good shooting is one of its most exciting aspects. What will follow is a progression of drills to improve that aspect of the game. This article will deal with the fundamental drills in the coaching progression.

Each coach will have to determine the amount of time spent on the drills with the capability of his players a big factor. The coach will also have to vary the drills over a period of time to keep maximum player interest.

Fundamental Level

Instep Drive

A. Emphases

- The part of the foot used must make clean contact with the ball;
- The kicking foot must be pointed downward, toes pulled to sole of the shoe (hard);
- The supporting foot should be approximately parallel to the ball and six to eight inches away;
- The kicking leg has a low windup from the knee;
- Use a low follow-through with the knee bent;
- Keep the head steady, which is more important than keeping the eye on the ball;
- The knee of the kicking foot is pointed at the target when the foot contacts the ball, thus the hips should also be facing the target upon contact;
- Kick through the equator of the ball so the ball will stay low;
- Hit the ball on the inside of the eyelets of the shoe (on the killer bone of the foot), not on the toe or laces.

A final note is to introduce players to all of these points gradually, and at first to disregard the pressure of an opponent or time.

B. Individual Practice

1. **Juggling.** The player must make good contact with the ball. He must juggle the ball, making contact so there is no spin on the ball, trying to hit the ball straight up on each juggle. For those having juggling problems, allow the ball to hit the ground between juggles.
2. **Striking Ball.** Now apply the means of good contact by hitting the ball over 10 yards distance to a second player.

Diagram 4-63

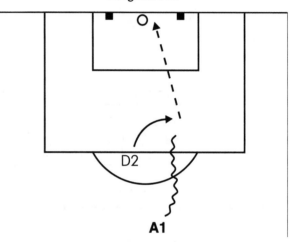

Diagram 4-64

3. **Volley Kicking in Pairs.** A1 volleys a selfdropped ball, aiming for the chest of A2, with A2 catching the ball. If skilled, A2 might try to trap the ball with his body. Players are 10 yards distant from each other. Switch roles.

Emphases

- Concentration! Make good contact with the ball with accuracy the first objective;
- Both knees are bent on contact, keep eyes on the ball;
- There can be some spin on the ball in this drill and more advanced players may want to learn to spin the ball using the instep and outside of the foot with the volleyed ball.

4. **Half-volley Kicking In Pairs.** Same drill as #3, but strike the dropped ball just as it makes contact with the ground.
5. **Kicking Dead Ball.** Dead ball with A1 taking a short run to the ball and kicking instep drive to A2, 15 yards distant. Switch roles.

Emphases

- Don't swing the foot in a circle before contact;
- The foot and leg go back in a straight line;

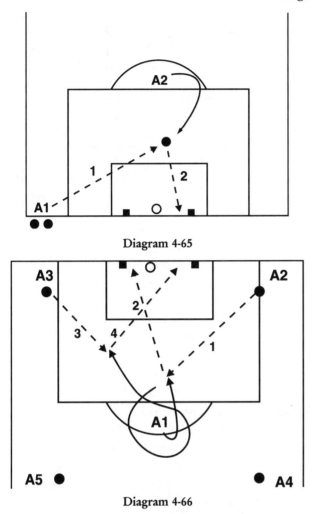

Diagram 4-65

Diagram 4-66

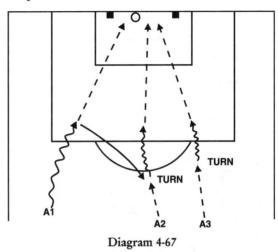

Diagram 4-67

• The swing and kick are straight through the equator or slightly below it with the followthrough straight and low.

6. **Goal-Shooting.** Now add running and apply the concepts as shooting takes place on the goal.

• Volley-shooting. A1 slowly runs and volleys a dropped ball at the goal, starting 25 yards from the goal and striking the ball 18 yards from goal. Gradually increase the running speed;

• Half-volley shooting. Same above but with half volley attempt;

• Shooting rolling ball. With ball at foot, 25 yards from goal, A1 pushes the ball ahead of himself, runs and makes contact with the ball at 18 yard line, emphasizing a low followthrough;

• Shooting in twos. A1 tosses the ball over A2's head. A2 is facing A1 and standing in the bubble of the penalty area. A2 must turn and sprint to the ball and shoot the first-time on goal from 18 yards. (Diagram 4-63) An option is for A1 to push a ground pass through the legs of A2 with A2 sprinting on for a first-time shot on goal;

• Shooting under pressure in twos A1 has the ball at

his feet facing the goal 25 yards away. D is sitting with his back to the goal in the bubble in front of A1. On a signal, A1 dribbles the ball with D1 jumping up to pressure the ball, attempting a tackle. For additional fitness have A1 repeat this three times and then switch roles with D1; (Diagram 4-64)

Another variation is to have D1 change his position by standing in the bubble with his back to A1;

A third variation is to have D1 standing next to A1 25 yards from goal. A third player pushes ground passes or lobs balls over head of A1 who selects right shooting technique while under pressure from D1;

A final variation would be for a third player to play balls over the heads of two players who contest for the ball (starting 25 yards from goal) in order to get off shot;

• Angled goal-shooting A1 serves balls from the goal line for A2 to run to and shoot with instep, using inside of or outside of the foot. Emphasis is on short strides with little windup and a low follow-through. (Diagram 4-65) Repeat three times and switch players. Also switch sides of the field;

• Angled goal shooting under pressure of time. Four players are serving balls at angles to A1 with A1 sprinting to ball served by A2 and shooting first-time and then alternately shooting balls served by A3, A4 and A5. All balls should be aimed by servers to the 18 yard line. Switch roles; (Diagram 4-66)

Variations of the above drill are for the servers to play air balls and bouncing balls and a final variation would be to have servers interchange air, bouncing and ground balls at their discretion;

• Turning and shooting under time pressure A final fundamental drill is to practice receiving and turning the ball for a shot at goal; (Diagram 4-67)

A1 dribbles and shoots the ball on goal and then sprints back to A2 to receive a ground ball. With back to goal, he turns ball quickly, dribbles and shoots ball, then repeats process with A3. Switch roles;

A variation would be to serve balls to receiver at

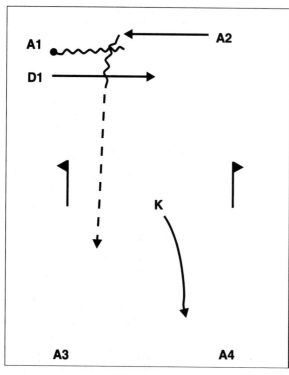

Diagram 4-68

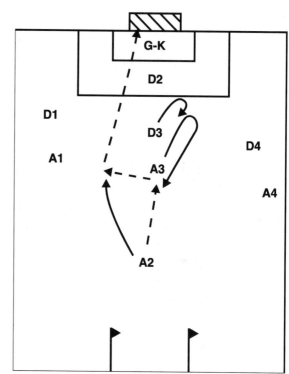

Diagram 4-69

varying heights and speeds.

MATCH-RELATED LEVEL

A. 2 v. 1 to a Central Goal: using stakes to make a fullsized open goal if two-sided goal not available

1. A1 and A2 create shooting opportunities v. defender by: (a) dribbling and beating the defender, (b) takeovers and fake takeovers, (c) 1-2 pass (wall pass), (d) takeover and spin turn (Diagram 4-63), (e) overlap run, (f) through pass. (Diagram 4-68)

   Shot should be taken from 12-18 yards out.

2. The shooter becomes the GK, the GK becomes the defender on the other side as the two new attackers play 2 v. 1 at the other side of the goal. The original defender (D1) and attacker (A1) remain and will become attackers when the ball returns to their side of the goal. Variations: add a second defender on the ball side. The procedure is the same except the other attacker goes to the other side, after the shot, as a defender when the ball goes over to the other side of the goal.

Coaching points

- Clean contact on the ball;
- Head steady;
- Hips over the ball;
- With an ankle locked, strike through the center of the ball using the "killer bone";
- Low follow-through;
- Concentrate only on the shot and beat the GK. Eliminate all distractions from your mind.

Advantages of the central goal

- Several goals can be set up on the field;
- Several players are shooting simultaneously;
- There is no lost time chasing balls that miss the goal.

Appoint a "captain" for each group to count the goals because each group will keep score.

B. 4 v. 4 to Goal: using full-sized goal

- The shooter must have the attitude to shoot;
- The shooter must recognize every shooting opportunity and shoot. He/she should not pass off the opportunity to shoot to someone else;
- Add a small goal at the halfway line for the defense to counter-attack;
- The coach should use the freeze-action method to make the appropriate coaching points;
- Restrictions can be placed on the game (one-touch shooting by midfielders, etc). (Diagram 4-69)

C. 6 v. 6 to an Open Triangle Goal: use stakes for the full-sized goal if necessary (Diagram 4-70)

- The GK serves the ball to the furthest player on the defensive team and the immediate transition is made from defense to attack and visa versa;
- Use the full length and width of the field;
- Emphasize mobility in attack by changing the direction of the ball;
- Build up the attack on one side of the goal and pass to a teammate "far away" for a shot on the opposite side of the goal;
- The goalkeeper can run through the goal to defend the other sides of the goal;

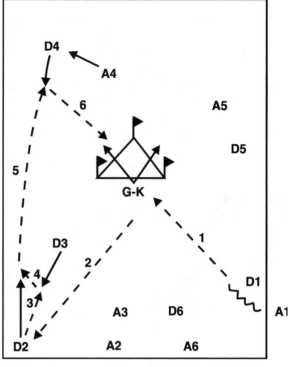

Diagram 4-70

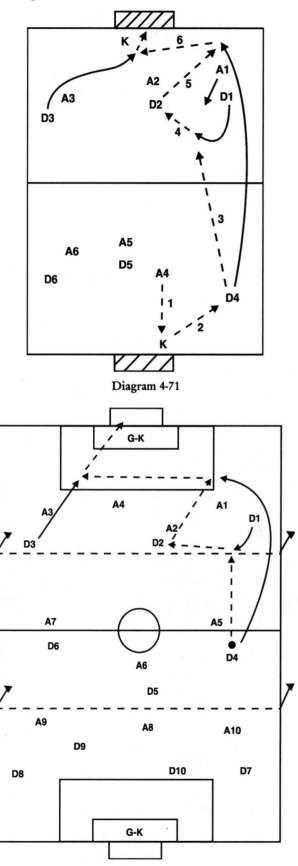

Diagram 4-71

• Progress to free play.

MATCH CONDITIONS

A. 3 v. 3 + 1 to Goal: full-sized goal. (Diagram 4-71)
• The field is half the regular field with full-sized goals;
• The objective is to develop the players' abilities to recognize chances to shoot;
• The field is divided into two zones: (a) the defenders cannot go into the other zone. (b) The player that passes the ball to a teammate in the other zone may cross over into that zone and support the attack. The defender may not follow. (c) If the goalkeeper distributes the ball over the half way line to an attacker, the closest attacking player can follow to support in the other zone;
• If the other team gets the ball or the keeper quickly distributes the ball, D5 and D6, must deal with a 3 v. 2 situation until D4 gets back on defense.

Progression: remove the zones and restrictions on the defenders and play 6 v. 6 to two goals.

Finish with free play.

B. 11 v. 11 in Three Zones to Goal
• The field is divided into three zones;
• The defenders cannot go into another zone;
• The player who passes the ball into another zone may enter that zone and support the attack. The defender may not follow; (Diagram 4-72)
• If the goalkeeper distributes the ball into another zone, the closest attacker will follow the ball into the zone and support the attack; (Diagram 4-72)
• If a pass crosses two zones, then the closest attacker

Diagram 4-72

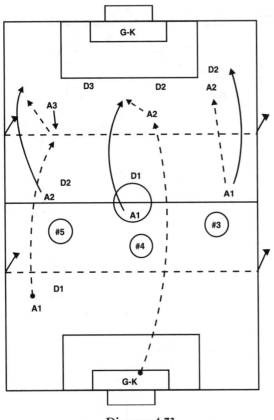

Diagram 4-73

follows the ball into the zone and supports the attack; (Diagram 4-73)

- The attacker (or one teammate) who goes forward into another zone must retreat quickly to his own zone when the ball is lost;
- Play full-field with full-sized goals;
- Stress recognizing the shooting opportunities and taking the shot rather than passing off the responsibility to someone else;
- Progression: remove the zones and restrictions on the defense and finish with free play.

CONCLUSION

Composure in shooting is very important. A shooter must be aware of time and space and the position of opponents, especially the goalkeeper. When shooting, the player must play with his eyes up to assess the situation and keep possession of the ball until a shot can be taken. Shooting is a mental and physical skill and the most important part of attacking play. Players must learn to take every opportunity possible to shoot. If players can achieve one goal in ten attempts, the ten attempts are definitely worth the goal. Use full-sized goals in all shooting practices to make them realistic.

Stress the following: (Charles F. Hughes, in *Tactics and Teamwork*, summarizes it very nicely!)

- Shots along the ground are more difficult for the goalkeeper to handle than shots in the air;

- Accuracy is stressed first and power second;
- Shots low and to the far post are usually more difficult for the goalkeeper to handle;
- All shots must be followed up, thus a goal can be scored easily when a goalkeeper knocks down the initial shot, but fails to hold it. Result: goal!
- The presence of players in the penalty area can distract the goalkeeper and a shot may deflect off a player thus changing the angle of the shot. The shot can result in a goal;
- Most shots in the penalty area will occur from bouncing balls or air balls, so shooting practice should center on them;
- Quickness of thought and action are very important for the shooter;
- The shooter must be able to control the ball with "first-touch positive" under pressure from an opponent and time. Space equals time. So the better the control, the less space is needed to work with the ball and to get the shot off;
- The main point is to "get the shot off."

METHODS OF DEVELOPING SOCCER SKILL

TEACHING THE GAME: EACH COACHING METHOD HAS ITS ADVANTAGES AND DISADVANTAGES
Jeff Tipping

*"Practice doesn't make perfect,
Practice makes permanent"*

Coaches have many means of addressing the teaching of the game of soccer in practice settings. I would like to offer the following methods as means of coping with the teaching of the game with the strengths and weaknesses of each approach listed as part of the discussion.

METHODS OF ON FIELD COACHING

1. Condition play

Dependent upon the desired outcome, coaches can seek to impose conditions on practice play. The following restrictions attempt to arrive at the following outcomes:

Restriction	Emphasis
1-Touch	Quality of support and passing
2-Touch	Quality of first touch and passing
3-Touch	Quality of shielding and dribbling

Condition Play: All attacking players must be over the half field in order for the attacking team to score. (Diagram 4-74)

The teams are playing 6 v. 6 soccer on a reduced pitch (44 X 60 yards) with the condition that the attacking players must all be in one half of the field for the goal to count. This develops compact team play.

Advantages

A. Coach controls aspect of play.

B. Habits ingrained in players to support the ball when on attack.

C. Normally played in game-like situation.

Disadvantages

A. Conditions of game become more important than good soccer (i.e., balancing the field defensively).

B. Takes away players' judgement.

C. How to punish player when condition is broken? Generally practice has to stop and flow of game is disrupted.

2. Drills

The players are practicing a basic wall pass drill which ends with a shot at goal. (Diagram 4-75)

Practice of certain techniques and skills by constant repetition and movement. This normally involves players forming line and it is generally not position specific, (i.e everybody performs same technique). It is normally done without opposition.

Advantages

A. Coach closely supervises large group or even two-three groups.

B. Isolation of special technique or movement.

C. Good for team spirit/morale.

D. Repetition takes place.

Disadvantages

A. Not position specific, i.e., not a lot of opportunities for backs to execute wall passes in central areas of field nor shoot from central positions per Diagram 4-75.

B. Lining up produces inactivity, cold weather could produce muscle strains, etc., if too much inactivity.

C. Lack of opposition makes practice unrealistic.

3. Repetitive Pressure Training

Pressure shooting by a CF. Usually the player receives a continuous supply of services with little time between serves. One player's shooting techniques are put under pressure by four feeders who give him continuous service in rotational order. (Diagram 4-76)

Advantages

A. Good for technical, functional training.

B. Initially enjoyable.

C. Good for fitness.

D. Good for imprinting habits.

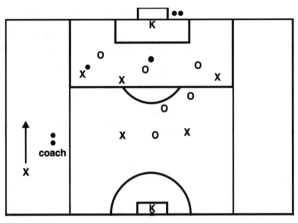

Diagram 4-74

Diagram 4-75

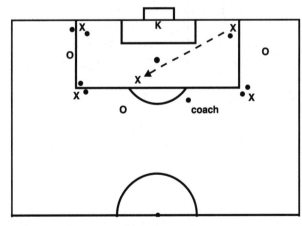

Diagram 4-76

Disadvantages

A. No opposition generally.

B. Servers are normally static.

C. Limited tactical choices.

D. Fatigue leads to sloppy technique.

E. Working player dependant on quality of services.

4. Shadow Play

Done in groups or over the whole field. Normally against imaginary opposition.

- Used to imprint a style of play (direct or indirect);
- Method used the day before a game to rehearse patterns of play, with guaranteed success (the confidence factor) and eliminating the danger of injury;
- Good for choreographing functional movements (e.g, fullback plays ball to winger and overlaps, winger dribble inside and reverses to the fullback who then crosses the ball to the center forward. CF heads to goal);
- Establishes a passing rhythm.

Advantages

A. Good warmup.

B. Good refresher in pattern play.

C. Players achieve success easily.

D. A good 'hurry up' technique when time is limited.

Disadvantages

A. Sometimes little transfer to competitive match.

B. Players get complacent.

C. Can create bad habits.

5. Functional Play

Play is 2 v. 2 down a narrow central channel. The coach can instruct either the functional play of center forwards or the functional play of center backs. (Diagram 4-77)

Coaching is done with small groups of players in specific area of field, e.g. two center forwards vs. two center backs at top of penalty box.

Advantages

A. Players get individual attention from coach.

B. Challenging and enjoyable as it is related to the technical and tactical demands of positions.

C. Can easily be incorporated into bigger game.

D. Coach works on very specific, functional weakness or strengths of players.

Disadvantages

A. Excludes large numbers of players.

B. Exercises are isolated from live game situation.

C. Physically burdensome if done to excess.

6. Phase Play

The prior functional practice has been enlarged to one third of the field where the attacking team plays v. the defensive unit. The services start with one of the central players receiving the ball. (Diagram 4-78)

A direct progression from functional play frequently used to highlight previously practiced small group functional play in a large game setting. Normally practiced over at least half of the field. Phase play would normally utilize a 'trigger-man' who begins each repetition or movement. This practice can be used to instruct either attacking or defending play.

Advantages

A. Realistic.

B. Easily supervised.

Diagram 4-77

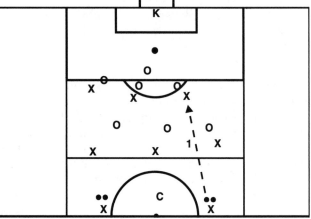

Diagram 4-78

C. Repetitive.

D. Involves large groups of players.

Disadvantages

A. Numerous stoppages to re-start exercise.

B. Defenders sometimes frustrated if they have no goal or reward.

C. Players 'cheat' knowing that 'trigger-man' re-starts with same service.

7. Coaching Grids

Gridwork: Grids are used to give meaningful practice to the squad. e.g. shooting and goalkeeping drills in area 40 x 30 yard (area A); 4 v. 2 possession play in 20 x 20 yard area (area B); and 1 v. 1 dribbling, counter-attack practice in area 10 x 20 yard (area C). (Diagram 4-79)

Squares or rectangles (normally 10 x 10 yards) marked on a training field. Utilize to work on various aspect of play giving coach easy flexibility to expand or combine squares. Used for effective teaching of techniques or basic tactical play.

Advantages

A. Easily organized and coach can easily view a lot of activity at one time.

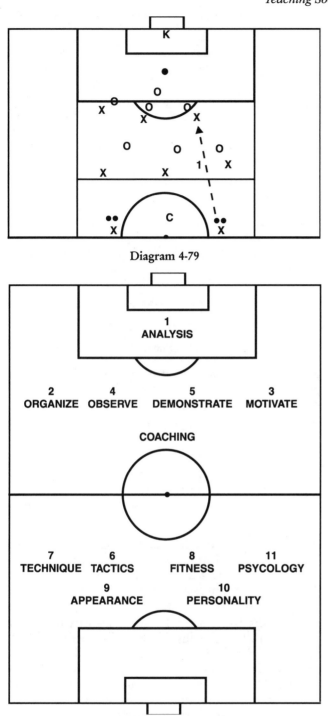

Diagram 4-79

Diagram 4-80

8. Coaching in the 11 v. 11 game

Coaches frequently finish a practice with an 11 v. 11 game. Can be used for testing to see if previous training has been effective or to highlight a particular team concept (e.g. defending as a team).

Coaching in the game: In an 11 v. 11 game the coach sets up an attacking situation from the defensive third of the field.

Advantages

A. Very realistic.

B. Players like it.

C. Facilitates team work and tactical understanding.

Disadvantages

A. Very dependent on coach's ability to break down complex situations in a complex setting.

B. Exposes poor technique, e.g., there are no tactics without technique or under pressure of opponents, technique fails.

C. Too much emphasis on the competitive aspect of the game diminishes learning.

D. Too complex for many coaches and players to analyze.

E. Communication can be difficult for players not near scene of stoppage. (Diagram 4-80)

Developing Passing Skill
5 v. 2
Dave Nicholas

Drill. Five players arrange themselves in a circle, approximately 10 yards in diameter. The size of the circle will vary depending on the players' ages and abilities. Within the circle are two defenders. The five players should play one or two-touch passing while attempting to keep the ball away from the two defenders. The offensive player who makes a mistake (i.e., ball out of area, too much pace on the ball, failing to control the ball) changes places with the defender who has been in the middle the longest. The first pass is always free, thus assuring that the drill gets underway.

This is a drill that can be used in warmup, but initially there must be some instruction. Following are some of the coaching points that need to be covered either in initial instruction or in subsequent practices.

Near Support. The players on either side of the player in ball possession are most important. They must be in a correct position for support by the time the player passed to receives the ball. Do not wait until he receives it! Anticipate! The supporting players

B. Good for specific training (e.g. 1 v. 1 in a 10 x 20 yd area).

C. Can be easily expanded.

Disadvantages

A. Players have difficulty 'transferring' how the practice fits into a full game.

B. Normally non-functional (e.g., wall passes by backs, etc.).

should almost be in a square position to support, while being as close as their skills will allow. (Diagram 4-81) The proximity of the defender is a consideration in terms of distance. Such positioning will result in a good many square passes which are possession passes. Possession is one objective of this game.

Far Support. While the near-supporting players are trying to disrupt the defensive arrangement with quick, short passing, the players on the far side of the circle are looking for the best position "away" from the ball that will allow for a pass to come to them between the two defenders. This drill builds the ability of the players to combine for the penetrating ball. In Diagram 4-81, we see that A1 has opened up for the ball, illustrating this principle.

For this to take place, the two-three players in close support are involved with quick, short passes. Three-five passes will hopefully lead to penetrating pass opportunities More passes will allow the two defenders to concentrate their efforts into a small space and deny the penetrating pass. Also, small spaces tend to limit play by the attackers, with play becoming very predictable. As the longer, penetrating pass is made, the two players closest to the receiver immediately take up their close support once more and try to repeat the same rhythm.

Rhythm. As players become familiar with the drill, we find a rhythm developing. This rhythm can be called short-short-long. The idea is to play a series of short passes, drawing the defenders to you, then switching the play to a far supporting player.

Vision. A lot of players ignore half of the field. This is evident in this exercise. If a player is receiving a ball from the right and his back is turned to the left half of the circle, he has cut his options in half. He must "front" the whole circle, opening up his body position so that he can see all of his possible passing outlets. (Diagram 4-82)

Disguise. In the previous example, the player will probably have to play the ball back to the right, thus being predictable. If he faces the entire circle, he could go left or right. With a quick foot, hip or shoulder movement in one direction (properly timed), he could unbalance the defender and play the ball in either direction.

Technique. Obviously various aspects of passing are going to emerge. The ball must be played to feet with accuracy to be stressed. Balls played behind a supporting player, and subsequently lost, means the player making the pass becomes a defender. Passes should be properly weighted. The strength of the pass is a judgement to be made by the passer. Again, if the ball is hit with too much strength (speed) it is the player of the ball who takes the middle on defense. Finally, players should strive for variety in their passing, using different parts of their feet. This lends itself to dis-

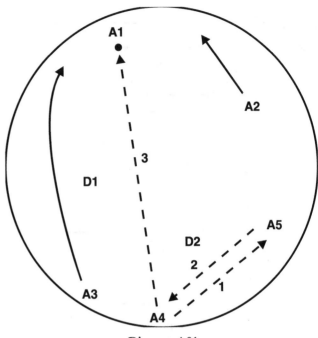

Diagram 4-81

guise and quicker foot movement with resultant greater speed and anticipation in the 5 v. 2 game.

Other coaching considerations

• Use players who play aroundeach other (strikers-midfielders; midfielders-backs; right side, central or left-sided players) together in 5 v. 2;

• Make competitions out of game (most penetrating passes in groups in five minutes);

• Use keepers as middle two defenders (with rest!);

• Limit to one-touch;

• Let the game move its location, with no stoppages for switching of attackers, to middle, with play continuous but with a limit of a 10-yard radius in effect as the group moves about.

Quick Feet (5 v. 2). Because of the limitation of space in this drill, you will begin to identify the better players on your team just through the use of this drill. Almost without fail, the poorer players will find themselves in the middle, defending against the ball. Part of the problem may lie in technique (poor control on reception or poor control in passing). Also it may be as a result of poor decision-making.

But players must build more time for decision-making by improving their "speed"; playing speed in this case. The faster the control can take place, the more time is on hand to decide which passing technique to apply the particular defensive problem to be overcome. So in control, passing (and dribbling), quickness of feet is important.

I have a couple of favorite ways of developing this particular area of concern. The first practice has nothing to do with the 5 v. 2 exercise. However it can serve

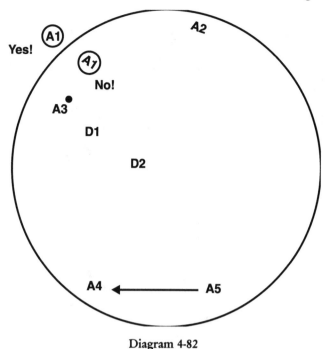

Diagram 4-82

as an indicator of the level and the improvement of quickness, as well as helping indirectly to improve the level of play in the 5 v. 2 exercise.

Start with one foot on the ground, bearing one's weight, and the ball of the other foot touching the top of the soccer ball. With a hopping motion, switch feet. Continue to repeat this movement. Everything must be done on the balls of the feet. Don't let the players get back on their heels. Demand speed with this drill. I have found that high school players should be able to touch the ball 90-120 times in 30 seconds if concentrating. Times can be varied on this drill, with limits of 10-30 seconds. Drilling longer than 30 seconds brings muscle fatigue which spoils the technique. Continually using this technique in practice will stimulate the neurological pathways necessary to improve quickness.

We can also work on quickness by implementing a condition on the exercise. Every player must touch the ball twice every time it comes to them no more, no less. After the player touches the ball once, a split-second will elapse before the second touch is possible. Strive to reduce the time between touches. By adding the mandatory second touch, the player's time and space is reduced. A defender now has a split-second longer to close down the player in possession.

The major fault of the players in this exercise is that they kill or stop the ball on the first touch. They must redirect the ball with the first touch, while maintaining the ball with their own space. However, here it is important to remember that disguise comes into play. He can play the ball back to the right (depending on the defender's position) with the inside of the left foot, the outside of the right foot, or he can backheel it.

Decision-Making. In the last example, which part of the foot is used? Which pass is made? Before a player is able to constantly make correct decisions, he must have certain tools at his disposal. We, as coaches, must give the players the opportunity to practice the types of passes being discussed.

Without acquiring these skills, players will lack the necessary confidence to quickly enact a decision. Also striving to improve quickness of feet allows players more time to analyze the situation and to make the correct choice. (More time sometimes means a fraction of a second; sometimes that is all that is necessary.) We must encourage players to "observe" the field while the ball is in motion. Upon receiving the ball, decision-making is made easier as the brain has already "taken" several pictures and has made a decision as to what is the best pass to make in relation to teammates' positions and the alignment of the defense.

Again, a coach can perhaps spot in the 5 v. 2 game, those players who have trouble with making the right decision. Usually they are in the middle! By reviewing the players' options in the 5 v. 2 game, the coach can begin to appreciate their thought process and help the player to make more correct passing decisions.

Changing Decisions. Sometimes a "mind set" is made by the player, but because of the speed of the game, that decision is no longer in effect as the ball approaches the player. In any case, even if the decision is changed by circumstance, the player must move to the ball. He can then use a second touch or disguise or both to buy time for a new decision to emerge. By demanding that a player move to the ball, the first rule of ball possession is instilled in 5 v. 2.

Reading the Game. After viewing your team playing the game for several practices, you will see that they all perceive the game differently. Unfortunately perception is one area of the game which is innate. It can be improved but not as readily as other aspect of the game. By improving the concentration of players and by working on their anticipation, a coach can perhaps overcome the lack of a player's innate ability to "read the game."

Concentration. This is an area of the game that can be improved by 80%. To improve concentration, we must give players very specific tasks. In the 5 v. 2 exercise, we can diversify the demands of concentration by imposing different conditions, but only one at a time. Examples would be: one-touch passing, two-touch passing, five passes equal one goal, all passes with the outside of the foot, etc. In other words, players are not just playing, but improving their concentration levels.

Anticipation. Anticipation is yet another area that can be drastically improved. Experience is certainly a factor in the development of anticipation, however one can begin to train players to disguise their own movements and look for cues from the opponent's movements.

DEVELOPING DEFENSIVE COORDINATION: 5 V. 2
Dave Nicholas

During the course of an earlier discussion we have noted many aspects of the 5 v. 2 exercise that need to be taught and thereafter practiced, for it is only through repetition (and correction by the coach) that a player will acquire these many, sometimes subtle, skills. We earlier examined anticipation, a skill necessary for a player to read the game more completely. For example, a player in possession may allow himself to be guided in a predictable direction by a defender. However, he may use this move to disguise his next movement which may be based on the anticipation of the defender's ensuing position and/or the movement of a teammate. Again, it is necessary to make the disguise realistic.

In order to create a realistic challenge for the five offensive players, the two defensive players must be taught their individual roles and responsibilities, as well as how to function in tandem.

Pressure. As soon as the first "free" pass is made, it is essential that one of the two defenders put pressure on the player in possession. If no pressure is applied, the player in possession and his immediate support should play a series of short passes until a defender is drawn to them. There should be no "diving in" or overcommitment unless there is a guarantee that the ball shall be won. In fact, in this particular exercise, defenders should utilize all their tactical ploys to win the ball and, if possible, remain on their feet throughout.

In approaching an opponent who has the ball, a defender must be ready to "check" his forward rush and momentum abruptly. Just as his opponent, the defender is trying to leave open various options in order to instill some decision-making in the mind of the attacker, for if he is unsure of the defender's next movement, the game is suddenly more difficult. The defender can fake a tackle, he can follow the pass or he can anticipate and intercept the pass.

Angle-Distance. Two considerations at this point are a) how close do we get to the player in possession,

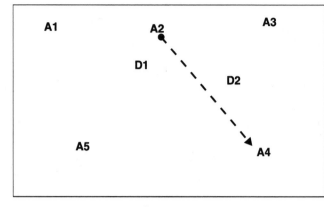

Diagram 4-83

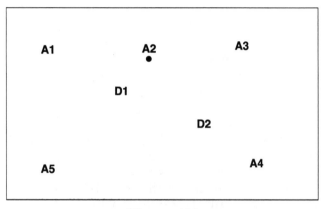

Diagram 4-84

and b) what is our angle of approach? Distance is dependent on defender's and/or attacker's ability. However, the defender should be close enough to tackle in case of poor control by the attacker and close enough to prevent/ intercept a forward pass. (This is usually in the region of 4-6 feet from the attacker.) In approaching the player, the defender must be examining his position by considering several factors: Where is his covering player located? What is the relative strength of the attacking players i.e., which are the weaker players? In which direction does he anticipate the play to move? Which are the attackers' good feet? In general we might state that if the defender approaches the attacker straight on, the at tacker has the option of playing to either his right or left. We must therefore teach the defender to "shepherd" or channel" play in the direction we want the play to go.

Cover. What is the role of the second defender? The one thing the defenders are trying to prevent is the "through ball", i.e., the pass played between the two defenders. The second defender therefore should not mark an opponent, but rather cover space. If he were to mark an opponent he would present a "square/ flat" formation (Diagram 4-83), and while his partner pressures an opponent, he must provide cover. (Diagram 4-84)

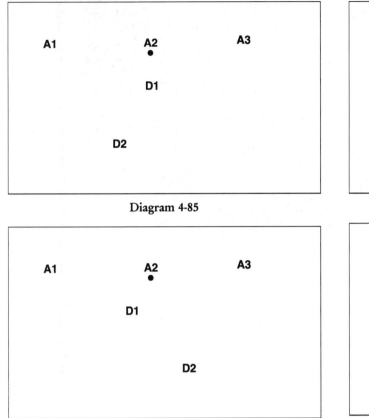

Diagram 4-85

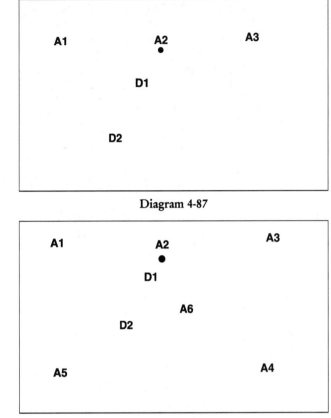

Diagram 4-87

Diagram 4-86

Diagram 4-88

Again, the question arises, how far behind the pressuring defender and at what angle does the second defender play? In terms of distance, the abilities of the players have to be taken into consideration. In a normal game, the second player should be close enough to intercept/tackle the onrushing attacker. In our particular exercise, where there is no attacker dribbling through, we still want to train the covering defender to be aware of this aspect of distance. In general he should be 6-8 feet behind the pressuring defender.

In looking at the covering angle, several aspects are considered, but above all, a "through ball" must not be allowed.

In Diagram 4-85, the pressuring defender has assumed a straight-on approach. The second defender has overplayed slightly to the left, and the ball will probably be played to A3. In Diagram 4-86, the pressuring defender has overplayed to the left, with the covering defender playing slightly to the right. Again, the ball will probably be played to A3. In Diagram 4-87, both defenders have overplayed to the left and the ball will again probably be played to A3. Remember, in stating that the ball will "probably" be played in a certain direction, the game of soccer is a game of "cat and mouse", where the attacker is aware of the defender's ploys and is trying to do other than the expected, and visa-versa.

The difference between Diagrams 4-85 and 4-86 is that in 4-85 the pressuring defender will move with the pass to A3 as he is the nearest defender, while in 4-86 the covering defender is closer so he is the one to apply the pressure to A3 with the other defender now assuming the covering role.

Communication. In this exercise communication is vital, especially in the early stages. Players may eventually play more instinctively once they are more familiar with the tactics of the game and with their teammates. However, for the time being, the covering defender, in general, should be "talking" to the pressuring defender.

Note: If you are working on defensive principles do not play one-touch passing, as the defenders will not have time to pressure and cover and therefore the coach will not have the opportunity to correct.

Anticipation. We also now refer back to anticipation. Let us look at Diagram 4-87 again (it could apply to 4-85 & 4-86 as well). If A2 looks up and sees both players overplaying on the same side, he will probably play to A3. But this could be a deliberate ploy by the covering defender. For once A2's head goes down and his foot initiates the backswing motion, the covering defender is already moving towards A3. This early movement by the covering defender should always take place before A3 receives the ball. The difference in time may be all an attacker needs to shoot or play a forward pass in a game. In this case, the covering defender has deliberately set up this play and is anticipating the next move.

Decision-making. Just as the defenders are trying to outwit attackers, the opposite is also true. With this in mind, defenders must never challenge with only one option in mind. They must have a backup should the attacker do something unpredictable. As was discussed earlier, a short, but very valuable amount of time passes before a second option can be initiated and enacted. However, the process can be speeded up if the backup option has already been initiated and is ready should the primary option be discarded.

In continuing the last notion, the pressuring defender can reach out with one leg to block a lateral pass by the attacker, but he must be ready to recoil and assume a good defensive position, if the attacker is faking a pass and brings the ball back to the other side.

OTHER VERSIONS

6 v. 2 (Diagram 4-88)

The placement of the players is the same as that for the 5 v. 2 exercise, with the addition of an extra attacking player who plays within the circle of five. The outer players still become defenders should they make an error, but the designated middle attacker stays in for a specific period of time, regardless of errors.

8 v. 3

Seven attackers form a circle (approximately 25 yards across) with three defenders inside the circle. The eight attackers play within the circle, as in the previous exercise.

Note: In any of these exercises, the coach can select the size of the playing area. This size will be determined by the age and ability of the players, plus the specific objective of the exercise.

By adding the "inside" attacker, in both 6 v. 2 and 8 v. 3 the exercises become more position-related. The inside player can offer constant close support to the player in possession, i.e., play as a midfielder. On the other hand, the player may position himself away from the ball and, playing as a striker, "show" himself at the approximate support angle, but more distant than in the previous example.

Open Play

Another variation allows a ball that has gone outside the area to be played back into the area with a one-touch pass by the attackers. The defenders can, however, intercept this return pass.

Summary. While 5 v. 2 is fun and a simple warmup, it is an exercise that initially demands that all the principles and subtle tactics involved in the game be taught.

Thereafter, the development of the game and the fun involved is as far-reaching as the players' imagination and creativity.

⚽

THE COACH'S SURVIVAL KIT:
DEFENSIVE PREPARATION
Jeff Tipping

There are three basic principles one applies to defensive problems:
- Pressure;
- Covering;
- Balance.

Good defensive attitudes are essential in the player in order for the person to play sound defense:
- Concentration on the task;
- A willingness to accept hard work;
- Patience under stress;
- Expectation — the ability to understand and anticipate opponents;
- Mental transition speed

LOOSE BALLS

One of the major defensive problems is contesting for loose balls. Success is dependent on the following factors:speed; low center of gravity;cutting and turning; dropping the shoulder in front of opponent. X represents the offensive player; O represents the defensive player. (Diagram 4-89)

Coach (C) midway between players X and O, tosses free ball out in front of them. Players X and O legally contest for ball. (Diagram 4-90)

Add cones (or flags) and have players run around cones as contest for the ball.

PRESSURIZING

How to apply pressure to an opponent from behind:
- Use the time the ball is in flight to close in on opponent;
- Control speed of approach so as not to overcommit;
- Use low center of gravity;
- Position one step off opponent;
- Practice patience;
- Tackle on opponent's turn;
- Tackle conservatively — poke tackle so as to not sell oneself.

Diagram 4-91 teaches points the above points as the coach serves balls for player to control (varying heights and speed of balls); player attempts control and defender uses time ball is on its way to pressurize the opponent.

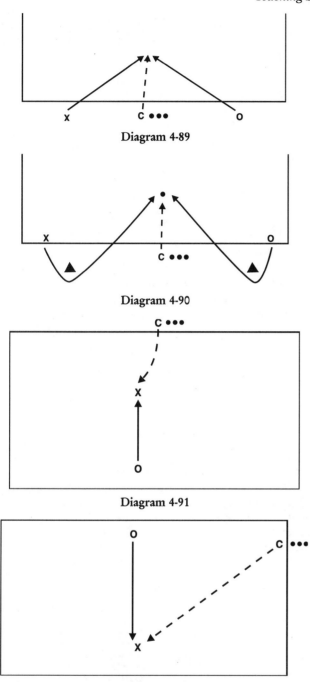

Diagram 4-89

Diagram 4-90

Diagram 4-91

Diagram 4-92

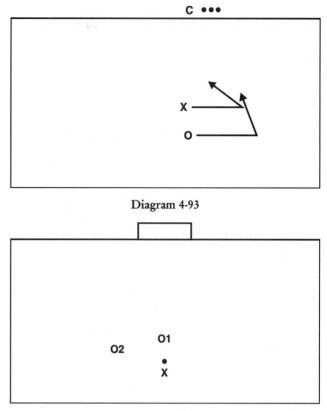

Diagram 4-93

Diagram 4-94

How to apply pressure to an opponent from the front:
- Use time of flight of the ball;
- Controlled approach — use feints;
- Assume a 45-degree body position relative to the opponent;
- Maintain a low center of gravity;
- Eyes on the ball;
- Feint tackle;
- Let attackers make the mistakes. (Diagram 4-92)

The coach again serves balls for player to control as they come at him. Defender applies frontal pres-

sure. (Use touch by the attacker to start defender in motion.)

How to apply pressure from the side:
- Use time of flight;
- Control angle of approach to invite him to go "outside";
- Control speed of approach so as not to overcommit yourself;
- Maintain a low body position, one foot forward.

TRACKING

Tracking the opponent so as not to lose him/her. Questions we need to ask are:
- Is there support for the attacking player?
- How will the attacker use the support?
- Are we being caught ball watching ?

We need to be prepared to: change pace; change direction; block shots and crosses.

Pressure tracking and transition can be taught through grid training. (Diagram 4-93)

One minute exercise. C serves many balls to keep transitional pressure on both X and O as he alternates receiver of his service.

COVER

Supplying cover for your teammate, who is pressurizing the man with the ball, can be taught with the following principles and exercises:
- See all the players and the ball;

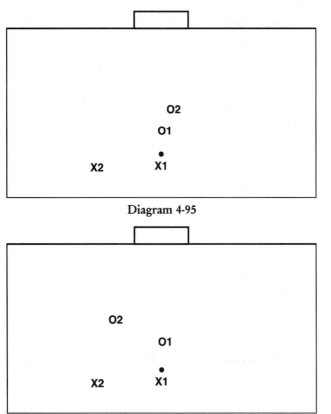

Diagram 4-95

Diagram 4-96a

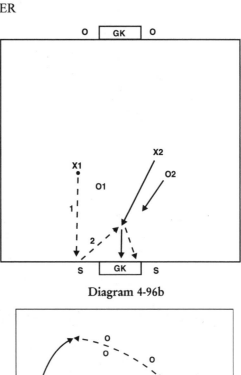

Diagram 4-96b

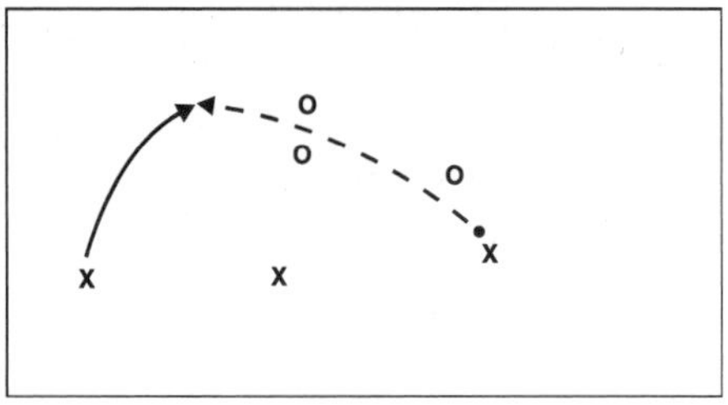

Diagram 4-97

• Support pressuring player so that he has confidence;
• Track a second attacker who shows as support for the first attacker.

Diagram 4-94 Incorrect
Diagram 4-95 Incorrect
Diagram 4-96a Correct!

Diagrams 4-94, 4-95 and 4-96a show wrong and right relationships of the covering player (O2) for his pressurizing player (O1). In Diagram 4-96a, O2 can see both opponents and ball and his cover is close enough so that O1 can pressurize with confidence.

Coach serves ball to X's and O's who must score using three-man combinations with supporting players (S) off the field. Defenders must track, cover and pressurize while outnumbered. (Diagram 4-96b)

BALANCE

Balance is an essential aspect of defense. Being caught over-shifted can leave one very vulnerable to quick goals.
We need to be watchful of the following:
• Always be in control of the space behind pressurizing players;
• Always be available to swing back to the opposite flank to cover;
• Track any third opponent who shows up.

Diagram 4-97 shows an excellent way to teach balance. Teams of three play in a grid and the coach must

look to see that the defenders are ready to remain balanced, dependent upon the position of the ball.

Diagram 4-98 shows three defenders playing in the penalty area. Seven offensive players will try to score on the three (plus keeper) inside the box. Pressure, cover and balance are a must if the defense is to be successful.

⚽

THE METHODICAL BUILD UP
OF DRIBBLING MOVES
Frans Van Balkom

1. At the beginning, all skills are learned with a dead or slow moving ball at a slow pace without any kind of pressure. Each player has one ball.
2. Players practice moves at high pace and work in pairs as in Diagram 4-99: Players perform same move at same time beating each other and then repeating in opposite direction.
3. Two players using one ball. In the beginning, player B is passive (does not try to win the ball). Later, B is allowed to move forward, put pressure on A and attempt to win the ball from A. (Diagram 4-100)
4. Four attackers (X), each with a ball and moving in a

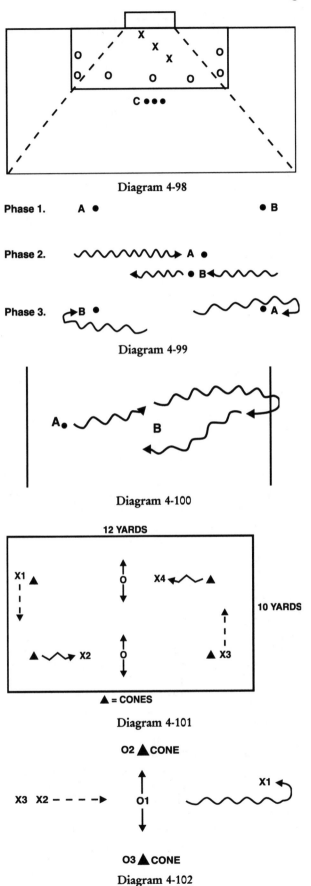

Diagram 4-98

Phase 1.   A ●   ● B

Phase 2.

Phase 3.

Diagram 4-99

Diagram 4-100

12 YARDS

10 YARDS

▲ = CONES

Diagram 4-101

O2 ▲CONE

X3   X2 - - - ➤   O1   X1

O3 ▲CONE

Diagram 4-102

counterclockwise direction, attack two defenders. At first, defenders are passive (standing), later, they may attempt to win the ball. Defenders, in attempting to win the ball, can only move to the left or right (not forward or backward). A defender who wins the ball changes place with the attacker who lost it. (Diagram 4-101)

5. Six players: three attackers (X), three defenders (0). A single defender defends along a line (5 yards) against a single attacker. 02 and 03 wait their turn by a cone at either end of the line. After 01 defends against X1, 02 comes in to defend against X2, etc. If the defender wins the ball, he/she changes places with the attacker.

   When all three attackers have played 1 v. 1 from one direction, they then attack from the opposite direction. (Diagram 4-102)

6. Combine dribbling moves with shielding and finishing work in restricted area 30 x 20 yards. 3 v. 3 and goalie, using goal at one end and a line between cones on other end as targets. Team in attack uses individual actions and combinations to score a goal. When a goal is scored, the attacking team keeps ball possession and attack line between cones. When ball is dribbled over line, attacking team attacks goal again. Defenders must allow attackers two yards to come out once they dribble over line. (Diagram 4-103)

7. 3 v. 3 and a neutral player (X) using two goals in a 30 x 20 yard confined area. Combine dribbling with shielding, feinting, finishing and counterattack. Neutral player plays with team in ball possession. (Diagram 4-104)

8. Same as #7 but neutral player plays with team defending.

9. One server (X) and three attackers play v. four defenders and goalie in confined area of 40 x 30 yards.

   Objectives: Attackers -Server dictates pace and controls attack. Attackers work on actions, ball possession, combination play, and finishing. Stressing individual actions is especially important

   Objectives: Defense — Winning and keeping ball possession, counterattack over line. After 10 minutes, attackers change role with defenders. (Diagram 4-105)

10. 8 v. 8 playing across one half of field using two goals.

    Objectives: Use individual actions in combination with feinting, shielding, finishing, and counterattack. Also, work on slow build-up, switching sides and pressuring. (Diagram 4-106)

    Once players have learned and are able to use skills at high pace, all dribbling must be performed in combination with all other skills in realistic game situations. A good deal of time must be spent during practice playing various types of games with and without goals such as 2 v. 2, 2 v. 3, 3 v. 3, 3 v. 4, 4 v. 5, 5 v. 6, 8 v. 8, and finally, players using dribbling skills in regular 11 v. 11 games.

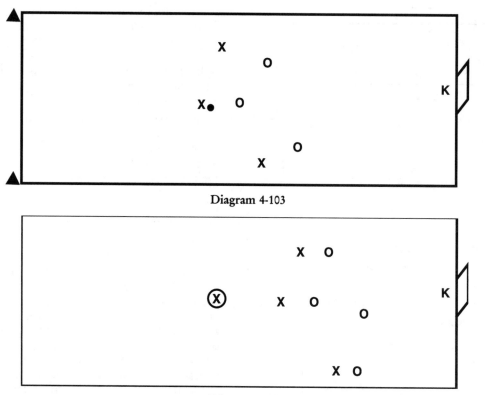

Diagram 4-103

Diagram 4-104

When And How to Practice Shielding
Frans Van Balkom

Once young players are fairly well-coordinated and have good basic skills, specific practice for shielding and playing the ball free should start. Important points when beginning shielding practice are:
• Sufficient space to work (10 players use an area the size of the penalty area);
• Each move is explained and demonstrated by the coach;
• Each player first works on the move individually in his own space and at his own pace;
• Up to six (6) moves are introduced and practiced in this fashion. Additional moves can be added later.
Further build-up is as follows:
• Practice the moves in pairs. Player with the ball is put under light pressure from the player without the ball. The players then alternate practicing the shielding moves;
• All the players, each with a ball, perform shielding moves in a restricted area (20 x 20 yards). They move

about at random and use each other to shield the ball and to play the ball free. The coach indicates which shielding move to use. Later the players can use any of the six shielding moves they have learned.
• Using their imagination, they can also use the lines or the restricted area as an "opponent" and shield the ball from the line;
• Before going into more realistic drills, the moves are practiced at the highest possible pace in various drills as follows:
1. Each player has a ball and they work in pairs. The pairs are spaced about six-seven yards apart and they are stationary. The drill begins with the last pair who sprint forward with the ball on the outside of the line. Each time they reach another pair, they execute a shielding move (shown by the @). In Diagram 4-107, the last pair would execute three moves and then take up a position six-seven yards in front of the lines. Then the next pair repeats the drill. The lines can move up and down the field or around the field. The same principle can be used with a single line in a zig-zag formation. (Diagram 4-107)
2. Each player has a ball in a 20 x 20 yard square. Any player can kick any other player's ball out of the square. Effective shielding of the ball is essential here. Once the player's ball is kicked out he/she retrieves it and reenters the game. To make it more competitive, players may not reenter the game once their ball is kicked out of the grid. The final two players remaining in the grid win the game. (Diagram 4-108)
3. Same drill as above with additional pressure. All

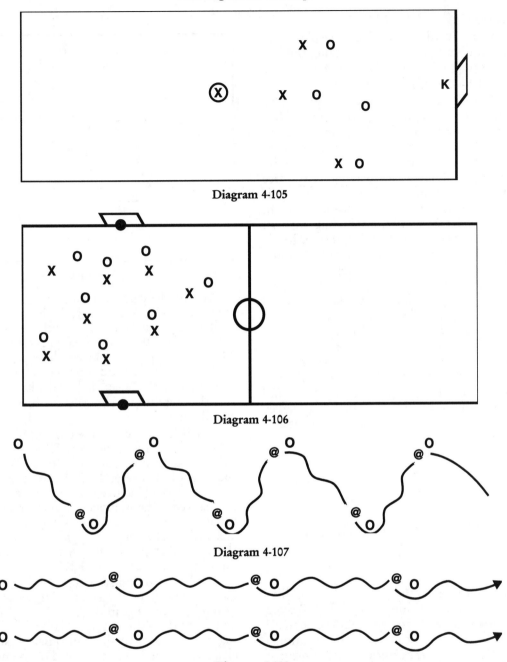

Diagram 4-105

Diagram 4-106

Diagram 4-107

Diagram 4-108

but three players have a ball. The three without a ball have one minute to kick out as many balls as possible. It is important that the defenders be instructed to tackle the ball, not the ankles or knees.

4. Three (3) players are positioned in a 10 x 10 yard square. One of the three (player C) does not have a ball and each of the three stand in a separate corner of the square. Player A dribbles to the empty corner. Defender C moves across to prevent A from getting to the corner. When they meet, A shields the ball from C and goes back to his corner. Then B dribbles his ball to the open/ empty corner and again C moves across to stop B. The role of C should be changed frequently to avoid fatigue.

5. Four (4) players are positioned in a 10 x 10 yard square. Inside the square, two players play 1 v. 1 and the player in possession keeps the ball by shielding. Outside the square, working along the length of the two opposite lines, the other players act as "walls". The player with the ball can pass to either one of the two wall players who must use one-touch only to pass it back. A player inside the square can change places with either wall player at any time, but you must have possession of the ball to change places.

6. 4 v. 3 in a 30 x 30 yard square. Four players in possession work on shielding and playing the ball free to keep it within the team. The three defenders apply full pressure. Watch or time the drill to ensure

that fatigue does not take over.

7. 3 v. 4 in a 30 x 30 yard square. The three players in possession combine shielding and playing the ball free with feinting, 1-2 combinations and takeovers. The four defenders apply full pressure.

8. 4 v. 5 in a 40 x 40 yard square using one goal and a goalkeeper. The keeper starts by throwing the ball to one of the four attackers who combine shielding and playing the ball free with takeovers, coming off the defender, 1-2 combinations, feinting and finishing. Once basic shielding and playing the ball free moves are mastered, more and more pressure is added in the various drills and special sessions. In these sessions, players combine shielding with all kinds of trapping skills (chest, knee, instep, inside and outside of the foot, etc.). Additionally, coming off of the opponent, feinting, takeovers, 1-2 combinations and finishing can be worked on. During all drills, while working to improve shielding technique and skills, playing the ball free, etc., the importance of keeping possession of the ball must be repeatedly stressed. Players who have the ability to shield and/or play the ball free under full pressure in actual game situations are of vital importance to their team. Players are judged on their ability to win the ball and to keep the ball in the team. Any player possessing these abilities will be able to play at any level, anywhere.

⚽

FINISHING: TECHNIQUE AND REPETITION
Sigi Schmid

The beauty of the sport and the game's most difficult art are embodied in finishing. The ability to score goals can make someone a hero overnight as evidenced by former UCLA All-American and current National Team player, Paul Caligiuri's critical goal that secured a spot in the '90 World Cup for the United States. But, as coaches, can we create a goal scorer through training? A true goal scorer is blessed with great instinct. This "nose for the goal" is inbred, not taught. As coaches, we can simplify the task and work on technique. Through this aid, we can improve a player's chances of scoring goals. But remember, we cannot make a diamond from a rock. The training methods herein described can only polish a diamond or, at best, clean up the rock.

CONSISTENT STRIKING OF THE BALL

Warmup

A warmup I use to work on striking is as follows. Players work in pairs with one partner serving the ball to the other from his hands. After ten to fifteen strikes

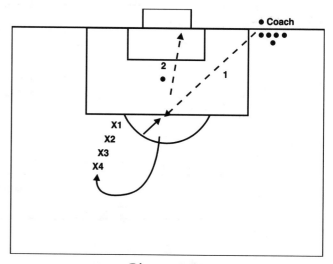

Diagram 4-109

of the ball, the partners change roles. Types of returns are instep volley, side volley, thigh trap and then instep volley (emphasis on trapping with one leg, striking the ball with the other), and finally, chest trap and volley. The coaching points to be emphasized include striking the ball cleanly, forward rotation on the ball, and power coming from the "snap" below the knee.

Another warmup, primarily for forwards, would be as follows.

The ball is served by the coaches with three to four players alternating as shooters. X1 jogs forward and hits the ball cleanly onto goal, and after shooting, X1 goes to the back of the line and X2 shoots. The types of shots practiced would include balls served on the ground and balls served in the air (volleys). This exercise can be done using both feet and from both sides. The coaching points are: striking the ball cleanly, hit the lower one-third of the net, and emphasis on how many clean strikes made out of ten tries. (Diagram 4-109)

Lastly, a reaction-striking warm-up would be: The ball is served by the coach. He varies the service (ground, bouncing, in the air, etc.). X1 faces the goal and, after 10-15 shots, a new player takes over. Coaching points: react to the ball quickly, strike the ball cleanly, hit the lower one-third of the net. Note that exercises are done without goalkeepers. (Diagram 4-110)

REPETITION TRAINING

Remember, training for finishing is practice for the forwards, not your goalkeepers. The exercises are set up to maximize the effectiveness of the forwards.

Use two goalkeepers and three to six shooters and have them switch every few shots. Set up cones 16 yards from the goal and one yard in from the goalpost. (Diagram 4-111)

X1 dribbles from an angle at the cone. As he nears the cone, he performs a feint and beats the cone to the outside, finishing with a shot on goal. X2 immediately follows while X1 retrieves his/her ball and goes to the back of the line. The group takes 10-15 shots then

Diagram 4-110

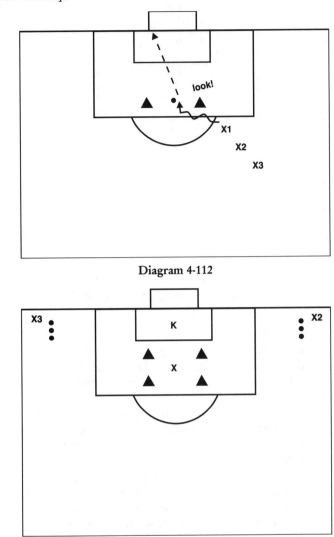

Diagram 4-112

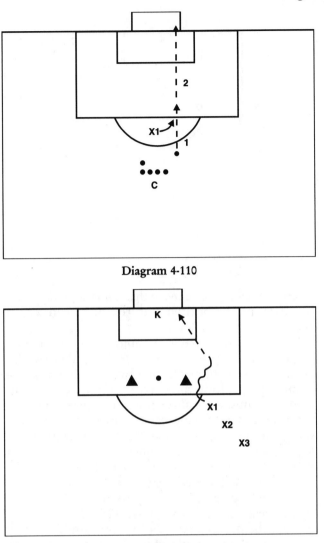

Diagram 4-111

Diagram 4-113

changes. Options include coming from both sides and beating the cone to the inside. The following are coaching points which are included. First, TAKE ONE LOOK. When beating the cone to the outside, take a look at the near post. If open, put the ball there. If the goalkeeper has it covered, shoot to the far post. You do not need to look and see if the far post is open.

When beating the cone to the inside, look at the post you are dribbling towards. If that post is open, put the ball there. If covered, you know where to shoot! Second, shoot to the right or left of the goalkeeper. If you miss-hit you will probably hit the corner. If you shoot for the corner, a slight miss-hit goes wide. React (shoot) quickly after your one look. The same coaching points are emphasized in the following two exercises. (Diagram 4-112)

Balls are served alternately by X2 and X3. X1 is to finish first time if possible. At most, two touch without going outside the square. Size of the square and positioning of the square are the option of the coach. When service comes from X2, player X1 needs only to look at post 'A' to see if that is open. Putting the ball back to

where it came from causes difficulties for goalkeepers. If post 'A' is covered, then he deflects to the other side. Again, ONE LOOK ONLY. (Diagram 4-113)

Player X1 starts by checking back from the penalty spot Coach serves a ball to the feet; X1 collects, turns and shoots. Immediately after the shot, the coach serves the second ball; X1 either first times or collects and then shoots the ball. A third ball follows. After three shots, another player goes in. Resting players collect balls. The service varies per the coach's discretion. Use the principles learned earlier: strike the ball cleanly and give one look, generally to the near post. (Diagram 4-114)

MATCH-CONDITION PHASE

5 v. 3 to one goal, use one-third to onehalf of a field. Coach starts each sequence with a service. Services vary with a long ball direct to strikers; a ball to wide players and a short ball to midfielders. After two to three minutes, change assignments. Coaching points include: watch how often players are shooting from positions practiced earlier on, clean strikes of the ball,

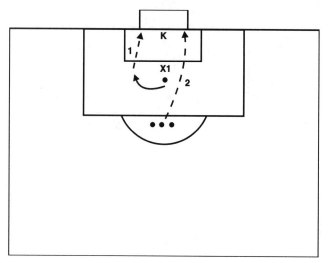

Diagram 4-114

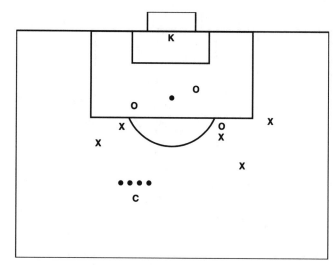

Diagram 4-115

ONE LOOK, and react and strike cleanly. (Diagram 4-115)

CONCLUSION

The above exercises try to improve the players' confidence in and ability to strike the ball cleanly, at first without pressure and later with self-imposed pressure and a goalkeeper.

Simplify the forward's task. Take ONE LOOK, preferably to the near post. There is no need for a second look because this slows down the time it takes to get the shot off.

Shoot to the right or left of the goalkeeper. Aiming for the post usually results in shots that are just wide. As a coach, conduct your shooting practice closer to goal from where most goals are scored anyway. Remember, these exercises are for your forwards, not the goalkeepers.

Finally, the pressure of a game can change everything. Hopefully a simplified thinking process and technical confidence can overcome game pressure. But remember, you can clean a rock, but you cannot make it a diamond.

FINISHING ACTIVITIES USING THE TWO-SIDED SOCCER GOAL

Andy Caruso

The following is a series of finishing activities which provides an economy of training. All activities employ the flat-faced goal and net which has been recommended by both Weil Coerver and Franz Van Balkom and used with great success in Holland. In general, we can achieve more than twice as many shots in a given period of time with this goal than with a traditional goal net.

The device is moved in the amount of time it takes to go from one place to another. If it takes twenty seconds to walk 100 feet, then twenty seconds is the required preparation time needed to relocate the flat-faced goal. Initial installation is about three minutes. The time lost retrieving balls "buried" in the net is totally eliminated, as well as the need to employ net pegs. The safety hazard of someone being struck by a ball while retrieving is also eliminated.

With the net fastened tightly on the two-sided goal, play can take place off both sides with no removal of the ball necessary. Also, there is a 4 foot rope running through the net to serve as a shooting guide. The actual goal is slightly reduced in size so as to promote accuracy. Virtually all shooting activities are aimed under the four foot rope that is hung in the netting and which runs parallel to the ground. The device is free standing and balls can be played through the net or off the face so as to simulate a target net or wall. In either case lines are eliminated and there is no delay in retrieving the ball.

Quality finishing requires many repeated trials at a full-size goal. Once shooting is technically sound without pressure, pressure is added and match conditions (short-sided games with specific restrictions) are the final stage for improving shooting ability.

TAKE-OVER AND SHOT

Activity one: (Net tied tight for balls dropping after contact.) Player A dribbles and leaves the ball for player B who shoots the shot with A taking the follow-up shot. Each returns to the opposite side of the goal; repeat. Adjust and vary distance to age of players; first occasion might be from 12-15 yards away (Diagram 4-116) Two other players can practice this drill on the other side of the goal.

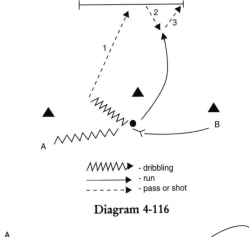

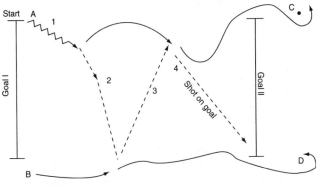

Diagram 4-116

MWWWW▶ - dribbling
———▶ - run
- - - -▶ - pass or shot

Diagram 4-117

1. Player A dribbles and leaves.
2. Player B takes-over and shoots.
3. Ball rebounds off net.
4. Player A shoots.
5. Ball rebounds off net.
6. Player A retrieves and dribbles ball to starting point.
7. Player A passes to player B.
8. The process is repeated.
9. After ten trials begin dribble from the right side.

Variations:

1. One touch shot.
2. Two touch shot.
3. Two touch, however change direction, then shoot
4. Either leave OR carry after feinted leave
5. One touch heel pass, other player shoots one or two-touch shot.

WALL PASS AND SHOT (DIAGRAM 4-117)

A and B attack Goal II. Player A dribbles with eye contact preceding the pass. Player B does not go out for the pass too early, bends his run and is accelerating on reception of the ball. Players must follow the shot. Players C and D go toward Goal I repeating the procedure. Six players may be ideal. The other sides of both goals can be used for keeper activities, penalty kicks, etc.

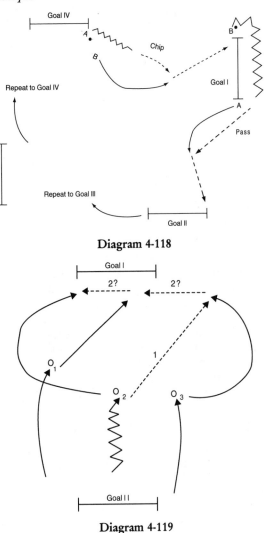

Diagram 4-118

Diagram 4-119

THROUGH BALL AND SHOT (DIAGRAM 4-118)

Player A dribbles, player B calls for the ball with an accelerated run. Player A chips the ball to space in front of B who controls the ball with ANY part of his body and hits a forceful low shot to the far post. If a one touch shot is possible, that is fine. The shot should be low, under the four foot marker rope on the goal. From two to 20 players can easily be accommodated. With fewer numbers, this can be turned into a form of interval training. Both players are to follow the shot and both players go around the goal posts before they go exchange roles and go to the next goal.

CROSSING AND HEADING (DIAGRAM 4-119)

The three Os start at Goal II, with O2 on the dribble (from half-field), move toward Goal I. O3 bends his run and O2 delivers a well-timed ball to the space at the goal line. O2 delivers either a hard-driven ball to O, who has run near post or to O2 who has bent his run to far post Each ball will be a header. Another group can repeat the drill to Goal II. Practice from either side should be insured. Defensive pressure

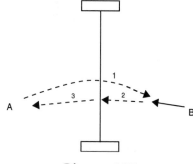

Diagram 4-120

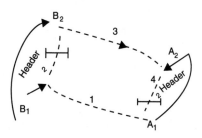

Diagram 4-121

(one to three players) can be introduced later in the practice sequence.

VOLLEY SHOT (DIAGRAM 4-120)

The ball is served over the net for a full volley shot. In this instance the net is tied loose and as the ball strikes the net, it is slowed down and comes to rest on the other side of the net.

Options: 1. Half volley; 2. Take ball with body on full run and second touch shot; 3. Heading shots; 4. Two receivers, the first player to touch the ball must control the air ball and attempt to set up his teammate for a strike at the goal; 5. Place a keeper in front of the goal and see if players can place the ball past the keeper.

LONG PASSING AND SHOT (DIAGRAM 4-121)

These circular activities provide innumerable repetitions of a skill in a short period of time. Again the net ties are set loose so the ball comes through the net with no retrieval necessary. It is good for development of accurate long passing with four players.

Options:

1. Chipped balls to central goal area (away from keeper).

2. 90' ground balls (move goal slightly for varied angles).

3. Driven balls to near post.

4. Driven balls to the chest.

5. Two receivers for flick-on heading practice.

There are many keeper activities that can be practiced, such as punting at the other side of each net, or throwing to a target on the net, or diving practice saves of kicked balls, etc. The array of activities are infinite.

GOALKEEPING

• •

Perhaps no area of coaching has been better defined in the recent history of American soccer than that pertaining to the goalkeeper.

Years ago coaches in this country would send their keepers to the other end of the field to "warm up." "Get ready, I'll call you when we're going to scrimmage" might be a parting comment by the coach.

Today that has all changed. Not long after soccer camps appeared on the scene in the 60s, specialized goalkeeper camps made their appearance. Concurrent with the focused instruction of the position, goalkeeper equipment was dramatically improved. Gloves, formerly an option for goalies, became a necessity. Not just a pair, but a pair for practice and a pair for the matches. Padded jerseys and pants were other additions to the keeper wardrobe.

Moving to the present one finds that at both the camp level and through clinic presentations, every aspect of the keeper's training has been dissected. Today innovative training exercises at both the individual and group level of play have been designed to prepare the keeper to deal with any situation in a match.

The chapter on goalkeeping will be divided into four areas of discussion. The first will introduce coaches to the psychology of the position, discuss evaluation, clarify the role of the keeper (including tactical concerns) within the team, even discuss what a coach should prepare for when a keeper is lost to the team.

Physical preparation of the keeper is the second area of concern here. Various drills that will provide the overload necessary for peak performance will be addressed in this segment.

Perhaps no area of goalkeeping has been given greater scrutiny than the techniques of the position. The third segment includes a discussion of diving, boxing, saving the breakaway and other specific skills needed by a keeper.

Finally a well-functioning team needs to integrate its keeper with its field players and the final part of the chapter addresses team tactics in relation to the goalkeeper.

The Psychological Dimensions of Goalkeeping

Mark Newman

What I always find is that as you go further in the game and you gain more success, then that brings more pressure on you to perform. But it's outside pressures, not the pressures of the game. The game is easy. It's when you get in front of big crowds and something's at stake like winning the match, that's when the mental side comes in.
— Pat Jennings

While a goalkeeper's performance involves such physical elements as quickness and power, it is often the psychological component which determines success. At every level, there are goalkeepers with exceptional quickness and great jumping ability, goalkeepers with good size and flexibility, and keepers who can make the great save. Goalkeeping, though, demands more than physical prowess.

The ways in which goalkeepers choose to deal with the pressure they experience, in part, determine their success. By virtue of their position, goalkeepers are put under enormous amounts of pressure to perform mistake-free, to not relinquish even a single goal. One mistake can lead to the goal being scored which may mean the loss of the game. How should goalkeepers cope with this kind of pressure? How should they deal with the fear of making mistakes and the expectations to play flawlessly? In short, how should goalkeepers think about keeping the goal to give themselves the best chance of being successful?

While it is true that goalkeepers must be physically able and ready to perform, equally important is their belief in that ability. At the moment of truth, goalkeepers must be able to remain focused and not be distracted by self-defeating thoughts. Simultaneously, they must be able to throw away fear and be decisive while remaining composed under the constant pressure of a 90-minute match. Goalkeepers must also have courage—a particular kind of courage. Of course, they need the physical courage required to sacrifice their body to stop breakaways and challenge

for crossed balls, but perhaps more important, they need the emotional courage to face adversity—the brutal slump, relentless expectations, mistakes and setbacks, the persistent injury—and cope with it in an effective manner.

In my various travels, I have had the opportunity to conduct extensive interviews regarding the psychological dimension of goalkeeping with several of the finest goalkeepers in the history of the game. The questions I asked each of these men stemmed from my own curiosity about what separated great goalkeepers from other goalkeepers. I wanted to know what these men possessed which enabled them to stand above all others. I wanted to find out, aside from talent and training, the most private thoughts, attitudes, and beliefs about goalkeeping that they were willing to share. My hope was that by asking the questions I did, I would elicit answers that would give others insight into aspects of thinking which might make them better goalkeepers. Due to the limitations of space allowed by this article I can only summarize a part of the information they shared.

If there is one predominant truth among the men I spoke to, it is that they have an unquestionable depth of belief about themselves as goalkeepers. They possess habits of thought that are consistent with their aspirations. Theirs is a deep enthusiasm for the game, a true love for what they do. It is an attitude which breeds greatness. For these men, goalkeeping is not about just stopping shots and distributing the ball; as Pat Jennings, the former Tottenham Hotspur, Arsenal, and Northern Ireland goalkeeper, said to me, it is about "Taking responsibility on the football field, making the confident call. It's being decisive." It is also about playing with a certain urgency and intensity: playing every shot and dealing with every situation that develops with the mindset that it is the last one that will ever be faced. In short, it is playing with a purpose.

These men spoke of thinking in ways which enabled them to grow in confidence, maintain composure in even the most trying of situations, and become deeply lost in concentration. Their confidence comes from the feeling of being able to control the outcome of the game on their own. "You look the part," said former Scottish International and Aberdeen goalkeeper Bobby Clark, "you know you're the part, and you let the opposition know it. You almost intimidate people by the way you do your job. You take balls with an air of pulling apples off a tree. It's a little bit of acting, but it's also you knowing you've got the ability too. It's having the confidence to meet any challenge. It's almost like treating things with a little contempt."

It is this supreme confidence which seems to separate the great goalkeepers from the mediocre. Perhaps Sepp Maier, the former Bayern Munich and West German National Team goalkeeper, said it best, "If

Michele Akers (10) scores one of her many goals for the U.S. National Women's Team. Being scored on is one part of goalkeeping; rebounding from that "defeat" and refocusing is a true measure of a goalkeeper's ability to cope.
(photo by J. Brett Whitesell)

you don't believe in yourself, you have no chance. It's very important within goalkeeping, in your whole life you have to believe in yourself. You must have a little...egoism. You must have that, otherwise you have no chance to move up. If you don't have it, you can't get out of the middle. You can't get to number one or be one of the best. You have to believe it when you say 'I can get it', 'I can make it', 'I have the possibility to get great'. It is not enough to just say it, you must believe it."

Along with confidence, these men possess the composure needed to deal with pressure, to cope with mistakes and setbacks. According to former Juventus and Italian National Team goalkeeper Dino Zoff, "The difference between a great goalkeeper and the others is the capacity of being calm when others just hurry to do something." Referring to his own disposition he said, "I am one who was very calm, who could use in a match his head. I was very cool in making decisions. This I think was my main characteristic." Bobby Clark spoke of composure as being about "How you handle the downs because you're going to get 'downs' as a goalkeeper." He added, "Anybody can handle the 'ups', but it's the real mark of a player in any sport if he can handle the disappointments; the lost games, the goals allowed if he's to blame. That's a true mark of a player."

The sort of pressure goalkeepers experience is in many ways different from that of field players. Since the goalkeeper "is an isolated person," as Pat Jennings called him, he stands, alone, constantly being exposed, while field players can hide if they do not want to move or pass. Field players also have the luxury of making mistakes and getting away with them, then making up for their mistakes in the 89th or 90th minute of the game by scoring the winning goal, or

by clearing a ball off the goal line to salvage a draw. Goalkeepers have no way out. One minute they can be the hero, the next minute the knave. If they make a mistake, there is nowhere to hide. If their mistakes result in goals scored against them, they must rely on their teammates to score for redemption.

If a goalkeeper relinquishes a goal early in the match, his responsibility becomes to make sure another one is not scored. If his team cannot equalize or go ahead, regardless of the number of saves he makes in the remaining minutes or his ability to initiate the attack, his efforts will have been for naught. That is the anomaly of goalkeeping. A goalkeeper, like a pitcher in baseball, is one of the most individual positions in sport. Every time a goalkeeper steps on the field of play, his reputation is at stake, as is the confidence of his team in him. A field player, or even a forward in basketball, or a lineman in American football can hide within his team if he makes a mistake; goalkeepers and pitchers, however, cannot. They must stand on their own.

After a mistake is committed that results in a goal scored, how must goalkeepers deal with that? What can they do to prevent mistakes from happening again? Or, at least, what can they do to reduce the chance of them recurring?

For the men I spoke to, composure meant striving for the perfectly played game, but being able to forgive themselves for a mistake made or a goal scored so they could go on with the rest of the match uninhibited. They spoke of playing with the confidence to make a mistake, of having the courage to face mistakes instead of fight them. "There's just no use in worrying if you make a mistake," said one-time Everton and Welsh National Team goalkeeper Neville Southall. "I mean, I don't think a goalkeeper can go through the League without making a mistake in a season." Early on in his career, if, Southall made a mistake he would usually make another just like it "Because I was so uptight about making the first one," he said. His experience, however, taught him to change that thinking. "I think now, now that I've done it, there's nothing I can do about it so I get on with it and make sure the rest of my game is spot on. I think you've got to do that or you won't make the next save. My thinking now is, let's see if I can make up for it."

Tony Meola, the former U.S. National Team goalkeeper, takes an analytical approach toward dealing with mistakes. "If I make a poor decision in a game and it leads to a goal," he said, "from the time that I pick the ball up out of the net 'til kick off, that little time, whatever it is, 15 seconds, 30 seconds, maybe a minute, while the other team's celebrating, or whatever, the time it takes the ref to get the ball to the halfway line is the time for me to evaluate what just happened." After he evaluates the situation, he banishes it from his mind. Instead of becoming discouraged or lost in self-worry or full of doubt, he uses the experience as a tool from which to learn. "My thinking is, 'Alright, what's just happened? How do I correct it for next time?' Once I've got it down, that's it. I've forgotten about it. The score is 0-0 again." Dino Zoff observed that, "You cannot be conditioned by mistakes or things that have happened because sometimes in a match it happens that you don't even see the ball and a goal is scored. Maybe it is your fault and maybe it is not. But you must have the strength of playing every instance as with the best concentration. You must not let things interfere with your concentration."

Concentration in goalkeeping is often the difference between making the save and not making it, making the right decision or making a wrong one, and making decisions without hesitation. For the goalkeepers I spoke to, there was a certain intensity of spirit, a youthful enthusiasm for the game which made it easy for them to fall into their concentration almost naturally. Tony Meola described it this way, "If you can't concentrate for 90 minutes and have fun then, then there's no other time to have fun. That's your time in the limelight. It's show time then. You show people what you can do."

Two elements were addressed by these men as factors affecting concentration: the fear of making mistakes and the fact that their livelihoods depended on their performances. While some people might suggest that factors such as these would detract from a person's focus, Pat Jennings referred to "mental pressure" as the thing which brought out the best in him. The more pressure he felt, the more effectively he was able to focus. "it gets me geared up to play," he said.

For the men I spoke to, concentration consisted of intense moments of both narrow and broad focus that were physically as well as emotionally draining.

Their's was not a total concentration for an entire 90 minutes. Rather, it was knowing when to turn the focus on and when to turn it off, when to increase its intensity and when to decrease it. Said Phil Parkes, the former England International and West Ham United goalkeeper, "When the ball is at the other end I might switch off a bit or when the game stops play I may have a look around or a laugh with the crowd. But when the whistle blows, I'm back on." Concentration amounts to recognizing a situation as it develops and responding without hesitation, seeing the shot and reacting. It is playing by instinct—trusting what the mind knows and simply letting the body take over.

The mental aspect of goalkeeping is several things, too many to be discussed with any depth in the space of this article. While it involves remaining confident, composed, and focused, it also entails doing what one must do to be the best he can be. That does not mean thinking as everyone else thinks; rather it is thinking in a way that provides the best chance of being successful. Neville Southall perhaps explained it better than any of the other goalkeepers I spoke to when he described his perspective on the psychological dimension of goalkeeping and goalkeeping in general. "You say it's psychology," he said, "but I do what I do. I mean I do the things that suit me, that work for me. You can't judge all goalkeepers by just one person, but that's what people do. They say, 'You've got to do exactly that!' But I've got my own style. I figure this is me. This is the enjoyment I get. It's what I do. I've got to enjoy the things I do."

⚽

Some Childhood Thoughts on Goalkeeping
Bobby Clark

Goalkeepers! What do I do with them? How often do soccer coaches ask themselves the above question!

One easy solution is to send them to a goalie camp for a week during the summer and then once team practices begin leave them off on their own somewhere until shooting practice. The other, possibly better solution, is to get a goalie coach and send them away to "Siberia" until, once again, it is time for shooting practice.

This isolation mentality will not totally stunt a young goalie's growth. In fact it might stimulate his fervor for the position. Often what happens is that the isolated goalies suddenly look on themselves as people apart. They see themselves as a separate little goalie club. This exclusive group can get so engrossed with their position that they get totally caught up with all the theoretical technicalities of their situation. Youngsters get so involved with the theory, the equipment, and somehow miss out on the most important factor: THE GAME!

Don't get me wrong, outfield players also get caught up in a similar fashion. The country abounds in fast footwork and dribbling drills. Like the goalkeeping drills, these are tremendous accessories. They promote skill, balance, and touch, but if not integrated into the GAME they are USELESS.

What is skill?

In my book it is applied technique; technique on its own is an impractical talent. Therefore, be it a goalie, a defender, a midfielder, or a forward, it is important that he accrues sufficient specific skill to carry out the duties inherent to his position, but it is equally important that he can apply these abilities within the team concept and not in isolation.

I look back on some of my contemporaries. Jim Cruickshank, Pat Jennings, Peter Shilton, Ronnie Simpson, Gordon Banks, Alan Rough, Ivo Victor, Sepp Maier, and Jongbloed to name but a few. I look at all these wonderful national team goalies and try to draw common bonds. All were quite different in size, shape, technique, and style. I think Jongbloed, a veteran of two World Cup finals for Holland, was possibly the most unorthodox. He was big, didn't wear gloves, was sort of stiff looking but, hey, don't tell me you get to play in two World Cup finals if you aren't a good goalie! All were different but the one linking factor was that they all KNEW THE GAME. They not only knew how to play but were able to apply their technical skills to solve the problems which the game presented in coordination with the rest of the team.

I think back to my own development and I often feel that the most beneficial drill I ever played was the little 3 v. 3 and 4 v. 4 pickup games which we played on a spare lot beside where I grew up. People are always asking me for my favorite drill. What helped you the most? What was your secret?

The big thing about these little games was that you played with "running goalies" or as we sometimes referred to the goalkeeper as a "back in goal". The key to this position was that you would become a field player when your team had possession and you became a combination of a defender and a goalkeeper when the opposition had the ball. Firstly you learned the game of football, and secondly, you learned naturally from the game what you had to do to be successful. Players developed naturally. Players who had a natural affinity for the position gravitated to playing the "back in goal", and because winning and losing was very serious in these early games, every game was a cup final in our young eyes, selection took on a very natural process.

There was, of course, one other very important factor in this stage of my development. It was role models. We didn't have television in these early years, so our role models were anything from the high school goalie, the local men's team goalie, or once I was old enough to travel, professional goalies. This again was natural growth, and I have tremendous memories of this romantic learning phase. As I previously mentioned, every game was a cup final and every victory was a celebration. I was a bit schizophrenic in these early days since one day I was Fred Martin; the next, I was Tommy Younger.

After all my above ramblings, I am sure you are wondering exactly what I am getting at. My main point is that the major priority in a goalkeeper's development is his basic knowledge of the game. I feel all good goalies would not be out of place on the field. Tony Meola is a classic example of a youngster who had ability to play the game. Catching and athletic skills are prerequisites. After that the game and ambition will soon start to dictate the areas which require most additional work. The goalkeeper is simply another player who has added responsibilities, but these extras do not detract from the fact that he is just one of the team.

Having outlined my argument, I would now like to come back to my original question. What does a coach do with his goalkeepers? Hopefully you will now come to the similar conclusion as me and agree that the goalkeeper should be part of the team and work with his teammates as often as possible.

Why should they warm up on their own? What do we use warmups for? If it is to get the team started, then, since I feel that the goalkeeper is a very vital part of the team, he should be present. If technique is involved, then why can't the goalkeepers be integrated using their specific skill in coordination with the other players. Use the goalies as targets in keepball. This is an ideal situation to develop distribution and understanding of how and when to receive and serve field players. Involve the goalie as a chaser in keepball. It's good practice for field players to evade a sprawling goalkeeper and it is also good practice for the goalie committing himself at the feet of field players. In this situation he will get a lot of one-on-ones. Shooting practices are natural times for a goalie to be part of the squad, but too often small goals are used in small-sided games. It is important that field players get into the habit of facing realistic situations, so use goalkeepers and full size goals so that everyone is getting worthwhile practice.

When coaching my college team at Dartmouth, I always outlined each practice for the team, and within this plan I make sure the goalkeeper is going to be catered to. I try to involve him, and find him a role within the various practices. It might be a player-directed warm up, and he might be asked to take the lead role. The goalkeeper must be the general of his defense and this will give him confidence directing and giving orders. I also try to find some time when they can get together and work on their own specific skills. Often I will assign one of my assistants or will take these specialist sessions myself. I feel the latter is very important since there is nothing better than when the head coach works with his goalkeepers. Take it from me, when the man who picks the team actually gets down and works with his goalies this provides tremendous motivation. My aim as coach is to develop the individual techniques of my goalkeepers but to do it within the context of the WHOLE TEAM.

THE EVALUATION OF GOALKEEPERS: COMPONENTS TO CONSIDER
Dan Gaspar and Tony DiCicco

PHYSICAL TRAITS

Strength & Power. Explosiveness to get to balls. Display stamina to withstand and absorb player contract.

Agility and Coordination. Harmonious action. Pay particular attention to hand-eye coordination and footwork movements.

Flexibility. The ability to challenge muscle groups to their maximum stretch. Changing body position and direction to make a save is not uncommon. These physical demands can only be accomplished with good flexibility.

Perception and Reaction-Speed. Acknowledge and respond quickly. Determine if the keeper is reacting with conviction or is there hesitation in decision-making.

Physical Limitations. Certainly, a keeper with good stature coupled with the above physical traits has the advantage over a smaller keeper with balance being equal. However, remember that skill, not size is what make the difference.

TECHNICAL ASPECTS

Catching and Boxing. As a result of the keepers' freedom to use their hands, catching and boxing must be mastered. Catching should be controlled and clean, with few rebounds allowed. Selective boxing with the purpose of achieving distance, height and width is of value.

Diving. Exciting and spectacular save. However, be aware of those goalkeepers who dive when it's not necessary, They tend to be risky. Evaluate reaction time, elevation of dive and extension. The ball breaks the fall and landing should not be on the stomach or back, as this will produce injuries.

The ability of a keeper to play high balls and protect themselves is an important goalkeeping technique. Here Houston goalie Keith Von Eron demonstrates the technique in 1978 NASL play. (photo by Milt Crossen)

Breakaways. Is there proper perception of this situation developing? Does the keeper (A) make the save before the shot is taken; (B) make the save as the shot is taken; or (C) make the save after the shot is taken. Does the keeper save under control or does the keeper sell himself too early? Is courage displayed?

High balls. The ability to control the box is crucial. Observe the keeper's timing, area covered and the ability to catch the ball at its highest point. Does he or she call "keeper" prior to making the save? How does the keeper absorb contact in the air? Is the knee up for protection?

Distribution. Is the keeper accepting the responsibility of initiating the attack or is distance the primary concern? Does the keeper switch play quickly and successfully? How many opposing players have been removed from defensive play as a result of effective distribution? Is the game's tempo being considered in the keeper's mode of distribution? Is short distribution being supported? Keepers should take their own goalkicks. Accurate distribution is determined by the ease in which a teammate is able to collect the ball.

Balance. Dynamic stability. Body should be in motion to overcome resting inertia. Body weight should be distributed equally. Notice if there is prestretch just prior to the shot. This gives the muscles that move levers of the body a better physiological advantage.

TACTICAL ASPECTS

Angle Play. Good positioning shows the keeper knows to reduce shooting angles by making the goal appear smaller. Analyze where the save is being made. Are they alert to their surroundings? Is the positioning three-dimensional? Are saves on ball line or are they consistently producing last minute desperate saves.

Communication. A keeper with organizational skills will reduce the number of shots taken on goal, thus allowing fewer goals. Communication must be specific and with authority. How does the keeper communicate on the restarts?

Anticipation. The ability to read the game. Especially, to recognize and prevent dangerous scoring opportunities from developing. Anticipation is a result of accumulation of match experiences.

PSYCHOLOGICAL FACTORS

Mental Discipline. This is attained through systematic training. Having the mind conditioned to cancel mistakes during the match. After the match those errors should be rehearsed and analyzed. Notice the keeper's body language after suffering a goal. Does that goal remain in the keeper's mind during the match and effect his play? The keeper must have a strong character to cope with this lonely position. Consistency in performance is a result of mental discipline. Certainly, physical, technical and tactical factors are important. However, without the proper attitude developed by a strong mind the other aspects are not nearly as effective.

Courage. Calmness and firmness in the face of danger from opposition. A courageous keeper can intimidate and disturb an opposing player's style of play.

Confidence. This is attained through achieving success. The keeper who has confidence in his play earns assurance and the respect from teammates and opponents. Be concerned about keepers who have excessive pride, who are overbearing and who do not accept fault. During the match are field players making keeper decisions or is the keeper in control?

Leadership. The quality of conducting guidance is of utmost importance.

Training Ethics. The various mental and physical demands placed on the keeper. Training principles must reflect the nature of the position. To achieve or maintain a high standard in knowledge or skill, the keeper must accept the training sacrifices. The keeper's fitness level must be excellent in order to be capable of responding when called upon. The keeper must assume responsibility.

Now, can that goalkeeper play for you? We hope these keeper considerations will guide you in evaluating a potential keeper.

MODERN TACTICAL CONCERNS FOR THE GOALKEEPER*
Frans Hoek

What I have tried to do for the last 10-15 years was to study goalkeeping. I played myself as a professional until recently when a bad injury ended my active career. But during those years I tried to not only play, but to study goalkeeping. I had a lot of meetings all over the world with other keepers, trainers of keepers, etc., while all the time collecting information on the subject of goalkeeping.

Because of that, I analyzed the games of goalkeepers all over the world. This included the great goalkeepers, so I will attempt to present the vision of goalkeeping which I made of my own experience; watching, talking with a lot goalkeepers, both great and little—and a lot of coaches all over the world.

So in the first part of this article I will try to share with you how I think about goalkeeping in terms of the tactics of the position. The first thing I was asking myself when I started to study goalkeeping was: "What is the job of goalkeeping? Stopping the ball? Dealing with crossed balls? Stopping shots?" Certainly there are a lot of correct answers here—but they are only part of what the keeper's job really is.

ORGANIZER OF THE DEFENSE

The goalkeeper's number one job is a defensive one. It is defensive because the first responsibility is to minimize goal-scoring chances and that's a lot different than dealing with crossed balls or stopping shots. Why? Well, because of the fact that a goalkeeper can play a perfect game without letting one ball in his goal and that's a bit different than a lot of people— the press, coaches and goalkeepers are thinking because they believe keepers play a great game when they make a lot of great saves or they make a lot of diving saves or when they save a lot of breakaways. Perfect. You can do a lot more before that. What can you do before that? How can you minimize goalscoring chances? The first thing you have to have is poise. Be able to organize and coach your defense because when I coach, when I as a keeper organize my defense well, it means mostly that I cut my work by 50%. I will give you an example. When my team has the ball, everybody, including the goalkeeper and including his defenders, are watching what is happen-

---

* *This article is a transcription by Joe Machnik of an audio tape recorded by the author.*

ing in and around the ball. When does the keeper start to coach? Generally he starts to coach when his team loses the ball.

When you have a smart attacker, the attacker has slipped away from the defender when the defender's team has the ball. When the ball is lost, a lot of times depth has been lost in coverage on the clever attacker and here comes a through ball and a breakaway situation. This is a realistic situation I've presented. But what happens when I, as a goalkeeper, organize my defense at the time that we have the ball? Now I make sure that everybody in the back—my defenders—are playing at least one against one. That means that when the attacker does free himself and the ball is coming over my defender's head, he turns and has a very good chance to defend. When the defender is standing in front of the attacker and the through ball is played, we now have a potential 1 v. 1 with me, the goalkeeper, and now the possibility that I may save that ball is not very good.

So first, the keeper's job is coaching and organizing. That starts before the game. Have conferences. Talk about how you will be using your voice. Review how you will use terms. What does it mean when you say "keeper"? What does it mean when you say "let", "close", etc. What does it mean when you say "you"? So goalkeeping coaching starts before the game. And then when we have the ball, I make sure all my defenders are concentrating in the back, 1 v. 1. In the midfield, I have the situation in my head. Then when we lose the ball, I know exactly where to place what player because the midfield players are also responsible for playing in the defensive third of the field. Then, of course, when we lose the ball a lot of things are already organized and as the opponents are coming closer to our goal, the more I become the keeper and less the organizer or coach of the defense.

So the first job is always organizing and coaching the defense. When you do that well it is 50% less work for you, the keeper.

How To Coach

The second thing that is important is to instruct keepers in how to coach. You have to coach them. Tell the keeper, "I want to hear you!" You have to tell them what you want to hear in various situations. They have to practice it! We saw two training games yesterday, the crossed ball game and the little game on the long, small field. Did you hear any coaching by the keepers? I didn't hear anything. In these games there are the moments you can start your teaching. Did you hear a little bit when the keeper came out for the cross ball and he had to only shout "keeper"? You see how difficult it is. You can't just say to your keeper "coach the defense!" No, he has to learn how to coach his defense. He has to practice it step by step by step.

Perfecting Positional Play

The second thing you have to do is perfect positional play. All the goalkeepers are going to prefer to stay on the line. On the line they are safe—or they think they are safe. They believe that nothing bad can happen. When I make the diving save and I touch the ball at the goal line, everybody says, "Oh, he's a very good athlete!" But who is telling me that I had a lot of choices before the great save—to scoop and catch the ball or perhaps to intercept it outside the area, or perhaps to play it away with the inside of the foot. The second thing is to perfect positional play and save yourself from having to make the desperate play.

The third thing which follows positional play is to try to get to the ball as soon as possible. Anticipation and getting to the ball means playing off the line. It mostly means trying to get to the ball outside of the penalty area. If that isn't possible, you have to do it inside of the penalty area, and when that isn't possible, you have to do it inside your six-yard box. When that isn't possible, you have the line to defend. What that means is that you give yourself a lot of chances—a lot of chances.

I showed you the work that the goalkeepers normally do. Direct danger is what a lot of keepers react to. Everybody recognizes those dangers — shots for goal in every situation are dangerous. That is what everybody says when you ask them what the goalkeepers' job is — making saves on the line. When goalkeepers practice, they always practice making saves. Saving shots at the goal is the last stage of keeping in my thinking because you have so many more opportunities for acting as a keeper before you let the opponents shoot the ball at your goal.

When you are on the line or a few steps in front of the line and you make a mistake, it's a goal. The line keeper is needed in cases of immediate danger. An example of immediate danger is the through pass. When I don't catch the first ball of a shot on the line, there must always be another opponent ready to score, but when I make the mistake on the through ball, it's not always a goal.

When I talk about getting the ball as early as possible, I mean trying to intercept the ball. Nobody ever trains for situations like this all over the world. And when you do train for this situation, you can solve the problem a lot earlier than waiting on the line.

Control Areas

You have to control areas. You need to know how big the area is that you can control. Controlling areas is important. I start with a small area and no goal. Train the keeper to not let the ball bounce. Have them try to get to it as soon as possible. When it's a ground ball, go outside of your area and play it with your feet. It will be the same with cross balls. We start in areas. What is your area? How far can you cover when the ball is there, and when the ball is there, and then there? We need the same with through passes, outside the penalty box, inside the penalty box. That means that area is your area. You're the boss! You know exactly what you can do. When you watch goalkeeping now, the areas covered are small. The line and perhaps a few steps in front of the line — but that's it. Why? Because the keepers are very, very afraid that they will make a mistake. A few steps too many in front of the goal, then the chip, a goal, and everybody's laughing. But when you know exactly where you can stand, then when the chip is coming, you are back early enough to deflect it, (or even better) catch it. Thus confidence is built in the keeper to even further expand his/her area of control.

CROSSES

Another immediate danger are crossed balls. We know that when you miss the ball, there is not always a goal. Normally there might be other opponents to help shoot the ball in. Practice must also mean crossed balls. And we know how difficult it is for the goalkeeper to intercept a cross ball. Everybody thinks it's easy. When the goalkeeper is intercepting a cross ball, everybody says "Okay, that's it. It's not spectacular." But when he misses the ball, everybody is shouting and yelling at him. He's not a good goalkeeper; he's a bad goalkeeper. You don't catch the cross ball. This is very, very difficult and goalkeepers need to be trained in how to check the flight of the ball to make the decision. I go or I don't go. All the opponents in front of you, including your own players in front of you, create confusion. You have to talk, you have to go, take off and make a good catch or a good box of the ball. The easiest thing to do is to stand on the line, let the person shoot, and hope you get to the ball. Then make believe you knew where it was going to be shot! That is a reflex. You don't need to do anything for that. You are born with that. But all the other things need practicing; they need building judgement. It means expanding your areas.

DISTRIBUTION

The only time the keeper is really the boss is when the ball is his/hers and they have to play it away with some intelligence. They have to make the right decision in terms of its distribution.

What we see all over the world today in terms of this part of the keeper's job is terrible. You see supposedly great keepers who, when they get a hold of the ball, delay play so the television cameras will focus on them I suppose, then bounce the ball and kick it away. Most of the time possession is lost when the main thrust of all of this is to see how far, not how accurately, they can play the ball.

In watching Bayern Munich play recently, I noted all the balls their keeper was punting and also noted how many were kept by his team. Out of 88 balls played, there were only between six and eight balls kept by his team. The rest he gave away. The first defensive job of the keeper is to minimize the goalscoring chances of the opponents. This is not being observed if that trend repeats itself match after match.

When I control the ball and I then give it away, the opponents have a good chance to score. In the first place, always try to do something useful. When you need to kick the ball as far and as high as possible that's okay, but don't do it because all of the attention is on you and television is watching you.

The first thing you always have to try is to keep possession of the ball for your team. For two reasons: one is when we have the ball, they can't score. The second is that when we have the ball, we have the possibility of scoring. We try to teach that when you have the ball, the strikers get to the defending line of your opponents where they then try to score. Another advantage for you as goalkeeper is that when your strikers get the ball in front, there is always the midfield for support and there are always our defenders who can try to get the ball again if it is lost. So always try to throw or kick the ball as far as possible, preferably to the strikers. Throwing is better than kicking due to its greater accuracy. When it isn't possible to reach your central strikers, try to reach the wings close by the defenders (outside midfielders). When that isn't possible, you always have the choice of kicking the ball. To dropkick or to punt are the choices you have to make. So then you have choice number one, far; choice number two, wings; choice number three, wing midfielders; and then finally, choice four, punting the ball.

FIELD CONDITIONS AND TACTICS

It might be that my best choice is to always punt the ball as this is the preferred tactic, depending on the circumstances. If our team is ahead with little time remaining, the tactics should call for long punts, not distribution of the ball close to our own goal. Our team tactics might be to use the long ball as played throughout much of England. There players are concentrated in the middle of the pitch and the fight is

> The first job of the goalkeeper is organizing and coaching the defense. When you do that well it is 50% less work for you.

on to control the keeper's punts. Flick-ons and passes to the wingers on the outside of the field off these punts are the tactics we see in the English game. Another obvious reason for punting is the weather conditions. When the field is very wet, throwing is difficult because you can misplay the ball close to your goal. It is then very useful to punt every ball as far as possible. So there are situations when you have to do things you normally don't do. Our Ajax team normally would have the keeper throw 98 of 100 balls he possesses. Only two balls would be kicked and he would use the drop kick to propel the ball. But in a game in Spain there was so much water, it was unbelievable. Throwing was very dangerous because the ball slid all over the place. When you wanted to bounce the ball, it stayed in the water. So the only thing you could do was to try to punt the ball as far as possible. So that's what was done.

⚽

The Role of a Goal Keeper as a Team Player
Dan Gaspar

The requirements of the goalkeeper position are uniquely different from the rest of the squad. Regardless of those distinctions, however, the goalkeeper is a team player. The skills that a goalkeeper masters must be practiced and integrated with the team. Harmony and interaction within the entire group, not just among the field players, is of utmost importance to a successful team performance. We all understand that the goalkeeper protects the goal area by mastering techniques for shot handling; we must also remember the keeper frequently starts the attack by effective and selective distribution of the ball. The goalkeeper also must possess the ability to direct players verbally and through use of physical signals. To capture and utilize these skills to their fullest, and to develop a sense of responsibility within the goalkeeper, he must be involved as a vital member of the team.

Here's the million dollar question: How important is your goalkeeper to your team's success? I'm sure you'll agree the goalkeeper is vital to team performance. Some would claim that the goalkeeper is the most important player on the team. I would have to agree that, while the goalkeeper is very important, his role is certainly no more dominant than any other individual. All players on the team are assigned crucial roles, and it is important that they understand how each functions in order to form a cohesive unit. Isolating the goalkeeper's training has merit, but total team training also provides results. Integration of all players is the key. So much attention has been given

Dan Gaspar (center) trains prospective MLS keepers at a preseason camp in 1996. Among the emphases in such training would be the role of the keeper within the team.
(photo by J. Brett Whitesell)

to training equipment that perhaps not enough attention has been given to the actual demands of the game itself.

Visualization

We need to do more than physically train the goalkeepers; we need to educate them to visualize the entire game. Accurate observation is a trained, learned visual skill. Nothing affects a keeper's actions and reactions more than the things he observes. Sight is a primary channel of information, and using this information in a positive, experienced manner is extremely important to the goalkeeper. Learning how to effectively observe through experiences, recollection, association and repetition is the basis for training more acute visual judgement. The goalkeeper needs to see, assess and act in an environment that is familiar and within the context of the game. There are several activities that will highlight the various aspects of goalkeeping, and how they work within the overall framework of the team game.

Warmup

Focus. The team prepares the goalkeeper to train

Challenge. Interaction among all players in the preparation process, with restrictions. Stretch between various restrictions.

Observations. Attain process in the areas of technical maintenance, the psychological component, and the physical elements of the game.

Activities

1. Each goalkeeper is in possession of the ball inside the goal box area. Field players move about creatively at a comfortable pace. Goalkeeper distributes a low ball to a field player. Player accurately pushes it back to keeper. The goalkeeper continues to distribute to and receive balls from other field players.

2. The keeper can now begin to serve air balls to field players. Field player then collect the services and strike ball back to the keeper within a comfortable saving distance. Field players must accomplish within three touches of the ball. After each service or save all players must perform an exercise (i.e. push-ups or forward rolls).

3. Expand the area and distance. We now ask the goalkeeper to find and locate the player farthest from the ball, and distribute it to that player. The player receives the distribution from the keeper (which may be a thrown, full or half-volleyed or struck dead ball) and serves the flighted balls into the goal box.

4. We can now begin to link up field players with combinations before we deliver the ball to the keeper. Example: field player receives the ball from the goalkeeper, who now locates another teammate, who strikes the ball at the keeper. The connection between field players can be in the form of wall pass, takeovers, one touch, seeking out furthest player, etc. What's important are the goalkeeper's movements with the ball. As we progress, the demands on the keeper increases. Let's reverse it, and have all field players involved in maintaining ownership of the magic object—the soccer ball.

5. We stress communication. The goalkeeper must signal—either visually or verbally—for the ball. The keeper then receives the ball, and sends it to the field player, who in turn sends it back to the keeper, constantly increasing the pace.

6. Players are dribbling. On the coach's signal, the player will sprint, with the ball, at least 10 yards. The goalkeeper, who is now ready for such activity, will perform breakaway saves.

7. You can link field players in groups of two to add pressure in many of these activities.

8. You can match goalkeepers to challenge each other, resulting in increased competition.

9. You can split the squad into two teams and play keep-away. Every third pass must go to the keeper.

These activities, and variations of them, are limited only by your imagination.

TECHNICAL PRACTICE

1. Focus. Absorbing low balls.

Challenge. Rapid fire.

Observations. Saving stance; the ability to drop; dynamic stability; and shooting signals.

Activity. All players outside of the goal box, keeper in goal. One serving player is in possession of all the balls. Other shooting players are lined up near the balls. The distributor touches the first ball to a shooter, who strikes it low and fast to a pre-determined side of the goal. This activity is performed rapidly and continuously. Once the save is made, and the keeper is in position, the next shooter fires.

Observe the keeper's starting position versus the saving position. The saving position should focus on the keeper getting closer to the ball. As soon as the shooter drops his head, and begins focusing on the ball, the keeper should be progressing forward. When the shot is just about to be delivered, the keeper gets balanced with equal distribution of body weight.

2. Focus. Handling bounced balls.

Challenge. One bounce only.

Observations. Foot skills; body and ball relationship; area covered.

Activity. Each goalkeeper has a ball, which they serve to a field player. The player strikes it away from the keeper, who has to chase and catch the ball before it bounces a second time. It's a lot of work—try it!

A variation is to have players juggling the ball 25-30 yards away. Keepers in goal area. Each player has a number. When the coach calls a number, that player serves an air ball anywhere into the goal area, and proceeds to chase it down. The keeper has to get to the ball first, as early as possible, preferably before the second bounce. The keeper distributes the ball to target players, and rotates to the end of the keeper line. Rotation must move rapidly, and the keeper must move aggressively forward toward the ball to make this exercise a success.

3. Focus. Flighted balls.

Challenge. 3 v. 3 + 1

Observations. Perception and action; communications

Activity. Keeper in goal, three offensive players, three defensive players, and one free player. All are outside the goal box. Free player serves to offensive players, who touch the ball back to the free player. The free player then serves a high ball into the box, and the offensive players chase it down. After making the save, the keeper distributes the ball to the defenders, who either find the free player or reload by returning the ball to the goalkeeper.

Note the keeper's evaluation of the high balls and his ability to direct defenders.

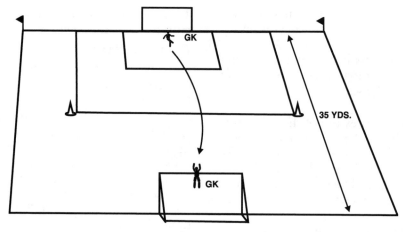

Diagram 5-1

4. Focus. Breakaway save.

Challenge. Solo save.

Observations. Attitude, anticipation and courage.

Activity. Keeper in goal, field players in groups of two with one ball. Assign numbers to each group. Players move freely, passing the ball to each other, 25-30 yards from the goal. Coach calls out a number. Player in possession quickly attacks the goal. After a two second delay, the second player in the group becomes the defender and pursues the attacker. Keeper has to decide whether to stay in goal or come out for the save. Should the keeper make the save, he distributes the ball to the pursuer.

Note if the keeper is projecting hands and body to the ball when saving; hands should be to the near post side unless the attack is coming straight down the middle. Down the middle, we go to the keeper's strongest side. Demand the keeper win the ball as early as possible (it's considered a win when the field player loses possession).

CONCLUSION

Our purpose in writing this article was not to highlight or break down in-depth technique. The goalkeeper will discover those by actually playing and developing in the position. The objective was to blend the goalkeeper and the field players, forming a bond between them. It is hoped that by visualizing the activities we discussed you can design others to help build improved communication in this area of team play.

⚽

GOALKEEPING
Dick Howard

COMBINATION DRILL FOR GOALKEEPERS

Equipment: 12 balls   12 players
                  2 portable goals   6 cones

DRILL I

1. The size of the playing area can be adapted to:
• Age of the players (e.g. younger players could play across the penalty area).
• Playing conditions (e.g. an indoor gym could be used in the winter months with the ball being thrown rather than kicked.
2. This can be a valuable practice for goalkeepers, but the coach must observe the goalkeeper(s) closely so that he can make relevant coaching points if possible through the WHOLE-PART-WHOLE Method.

1 v. 1 - TWO GOALKEEPERS

Goalkeepers restricted to own half of the field. Goalkeeper tries to score goals using volley, half volley and instep drive kicks. (Diagram 5-1)

Coaching Point. Emphasize good ball handling techniques — no rebounds.

DRILL II

2 v. 2 GOALKEEPER & SHOOTER
(IN FRONT OF GOALKEEPER)

Players restricted to own half of field.
2-touch restriction for shooter.
Each team tries to score in the opposing goal using various shots. (Diagram 5-2)
Coaching Point. Emphasize good shot stopping techniques.

DRILL III

2 v. 2 GOALKEEPER & SHOOTER
(BEHIND GOALKEEPER)

Players restricted to own half of the field.
Two touch restriction for shooter.
Each team tries to score in the opposing goal using various types of shots. (Diagram 5-3)
Coaching Point. Emphasize good positional play by the goalkeeper to reduce the area of the goal to the shooter. Fast feet to get into good positions.

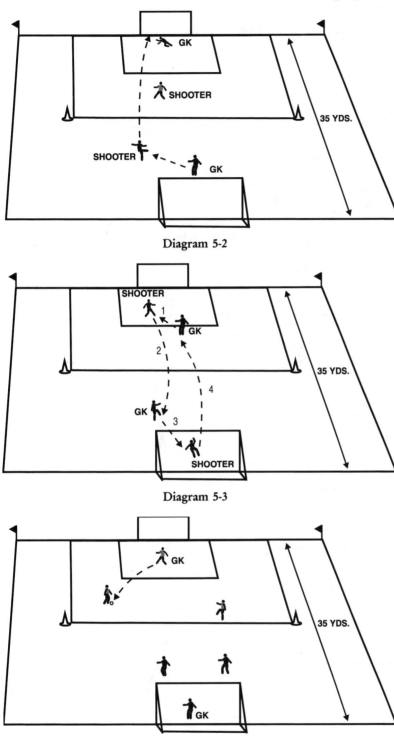

Diagram 5-2

Diagram 5-3

Diagram 5-4

DRILL IV

3 v. 3 GOALKEEPER — 2 SHOOTERS

Each team must shoot from own half of the field.

One touch per player - three touches maximum before shooting. (Diagram 5-4)

Coaching Point. Emphasize good positional adjustment as the ball is passed between the players prior to the shot on goal.

WHAT TO DO WHEN YOU LOSE YOUR KEEPER
Tony DiCicco

If you have a couple of days to prepare:

- Try several different players in goal. One may have better instincts than the others, and become the obvious choice.
- Don't try to develop a keeper in one session. Attempting to teach everything about goalkeeping will only confuse or intimidate the player.
- Look at the player's "style," and concentrate on one or two key points that may help him or her become a more effective keeper.
- Build confidence, by reassuring the player that no one expects him or her to win the game alone.
- Appeal to the rest of the team to improve the other players' game, or raise it to a higher level—especially defensively—to compensate for the lack of keeper experience. (This usually happens!)
- Be positive before and during the game, and at halftime. Make simple suggestions — and not too many of them.

If you must use a non-keeper during the game, without any preparation time at all:

- Pick one of your best athletes, with good anticipation and leadership skills, to fill the spot.
- Reassure the player that he or she can do the job.
- Give one—and only one!—piece of advice, probably pertaining to distribution.
- Build confidence during the match. Every time the player handles the ball successfully, give encouragement.
- Make very simple adjustments. Do not try to overcompensate by moving many people around, or changing strategy drastically.
- Have a positive conversation with the player after the game.

Note: If you think that, for any reason, you may find yourself "keeper-less" during a season, dedicate one practice to goalkeeping. Bring in an expert to train the entire team as keepers. Who knows? A star may be born!

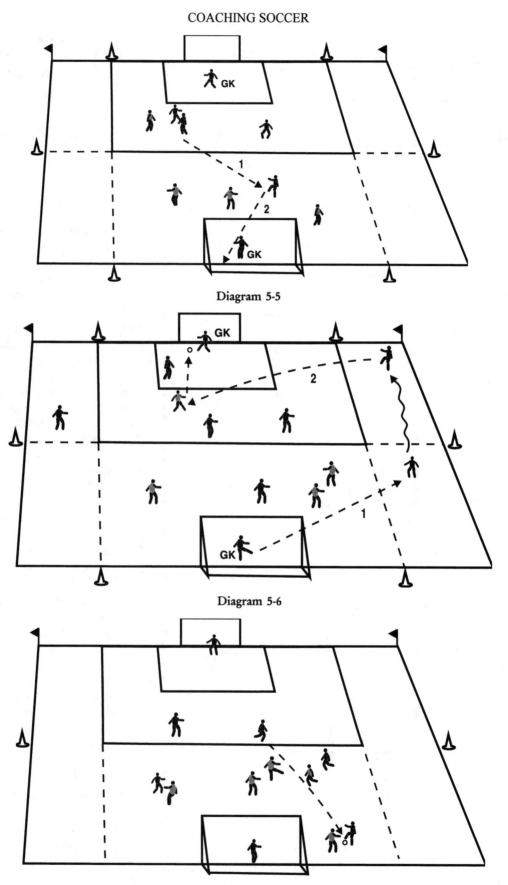

Diagram 5-5

Diagram 5-6

Diagram 5-7

DRILL V

4 v. 1, Goalkeeper & 3 v. 1

One player is allowed to play the ball in the opposing half of the field — one-touch restriction.

The remaining three shooters on the team are still restricted to their own half of the field with one touch allowed per player up to a maximum of three touches prior to the shot on goal. The opposing player is not allowed to challenge for the ball as it is being passed around.

The goalkeeper after saving the shot is allowed to:

• Throw the ball to any player on his team prior to a shot on goal;

• Kick or throw the ball to his teammate in the opposing half of the field to deflect into goal. (Diagram 5-5)

Coaching Point. Emphasize through balls:

• Good decision-making to anticipate as well as shots on goal;

• Good communication with teammates.

DRILL VI

4 v. 1 (+2) Goalkeeper + 3 v. 1 + 2

NEUTRAL PLAYERS

The rules for the previous practice still apply, but now the goalkeeper is also allowed to throw the ball to either of the two neutral players who are allowed to make unopposed runs down the side of the field prior to crossing the ball for the sole attacking player to deflect into goal. (Diagram 5-6)

Coaching Point. Emphasize all the previous coaching points with increased emphasis on the quality of play of the goalkeeper in attack and defense.

DRILL VII

"KING LOUIS" — 6 v. 6, Goalkeepers + 5 v. 5 (Diagram 5-7)

One-touch restriction inside penalty area.
No-touch restriction outside penalty area.
First team to score:

• 5 goals;

• The most goals in 10 minutes wins the game.

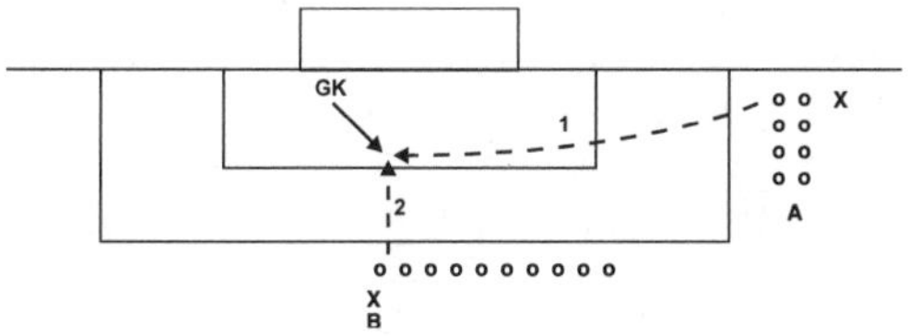

Complex Training Drills For Goalkeepers
Joe Machnik and Frans Hoek

1. **Objective.** Improvement in dealing with crosses and the reaction to a second shot at goal.

The coach (A) serves the ball and the goalkeeper catches, distributes to the side and gets ready for a second shot that is delivered by player (B). (Diagram 5-8)

NOTE: Player B should not lob the ball over the goalkeeper's head. This destroys the purpose of the exercise and discourages the goalkeeper. If the goalkeeper does not catch the ball, but is able to box it and continue its direction, player B should also shoot.

2. **Objective.** Improvement of reaction time, courage, mental and physical toughness.

The coach and a player line up at a distance of approximately six yards from the goal to the outside of each post, each with several soccer balls. Starting from the middle, the goalkeeper adjusts his position to save a direct shot at goal by the coach and then immediately runs across the goal to save a shot from the other player. (Diagram 5-9)

NOTE: 1. The coach and player shoot at full strength to the short corner, then long corner and then to an unannounced corner; 2. The exercise should continue whether or not the goalkeeper saves and how he saves in the emergency situation is unimportant. Remember, of course, that proper technique is the best route to success; 3. The coach and player should give the goalkeeper a tempting amount of time to regain his position for the new situation.

3. **Objective.** Quick movement in the goal in dealing with high and low shots (Diagram 5-10).

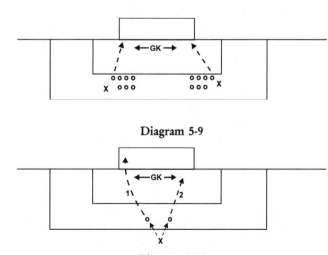

Diagram 5-9

Diagram 5-8

Diagram 5-10

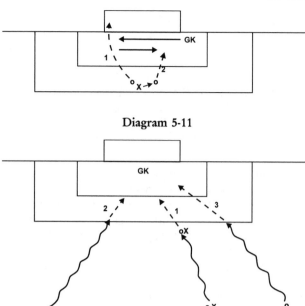

Diagram 5-11

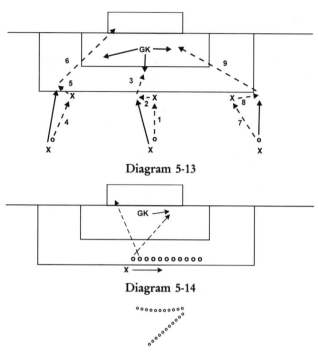

Diagram 5-13

Diagram 5-12

Diagram 5-14

Diagram 5-15

A. The coach plays a high ball to the right of the goalkeeper. The keeper saves and rolls the ball back to the coach who in the meantime has shot a second ball low to the other corner which the keeper moves quickly to save.

B. Change sides - high and low.

NOTE: The goalkeeper must try not to fail ... the coach must demand effort and quickness in the goal.

4. Objective. The improvement of quick movement in the goal and agility. (violent change of direction — Diagram 5-11)

A. The goalkeeper stands to the side of the goal and runs across the goal to catch a ball out of the air served high by the coach; then turns around quickly to save a low ball tossed into the corner. The coach serves from about the penalty spot.

B. Repeat A, but change sides.

5. Objective. Intensive training for the maintenance of reaction time and the improvement of overall conditioning.

A. From the center of the field players dribble towards the goal. Shots are taken from the top of the penalty area. Goalkeeper saves first shot and immediately gets ready for the second. Third player hunts rebounds or can be a third shooting player. (Diagram 5-12)

B. From the center line again, balls are played forward to a target player who squares the ball off and the passing player shoots first time. Goalkeeper saves and gets up quickly for the second and third shots. (Diagram 5-13) As in A above, the tempo is kept fast.

C. Diagram 5-14. The coach plays the first ball into a decided corner. The goalkeeper knows the corner

and the pressure is to catch the ball. The second ball is shot into the opposite corner, and the demand is the same, as the goalkeeper must get up quickly and save at the opposite corner.

D. Same as C above, but the balls are placed in different order and line as in the two examples in Diagram 5-15.

6. Objective. Sharpening and maintaining reflexes.

A. Coach shoots the balls quickly at full strength to the goalkeeper's body or just to the side of the goalkeeper with rapid repetition. The keeper saves with his feet, legs, body, arms, hands, whatever. Technical saving is not important, but the defending is what counts (Diagram 5-16). Exercise can also be done with a screening player interfering with the goalkeeper's vision.

B. Same as 6 above, but with a drop-kick.

7. Objective. Improvement of quick movement in front of the goal.

A. Player A serves a low shot along the ground to the post; the goalkeeper, with footwork, dives to save the ball and quickly returns the ball to shooter A while at the same time a ball is shot by player B low to the opposite post. The keeper continues to save at both posts. (Diagram 5-17)

B. On the signal from the coach, the goalkeeper starts at the center, runs over to touch the goalpost then goes full length across the goal to save a low ball delivered by the coach to the opposite post. The goalkeeper then returns the ball to the coach, resumes his position in the middle of the goal and waits for the next signal. (Diagram 5-18)

C. Same as B above, but the starting position changes to include starting from a sitting position,

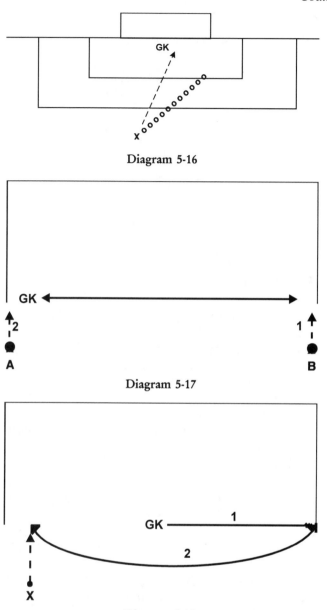

Diagram 5-16

Diagram 5-17

Diagram 5-18

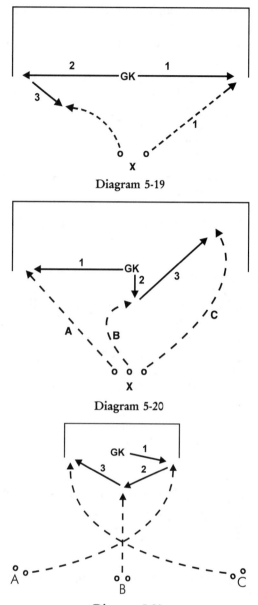

Diagram 5-19

Diagram 5-20

Diagram 5-21

lying on the stomach, lying on the back, push-up position, etc.

D. Same as B above, but the ball is served at varying heights. This way the goalkeeper must fall, dive, fly and catch, tip or box the ball.

E. Same as D above, but change starting positions as in C above.

NOTE: Training must be done to both sides — left and right.

F. The coach serves a ball low to one of two sides. The goalkeeper saves accordingly and plays back to the coach. The goalkeeper immediately gets up, runs to touch the other post and saves a ball thrown high in the air by the coach before it bounces a second time. (Diagram 5-19)

Variation: The goalkeeper, standing at one post, serves a ball as high and straight in the air as possible,

then runs across the goal to save a low ball thrown by the coach. The goalkeeper returns the saved ball to the coach and immediately gets up to catch the first ball which he threw high before it bounces a second time.

G. Same as F, but change starting sides.

H. Diagram 5-20. A ball is played into the corner, then; a ball is served with an arch which the keeper must come out and get before it bounces, then; a lob is put over the goalkeeper's head and he must run back quickly to either tip the ball, box or catch it.

I. Same as H above, but change starting sides.

J. Diagram 5-21. Player A plays the ball high near the far post. Player B shoots a straight shot along the ground down the center of the goal. The goalkeeper runs diagonally forward to save the low shot. Player C plays a high ball to the far post with which the goalkeeper must deal. The keeper then returns to the middle to start over.

K. Repeat J above, but start in the opposite direction.

L. See Diagram 5-22. Ball A is shot into the corner of the goal. Ball B is tossed with an arch to get the goalkeeper out of the goal. He should attempt to catch the ball before it bounces. Ball C is lobbed or bent around the keeper. Ball D is played to the other corner.

The goalkeeper should work hard in these intensive training exercises for a period of 40 seconds of non-stop activity. He should then rest for 40 seconds while the backup goalkeeper is put through the same routine. Each exercise must be worked to both the right and left.

If each goalkeeper participates in ten exercises to the right and ten to the left for a 40 second period in between exercises to set up each new drill, retrieve balls, change keepers, etc., the total time consumed should amount to approximately 40 minutes. This is a terrific training session for both goalkeepers. Many goalkeepers who believe they are fit have difficulty with six to 10 stints. Twenty is the objective, ten to each side.

OVERLOAD TRAINING FOR GOALKEEPERS: DOUBLE GOAL THEORY
Joe Machnik

Changes in the laws of the game which affect the goalkeeper:

• Anti-parry law — parry is possession;

• Anti-handling law — goalkeepers may not handle balls played to them by teammates;

• Strict interpretation of serious foul play — ejection for deliberate hand ball outside of penalty area when used to deny clear goal-scoring chance or other similar violation of Law XII.

These changes place a greater demand on the goalkeeper to be a skillful soccer player in terms of the skills which normally apply to field players in the defensive third of the field.

This greater demand may be met through the application of the overload theory of training for the soccer goalkeeper. There are numerous uses of this theory in other sports, i.e., the baseball swing uses a weighted doughnut, speed is addressed with a parachute device, jumping is increased with plyometrics.

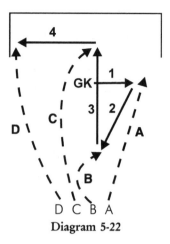

Diagram 5-22

SOCCER GOALKEEPER: DOUBLE-GOAL THEORY (OVERLOAD)

Phase 1
Goalkeeper defends double-goal (48 foot goal line) against long range shooting appropriately placed at a distance relative to the ability of the goalkeeper. Normal distance for senior – 35 yards. Goalkeepers may use any skill to defend the goal.

Phase 2
Similar exercise but now the overload is increased by restricting the goalkeeper to defend without diving.

Phase 3
Similar exercise but now the overload is further increased to restrict the goalkeeper — no diving — no hands — except for balls head height or above.

Phase 4
Remove the overload to include but a single goal (24 feet).

From the same distance, goalkeeper now decides which balls are playable without hands when shots are on target.

For practice, shots off target are deemed to be "pass backs" and may not be played with hands.

In each case goalkeeper distributes according to the laws of the game.

Phase 5
Practice of game situations whereby the goalkeeper gets used to playing without hands at the top of the penalty area and beyond.

• Through passes on ground

• Bouncing

• Pressure of opponent

• Heading requirements

Phase 6 - Game Situation
Diagram 5-23 illustrates a game that enables the goalkeeper to practice under pressure the responses

to the various new demands placed upon the goal-keeper in modern soccer.

- Goalkeeper A may only handle the ball in the goal area;
- Goalkeeper B may only handle the ball in the semi-center circle;
- Coach C positions self at halfway line to call offsides;
- Teams X and 0 play 3 v. 3 or 4 v. 4 as size of field allows, and are instructed to play offside trap at imaginary center line;
- Goalkeepers may not handle pass back from team-mates anywhere (new rule);
- Goalkeepers are encouraged to play "goal sweeper" and participate as much as possible in support of defense and attack;
- Goalkeepers get bonus points for encouraging op-ponents to chip ball over head when such ball is either saved and held or causes opponent's loss of possession — no bonus point for corners.

* This article is based on Dr. Machnik's lecture at the annual Westchester Sports Clinic, January, 1993.

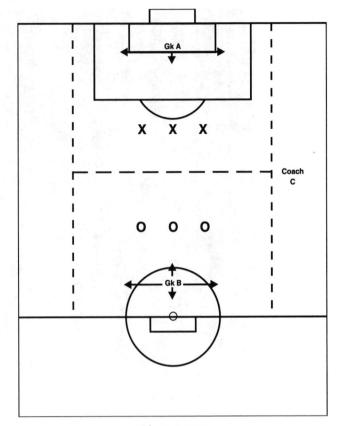

Diagram 5-23

⚽

TECHNICAL TRAINING FOR THE GOALKEEPER

THE BALL STOPS HERE: THE ART OF DIVING
Dan Gaspar & Jeff Sturges

OVERVIEW

The diving save is probably the most spectacular technique that the goalkeeper can use. A great save made by diving can increase the self confidence of the goalkeeper, inspire respect from all the players and most certainly entertain the fans. It is likely that sev-eral saves in any one game will have to be made by diving. Let's explore ways to improve this essential technique.

The technique of diving is necessary to reach balls that cannot be reached by any other method. Some young or inexperienced players might have a fear of diving. If it's done incorrectly, that fear might be jus-tified. If it's done correctly, they will quickly over-come that reservation. Every goalkeeper must become competent at making the diving save. Good goalkeep-ers look forward to the opportunity to demonstrate this unique skill. Great goalkeepers always seem to

have their best action photos taken while they are in mid-flight!

TECHNICAL CONSIDERATIONS

First, pick a soft training area whenever possible to minimize scrapes and bruises caused by mistakes in technique. Soft landing areas include beaches, sand pits or moist grassy areas.

The best way to learn diving is to start in the sit-ting position. This allows the keeper to learn the proper position of the hands and arms. It also allows the teaching of making ground contact while mini-mizing the chance of injury. Proper hand position allows the keeper to use the ball to absorb much of the impact of the dive.

(Remember the old joke, it wasn't the fall that killed the fellow who jumped off the building, it was the sudden stop at the end.)

Hand position should be as follows. When saving a low to medium height ball, the dive-side or lower hand should be the barrier behind the ball. Get the wrist involved as well. If you can curl your fingers around the ball, you eliminate the inherent weakness of the wrist joint. The forearm provides greater strength and offers an additional barrier. Furthermore, should the ball slip away, the fingers will tend to guide the ball toward the chest. The far-side or upper hand should be on top of the ball and should be used to clamp the ball to the ground. When saving a high

Jim Brown (1) of the then Washington Diplomats begins his drive to control a shot by the Cosmos' Peter Baralic.
(Photo by Gere DiSilva)

ball, the keeper may need to use the far side, that is, the non-ball side arm and hand to deflect the ball. The eyes should be "connected" to the ball at all times. By "connected", we mean always looking at the ball. The head should be behind the arms and therefore be protected by them. If it is not possible to make a clean save then deflection technique must be used. It is desirable to get as much of the hand on the ball as possible in order to have enough power to deflect the ball beyond the post.

The keeper should receive multiple services to either side from the sitting position. Gradually the services should be made further away from the keeper so that greater stretch and extension is required. After your keeper has learned the hand and arm positioning and mastered the technique of using the ball to break the fall, we can progress to the kneeling position. Slightly more impact will need to be absorbed so technique will need to be perfected. The final passive starting position will be squatting. This will be similar to some actual diving save situations.

TYPES OF DIVES

Next in the logical teaching progression is the collapse dive. The collapse dive is executed from a standing position. The inside (dive side) leg gradually bends or collapses to lower the body to the ground with a minimum of impact. This technique should be practiced frequently and is always a good warm-up to full speed diving exercises. The Grass Cutter dive is used for saving low shots. Make sure to reduce airspace

between the ground and the outstretched body to provide a long, low barrier that will not allow the ball to slip underneath. Avoid what we sometimes view as windmill action. Here, the keeper projects too high, tries to get low, and generates a lot of air that won't stop anything!

The final and most spectacular dive is the Soaring or Rocket Dive. This dive is used when it is necessary to save a high ball or deflect the ball over the cross bar. Height is generated from the explosive power generated by uncoiling of the springing legs and the momentum of the arms and hands reaching skyward. This full power dive may be preceded by a single sideways shuffle step or, if greater range is required, by a cross-over step. This shuffle step will add additional width because of the distance covered by the shuffle itself and the momentum it generates. The cross-over step, followed by as many shuffle steps as necessary, can cover even greater distance and generate more power. The shuffle step is preferred if the ball is traveling at a slow rate or if there is little distance which must be covered. The cross-over step must be used when it is necessary to quickly move beyond one's body length.

There are two common errors that are made by many goalkeepers that significantly diminish the effectiveness of their dives even though their technical form may be correct. Number one, some goalkeepers dive backward. Number two, some keepers always dive parallel to the goal line. This diminishes the maximum effective width that the keeper can cover. The dive should be made perpendicular to the flight of the ball to achieve the greatest coverage width. This usually means going slightly forward. To avoid going backward or parallel to the line, the keeper must step into the dive. The body should be driven to the side and forward by the inside (dive side) leg. If diving right, the right leg steps slightly forward and to the right and then is planted to become the foundation of the extending leg that drives the body into the air. The head, shoulders, arms and hands are projected towards the ball with an attacking attitude. Similarly, when diving left, the left foot becomes the springboard and that leg is extended to create the diving power.

As we stated, in order to get power and width, the inside (dive-side) foot is driven into the ground and that leg is explosively extended. In order to get height and help insure that the ball and arms land the first, the outside knee is driven up and over the inside shoulder. When coming back down, the hips are extended outward and the toes are pointed toward the sky. The objective when landing is to touch down in the following order: ball, arms, shoulders, hips, and legs. You always want to land on your side, not on your stomach or your back. Often the shoulders will land at almost the same time as the ball and the arms. Remember the ball doesn't get tired or injured. It won't break and it never has to go to the hospital. Effectively use the ball to make sure that you don't have to go either. Use the ball to break the fall. We only have one body and we have to protect it.

After you land there are three considerations. The first is protecting the ball. The second is protecting your body. The third is reloading if the save was not completed and the ball is still in play. We call the act of completing the save with a caught ball "terminating the save."

- **Protecting the Ball.** After the keeper lands the ball should be protected by having the forearms, as well as the hands, behind and on top of the ball. As soon as sufficient ball control is obtained the ball should be brought in to the chest area with your arms wrapped around it. The top knee should be drawn up to a modified fetal position to protect the ball as well as the keeper.

- **Protecting Yourself.** The arm that is now on top of the ball should also be used to protect the face. This happens naturally when the arm is extended for the dive. The outside, now top, leg should remain raised to protect the mid section and lower body area as stated above. This leg position is similar to the position of the raised leg when jumping to make a high save.

- **Reloading.** Finally you must regain your feet quickly and assume the ready position if the save is

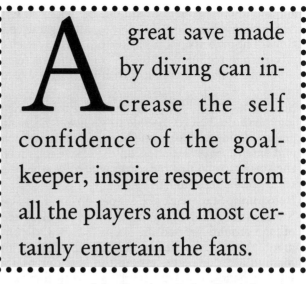

A great save made by diving can increase the self confidence of the goalkeeper, inspire respect from all the players and most certainly entertain the fans.

not terminated the first time. Reloading is best done without using the hands to push off from the ground. Reloading in this manner leaves the hands free in front of the body to make the follow-up save. For example, after diving to your right you are lying out-stretched along the ground on the right side of your body. You must immediately propel your head, arms and shoulders using your counter-balanced leg to explosively move to the left to obtain three points of contact for reloading to the dynamic ready position. In this case these three points of contact include the right knee, the right instep, and the sole of the left foot. Once these three points are in contact with the ground, push explosively! If the save cannot be made on the first ball contact, then reloading speed becomes very important.

- **Rollout.** To reduce the impact of some very high dives and assume a dynamic distribution position quickly, the roll-out is very effective. The roll-out is initiated by planting the ball as usual and then executing a shoulder roll over the ball. This allows the diving momentum to be converted into energy that helps the keeper regain his/her feet immediately. The keeper can now surprise the opposition by a quick distribution to initiate the attack.

- **The Diving Decision.** The decision as to when to use the dive is very simple. You should use the dive to make a save when there is no other way to reach the ball. Why some reluctance to diving? If you stay on your feet you can change directions. Once you leave your feet it's a total commitment. You cannot change your direction in mid-dive. You must make the correct decision the first time. You should use the Grass Cutter Save for low balls and the Soaring or Rocket Save when a high ball requires a high trajectory.

TRAINING METHODS

Begin with the technical progression that was described earlier which includes; sitting, kneeling, squatting, and standing. Service should be a kicked ball whenever possible to most closely simulate game conditions. The objective of the initial phase is to develop confidence in technique through gradual increases in tempo and intensity coupled with successful execution.

- **Service right and left— Easy Dive.** From an easy jog, serve the ball to the side to yourself and make an easy diving save after one bounce. Work on form and extension. A variation on the above is to have the keeper jog behind the server who tosses the balls to the side at random.

- **Reloading.** Start with the keeper on his/her side. Server kneels and holds the ball two to three feet off the ground beyond the keeper's feet. On command the keeper reloads and attacks the ball by making a diving save, taking the ball out of the server's hands. Intensity can be added to this exercise by increasing the height of the ball or by having the server drop the ball at the appropriate moment so that the keeper must make the save before the ball hits the ground.

- **Service right and left — Full Dive.** Random Service. As confidence increases and form improves, increase tempo, ball pace, and intensity.

- **Double Fly.** Keepers line up next to one post. Service is made to mid-goal for a diving save. Keeper reloads and is given a service to the far post.

- **Post to Post.** Start keepers at mid-goal. Keeper shuffles right or left, touches a post, then service is made requiring a dive off the goal line. Exercise is repeated emphasizing lateral movement, reversal of direction, diving form, and rapid reloading.

- **Classic Extension Practice.** One way to increase extension is to practice diving over obstacles. Perhaps the best obstacle is a rope strung to one of the goal posts. It can easily be raised as proficiency increases and if technique is off during the learning stages, it would hurt less than hard obstacles. The receiving keeper does a forward roll over the obstacle, the keeper reloads, and the server serves a ball that requires the keeper to dive back over the obstacle.

- **Spin Dive.** Another exercise to practice extension starts with the keeper at mid-goal on the goal line, facing into the goal, back to the server. The goalkeeper points in the direction that he/she wants the service. If the keeper points right, he/she pivots on the right foot and opens up toward the server with the left leg so that the dive is made at an angle from the goal line.

- **Gaspar's Pit.** Create the pit by making an eight yard by eight yard square with four balls. This may be adjusted slightly smaller for junior players. Number each ball. This very popular exercise starts with the keeper in the middle of the pit and the coach anywhere outside the pit with additional balls The objective in this exercise is to gain practice diving for low balls, reloading, and diving for medium or high balls. The exercise starts when the coach calls out a numbered ball. The keeper must immediately shuffle toward it and make a Grass Cutter Dive to capture the ball. The keeper leaves the ball, reloads, and dives to save a medium or high ball delivered for full extension anywhere in the pit by the server.

- **Airborne.** This next exercise is designed to practice extension, facilitate movement through other players, and add inches to the dive. This will help demonstrate to keepers that they can dive farther than they may have imagined. The keeper lines up behind and slightly to the side of a stationary player. In order to make the save, the keeper must step in front of the stationary player. Once again we reinforce the keeper to step into the save. Now we add challenge by limiting the keeper's use of hands. The save must be made with the head, chest, or other part of the body. This requires some courage, but after just a few times the keepers are always amazed at how much ground that they can cover. Once they've learned to provide coverage without the hands, extend the range by allowing hands and extending the service.

- **Two Goal Save.** Place two cones on the six yard line immediately opposite the two goal posts. Use two servers. Position the first server along the goal line just outside the penalty area on the right side. Position the second server inside the crescent at the top of the eighteen. Start the keeper on the right post facing server one. Server one directs a low ball toward the cone. The keeper makes a Grass Cutter Save and immediately reloads. Server two then sends a flighted ball toward the upper corner of the far post. The keeper must then use a cross-over run and a high ball technique to terminate the save. This sequence is repeated several times. Then the mirror image situation is set up on the left side of the goal and repeated.

- **Power Fly.** The Power Fly exercise starts with an imaginary cross from the wing. The goalkeeper starts on the goalpost nearest to the imaginary cross. The server is positioned near the penalty spot. The keeper starts the exercise by drifting toward the opposite post to cover the cross. The server "redirects" the ball toward the far post. Immediately after the recovery a second serve is made to the near post. After several repetitions from one post, the exercise is repeated starting from the other post.

- **Rapid Fly.** Six balls are placed on the eighteen yard line, three in front of each post. Two servers position themselves behind the two groups of three balls. The six balls are kicked in fairly rapid succession in the following manner: The keeper starts on the right post. Server one kicks a low Grass Cutter to the opposite post.

Server two kicks low back to the starting post. The next two balls are served in the same manner at medium height and the final two are served high flighted in the same sequence.

- **Roll-Out.** Goalkeeper squats holding the ball on the ground to the right of the shoulder. The goalkeeper executes a shoulder roll to the right and comes up into a distribution stance ready to throw the ball. Repeat to the left. Increase intensity and difficult by initiating from a standing position. Then initiate after a shuffle step, after a cross-over step, after a shuffle and a cross-over step.

CONCLUSION

Soaring to make the diving save can be spectacular and effective. However, fly only when necessary. Unnecessary flying is high risk keeping. Change of direction is impossible. Injuries are increased and so are rebounds. Get the goalkeeper as much experience in the net as possible saving kicked balls. Another goalkeeper is often the ideal training partner, but a field player will do too. Good luck. We hope that we have helped you or your keeper soar to new heights.

BOXING TECHNIQUE FOR GOALKEEPERS
Bob Barry

Many of today's coaches are presently teaching their goalkeepers the proper or correct fundamentals of catching all types of balls shot at goal. This must also be supplemented with teaching the keeper to box or punch balls. It is incorrect to presume that a goalkeeper will automatically box a ball properly if he cannot catch it! It is a part of the keeper's game that is going to have to be dealt with in practice with and without opposition in order to be able to use it in a game situation. Not all balls can be caught and every goalkeeper must know how to deal with each shot. The basic rule is if he cannot catch the ball he should box or deflect it.

Why box? There are three basic reasons why a keeper should box shots on goal. Weather conditions might be such that the ball is wet and too slippery to catch or the sun makes it difficult to see the ball clearly. The type of shot will also have a bearing on whether the keeper catches or boxes. Is the shot too hard or taken too close to goal for the keeper to catch it? Is there too much spin on the shot? These are questions which must be answered by each keeper because each has a different skill level. Some have the ability to catch well hit balls because of their strength and ability to relax and take the pace off the shot. The third reason to box the ball is because of the number of players in the area in front of the goal, better known as traffic in the box. Often it is physically impossible

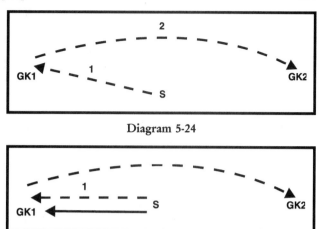

Diagram 5-24

Diagram 5-25

to reach the ball in a crowded goalmouth in order to safely catch it.

Where does the GK box the ball? All shots should be boxed high, far, wide and with accuracy.

How does the GK box? Balls should be boxed with two hands to change the direction and with one hand to carry the ball in the same direction.

What is the technique of boxing? Make a tight fist with each hand and bring them together, keeping the wrists straight. You will see a flat surface formed by the two hands. This is where the ball is to be boxed. The GK should strike through the bottom half of the ball with a short but explosive motion which begins at the chest. It should also be remembered that the arms should be bent so that when the fist(s) are thrust toward the ball the effect is to develop power as the arms are straightened.

Remember to box forward when moving forward and to box backward when moving backwards.

DRILLS

1. Warmup

(a) - Keep ball in the air using two-hand boxing; (b) - Same as (a) but alternate each hand; (c) - in pairs, box to each other using two hands; (d) - Same as (c) using two touch boxing with two hands.

2. Sitting

(e) - Coach serves ball to GK who boxes it back to him, concentrate on technique and timing; (f) - Alternate boxing with left, right, then two hands in same drill as (e).

3. Kneeling

(f) - In groups of three strike ball using upper body for power and distance. Keep eyes on ball at all times. GK should fall forward to ground after making contact; (g) - Same as (f). Server follows ball to give pressure to GK. (Diagrams 5-24 & 5-25)

4. Standing

(h) - Box air ball for distance and accuracy, making contact at highest point possible. Alternate taking off

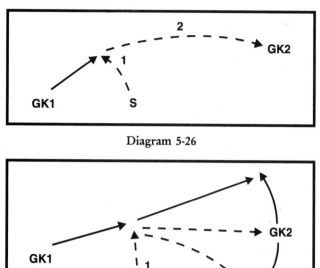

Diagram 5-26

Diagram 5-27

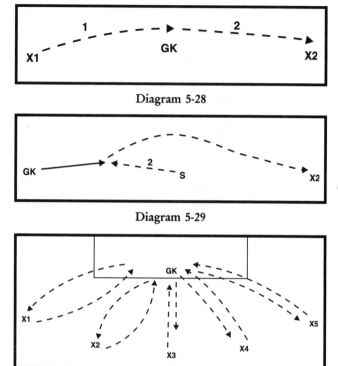

Diagram 5-28

Diagram 5-29

Diagram 5-30

with left and right leg; (i) - Same as (h) but target player moves to different positions. (Diagrams 5-26 & 5-27)

5. One hand boxing (keep distance)
(j) - In groups of three GK boxes from one server to the other using the nearest hand to the ball. Start from kneeling position; (k) - Same as (j) but from the standing position. (Diagram 5-28)

6. Forward boxing
Many times the keeper is going to have to dive forward to reach balls that are going to drop in front of him in the penalty box. It is important for the GK to practice this dive to eliminate any fear of injury and to concentrate on his technique of boxing; (l) - GK dives forward to box ball to X2. (Diagram 5-29)

7. Goal Mouth Play
(m) - Same as (l) but GK dives over obstacle or teammate; (n) - Go to goal and practice all types of services from around the penalty box. The services must be good and the ball will determine the type of box to use; (o) - Same as (n) but to add opposition in front of the goal. (Diagram 5-30)

SAVING THE BREAKAWAY
Tony DiCicco and Dan Gaspar

DEFINITION
A keeper is involved in a breakaway situation when an offensive player has released himself from the op-

posing players and the goalkeeper is the last line of defense. In essence, a 1 v. 1 situation is created. The importance of accomplishing the save successfully will create a positive impact on the team and at times even possibly change the flow or rhythm of the team's play.

COACHING CONSIDERATION

1. Advise your goalkeeper, a day in advance, prior to training for breakaways. This is necessary so that the goalkeepers may prepare themselves by wearing protective gear and will have time to establish a proper mental attitude.

2. During training sessions, attempt to form a correlation between the technical, physical and tactical components that this save will require. Observe and evaluate these components and then design your training program based on your goalkeeper's needs.

3. Motivation is a must. This "big time" save requires confidence and courage and you can help your goalkeeper with words of encouragement so that he/she may find the energy and desire to achieve success on this crucial save.

4. Other than the strikers avoiding contact while going for a goal, the drills should be realistic.

5. As a result of making the save, the goalkeepers, through their excitement, will in many cases demonstrate poor decision-making with regards to distribution. A successful save is not only determined by keeping the ball out of the net, but equally important is the ability to maintain possession. Be aware of your goalkeeper's emotional makeup. The

The keeper (#1) must have exquisite timing. Here the Norwegian keeper attempts to thwart U.S. National Team player Mia Hamm (#9). (photo by Brett Whitesell)

keeper must exhibit poise.

6. For the goalkeeper to get a good picture, let him handle the breakaway as a field player.

GOALKEEPER ALTERNATIVES

The goalkeeper has three basic options in regard to the save:

- Make the save before the shot is taken;
- Make the save as the shot is taken;
- Make the save after the shot is taken.

Your goalkeeper should be made aware of the following considerations:

1. When the ball is exposed (naked) and the goal keeper can win the ball before the oncoming opposing player, that's the signal to attack quickly.
2. Determine the distance and pace of the striker and the ball.
3. Evaluate the angle of approach and reduce it by good positioning.
4. Maintain dynamic stability by proper distribution of weight. The goalkeeper should not sell himself or over-commit. Try to force the attacker to make a decision.
5. Present the largest barrier. Make the body appear as large as possible.
6. Win time. By delaying the attacker, the defenders will have a chance to recover and apply pressure.
7. Be aware of surroundings before the save and after the save.
8. He must understand the difference between handling breakaways when the attacker is marked or unmarked.

9. Examine the perception and execution of action towards the save.

TRAINING SESSION PROGRESSION

We attempt to utilize the ball in all our activities. Our warmups consist of various exercises, ball gymnastics and strength exercises. We stress maximum flexibility, agility and hand, eye and ball coordination, as well as proper execution of technique. When the keepers are physically, as well as mentally, prepared we now increase the pressure in all aspects of this demanding position, including the decision-making process.

1. Within a restricted area, an unlimited number of goalkeepers perform various activities at a controlled and comfortable pace. Examples: (a) roll the ball and get behind (b) bouncing the ball while moving (c) goalkeepers interchange various services while moving (d) designate different numbers to represent various exercises and, on command, goalkeepers perform the exercises.
2. The ball is placed with two hands behind the head, while lying down on back. Lift legs behind the ball. Using your feet, attempt to move your legs as far right and left as possible. Try to maintain balance.
3. While sitting, lift legs and pass the ball from hand to hand between the legs, forming a figure eight around the knees. Feet should not touch the ground.
4. Standing with legs spread at shoulder width apart and with ball in hands, bend down and roll ball between legs as far as possible and hold position for ten seconds. Proceed to roll the ball forward

into a push-up position. Perform push-ups and repeat again.

5. Lie down on side and strike the ball with instep, sit-up and repeat to opposite side. Strike the ball harder each time. Concentrate on hand positioning.

6. Hold the ball in one hand and turn to full extension while standing. Drop the ball and quickly turn to the opposite direction for the smoother save. Eyes must follow the ball as much as possible. When sight of ball is lost, find it quickly.

7. Lie down on stomach. Rock back and forth while rolling the ball underneath the chest area. Arch back and establish a rhythm.

8. Have two goalkeepers both moving and facing each other while touching the ball back and forth between their hands. Select a leader, who then pushes the ball to one direction, the other goalkeeper responds by pushing his ball in the opposite direction. Both keepers save the other's ball as quickly or early as possible, whichever is faster!

9. Use one ball, two goalkeepers and one field player. The keeper is in possession of the ball and is followed by the partner. The keeper in possession pushes the ball. This is the signal for both field player and keeper to attack the ball. There is only a token challenge by the field player initially.

10. Maze drill. Stagger about 8-10 balls in various positions and distances. One keeper begins by saving each stationary ball randomly. Same drill but now add another keeper. In third drill include field players to make contact with the ball as soon as the keeper saves. The purpose of this drill is to complicate the environment.

11. Use one goalkeeper and one field player. The keeper lies down on one side. From this position he strikes the ball to the field player. The keeper gets up quickly and saves off the feet of the field player.

12. Use two regulation goals, with one keeper in each goal approximately 18-20 yards apart. They both serve and challenge each other.

13. Use two goalkeepers and two field players. One keeper is in the push-up position and the other keeper will serve the ball through the hands and feet of the keeper in the push-up position. As soon as the ball passes under the keeper he moves quickly to make the save. Goalkeepers alternate roles each time. At the end of every service, there will be a field player attempting to shoot the ball past the keeper into a regulation goal.

14. Use one keeper, one server, one field player and two target players. Keeper is in a regulation goal. The server is behind the field player and sends various services towards the goal. Both the attacker and the goalkeeper react to the serve. The attacker attempts to score while the keeper attempts to save. Should the keeper make the save,

he now distributes to target players. This drill should be expanded upon by including a defender and by marking up the target players.

15. Field players dribble and interchange positions within a restricted area. Each player is assigned a number. When the number is called out by the coach, the respective player bursts with speed towards the goal. The keeper concentrates to make the save. Introduce defenders and targets and use them creatively. These types of drills will help the coach and the keeper sort things out tactically as well as technically.

16. Use two regulation goals approximately 20-30 yards apart. There is a keeper in each goal. Begin with a 2 v. 2 situation and increase the number of field players accordingly. The keeper may leave his goal to support the attack. The team now is involved in the training of the goalkeepers. The keeper now feels part of the team, rather than constantly being trained on an isolated basis.

Our purpose in these drills is to provide the basis for the evaluation of the keeper, thus improving his ability. Not all of these drills should be part of one training session. We suggest you use a combination of these drills. Goalkeepers' skills and decisions should not only be evaluated during training sessions, but also tested during match-related situations. The match itself is the best indicator of the goalkeeper's ability. Being capable of successfully performing under match conditions is the goalkeeper's and coach's reward.

THE GOALKEEPER: "HEEL OF THE HAND" SAVE
by Tony DiCicco

Look at your hand! If you're a goalkeeper or a goalkeeper coach you must identify a part of the hand important to success. It is the heel of the hand and it is a tremendous tool for the goalkeeper when used as a saving surface.

What makes the heel of the hand important? The heel of the hand offers a hard surface for shot deflection. This is important because on strong, powerful shots, finger tips have little effect on altering the path of the ball. Soft areas of the hand will not sufficiently clear the shot, but will probably allow a rebound that can be easily converted to a goal if an opponent is available to touch it into the net.

The heel of the hand will have the same effect on a shot as the fist does on a crossed ball. It will safely clear the shot.

Note the wrist position as the goalkeeper deflects the ball wide of the post. (photo courtesy of Tony DiCicco)

To execute this skill correctly, the wrist joint must be fully extended. Because of this extended position, the wrist is rigid, which adds to the positive clearing effect from the heel of the hand saves. The fully extended wrist also serves another important function. When a hard shot is saved with the heel (wrist extended), the ball is often given spin. This spin causes the ball to move away from the center of the goal after it lands, often safely over the goal line for a corner kick.

WHY NOT USE THE FIST?

Some very successful goalkeepers do save shots by fisting. However, I believe and teach to deflect hard shots with the heel of the hand. Clear crossed balls that cannot be caught with your fist or fists. The reason is simple. Refer once again to photo #1. Visualize this: a goalkeeper attempts to save a hard shot with the heel of the hand. If the goalkeeper's perception is off, there is a margin of error. The save still could be made with the rest of the hand. Yes, the rebound may be dangerous, but it is still out of the net. With the fist, especially when diving to save, there is no margin of error. If the shot grazes the fist it will end up in the back of the net. If your goalkeeper is successful and comfortable saving shots with the fist, don't insist on change. Otherwise save shots with the heel; clear crosses with the fists.

WHEN DOES A GOALKEEPER USE THE HEEL OF THE HAND?

On a strong shot low to the goalkeeper's left, the goalkeeper may not have time to get both hands in position. The left hand extends out to parry the ball away by using the heel portion of the hand. There is no swinging of the arm from posterior to anterior to meet the ball. Just extend the arm straight out to meet the ball. The strength of the shot and the rigidness of the heel will clear the shot.

Also saving with one hand instead of two hands gives the goalkeeper added inches of reach to get to the ball.

The heel save is also used on a high, hard shot. If the shot is also to the goalkeeper's left, requiring a diving save, the goalkeeper uses the heel of the top hand or, in this case, the right hand. This save is world class because getting and saving shots towards the upper corners requires a special athlete. Our recommendation is to spend much more time working on the heel save to the lower corners. Once the goalkeeper can protect those low corners effectively, then start to train in the upper corners.

TEACHING PROGRESSION

The following is a progression of exercises to teach heel of the hand shot saving:

1. Using the coach or another goalkeeper as a server, a goalkeeper on his or her knees (three yards from line) and another goalkeeper outside the post, serve hard rolling balls to the goalkeeper's right. When the goalkeeper falls to save, they should require full arm extension. As the ball is deflected with the heel, the ball will deflect wide of the goal and as it lands the ball's spin will keep it wide or take it over the goal line for a corner. Work both sides.

2. Now the goalkeeper stands and works one side at a time. Again use a firmly served ball. Coaching point: Teach your keeper to dive slightly forward in the saving motion.

3. Once the goalkeeper is technically sound, bring in some field players. The field players shoot moving balls, aiming for the lower corner. The goalkeeper must make proper decisions. When to catch, when to touch and when to heel shots must be decided.

Repetition will condition the goalkeeper to react correctly to shots that require heel of the hand saves. Train properly and add this potential save to your goalkeeper's arsenal.

●

TACTICAL CONSIDERATIONS FOR THE GOALKEEPER

DOMINATE THE BOX!
Tony DiCicco and Dan Gaspar

What is "controlling the box"?

Picture this: The through pass beats the defense. The speedy winger is running onto the ball; a shot is imminent. Then, out of nowhere, the goalkeeper courageously slides through and intercepts the ball just as the winger is reaching it.

Statistically, is it a save? No. Was a shot even taken? No. But was it possibly a game-saving play? You bet!

Or: A winger dribbles past his defender and curls a dangerous cross into the penalty area. The center forward approaches the ball to head it into the goal. The goalkeeper steps in and, using the privilege of the position, snatches the ball just before the forward can get his head to it. No save! No shot! Is this keeper dominating the box? You bet!

That is "dominating the box."

The "box" refers to the penalty area (18 yds. x 44 yds.). "Dominating the box" is an asset possessed by most top goalkeepers which enables them to intercept or extinguish a potentially dangerous situation before it materializes. Top goalkeepers who do not dominate the penalty area have the ability to dominate the smaller box, the goal box.

A goalkeeper who dominates the box should see fewer shots and, hopefully, allow fewer goals than one who does not rule the box.

However, other ramifications exist too. Teams playing against a box-dominating goalie will have a tendency to cross less, or cross to the top of the area.

Wisconsin goalkeeper Jon Belskis demonstrates dominance of the box versus Duke in the 1995 NCAA Division I championship match. (photo by Brett Whitesell)

They'll overlook the through pass, and push the ball wide instead. They'll shoot from further out and, when they finally penetrate into the penalty area, will always feel the pressure of the dominating keeper.

All this helps the goaltender's defenders, too. The box belongs to the keeper and opponents will sense this and, consciously or unconsciously, will alter their game.

As a goalkeeper, you should strive to become more dominant in the area. As a coach, you want to assist your goalkeeper in developing this ability. But how?

First, does the goalkeeper have the qualities necessary to dominate the box? The dominating goalkeeper must be courageous, often diving at the feet of onrushing opponents. This dive has to be technically sound, creating the "body barrier" for safety as well as success.

The keeper must possess two types of quickness: perceptual quickness (to see the play developing and be able to anticipate the pass), and reaction quickness (so that once the move is initiated it is done with a burst of speed and conviction that can neutralize a seemingly dangerous situation).

Certainly, the goalkeeper has to be able to make correct decisions, not just "decisions." The keeper who goes for the through pass, but misjudges the speed of the winger and gets to the ball second, will suffer many goals.

The dominant keeper sees the situation an instant before it actually takes shape, and has initiated movement before the ball is delivered. This is anticipation. It comes from inborn qualities, to some degree, but also from a goalkeeper learning how to read the game, to understand the alternatives an opponent with the ball has, and then to determine which reaction he will choose.

What can the goalkeeper and coach do to help the goalkeeper reach this ability to dominate the box? Match condition challenges are paramount.

In practice, offer 4 v. 4 drills, with two goalkeepers in full goals over a 40-yard field. Let the goalkeeper see crossed balls daily - sometimes with no pressure, sometimes with congestion and challenges.

Train the goalkeeper technically. Have him create a "body barrier" when going for the ball in different situations (where he or she may get to the ball slightly ahead, at the same time, or even slightly after the opponent).

With this type of training, the body reacts well under the pressure of a match, just as it was conditioned to react in practice.

All this training, over the course of a season, develops the confidence a keeper needs to "dominate the box."

THE GOALKEEPER ON ATTACK
Jim DiNoble

The ability of the goalkeeper to initiate and control the attack from the defensive third of the field can and will determine the outcome of a team's offense during a game and throughout a season.

The attacking goalkeeper should aggressively determine the how, where and when of the distribution while always considering their own abilities and the potential of the team and its players.

The basic requirement of the goalkeeper is one of overall fitness and the capability to initiate the attack bears no exception. The combination of flexibility and strength will determine the effectiveness to execute the technical requirements. The major muscle groups of the legs, lower and upper back, stomach,

chest, shoulders and arms, and the smaller muscle groups of the feet, ankles, hand and wrists must all be well conditioned to meet the demands for maximizing the range of motion necessary and the amount of power needed to achieve the desired results in the goalkeeper's distribution.

The variety of skills for the attacking goalkeeper include punting, dropkick, goalkick, throwing (bowling, overhand, sling), dribbling and heading. Each of these skills have their own individual technical aspects but all depend on proper footwork, leg and arm speed, contact on the ball and the timing necessary to produce the accuracy and distance required to start the team's attack.

These technical skills all must be developed over time and through repeated practices to gain a certain level of proficiency that when introduced into a match situation will produce the results expected.

The technical abilities of the goalkeeper on attack will be best measured on how they are utilized during the pressure of a match. Given the abilities to distribute effectively the goalkeeper must base his/her decisions on numerous factors, many of which are occurring simultaneously.

The goalkeeper that will enhance the team's capability to attack from the defensive third of the field must look for, identify and react to many situations.

KEY CONSIDERATIONS FOR DISTRIBUTION

1. Field Conditions

Every soccer field is different and each make their own demands on play.

• The length and width will determine how much time and space is available.

• Smooth v. bumpy field will give an indication how well the field players will be able to control the ball.

• Hard vs. soft field will determine the degree of speed and bounce of the ball.

• Wet v. dry field will also indicate speed, bounce and ability of field players to control the ball.

2. Weather Conditions

Soccer is played during all types of weather conditions. Rain and snow, heat and cold, humidity and dry air, high altitude and sea level, windy and calm conditions and everything in between. These conditions on game day must be evaluated as to what effect they will have on distribution.

3. Direct v. indirect style of play

Each team should have a particular idea on how they will develop their style of play. This style is generally based on the total player ability considering such factors as their physical, technical and tactical competence.

The coach, goalkeeper and the field players should develop an attacking strategy based on the strengths and weaknesses of the team. Direct, indirect or a combination of both styles should be identified so there is a general understanding of how the goalkeeper will initiate the attack.

4. Danger v. safe areas of the field

The goalkeeper must continually weigh the risk and safety factors of the distribution in relationship to the areas on the soccer field. Many factors can be considered but generally distribution should be made to the outside of the field given the time and space available. Distribution in the middle of the defensive half is a high risk and quickly can turn from a seemingly safe situation into a goal for the other team. Long distributions into the offensive half can be considered safe and effective.

5. Controlling the tempo and pace of the game

- Score of the game. When a team is ahead in a game the distribution should be deliberate without any unnecessary risks that may result in a loss of possession, while maintaining a confident and not a tentative attitude. When a team is down in the score the distribution should be made quickly to utilize the time left in the game but not rushed to be made unaware of the risks involved.
- Time in game. When a team is ahead in the score the distribution again should be deliberate and avoid risks If down in the score, the time should be used effectively, the less time the more the urgency for immediate distribution.
- Transition. Depending on how quickly or slowly the opponent adjusts to a loss of possession and how they make the transition to defense will indicate at what speed you will play at to take advantage of the situation.
- Changing the speed. Changing the speed of play from slow to quick in distribution can be used to unsettle the defense and force them to make adjustments.

6. Key target players

The goalkeeper should have primary players (defenders, midfielders and forwards) that he/she looks to for immediate distribution. These players should basically want to have the ball distributed to them and have the ability to receive, turn and go forward with the ball.

7. Balls that field players can receive.

The goalkeeper must give the field player the best chance to receive the ball which will provide the most time and space to continue the attack.

- Play to feet - balls should be played that can be controlled easily and quickly. Balls played above the waist are more difficult to control.
- Play to the front of the player — the distribution should be played to the front and hit the player in stride as opposed to being played behind.
- Away from the defender — balls should be played to the opposite side from where the defender is able to close down the receiving player.

8. Pace of the ball.

The speed of the ball should be as such that the field player can effectively control the ball and at the same time eliminate the defender and put him behind or out of the play.

If the ball is played too strong it can be difficult to control and if it is played too softly it can be intercepted by the defender.

9. Reading the game.

The critical part of distribution is quickly identifying situations and taking advantage of them. The goalkeeper must look for numerical superiority and make the correct distribution and maximize the opportunity. Conversely the goalkeeper must read numbers down situations and not make unnecessary risky distributions.

The ability to make quick decisions in the defense transition and analyze the numbers up and the numbers down situations can quickly result in a goal.

10. Changing the point of attack.

Generally speaking when the goalkeeper receives the ball from one side he/she should change the attack to the other side to take advantage of the defense's transition in their attempt to pressure the ball and provide cover and balance.

The goalkeeper should identify numbers up and numbers down (as mentioned above) situations across the field and distribute the ball to the point that will cause the defense to make the most adjustments.

11. Identifying weaknesses.

Throughout the match the goalkeeper should be looking for individuals or areas on the field that may be exposed. Players who are slow, tired, deficient, or areas on the field in and behind the defense that are being left unprotected. These players and situations will continually change during a match and should be taken advantage of when the opportunity presents itself.

12. Communication.

Communication in distribution as in all aspects of soccer is essential. When a goalkeeper is under pressure and/or in heavy traffic a call directly from a player who wants the ball or a player directing a distribution to another player or area is very important.

The goalkeeper must after a distribution, give a command to help the field player continue the attack i.e., "turn, hold, time, line," etc.

Also, a goalkeeper should develop the ability to initiate eye contact with the player he is distributing to, so to give quicker distribution and deception.

In conclusion, the attacking goalkeeper must be opportunistic and be continually looking to seek an advantage. In order to create attacking situations from

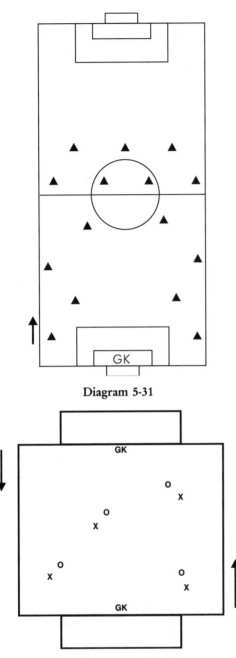

Diagram 5-31

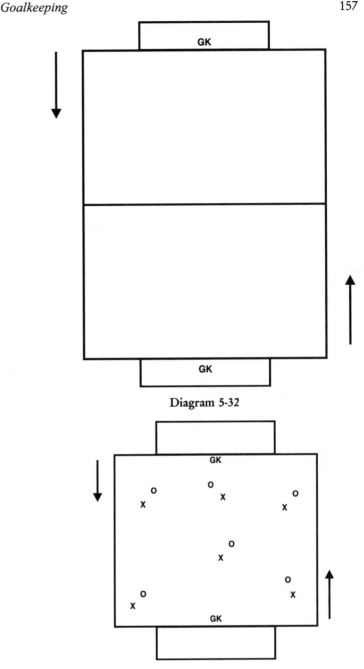

Diagram 5-32

Diagram 5-33

Diagram 5-34

the defensive third, the goalkeeper must be aggressive and confident to react to the situations as they present themselves and then have the skill and courage to make them happen.

The goalkeepers who have the ability to develop the attack become a tremendous asset to a team. It is when all is equal that the goalkeeper on the attack can be the difference!

TRAINING SITUATIONS

1. Hitting Targets

Place targets throughout the field using markers, cones, etc. and try to hit the targets with various throws and kicks. (Diagram 5-31)

2. Goalie Wars

Field. Field is 25 x 25 yards, two full-sized goals.

Objective. Goalkeepers try to score on each other with throws and kicks. Throws and kicks are taken from goal line or where save is made. (Diagram 5-32)

3. 4 v. 4 w/Goalkeepers

Field. 40 x 50 yd.

Purpose. Reading the game, quick, short and medium distributions. (Diagram 5-33)

4. 6 v. 6 w/Goalkeepers

Field. 70 x 70 yards

Purpose. Read the game numbers up, numbers down, short, medium and long distributions. (Diagram 5-34)

Situational Performance Training For The Goalkeeper
David M. Smart

What is the most important attribute of a quality goalkeeper? The question is often posed to me. My answer is simply that he or she have the ability to get the job done. There is nothing profound in this statement, and most goalkeepers are technically and physically adequate. Yet while field players are asked to be effective in tactically demanding training environments, most keepers are sent off to one side to train themselves until needed for the final practice progressions. This provides minimal tactical development for goalkeepers and therefore does little to increase their match effectiveness. It is not only important for goalkeepers to know the techniques of goalkeeping, but more importantly, when, where and how to apply a particular one.

There are basically three arenas available through which improvement can be made. They are: individually motivated training either alone or with friends; specialized instruction at summer camps; training for and playing games with their own team. Each is necessary and holds valuable benefits, yet each is also marked with certain limitations and hindrances.

Self-training results are limited. The player is attempting to improve without guidance, instruction, encouragement and goals.

Few summer goalkeeper camps offer truly specialized training whereby field players create a tactically realistic environment for keepers and visa versa. To be effective such camps need to merge their specialized training sessions into quality instruction for both groups in a match related learning environment.

In as much as the game can teach, team training sessions need to be the forum in which the goalkeeper and team obtain consistent effectiveness. Yet, as noted earlier, coaches are knowledgeable enough or haven't the time to devote to the training of their goalkeepers.

The answer is for coaches to employ "Situational Performance Training" during practices. It is a simple concept and many coaches are just one step short of implementing it even now. Situational Performance Training has the coach designing certain tactical training sessions for the team that include the goalkeeper. Next, the coach must be able to recognize where the keeper is less than effective and make corrections as part of the session.

Coaches often ask me for examples of both tasks. The following excerpt is from my "Complete Guide to Situational Performance" for the goalkeeper. Keep in mind the purpose of the guide is to enlighten the coach in terms of what to look for when evaluating goalkeeper's tactical performance. These guidelines can be applied to any lesson the coach chooses to impart to the team. The field player progressions provided are only one possibility — but they also involve the goalkeeper making for a very effective training session.

The Air Game in front of the goal is increasingly becoming the vital space which must be controlled if games are to be won. The Guide offers a training session addressing flank serves and attacking runs. At the same time the defensive side of play also needs to be coached. Performance priorities for the attack, defense and the goalkeeper are listed.

Situational Performance Training

Flank Serves: Warmup (Diagram 5-35)

Moving in pairs around one half the field, players serve 10 to 30 yard air balls to each other, collecting and reserving quickly. The flight of the balls should be varied in height, pace and spin. Each keeper should pair up with a field player, receiving the ball with his hands then quickly distributing to his partner. Have

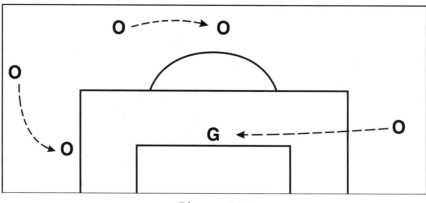

Diagram 5-35

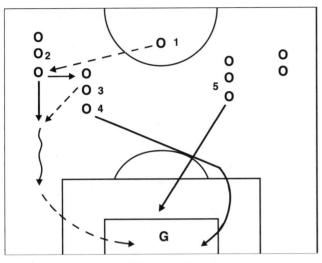

Diagram 5-36

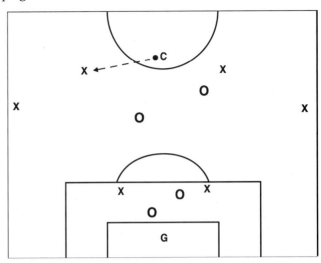

Diagram 5-37

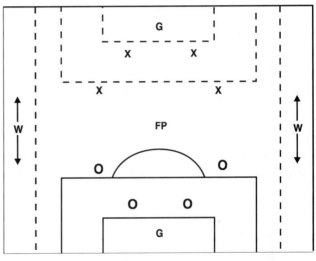

Diagram 5-38

the keeper locate himself/herself in the penalty area during this phase. In addition, the goalkeeper should be required to call for every ball loudly and clearly. (See the "Troubleshooting" section, items 3-7 for the coaching points to be stressed here).

Serves and Runs (Diagram 5-36)

O1 with a supply of balls, plays to O2. O2 combines with O3 then carries the ball up the flank, timing a near or far post serve with the runs of O4 and O5. Alternate sides and runs.

Attacking priorities:

• Speed on attack

• Quality serves, away from the keeper

• Timing and accuracy of serves

• Correct timing and path of runs

• Effective finishing

Goalkeeping priorities: Because the goalkeeper has no defenders, he/she must try to play every ball possible. Also, the keeper cannot be indecisive and attempt to cover both posts. He should position himself at the near post to cover the immediate danger while encouraging the server to choose the far post. An open stance is essential for proper vision and mobility. (See "Troubleshooting", items 1-8)

6 v. 4 (Diagram 5-37)

Coach (C) plays a ball in to the attacking six, who start each attack 40 to 50 yards from goal. Goals can only be scored as a result of a flank serve. Require the flank attackers to stay wide.

Attacking priorities:

• Keep width to stretch the defense;

• Quality of path and timing of run;

• Quality of timing and flight of ball;

• Attackers making clearing runs for midfielders;

• Effective finishing.

Defensive priorities:

• Pressure on the ball with cover and width;

• Compactness in the central danger area;

• Tracking attacking runs;

• Destroy, disrupt, or delay the attack.

Goalkeeper priorities: With the addition of defenders, it is important for the keeper to read the attack and direct his defense with authority. Also, the goalkeeper must coordinate his/her efforts with those of his defenders when coming to win a ball.

4 v. 4 + Free Player and Two Non-Penetrating Wingers (Diagram 5-38)

With a second goal at midfield (shorter for younger players), four play against four with an extra player (FP) always playing with the team on attack. Two wingers stay wide, serving crosses back to whichever team they received it from. Again, goals must be scored from flank serves at first. Later the restriction may be dropped. (The second box should be marked off to aid for keeper's spatial awareness.)

Attacking priorities:

• Same as those in previous drill;
• Quality passes wide with speed;
• If after the initial serve, the area becomes congested and the runs dead, get the ball wide again, clear the box and retake the runs.

Defensive priorities:

• Same as those in previous drill;
• Reorganize the defense after the ball is reloaded wide;
• Quick transition to attack once possession is won.

Goalkeeper priorities: Same as in previous drill with the addition of quick attacking distribution once possession is gained. At this point, the goalkeeper should work on analyzing the team's strength in the air in relation to the that of the opponent's. Does the opponent prefer the near or far post? Do they place someone in close to the keeper? Are their runs in the box organized and with purpose? Are their kicks taken quickly? Taken short?

TROUBLESHOOTING YOUR GOALKEEPER'S EFFECTIVENESS

When analyzing a breakdown in your keeper's performance, you should ask yourself the following questions:

1) Was the goalkeeper's positioning at the time of the service correct?
• Was their position too far off or hiding too much on their line based on their personal abilities?
• Closeness to the near post is determined by the angle and distance the player with the ball is from the near post; nearer making a shot or flick-on to goal more likely.
• Was their stance too closed, limiting movement and vision?
2) Was the keeper's decision to go or stay correct?
• Was the ball within their ability range?
• Was the path to the ball clear enough?
• Was the ball one they could handle? (speed, spin, trajectory, etc.)
• Were weather conditions a factor? (sun, mud, wind, rain, etc.)
3) Was the keeper's path to the ball correct?
• Was the path the most direct? (many take a curved path)
• Was the path choice correct to meet the ball at the highest point?
• Was the path chosen as to beat any attacker to the ball?
4) Was their footwork to the ball of adequate quality?
• Was the run coordinated with speed and agility?

5) Was the transition from run to jump smooth for maximum transfer of momentum?
• Was the keeper there too early, having to wait to jump?
• Was the width of each stride adjusted properly?
6) Was the quality of the jump adequate?
• Was the technique of the jump correct? (correct leg, body square, etc.)
• Was the keeper's body weight forward and carried through where contact with the ball was made? (to ensure strength in any contact)
• Was the keeper at full extension?
7) Did the keeper make a strong catch and hold the ball tightly throughout any contact with a player or the ground?
• Was the ball held high for a second to avoid bringing it down on an attacker?
• If falling to the ground, was the ball brought in to a basket catch?
8) If the keeper was not able to catch the ball well, was an EFFECTIVE contact with the ball made?
• Was the ball sent with sufficient force to a safe location, high, far, wide, or out of play?
• If the ball could not be cleared sufficiently, was the keeper able to disrupt the flight of the ball enough to prevent an attacker's play on the ball
• Was the ball at least sent high to buy time?

The above troubleshooting questions relate specifically to the goalkeeping actions necessary to effectively handle flank serves. There are additional factors related to the tone, tempo and psychological control of the game which warrant mention.

First play of the game. Quite often an opponent will challenge your keeper for an air ball early in the match to destroy confidence. It is essential for the keeper to train with absolute commitment to ensure an unwavering performance at any time.

Pressure in a game. The stress, tension and nervousness found during the course of a game will have a greater negative influence on the keeper's performance if they are unsure of their abilities. Training sessions must therefore expose the keeper to many repetitions of varied services until they have clear understanding of which crosses they can and cannot handle.

Play to your strengths and protect your weaknesses. A friend of mine is five-foot-seven. Too short you might think to be effective on a top college team. His team protected him by denying serves as much as possible and by being strong in the air themselves. He played to his strengths of shot-stopping, controlling breakaways, excellent distribution and by demonstrating a fierce competitive intensity. As a result, he helped his team to two national championships.

Corner Kick Adjustments. Because the ball is served from the end line at its farthest point, offsides

Communication with one's team becomes even more important for the goalkeeper with "the no pass back" rule in effect.
(photo by Perry McIntyre, Jr.)

is not a factor on the initial serve. This allows a greater number of opponents increased access to the goalmouth. Before the serve the keeper must take a mental picture of player placement and anticipate probable runs. Using this along with the "trouble-shooting" factors, a better decision can be made on whether to come for the ball and which path to take. The position the keeper takes along the goal line will also be determined by where the anticipated danger will surface. A scouting report may indicate inswingers to the near post, flick-ons at the near post, and other tactics for which adjustments in defense can be made.

Flick-ons. A tall defender should be stationed off the near post to attack these. The keeper should position himself to protect the near post and to have a possible play at the ball if it is flicked-on across the goalmouth.

An attacker standing in front of the keeper. Recognizing the obstruction the keeper should "cre-ate space" by stepping closer to the near post. The opponent will try to stay in front of the keeper. Place a strong defender in front of him. Just before the ball is served, step back into the space you created.

SUMMARY

Because the vast majority of goals are scored from the area in front of the goal, it is imperative for the goalkeeper to control and command this area. Having the best view and therefore perception of a given

situation, he or she must take responsibility. Here are a few steps I would encourage to follow for coaches interested in the "Situational Performance Training" concept:

- Provide your goalkeeper with a sound technical base. Summer camps, video tapes and local clinics can provide this;
- At home, watch a videotape of a game and analyze the keeper's performance based on the troubleshooting framework provided. Also consider the additional tactical aspects mentioned;
- Design your training sessions to include your keepers as much as possible. Place yourself in a coaching position as to best view their performance. Be supportive and demanding, encouraging keepers to always identify and then to extend their limits.

THE BACK PASS RULE AND THE GOALKEEPER
Tony DiCicco

Ever since the back pass rule was introduced by FIFA, it has undergone an evolution. I have had the opportunity to study the effects of the rule during the U-20 men's world championship in Australia, and at many full internationals played by the U.S. women's and men's U-20 teams. Here's what I've found.

For defenders, obviously the biggest fear has always been scoring on their own goals. The back pass rule has raised defenders' stress levels to new heights. A back pass is no longer a ball safely played to a keeper's hands; now it must be properly weighted as well. If hit too hard the keeper will have a problem controlling it or playing it one-touch; if hit too softly, a striker may challenge the keeper for possession.

Now more than ever, defenders need early, simple and concise communication from keepers on what to do ("Play it back!" "Turn it outside!"). Without this information confusion reigns — and goals result. In a recent match between our women's national team and the U.S. amateur squad, our national women gave up a goal because of just such confusion. A ball played to the top of the area was tackled away from goalkeeper Mary Harvey when it could have been cleared by Carla Overback, our sweeper. Communication was not made early enough, and the striker took full advantage of the indecision between the two players.

Defenders will most often prefer to take the ball wide and try to turn it upfield, rather than risk a too-soft or over-hit ball back to the keeper.

This is important information for coaches and goalkeepers, as they work out the strategies involved in the back pass rule.

How does the rule affect attacking players? Attacking players who are naturally aggressive defenders in the final third will benefit from the new rule. The pressure they put on defenders will not be relieved as easily as before by the pass to the goalkeeper. In the Women's World Championship final in China before the rule went into effect, Norway used the back pass to the keeper's hands to relieve all pressure from our attackers. It was not very attractive — but it was an effective game plan for them. With the back pass rule, that tactic will not work nearly as well.

The best attackers will study every keeper, and find out which ones struggle with foot skills. They will know which is each keeper's weak kicking foot. They will know which keepers are tactically safe, and which take occasional risks. They will also be selective with their chances, picking the right opportunity to pressure the keeper. These strikers will create goals because of poor defensive decisions or unnecessary risks on the part of the keeper.

How does the rule affect coaching? First, strikers will be coached to capitalize on defensive mistakes. In Ohio, our national amateur team played Italy. We played an excellent first half, and the score was 0-0. In the second half Italy scored twice, both on back passes, and the final score was 4-1. They used a team tactic I thought was excellent: When the U.S. had the ball in our defensive third, Italy allowed the keeper to receive the ball. They did not cut off the back pass to the keeper; instead they encouraged it. Once it was made and the right opportunity created, a first attacker sprinted to the keeper. Attacker #2 was right behind his teammate, and the rest of the team surged forward to cover outlets and fill spaces where the keeper's clear would likely go.

In that game, the first attacker tackled the ball from the keeper. The U.S. keeper went strongly into the tackle and won the duel. The ball sprung free, at which point the keeper had full use of her hands because the attacker had made contact with the ball. The back pass rule was no longer in effect, and she could have dove or scooped up the ball without penalty. But she did not, and her attempted clear was blocked by attacker #2. The ensuing penalty area scramble resulted in an Italian goal.

It terms of coaching defenders and goalkeepers, every coach must create a structure on how to play when defenders are facing their own goal and in possession, or chasing down the ball with pressure from behind. We have initiated the following on the U.S. women's national team:

- Whenever possible, have the defender take the ball wide with a self-pass toward the touchline. This allows the defender to assess the pressure, and decide either to pass the ball up the line or play it out of touch for a throw-in. The defender can never be dispossessed in this situation.

- The keeper must adopt this philosophy, and communicate as early as possible with either a "back" or "outside" call. This communication should come before the defender reaches the ball — the earlier the call, the better for the defender. The keeper should not use "Keeper! when desiring to have the ball played back. "Keeper!" has one meaning to teammates: "Leave the ball; I will get to it."

- Whenever possible have the defender turn it outside. The risk of passing it back to the keeper is in most cases not worth the gain.

- The keeper must assess which shoulder the attacking player is pressuring the defender on. If it is the inside shoulder (toward the middle of the field), the keeper should always have the defender turn to the outside. If it is the outside shoulder (toward the touchline), then the keeper should in most cases call for the back pass, rather than have the defender turn into the center.

What does the keeper do when the ball is played back? This will evolve into a more controlled possession approach, but currently the keeper should run onto and one-touch a long, high kick upfield to a front runner. Though possession may not be obtained, the keeper avoids risk while discouraging attacking players from chasing down back passes. If the keeper has a tendency to hold back passes and then distribute, the first attacker will most likely always consider following the pass in, hoping for a mistouch by the keeper.

If the keeper is challenged and being closed down, it is better to give up a throw-in rather than kick the ball into the advancing opponent.

I also think the coach should show confidence that the keeper can receive a back pass and deal with it effectively. The coach's expectation that this is a sequence that must be played soon becomes the mentality of the goalkeeper and defenders as well.

The coach must, however, put defenders and keepers into this decision-making environment — under pressure — to avoid costly mistakes that will lead to goals and losses. And the coach must continue to develop keepers as soccer players with solid foot skills, as well as good goalkeeper skills.

The team that is most prepared, both offensively and defensively, will take best advantage of the new back pass rule.

Finally, how does this rule affect the goalkeeper? The keeper should approach the rule positively, because it brings the keeper further into the team. Certainly the keeper must understand the coaching structure outlined above on how to handle back passes. The keeper must also work at foot skills, specifically clearing balls with both feet.

Communication, decisions and confidence will become vital tools for the keeper with the new back pass rule. One point I strongly encourage is that keepers can help reduce the stress levels of defenders. This can be accomplished by not making every back pass a crisis, especially when the ball is misplayed back.

Last summer Michelle Akers played a back pass to Mary Harvey's chest. Of course, Michelle had forgotten that Mary could not use her hands. Under pressure Mary took the ball down with her chest and volleyed it out of danger. Michelle apologized, but Mary's response was that it was no problem, and not to worry. This is good leadership; it contributes to the team's overall confidence that they can handle the back pass dilemma easily and effectively.

The keeper should have balls passed back as if to a sweeper — in other words, to feet. The ball should not be passed back into space on the outside of the goal, unless there is plenty of space between the pressuring attacker and the keeper. Balls weighted improperly outside the goal frame have a tendency to limit

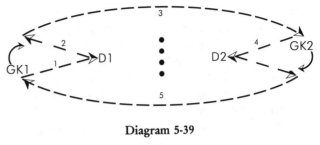

Diagram 5-39

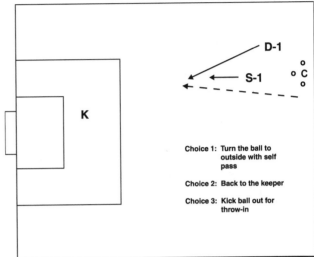

Diagram 5-40

the keeper's options to distribute, or even kick upfield effectively.

Finally, of course, the most important elements in dealing with this rule are practice and confidence.

EXERCISES TO IMPROVE HANDLING OF THE BACK PASS RULE

This is a progression I have used with our U.S. national team.

Exercise 1 — Diagram 5-39

Line up two keepers and two defenders as in Diagram 5-39. Keeper 1 starts with the ball, then hand-outlets it to Defender 1. Defender 1 touches a ball back to the keeper, it is played one-touch over the top of both defenders, to the hands of Keeper 2. Keeper 2 then distributes to Defender 2, and continues the same as Keeper 1. (Keepers should clear with both feet.)

Next, have the defenders apply pressure to the keeper, after playing the ball back.

Exercise 2 — Diagram 5-40

Start at midfield. Play a ball into space with the Defender (D1) chasing the ball back toward his or her own goal while under pressure from an attacking player (S1).

The keeper must communicate early to the defender about whether to play the ball back or take it outside. It also helps if the keeper points to the outside when directing the defender to turn it there.

Add numbers, and play the ball in various spots behind the last defender. The keeper must call early, so the defender knows what to do before he/she reaches the ball. When the ball is cleared weakly, it allows the attacking team the opportunity to score.

Restart the exercise from midfield, forcing the defending unit to play flat so that balls can be played over their heads.

Option 1. Turn the ball to the outside with a self-pass.

Option 2. Go back to the keeper.

Option 3. Kick the ball out for a throw-in.

Note: Each situation is different; there is no simple best choice.

DEVELOPING INDIVIDUAL AND TEAM TACTICS: AN ACTION PLAN FOR THE GAME

Tactics can be thought of in coaching terms as the collective approach to the playing of the game. That development of that team blueprint is of course a major decision for the coach. Basic to the decision of "how to play" is an evaluation of the talent existent in the individuals who comprise the team.

The chapter focusing on individual and team tactics offers coaches a means of developing a varied approach to the teaching of the tactical side of soccer. The degree to which players can translate soccer technique into skill under game conditions is the true measure of an individual's ability to play the game. Once each individual is trained to properly play the game, a collective strategy can be adopted for the team.

Our selection of editorial will offer coaches expertise in how to tackle this problem. Jim Lennox explains how to build a practice around the correct tactical progression. Andy Roxburgh offers readers small game exercises that seek to isolate various techniques and improve them in pressure situations. Scoring is something that coaches are always seeking answers in terms of team performance and Jack Detchon identifies means to that end for us. The 6 v. 6 training model espoused by many as the ideal coaching environment to develop tactical awareness, is dissected by coach Jeff Tipping. Possession of the ball and how to achieve it is the subject of one of Bob Dikranian's presentations. The second seeks to break down 1 v. 1 to its essential components. Once players are taught individual defense, a coach needs to teach collective defending and Jeff Tipping discusses zonal defending in his article.

Modern wing play is the focus of Bob Gansler's offering while Mike Russo talks about how to counter attack off an opponent that overlaps from the back. Jay Miller continues the counter-attack theme in his article. Clive Charles and Tom Rowney offer ideas on how to develop attacking play in your team while Ron McEachen's piece relates to that as he focuses on collective play in the final third of the field.

Some very specialized presentations conclude the chapter including a discussion by Manual Lagos on the topic of developing better verbal communication skill in the team. Tom Martin offers ideas on how to collectively combat the offside trap while irregular fields and how to deal *with them tactically are addressed by Hubert Vogelsinger.*

Finally, Alan Maher has selected 20 top questions from the popular "Soccer Situation Tests" which appeared in Soccer Journal. These to sharpen your soccer intelligence.

⚽

TACTICAL PROGRESSIONS
Jim Lennox

I. Introduction

A. Tactics are built from the simple to the complex.

B. Begin with one player, then complicate the environment by adding players, which increases the number of choices a player must make.

C. Build up your progressions. Players must learn, play in situations where they are out-numbered as this is what occurs most often in a match.

II. Technical Points *(During Jim's session he made a number of technical points worth noting)*

A. A player with the ball should not get caught in possession of it.

B. Prepare balls as you receive them to pass, dribble, or shoot. Do not "trap"/stop a ball.

C. On wall passes, the player with the ball must take the defender on, playing the ball when he/ she is as close to the defender as possible. The player without the ball must "show" for the pass in a "sideways on" (at an angle) to the player with the ball and on an almost level position relative to the defender. The player without the ball must have a view of the defender.

D. Attempt to play balls to the player's preferred (strong) foot and space. Play passes to the foot farthest from the defender.

E. Receive all balls across your body (across your support foot) to obtain proper vision of supporting and defending players.

F. Move a ball when running (vertically) with the toe down; move sideways (laterally) with the toe up.

G. When a player is standing or moving to you, play the ball to his/her feet so that he/she can play it into the space more quickly.

H. Center back (stopper) should not mark by being directly behind a center forward. The back should stand sideways or perpendicular to the forward aligning the opposite shoulder alongside the forward shoulder. Cut off a bad pass or move behind the foot receiving the ball if a good pass. (Diagram 6-1)

III. Tactical Progression

A. 2 v. 1

1. RW wants to get behind LB. RW comes out (checks back) to make room behind defense. Come out in a "sideways on" position to see the defense and to see behind it. RW must maintain width. (Diagram 6-2A)

(a) LB stays off on check back run. RW receives ball, turns and attacks the LB. Coach must encourage forwards to attack defending players. Attack the forward leg of the defender, as most

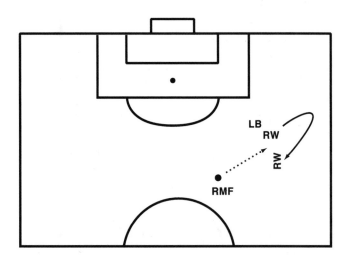

Diagram 6-2A: 2 v. 1

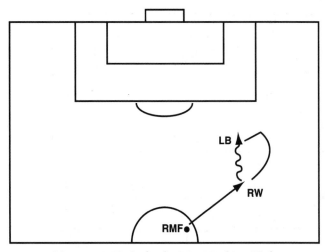

Diagram 6-2B: Defender Not Marking Tight

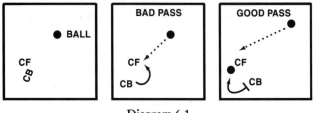

Diagram 6-1

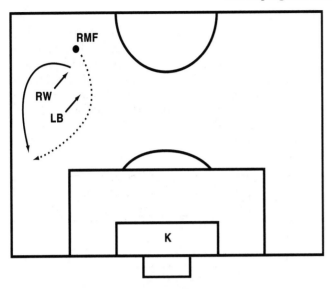

Diagram 6-3: Defender Marking Tight

defenders force the forward outside, and EXPLODE by the defender. (Diagram 6-2B)

(b) LB stays with RW on check back run. RW turns and runs behind defender to a pass from the RMF (Diagram 6-3)

2. RMF can play the ball to the RW and support the wing behind of square and not too vertical. This allows a better angle to pass into the RW. By narrowing the angle of the pass it keeps it from a covering defender (sweeper). (Diagrams 6-4A and 6-4B)

3. RMF can play the ball to the RW and run behind (overlap) the RW.

4. RMF can play a wall pass with the RW.

B. 4 v. 3

1. If the decision is not to attack on one side, then change the point of attack to the other side. (Diagram 6-5A)

2. The offside wing is positioned to pinch in field and push up towards the halfway line as much aspossible. WHY? Because, if the other side (ball

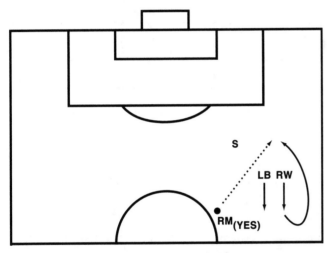

Diagram 6-4A: Correct Angle of Support

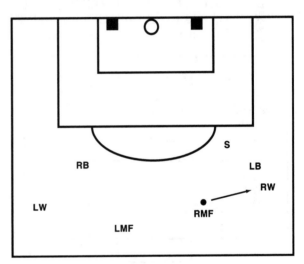

Diagram 6-5A: 4 v. 3

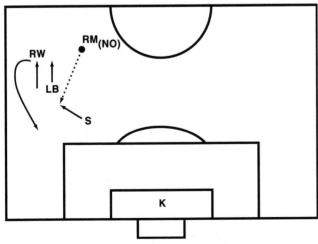

Diagram 6-4B: Incorrect Angle of Support

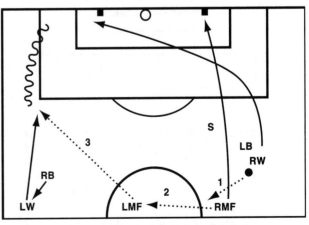

Diagram 6-5B: Switch Point of Attack
(Backs Mark Tight)

side) players get through, the offside players can move into the box more quickly to score. On runs, the farthest player from the ball generally goes to the near post. (Diagram 6-5B) The player next to arrive goes to the far post.

3. As the ball changes sides, the-original offside wing moves out from goal back to the level of the ball and goes wide. If this is done quickly, space is created as the sweeper attempts to change sides to support the "new" ball side. As the wing does this and if the fullback marks tight, the wing breaks through. (Diagram 6-6) If the fullback is loose, the wing turns and attacks the fullback.

C. 6 v. 2

1. The CF can compact or pull apart the center of a defense. Decisions must be made about the characteristics of a CF and the tactical implications of a coach's decision about the role of the CF.

2. Begin with the CF making runs (CF is a mobile player and pulls apart the center of the defense) to the MFs who play vertical balls to the CF's feet. In Diagram 6-7 we see the CMF passing to CF (as he checks to the ball), CF plays to RMF, RMF to LW on a diagonal run through.

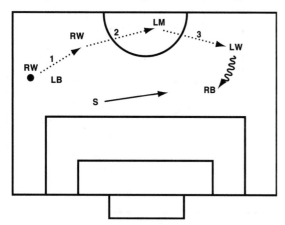

Diagram 6-6: Switch Point of Attack
Backs Mark Loose

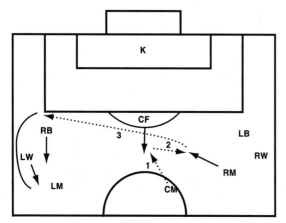

Diagram 6-7: 6 v. 2
CF Opens Up Space

D. 6 v. 3

1. A CB is added to the progression with the CF now pressured to make decisions. In Diagram 6-8 CF checks away with CB marking, RM plays to feet of the CF, if he can turn on the CB, CF may play through ball to RW who has taken his defender away to create space for ball to be played to; if CB marks tightly, then CF may be forced to play first time ball back to his CM and restart movement again.

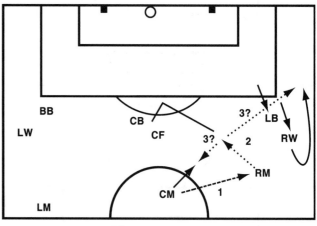

Diagram 6-8: 6 v. 3

E. 6 v.4

1. A sweeper is added to the defense and all play depends on how the CB and S play in relation to CF.

• Must read the reaction of the central defenders.

• CB loose, SWPR loose - CF turns.

• CB tight, SWPR tight - play through behind defense to a W.

• CB tight, SWPR loose - play to space behind CB but in front of SWPR - wall pass, etc.

2. In Diagram 6-9 we see the CB and S playing tightly, then a combination might be to play to space for LW to run into.

F. Full Field — 3 v. 3 — 2 MFs — 3 v. 3

1. MFs always play on the team with the ball and ball is played to one of them when won by a defender. Can play with or without keepers. Can add a SWPR to get numbers down situation. MF can only support strikers - no penetrating runs. Can lift restrictions on MF as progression continues. (Diagram 6-10)

IV. Summary of Progressions

A. One wing + 1 midfielder player v. one defender (2 v. 1).

• Attack defender with the ball.

• 1-2/wall movements.

B. Two wings + 2 midfield players v. two defenders (4 v. 2).

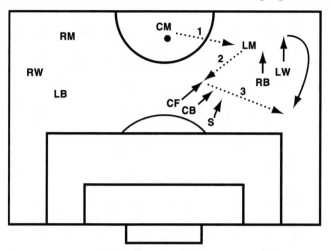

Diagram 6-9: 6 v. 4
Tight Marking by Central Defenders

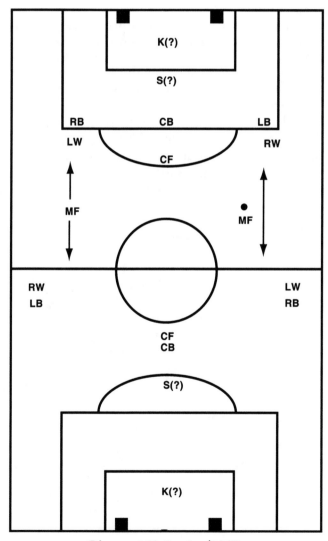

Diagram 6-10: 3 v. 3 w/2 MFs

- Defeating the defender.
- Opposite wing get into the box to finish.
  C. Two wings + 1 center forward + MFs v. two defenders (5 v. 2)
- Center forward shows for 1-2 movements.
- Maintain possession and change the point of attack through the center forward.
  D. Add a third defender to mark the center forward.
  E. Add third midfielder player
  F. Add sweeper — now 2 wings + 1 center forward + 3 midfielders v. 3 defenders + sweeper (6 v. 4).
  G. Allow one MF to penetrate.
  H. Add a defensive MF.
  I. Full field 3 v. 3 + 2 to both ends (with or without keepers).
  J. Add a sweeper to both teams.
    * as reported by Jeff Vennell

🌐

INDIVIDUAL SKILLS
Andy Roxburgh

One of the highlights of the January 1988 NSCAA convention in Washington, D.C. was the appearance of guest clinician Andy Roxburgh. Andy gave his insight into the game of soccer at three sessions. It was a privilege to learn Andy's coaching philosophy and watch his coaching style in demonstrations at each session.

Individual skill training sessions should be well-structured, noted the Scottish National Team coach. Players need training goals set for them in order to create interest and concentration. Practice time should simulate the game as much as possible, giving each player the maximum amount of ball contact time. Problem-solving in training sessions will create both player interest and concentration resulting in a good training environment.

Cues for good technique need to be given to the players to guide them. The coach needs to focus on the individual technique of each player during training. The following suggestions and activities were presented by Andy.

HELPFUL CUES FOR GOOD TECHNIQUE

- When in soccer do you run in circles?...you don't! Keep changing direction!
- When you dribble the ball, look beyond the ball and keep your head up.
- Do not only see the ball, but be aware of it.

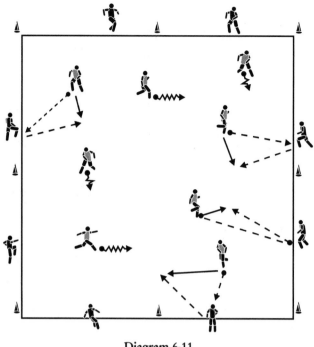

Diagram 6-11

- When cushioning a ball, relax upon impact. Remain in balance to better cushion and then play the ball.
- Soccer is a sequence of skills. With only one skill, you are limited.
- In soccer, the body must have a rhythmic flow.
- If a team player moves toward you, he/she wants to give you the ball.
- There are two ways to lose a defender. You can either outrun (speed) or outsmart the defender (direction). A change of direction will lose the defender every time. Using speed will not have the odds in your favor to lose a defender.
- To gain space a player must first go away from the ball.
- When you play a pass, make sure you give support. You cannot always run forward.
- Each player is different, requiring individual help, guidance, and stimulation.
- Well planned training sessions, keying on individual skills with positive reinforcement, will turn the wheel of individual soccer development.
- Individual players need to be given responsibility to initiate action in carrying out a task.
- And lastly, give the player homework to keep the wheels rolling.

Roxburgh then demonstrated several practical sessions he has used to develop technical and tactical awareness in players. The basic skills are emphasized in small-sided games. He identified them as follows: 1. The windows; 3. Possession game; 4. Winger's game;

5. Numbers game.

Group skills came into play in games which Roxburgh labeled: 6. Off the wall; 2. Schemer and striker play; 7. Schemer's game; 8. Pressing game.

1. THE WINDOWS (PASSING/COMBINATION PLAY)

One player stands in the gap between two markers (the windows). His/her partner runs freely inside the box.

- The window player passes the ball. Middle players play (a) one-touch; (b) turn and pass; (c) control and pass, etc. Change roles after one minute.
- The middle player dribbles with the ball, passes to a window player who plays (a) wall pass; (b) two-touch. The side players, when receiving a short pass, should then play a longer one and vice versa. (Diagram 6-11)

2. SCHEMER AND STRIKER PLAY (SHOOTING)

LEADUP ACTIVITY

Tactical Shouts

"Man On" — The schemer A plays an angled ball forward. The receiving player B plays it back to the schemer who then plays a ball forward to the target player C. The target player lays the ball off and B completes the sequence with a shot at goal (Diagram 6-12).

"Turn" — The player receiving the ball turns away from the schemer A who delivered the pass and passes the ball forward to player C. The target player lays the ball off to B who shoots at goal. (Diagram 6-13)

"Hold It" — The schemer A passes the ball and then sprints around the outside of receiving player B.

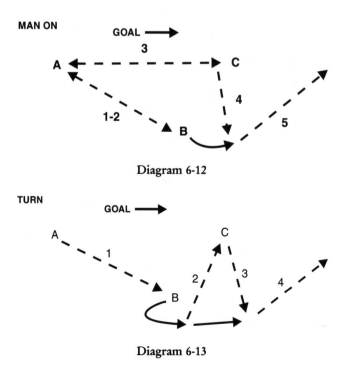

Diagram 6-12

Diagram 6-13

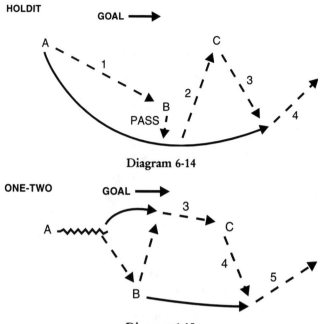

Diagram 6-14

Diagram 6-15

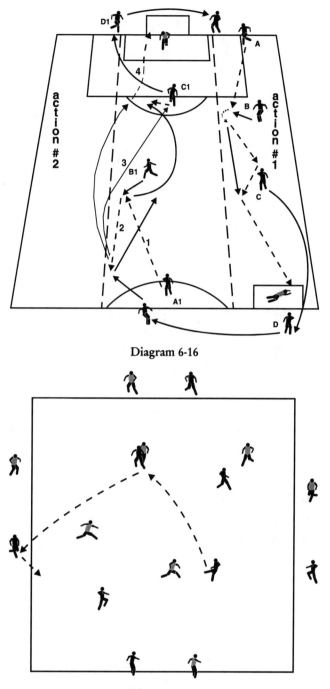

Diagram 6-16

Diagram 6-17

At the appropriate moment, B lays the ball into the path of A who then plays a 1-2 with C and shoots for goal (Diagram 6-14).

"1-2" — The schemer dribbles forward and plays a short 1-2 off the receiver or wall B and then passes to the target player C who lays a ball off for B to shoot at goal. (Diagram 6-15)

SHOOTING ACTIVITY

Action #1

• The schemer (A) plays an angled pass forward to B. The receiving player (B) reacts to the tactical shout (turn, hold it, etc.) given by A. B turns and plays a forward pass to the target player (C). The target player lays the ball off and (B) completes the move with a shot at goal. D recovers the ball and moves across to join the line waiting to go in the opposite direction. A now moves to position B, B moves to position C and C becomes the ball person. The exercise is now repeated. Both channels are working simultaneously. (Diagram 6-16, right side)

Action #2

• The schemer A1 plays the ball forward. The receiving player B1 plays it back at an angle to the schemer who then plays a forward pass to target player C1. The target player lays the ball off for B1 who completes the move with a shot on goal (Diagram 6-16, left side).

3. THE POSSESSION GAME (WALL PASSING)

8 v. 8 on a 40 x 40 yard field — Each team has four outfield players and four wall players, one on each side of the box. The latter cannot enter the field.

Ten consecutive passes equals one goal. The wall players have only one-touch. A wall player cannot play the ball back to the player who last passed the ball to him/her. The ball cannot be passed directly from one wall player to another. Wall players cannot tackle the opposition. (Diagram 6-17)

4. 3 v. 3 WINGERS' GAME (CROSSING/COMBINATION PLAY)

3 v. 3 plus goalkeepers and wingers on a 50 yd. long by 60 yd. wide field. One winger with the ball begins from a position deeper and wider than the at-

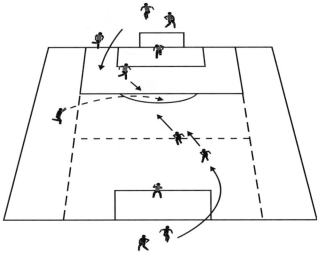

Diagram 6-18

tacking penalty box one-touch forward and cross. 3 v.
3 play normal soccer until the ball goes out of play or
a goal is scored. If the group defending wins the ball,
they can counter attack and score without involving
either of their wingers. Once the phase of play is completed, a winger at the other end of the field immediately starts a new attack. This continues alternately.
Change the players' roles regularly; normal scoring.
(Diagram 6-18)

5. NUMBERS GAME (TACTICS OF PLAY)

Two teams, four or more players plus goalkeepers
on a 50 yd. long by 60 yd. wide field. The coach at
midfield calls a number and a side (left or right). The
required number of players enter the field from the
right or left-hand side of the goal as requested. The
ball is kicked into the field of play by the coach. When
a goal is scored or the ball goes out, the phase of play
is over and the players immediately run to the rear of
their respective teams. The coach re-starts the game.
(Diagram 6-19)

6. OFF THE WALL (COMBINATION/FREE PLAY)

Four pairs in the field 50 yd. long by 60 yd. wide, a
ball between two, two neutral goalkeepers, eight side
players, one to each side of the goal on each end and
two on each touchline. A player with the ball on the
field of play passes the ball to a side player who plays
a one-touch pass to the player's partner. The side players should vary the angle and length of the pass, i.e.,
receive a short pass, then play a long one. The receiving player can (a) turn and dribble, (b) shoot at goal,
or (c) pass to another side player. The pairs in the field
can also combine with 1-2s and takeovers. After two
minutes those in the field change places with the side
players. (Diagram 6-20)

7. SCHEMERS' GAME (3 V. 2)

Exercises focus on play in the final third of the

Diagram 6-19

Diagram 6-20

field. Field 50 x 60 yard (3-20 yard grids). 6 v. 6 plus
goalkeepers, two attackers, two defenders and two
schemers in each third of the field. All must remain in
their areas except one schemer from the team in possession can enter the attacking third in order to support the strikers. The schemer must return to the
middle area immediately after possession is lost; normal scoring. (Diagram 6-21)

8. 5 V. 5 PRESSING (POSSESSION/PRESSURE TACTICS)

Two teams of five plus goalkeepers on a 44 yd. wide
by 50 yd. long field. Normal game until a team scores.
When a team scores they cannot score again until they
lose a goal. The winning team at this point tries to
play possession football. The losing team, using the

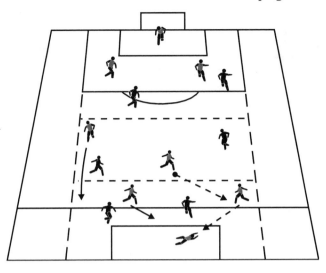

Diagram 6-21

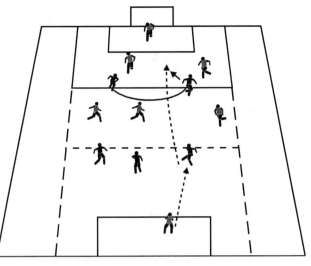

Diagram 6-22

goalkeeper as an outfield player (effectively 6 v. 5), tries to gain possession and score. When an equalizer is scored, the game returns to normal. All restarts for balls out of field via throw-ins. (Diagram 6-22)

A team wins by (a.) being one goal ahead at full time, or (b.) being one goal ahead for a five minute period.

> * *The preceding article was written after a presentation by Scottish National Coach Andy Roxburgh at the 1988 NSCAA Convention in Washington. The article was prepared by Ray Kiddy, coach at Catonsville Junior College (MD).*

⚽

A DYNAMIC MODEL FOR TEACHING — 6 V. 6
Jeff Tipping with Matt Robinson

Although 3 v. 3 and 4 v. 4 are effective in teaching key offensive concepts, 6 v. 6 (5 v. 5 plus goalkeepers) is a tremendous small-sided shape for teaching the more advanced tactical concepts of the game.

The advanced concepts that can be emphasized in the 6 v. 6 model include:
• Player movement through thirds of the field. (Movement from the back defensive third to the middle third, and middle third to the front third);
• Simulating a piece of the game. (Play between three backs and two center midfielders or three midfielders and two center forwards);
• Opportunity for players to work on holding the ball until there is an opportunity to play it to a target;
• Effective play and communication between two front players;
• Effective combination play between front players and players advancing from rear positions. (Overlaps, double passes and three-man combinations can be emphasized).

The stages of a typical practice session using this concept will be outlined for implementation purposes.

A. WARMUP

A model 6 v. 6 training session will move through a logical progression from simple to advanced. The five-stage warmup session will begin with three players with a ball in an area of 30 x 20 yards.

In Stage A, as two support players, A1 and A2, pass between themselves, a target player, A3, will check and receive a pass from a support player. The target player will then one-touch the ball to the second support player for a three-man combination.

In this warmup the target player is working on checking with special emphasis on eye contact with the person who is best suited from a timing standpoint to deliver the ball to his checking run. The support players are also working on eye contact with the checking player which helps the timing of the pass. They also must focus on the pace of the pass relative to the check of the target player. The coach should rotate the players so each will have equal time to perform both as the checking player and as a supporting player. (Diagram 6-23).

In Stage B, the support player, A1, passes to the target player, A3, and remains stationary after the pass. The other support player, A2, moves to support the target player, and thus those two become the support players while player A1 becomes the target player. A key coaching point in this exercise is to watch the angle and timing of the support run by A2. It should be timed such that as the ball is played forward the run is

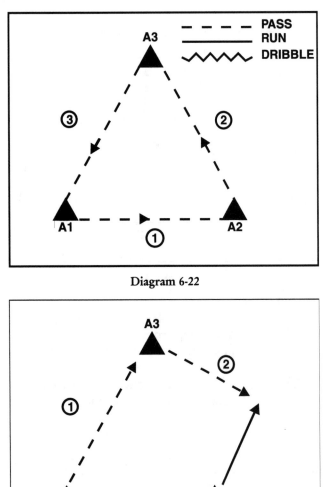

Diagram 6-22

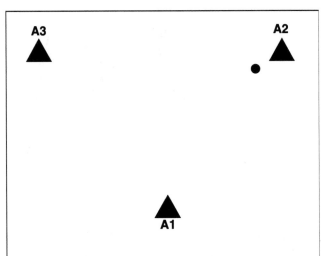

Diagram 6-23b

Diagram 6-23a

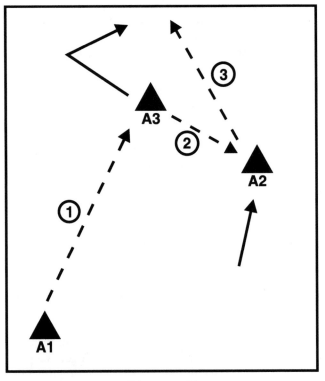

Diagram 6-24

made with the idea being a one-touch pass to the support player as he/she arrives. If the supporting run is made too late, the target player will have to hold the ball and he/she may be tackled (Diagrams 6-23a and 6-23b).

In Stage C of the warmup, the three players will work to execute a three-man combination that incorporates a double pass. In this segment player A1 will play the ball to the target player A3. Player A3 will lay the ball off at a slight angle to the other support player, A2. After laying the ball off, A3 will spin right and receive the ball on the left side of an imaginary defender. This stage acclimates the players to the concept of getting behind the defender. Once completed, the player who played the ball to the target player, in this case A1, becomes the target player. (Diagram 6-24)

Stage D of the warmup has the two supporting players, Players A1 and A2, using the target player, A3, to create a three-man combination with an overlap in-

corporated. A2 plays ball to A3, while A1 makes an overlapping run and receives the pass to complete the three-man combination. Once completed, the player who played the ball to the target player, in this case A2, becomes the target player. (Diagram 6-25)

B. MATCH-RELATED PRACTICE

Now that the players have executed a warmup and have been acclimated to concepts that will be utilized in the practice session, defensive pressure can be introduced and the session can progress towards the full 6 v. 6 training game.

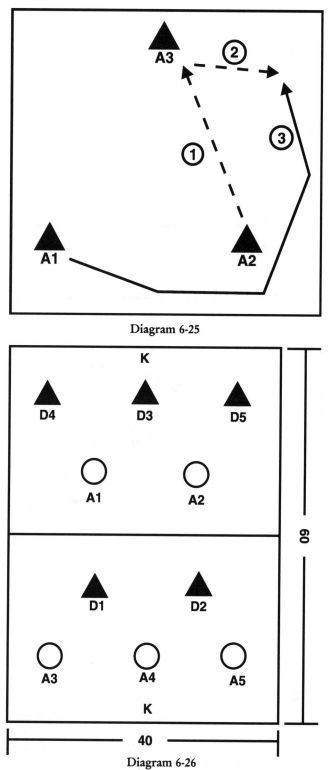

Diagram 6-25

Diagram 6-26

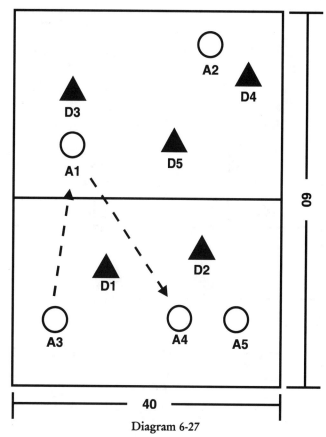

Diagram 6-27

ball away from Players D1 and D2. The "A" players may play the ball to Players A4 and A5 for three-man combinations, but A1 and A2 are limited to two touches and may not cross over the halfway line.

If D1 or D2 win the ball they play the ball to D3, D4 or D5. When either team has the ball, the playing objective is to maintain possession. The back players should focus upon their angle and distance of support in relation to one another in order to keep ball possession. The angle should be square or back of square and the distance should not be too close that an advantage is not gained by the pass or that the distance is so far that a defender can intercept. They should also be conscious of moving to receive a ball if it is played to A1 or A2. (Diagram 6-27)

In Stage B, players A1 and A2 will be working on receiving the ball with their backs to the goal. Focus is placed upon the forward making good decisions with his/her back to the goal. Player D4 marks either A1 or A2. The other players, D3 and D5, are idle. Players A3, A4 and A5 must play the ball to the marked forward, A1. This forward can use his/her partner, A2, to free himself up for a 1-2 combination.

The support player, A2, has only one-touch. It should be stressed to the forwards that they should be making the decision on whether to attack with the ball or to play the 1-2 or wall pass combination before

Organize the playing space into a field 60 x 40 yards with a clearly marked halfway line. Players should be organized into teams of five with a 3 v. 2 situation in the defensive half, and 2 v. 3 in the offensive half. Each team will have a goalkeeper. (Diagram 6-26)

In Stage A, Players A3, A4 and A5 are keeping the

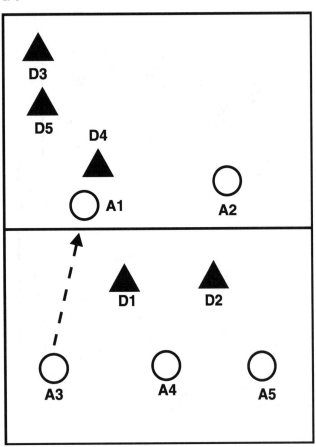

Diagram 6-28a

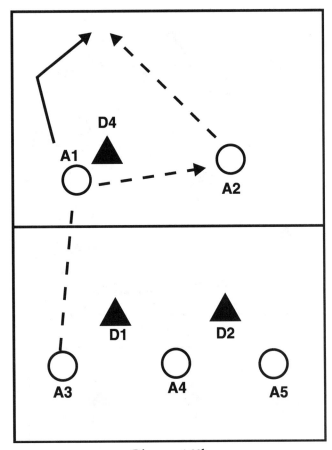

Diagram 6-28b

he/she receives the ball. Once he/she makes contact with the ball he/she can act. Vision and communication with other players will provide the player with that information. (Diagrams 6-28a and 6-28b)

In Stage C, another defender becomes involved to make the game a 3 v. 2 for the A team in the defensive half and 2 v. 2 in the offensive half. The idle defender, D4, only becomes active if his/her team wins the ball. Now the two forwards must work in opposition (if one checks, the other remains away) to create space to receive the ball. There are several key points that can be focused upon in this stage.

Again it should be stressed that the checking player should be making a decision before receiving the ball. Also of importance is that at times it is the pass that initiates the check. If the passer is under pressure, the ball may be played and the forward must move to receive it prior to any checking away run takes place. If the forward opts to play the ball back, he/she should then try to get behind the defenders to receive a subsequent pass in that vital attacking space.

For the back players, it should be stressed that the ball they do play forward must have the proper pace, and preferably split the two defenders. It should also be emphasized that the best pass is always the longest

pass where possession can be maintained. The back players must also move into position of support to receive a back pass from a forward. (Diagram 6-29)

A final defender is added in Stage D. Now the back players are permitted to cross the halfway line, if that player is participating in a 1-2 combination or a three man combination. It must be stressed to the back players that they must anticipate the potential for the 1-2 or three-man combination and begin moving with the proper timing. The wrong delay in the run by the back player can prevent a successful execution of the combination. (Diagram 6-30)

C. Match Condition

In Stage A, players are permitted to carry the ball over the line untracked, and finally free play in the area is permitted in Stage B. Even though free play is permitted, the players should not abandon the concepts being stressed earlier when play was restricted.

Conclusion

Again the 6 v. 6 game is an excellent model to address important advanced offensive concepts. There are several important teaching points a coach can focus upon while conducting the session with a team. They include:

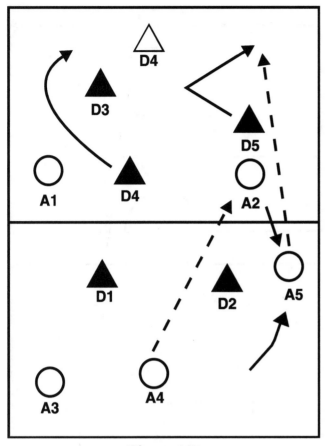

Diagram 6-29

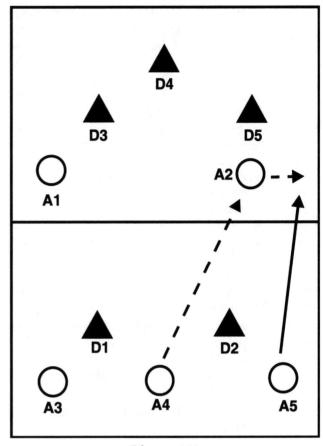

Diagram 6-30

- Possess the ball by playing backwards or sideways until it can be played forward. Support must be given to the first attacker either square or back- wards of square;
- Whenever possible, play the ball forward between two defenders;
- The best pass is always the longest as long as possession can be maintained;
- As the ball is moving between back players, the forwards should anticipate a window opening up between two defenders;
- Look for the second center forward when passing;
- Pace of the pass is vital;
- Sometimes the pass initiates the check, especially when the passer is under pressure;
- Center forwards check and work in opposition before a first attacker gets ball, especially if first attacker is under pressure;
- A checking player must read the defense as the ball is being played to him/her;
    - Can the player turn?
    - If not, must the player hold, or play back?
    - Can the player use the second forward?
- Center forwards must read when to support as ball

is traveling to them;
- Angle and distance of support as well as timing of support runs are vital;
- Back players try and move with correct timing for three-man combinations to work most effectively;
- Center forwards must try and get behind defenders once they have played the ball backwards.

TEACHING ATTACKING SOCCER
Jack Detchon

Following is a teaching progression that focuses on development of team attacking tactics in the final half of the field.

There are some assumptions made in this presentation.

- The double center striker setup is the alignment chosen by the coach;
- That functional training of the two forwards precedes the implementation of this exercise. That is,

there is a bit of understanding as to when the supporting forward should create space for his teammate, when he/she will show for a 1-2, when a possible through ball is "on" as well as when a possible overlap or takeover might take place;

In other words, combination play has been taught, and implemented in the overall coaching scheme.

• There has been functional/technical training between the midfielders and the strikers in terms of playing balls to feet or space with the strikers making the proper decisions based on: 1.) the pressure by the defender, or, 2.) their position relative to the defender's positioning;

• Some time has been spent on playing the ball wide to outside players with proper supporting runs then made by both strikers and supporting midfielders in order to connect with flighted balls to either the near or far posts or balls played behind the defense to withdrawn attackers.

Once these technical/tactical building blocks have been established (they actually might serve as the basis for the warmup leading into this activity!), then the coach can seek to coach to perceived problems that are exhibited as these exercises are implemented.

EXERCISE I. 2 v. 2 IN RESTRICTED GOAL AREA (DIAGRAM 6-31)

Organization:

Use flat cones to define the restricted areas with server playing balls to either of the two forwards to initiate play.

To begin play the server plays balls to the strikers and 2 v. 2 play takes place in the restricted area shown.

Objectives:

• To review the various phases of combination play between the two strikers;

• To develop an aggressive attitude to score within players;

• Creation of space by the forward based on quick checks to the ball or by a good first touch of the ball;

• Use of quick changes of direction or changes of pace to free selves;

• Develop judgement of angles and distances both from each other as well as in relation to goal and keeper;

• Exhibit quality passing throughout exercise.

Coaching Points to be Emphasized/Observed:

• Can A9 or A10 turn quickly on defender & shoot?

• Can they receive, turn and dribble to shoot?

• Can they receive, turn and recognize when to play a 1-2 combination?

• Can they receive, turn and play partner into a scor-

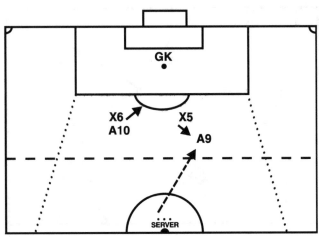

Diagram 6-31

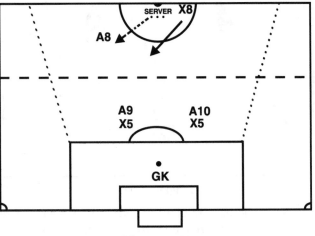

Diagram 6-32

ing position via a through ball, via an overlap or initiate a takeover?

EXERCISE II. 3 v. 2 IN RESTRICTED AREA (DIAGRAM 6-32)

Organization:

Server plays balls to A8 creating a 3 v. 2; X8 recovers on the second touch of A8.

Objectives:

• build on Exercise I;

• A8 takes long range shot;

• A8 overlaps or

• decoy overlaps creating a 2 v. 1 and allowing A9 or A10 to turn.

Coaching Points to be Emphasized/Observed:

• Do the players take advantage of their numerical superiority?

• By attacking aggressively with at speed, with pace?

• Does the player furthest from the ball pull wide to create space?

• Can the attacking team maintain the momentum of the attack?

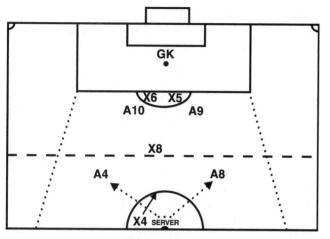

Diagram 6-33

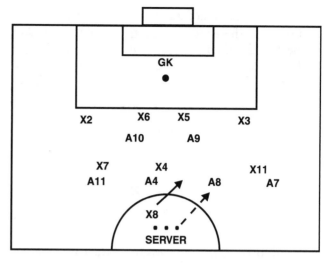

Diagram 6-35

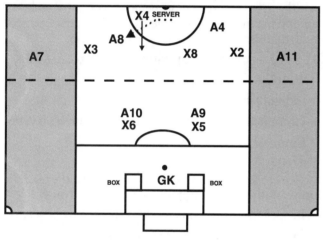

Diagram 6-34

EXERCISE III. 4 v. 3 IN RESTRICTED AREA (DIAGRAM 6-33)

Organization:

Server plays balls to A4 or A8 and they combine with A9 & A10 v. three defenders (X5, X6 and X8) with X4 a recovering defender (on second touch of ball by A4 or A8).

Objectives:

• Play the ball forward into the danger area with controlled speed.

Coaching Points to be Emphasized/Observed:

• Do attacking players maintain maximum width but attack as centrally as possible?
• Are early decisions made by midfielders to run with or pass the ball?
• Does the team maintain its attacking momentum?

EXERCISE IV. 4 v. 4 WITH WINGERS (DIAGRAM 6-34)

Organization:

Server plays to 2 v. 2 midfield situation with X2 &

X3 acting as recovering wing backs. A7 and A11 are wingers and are the only attacking players who may play in the shaded area (use flat cones to designate). At a point allow X2 or X3 to chase a winger as exercise concludes.

Objectives:

• Attack with pace centrally to take advantage of the bad positions of X2 & X3 (they can recover to defend centrally);
• Play wide to A7 or A11 only as a last resort;

Key Coaching Points/Observations:

• If the attack is slowed and ball is played wide, is the service of the ball EARLY with PACE into the second six yard boxes (labeled "box" on the diagram)?;
• Is the early ball played preferably between knee and head height?

EXERCISE V. 6 v. 8 (DIAGRAM 6-35)

Organization:

Use the full width, half field, six attackers, eight defenders (one recovering at the start). Whether X8 recovers to mark A8 and the Xs play with a back four or X3 pushes forward to mark A8 and they play with two defenders and a sweeper is up to the defenders.

Objective:

• Can the attacking players make decisions when to attack centrally and when to attack wide?

In conclusion, this practice session, which is part of the NSCAA Advanced National Diploma curriculum, demands high organization and a keen sense of observation by the coach in order that it be of value to the players and the team.

When to halt the exercise, when to move on to the next stage, when to place restrictions on players, etc., must be part of the coach's methodology in order for this to be imparted accurately to the team.

Finally, if there are repeated technical breakdowns in the exercise then the coach and the team must get back to fundamentals and correct those errors. As often stated: "There are no tactics if there is no technique!"

⚽

POSSESSION
Bob Dikranian

In all soccer games, possession of the ball, whether in counter-attack situations or the methodical building of an attack, is vital in creating scoring chances and goals. Controlling the ball individuality and keeping control collectively, is a big problem today in U.S. soccer. In this country we do not see teams consistently stringing together passes throughout a typical match. Technical problems in receiving, dribbling, and distribution of the ball are major obstacles to ball possession. Tactical problems, i.e. , proper movement, timing of runs, and mobility in creating space, further contribute to the possession problem. Lack of individual composure and patience also contributes to the lack of ball possession by teams in this country.

Possession in building an attack usually begins with effective use of the extra player or players in the defensive zone. The team objective in possession soccer is to safely move the ball from the back third to the middle third as quickly and through the best avenue possible with the ultimate aim of penetrating the final third of the field for an attempt at goal. By having back players coming forward and supporting the at-

tack, numerical advantages can be created to enhance possession and penetration. The more times we can enter the front third of the field with full possession, the more we can create scoring chances on goal.

Tactical exercises such as 2 v. 1, 3 v. 1, 4 v. 2, 5 v. 2, 5 v. 3, 6 v. 6, etc., are important to teach various principles of play (mobility, support, etc.). The exercises that follow complement the aforementioned activities. They encourage patience in play as well as improving a team's tactical awareness and decision-making, thus establishing better possessional play. Technically, the skills of receiving, dribbling, and passing are being used and hopefully improved under pressure in realistic game-like conditions. These exercises and others are virtually worthless unless the coach has full understanding of the principles of play (mobility, support, width, improvisation, and penetration) on attack, or an understanding of the role of the first attacker, second attacker and third attacker on offense.

1) 3 v. 3 IN GRID + 4 OUTSIDE GRID (DIAGRAM 6-36)

Objectives
• Individual and collective possession;

• Combination play between two and three players;

• Emphasis on safety versus risk.

Exercise
In an area approximately 20 x 25 yards, the team in possession of ball maintains possession through:

• Proper timing of runs to open space;

• Proper technique in receiving ball;

• Individual dribbling and deceptive moves to escape pressure for passing options or combination play.

They use players outside grid when other options aren't available or the risk in losing possession increases.

In the above exercise, X1 moves correctly towards outside player with ball. After proper reception, X1 uses dribbling and passing options with players inside and outside grid area. Players inside grid are encouraged to dribble and use whatever appropriate maneuvers to escape pressure to keep possession. As players increase their confidence and ability in dribbling, they are then encouraged to determine which dribbling, passing or combination play options are "on" within grid. The area of the grid may be larger or smaller depending on the ability of the players.

If the initial defending team gains possession, they then try to maintain possession.

2) 4 v. 4 PLUS ONE FREE PLAYER OR 5 v. 5 WITH ONE FREE PLAYER (DIAGRAM 6-37)

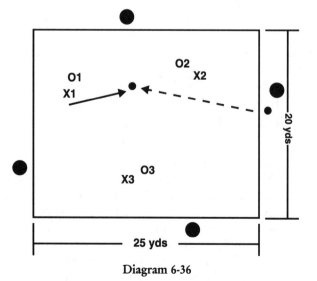

Diagram 6-36

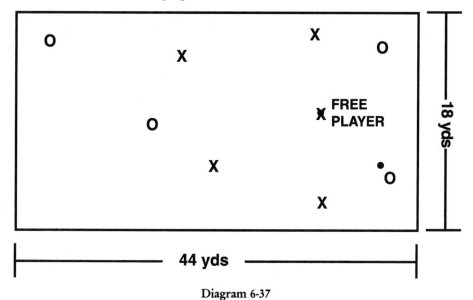

Diagram 6-37

Objectives

- Individual and collective possession;
- Combination play between two and three players;
- Decision when to dribble, when to pass or when to play quickly;
- Switching the play;
- Safety v. risk.

Exercise

This exercise can be performed inside the penalty box. The team in possession uses the free player to keep possession of the ball, through dribbling, passing or combination play (wall pass, take over, etc.). Players are encouraged to dribble, when passing options don't exist. Players are also encouraged to play one- or two-touch to escape pressure. The player with the ball is constantly looking for the best options to keep possession and relieve defensive pressure. Switching the play is another option.

Progression

- Unlimited touches;
- Three-touch then two-touch for the free player;
- One-touch game with dribbling - players get a point for every time a one-touch pass is made. Twenty points wins the game. When players can't play one-touch, they are encouraged to dribble and maintain possession until one-touch interpassing is possible. Hopefully players will develop quick and safe decisions with the ball, when to dribble and when to pass;
- 5 v. 5 plus free player (more difficult - less space)

3)6 v. 3, FIVE PLAYERS ON THE OUTSIDE AND ONE PLAYER IN THE MIDDLE V. THREE DEFENDERS (DIAGRAMS 6-38A AND 6-38B)

Objectives

- To possess ball through passing and proper support (passing angles);
- Switching the play;
- Dribbling and passing options (center player or players);
- Combination play;
- Safety v. risk.

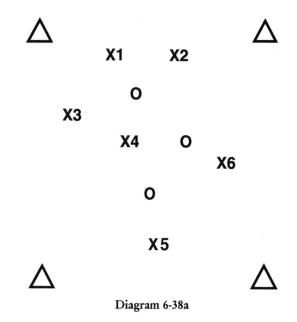

Diagram 6-38a

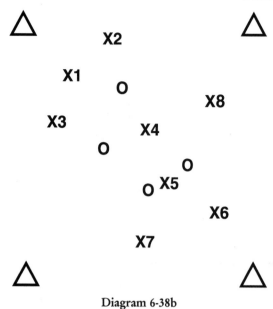

Diagram 6-38b

Exercise

This exercise can be played in an area approximately 30 x 30 yards. The area can vary depending on the ability of the players. Making the area smaller puts more pressure on the team trying to maintain possession. In 8 v. 4 exercises, increase size of the area slightly.

Progression

• Unlimited touches;
• Two-touch restriction on the outside players, unlimited inside players X4, X5 and X6;
• Defenders win the ball, one-touch v. the midfielders (three touches in 6 v. 3; four touches v. X7 or X8 in 8 v. 4).

4) 1 + 6 v. 6 + 1 (7 v. 6) (DIAGRAM 6-39)

Objective

To possess the ball through dribbling, interpassing, and combination play until attacking team can dribble ball under control over opponent's endline.

Exercise

In an area approximately 40 x 70 yards, the attacking team makes use of extra players to maintain pos-

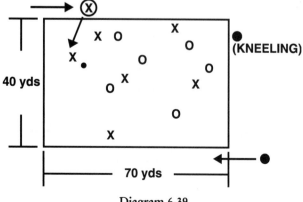

(KNEELING)

40 yds

70 yds

Diagram 6-39

session and gain penetration. The extra player is only active when their team has possession of the ball. When possession is lost, extra player kneels down (not active).

Progression

• Unlimited touches ;
• Three-touch everyone – two-touch for the extra player;
• Two-touch everyone – one-touch for the free player; Player attacking end line may have more than two touches;
• Use of goalkeepers with shooting to score goals.

5) 3 v. 3 or 4 v. 4 (DIAGRAM 6-40)

Objective

To maintain control of the ball mainly through dribbling (shielding, deceptive maneuvers, etc.), passing, combination play.

Exercise

The team in control will try to maintain possession in an area 25 x 25 yards until they can successfully dribble from zone A to zone B. When all attacking players have moved over, they will then try to successfully penetrate back to the initial area. Team in possession of the ball may not pass the ball from one zone to another; however, they may pass in their existing zone until they can dribble to the opposite area.

6) 4 v. 3/ 1 v. 1/ 3 v. 4 (8 v. 8) with Goalkeepers (DIAGRAM 6-41)

Objective

Keep possession of the ball and penetrate towards your opponent's goal until you can create goal scoring chances. Emphasis is placed on successfully getting out of the back third safely, preparing and entering the front third.

Exercise

Area approximately 70 yds. wide by 85 yds. in length. Players are restricted to zones. One defender may attack or leave defensive third. Midfielders can go into any zone. In the diagram, X1 midfielder helps get X2 (leftback) into midfield. X2 will penetrate and work with the three forwards and one defender to create chances to score. When the O defenders win the ball, X2 will retreat back to his/her back third while the O team will control the ball and gain penetration towards their opponent's goal.

7) 8 v. 8 + 2 Free Midfielders with Goalkeepers (10 v. 8) (DIAGRAM 6-42)

Objective

Maintain possession with the use of two extra midfielders. Penetrate until scoring chances are created. Special emphasis is placed on the two free

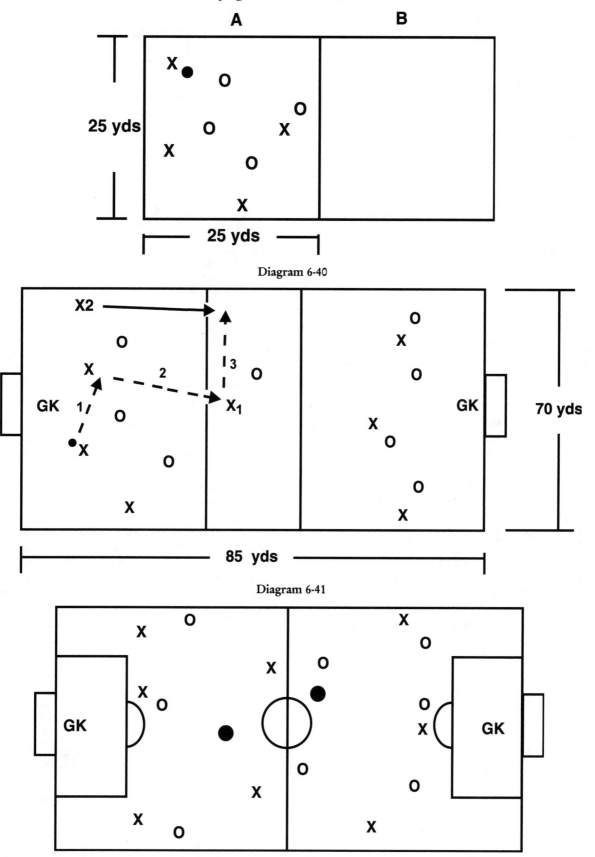

Diagram 6-40

Diagram 6-41

Diagram 6-42

midfielders to support the ball, maintain control of the ball, and distribute accurately and intelligently.

Exercise

Full field or an area 70 x 100 yards Safe passing from the defensive zone to the midfield zone. More risk in the attacking third of the field. All principles of play are applied.

Progression

- Unlimited touches;
- Touch limitations (especially the two free midfielders);
- Scoring chances - everyone should be at the midfield line or beyond;
- Backs must assist or score goals.

⚽

MODERN WING PLAY
*Bob Gansler**

If you were at the 1992 NSCAA convention and didn't catch Bob Gansler's session on modern wing play, you missed a classic example of both progressive and effective coaching by our former national team coach.

Coach Gansler began the session by telling that he had done a similar session in 1979. "Not all that much has changed since that clinic," he said. His contention was that most goals are scored in one of two ways: set plays and crosses. The objective of this session was to improve the quality of wing play.

The warmup consisted of pairs of players going 1 v. 1, with the emphasis on the attacker's ability to get behind their defender. Gansler made the important insight that "once you beat the defender on the wing, you need to go to goal to seal off the marker" as opposed to running parallel to the touch line.

- **Step 1.** Coach Gansler progressed to two unopposed attackers, introducing overlaps, wall passes, and take-overs. It was clear that he was interested in the small, two-man games that are so important in getting players free on the flanks. "Timing is critical, insist on quality," he told his charges. Gansler also stressed that "the first step of the wall pass is also the pass itself." As you make your first stride you strike the ball." As with all his progression, Gansler jumped in and demonstrated each new combination, thus giving the players a visual standard to reach. Double passes were introduced, and the players started to create their own rhythm. The convention center was quiet, save for the tap-tap-tap of the soccer balls.

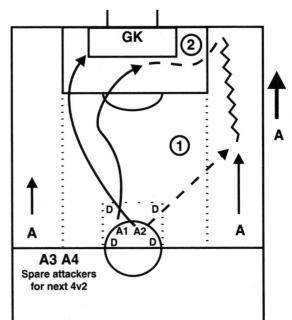

Diagram 6-43: In small field settings two attackers win ball from four defenders in central grid and play the ball wide to either side and then make runs to near and far posts respectively. Game restarts with four defenders playing keep away from two new attackers in grid.

- **Step 2.** It was time to introduce defenders. A game of 4 v. 2 was set-up at midfield, with a winger stationed wide on each side. (Diagram 6-43) When the two win it, they play to either wing and get in to finish. This provided realistic transition play for frontrunners, and gave the wingers functional training on service. Gansler stressed the importance of getting around the defender and playing quality balls at game speed. "Chris Henderson is the only player on our national team to consistently get around and play quality ball from both sides," he said about the former UCLA NSCAA/Umbro All-America player.

- **Step 3.** Gansler then added another wide player on each side, re-introducing the two man games. He also added a pair of unmarked strikers. The first option presented has the second attacker overlapping the dribbler, receiving the ball and serving it to either post. (Diagram 6-44a) The second option was a three-man combination with the first wide player to get it, play to a striker, and make a run to goal. The second wide player overlaps, gets the ball from the striker and serves a first-time ball. (Diagram 6-44b) After the players got a clear picture, Gansler introduced man markers on the strikers. This variation gave a sense of game conditions to the session, with a wide player getting around the defense. The winger would play the ball to the striker's feet, then get the return pass near the end line, setting up some quality chances.

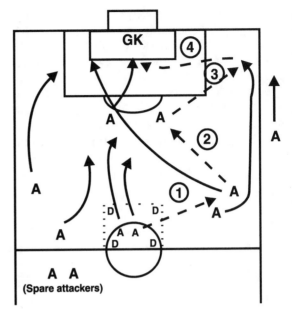

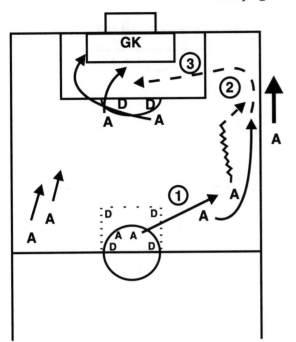

Diagram 6-44a: Two-man play with overlapping winger serving ball.

Diagram 6-44b: Three-man play with first pass to winger who plays to feet of striker with overlapping winger receiving striker's pass for service to near or far post. Resume with 4 v. 2. Switch sides to play it both left and right.

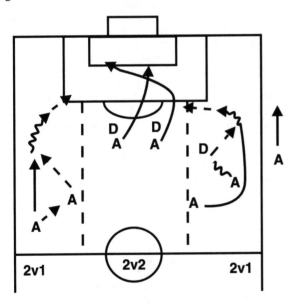

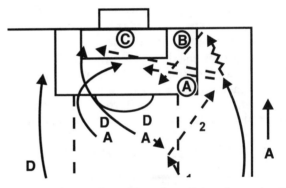

Diagram 6-45a: 2 v. 2 in central area; 2 v. 1 on flanks. Overlap shown on right flank; wall pass combination shown on left flank.

Diagram 6-45b: Overlap with options of A-early service; B-pullback; C-far post service. Alternate sides of the field. Restart with clearances by defense if it wins ball to attackers on side opposite from the initial attacker or new attackers themselves if goal is scored or shot attempt is off target. Spare balls should be available on each side of the field.

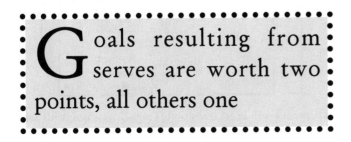

- **Step 4.** Next he played 2 v. 2 in front of goal, with 2 v. 1 out wide. (Diagram 6-45a) The wide players could work various combinations to beat the single defender. This worked well as did with the flank players interpassing looking for the striker showing for the ball. (Diagram 6-45b) Some good combinations ensued in this match-condition practice and the session took on a quicker pace. In order to concentrate on wing play, he made goals resulting from serves worth two points, all others one.

- **Step 5.** Gansler then introduced a second goal, with a spare player joining with the old defender in the flank area to form the two new attackers going the other way. (Diagram 6-46a) Once the session went to two goals, the intensity and creativity improved dramatically. The field had two offset goals, and each attacking team continued to play 2 v. 1 in the flank grid and 2 v. 2 in the central grid. Both teams enjoyed this "numbers up" out wide, and a new defender took the attacker's place to defend against the two new attackers going the other way. (Diagram 6-46b) Although the rotation is a bit confusing, each player takes two repetitions, then steps out. (Diagram 6-46c) The coach had created the proper environment, he "had set up, in a repetitive nature, wing options."

• **Step 6.** The last progression was a 5 v. 5 game with keepers. "I've done my teaching, now we play 5 v. 5 and I assess," he said. For the first time in the session, the goals were placed in their natural positions. (Diagram 6-47) With the scoring system still in place (two for goals off crosses, one for central strikes), the players looked for quality chances out wide, and took full advantage of the ensuing service. The action was quick paced, and the players finally broke their session-long silence. They called for balls, shouted out warnings, and provided the coaches on hand with plenty of "good pictures."

In retrospect, the theory of progression was in clear evidence. We say the activities increase in technical and tactical demand, going from no goals to one, and finally to two. The session started with fundamental technical training, and progressed into match-condi-

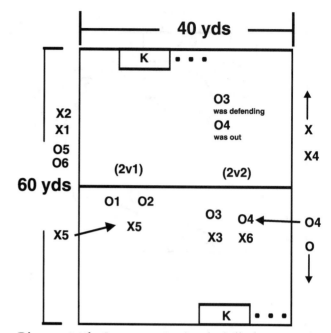

Diagram 6-46b: Once team O wins the ball, the two O defenders (O1 and O2) become the two O attacking flank players who go 2 v. 1 against X5 (who was a spare player in diagram 4A). O3 (who was defending in Diagram 4A) and O4 (who was a spare player) go to goal against X3 and X6 (who was a spare player) 2 v. 2. Drill is continuous with defenders (including keepers) seeking to find teammates with outlet passes if they dispossess the attacking team. If shot by the attacking team is wide, then keeper uses spare balls to initiate attack. Initially play has the restriction that the two attackers in the 2 v. 2 game must play the ball wide into the 2 v. 1 game seeking the crossing ball as the end result. Later the play can be free.

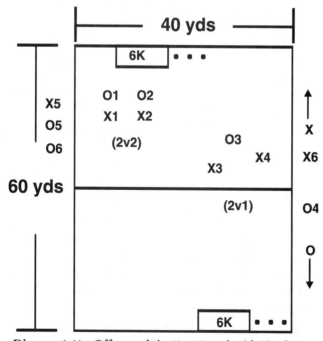

Diagram 6-46a: Offset goals in 60 x 40 yard grid. Six players on each team. 2 v. 1 on flank; 2 v. 2 central. Team X has possession of ball. X1 and X2 play 2 v. 2 central; X3 and X4 play 2 v. 1 on flank. Spare players shown outside field.

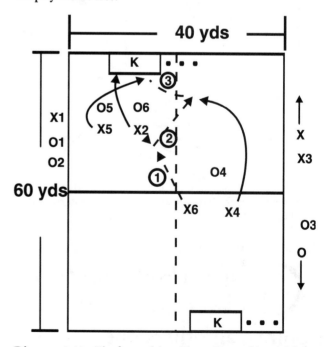

Diagram 6-46c: Final transition. Team X attacking with X4 and X6 playing 2 v. 1 versus O4. X2 and X5 play 2 v. 2 versus O5 and O6.

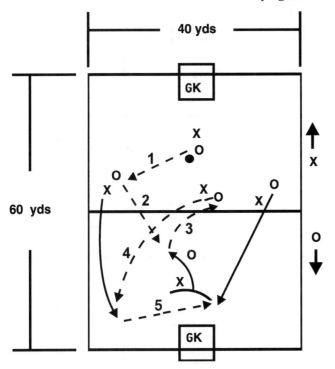

40 yds

60 yds

GK

GK

X
O
1
O
X
2
X
O
X
O
3
X
4
O
X
5

X

X

O

O

Diagram 6-47: 5 v. 5 with goalkeepers.

tion activities. With the limited space available, the 6 v. 6 was as close as Gansler could get to match conditions. The tactical demands increased as the numbers did, with the various choices presented to the wingers (driven near post, chipped far post, pulled back to the top of the box, early cross) becoming more and more real. All of the flank players had many repetitions serving, and it was clear to all the players that improving wing play was the goal of the session.

* Reported by Rocky Harmon

ONE V. ONE
Bob Dikranian

There are many tactical situations that occur in the game of soccer. The most common situation is the one versus one confrontation.

One attacker challenged and pressured by a single defender occurs more often than any other situation in a soccer game. The winners of these individual duels have a critical impact on the outcome of the game. Usually the ability to collect and possess the ball offensively, coupled with a similar capacity to play the ball in a positive manner forward, will enhance a team's chances of creating scoring opportunities. Defensively, the skill to win the ball directly on a pass or dribble and immediately start a counter attack will help cre-

ate quick penetration and anticipated scoring chances.

COACHING POINTS

Offensively

- **Use of Mobility** – Attackers should use different types of runs to get free and create space for themselves to receive the ball under the least amount of pressure possible.

- **Receiving** – Attacker should correctly receive the ball and attempt to turn as quickly as possible and play (dribble, pass) forward for penetration.

- **Deception** – should be encouraged; especially turning maneuvers (spin turns, step-overs, etc.) which enable the player to face forward (towards his/her attacking goal) and be able to play in that direction.

- **Tactical Application** – Depending on the situation and position of the ball on the field of play, the attacker should selectively pass or dribble for penetration. Safe passing or dribbling in the back third is the general tactical rule. Greater risk is progressively taken as players move from the middle third into the front (attacking) third of the field.

In the front third deceptive dribbling with the ball to beat defenders should be encouraged to penetrate defenses and create scoring chances.

Defensively

- **Positioning** - When the ball is lost, take a defensive position goalside of the ball and your attacker.

- **Interception** – On a pass, try to win the ball cleanly and start the counter attack.

- **Destroy play** – If you cannot win the ball cleanly, destroy the play (i.e., clearing the ball, kicking the ball out-of-bounds).

- **Timing** – If a pass is made to an attacker, close down and pressure from behind. Deny the attacker an immediate turn. As a pass is being made, the defender should use that time to "make up ground" - lessen the distance between the themselves and the attacker.

- **Deny Turning** – by pressuring at arm's distance (not chest to back) and force backward dribbling or passing.

- **Delay by Using Control and Restraint** – Do not step or dive in while out of control nor jump in to any feint or fake by the attacker.

- **Cover** – Wait for help from a supporting (covering) defender so you can exert more pressure on the attacking player with the ball. At the right time, tackle intelligently and courageously to win the ball.

ONE V. ONE TRAINING EXERCISES

I. One v. One – Two or four goals (two goals can be with or without keepers). Attacker X can score at

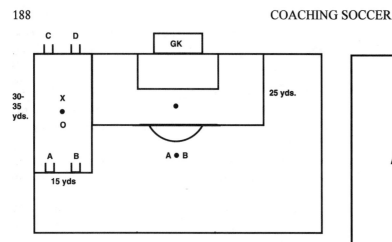

Diagram 6-47 & 6-48

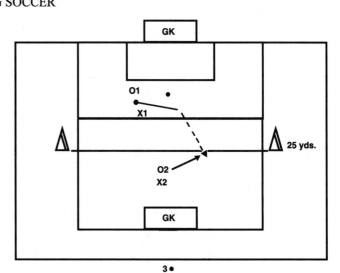

3●

Diagram 6-49

small goals A or B while O can score to goals C or D. (Diagram 6-47)

II. One v. One – Draw. On command, both players compete for the ball. Whichever wins the ball becomes the attacker; the other the defender. (Diagram 6-48) Variations: play to one goal with keeper, to two goals with keepers, no goals. Emphasis should be on shielding and escaping.

III. One v. One – Zonal. Use two zones with 1 v. 1 in each zone. Defensive player O1 tries to play the ball to teammate O2, who then attempts to turn and score. Players are restricted to the zone they start in. If the X team win the ball they immediately counter attack. (Diagram 6-49)

IV. One v. One v. One – Players change roles and zones. O1 attacks defender X2 with the ball. When a goal is scored or X2 wins the ball, he/she then becomes the attacker and dribbles to the neutral zone before attacking A3. (Diagram 6-50)

V. One v. One – Central Goal. Use two zones with 1 v. 1 in each zone. The goalkeeper is in a central goal. X1 starts by dribbling while O2 defends and tries to win the ball. X1 attempts to score. If the ball goes to the opposite side, the first player to the ball becomes the attacker and the other the defender. (Diagram 6-51)

VI. One v. One – Alternating. X1 dribbles and attempts to beat defender O2. After that attempt, O1 takes on X2. Players exchange roles in the next round. (Diagram 6-52)

VII. One v. One – Three Zones. Use six players. O1 has the option of dribbling to penetrate or passing to flank players O3 or X4. Attackers with the ball are encouraged to use safe dribbling in their defensive third and use their flank players accordingly. Attackers are encouraged to take risks and beat defenders in the attacking third of the field. If defender X2 wins the ball, he/she becomes the attacker and O1 the defender. (Diagram 6-53)

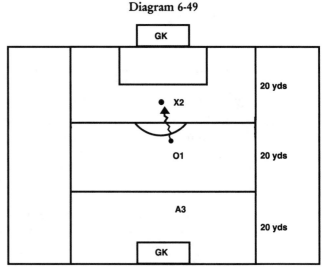

Diagram 6-50

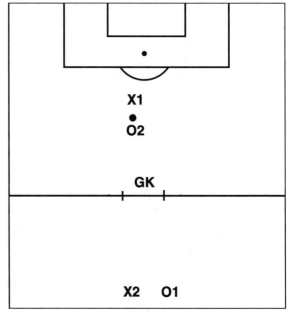

Diagram 6-51

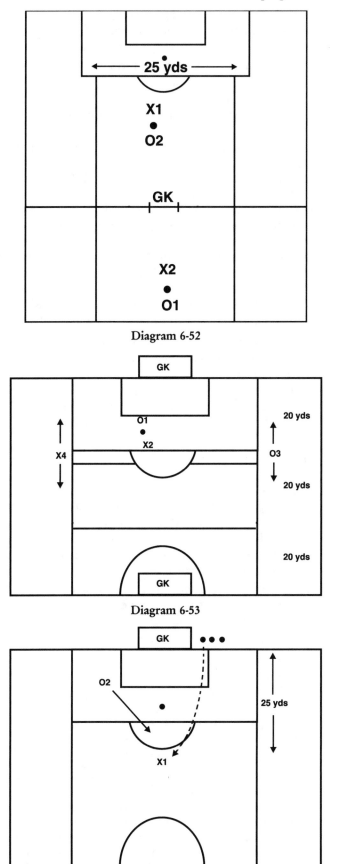

Diagram 6-52

Diagram 6-53

Diagram 6-54a

VIII. One v. One to Goal. With emphasis on defensive play, particularly on closing down attackers. In Diagram 6-54a the ball is played to X1. As the ball is in flight, O2 makes up ground, closes down X1 and pressurizes him/her.

In Diagram 6-54b the ball is played to O1 (with his back to goal). X2 closes down and denies O1 the turn.

In Diagram 6-54c the ball is served to attacker X1 on the flank. Defender O2 carefully closes down, contains and denies a service from X1 to X3. O4 is positioned to correctly cover attacker X3.

In Diagram 6-54d the ball is played to attacker X1 who tries to turn and play forward to teammate X3. Defender O2 closes down and denies the attacker from playing forward. If attacker X2 is able to turn and play to X3, defender O4 should try to anticipate the pass and win the ball cleanly.

IX. Half or Full Field Play. Finally, half field (6 v. 6) or full field (8 v. 8 or 11 v. 11) scrimmages should be used to emphasize attacking play as well as 1 v. 1 defensive play in different zones of the field.

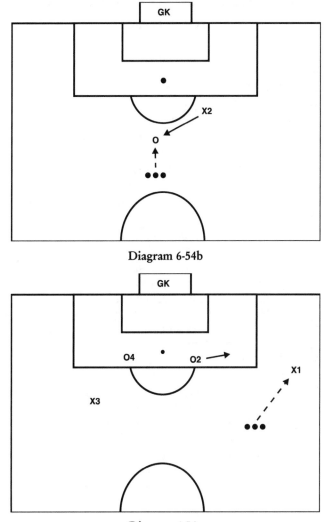

Diagram 6-54b

Diagram 6-54c

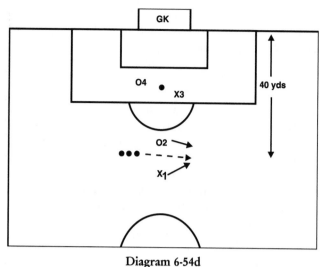

Diagram 6-54d

ZONAL DEFENDING: IS IT RIGHT FOR YOUR TEAM?

Jeff Tipping

This presentation deals with methods of teaching zonal defending. We are primarily concerned here with two major characteristics of zonal defending:

• Concern with space defending rather than man-to-man. The decision whether to mark a man tightly or to cover a teammate is highlighted in zonal defending more than man-to-man.

• Maintaining an effective team shape from which to defend. Collective defending is important in zonal systems. Keeping zones small and tight is critical if this system is to be effective.

It should be noted that most zonal teams play out of a 4-4-2 formation. It is generally accepted that four players can cover the dangerous spaces across the field. In the '94 World Cup Brazil, Italy and Sweden employed a zonal defense and all utilized a 4-4-2. Closer to home, in the recent 1993 NCAA Division I Final Four, Princeton and South Carolina defended zonally, again utilizing a 4-4-2 formation.

Team managers and trainers adopt zonal tactics for a number of reasons, some of which include:

1. **Team shape.** It is easier to keep a good defending shape out of a zone. Players are less inclined to get pulled out of important positions.

2. **Fitness.** Players in zones generally do less running and tracking of opponents around the field.

3. **Weaknesses.** It is easier to hide a weak defender in a zone than in man-to-man.

4. **Attack.** Teams which have maintained a good shape defensively can attack more efficiently from an organized shape after gaining possession.

The disadvantages in zonal defending may include:

1. **Assignment marking.** It is difficult to pull a player out of a zone to "assignment mark" an outstanding opponent. (Maradona v. England 1986 World Cup, Claudio Reyna v. Princeton 1993 NCAA).

2. **Demands verbal communication.** "When in doubt give a shout" is never more true than in zonal defending. Talking is indispensable and yet many of our players do not talk.

3. **Square back four.** The back four get caught flat, especially when the ball is in the middle of the field, or with long flighted balls.

4. **Decision-making.** Emphasizes the burden on defenders of deciding whether to pressure a player or cover for a teammate. This leads to looser marking than in man-to-man. (Ian Rush v. Everton 1989 FA Cup Final goals #2 and #3).

KEYS TO GOOD ZONAL DEFENDING

1. The work of the two central defenders is vital, The whole team pivots around these two.

2. Defenders generally do not cross in front of each other except in emergency situations. They may cross behind a teammate to cover for him or to cut out a through pass.

3. Teams must be compact and "travel with the ball." Defenders must move as a block to minimize spaces. (Roxburgh)

4. The ball should be forced wide and kept wide. This helps the "stepping" effect of back four and midfield.

5. There must be constant pressure on the ball to prevent vertical service.

6. If no pressure on ball, the two central defenders must decide whether to drop off or possibly step up to catch opponents offside.

WARMUPS*

1. **Handball** – Game normally promotes lots of verbal communication between players. 5 v. 5 in each half of the field. One defender goes in goal when opponents come over halfway line. Defense plays a 4 v. 5. Nobody allowed over halfway line, but when defense wins ball they pass to teammates in other half. Passing is by the hand only. (Diagram6-55)

2. **"Fire" exercise** – This exercise (designed by coach Mike Berticelli of Notre Dame) is good for team morale and also teaching defenders important zonal principles. Split team into three groups of three defenders and two groups of seven attackers. Three defenders stand in the "D". Goalkeeper punts the ball to seven attackers waiting at the halfway line.

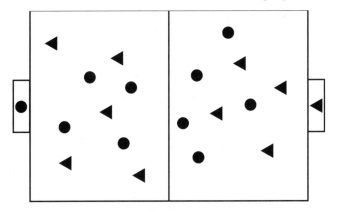

Diagram 6-55

As GK punts ball the two outside defenders sprint to opposite touchlines, and the central defender runs around the goal. The attackers must wait for a teammate to touch the ball before they can go over the halfway line and attack. All three defenders must sprint to get back into a defensive triangle to deal with the oncoming seven attackers. Alternate groups and keep score. If defenders intercept the ball and play it out of bounds, they get a goal; attackers get a goal if they score. (Diagram 6-56)

*Any exercise in which defense is outnumbered becomes a zonal exercise.

Teaching zonal coverage

1. **Training the two center backs.** The pivoting of the center backs is a good place to start when introducing zonal defending. Each center back just decide when to pressure and when to drop off and cover.

Organization (Diagram 6-57)

- Two center backs v. one center forward in central half of one field. The center backs are responsible for one goal each. When they win the ball they play ball to side servers or straight to their center forward;

- Center forward can score in either goal;

- Introduce second center forward.

Coaching Points

- Two center backs must be concerned with their zone;

- Verbal communication with each other especially when switching;

- Tactical decision-making as to who shall pressure or who shall cover;

- Center backs should not cross in front of each other — "pass on" the attackers to each other.

It is important to introduce a second center forward, as center backs in a zonal system frequently do play 2 v. 2. Communication is even more important as the covering and pressuring decisions become more

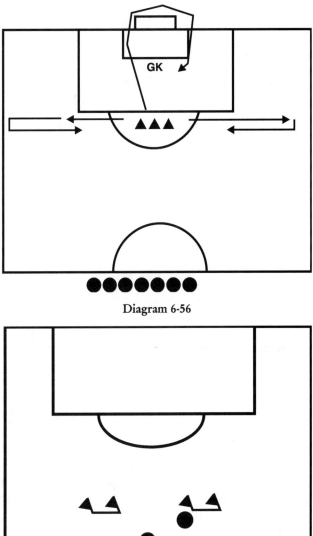

Diagram 6-56

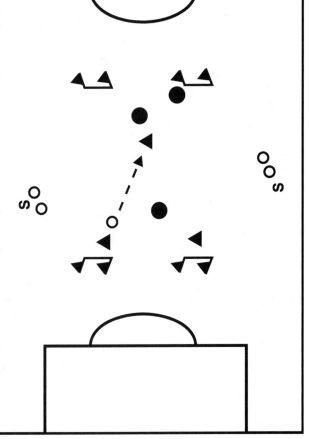

Diagram 6-57

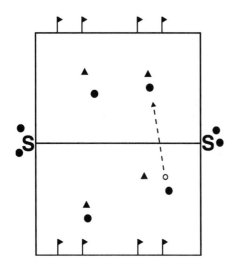

Diagram 6-58a

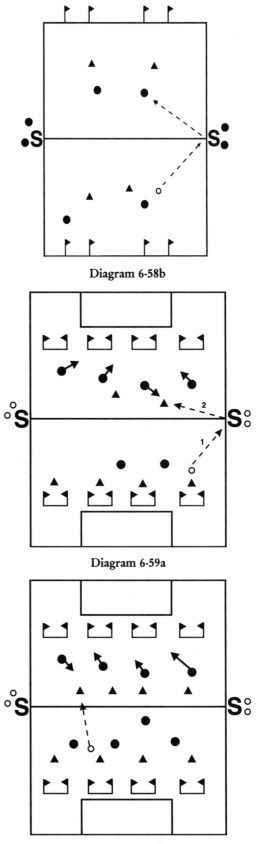

Diagram 6-58b

complex with the second striker to deal with.

Organization (Diagram 6-58a & 6-58b)

Play four goals, two in each half of central field area with teams allowed to play directly to their center forwards or play to server who then dictates passes. Each back is assigned a goal to defend.

2. **Introduction of outside backs.** Organization (Diagrams 6-59a & 6-59b) Two outside backs who also must defend a goal are introduced. The back four now must each defend a goal while still covering for each other. Support players are placed at corners of the halfway line to help the two center forwards. (Goals should be at least four yards wide to prevent defenders from retreating into goals and not pressuring.)

• Nobody allowed over halfway line;
• Defenders play balls into other half once ball is won, or to side support players;
• Build up to 4 v. 4 + 4 v. 4.

Coaching Points

1. Defender must decide when to tackle/pressure and when to drop off/cover;
2. Outside backs pinch in to help center backs when ball is central (Diagram 6-59a);
3. Try to force ball outside;
4. Defenders "step" themselves when ball is in wide position (Diagram 6-59b).

TRAVELING WITH THE BALL

These exercises were used by former Scotland coach Andy Roxburgh and are designed to help the defenders keep their zonal shape laterally across the field and also establish compactness vertically up and down the field.

Diagram 6-59a

Diagram 6-59b

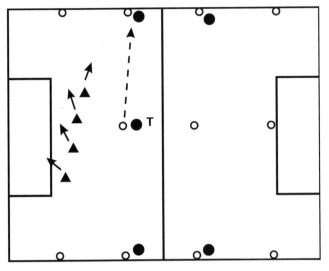

Diagram 6-60

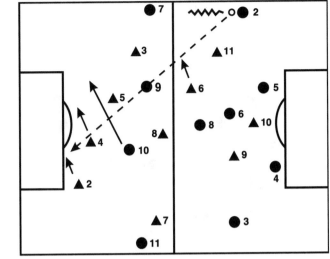

Diagram 6-61

Organization (Diagram 6-60)

- On a full field, the trainer (T) has a ball and is alone with the back four. Trainer establishes an acceptable distance between himself and the back four (25-30 yards) and puts markers down every 25-30 yards downfield. Trainer moves with the ball and back four maintain that distance between themselves and trainer up to halfway line.

- Flank players placed at pinnies at four wide positions. When ball played to players in wide position the back four must swivel.

- Two attacking center forwards are introduced. Four defensive midfielders are introduced.

- Midfield players must do the same as back four and travel with the ball, no more than five yards away. When ball is played to wide players the whole team must swivel.

- Wide players can play ball into center forwards and then the game is live.

- Add more numbers to make it more like a game. Trainer is replaced by central midfielders.

Coaching Points

- Keep correct spacing between ball and the two "lines" of defenders.

- When ball is played to a wide attacker both lines must swivel and employ "stepping" in their positioning.

- Angles of approach are such that attackers are forced down the touchline.

- Midfielders try and screen opposing center forwards by "stepping" into passing lanes, especially when ball is in wide position.

- Midfielders try and push up on opposing outside backs when those backs are retreating to retrieve a

ball. Center backs must push the whole team forward.

Stepping — and the offside factor (Diagram 6-61)

The stepping effect of the back four and midfield enables covering defenders to:

- Slide behind a beaten defender (e.g. triangle #11 is beaten by attacker #2, T#6 can slide behind to contain attacker);

- Be well positioned to cut out balls to the feet of the center forward (e.g. T#6 may be able to cut out a pass to attacking #9);

- Pick off a pass played over the heads of pressuring or second defenders (e.g. a ball floated over T#4 can be attacked by T#2);

- Positioned to be able to see ball and detect a vertical or diagonal run by attacker (e.g. T#4 can track a run by attacking #10 and still see flight of the ball).

A critical point which a trainer must now wrestle with is the positioning of defenders relative to attacking players and offside space. Teams which high-pressure opponents must be pushed up from the rear to maintain compactness, therefore space behind the back four could be exploited by attackers making vertical/diagonal runs. The decision for the back four, especially, is whether to track these runs, or hold their position in the hope that players will run into offside positions.

Baressi, the Italian defender, is the supreme example of a defender who uses the offside line by stepping up or dropping off as the ball is about to be struck. In Diagram 6-62, T#2 and T#4 have flattened their "stepped" position. This positioning makes attackers #9 and #10 much more reluctant to make a vertical run as they are not being kept onside by #2 as they are in Diagram 6-61. However, if attacking #10 beats the

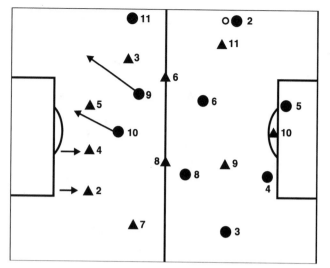

Diagram 6-62

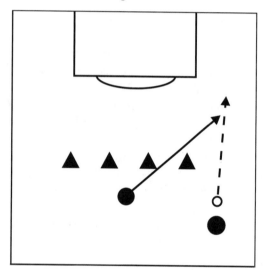

Diagram 6-63

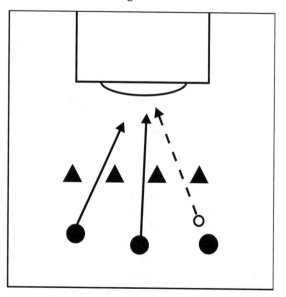

Diagram 6-64

offside line, the defending team is in a very poor position to recover. The other threat to an offside line is the run of attackers #6 or #8 from a deep position (Diagram 6-62).

Steve McMahon, formerly of Liverpool, was a master of beating the offside line from a deep position.

When holding an offside line, some consideration must be given to the following:

• Players making runs from deep positions are liable to beat the offside line;

• Players coming from weak-side blind positions are liable to beat the line;

• Generally, the shorter the distance of the pass the more an official's judgement is clouded;

• Runs from inside to out are easier to recover from (Diagram 6-63) than outside in, or straight vertical runs. (Diagram 6-64) The angle of the run is of considerable importance if the runner beats the offside line.

The decision as to whether to hold an offside line or track a vertical run is a split-second one. It demands not only good judgment but also perfect coordination between teammates. A well orchestrated offside line, while being annoying to the spectator, can keep opponents squeezed into very small places, and is very useful, if a somewhat dangerous tactic.

The question of who shall adopt a zonal system is of particular interest to those coaches who wrestle with the concept of which system is preferable for them. Those choices do depend on the qualities of the players available to a coach, yet both systems have inherent strengths and weaknesses, which were highlighted for all to see in World Cup '94.

QUICK AND EFFECTIVE COUNTERATTACKS
Jay Miller*

Following is a report of a session given by coach Jay Miller at the 1993 NSCAA Convention in Baltimore.

There were some outstanding coaches conducting clinics at the Baltimore convention, but none got the job done any more effectively than Jay Miller. Combining a mixture of humor with the correct teaching progression, Miller effectively charted how to develop effective counterattacks. This is not to imply that Miller was not all business, for his session was quick paced and action-packed. But Miller's approach is a

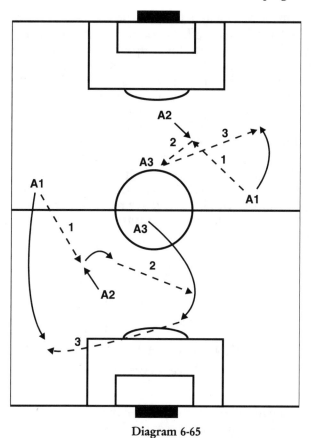

Diagram 6-65

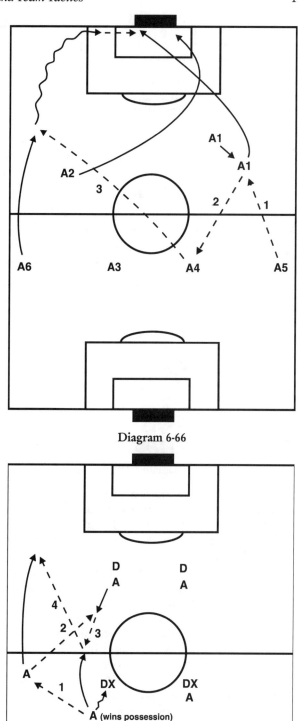

Diagram 6-66

classic example of one who believes that soccer is still a game, and that the players should have fun in their sessions. His quick wit made both coaches and players smile, but he got his point across in the process.

The session started with two simple three-man patterns. (Diagram 6-65) Both were designed to play the ball forward as quickly as possible, specifically to the deepest player available. Miller then demonstrated six-man patterns, and introduced a change of field exercise as well. (Diagram 6-66)

The progression then called for two defenders to mark the two forwards, and the addition of another center-midfielder to play on the attacking team. The resulting 6 v. 2 started with the outside midfielders playing the ball to a marked forward. The three patterns that were introduced earlier came through with the introduction of pressure.

Next Miller placed two small goals on the width of the field, and added one, and then two "Dribbleinos" to play against the attackers. The restriction was placed on the Dribbleinos that they could only pass to each other or take on the opposing midfielders with the object being to score through the small goals. (Diagram 6-67) When the midfielders dispossessed the Dribbleinos, they countered to goal. The ensuing 6 v. 4 was quite realistic and provided many teachable moments for Miller. A main objective was for target player to play it back to the middle, not out wide.

Diagram 6-67

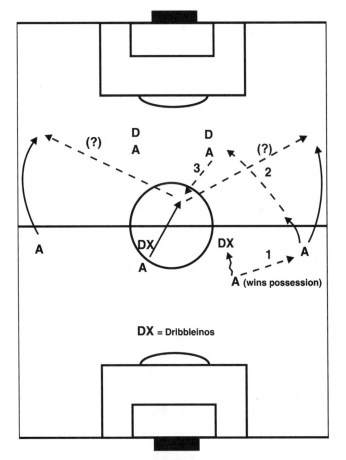

DX = Dribbleinos

Diagram 6-68

This gave the CM the option of switching fields or playing down the wing. (Diagram 6-68) game. Miller noted that the pass from the CM "must have perfect weight." Good goals started to come, with one particular OM getting praise.

By having the Dribbleinos start with the ball, the activity provided real counters, and the simple patterns demonstrated earlier proved very realistic in terms of having application to the counter-attack sequence. The session went from simple to complex, from no pressure to pressure, and from no goals to one, and eventually two goals. he explained.

In closing, Miller addressed the four aspects of training. As for the physical aspect, ne noted that the first thing to get right, from the organizational standpoint, was to get players with pace on the flanks. The technical aspect was addressed in three and five player patterns. Miller reminded the crowd that the way to improve technique is through repetition.

"Once the players feel comfortable with their technical execution, then we introduce tactical decisions," he told the crowd. This was achieved by introducing pressure in the form of the two marking backs. Miller made sure that the attacking team provide the server with both near and far post runs, and tactical deci-

sions made as to where to serve the ball.

Perhaps the most effective aspect of Miller's coaching style has to do with his grasp of the psychological aspect of the game. "How do you make your players believe?" he asked the crowd. "By success" was his answer. Miller had set up a session that got increasingly more difficult, but one that ensured success in the early stages. Combined with his humorous and good-natured demeanor, the players were put at ease and challenged in a positive environment.

"We call it the sandwich effect," said Miller of his positive enforcement. "You give the success and positive reinforcement, then negative remarks in order to correct, and finish with the positive remarks" he explained.

⚽

COUNTER TO EXPLOIT THE
WING BACK OVERLAP
Mike Russo

In the most recent World Cup, Italy demonstrated that counter-attacking soccer can be skillful, exciting, and successful. If coaches approach the use of the counter-attack not as a kick and run method of play, but rather as a distinct style that is characterized by skillful, direct, and quick play, then dangerous scoring chances may be created. Many of the better teams use a combination of buildup and counter in their play, therefore it makes good sense to train our players when to counter and when to buildup.

One situation when the counter can be used effectively is against the wing defender's overlap run when it is not covered by the sweeper or a midfield player. If you are playing a team that employs their wing backs frequently in attack, then you might consider playing your wingers in a more traditional sense by freeing them from defensive responsibilities when the wing back on their side of the field goes forward in attack.

A tactical decision must be made defensively to combat the overlap run by playing more zonally through midfield as did many teams in the 1982 World Cup. If the ball is played to the overlapping wing back the right midfield player is asked to track the wing back and the other midfield players slide over to seal off space in the central part of the defense. The offball winger is asked defensively to drop back looking for any change in the direction of the attack. (Diagram 6-69)

The player who regains possession of the ball must be instructed to play the ball immediately to the winger at midfield. Both field players and goalkeepers must work on distributing the ball quickly and accurately to that part of the field. The winger must be trained to receive the ball fluidly and take it toward the center of the field at top speed to attack the sweeper. (Diagram 6-70)

As the winger begins his run, the central striker makes a key tactical run away from the ball trying to get blindside of the center back. If the center back tracks him, then the winger should be encouraged to challenge the sweeper. (Diagram 6-71a) If the sweeper retreats intelligently (Diagram 6-71b), then the center forward should be prepared to receive a possible through pass from the winger. If, as in Diagram 6-71c, the center back is drawn toward the ball, then a possible through pass over the top to the center forward

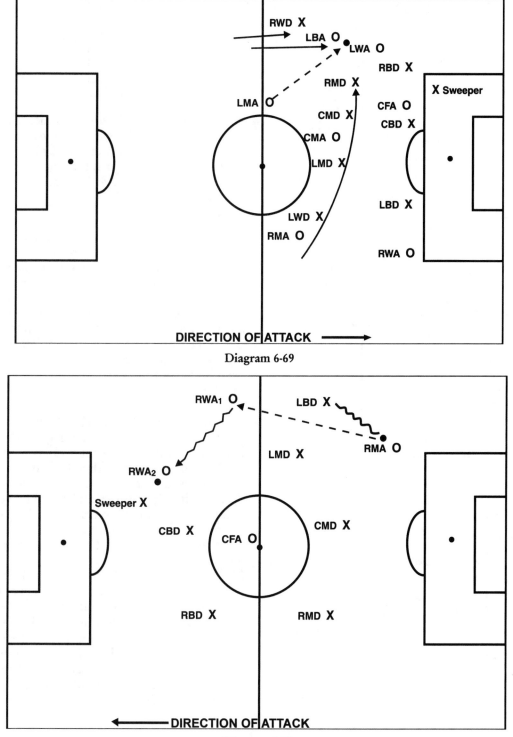

Diagram 6-69

Diagram 6-70

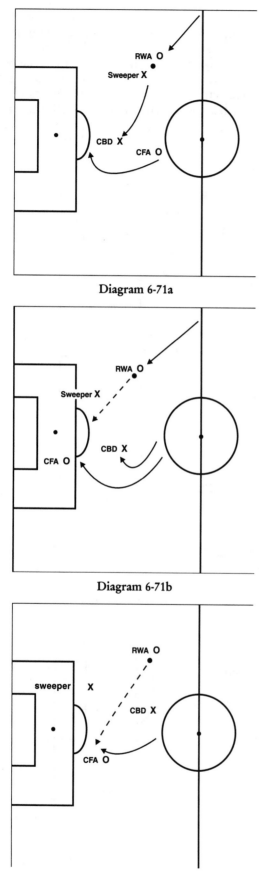

Diagram 6-71a

Diagram 6-71b

Diagram 6-71c

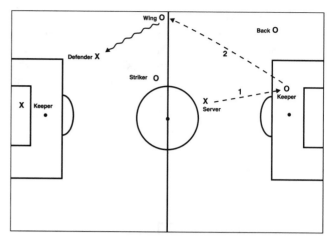

Diagram 6-72

may be attempted. Obviously, quick 1-2 pass or any other combination between the two attacking players can be utilized. The advantage of playing the ball immediately to the winger is that there is the possibility of getting a 1 v. 1 or 2 v. 2 situation in the entire attacking half of the field.

TRAINING SESSIONS

Training sessions can be designed to develop the skill and speed necessary to make the counter attack effective. In Diagram 6-72 a server plays the ball immediately to the winger. The winger is asked to receive the ball quickly and fluidly and move off with it at speed. The center forward without opposition bends away as the winger attacks the sweeper. The options mentioned previously can be implemented in training sessions until success is achieved. At that point the exercise can be functionally developed by initially adding the center back and the supporting midfield players.

The counter attack obviously should not be used all the time. However, if your goalkeeper and field player are trained to distribute quickly and accurately to the wing areas of midfield, then goal-scoring opportunities can be created. Many teams attack randomly with their backs and are thus vulnerable to counters. Also, most players after making several overlap runs will be slow in making the transition to defense. Another factor to be considered by playing the winger wide at midfield and free of defensive responsibilities is that teams who employ their wing backs in their attack may be forced to change their style of play when they realize your winger is not tracking.

Italy was very skillful in using the counter attack game, and I found them entertaining to watch. If you train your players to look for counter attack in certain situations, I believe that you will be pleasantly surprised as to the number of goal-scoring opportunities that will be created.

PLAYING IN THE FINAL THIRD
Ron McEachon

Developing play in the front third and building a successful attack takes many hours of training but it can and must be achieved. The vital point for the coach to keep in mind is that while there is a need for certain structural guidelines, soccer is a highly creative game and there must be ample room for the players to improvise and utilize individual flair. The coach must have the confidence to stand back and give his players a chance to make mistakes and then learn what will be successful as part of an overall several man attack. Training, as we will describe it, is designed with this end in mind and, if properly implemented, can bring about dynamic positive results.

I. PRIMARY OBJECTIVE: PENETRATE AND SCORE GOALS

We must always remember that the primary attacking objective is to penetrate and score goals. There are other "secondary" objectives such as ball possession, width, and support, but we must never lose sight of the vital fact that soccer is about scoring goals and therefore, we must train our players.

II. SECONDARY OBJECTIVES: POSSESSION, PATIENCE (WIDTH AND UNBALANCE DEFENSE), PROBE, POSITIONING (SUPPORT)

These secondary objectives can be accomplished through a variety of isolated training processes. Emphasis on mobility, combination play (creativity), improvisation (the unexpected), width, depth, support, and the mechanism of finishing (shooting) all lead to a development of the secondary objectives, thus leading to a stronger probability of achieving the primary objective.

The purpose of this article is to develop more coaching mechanisms by which you, the coach, will develop a more effective execution of the primary objective - goals.

III. METHODOLOGY: COACHING CONCERNS

How does a coach achieve these ends in actual coaching processes? This article will detail coaching concerns in terms of player decision-making and coaching evaluation of field execution with respect to the appropriate parameters for integrating necessary variability.

No single coaching session can contain the wide variability inherent to the options facing a player on the field. The tactical maturity of a player is viewed in his/her ability to see options and, subsequently, facilitate their execution. Player movement (e.g. changing positions, timing their runs, attacking from behind) combined with combination play (e.g. takeovers, wall passes, overlaps, and third man sequences) impose on the players the pressure of reading the appropriateness of these various options as they present themselves. Each, in its own right, is a necessary coaching concern, especially when viewed from player psychology (risk-taking versus safety and predictability) or his/her ability to view "first touch" sequences in a positive and negative fashion.

It goes without saying that we are assuming technical competency, although this is without a doubt a major American concern. The ability to play a ball with appropriate pace to space or feet, or being capable of doing so under the pressure of limited time and space needs is a continuous coaching objective.

IV. COACHING SEQUENCES

A. The Warm-up

A warm-up should always be related to the theme of the practice; therefore, the coach who wishes to develop play in the front third must use the warm-up as added emphasis for the above concerns (i.e., involving combination play between the various groups on the field). One suitable approach may be to create groups of four and ask the players to look for such possibilities as 1-2s (Diagram 6-73), overlapping runs (Diagram 6-74) and/or diagonal runs. (Diagram 6-75)

The players thus develop an attacking rhythm. It is important to organize the practice so that everything is directed towards a goal. These groups of four players should look for combinations which will produce scoring opportunities. An important consideration is that the players have as much opportunity as possible to achieve success. Initially the attack works against only one defender (or for younger players, perhaps initially there may be no defender present), then subsequently add a second and third defender as the offense becomes more and more successful. The goal of each sequence is to apply combinations that will result in a successful finish.

While it is necessary for the coach to initially structure, once this has been done, the coach must allow the players to play (fail and succeed) on their own. It takes time and coaching patience to develop a successful attack. The players must experiment and get used to each other's style and tendencies in order to develop a successful attack in the final third. Time and space are often limited by the opponents' marking so the players must play quickly and be sufficiently creative to add the element of disguise and surprise to their attack.

Diagram 6-73 - One player starts with the ball and looks to complete a 1-2 with every other teammate, a total of three combination passes. Work your way

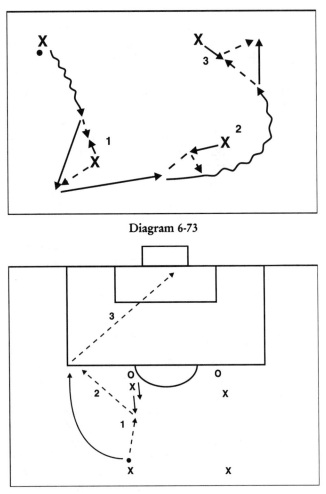

Diagram 6-73

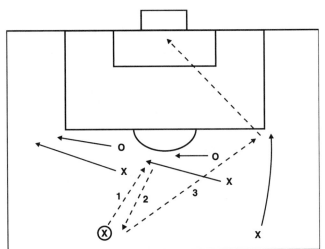

Diagram 6-75

Diagram 6-74

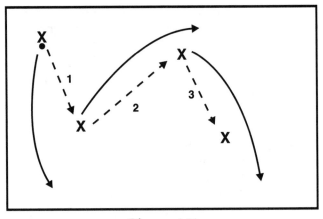

Diagram 6-76

through the entire group with players #1, #2 and #3 doing the same.

Diagram 6-74 - A basic overlap with the player with the ball playing to a front runner and then running past him/her to receive a return pass for a shot on goal. The objective is to create a 2 v. 1, isolating one defender.

Diagram 6-75 - Frontrunners make diagonal runs to one side, drawing defenders to that side. The man with the ball plays up to the second striker and then receives a return pass and plays it through to a teammate overlapping on the side away from the ball. The objective is to build play on one side, drawing the defense to that side and then change the point of attack to the opposite side.

The coach should not constantly stop and restart play. Rather he should occasionally step in and point out possibilities. He/she should try to make his players aware of as many options as possible by giving them the chance to see the options and then to make their own choices. Two such possibilities are illustrated in Diagrams 6-76 and 6-77.

Diagram 6-76 - One player starts with the ball and passes to a teammate. Then he/she makes an over-

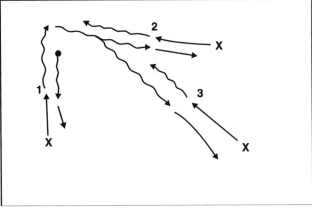

Diagram 6-77

lapping run past that teammate. Play continues with further passing and overlapping.

B. Coaching Progressions

Once the players have a sense of how their attacking partners will play, then it is necessary to initiate, within the coaching sequences, what focus the coach would like to emphasize in his/her assessment of the strengths and weaknesses of his players. This progres-

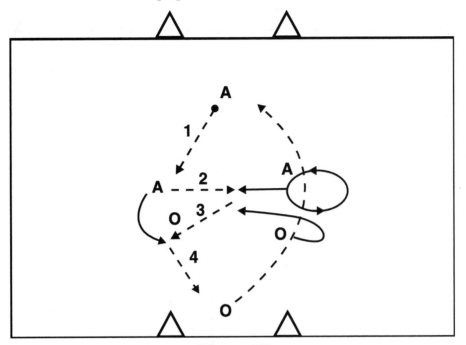

Diagram 6-78

sion should be gradual and always geared towards success.

Diagram 6-77 - One player starts with the ball, dribbling toward a teammate who performs a takeover. This teammate then works a takeover with another teammate, etc.

Individual offensive play is of initial concern (e.g. 1 v. 1 opportunities, feints, and fakes) as well as technical decision-making (e.g. pace on ball, and bending of ball). This should be combined with far, near, and slot-timed runs.

Once the individual has a good perception of what has been sufficiently expressed to the players, then 2 v. 2 + 1 and 3 v. 3 + 1 (Diagrams 6-78–6-80) playmaking situations (using the MF or support backs) should predominate in the coaching scheme. Initially, with the two defenders, the emphasis should be focused on the timing of the runs, the quality of the service, and the decision-making that goes into when the services should and should not be delivered. As competency grows, added defenders will complicate the environment for the server and for the marked defenders as they will then need to add their own calculations into the probabilities necessary for successful execution of any particular sequence.

Half field sequences starting with 6 v. 0 (shadow play) to 6 v. 2, 6 v. 3, and 6 v. 4 orient the total offensive sequences. The services of the MF and the wings should be a constant concern of the coach during these progressions. Additionally the timing of the runs, where the runs go, and finally the finish are objectives that the coach, given the primary objective, must make of absolute importance.

Once the players understand their roles under limited pressure, the system needs to be put under greater, and more game-like stress, adding first an equal number of defenders and then adding defenders so that 6 v. 7 and 6 v. 8 situations arise as they would in a normal game situation. While initially the ball may be returned directly to the attacking team, eventually the defenders need to be given goals and the attackers given the orientation which will result in opportunities caused by the counters associated with the winning of balls by the strikers and midfielders. They should learn to execute in these transition situations.

Diagram 6-78 - 2 v. 2 + 1 is shown in this diagram. The two A players are seeking to penetrate by using a combination play with each other and the supporting player. The supporting player is restricted initially to supplying passes only. The third O player acts as keeper and continually throws back missed chances to A's supporting player. Later the O team can counter-attack with the A team defender as keeper. Another variation would be to allow the supporting player to move forward with overlapping runs, etc. Depth on attack must be emphasized should forward runs by the support player be allowed.

Diagram 6-79 - The supporting player is shown here in a frontal support position. The player would play 1-2 touch passes to onrushing teammates with penetration passes and possible third-man options as objectives of this sequence.

Diagram 6-80 - 3 v. 3 + 1 - Much like 2 v. 2 + 1 training with the exception that the role of the third attacker (A3 here) is stressed. Balance and width are emphasized for that player.

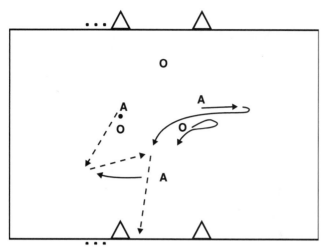

Diagram 6-79

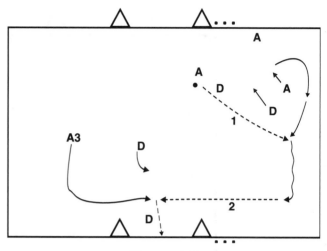

Diagram 6-80

C. Styles of Play

Once the attack achieves a sufficiently high rate of success so that the offense can perform with confidence, then the concept of "team" attacking styles needs to be added. The basic options that have been worked upon need to be reemphasized so that the players do not lose sight of the work they have accomplished in group and team tactical situations after this extrapolation into a full-field situation.

The three midfielders (left, right and center) should initially be limited to two options. They must learn how best to implement the options that they are going to express. Additionally, it is necessary that the other players understand what the options of the midfielders are and what they should be doing, given the decisions that they see the midfielders are taking. Initially, the play will be predictable, but this should lend itself to a high level of team understanding. Finally, when the players have experienced a high level of understanding, situations should be created where the midfielders and strikers must react and improvise. This will then necessitate creative reading of the game on behalf of the other players on the field. This is the true sense of a learning situation and will provide a creativity and enjoyment which will be seen, not only by the players themselves, but by the audiences who will be watching the game. Such satisfaction is generally lacking from American soccer as we know it today, but must be added if we are going to develop a sport which will be appealing to the American sports fan.

V. Conclusions

It is essential that we keep in mind that the primary aim of soccer is to score goals. Scoring not only makes the game interesting for all those who watch, but interesting for the players themselves. Scoring goals, however, is the most difficult aspect of the game. Unlike many American sports where goals or points occur regularly, soccer provides fewer occasions for this ultimate climax; therefore, it should be our objective to optimize the number of opportunities and then accentuate not only the number of opportunities but also the success rate for those opportunities that present themselves. Scoreless soccer may be occasionally successful in the short run, but fails in the long run. We must be willing to orient our teams with an offensive goal-scoring attack. After all, what else can be more satisfying than putting the ball in the net?

⚽

Creating and Developing Attacking Situations
Clive Charles and Tom Rowney

Using small-sided games is an effective way for coaches to structure practice sessions so that players are required to function under realistic conditions. Such games foster economical use of time and resources so that a number of technical, tactical, psychological, and fitness objectives can be effectively achieved at the same time.

The following practice progression was designed to facilitate the creation and development of a variety of attacking situations for intermediate-advanced players.

The organization and progression of these particular practices allows several objectives to be addressed:

Technical & Tactical

• Combining with teammates to create and exploit space;

• Penetrating from deep positions with and without the ball;

• Repeated functional training, e.g. forwards receiving the ball with back to opponents' goal; backs

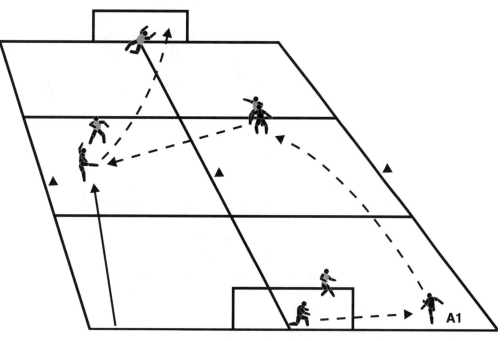

Diagram 6-81

receiving passes "wide and deep" from goalkeepers; repeated opportunities to strike at goal;

FITNESS

• Continuous physical workload in a game-related environment.

PSYCHOLOGICAL

• Improving the speed and quality of players' thought processes and decision-making.

PRACTICE 1 (DIAGRAM 6-81)

Organization

Play is 3 v. 3 in 20 x 30 yard area with goalkeepers. Area is divided into two halves. In each half a 2 (defenders) v. 1 (attacker) exists. Players are conditioned to remain in their assigned halves. Practice starts with one of the goalkeepers in possession of the ball. The ball must first be played to either back who has moved into a wide and deep position to support the keeper.

The ball should then be played towards the forward teammate in the attacking half of the area. Once the ball has been played forward the non-passing defender may move into the attacking half to support his/her forward teammate, thus creating a 2 v. 2 situation.

If the defending team wins the ball, they must look to play it quickly to their forward teammate.

Key Coaching Points

• As the keeper receives possession, backs must immediately position wide and deep to receive throw from the keeper.

• Defender should control the pass so that a forward pass can be made on the second touch.

• Forward players must attempt to gain space, e.g. by making a checking run before "showing" for the ball from the fullback.

• The free defender must support the forward quickly.

• Forwards receiving the ball must be aware of the possible options: a) If defender comes too tight, turn with the ball and look to shoot; b) If defender adopts solid defensive position look to lay the ball off quickly to a supporting player; c) If no support is immediately available, shield, then turn or shield, then pass.

• Forward player on the defending team must chase down and defend against the backs. Once the ball has been played out of the area, he must position to receive a possible interception.

• Look to get a strike on goal at all times.

PRACTICE 2 (DIAGRAM 6-82

Organization

Play is 4 v. 4 in 30 x 40 yard area with goalkeepers. Area is divided into two halves. In each half a 2 (defenders) v. 2 (attackers) exists. Players are conditioned. to remain in their assigned halves. Practice starts with one of the goalkeepers in possession of the ball. The ball must first be played to either back who has moved into a wide and deep position to support the keeper. Forwards in that half must remain in a central position until the backs' first touch on the ball.

The ball should then be played quickly to a forward teammate in the attacking half of the area. Once the ball has been played forward, the non-passing defender may move into the attacking half to support

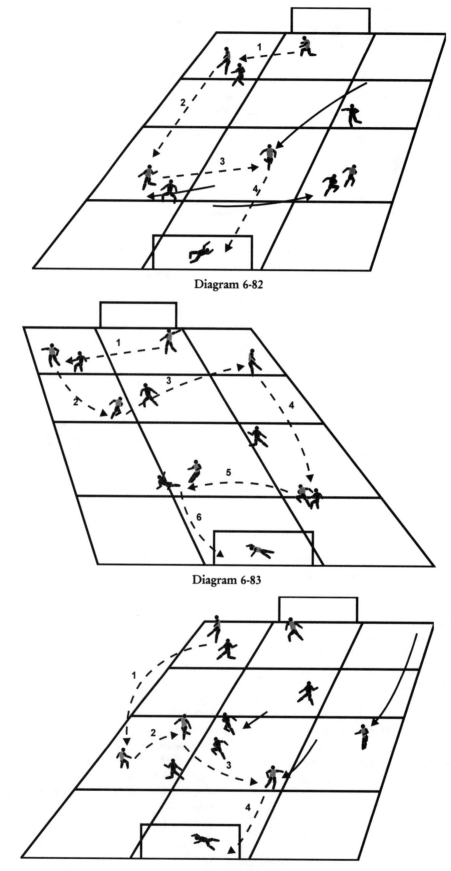

Diagram 6-82

Diagram 6-83

Diagram 6-84

his/her forward teammates, thus creating a 3 v. 2 situation. If defending team wins the ball, they must look to play it quickly to a forward teammate.

Key Coaching Points:

- Forward teammates can combine to create space using the following: a) split run creating space in the central area for a player coming from deep; b) crossover runs creating space in central and wing positions.

- If the penetrating pass cannot be made safely to the nearest forward, it should be made to the furthest forward.

- The free defender must move quickly to support his/her forward teammate and exploit the space created by them.

- If possession is gained by the defending team, they must look to play the ball quickly forward into their attacking half.

Practice 3 (Diagram 6-83)

Organization

A midfield player is now added to each team creating a 5 v. 5 in the 30 x 40 yard area. In each half 2 (defenders) plus 1 (midfielder) v. 2 (attackers) exists. Midfielders only may move into their attacking half when in possession.

A goalkeeper begins the practice by serving to either a defending or midfield teammate. At least one other pass must be made in the defending half of the field before a forward pass into the attacking half can be made.

The ball can then be played towards a forward teammate in the attacking half. The midfield player may now move into the attacking half to support his/her forward teammates, thus creating a 3 v. 3 situation. If the defending team wins possession, they should look to play a penetrating pass to their forward teammates.

Key Coaching Points

- Midfield players should move quickly to support forward teammates and to a position to prevent the opposing midfield player from covering defending teammates.

- Forwards must move and position to prevent the opposing midfield player from intercepting the penetrating pass.

- If attacking players intercept the ball in the opposition's half, they should look to shoot on goal as quickly as possible.

Practice 4 (Diagram 6-84)

Organization

Midfield players are now conditioned to start the practice on the halfway line while a 2 (defenders) v. 2 (attackers) situation exists in each half of the field.

Midfielders only may move into either half of the field. A goalkeeper begins the practice by either serving to a fullback, who must play a long pass to a forward teammate, or using the long throw directly to a forward teammate, thus by-passing the midfield player.

Once the ball reaches the attacking half, the attacking midfielder may enter that half to support his/her forward teammates. After the attacking midfielder has touched the ball at least once, the opposing midfield player may move from the center line to challenge.

Progression

As above, but passes from defenders and goalkeeper can be either long (to forwards) or short (to midfield teammate). Objective is to keep possession but look to penetrate with the long or short passing option.

Key Coaching Points

- Passes from the keeper and defending players to forward teammates should be accurate and correctly paced. A variety of lofted and ground passes should be made.

- Forward players must continually look to "show for the ball."

- Midfield players should make supporting runs quickly into a position from which a shot on goal or forward pass to a teammate can be made.

- Forward players should look to lay off a first-time pass to the supporting midfield teammate.

- The three attacking teammates should coordinate their runs to create space in which to shoot on goal.

- Defending teammates should look to win possession and counter-attack quickly.

Practice 5 (Diagram 6-85)

Organization

A 50 x 30 yard grid is divided into three areas. In each of the end 20 x 30 yard areas, a 3 (defenders) v. 2 (attackers) situation exists. In the central 10 x 30 yard channel (shaded), a midfield 3 v. 1 exists. Players are conditioned to remain in their assigned halves. The 3 midfield players float with whichever team is in possession.

Practice starts with one of the goalkeepers passing to a teammate in the wide fullback position. A pass must then be made to one of the three midfield players in the central channel.

Attacking in the same direction, at least two passes must be made within the midfield channel before a pass can be made into the attacking end. Midfield players may then move into the attacking end to support forwards.

Progression

1. The three midfield teammates may attack in any direction after receiving the ball.
2. 6 v. 6 game emphasizing key coaching points.

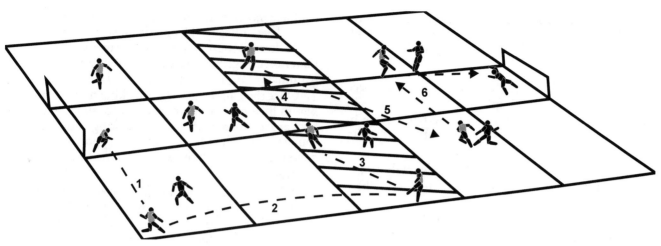

Diagram 6-85

Key Coaching Points

• Midfield players receiving the ball from fullbacks must control and turn in one movement.

• After turning with the ball, midfield players must look to pass quickly and accurately if under immediate pressure from an opponent.

• Midfield teammates must adopt wide-angled supporting positions to effectively support a teammate in possession.

CONCLUSION

In most small-sided games a single condition is typically applied to focus on a particular aspect of the game. In the above practices a number of different conditions are placed on the players. However, while the restrictions set in practices should not be too complicated, for advanced players they should be more challenging to facilitate improvement.

For less advanced players the above progression may be attempted over several practice sessions beginning with Practices 1 and 2. As players become more familiar with each stage of the progression, the next level may be added. Other changes in the organization of the practices may be made. For example, the practice area may be increased or decreased to allow players more or less space and time to perform individual functions.

Finally, having used these practices with several groups, invariably the players find them challenging and fun. Although each individual coach may wish to focus on a specific aspect of the game, maintaining the basic practice procedure will ensure that all the players in the drill are continually active and have repeated opportunities to shoot on goal.

BEATING THE OFFSIDE TRAP
Tom Martin

INTRODUCTION

The offside trap is a highly successful tactic used the world over. It is not uncommon to see two top teams employing the trap with twenty players all in close proximity to the half-line. Nothing can frustrate an attack-oriented team more than constantly getting caught offsides by intelligent defensive play. Much time in training is devoted to perfecting and coordinating an effective offside trap. Of equal importance is the tactical knowledge required to beat the trap. It is the intent of this article to illustrate methods to beat the offside trapping defense, and to offer training situations designed to teach and perfect these methods.

BEATING THE TRAP

The first method to beat the offside trap is for a player to "go it alone". Usually a deep lying forward or a midfield player attempts to either dribble through the trapping defense, or play a pass to oneself in space behind the defense. In this situation the player not only needs the technical ability to take on defenders, but the personality to take them on as well. This is a particularly good method against slow defenders and teams that don't apply pressure on the ball. (Diagram 6-86)

A second way to attack the offside trap is to send deep lying players on diagonal runs through the defense, either playing a through ball or going over the top to them. Forwards are coming back (baiting the defense), and the timing of the pass is critical. Smart, intelligent timing—both of the run and of the release

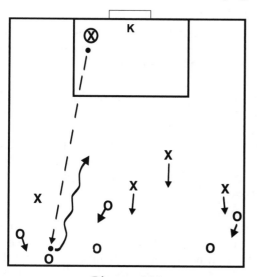

Diagram 6-86

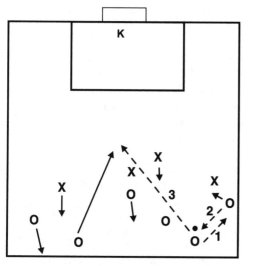

Diagram 6-87

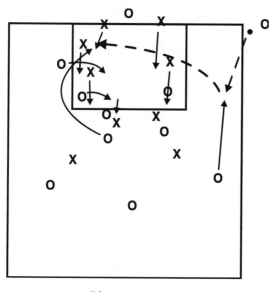

Diagram 6-88

of the pass— are keys. This is also an exceptionally good method of attacking teams that try to trap on variations of short corner kicks and similar restart situations. (Diagrams 6-87 and 6-88)

Lazy forwards not checking back enough when the attack breaks down in its own half present a very common situation that catches players offsides. In this instance intelligent play is required of the player receiving the ball. His choices are these: 1) hold the ball until the forwards get back, 2) play the ball square or back to a teammate, or 3) try and dribble through on his own. Method three is again a good choice, as it is very difficult, if not impossible, for a player to be offsides when another player is dribbling the ball on his own.

Quick, fast players may make special use of their talents to beat a trapping defense, especially when going against defenders slow on the turn. As the midfield or back players are building up the attack, flat or bent cross-over runs off the ball can prove very effective at finding space at the back of the defense. Intelligent change of speed by the forwards and timing of the forward pass are crucial elements. The quick reverse pass is a similar tactic that is also effective. (Diagrams 6-89 and 6-90)

A final method has been suggested by Vogelsinger as possibly the best method to beat a trapping defense. Quick 1-2 combinations, especially between midfielders and forwards, are very effective. Following the same thinking, the up-back-through sequence to a third man running off the ball will also prove effective. Quick, early playing of the ball is vital, but more important is the technical ability of the players to play one-touch soccer. This technical ability in itself is successful against a trapping defense. (Diagrams 6-91 and 6-92)

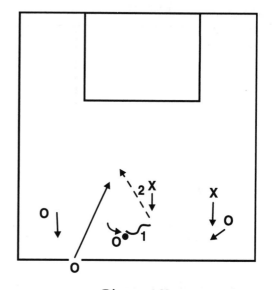

Diagram 6-89

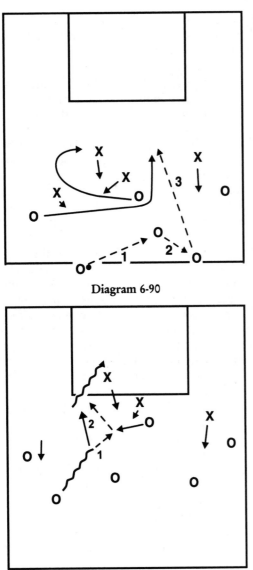

Diagram 6-90

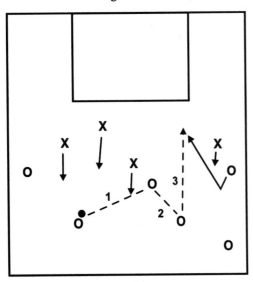

Diagram 6-91

Diagram 6-92

TRAINING/TEACHING SESSIONS

All of the methods mentioned above can be developed following a progression from a small number of grid training situations up to a full field 11 v. 11 situation.

- **Grid training** – any of the previous methods begin here. First, with passive resistance, then with active 100% resistance. The size of the grid must change to suit the purpose and number of players involved. (1 v. 1, 2 v. 1, 3 v. 1, 3 v. 2,...6 v. 4) Once the concept is understood and players become proficient, the coach moves on.

- **1/2 - 3/4 field work** – six attackers v. four defenders of a regulation goal. Each method of attacking the trap is developed from the passive to active phase. Balls are initially cleared from the goal by the defense (or a coach) to start the drill. The attacking team attempts to beat the trap by a specific tactical method and go to goal. Restrictions as to which method used should be placed on the attacking team by the coach. At the end of this phase, players are "set free" to make their own choices as to how to beat the trapping defense.

- **11 v. 11 full field** – Two complete teams play either on a 3/4 field or an entire field with regulation goals. Simple restrictions emphasize the theme of beating the trap. First, team A traps and team B has no restrictions. After execution, teams reverse roles. Second, both teams are asked to employ an offside trap. At this phase intelligent team and individual decisions are required, as the game situation becomes the true "acid-test" in dealing with the offside trap. Finally, two teams continue 11 v. 11 full field, trapping intermittently under instructions from the coach or defensive leader, as determined by the situations of play. An intelligent defender occupying a central position usually keys the trap.

CONCLUSIONS

The tactic of beating the offside trap is one which should be an integral segment of any team's training. Intelligent players must develop their ability to read the defensive offside trap and make the necessary adjustments to successfully attack it. Scouting gives a coach the luxury of knowing when an opponent uses an offside trap. Some opponents are not so predictable. One opponent may only trap in specific situations. Others may only trap in the second half, not affording you the chance to make adjustments with your team at the interval. All good teams must make preparations during training to combat the trap.

In summary, all types of combinations which come from the midfield and rear work to beat the trap. They must be rehearsed in training so that the timing is correct. Also, it is sound practice to train your team so a second player will support the attack once the defense is beaten. This tactic increases a team's chances of further exploiting the offside trap and creating scoring opportunities. The methods in this article and variations of them can prove very successful in situations where your opponents choose to use an offside trap.

REFERENCES

The following references provide valuable information to give additional insight in dealing with the offside situation.

1) Chyzowych, Walter. *The Official Soccer Book of the USSF.* Rand McNally and Company, New York, NY, 1978.

2) Herbin, Robert. *Soccer the Way the Pros Play.* Sterling Publishing Company. London, 1978.

3) Hughes, Charles. *The FA Coaching Book of Soccer Tactics and Skills.* BBC, London, 1980.

4) Lodziak, Conrad. *Understanding Soccer Tactics.* Faber and Faber, London, 1974.

5) Maher, Alan E. *Complete Soccer Handbook.* Parker Publishing Company. Inc.. West Nyack, NY, 1983.

6) Tassara, Hugo and Pila, Augusto. *Functional Modern Soccer.* Editorial Augusto E. Pila Telena, Madrid, Spain, 1983.

7) Vogelsinger, Hubert. *The Challenge of Soccer.* Allyn and Bacon. Inc., Boston, 1973.

One of the prerequisite skills for a goalkeeper is effective communication with the team.

(photo by Perry McIntrye, Jr.)

COMMUNICATION IN ATTACK
Manuel Lagos

Passing is the physical skill which ties together eleven soccer players in attack. Communication is the mental link which unites their minds through common understandings. Eleven attacking players connected by effective passing using intelligent communication is perhaps the most beautiful aspect of the game. How can a coach develop this communicative ability? Following are a potpourri of ideas and drills for developing effective communication among attacking players.

How often have you heard a coach reprimand his players for not talking during the game? Most players respond by going back on the field and yelling standard phrases like, "come on let's hustle", "nice try", "we've got to really want it", or "let's not let up now". Such communication is primarily supportive. It provides teammates with emotional motivation. It is important, but is not the type of communication which will improve our team's control of the ball.

Another verbal cue that is commonly used by certain players and coaches is the "don't" phrase. "Don't

hold the ball so long", "don't dribble so much", "don't lose the ball", "don't sell yourself", or "don't pass it to her" are some phrases that are often heard. The shortcoming here is that it doesn't tell a player what to do if he decides to follow the advice.

In what manner should players try to communicate? Communication among players should be centered around giving information about what is going on in the game. A player should inform another about his/her intentions. They should also alert teammates of something of which the other player might not be aware. Phrases like "man on", "Sam's open", "time", "support", or "overlap" let another player know what is happening around him. It is then up to the player to make correct decisions with the aid of this information. Often players give information in terms of simple commands like "turn", "go through", "One-two", "hold it", "pass it to me", or "clear it". If a player holds the view that he must do this because he was told to by his teammate then this form of communication loses some of its effectiveness. If a player realizes that there is a hidden phrase before each command, "you have the option to turn", or "you have the option for a 1-2 pass", then these command phrases fall into the information-giving category. With this information the player can choose which is the best of his options.

Coaches can easily teach players the phrases but players will remain silent on the field unless they are taught where and when to give the information. They need to be able to recognize situations and have confidence in their assessment of what is occurring. With good assessment will come the confidence to offer information and give advice to teammates. This confidence can be developed in training sessions in which verbal communication is used in a variety of match-related drills.

Verbal communication is essential to developing teamwork among players. Its shortcoming however is that it also informs the opponent about your team's options. When a player moves into a supporting position and yells "support", players on the other team will quickly move in to mark him and take away his advantage. Can a team change its communication to a non-verbal form thus avoiding letting the opponent know their intentions? As a team trains effectively under the watchful eye of the coach, much of the verbal communication will hopefully be unnecessary, for players will begin to read each other. They will develop understandings of teammates' tendencies, positioning, etc. Eliminating some of the verbal communication also forces each player to be more aware of accurate in assessment of the situation. For example, a player who is receiving the ball must first look around to see if opponents are near so he can turn quickly with the ball. If teammates are always telling him when to turn, he may never develop this valuable expansion of his field vision.

What are some non-verbal ways beyond the general team understanding that enable players to communicate? Pointing can be used at times to indicate the space to which a player wants the ball played, or to where he should run, or to what teammate the ball should be passed. Although this visual form can be picked up by opponents, it can be done in a subtle and inconspicuous manner. A player can also call for the ball by making a sudden sprint or a change of direction. Eye contact is another very important way to communicate especially for a passer and receiver. The ball can be used by a player to indicate to his teammate what he should do. Playing a the ball to one foot or the other suggests which way to turn. By playing a the ball to certain spaces the passer tells a player where to run and where defenders are positioned. In addition to disguising one's intentions from your opponent, another fringe benefit for communication in these nonverbal ways is that it forces the player on the ball to play with his "head up" further developing his field vision.

Once a sound team understanding has been established with minimal reliance on verbal communication, then a coach can reintroduce verbal communication. However the intent of the communication will be to deceive one's opponents. A player can call to a teammate with information that is meant to mislead the other team. A high level of awareness allows his teammate to see through the ploy and make use of the other options that are available. Often the opponent is fooled, it opens up excellent opportunities to develop the attack. Some examples of situations where such communication can be effective are in a wall pass where the passing player shouts "1-2," fakes the return pass, then turns quickly in the opposite direction. Or a player makes a near post run yelling "near post" opening up space in the center and at the far post. Perhaps a player runs past the ball carrier calling for the ball causing the defense to shift and allowing a teammate from behind to move into the open space. A high level of sophistication is required of a team if its attacking players are to by-pass the announced verbal cue and choose another option. At each moment every player must have a global rather than a local awareness of their role in the match.

Communication is an important part of the game and a coach must spend time developing it among the players. In such development the coach must start with verbal communication, for initially this form is the most effective among players who are learning about each other. After a high level of verbal communication is being passed among players and players are beginning to read one another, then the coach can begin to insist on less verbal information being given. He can suggest several nonverbal cues and players will devise some of their own. After a certain level of sophistication in the team's play is reached under these constraints, then verbal deceptive information can be introduced.

⚽

Tactical Use of the Size and Shape of Soccer Fields
Hubert Vogelsinger

The size and shape of a soccer field can greatly influence the style of play. Diversity in existing facilities necessitates tactical versatility.

As the game has grown in popularity at all levels — club, school, college and professional — we are pleased to have any field to play on; we make do with what is made available. With increased prestige, doors are opening to the big stadiums previously reserved for other sports. This has resulted in diversity in shapes

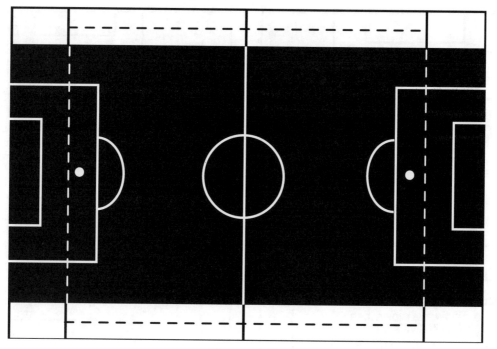

Diagram 6-93

and sizes of fields being used for soccer, all the way from long narrow football fields to baseball outfields that are short, wide almost square.

The rules of soccer allow for this diversity. The length of the field may be 130 yards maximum and 100 yards minimum, with the width 100 yards maximum and 50 yards minimum. (Diagram 6-93) The shape and size of a field can require a change in the basic system of play. For example, if a team usually operates out of 4-2-4 and has to play on a long, narrow, football-shaped field, it is wise to play with only three attackers because (a) there's not enough space for fluid interaction of the forwards, and just as important, (b) the midfield is long, requiring an additional midfield player to prevent a gap in midfield and ensure control there.

Physical conditioning of players is also affected by changes in size of fields. When a team comes from a small field to one of maximum size, the work rate of every player is increased tremendously. Without necessary preparation, players would tire too soon.

Following are some considerations coaches may want to keep in mind as they prepare their teams tactically, in relation to field size.

PLAYING ON A LARGE FIELD – MAXIMUM OR NEARLY MAXIMUM DIMENSIONS

Soccer is an artistic game and players need space and time to express their individual skills. That must have been in the minds of the originators of the game when they determined the size of the field. If you are fortunate enough to have a field of maximum dimensions, it will be clear that the better-conditioned team

has a definite advantage. Midfielders particularly must be robust, with lungs like iron.

On large fields the team has to be disciplined and organized in order to cover the entire territory. A quick and open style of play is advised, where the ball is used to take advantage of the size of the field. This necessitates having a midfield player or two with the vision and skill to spread the game over the entire width of the field and deliver the long pass. I have coached teams that played on football-shaped fields. When our team then played away on fields 29 to 30 yards wider we had tremendous difficulty keeping our defense organized and compact. The tendency is to get drawn too much to the side of the ball and become vulnerable to quick cross-field passes. Sometimes teams take too long to make the necessary adjustments and are often caught square and spread out — fatal defensive mistakes that a team can't afford.

Moreover, I like an offensively oriented team, one that overlaps frequently. This can really hurt a team on the larger field. It is difficult to make the adjustment and cover up for each other, distances between players being longer. Bringing the winger into play with long, rangy lead passes utilizes the width of the field to its fullest and an effective wing attack is essential. The same attacking style on a narrow field will not be effective because the ball will frequently be out of touch.

PLAYING ON EXTREMELY LONG, NARROW FIELD — SHAPED LIKE A FOOTBALL FIELD

The narrow field is an obvious home advantage. It was always interesting to me to see how opposing teams struggle, particularly at the beginning of the game. Play-

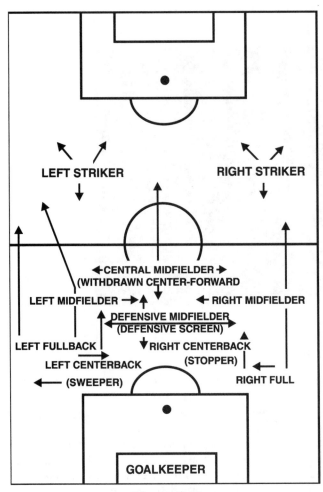

Diagram 6-94

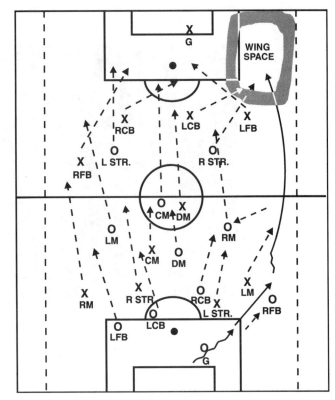

Diagram 6-95

ers begin to even turn to each other in disbelief when they see apparent chances disappear because beautiful lead passes ran out of touch. Some teams actually can't adjust throughout the game to narrow pitches.

The system of play must be such that the number of attackers does not exceed three, while the number of midfield players should not be fewer than three. (Diagram 6-94)

Three attackers is the maximum number that can be used effectively. I prefer just two in order to ensure space to move about freely and effectively. But then it is essential that players come through on overlaps from the back and midfield.

Since the midfield is rather long, at least three players are needed to cover the territory. Otherwise there is a danger of creating a large gap between offense and defense. The tendency then is to bridge this space with long lead passes, resulting in a kick-and-rush style of play.

Defenders on such narrow fields have the advantage, for it is easy to stay compact and well organized. The offense is faced with the real task as it is difficult to spread and penetrate a well-organized defense because of the lack of width and consequently, space. Offensively, it is essential to:

- Use the fast counter attack with a minimum of pinpoint passes, and finish with a desirable strike at goal.

- Play to the wings rather than from the wings. It is difficult for the winger to wait out on the wing and then try to do something with the ball when he/she has tremendous pressure on from both the defenders and the touchline. Playing to the wings means to leave the-wing-space apparently open (without having a player assigned to it). Apparently, but not actually, for the strikers move frequently to the wing as do the midfield players and occasionally even the fullback comes through on a timely overlap.

The most effective attacking pattern is to counter quickly with a long pass along the touchline from the fullback to the wing space for the striker to run onto. Quick strikers should then be able to take advantage of the temporarily unsettled defense and score! (Diagram 6-95) Maximum positional interchanging will loosen up the tight defense or cause it to make mistakes.

A quick striker should be able to take advantage of this situation either through a) a quick cross into the goalmouth for the second striker to head home or b) by beating the centerback thereby turning the defense, sot that he/she can lay the ball back to a supporting player to have a shot at goal.

PLAYING ON SHORT, WIDE FIELDS – BASEBALL OUTFIELD

I'll never forget the shock I experienced in my first

season with the pros when we played in Baltimore. My scout had neglected to mention in his report that Baltimore played in a baseball stadium where the field was very wide and short, almost square.

The goalkeepers could kick the ball easily from one end of the field to the other. The horror started with the opening kick-off. Baltimore, using a football type of kick-off, booted the ball downfield high and five or six players ran after to recover it. They almost scored because my defenders, including the goalkeeper, were spellbound.

The first 20 minutes were a nightmare. My defense cleared out as we were accustomed to do on other fields in order to catch the opponent offsides. Baltimore just put the ball over our defense and chased after it. My defense must have felt like revolving doors they were turned so frequently. Before we knew what hit us and could make an adjustment, we were down 2-0. We made the right adaptation and pulled even at 2-2 but then lost the game 3-2.

On such a field it is obvious that any long boot downfield is an attacking threat, even out of defense, even a goalkick, for that matter. It is safer not to lay the offsides trap, clear much upfield, if at all, and to organize the defense in depth to negate the long balls into space behind the defenders.

It's advisable to prepare the attack on one side of the field by short, quick interpassing. Then play the long, square ball unexpectedly and timely to the other side of the field. This is a most effective maneuver to loosen up the defense. Though of course it has to be followed by the payoff, the through pass.

PLAYING ON A SMALL FIELD

The premium here is on individual skill and fluid play. Since space and time make it impossible for the players to express themselves, teamwork becomes important. The ball should be moved about quickly, if possible with one-touch passing. Long balls won't lead to much success; a short passing game is more effective. Passes should be made to the players' feet rather than into space. And shots should be taken frequently from any position.

Skillful quick players are more effective on small fields than the physical, cumbersome player who lacks finesse. But overall a team has to be skillful, sure of itself, and well poised to maintain its own pace, rhythm and style of play. A physically aggressive team lacking finesse could offset the opponent's skill by high pressuring them, eventually forcing them to give up their game plan.

CONCLUSION:

The key to winning coaching lies in thorough preparation of even the smallest detail. The size and shape of the playing field are not the least among your concerns. You will want to surprise your opponents

tactically so as to throw off their game plan. Since that's what the rival coach will also be trying to do, you'll have to be ready for anything and everything.

THE TACTICS QUIZZES: SHARPENING YOUR SOCCER BRAIN!
Alan Maher

Member Gene Chyzowych initiated a very popular series in *Soccer Journal* in 1980 called "Tactical Soccer Situations Test for Players and Coaches."

The idea was to offer in diagram form various tactical options for players and coaches based on position of the ball, teammates' support positioning, placement of defenders, etc.

The first quizzes were designed by East German coach T.K. Trapp and administered to a group of U.S. Soccer staff coaches in the spring of 1988. The 30-part series was reproduced in subsequent issues of the magazine and then, over a period of several years, coach Chyzowych, several other U.S. coaches and James Prunier submitted other quizzes of their own design to stump members.

Eventually 190 questions were formulated and produced for coaches and Alan Maher has examined each and collected what he feels are the top 20 questions that appeared in the series.

The darkened player is always the player you must make the decision for and the arrow designates the direction in which the team with the ball is moving.

On the diagrams a straight line indicates a run, a dotted line a pass and an irregular line a creative dribble. Defenders are shown in circles while triangular-shaped figures represent attacking players.

Members wishing to procure the entire set of the quizzes can do so by writing the editor and enclosing a check (endorsed to NSCAA) in the amount of $25.

THE QUIZ

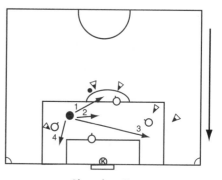

Situation One

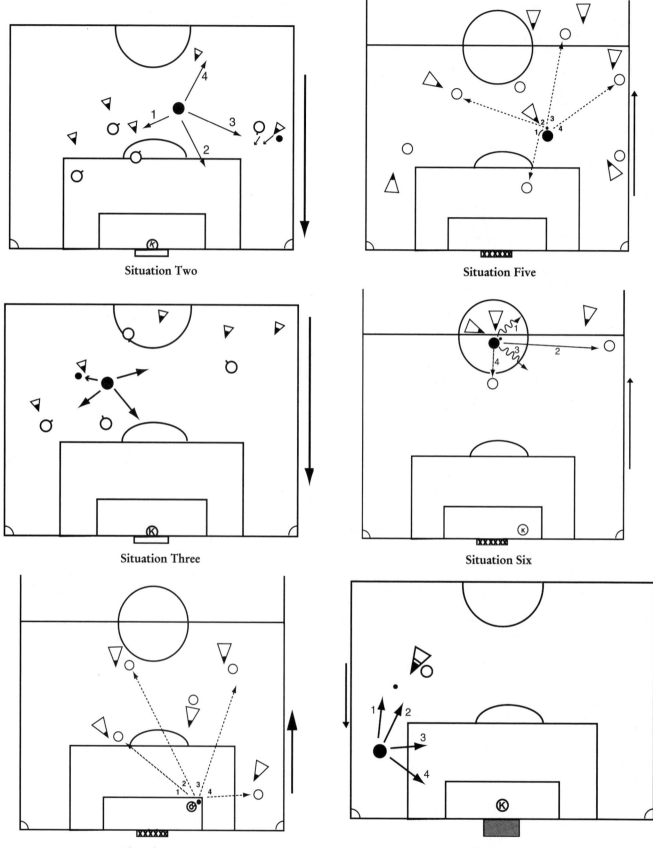

Situation Two

Situation Five

Situation Three

Situation Six

Situation Four

Situation Seven

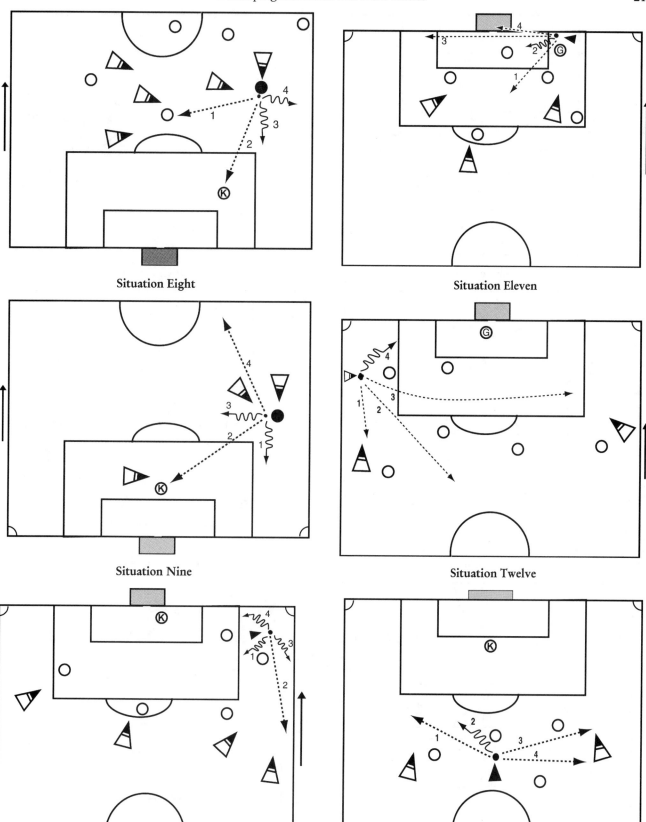

Situation Eight

Situation Eleven

Situation Nine

Situation Twelve

Situation Ten

Situation Thirteen

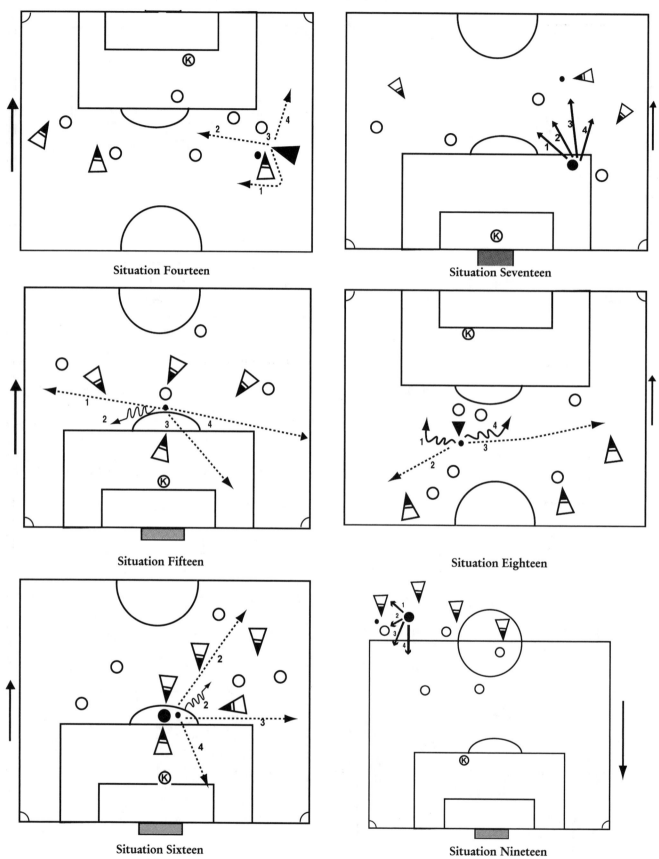

Situation Fourteen

Situation Seventeen

Situation Fifteen

Situation Eighteen

Situation Sixteen

Situation Nineteen

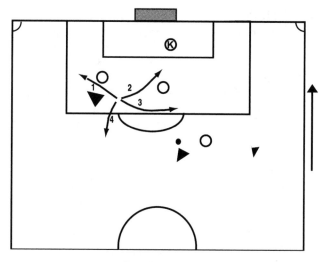

Situation Twenty

ANSWERS TO TACTICAL QUIZ:

1) **#1 IS CORRECT OPTION.** Pressure must be put on the ball at all times in and about penalty area; approach should be at angle to cut down shooter's opening to goal. #2 allows for shot. #4 -teammate already making the attacker and there is no need to cover defender whose attacker does not have ball. #3-same as #4-teammate already marking the ball

2) **OPTIONS #2 AND #3 ARE CORRECT.** #2 allows for coverage of attacking space by the defender while #3 might become a good covering position for defender if he arrives in time for goal side position. Also it affords possible offside trap positioning by defensive unit should dribbler look to pass ball behind defense. #4 is not option as it creates a 4 v.4 situation for attackers in final third; "numbers up" is to be preferred. #1 takes defender into space where he is not needed as the attacker is marked by another defender.

3) **OPTION 4 IS CORRECT.** Approach ball at angle to channel play to touchline. #3 is "no pressure" situation — too far from the player with the ball. #2 is not a good option as deeper defender (sweeper) is already in position to defend space. #1 is worst option. The player makes no contribution to the team defense with the move.

4) **OPTION 3 IS CORRECT.** Prepared by Don Schwartz, Ann Arbor, MI. Options 1 and 4 are the same in that they are risky short passes to marked players in the final third of the field. Option 2 is a long pass to marked player in the center. While the long pass is more playable by the receiving defender because of the available time and space, it breaks the axiom of not sending the ball down the center. Such a pass, if lost, greatly benefits the attacking team. The lack of playing space in options 1 and 4 would require the goalkeeper be available for a back pass, the safest continuation. Option 3 offers a long

distance from the goal, playing space to settle the ball and the security of laying away from the center of the field.

5) **OPTION 1 IS CORRECT.** Prepared by Jay Miller, University of South Florida. The pass back to the goalkeeper is apt because the only other realistic options open to the defender are long, the receiver being well-contested for possession. The defender should recognize that there are no immediate outlets and thus should not try to maintain possession too long. Option 1 is a sound, practical tactical decision.

6) **OPTION 4 IS CORRECT.** Jim Prunier and Gene Chyzowych. All the options shown have positive merit. The best is Option 4, a pass back to the supporting defender who has both time and visibility to make the best decision. Option 3, a backward dribble in order to gain both time to observe and select the pass is good, but amounts to a slower version of Option 4. Option 2 has the ball going wide to a player who has space in which to play the ball forward. This however takes the ball out of the center, which is the best distribution point. A dribble forward, as in option 1, seems to be a slight risk, but the result of this maneuver is unclear.

7) **OPTION 2 IS CORRECT.** Prepared by Jim Prunier and Gene Chyzowych. Moving to stay close and stay between the ball and the goal is the embodiment of option 2. Option 1 takes the defender too far from the center. Option 2 and 4 simply take the defender too far from the action. They both relieve the attacker of pressure.

8) **OPTION 2 IS CORRECT.** It is always best for defenders to move out-of goal by taking the outside route. The pass to the center, 1, defies this principle and incurs a great risk. A dribble away from opponents towards the goalie, option 3, is slowing and non-purposeful. It lacks construction. The dribble to the outside, 4, presumes that an outlet up the wing will remain a possibility even though the threat of being double-teamed is present danger. By sending the ball back to the goalie the opportunity for a long-reaching kick delivering the ball to open receivers is realized. Where the goalie is not able to sent the ball that far, the team must fall back and give realistic support. For intermediate and advanced players option 2 is correct play.

9) **OPTION 1 IS CORRECT.** This is an unusual circumstance where the defenders are outnumbered and under immediate pressure. In such a condition sending of the ball "away" is compelling, as in choice 4. However, there seems to be enough time to recognize that this direction of the ball from its lie would be difficult, and therefore not a good choice, it is only necessary for one to slow or some how hamper the dribble in order to give the other oppo-

nent a good chance to tackle for the ball. The election of a pass back to the goalkeeper in a marked position, choice 2, represents an exceptional hazard. Therefore, the choice of shielding the ball and moving away safely is the best play for the moment.

10) OPTION 4 IS CORRECT. Choice 1 is a move into a defender which can be ruled out as a surprise which will produce dividends because of the more likely possibility of being double-teamed. The pass play, 2, a link-up to a player better disposed by the dribble to the outside for room: number 3, However, the success of 2 alone or the success of 3 followed by 2 will not compare to choice 4, the straight forward spin away from opposition. The potential for creating a chance to strike on goal is excellent with the ball in this position and attackers arrayed in such fine fashion.

11) OPTION 4 IS CORRECT. Though the angle is unfavorable, the goal is momentarily open and this demands a ball be played centrally, option 4. Option 1, a pullback pass, will center the ball in center of the goal, but is speculative, kills the immediate attack and could cause the defense to regroup. The choice of dribbling forward, option 2, would significantly improve the shooting angle... if it succeeds. It seems most certain that the defenders could thwart the tactic.

12) OPTION 3 IS CORRECT: In this situation of 4 v. 7, the choice of the best pass is crucial. The four defenders closest to the ball are massed in relatively good positions. Choice 1 is a safe enough play but, clearly, penetration down the wings finds the defense ready to combat it. Choice 2, a penetrating through ball, is difficult to make but offers the potential of a strike at goal or switch in play to the right side of the field. Option 4, the dribble, will find the sweeper covering creating a 1 v. 2 situation. Option 4, the long penetrating pass, will find the weak side defense square and if successful will result in a clear opportunity for goal.

13) OPTION 2 IS CORRECT: In an open area the choices for successful continuation of the 3 v. 3 situation are all tempting. The pass to the outside, shown as option 4, is safe, but more direct play is called for. Option 3 is a penetration along the wing, a promising possibility as it does take advantage of the numerical equality by advancing the attack quickly before more defenders can recover. The through pass on the left, shown as option 1, could be an explosive move toward goal, but calls for perfect execution without which the defender might get to the ball first. Without a covering defender the attacker must try to beat the single defender and achieve a one-on-one with the goalkeeper. Option 2 defines this choice.

14) OPTION 2 IS CORRECT: The three immediate defenders outnumber the attacker, 3 v. 2 in the vicinity of the ball. How can the player in question relieve some of this pressure? Option 1 keeps the player in front of the defense and poses no problem for it. Option 4 seeks to expand the tightness on the right by a run down the wing. This doesn't satisfy the need for interactive passing at speed and doesn't commend itself as a solo attack. Option 3, if not an obstruction foul is worse than standing still because it offers nothing to the ballplayer. Option 2, a central, lateral run is the best move, drawing the attention of the defense and opening the possibility for a penetrating dribble using the vacated space. Action could lead to a strike on goal.

15) OPTION 2 IS CORRECT: No defender wants to risk being caught in possession in the defensive third of the field. The challenge here is to avoid risk. Sending the ball back to a marked goalkeeper, option 3, with a defender in place to intercept, is the gravest risk. Kicking the ball into touch, shown as option 4, must be considered panic play. A team is required to have better poise than that. The kick to an open teammate would be quite right if the player was within his/her vision; he/she is not and the proposed pass is a nearly square ball, a tactical error never to be committed in the defensive final third. There is some space for a short dribble to buy some to me for a possible pass. This is the essence of option 2; there's time, so use it. Find out where help is or isn't. If there's no sensible pass to be made, at least the defender is better positioned for a clearance kick up field or out-of-bounds.

16) OPTION 3 IS CORRECT: The defender is under severe pressure and open teammates are not in sight. Option 2 is a dribble into strength in hope of finding an outlet. This is a double risk: going against strength, hoping for help. It is a bad tactical choice. Option 1 appears safest for a time; until the opponents gain possession and go forward with a quite well-placed attacker. It may be a safe pass but it is a predictable, long pass which is easily read. The pass back to space for the goalie is reasonable, but with a defender positioned to intercept, is questionable. A kick to the touchline, indicated as option 3, is easy to execute and tactically correct. "Hit the ball high and wide."

17) OPTION 2 IS CORRECT: The problem is lack of defensive concentration in the area of the ball. Choosing option 4 will put the open attacker under some marking pressure and thereby reduce the dangerous one-two passing in this situation. It would, however allow for a blind-sided run by the open, supporting attacker. Option 3 presents a pres-

suring of the ball but has to be regarded as a serious over-commitment as it leaves an open attacker if mistimed. Option 1 covers the first defender, but is too deep a position to do much good and again leaves an open attacker. Option 2 is a compromise of positioning by supporting the first defender and staying nearer to the open attacker. This is the best resolution.

18) OPTION 2 IS CORRECT: There is no attack for the moment, so how to maintain possession in a 4 v. 6 situation and penetrating and lateral dribbling around two well-positioned center defenders does not offer much in the way of odds of possession and support of the other three attackers is not evident. Option 4, seeking to keep the ball in center while awaiting team support, is the best of the two dribbling choices. Option 3, the long pass to the outside is an improvement for penetration play if it reaches the target. It would then create a 1 v. 1 on the outside of the field. Option 2 plays the ball to space where the supporting player now can focus on subsequent runs by the other players and possibly link with the passer of the ball to create a 2 v. 2 situation.

19) OPTION 4 IS CORRECT: The attackers are outnumbered 4 v. 6 and the question revolves around what is the best covering position for the player under consideration. Option 1, cutting off communication with the nearest attacker and forcing the ballplayer to the outside, in fact sets up a one-on-one for the ballplayer. Option 2, double-teaming the ball, is not a bad choice this far from the goal. There is a risk that the ball might be played to space in along the touchline for a supporting player to run onto, but the depth in defense should take care of that option. Improving the defensive posture is appropriate. Option 3 does this by denying the possibility of penetration on the outside. Option 4 supports the first defender, provides cover for both pathways around the first defender, and keeps the supporting attacker in view. Option 4 is preferred tactically, as the rule of thumb is that the further you are on the field from your defensive goal, the longer is the distance for covering your pressurizing defender. Option 4 is the choice for this reason.

20) OPTION 1 IS CORRECT: In this situation, the attacking team appears to be moving towards a 2 v. 2 situation in its attacking third. The defense wants to become compact. The attacking team wants to penetrate. Option 2 offers the potential for an offside trap by the defense. Option 3 is a possibility, but a pass to the position would delay matters and also bring the defender with him to the central area of the field. Option 4 helps the defense in that it knows where the supporting player is located; namely right in front of them. Run 1 must be made with the idea of staying wide (and outside). It occupies the second defender. That player must now elect to stay with the run or cover for the teammate who must now confront the player with the ball. Run 1 thus causes the most problems for the defense.

RESTARTS

• •

Estimates vary according to the statistician cited, but soccer coaches everywhere are familiar with the fact that restarts account for nearly half the goals scored in matches.

This chapter will offer ideas from the simple principles of set pieces to an indepth look at the psychology of taking penalty kicks. It will also include ideas on restarts from an offensive and defensive viewpoint from all points on the field. Finally, specific strategies on defending at corners, trapping on free kicks as well as a creative dead ball practice session will conclude the chapter's discussion for coaches.

SCORING FROM SET PLAYS
Gordon Jago

Well planned and executed set plays are, in my opinion, a top priority in game preparation. The situation of a stationary ball, no opponent allowed within ten yards of the ball, and time to act is too good an opportunity for a "kick and hope" effort.

From my experience, players like to be organized at set plays, although you must always allow for indi-

viduality. The first priority is to take any advantage one can gain. A quickly taken free kick can catch opponents unprepared.

Planning of set plays is a joint effort between coaches and players. The coach can "sow a seed" by presenting a play and then allow his players to add or subtract. In this way you will develop the best suited plays for your team and more importantly, your players will have a good psychological feeling that they have contributed, for at the end of the day it is the players who will have to execute the plays.

The following are basic fundamentals in the planning of set plays.

1. Utilize Individual Ability

A powerful shot the skill of curving a ball around or over a defensive wall, a lob over the wall, a powerful header of the ball, or the quick speed of a player can all be used to good effect. Take an inventory of the technical abilities within your team and place them into your "pieces."

2. Minimize the number of passes before goal attempt and the number of players involved with the ball

Some principles in this regard are:
• The more players—the more passes—the greater the error factor;
• Obviously the very best situation is a direct shot—one player—one kick;
• Attempt to plan one-pass attempts in on-goal situations.

For myself I allow a maximum of two passes before the shot, thus a maximum of three players involved with the ball.

3. Target Areas

Most free kicks around the penalty areas are defended by a wall of players either placed to cover near post, or far post and sometimes a split wall depending on the desires of the coach. However basically most defending walls are placed to cover the near post and the goalkeeper defends the far post area.

The main object is to play the ball into the area which gives you the greater target of the goal. A ball played wide of the wall towards the center of the goal is far better than the ball played wide and away from the goal if you are attempting a one-pass shot situation. A ball played over the wall or to the side of the wall puts you into a good central position on goal.

The ability to bend a ball is one of those qualities in a player that a coach should seek to utilize in designing restarts.
(photo by Perry McIntyre, Jr.)

A ball played into the area in front of the goal between the six yard area line and the penalty spot is the most dangerous area to exploit.

In the use of two-pass shot situations, one often plays the ball away from those vital areas on the first pass, (in order to move opponents away from guarding them) and then back into those areas on the second pass, ready for the goal attempt.

4. Decoys

I have stated that for obvious reasons it is best to minimize the number of players to be involved with the ball in set plays, but except for your goalkeeper all your players must be involved as decoys or to require the marking attention of an opponent.

By positioning your players you can attempt to control each opponent's position at a set plan and you may be able to have those vital areas you wish to use left unguarded. If a team places four and five players in a defensive wall, it is impossible for them to mark all your players. You must finish with at least one or two spare men and/or free areas.

Movement by decoys can take opponents out of areas you wish to use and create space and unmarked players.

5. Signals

When set plays are planned and accepted by both you and your players, you must have a manner/signal/words to indicate to all your players which play you are to attempt. Every single player, even your goalkeeper, should know your signals. Keep your signals simple.

6. Selection

The most important task. Once the ball is placed, one of your players must have the responsibility to decide which of your plays is best suited for that moment. Position of wall, position of opponents and position of his teammates must quickly be assessed and a decision made—then the signal. More than one player should be proficient in case of injury.

Do not design too many set plays, three or four with variations should be sufficient. Too many cause confusion.

Even though a signal is given and players know what is to be attempted, all must be prepared to receive the ball, for the best made plans can go astray.

If you wish, the coach can decide which play should be attempted and he can signal to his "quarterback" what he wants.

7. Execution

Practice makes perfect. A successful set play needs correct selection, signals, movement, timing, passing and shot or header.

Only by continual practice can all these demands be achieved. Perfection is the key word and the joy shown by all when a set play is successful is a fine reward for the planning and work of all concerned.

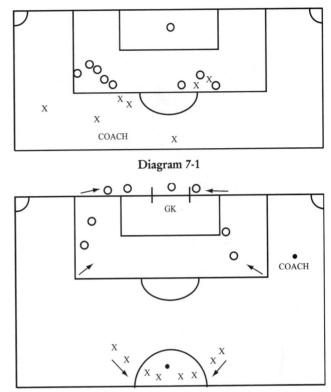

Diagram 7-1

Diagram 7-2

TEACHING INGENUITY AT RESTARTS
Tom Turner

Every now and again, we see another coach in action, presenting some aspect of the game just that little bit different, and just that little bit better.

In the summer of 1993, at the Olympic Development Regional camp in Ames, IA, Michigan's U-15 coach, Mark Christensen, trained his team on restarts in a manner which alleviated most of the major problems associated with the "traditional" approach of lining up walls and taking endless re-kicks until either limited realistic success is attained, or boredom prevails. The Christensen Method allows for repetition, and competition, and produces an environment in which players can improve their technical and tactical execution at restarts, and have a challenging experience in the process. Not a bad combination!

I would like to pass his basic method along in the hope that others will benefit from his innovation. I have provided an alternative grouping and teaching method to incorporate different team situations, and have also included additional suggestions on how to conclude each attack. Finally, there are some ideas on different options relative to the position of the ball.

METHOD I FOR TEACHING IMPROVISATION

1. Divide the team into two even groups.
2. Give each group one end of the field and allow for 20-30 minutes "experimentation" with no opposition. Tell the groups that they will have an arbitrary number of "live" attempts (e.g., 10) against the other group, and that they should develop and practice their restarts from inside and around the box, and from corner kicks and throw-ins. Older players will probably need much less adult intervention and guidance than younger ones in these initial stages. As ideas are developed in successive practices, different options, and the timing and shape of runs should be coached more extensively. With younger players, a questioning approach would probably best spark the creative mind. For example, questions such as: "From this position, can you find a way to attack around the outside of the wall?"; "From this position, can you find a way to use Robert's height and heading abilities?"; "How can you give Wendy a better shot at goal from this position outside the box?"; give enough of the answer away while still allowing the players to come up with their own solutions. As a general principle, it is advisable to require that attempts at goal be generated in three passes or less. The old adage of Keep It Simple Stupid (KISS) is a useful philosophy for most restarts.

3. The next step after practice is competition. Begin the exercise with the teams distinguished by scrimmage vests and the ball placed in any position in the attacking third. (Diagram 7-1) The attacking team (selected by the toss of a coin) has one attempt at the restart, and the attempt ends when either a goal is scored, or the ball is cleared out of the attacking area. If the defense plays the ball over the goal line, the attacking team continues the attack with a corner kick.

4. When the attempt ends, the attacking team turns and jogs around a marker at the near end of the center circle, while the defending team turns to jog around behind the goal. (Diagram 7-2) This clearance is important in that it forces each team to adapt to a completely new situation. When the teams re-enter the field, a new ball is in place (placed in a different position by the coach) at the site of the next restart. The ball can be placed in any position and can include: indirect or direct free kicks inside and outside the box; corner kicks; and, occasionally, throw-ins. The teams prepare their strategies relative to the position of the ball, and the attacking team again attempts to find the net.

If the ball is only partially cleared, and the attacking team has possession it is important to allow the

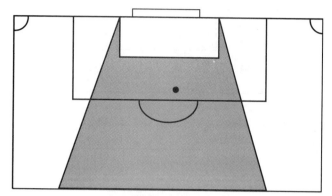

Diagram 7-3

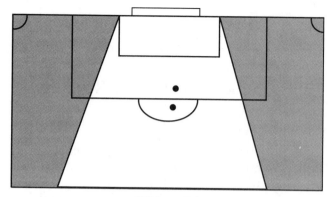

Diagram 7-4

attack to reach a conclusion. When the ball is only partially cleared and the defenders have possession, a recognized outlet (i.e. crossing the half way line in possession, passing to a target player or space, etc.) should be conditioned, along with the habit of pushing out of the defensive third as a group.

5. When the attacking group have had their designated number of attempts, the teams change places and try to outmatch their opponent's efforts. It follows that if one team is attacking at a restart, another must be defending. This exercise offers a perfect opportunity to change the focus of a subsequent practice to the defense, and coach the players on how to defend a variety of different situations.

METHOD II FOR TEAMS WITH ESTABLISHED "FREE KICK SPECIALISTS"

Divide the players into two groups: (by contrasting shirt colors).

1. An attacking group, consisting of players who would normally be involved in restarts, i.e. good strikers of the ball, good headers, players who will attack the ball in the box, the best passer, players with the ability to time runs well, etc. This group will number around seven or eight players.

2. A defensive group, which will consist of all the other players (normally at least as many as the attacking team).

3. Repeat steps three to five from Method I. It is important to allow the defensive group to have their turn at beating the attacking groups' goals total. There will be much more motivation to defend if pride and competition are at stake.

The advantages of this method lie in its realism. Each new restart is from a different position. There may be corner kicks, direct and indirect free kicks, kicks from inside and outside the penalty box, throw-ins, goal-line stands, and restarts where the attacking team might be more likely to simply possess the ball and build into an attack. The number of options is infinite, and each situation allows the attackers to evaluate their options in search of the best route to a scoring chance.

In the early stages it will be more appropriate for the coach to provide some direction to the players on which options are available to them given the personnel, and which possibilities exist from any particular position. The coach may also ask specific players to do specific things in certain situations. These tendencies can then be developed by including extra restarts from near that same position. The concern of too much coaching however, is that players are not given the option to try something on their own, that they are so conditioned to "hit and shoot" that they never look for the quick pass or shot, the subtle little ball to the front or back post, or the ball down the outside of an unwary wall. It is the simple and unexpected which can have the biggest returns and as this coach jokingly once said, "If my players aren't sometimes smarter than me when they get on the field, we're in trouble!" Let them experiment, . . .and fail. They will be wiser for the experience in the long run.

COACHING STRATEGIES

As the person in control of placement, the coach has the ability to respot the ball in any position. In this way, opportunities can be provided to repeat any re-start if necessary. A quiet word in the ear of a particular player might be all that is needed to produce a better attempt at goal next time around.

The following are some options which can be developed given the position of the ball in relation to the box.

Balls in Central Position (Diagram 7-3)

1. Can a player accurately shoot from that position?

2. Can a player bend the ball around the wall?

3. By playing the ball to a second player within one to three yards of the restart, can a player execute steps one or two listed above? The shooter might be a third player or the original kicker.

4. Can the ball be lifted to a second player for a volley or half volley?

5. Can the ball be shot directly at, or through the wall?

6. Can a mini-wall of two or three players be erected four-six yards from the ball to obscure the view of

Here we see a corner kick taken by the light shirted squad. Note that the defensive team does not have a player designated to defend against a "short corner." Author Kline discusses zonal defending of the corner kick. (photo by Brett Whitesell)

the defense and provide an option for a player to execute step one or two?

7. Can a player, or players, be inserted into the wall to cause confusion or possibly a hole?

8. Combine steps six and seven?

Balls in Flank Positions (Diagram 7-4)

1. Can a player accurately shoot from that position?

2. Who are the best headers of the ball, and are they best suited to attacking the near-post, mid-goal or back-post areas? How can space be created by other players for these runs?

3. Are there possibilities for a cross-field pass and a shot?

4. Are there possibilities to get a player behind the defense either directly, down the outside of the wall, or with a two-, or three-player combination?

5. Are there possibilities of playing the ball into feet for a two-, or three-player combination resulting in a shot or a cross?

6. Are there possibilities for playing short and creating space for a late run to the back post?

7. Is the best option to keep possession?

In conclusion, The Christensen Method provides a wonderful opportunity to practice restarts in a new and interesting way. The time spent evaluating and repeating attacking options in training is the key to improving match day performance. In the real game it is the players who make tactical decisions. As coaches, it is our job to help players make better evalu-

ations of match situations: I think this method helps our cause.

⚽

ZONE DEFENSE OF THE CORNER KICK
Loren E. Kline

The corner kick in soccer has traditionally been a tremendous scoring opportunity for the attacking team and a very dangerous situation for the defending team. The rules of the game dictate that the ball be placed in the corner arc, that the defenders must be 10 yards away, that the kick is direct (can score without a second touch) and that there can be no offsides on the kick. These rules give an advantage to the attacking team. Along with the rule advantage, the attacking team has an opportunity to run predetermined plays, kicking the ball to a specific spot and running players to assigned positions. Many goals have been scored from the corner kick. According to Charles Hughes, one of the five reasons goals are scored as set plays. Probably the most dangerous of the set plays is the corner kick.

In defending the corner kick it is important to first understand the offensive strategy. The attacking team can either kick a short corner or a long corner. The short kick attempts to take advantage of the elements

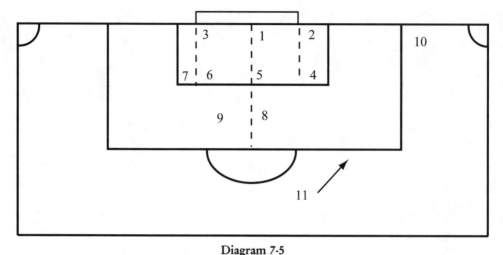

Diagram 7-5

of surprise and numerical advantage, to draw defenders out of position and to find an opening closer to the goal. The long corner attempts to place the ball in a dangerous area in front of the goal or somewhere out from the far goal post. The long kick may be either an inswinger or an outswinger depending on the attacking team's strategy of scoring directly or indirectly and conditions of wind, sun, wet ball, etc.

Since the attacking team will utilize well rehearsed plays and has many advantages to score goals off the corner kick, the defending team must work hard at practicing defense on the corner kick. The defense has to consider the use of either a man-to-man or zone system to minimize the opposition's scoring chances. Over the years most teams have employed tight man-to-man marking and the placement of two defenders on the post to help the keeper. The man-to-man marking requires players to follow the flight of the ball at the same time they see their man and attempt to play the ball out of the area. While working on corner kick defense at Delaware, I find that many players' idea of tight marking does not match mine. They feel they have a man when he is actually free. Another problem is that players watching the flight of the ball have difficulty keeping track of their man. A third problem of man-to-man defense is a mismatch in size or an offensive player running our best defenders away from the dangerous area.

While coaching at the University of Delaware, our change to zone defense against the corner kick was made because the zone had some obvious advantages versus playing man-to-man. Amongst the advantages are:

• We can assign our best headers to specific areas;

• We can place smaller players where size is not so important;

• Our defenders need only key on the ball coming into their area and need not split their attention between the ball and a man;

• Our defensive assignments can remain the same for

any type of corner kick of the attacking team.

Our player positions and responsibilities for defending the corner kick are as follows (Diagram 7-5):

1. The goalkeeper: The keeper should position himself in the middle of the goal one step off the line facing the field of play. By being in the middle of the goal he will be in a better position to come out and collect air balls. The keeper should not leave his position until he can judge the distance, arc and swerve or spin of the kicked ball. He should be able to see the kicker's foot, approach, run and flight of the ball. If the goalkeeper can safely reach the ball he must call "keeper" and collect the ball or punch it clear and wide of the penalty area. He must not allow the ball to come down to the ground. If the keeper cannot reach the ball he must call "clear," hold his position and depend on his teammates to clear the ball from the area.

2. Defending the near post: This position will be taken by one of our midfielders. Size and heading ability are helpful but not of prime importance for this spot. This player must protect the near post area in case of a hard driven ball or sharp inswinger. He cannot leave his post until he hears the keeper's command. If the keeper calls for the ball the near post defender must "lock in" behind the keeper and protect the goal. If the keeper calls "clear" he shall head any ball near the post, protect the post area from a shot and then move out.

3. Defending the far post: This position will probably be taken by another midfielder. Again, size and heading ability are helpful but not of prime importance. The player may be one step from the post since he has more time to read the flight of the ball. His prime responsibility is to protect the far post area from a long inswinger or shot off the long cross. If the keeper calls for the ball this defender must "lock in" behind the keeper and protect the goal line. If the ball is played out front he should be alert for a deflection and then move out!

4. Defending the zone inside the goal area from the near post to the near corner of the goal area: Number four will position himself in line with the near post and one or two steps from the six yard line. This player should have good size and good heading skills. He will probably be one of our wing defenders. This player must be the first player to reach any ball in his zone. He should use his head to clear any ball he can prevent from coming across the goal area.

5. Goal area from center of goal to near post: This player will be one of our two best headers and have good size. He will probably be a central defender. His position is in line with the center of the goal about two steps from the six yard line. He must be alert to the goalkeeper's command and not allow any ball to come down in front of the goal.

6. Far post to center of goal mouth: This player will be the other one of our two best headers and have good size. He must be a strong aggressive player who will listen to his keeper and win any head ball in his zone in front of the goal.

7. Far quarter area to far post: This player will position himself on the far corner of the goal area. He will probably be another wing defender. He must win any head ball in his area, being alert to the long cross and at least skip it off his head to the far side line. If the ball comes to the ground on the farside, he must go out and close down any shot.

8. Penalty area from penalty mark to near side of box: This player will be our third best header. He should have good size and speed to win any balls in front of the goal area. He must be alert to any balls that come to ground or rebound. He will probably be a center halfback or center fullback.

9. Penalty area from penalty mark to far side of penalty box: This player will position himself in line with the far post, halfway between the top of the six yard line and the top of the 18 yard area. He will probably be our forward with the best heading skills. His job will be to clear any ball falling in the far side of the penalty box. He must also be alert to move out on balls which come to ground and block shots from the far side of the penalty box.

10. 10 yards in front of the ball before the corner kick This position will be assumed by one of our forwards. Size and heading skills are not important. His responsibility is to distract the kicker and perhaps even block the kick if it is low. Another reason for being there is to discourage the short corner by marking any man running to the kick and calling for help. This player should cue on the kicker's approach to determine if the kick will be an inswinger or outswinger. For an inswinger, his position should be about three or four yards into the field of play from the end line. For an outswinger, his position should be right on the end line in an attempt to stand in the path of the kicked ball.

11. Half way between the penalty box and midfield line toward the ball: This position will be assumed by one of our forwards. He is a target man for the outlet pass and should win any ball played out of the danger area. We would want him to start the counter-attack after the kick. This man must also be alert to a short kick. If it develops, he must run back and help #10 fronting the ball and create an even up situation.

Our defensive strategy for zone defense of the corner kick requires first a clear verbal commitment from our goalkeeper. He must win the ball and everyone else hold, or he must hold his position and depend on his teammates to play the ball out. All players must hold their zone until the ball clears the penalty box. All players must concentrate on the ball and give a total commitment to being first to the ball if it comes in their zone. As soon as the ball is played out of the area all players must move forward to catch slow reacting opponents in an offside trap and move into counter-attack positions. Positions #8 and #9 must work hard to win deflections and begin a counter-attack. If the ball comes to ground in the penalty box, all defensive players must immediately become conscious of unmarked players in their zones, match up and communicate to achieve close marking. If a second offensive player moves to the corner for a short kick play, the player in the number 11 position must immediately come back to the corner and prevent the play from developing.

This defensive system gives all eleven players a predetermined position and assignment. They know exactly where to go and what to do. This allows the defense to set up quickly before the offensive play begins. This system should not be confused by running players, switching or overloading. This system can work equally well against a long throw-in or any free kick near the corner of the field which is played like a corner.

⚽

PENALTY KICKS AND SPORTS PSYCHOLOGY
Stuart Barbour

The importance of penalty kicks has increased steadily over the last three World Cups. The 1990 World Cup saw 56 penalty kicks taken in both regulation play and in shootout competitions. During standard play, PKs accounted for five percent of the goals in Spain in '82, nine percent in Mexico in '86 and 11.3

TABLE 7-1: PENALTY SHOT TECHNIQUE AND OUTCOME				
Type of Shot	**Number**	**Outcome**		
		Goal	Save	Miss
Power	19 34.5%	14 73.6%	2 10.5%	3 15.7%
Side-Foot	21 38.1%	14 66.6%	5 23.8%	2 9.5%
Instep	14 25.4%	12 85.7%	1 7.1%	1 7.1%
Chip	1 1.8%		1 100%	

percent in Italia in '90. In 1986 three of the quarter-final matches were decided by penalty shootouts. In Italy there were four shootouts, one in the second round match, one in the quarterfinal and in both of the semifinal match-ups.

With the increase in significance of the penalty shot there is a need for detailed study of one of soccer's more controversial, yet incredibly dramatic, traditions.

ITALIA '90 ANALYSIS

Examining the penalty kicks in the 1990 World Cup we see that the shooter was able to convert 41 of 56 attempts, a success rate of 73.2 percent. Of the 15 unsuccessful shots, nine (16 percent) were saved and 6 (10.7 percent) either missed the net or hit the woodwork.

Three main types of shots were identified from the video analysis. The first type can be referred to as the power shot. This shot is struck with the laces and the knee is directly over the ball. The speed of the shot appears to be the dominant factor as the kicker shows little sign of careful aiming. According to Werner Kuhn's research (1987) this type of shot is traveling between 75 and 100 km/hr and takes between 600 and 400 ms to cross the goal line.

The second type of shot is the side-foot shot and resembles the push pass. The dominant factor in this approach is accuracy. In some cases the shooter appears to process feedback from the positioning of the keeper.

The third category of shot may be termed the instep shot. In this strategy, the ball is hit with a fair degree of force and contact is made just behind the big toe on the inside of the foot. This technique usually means the ball is "cut" and has a degree of side spin on it. There was also a fourth strategy used but it has been known to give coaches ulcers.

The chip shot, if successful, is a sign of arrogance, but if saved is the ultimate form of embarrassment. Just ask Bilek of Czechoslovakia .

The side-foot technique accounted for 21 of the tournament's penalty kicks, yet had the lowest success rate at only 66.6 percent. (Table 7-1) This can be attributed to the ease at which this type of shot is "read" by the keeper (Table 7-2) and poor placement by the shooter. When this shot is hit correctly, it is unstoppable as Andres Brehme demonstrated in the tournament final.

The power shot accounted for 19 of the tournament's penalty kicks and had a conversion rate of 73.6 percent. While virtually unstoppable when hit with a relative degree of accuracy, the biggest risk with this technique is missing the net entirely. (Table 7-1) The power shot offers virtually no clues to the keeper as to the placement of the shot and in some instances the player himself is even surprised as to where the ball ends up. The World Cup keepers were only able to read the direction of the power shot correctly 26 percent of the time. (Table 7-2) The rest of the time they were off flying in the wrong direction.

The instep shot was the least popular of the techniques and was only selected on 14 occasions, yet conversely, had a success rate of 85.7 percent. While the shot may have a high success rate, it is evident that the keeper finds it easy to predict the direction of the shot and "guessed" correctly 50 percent of the time. (Table 7-2) This technique offers a nice trade-off between power and accuracy.

The goalkeeper has a choice of two strategies. The first strategy involves decision-making before ball contact is made by the penalty shooter. In this strategy, the keeper reads the pre-contact cues (angle of the approach run and body orientation in addressing the ball) of the shooter and dives early. The second strategy

TABLE 7-2: SHOT "READABILITY" BY GOALKEEPER			
Type of Shot	"Guess" Correctly	"Guess" Incorrectly	Hold
Power	5 26%	13 68.4%	1 5.2%
Side-Foot	7 33.3%	7 33.3%	7 33.3%
Instep	7 50%	4 28.5%	3 21.4%

TABLE 7-3: GOALKEEPER DECISIONS AND "SAVE-ABILITY"		
	"Guess" Correctly	"Guess" Incorrectly
	19/44 = 43%	25/44 = 56.8%
Stoppable: Yes No Miss	5/19 = 26.2% 12/19 = 63% 2/19 = 10.5%	16/25 = 64% 6/25 = 24% 2/19 = 16%

involves the keeper holding his ground and reacting to the flight of the ball.

It is evident from the 1990 World Cup that the most popular strategy employed by the keepers involved "guessing" the direction of the shot and diving early. From the video analysis a "guess" was defined as any time the goalkeeper shifted his upper body weight off center prior to contact of the ball. In other words, he initiated a movement either to his left or right. In all, goalkeepers "guessed" on 44 of the tournament's 56 penalty shots. Now remember, these are not just wild flings across the net but the result of a careful reading of the pre-contact cues of the shooter.

The world's best keepers "guessed" correctly only 43 percent of the time (see Table 7-3). Of the nine saves made by goalkeepers during Italia '90, five were the result of this guessing technique for a save percentage of 11 percent. One of the five saves actually occurred when the keeper had gone the wrong way, but the poor quality of the shot gave him time to readjust and make the stop. The least popular strategy involved the keeper holding his ground and reacting to the flight of the ball. This only occurred 11 times yet resulted in four saves for a save percentage of 36 percent.

Studying the placement of penalty kicks from Italia '90 (Diagram 7-6) we can see that six of the fifty-six shots may be deemed totally stoppable as they were within four feet of either side of the keeper (zone A). Twenty of the shots may be deemed stoppable, as they were between four and eight feet away from the keeper. (zone B) The remainder are considered unstoppable. (zone C) Hypothetically if the keeper were standing still and reacting simply to the flight of the ball, he would have had a very good chance to stop all the shots in zones A and B.

The most vivid example of these opposing strategies was presented in the Republic of Ireland-Romania shootout. Pat Bonner, the Irish keeper, guessed correctly on the first shot but did not make the save. He then held his ground on the remaining four shots and made one save off Timofte, the final Romanian shooter. Lung, the Romanian goalkeeper, elected to guess on every Irish shot. He was incorrect on four of the five occasions. The Romanian shots were far better taken. Four of the five were considered unstoppable while all five of the Irish shots were deemed totally stoppable. Fortunately for Ireland, Lung was already jumping away from the shot on four of the five occasions. The one time he did guess correctly, he essentially dove over the ball.

PSYCHOLOGICAL COMPONENTS OF A PENALTY KICK

The actual physical task of taking a penalty shot is relatively easy, yet somehow players manage to miss. Missed penalty shots can be attributed to a number of

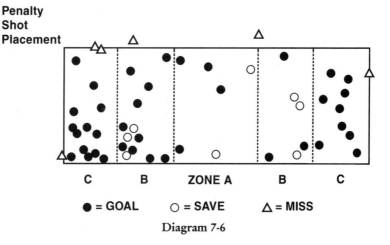

Diagram 7-6

factors, some of which are beyond our control while others are not. Penalty shootouts occur at the end of 120 minutes of grueling play. During this time the average player will have run over 12,000 meters. To say that fatigue is not a factor would be shortsighted.

Psychologically speaking, soccer players tend to be very strong in terms of their broad external focus. The very nature of the game requires the players to assess and read a very complex and dynamic environment. A penalty shot is a lot like skeet shooting or a free throw in basketball where the player is required to use a narrow internal focus. The athlete taking the penalty shot is in a position to dictate the flow of the game. He is also given a reasonable amount of time to prepare and take the shot. The penalty kick is a standard situation since the distances and dimensions are fixed. The player's only job is to score. Thus, they must take time to prepare, centering in order to adjust tension levels so excess muscle tension does not interfere with the execution of the shot. One should expect that some players will find penalty shots difficult, since the very psychological nature of a penalty shot is very different from that of the game in which the player excels.

The physical execution of a penalty shot is rather stress free. However, Friedman and Bar Eli (1988) identify seven interdependent factors that may be viewed as related to the performance of the penalty kick. These factors are: team, coach, management, opponent, spectators, media and the player himself (I would also add family members). They claim that when these factors become social pressures they can enhance the level of stress the player is already experiencing and this will negatively affect task performance. One begins to feel social pressure when these significant others let the player know, either directly or indirectly, that they have a vested interest in the player's performance. This external stress is magnified and can create a performance decline which is evident the moment the penalty kick is struck.

Players must realize that they have total control over only one of these seven—themselves. Worrying about others' expectations, the crowd, teammate's ability to take penalties or reflecting on the game just played will detract from performance. During the 1984 Olympic quarter-finals, Brazil came from behind to tie a very solid Canadian team. In the ensuing shootout, the Brazilians won 4-2. Ian Bridge had volunteered to take a penalty for Canada which was easily stopped by the keeper. He explains that while waiting in the center circle for his turn to shoot, he was "very satisfied with our [Canada's] performance up to that moment and if we lost in the penalties it wouldn't be that bad because our team had made a very good showing." In hindsight, he claims that "my biggest fault was reflecting that we had done so well prior to tak-

ing my shot." Undoubtedly, this lack of internal focus adversely affected Ian's penalty shot performance.

Another source of internal stress occurs when the athlete experiences indecision as to which way to shoot. It is very important for the penalty shooter to pick his or her spot and stick to it. As Gerry Gray, one of Canada's successful shooters during the Olympics, states, "Do what you do normally, do the thing you know you do best." These few words may have helped Dale Mitchell prior to his penalty kick against Brazil. In the last game of the opening round, Dale successfully converted a penalty during the run of play against Cameroon. On his approach to the penalty kick against Brazil, Dale became worried that the previous match had been scouted. "I normally shoot to my right as I did against Cameroon but...I decided to go the other way and as a result, I did not hit the shot as confidently as I had against Cameroon. The keeper guessed the right way and saved it." Dale admits that had he taken more time to analyze the situation, he would have realized there was no way that Brazil could have scouted the game. Canada had played their opening group in Boston and Brazil had been playing in California so it was very unlikely that any Brazilian had seen his penalty kick. This is a very easy thing to reflect about later but in the heat of the moment sometimes logic is the furthest thing from your mind. This is why it is so important that the whole procedure becomes automatic.

During a penalty shootout, effective communication between players and coaches is very important. If a team has been ideally prepared for their elimination rounds, they should have at least five competent and confident shooters. Failing this, the coach is usually left searching the team for five kickers. The best approach is to ask for volunteers to take the shots, as opposed to telling players they are shooting. As Bruce Wilson, captain of Canada's Olympic team, explains, "It's a confidence thing; you're in the Olympics, it's the quarter-finals, the game is being broadcast to 45 million Brazilians, let alone the rest of the world... It comes down to someone having enough confidence to do it on the spur of the moment when the pressure is on." By asking for volunteers, the more confident players should come forward to take responsibility. Players should realize that if they are confident in their ability to score, they should speak up immediately. There is nothing more frustrating than finding out from a player a week after a loss that they were really confident on match day and would have liked the opportunity to shoot.

Communication problems between the captain, his or her teammates and the officials will create unnecessary stress that can result in less than peak performance. It is very important that every shooter knows the order of the shots and that this information has been double-checked with the officials. During the quarter-

APPENDIX B: SOCCER PLAYER
INTERVIEW GUIDE

1. How clearly do you recall the penalty shoot-out you were involved in during the 1984 Olympics?

2. What was your first reaction when you realized that you had to take one of the five penalty shots?

3. What was going through your mind as you waited in the center circle for your turn to shoot?

4. When you walked up to take your penalty shot: How confident were you? What were you saying to yourself? Did you have any visions of yourself missing/scoring?

5. When did you decide where you were going to place your shot?

6. Do you regularly take penalty shots for your country or club?

7. After you had taken your shot how did you feel? What thoughts raced through your mind?

8. During your training camps, did you practice penalty shots? How did you practice them? Did you attempt any mental imagery?

9. If you could go back and change anything about your training for the penalty shootout, what would you do differently?

10. Was the loss to Brazil viewed as a team or an individual loss?

final penalty shootout between Argentina and Yugoslavia, a critical communication error occurred that may have changed the result of Italia '90. The shootout was tied at 2-2, Yugoslavia had two shooters left to Argentina's one and was in a superb position to knock out the reigning world champions. Hadzibegic came forward to shoot for Yugoslavia. He got all the way to the penalty spot and was then told by the of official that he was listed as the fifth kicker. This brought forward a surprised looking Brnovic. Both Brnovic's and Hadzibegic's shots lacked conviction and were easily saved by Goycochea. Dezotti's goal paved the way to a semi final match against Italy and another penalty shootout.

In summary, most missed penalty shots can be attributed to improper preparation either technically or mentally. Some players and coaches, such as Bruce Wilson, are of the opinion that penalty shots "come down to something you cannot coach... [or] really train. It's experience, professionalism and being able to carry through. That is what you get paid for." But to accept this is to say that one cannot learn. If players truly want to achieve excellence and are willing to toss aside those psychological shackles that inhibit them then all they need is a plan to follow that will allow them to became clutch penalty shooters. The following plan will improve one's technical ability to take penalty shots as well as develop the mental strength required to succeed under intense pressure.

A TRAINING PLAN

The first thing a player must gain is confidence in his or her technical ability to strike a penalty. Once a player is technically competent we can then improve the mental side of his or her penalty taking. The first practice involves taking shots from the penalty spot on an empty net. Two corner flags are placed a yard in from each post and the player works at putting the ball between the flag and the post. It is important that the player works on a routine that he or she will follow in a match situation. The kick should be divided into five steps:

Placement. Ensure that the ball is sitting securely on the penalty spot. Make sure the ball is not in a depression and clear away any dirt or pebbles in front of the ball.

Decision. You should be 100 percent sure where and how you are hitting the ball before you start your run to the ball.

Focus. Before you start your approach to the ball take a moment to focus on the task ahead of you. Approach: Your approach to the ball must be smooth and natural and should be performed at a speed that would occur in a match.

Strike. Your shot should be clean and sharp and feel "sweet" coming off your foot.

After players are confident in their technical ability, a keeper is then introduced to the training. At first, the flags are left in place so shooters still know their target. Prior to removing the flags, players should adjust their aiming to a spot on the net that will result in the same degree of accuracy. One shot should be mastered, "playing around" with different types of shots and approaches should be avoided. Shots should be taken at game speed and avoid rapid fire shooting. It is the quality of the shots which is important, not the quantity (you only get one chance in a game).

The goalkeeper should be educated as to the success rate of the two strategies employed by keepers. He should then be given the opportunity to study the pre-contact cues, such as the angle of the approach and the angle of the ankle, which can aid in the diving decision. This can be achieved by studying either professional or amateur video tapes of penalty shots. The goalkeeper should never dive early, make the shooter beat you. In training, improvements in reaction and movement times should be emphasized. According to Kuhn (1987), this can be achieved by "under loading" the keeper (use distances of 13 and 14 yards) and then switch to an "overload" situation (use distances of 10 and 11 yards). Once improvements in these physical attributes have been made, practice should switch to game-like situations which allow the keeper an appropriate rest between shots. Bombarding keepers does nothing for either their skill or confidence.

The most valuable strategy in coping mentally with a penalty shot situation is to put the whole game in perspective. If a player associates his or her success in soccer with his or her identity and self worth, then that player runs the risk of putting a gigantic amount of strain on him or herself which will decrease the chances of success. "If you can approach anxiety provoking situations with a healthy perspective, then the most debilitating anxiety will not surface." (Orlick, 1990 p. 36). Remember, it is only a game. The Canadian Olympic players that were interviewed were unanimous that their penalty shot loss to Brazil was a team loss rather than an individual loss. Dale Mitchell claims, "It was more like a team victory...we were more pleased with our performance than devastated by the loss to Brazil."

Not only is it important to educate soccer players about the technical side of penalty shots, but they must also fully understand the mental side. Players must realize that important penalty shots will create a degree of anxiety and they should be taught to identify the early physical symptoms of anxiety and learn how to channel it to improve performance. One could easily become preoccupied with their feeling of stress and start to worry about being nervous. These self defeating thoughts will usually result in a missed shot. An elite athlete will interpret the early signs of stress in a positive manner. By relabeling your signs of stress as a cue to yourself that you are ready, activated or pumped, you can channel your anxiety to improve your performance. Essentially players must realize that they are in total control of their own thought patterns and it is up to them to direct them for maximum results.

If players still find it difficult to attain a balance between anxiety and arousal, then they should have the opportunity to practice different relaxation techniques to discover what works best for them. Players should be taught progressive muscular relaxation techniques, controlled breathing techniques and how to use self-directed thoughts to control anxiety. It is of paramount importance that the player discovers a technique that works best for him or her. For example, a player may find that extra leg stretching and a quick shoulder massage puts him in the best mental frame for a shootout. He should then have no hesitation in asking one of his teammates to assist in the procedure (preferably one who is not shooting).

The importance of staying mentally relaxed was demonstrated during the Los Angeles Olympics. After the coin toss for the penalty kicks in the Canada-Brazil match, there was an unexplained delay in getting the shootout started. Bruce Wilson faced a one and a half minute delay prior to his shot. If this does not seem like a long time to you, stop reading and watch the clock for 90 seconds. How many times did your thoughts wander in that time? Now, could you imagine that same delay in a packed stadium while you are standing alone on the penalty spot? Fortunately for Canada, Bruce was able to use the delay as a positive event: " I think it worked to my advantage because I had a chance to talk to the referee and make a joke or two with him and as a result I was quite relaxed."

Players also need to be trained to monitor their self statements. Self statements are negative or positive statements that persons say to themselves either out loud or internally. The key thing is to replace negative statements such as, "I am going to miss," "This keeper is awesome," or "This one is going over the bar like my last shot," with positive statements like, "This one is going in," and "My shots are unstoppable." Gerry Gray's first thoughts during Canada's Olympic campaign clearly illustrate positive cognitive coping strategies. When it was decided he would take a penalty, the first thing that he thought was, "I am going to score this bloody thing." Five years after the event his voice still parallels the conviction with which he scored his spot-kick. During training sessions players should pay attention to their self statements and attempt to enhance their cognitive coping capabilities.

Given the extreme importance that is placed on every kick of the ball during a penalty shootout, coaches and players should be encouraged to jointly prepare a "Penalty Kick Focus Plan" (see appendix A).

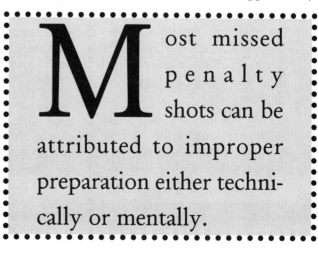

Most missed penalty shots can be attributed to improper preparation either technically or mentally.

One should never play a game hoping for penalty shots, but it is nice to know that one is prepared. Confidence and attitude are often considered the most important factors in penalty shots and it is the intent of the planning sheet to improve these attributes. The penalty shot may be broken down to four critical stages: the wait in the center circle, the walk up, the time at the spot and the final approach. It is important for athletes to develop an effective mental focus for each stage that will enhance their own performance and this should be developed according to individual differences. The key is to decide how you want to feel in each of the stages prior to taking a penalty kick and devise a plan that will ensure this will occur. Use positive self statements and the plan should be free from technical jargon. "Competition is not the time for technical instruction, it is the time to trust your body, to focus ahead and go." (Orlick, 1986 pg. 43). Practice and refine your plan.

The second stage of planning for a penalty shot involves developing a refocusing plan. The player must identify potential problems or negative intrusions that could occur which would have a critical effect on the outcome of the shot. Werner Kuhn, in his study of the German Bundesliga, reported that "some players engaged in what may be termed psycho regulative measures. Examples are deliberately delaying the execution of the kick by walking around the penalty area, telling the shooter which corner is his favorite or making allusions about the morality of the shooter's wife!" (1987 pg. 491). Players should also have a plan about what to do if they are awarded a second penalty in a match or granted a retake if the keeper moves early and stops their first shot.

The final stage of this training plan is the application stage. During this stage the player who is committed to excellence will follow these basic guidelines:

• Commit yourself to executing your penalty shots with the highest degree of effort and skill;

• Simulate what you want to do in competition. Go through the entire penalty shot sequence as it would occur in a match;

• Commit yourself to focusing 100 per cent on each penalty shot;

• Visualize executing the penalty shot in the stadium where it will occur. (Adapted from Orlick, 1990 p.13).

Simulating Game-Like Conditions

The key in training is to create an atmosphere that is as close to a game-like condition as possible. Simply standing around the penalty spot after training and taking rapid fire penalties on a helpless keeper is far from reality. Some form of stress must be introduced that the players must work at coping with. Gerry Gray overloads himself in practice by telling the goalkeeper where he is putting his shot. Gerry explains, "That way, in a game, if the keeper guesses right I'll still have to beat him. If the keeper guesses correctly your shot should still beat him."

During training sessions, any time the opportunity for a penalty kick occurs, seize the teachable moment. This approach will have three major benefits. The fouling player will be appropriately punished for his or her actions and this should transfer to your games. Both the goalkeeper and shooter are presented with opportunities to refine their penalty-kick routines. The coach is also given the opportunity to instruct the non-shooting players as to their roles during a penalty-kick. A great opportunity to simulate a penalty shootout occurs in training during 6 v. 6 tournaments or games. Any time a match ends in a tie, decide the outcome with a FIFA shootout. Make every attempt to simulate the real thing. The coach can act as referee, the players should wait at the center circle for their turn to shoot and one may even encourage some gamesmanship in order to practice overcoming obstacles.

An enjoyable alternative for older players is a cash penalty shootout. Each player brings a couple of dollars to practice. The players take turns shooting from the spot while the goalkeepers rotate. A missed shot costs the player a dollar to the pot for the shooters and every save or goalpost hit is dollar into the keepers' pot. Once a player has lost the two dollars, he or she is eliminated. Eventually, one winner emerges and he or she keeps the pot. This sort of activity creates plenty of opportunities for the players to apply and to refine their penalty kick focus plans.

Preseason and exhibition matches offer another opportunity for teams to simulate penalty shootouts. Arrange an exhibition match that is a two out of three affair. The game itself and two separate penalty shootouts after the match represent the three events. The shootouts can be conducted simultaneously at either end of the field. This will overload the shooters with distraction and really force them to draw on their coping strategies. Each team divides its 10 field players into two groups and uses the goalkeeper and his back-up from the bench. If this game is arranged well in advance, it can represent an incentive for the players to work on their penalty shot routines and planning sheets because they will know there is no escape from having to take a spot-kick. A post event discussion between coach and players will help draw out some of the problems that the unsuccessful shooters encountered.

Victory in soccer is often decided by the narrowest of margins. By implementing a technical and mental training plan for penalty shots, hopefully more of these tight matches may become clutch wins for your team. If every team were to follow this training plan for penalty shootouts then it would only be 50 percent successful. To win at soccer requires a team to be better than its opposition in all elements of the game and penalty shots are one more element of the world's simplest game. Critics may feel that all this planning is far too elaborate for one kick of the ball, but if you have the knowledge, can you afford not to use it?

REFERENCES

F.I.F.A. (1990). *F.I.F.A. Report: World Cup '90 Italia.* F.I.F.A. House: Zurich, Switzerland.

Klein, A. & Friedman, Z. *Soccer For Everyone: Penalty Kicks.* West Hills, California, USA.

Klein, A. & Friedman, Z. (November/December 1988). "Psychological Stress in Soccer: The Case of Penalty Kicks." *Soccer Journal.* pp. 49-52.

Kuhn, W. (1987) "Penalty Kick Strategies For Shooters and Goalkeepers." *Science and Football* pp. 489-492. E. & F. Spon: London.

Malone, C. (February 1981). "The Psychology of Penalty Kicking." *Soccer Corner* pp. 46-48.

Mazzei, J. (1982). *Pelé Soccer Training Program.* Unicorn Publishing House: Verona, NJ.

Orlick, T. (1986). *Coaches Training Manual to Psyching For Sport.* Champaign: Leisure Press.

Orlick, T. (1986a). *Psyching For Sport Mental Training for Athletes.* Champaign: Leisure Press.

Orlick, T. (1990). *In Pursuit of Excellence. Second Edition.* Champaign: Leisure Press.

RESTARTS: PRINCIPLES & PLANNING
Tim Schum and Chris Dimitriou

One of the intriguing features of soccer is the fact that once the game begins there is very little control over its outcome by the coach of either team.

Outside of good preparation in practice for the free play aspects of the sport, the soccer coach is not empowered to affect the flow of play. Some might argue that substitutions can dictate the course of a match, but others would contend that those same substitutes disrupt play rather than complement it.

The one area that does lend itself to some degree of control by the coach is the restart situations. Estimates vary depending on the study, but certainly near half of the goals scored in soccer are either the direct or indirect result of a restart situation. Time spent understanding the principles governing restarts and planning for team implementation in the game can reap major dividends for the coach and the team.

UNDERLYING FUNDAMENTALS GOVERNING RESTARTS

Gordan Jago of the CISL Dallas Sidekicks outlined some basic ideas regarding restarts in a 1980 presentation at the NSCAA Convention in Philadelphia. Soccer Journal would later published Gordon's thoughts in an article titled "Scoring from Set Plays" in the 1983 May-June issue (pp. 33-34).

Among coach Jago's thoughts:

- Utilize individual ability: Take an inventory of the technical abilities within your team and utilize them in your planning (i.e., accurate strikers of the ball, heading ability, powerful shooting);
- Minimize the number of passes before attempts on goal and also the number of players involved over the ball: The more the players, the more the passes, the greater the chances for error. The simplest idea is one player, one shot;
- Know the area you want to exploit: Play the ball to the area which gives you the largest target to goal (i.e., generally a defensive wall covers the near post, the far post is therefore your target area). Generally in a two-pass sequence the first touch is away from the target area, the second is played to the target area. For example, the first touch may turn a defender's attention away from the intended target area, allowing for the attacker to get in a good position for an attempt on goal in the intended target area. The area between the six yard and 12 yard lines is a second area that is difficult to defend;
- Decoys are needed in order to distract the defense or take defenders away from the zones your team wishes to attack. The attacking team should always have a one or two free men based on the fact that the defense deploys players in the walls. By occupying other defenders with either runs or placement, the attacking team can exploit its "man up" situations;
- Signals are needed in terms of which set piece will be operative. Keep them simple. All players, including your goalkeeper should know them;
- Selection of which set piece to put into action needs to be centralized (i.e., your captain, your best "thinker," or the coach himself giving the signal to the captain);
- Do not design too many plays. Keep them simple and offer options. All players must be ready to react to the play;
- Execution demands practice and repetition of the fundamentals of correct selection, signals, movement, timing, and passing will result in a quality attempt at goal.

Additionally as the coach and the team begin to cooperatively develop strategies for restart situations other individual and group objectives will emerge including:

- The process of preparing for restarts builds both individual assurance and poise and team trust in terms of role-sharing with the coach;
- Player leadership roles can be identified and responsibility assigned within the team;

- The development of dead ball strategies can call on the creative energies throughout the team and the twin elements of concentration and surprise applied if preparation is thorough.

Unstated is the fact that restarts are the lone time in the game that opponents are a prescribed distance (10 yards) from the ball and the ball is at rest.

Following are some thoughts on the various dead ball situations and how we as coaches might choose to deal with them.

I. KICKOFF

In salesmanship, one of the tactics to finalize a contract is to give the buyer a "throwaway," some item that is not going to cost the seller much while heightening the buyer's interest in signing on the dotted line.

In soccer, unfortunately, the kickoff is viewed by many coaches as a "throwaway" with a little attention given to it in terms of team planning.

A new twist on a business dictum at this point might be appropriate - changing "let the buyer beware" to "let coaches beware" of neglecting attention to the kickoff in team preparation.

GAME SITUATIONS

Situation 1

Before the first scrimmage match of the season, the coaches have spent some time planning some restart strategy. Included in the practice session was initial setup work on the kickoff.

With no decided advantage to taking a side of the field to defend due to wind, sun or other playing factors, the team elects to take the kickoff at the outset of the scrimmage.

Setting its fastest, most talented (and tallest) striker on the left outside of the field, the team plays the kickoff back to the right midfielder, a strong, accurate long passer of the ball. With the striker splitting an unprepared, square defense, the ball is played behind the defense into open space where it collected by the striker and struck past the keeper for a goal — 10 seconds into the match.

Situation #2

The defensive team hurriedly takes the field following the half-time break. A new sub at left back has not had a chance to properly warm up or get into the flow of the match. The opposition, with a wind advantage, sends its outside striker on a run at the left back and plays the ball into the space in back of him. The winger collects the ball and with the sweeper now out of the middle while covering his left back, sends the ball into the goal mouth for the center striker to nod on for a goal.

HAPPENSTANCE? LUCK? UNIMPORTANT?

As some are so fond of quoting — "Luck is the residue of design." or — "The harder I work and plan, the luckier I seem to be."

The situations cited have either been experienced or observed by the authors in their coaching roles. All point out the importance of one of soccer's least-planned restarts — the kickoff.

ATTACKING STRATEGIES

Planning for the kickoff in terms of offensive strategy includes taking into consideration the following factors:

- What particular abilities of your players can be featured or highlighted in taking the kick?
- What are the tactical decisions available when the kickoff is awarded?
- What outside factors need to be taken into consideration in relation to the kickoff - weather, field conditions, referee, ball, crowd, etc.?

Most importantly, after inventory of all the above, the basic question for the coach in relation to the offensive kickoff is: What is the objective for the team now that we do have the ball?

If there is no score (the ball is awarded without any momentum having been built up as a result of an opposition's score), then the basic question might be: Do we want to possess the ball and maintain our normal scheme of playing the ball forward? Or do we want to play a slow, rhythmical game, having everyone on the team get a touch on the ball to some degree? Or, do we want to place immediate high pressure on the opposition by opening up spaces for our best offensive players to run onto for the highly speculative score or thrust on goal?

POSSESSION AND PENETRATION

As Vogelsinger points out in his book, *The Challenge of Soccer*, offensive vulnerability on the kickoff is a fact of soccer life. One of the basic elements involved in penetrating offensive play, namely depth, is missing on the initial kickoff. This is the reason why most teams elect to buy some time for the creation of offensive balance on the field by playing the kickoff back into their defensive half, allowing time for the strikers to move into the defense to offer penetrating potential. The principles of play that need to be emphasized if the "possession" objective is elected by the team are:

- Immediate penetration to provide depth on attack;
- Creation of width on the attack;
- Players near the ball recognizing the need for support around the ball while those off the ball must maintain a good defensive posture in terms of balance and depth.

POSSESSION KICKOFF

Player Roles

The players over the ball at kickoff must be good decision-makers and concentrate on good passing at the kickoff. We have placed the CF and CM over the

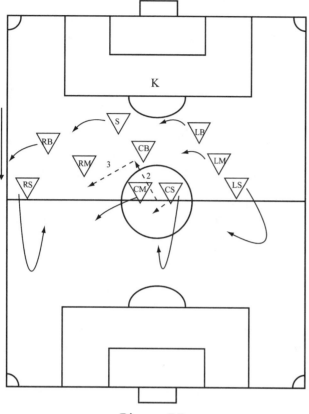

Diagram 7-7

ball in Diagram 7-7. We like to have one of the players blessed with good shielding skills in case he is high pressurized by two or more defenders. The CF's job is to find open space downfield as quickly and in as central a position as possible. Meanwhile one outside striker (RS) moves downfield and checks to the ball on the outside of the field while the other (LS) pinches in a bit while moving downfield.

Once the CM is in possession he could buy time with shielding though it is clear that numerically the attacking team's advantage lies in the middle of the field, particularly in the RM-CB-LM triangle. Dependent upon the strength of the opposition and matchups, the attacking team may be able to determine which side of the field its attack will be focused in advance of kickoff. In Diagram 7-7 we see how players might be positioned were the ball to be played down the right side of the field. Note the positioning of the left-sided players relative to the ball. If the ball is played back to the CB, then the supporting midfielders to either side of the CB must read the situation and offer themselves in the best spaces for subsequent passes to be made forward. The CM in turn must look to support in a forward attacking position once that ball has been played back to the CB, in a sense acting as the link between the ball forward to the attackers and to bring the entire team unit into attack in the opposition half of the field.

As mentioned, it may be that the team recognizes that its best strategy would be to attack one side of the field (the right side in Diagram 7-7) for any number of reasons. In that case the second play of the ball would be to the supporting midfielder, with the CF, the RS and CM all combining to create a hoped-for numerical advantage on the intended target side of the field.

The roles of the backs would be to offer themselves for support in terms of width, although it is poor strategy to have both backs offering width at kickoff as it would leave the team unbalanced and vulnerable to a counter-attack. It is better to determine in advance which back would move forward, though obviously an attack to the right side of the field would have the outside back on that side moving forward to maintain offensive compactness while the off-ball outside back would drop back and in and combine with the sweeper to insure defensive depth and balance off the ball.

Should the kickoff be played into the midfielder-CB triangle, the sweeper's role is to offer support for the player in possession if the ball is to be played back, and to move to that side of the field if the ball is played to a given side - again to provide the twin objectives of offensive support and team balance defensively.

The role of the keeper cannot be minimized. He/she should definitely not be on goal line. A good position would be on the 12-yard line, central to all the field. The keeper must be alert to the fact that if there is an offensive breakdown, his team's numbers up advantage lies with the keeper (he is the least vulnerable player in teams of being marked) as the team can use him for support.

At this point in the possession process, the normal playing roles and abilities on the team must be implemented. Checking runs, runs to open spaces for attacks, dribbling opportunities, mobility in attack in terms of switch of play to the other side of the field are all distinct possibilities, as all of the elements of attack have been put into place - width, depth, balance and concentration.

QUICK PENETRATION

Perhaps it wasn't too many years ago that a standard kickoff ploy (not play!) observed in American soccer circles where the game was in its infancy, was for the ball to be played off to the central midfielder whose singular thought was to boom the ball as long and deep into the opponent's half of the field as possible. The forwards all rushed quickly downfield in hopes of collecting a poorly played rebound off a defender or a misskick of subsequently played balls. Distrustful of their ability to maintain possession in their own half of the field, the idea was quite simplistic: put the pressure on the other team to control the ball. If the opposition couldn't execute, the attacking team might be the beneficiary.

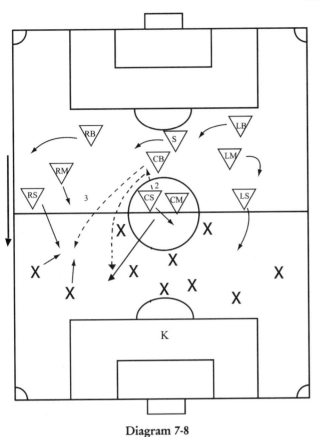

Diagram 7-8

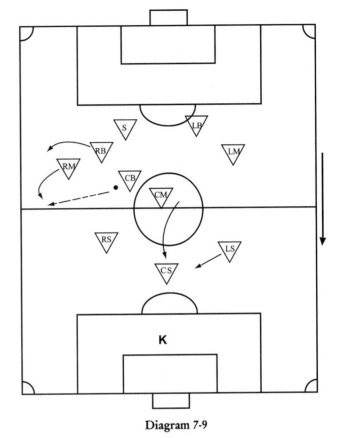

Diagram 7-9

With more organization, the quick strike into the attacking third of the field has the element of surprise working for its success. Also the attacking team's psyche at the kickoff is positive (we are going forward quickly!) and that attitude cannot be minimized.

Diagram 7-8 shows the RS being played to, with the pass coming from the CB, who had received the pass back on the kickoff. The strong run by the RS inside the defensive midfielders splits the defense. The attacking RM while clearly having the intended target out in front and the RB of the kickoff team are also depicted. The CS's run should attract some of the defensive team's attention away from the intended target area and offers the potential for an even more incisive penetrating pass by the CB.

The RS should be a player with good control of the ball and a good sense of forward support. Speed and dribbling ability should be additional talents of the person selection to make the run from the RS position.

Often the failure of such a tactic is the result of incorrect positioning and play back of the ball at the kickoff. Diagram 7-8 shows the ball being played back into space in front of the CB in such a way that the ball player has the ball in a position where it can be moved onto such that he can evaluate in terms of other choices that may be more obvious. It may be that the run of the RS is anticipated by the opponents. In which

case the CB can elect to play the ball to the RM (who is moving into the open space created by the RS run) or even to the RB. This is shown in Diagram 7-9.

The simplest penetration is to send a long ball into the spaces on the perimeter of the field with the intended objective of isolating an attacker on an uncovered back. Again the quick attacker keeps to the touch line on the immediate run at the LB of the opposition. The CS runs into a central position to draw the attention of the central defender. If the ball can be played long and accurately into the final third, it may isolate the attacker 1 v. 1 against the opponent's outside back. The run of the LS to a central position offers the depth necessary should the RS win the ball and subsequently penetrate to cross the ball. Additionally, the LS's run might freeze the sweeper to cover him as the CF's run to the support of the RS should find the defensive CB moving out to cover him. Note that the attacking team has a support triangle for the CM should the ball need to be played backwards due to good defensive pressure. The RB-CB-S are in a good position to offer support for the attack and concentration defensively for any counter-attack of a central nature. The LB and LM offer balance and width for the team.

There are a number of factors which would make this "quick strike" strategy inoperable or a poor tactical choice:

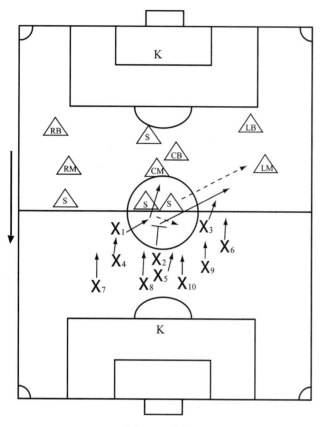

Diagram 7-10

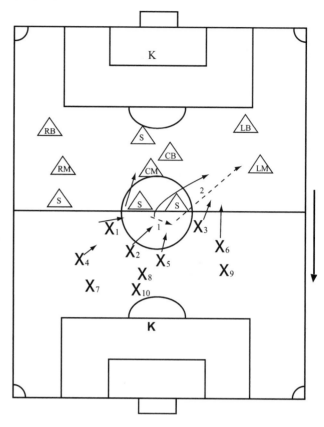

Diagram 7-11

• A low pressure defense which is concentrated centrally;
• Weather conditions where wind or other factors may preclude such strategy;
• The objective of conserving time is not achieved with the penetrating kickoff.

Basically, the long-penetrating kickoff strategy should be used as a surprise maneuver, but properly instituted it may enable a team to initially unnerve another team and indicate to all concerned that play by the offensive team is to be upbeat and attacking in nature.

The long-penetrating kickoff may also be selected when a team is trying to get back into the match following an opponent's score. Immediate attack deep into the opponents's final third may find just that moment of disorganization that typically occurs after a team scores a goal. As those involved with the game can statistically prove, one of the most vulnerable times for a team to give up a score is just after it has scored a goal itself.

The movement of the defensive team on the kickoff can be noted by any number of players and staff on the offensive team, including the keeper and substitutes on the bench.

DEFENSIVE TACTICS

The major emphases on the kickoff should include:
• Pressurizing the kickoff such that a long penetra-

tion by the opposing team is minimized;
• Defensive matchups (here the premise is that a team will be playing combined man-to-man defense with zonal principles) are picked up at the onset of play;
• The potential for counter-attack is understood;
• There is sufficient cover for the point of the opposition's attack;
• There is compactness to the team defensively.
• Strength of the opposition.

Matchup Pressurizing

Diagram 7-10 illustrates all the emphases being put into operation in a high pressure situation. Three players (X1, X2 and X3) are placed on the circle, each with a specific responsibility. X1 and X2 will pressurize the ball and seek to have it played in a predictable fashion, backward and into the opponent's left attacking side of the field, while X2 will put pressure on the ball. X3 will hold and not allow for the ball to be played forward. Sometimes overanxious pressure by X1 and X2 can result in a quick 1-2 by the opposition or that player being beaten by a subsequent dribble. X5 (the CM) minimizes this by covering the middle and additional depth is provided by the X8 (the CB). The outside midfielders (X4 and X6) pinch in towards the middle to give the team compactness with X6 looking to move forward. X7, X8, X9 (marking backs) and X10 (the sweeper) would also be moving forward should the proper pressure be applied by their strik-

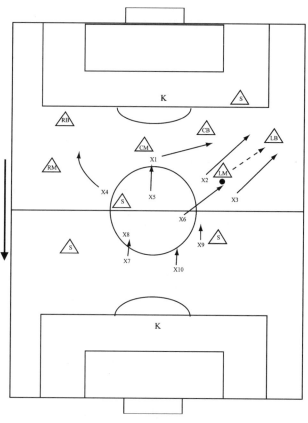

Diagram 7-12

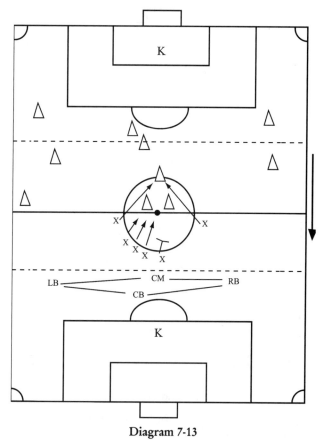

Diagram 7-13

ers on the kickoff and to watch to mark the opposing forwards as they move downfield.

If the ball is played back for possession by the attacking team, Diagram 7-11 shows how the defending team would align itself. X2 or X3 (depending on the distance to be covered) would move to pressurize the opponent's LM with one pressurizing and the other covering. X1 would compact play with attention to the opponent's CM. The three defensive midfielders (X4, X5, X6) would step up to seal off the middle of the field. Defenders X7, X8 and X9 would pick up their defensive assignments on the opposing strikers with X7 shown in offering defensive balance with his/her position in the diagram. X10 would offer depth with the positioning shown as would the forward position in the box by the keeper. With this collective positioning the defensive team is now in a good alignment in terms of countering any ball movement in any direction by the attacking team. It has compactness, pressure on the ball and its marking responsibilities have been assumed.

An additional advantage of this defensive plan is that it places the defensive team in good positions to counter-attack should the ball be won. Two crucial tactical principles, namely those of depth and width on attack, are in place.

Diagram 7-12 also shows one more backward play by the attacking team and how this would be handled

defensively. Both X2 and X3 would pressure the opposing left back with X1 moving to further "squeeze" play into the corner of the field. X5 and X6 matchup against their midfield counterparts while X4 offers midfield depth with his/her positioning. All the backs and sweeper would also "push up" with the ideal of compactness.

With this in place the counter-attack potential available to the defending team at kickoff needs to be emphasized. Basically, the defending team must be alert that if the ball is won, that player winning the ball must look for immediate penetration via the dribble or penetrating pass. That not available, switching the point of attack with off-the-ball runs by X4 and X5 might be a coaching emphasis.

HIGH PRESSURE

An example of extreme high pressure defending was sprung by the long, penetrating pass at kickoff. The defending team can anticipate this tactic and put overwhelming numbers of players on the circle at kickoff. The objective of such a tactic would be to double-team the likely target players thus preventing any dangerous penetration of the ball into the attacking zone at kickoff.

Diagram 7-13 shows two players assigned to attack the likely midfielder on the kickoff while three players attack the players combining to start play. One player stays on the circle to stop any penetration and

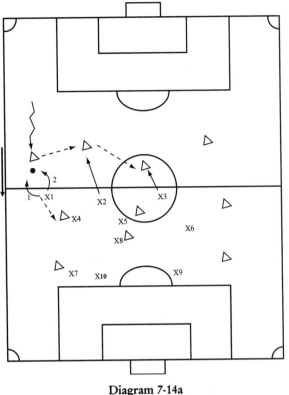

Diagram 7-14a

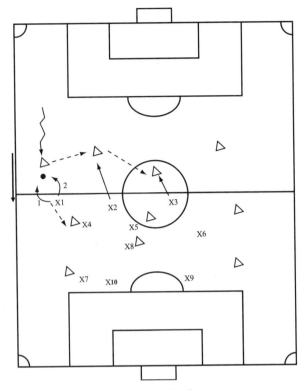

Diagram 7-14b

offer support if the ball should be won at kickoff. The four backs form a deep triangle to stop any direct attack centrally.

This tactic was first viewed in the 1982 World Cup semifinal between Germany and France in Seville. Germany had rebounded from a 1-3 deficit to tie the match with a late overtime goal and with the final seconds ticking away and clearly the game's momentum on their side, the Germans defended the kickoff in an unusual fashion. The tired French team had the obvious tactic of playing a long ball into the Germany zone in order to generate a last second attempt to score the winning goal. Also in hopes of keeping play in the German half and taking away that team's impetus. A third reason for the intended long ball tactic might have been to ensure that the game moved to penalty shots. Germany's tactical counter at kickoff stymied any thoughts the French had of penetration and resulted in the ball being kept in the midfield area. At that point the result played more into the hands of the German team than the French. As most followers of WC history know, Germany moved to the '82 WC final via the subsequent penalty kick route.

Low Pressure Defense

At times a low pressure defense may be the tactic chosen for the kickoff. While X2 will pressurize the ball and seek to channel play into a predictable area of the field as per high pressure tactics, X1 and X3 will clog the middle with their positioning, hopefully then inviting the attacking team to play wide or back. The

remainder of the team will remain compact and will elect to defend in the defensive half of the field, closing off passing lanes based on the opponents' use of the ball. Diagram 7-14a illustrates how this can be accomplished. Once the ball is played the defending team will:

• Maintain its compactness;
•Channel play into wide spaces and "make them smaller";
• Defend ball side of all attacking players near the ball centrally, goal side of the ball on the width of the field, defend spaces away from the ball (zone);
• Keep the ball in front of the defense as much as possible.

We see these principles in operation in Diagram 7-14b. X1's position relative to channeling play will dictate the positioning of the rest of the team. There are two possible positions that the pressurizing players can assume. Note the goalside or ballsided positioning of players behind the ball as well as the zonal coverage away from the ball. Option #1 shows the pressure being applied with the objective of making play predictable with a backward pass. Option #2 offers the attacking team a forward pass or a dribble on the flank area.

Once players come into the attacking half of the field, immediate pressure will be put on these players by their assigned markers. The roles of the three attackers (X1, X2, X3) is also important in attack as the low pressure defense has the intent of luring the at-

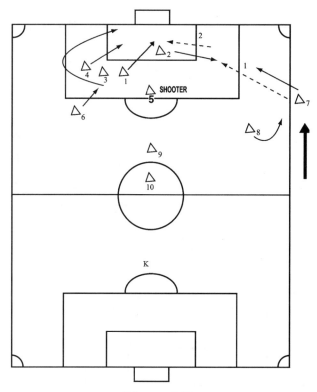

Diagram 7-15a

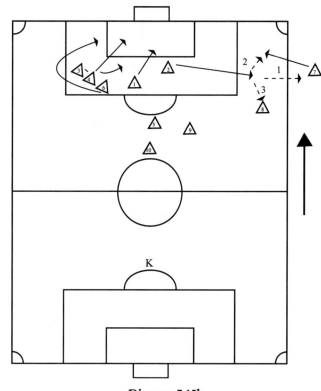

Diagram 7-15b

tacking team to come forward out of the back. This opens up the potential for the quick counter-attack should the ball be won. The ability of the three strikers to read where the open space is for the initial "killer pass" is vital in this planning process.

If the low pressure approach to kickoff defense has its intended tactical impact, the opposition may try to penetrate with long, speculative passing. Therefore the role of the sweeper and keeper is to offer cover for the defensive. Both must be alert for the long pass to space and with good reading of the situation, work to "soak up" this type of pressure by the attacking team.

FURTHER COACHING REMINDERS — KICKOFF

1. Scouting the opposition should include notes on their defensive and attacking strategies at kickoff.

2. Have players on the bench observe the movements offensively and defensively of their counterparts on the opposing team at kickoff. This can help in later planning of your team's strategy.

3. Kickoffs are an apt time to substitute players. But they should be reminded of their responsibilities (especially defensive matchups) before they take the field.

4. It is a good idea to remind players of their responsibilities on the kickoff as part of the short team meeting at the huddle before they take the field. At that time new substitutes ought to be verbally reminded of what is expected from them at the restart.

5. The keeper's role ought be examined to make certain that correct positioning is taking place.

6. Variation at kickoff is important; don't repeat anything, if possible.

II. THROWINS

Offensive Half of Field

With our hand-eye sport emphasis in this country, a good many teams today find themselves with throw-in specialists, players with the ability to reach the center of the goalmouth with the ball. So it is important for coaches to plan for inclusion of such individuals in the restart planning process. In many ways a strong throwin is to be preferred to a corner kick in terms of its accuracy. Player placement to nod on or redirect a ball on goal will be achieved more readily via the throwin than with a kicked ball.

Diagram 7-15a shows one situation where the thrower tries to hit target Δ2 for a flickon to Δ1 at the near post or either Δ4 or Δ3 who make criss-crossing runs to the middle and far post zones of the goal respectively. Δ5 and Δ6 are positioned for dropped balls and poor clearances while Δ8 offers support for the short throw. Δ8 and Δ9 are selected as defensive cover with good speed and tackling ability as possible prerequisites. Note the keeper's forward position. A final note is that the coach may elect to take a player (Δ6?) and place that individual on the goalkeeper.

Diagram 7-15b offers the possibility of a dummied header by Δ2 with Δ1 looking for a shot at the near

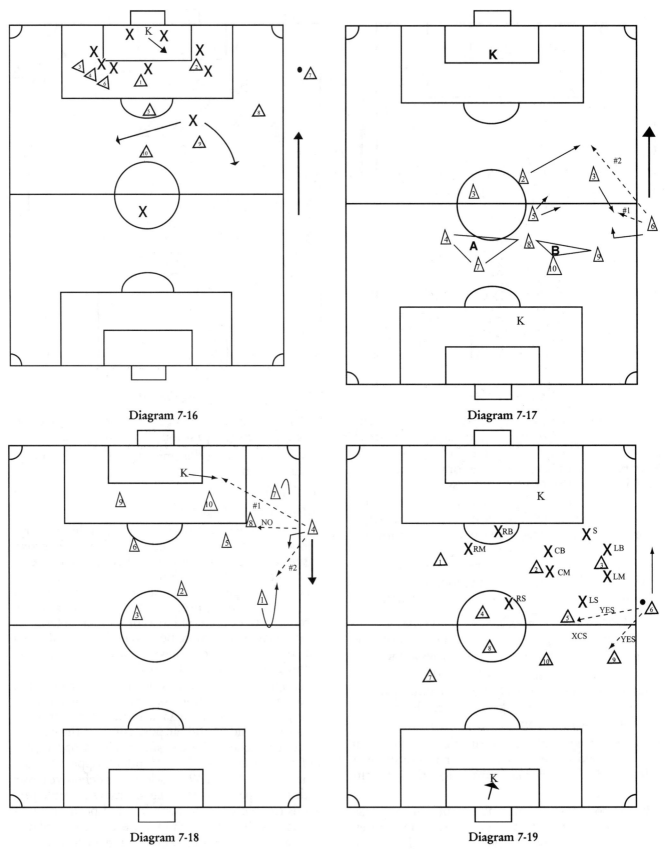

Diagram 7-16

Diagram 7-17

Diagram 7-18

Diagram 7-19

Defensively, teams must be ready to mark the most likely target player and assign their best headers and clearers of the ball to the most dangerous goal area zones.

post. In the meantime Δs 3, 4, and 6 will be looking for half chances at the far post. Note the blind side run by Δ6. Other options (#1) would be for Δ2 to play back to the thrower; (#2) to pass forward to the thrower or (#3) to have Δ2 play to Δ8. All three options would be looking for crosses to the near or far post areas. In scouting teams and their defensive positioning against such throwin situations, note should be made of zonal or man-to-man team defense, how the posts are covered, general balancing of the defense, whether the thrower is marked and which spaces (six yards, 12 yard and 18 yard) are most vulnerable.

Defensively, teams must be ready to mark (perhaps double team) the most likely target player and assign their best headers and clearers of ball to the most dangerous goal area zones. The width of the field must be noted and if a field is less wide than your own, dealing with throws that arrive slightly earlier and deeper into the goal mouth must be practiced prior to playing on such a pitch. The decision to play the thrower must be calculated by the coach and a player assigned to that role. A short throw played back to the thrower who penetrates via the dribble can badly disrupt the defensive team. Care must be taken to cover this eventuality. A dummied or flicked-on throwin can be very effective (selection of a player who can flickon is one important first step). The attacking team's goalkeeper should be analyzing what the defensive tendencies of the defending team are in order to offer suggestions for future restart possibilities later in the match.

Diagram 7-16 details the initial defensive setup of a team with defense of the near post highlighted. The setup features four players in and about the near post. One is at the post itself while players double team the likely target player. Note that one defender fronts the receiver while the other is goal side of the receiver (don't have the second player play behind the receiver!) so that he/she can compete for the ball. It is open to debate whether to place a player on the thrower. All other defenders are ball side of the players they are marking. Meanwhile the far post features three players also marking ball side of their assigned attackers as well as one player on the far post. Both post players step in and out one step once play is underway to cover areas vacated by the keeper as he/she competes for

the throw. Note also that Diagram 7-16 indicates that the furthest defending player is ready to spring forward in order to offer a target for counter-attack should the ball be won or cleared cleanly by teammates.

Diagram 7-17 shows offensive possibilities on a throwin in the middle third of the field. It is recommended that the outside midfielder take the toss with the outside back on that side of the field offering depth and positioning for the back throw. In most cases it is advised that the play be made "forward." (options #1 and #2). Square passes are to be avoided at all costs as oftentimes dispossession will find the defense unbalanced and vulnerable to a quick counter-attack. Diagram 17 also indicates two defensive triangles (A & B) insuring that there is good depth. Obviously the five players in those triangle would move forward as possession is obtained to support the ball.

The first option (Diagram 7-18) for a throwin in the defensive third of the field (final third) should be a quick toss to the keeper (#1) or a fast forward throw for possession. Barring that, at all costs the ball should be thrown forward into the outer quarter of the field. Perhaps, if talent is limited on the team, the forward or midfielder (Δ1) with the best ball control can be positioned to receive the ball (option #2). The ability to free themselves and turn the ball, play it back to an unmarked thrower or flick it on to teammate cutting into forward space are technical skills required here. Obviously if a long throwin specialist is available, a deep throw down the touchline "is on."

In no case should a square ball be attempted in this area of the field!

DEFENSIVE TACTICS ON THROWINS

Defending the throw in the middle and attacking thirds of the field demands certain understandings by all players involved, particularly in terms of maintaining compactness. In Diagram 7-19 the midfielder and back on the ball side of the field should try, if possible, to double team the most logical receiver of the ball. They, along with the CM, CB and S form a tight cohesive unit with the RB and RM offering weakside depth and balance to the team. The defending team "invites" throws back or square and are ready to pressurize the ball once it is on its way. If the ball is played back to the thrower, the midfielder releases from the double team to pressurize the ball.

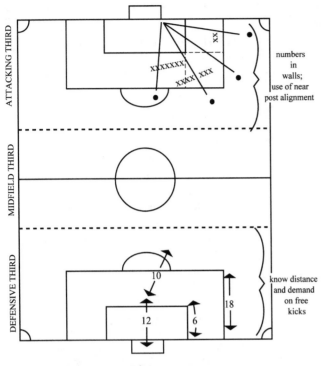

Diagram 7-20

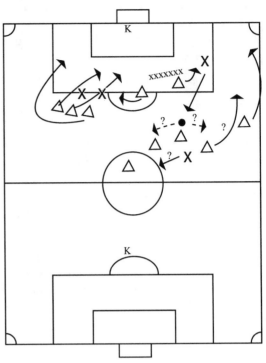

Diagram 7-21

The defensive team is shown with a 4-3-3 formation. Obviously coaches can work out the tactics discussed with other tactical player placement.

By balancing the field a bit, the defending team should recognize that its team is well-positioned (CS, RS) to counter-attack centrally and in the space away from play should the ball be repossessed at the throwin.

III. FREE KICK RESTARTS - ATTACKING THIRD

The most dangerous opportunities for the attacking team are those that take place within 20-25 yards of the a team's goal. Diagram 7-20 indicates any time that a team finds itself defending from the "D" vertically back to the goal, 5-6 players are needed in a wall. Subsequently the number in the wall diminishes as the placement of the ball becomes more acute. The wall should always be set by the keeper in a line through the second man in the wall, this in order to possibly foil a bent ball defeating the wall. In any case in setting walls, defensive teams should be familiar with the markings on the field to help them gauge "where" to set the wall. Finally it must be understood who is going to "rush" or pressurize the ball.

Diagram 7-21 illustrates coach Jago's principles of restarts in action. In total there are eight attacking players playing versus nine defenders (note the "lone ranger" hanging out about midfield). As six players are occupied in the wall itself, that leaves the attacking team with man up advantages in at least two other areas of the field. The four players around the ball are key. The attacking players in the wall might be a good-sized player who lines up on the end of the wall. They

can move laterally in hopes that the wall "will break" and the ball can be struck through the vacated space.

The three players at the ball must be in sync. If the ball is to be played laterally for a shot, it is very important that it be played slightly back at an angle for the second player then to strike it on goal. In this way the pressurizing player isn't advantaged by having to move less than 10 yards in order to disrupt play.

In the meantime the other four attacking players all find themselves with roles. The single attacker to the right of the ball must "shout" for the ball to distract the wall while the three players away from the ball must exploit their 3 v. 2 advantage (does the coach bring his "lone ranger" back? Probably so.) through penetrating and blind-sided wide runs. Sometimes a fake kick at the ball when coupled with these runs can identify how the defense will react. Based on the reaction of the defense, this could lead to a ball to the side and a cross to the near or far post

In any case, it is obvious, per coach Jago's recommendation, that if the team's best schemers are at the ball, plenty of opportunities to read which option to exploit will result in good shots at goal. Hopefully "on goal" and even more to the point, "in goal!"

MIDDLE THIRD

Offensively two restarts are shown in Diagram 7-22. The first is a short ball to a player who would be chosen for his/her dribbling skill and ability to play an accurate ball into the space between the 18 yard line and the goalie box.

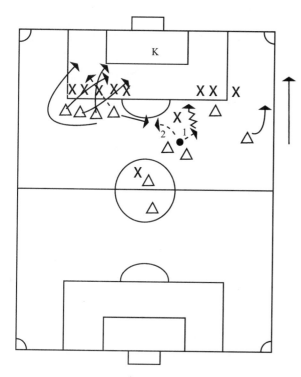

Diagram 7-22

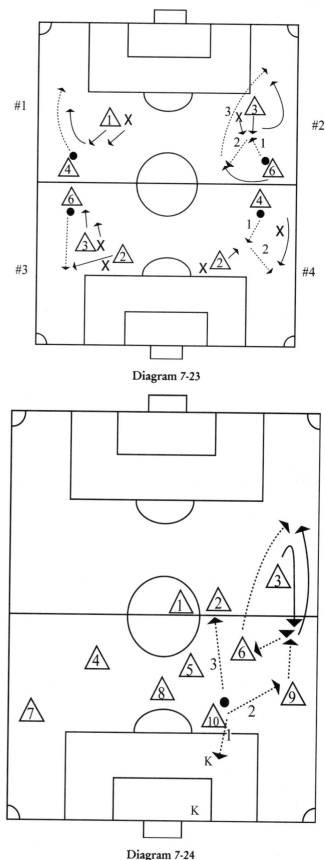

Diagram 7-23

The second would be a ball into a talented header for that individual to head the ball against the grain of play on goal. In the latter situation we see runs by fellow players opening the space for our most talented header to run blind side for an attempt on goal. As noted by coach Jago, spaces must be emptied of defenders so that the targeted space can be used effectively. Generally a shorter team lacking good headers in the box might more effectively try "short balls" while a taller team might rely on flighted balls.

Defensively teams must try to hold a line against opponents' free kicks from the middle third of the field. In Diagram 7-22 we see the line at 18 yards. If scouting a team has denoted one player as being the target of free kicks that individual might be double-teamed. Note that all defenders should be prepared to drop back if the ball is flighted behind them. Meanwhile one defender is ready to challenge the short ball by the attackers and three others mark the weak side of the ball. Another defensive tactic to impart in this situation would be for the backs to exercise the off-sides trap as the kicker runs up to strike the ball into the box.

Diagram 7-23 also details four restarts that can be used offensively on the outside of the field. Option #1 would be a hard check back to the ball followed by a ball over the top of the defender to space. The second would be a simple 1-2 followed by the ball to space. Option #3 depicts a "clearout" whereby a team sends players away from the wide space and then the team's best striker checks into the space to play 1 v. 1 in hopes of crossing or shooting the ball on goal, not unlike

Diagram 7-24

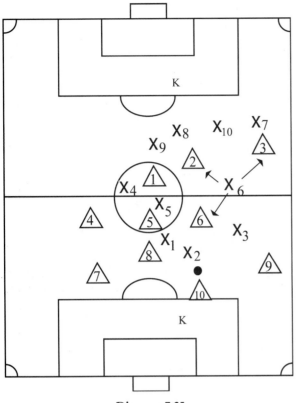

Diagram 7-25

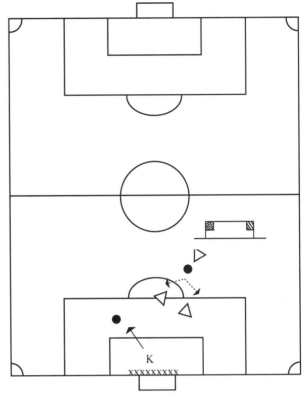

Diagram 7-26

what is frequently viewed in professional basketball. Finally option #4 shows two checking runs coordinated such that a wall pass is played into space for the striker to run onto.

In Diagram 7-24 we see outlined various possibilities for free kicks taken in one's defensive third of the field. Basic to taking the kick is the degree of pressure exerted on the kick by the defensive team. If the defenders high pressure then the ball should be played long (#3). If there is low pressure being applied, teams might look to play for possession and build out of the back with shorter passes.

Prior to the change in the "backpass to keeper rule," the obvious first play would have been to the keeper. It still has potential depending on the foot skills of the keeper. A second option would be a short ball to the outside back ($\Delta 9$) to play to a checking striker ($\Delta 3$) supported by the RM ($\Delta 6$). A ball into the space by the RM could follow. A third choice might be similar to the second with the CF ($\Delta 2$) getting on the end of the ball out of the back supported by the CM and RM ($\Delta 5$ and $\Delta 6$) who might play the ball to central space or switch play to the left side. Here the strikers must gauge the typical distance the taker of the free kick has and locate themselves in those areas of the field. Also important is that such target players "play into" their defenders in a physical sense, thus being able to better compete for possession or flickons of such free kicks.

In defending free kicks by the opposition from deep in its defensive half of the field, teams must try to remain compact and highly pressure likely target players. By placing a mobile player with good heading ability in a zone where this double-teaming could take place a team can win a lot of such balls. In Diagram 7-25 the coach has given X6 this role. That player can "cut out" balls to the opposing strikers, could double team at the outset either player (perhaps scouting could help dictate such a positioning) or mark or be ready to mark the opposing CM ($\Delta 6$). X3 in the meantime zones the left side area, ready to channel the opposition left back ($\Delta 9$) should the ball be played short. Meantime the two other strikers, X1 and X2 defend against short balls and funnel back to become target players once possession is regained.

INDIRECT KICK INSIDE THE BOX

In Diagram 7-26 we see outlined both offensively and defensively the indirect free kick inside the 12 yard line. In terms of attack, the ball needs to be angled a bit away from the onrushing defenders rather than towards them. Every millisecond counts! The shot itself has its best chance to either upper corner of the goal though some coaches prefer to hit it hard at a defender's head and hope for the "ducking head."

Decisiveness in what the team is going to do in this situation is a coaching "must" and players' roles should be clear relative to this offensive situation. Defensively,

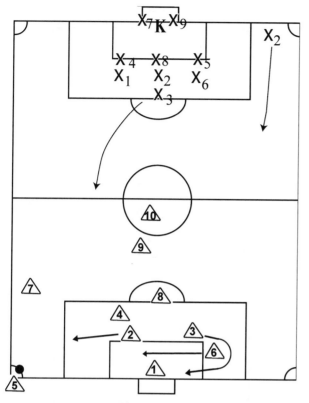

Diagram 7-27

the wall should have its tallest players at the near corner, hopefully to dissuade play into that area. Unless prevented by a kick taken at a distance of less than 10 yards, the keeper should be positioned in front of the wall and be ready to challenge the kick the moment the ball moves. Generally the more central the ball is placed on an indirect kick, the more aggressive the team and the keeper must be. Again, the positioning of the keeper is a bit dependent on one's coaching philosophy. In addition to defining a keeper's role, a quick, aggressive second player should be positioned at ten yards distance to also pressure the kick.

IV. CORNER KICKS

Offensively coaches may want to keep things simple and in a sense they can "double dip" tactically. When planning their team's strategy for the long throwin they can transfer this same information to apply for attacking on the corner kick. Several of the same factors for a coach to be concerned with as they selected players for attacking and defending roles at the throwin apply for corner kicks. Offensively one wants to place the best headers at key positions within the near and far post zones. Strong shooters must patrol positions in and about the box. A players with an accurate, consistent service should take the kick itself. A good dribbler with the ability to size up a weakness in a crowded area is needed if a short corner is taken.

Several factors influence the selection of set pieces for corners. Obviously a short defending team would

be vulnerable to high services as would a team with and "on line" goalkeeper. A team that doesn't defend the corner with a defender 10 yards from the ball is vulnerable to a short corner. A team is also vulnerable if its players are forced to defend balls that are played into the spaces behind them or if they are forced to defend while running towards their own goal. There are enough "self goals" to attest to that fact!

The ability to penetrate 2 v. 1 with a short corner is a valuable weapon for an attacking team due to the diffused focus it causes for the defense. If defenders focus on the ball as the dribbler moves toward goal, it may allow an attacker to blindside them and become free to attack the ball offensively.

Teams should never become too predictable at taking corners. They should change the rhythm of their set pieces, first playing a ball to the near post, then taking a short corner, followed by a ball to the far post, etc. Diagram 7-27 (bottom) shows an attacking player running on to a low corner for a flick on to the near post or far post (resembles the throwin, doesn't it?). If that piece had not been introduced until late in a match it may result in the decisive goal being scored. Options that allow for variety include a ball back to a supporting player for a ball to the far post; inswinging balls versus outswinging balls (outswingers are more easily and accurately headed by attacking players, but not defensive players trying for clearances); short or near post balls. Finally, if a team does not leave a player forward as a target for its counter-attack, then the attacking team may elect to put one more of its players into a corner kick attacking position. This is true especially late in a match where a tying goal is needed.

Intermingled with such tactics is the need for uniform signals to be adopted by the team/coach so everyone understands how and where the service is going to impact on the kick. Signals from the bench or captain or taker of the corner (one reason to keep but one or two persons taking all the attempts) should allow all players concerned as to the tactic being invoked.

Generally weather conditions might also help dictate what "is on." Certainly wet, windy days may not be the time to try anything "too cute." Make the other team make the play by putting the ball into the goalmouth!

Scouting is very important in terms of evaluating the key individuals in terms of a team's offensive organization for corners.

Offensively it is important to realize whether a team plays zone or man-to-man in terms of its defensive system of play. If in doubt run a player to the ball and watch a team's reaction. Not many teams play man-to-man but if they do then runs can open up spaces for the ball to be played to. A zone defense alignment is shown in Diagram 7-27 (top). It depicts players on both posts to assist the kicker (this is de-

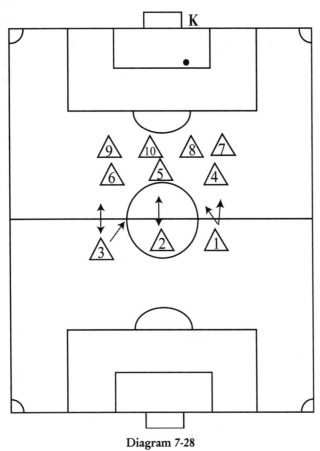

Diagram 7-28

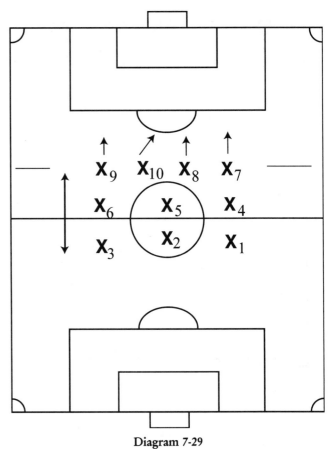

Diagram 7-29

pendent upon one's coaching philosophy also; some coaches place a defender on the more vulnerable near post). X5 should be the team's best header as, again, the near post is the team's most difficult zone to defend. X2 should be a good defender with the ability to deal with both 1 v. 1 and 2 v. 1 situations. Also X2 will move upfield after dealing with the short kick situation and become the intended target player for the defending team. Such a player must be very mobile and seek to latch onto any clearances and "buy time" for his teammates to move to him and attack in a cohesive manner upfield or also recognize when to take the opportunity to effectuate a quick counterattack.

As one can see, all 11 players are needed to defensively deal with the corner kick. Player X3 can assume the position indicated or could mark up against an obvious target player of the attacking team. This role could also be assigned to the far post defender by the coach. Unstated here is the fact that when a ball is cleared all players must sprint out a top speed to effect a possible offside trap and also in order to double-team players who might strike a long shot back into the goal area "against the flow" of play. Defensive tactics vary but some decisions need to be made by the coach and other items constantly practiced by the team. They include:

- Use a taller player or a good 1 v. 2 player to defend at 10 yards from the corner?
- It is thought that the keeper should be able to "clean up" far post crosses; near post is where more serious damage can be done by the attacking team;
- The keeper's initial positioning should be a yard or two off the line and about in the middle of the posts;
- An "open defensive posture" should be assumed by players prior to the ball being struck such as to see both ball and opponents and for added jumping power;
- Balls being cleared should be "high, wide and handsome (accurate)" in terms of priority;
- A commanding voice and presence by the keeper needs to be acknowledged and coordinated if balls are to be secured.

V. GOAL KICKS/KEEPER'S PUNTS

Offensively it is preferable for the goalkeeper to take the goal kick as it releases one more player to move forward in attack. In reality, coaches can simply transfer information from Diagram 7-25, which details possible attacking moves on kicks taken from within the team's defensive third, to the goal kick situation. Obviously persons who can accurately both flight and fight for the ball on a goal kick are invaluable and selection of those players and coordinating their talents is of utmost importance. Diagram 7-28

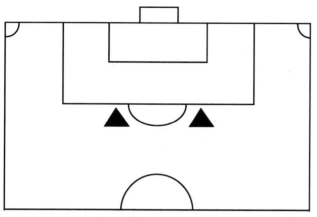

Diagram 7-30

does show how teams can align themselves offensively to deal with the long balls coming out of the back either by the goal kick or punt. Obviously Δ1, Δ2, and Δ3 are shown in a compacted central area of the field and they must know the range of the taker of the kick and adjust their positioning in order to be first to the ball as it drops. The concentration of the three forwards in the central area of the field now allows for effective flickons as the two forwards not dealing with the header can begin to get themselves in good forward support positions to run onto the flicks by their teammate. One or two of the supporting midfielders (Δ4, Δ5 and Δ6) all may or may not move into the "receiving area" to compete for possession of long clearances out of the back or more commonly, seek to assume good supporting positions for their forwards to play to for possession purposes. The backs and sweeper assume a line at about the 35 yard mark to maintain team compactness.

Defensively on the goal kick it is recommended that the team assume a very compacted positioning and that "a defensive line" be established depending on the strength of an opponent's kicking range. It should be mentioned that the recommended alignment would hold true for dealing with an opponent's keeper's punts. Diagram 7-29 indicates a typical defensive alignment. As a kick were taken, the backs would drop back if they anticipate the ball will be flighted behind them. The sweeper, X10, if not attacking the ball, would provide the usual defensive cover for the team. The forwards would try to anticipate balls being played to them and assume good supporting positions for the counter-attack to take place. Were the ball to be played short, the closest pressurizing attacker would assume a channeling role and the collective unit would take its most effective postures as discussed earlier.

VI. DROPPED BALLS

Reminders for coaches:
- Know the rule regarding offsides;
- Use your quick-footed players in these situations;
- Don't expose stars to these situations!

VII. PENALTY KICKS

Offensive Reminders:
- Selection of shooters via constant competitions;
- Take practice shots with balls used in matches; procure game balls of opponents if match is away for practice purposes;
- Note in Diagram 7-30 the key positions that your team needs to try and win prior to kick;
- As practice, cite rules on PK as regards balls rebounding off posts or goalkeepers and who is eligible to play them;
- Notify team before hand which player(s) will take PKs in game and/or in the overtime.

Defensive reminders:
- Get to key spots on D first!;
- Make certain have enough players back to avoid problem with counter attack by opposition.

PREPARING PLAYERS FOR THE PHYSICAL DEMANDS OF SOCCER

training meal exemplifies this. The typical pre-game meal served athletes, namely steak and eggs, is a relic of the past.

In this chapter several articles will take the reader through understanding various components of preparing the player to meet the challenges of the modern game. There will be exposure to an objective analysis of the demands of the sport of soccer. Among the other related subjects discussed will be proper nutrition, sports drinks and their impact, how to develop the elements of power, flexibility and speed in a player and an overview of interval training.

Modern coaching has stressed the need to train players "economically." This has meant that instead of performing situps as a singular exercise we now find players doing situps and heading the ball at the height of their situp. In this segment of the book we'll see how Warm-Ups can be conducted in a small field (a grid) with the ball.

Finally not all goes well in a player's season and when injury strikes, coaches must know how to treat that individual from both a physical and psychological viewpoint.

PHYSICAL AND TACTICAL DEMANDS OF SOCCER
Donald T Kirkendall, Ph.D.

Early coaching of the game of soccer in this country could be termed rudimentary. The coach primarily sought to motivate his charges and focus on the physical preparation of players. "Get them in shape and let them play" was the motto of more than one coach of soccer during its infancy in this country.

Some of the early collegiate powerhouses earned their stripes in part through skill but just as often through vigorous physical preparation.

Much has changed in terms of the science of coaching soccer and no area exemplifies this more than the approach to coaching players. Perhaps something as simple as the

Every coach continually questions himself. How to improve so and so's skill? Is this the best player for a position (or vice versa)? Why do we have problems counter-attacking? Are my players match-fit?

If questions are not asked, improvements cannot be planned, expected or obtained. Coaching schools address the fitness-technique-tactics triad and most references for coaching are heavily weighted in the latter two. The belief is that most aspects of the well-organized, efficient training session will encompass at least two facets of the triad and fitness will develop specifically due to controlled individual, small, and large group training.

For the most part, this confidence in a well-organized regime will be rewarded by having players who are of sufficient specific fitness to execute the necessary skills which will allow for a successful tactical performance. The question of match fitness is regularly raised, especially when your opponent displays greater fitness than your own team. But, in any game, not just soccer, to understand match fitness, the work requirements of the game must first be understood. Most books on soccer make statements about the work requirements, mainly in terms of total yardage. Ranges of 3,000-15,000 meters can be found! Total distances are a bit hard to interpret.

If, for argument's sake, you believe a player covers 10,000 meters (6.2 miles) in a full 90-minute match, at a constant jog, that is a 15:00 mile pace. The game is obviously an accumulation of repeated short runs at a variety of paces. Given 90 minutes the distances add up. Two good references on total distances may shed some light. The papers of Withers (1982) and Reilly (1976) involved detailed analysis by professionals to arrive at their results. Both further analyze their results by type of run. These two studies will be discussed. (See Diagram 8-1)

Each author divides running intensities into five categories: walking, jogging, backing, cruising (or striding - running with manifest purpose and effort), and sprinting. (Withers subdivided further to backwards jogging and walking, along with sideways running.) Figure 1 depicts the distances covered and percent of total distance for each type of running. As you can see, the English average just under 9,000 meters while the Australians averaged just over 11,500 meters. Notice the largest variation was in the distance jogged, while total distances of other types of running seem to be somewhat similar.

Both studies further divided their data by outfield positions. Reilly found significant differences between positions (midfielders covered the most, central defenders the least distance), but Withers found no positional differences in distance covered. In fact, the only positional difference found by Withers was in the distance sprinted, with fullback the highest and central defenders the lowest. We should not forget the pauses during a game. Reilly showed individual pauses of between 11-120 seconds for field players during play and 13 minutes total, while Withers reported that the ball was out of play for 16 minutes from kickoff to closing whistle.

Frequency of movements was also described by Reilly. Given a 90-minute game, a change of speed or direction occurred about once every 5-6 seconds. The player was called to work at the higher intensities (cruise and sprint) once every 30 seconds with a sprint once every 90 seconds (at about 15-20 meters per activity).

IMPLICATIONS FOR COACHING

If, as we were taught in exercise physiology, the body adapts to a specific type of stimulus, then on or off the ball training should include changes of direction and, frequent work at higher intensities over short distances. In-season distance running, while a necessity in the off-season, would probably be taking time away from more valuable lessons. Also, extended, unrestricted full-time full-field work in practice would probably not overload the player, leaving a sufficient fitness reserve when it is needed in competition. (The old axiom of "play your way into shape" only works if one plays above the physical intensity needed for a match. Thus the newer axiom "don't play the game to get into shape, get in shape to play the game".) If the game requires

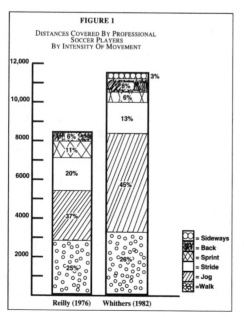

Diagram 8-1

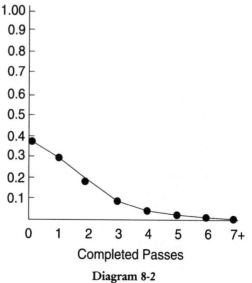

Diagram 8-2

frequent changes of direction and repeated high intensity work, then that's the way to train.

All that has been discussed has been distances covered. How about some simple tactics? Not methods of developing individual, small or large group tactics with which coaches try to keep current, but things that develop ball control, shooting and scoring opportunities. An English mathematician recorded a phenomenal amount of data between 1953-1967 on 578 miscellaneous, first division and World Cup matches. Diagram 8-2 shows the percentage of completed passes.

Notice that nearly 40% of all possessions of the ball began and ended without a completed pass and that just over 90% of all ball possessions were of three passes or less (add up the percentages for 0,1,2,3 completed passes). This pictured distribution is nearly a perfect fit to an expected mathematical distribution. This would not surprise a statistician who expects an element of chance in everything, including ballgames. (The authors have shown in another paper that a similar mathematical fit also occurs in various aspects of American football, baseball, ice hockey, tennis and cricket.)

Strategically, a 10:1 shots:goal ratio was reported. They divided the field into quarters with the offensive quarter being called the "shooting area". Just over 50% of all goals came from passing combinations that began there; 30% of all attacks that reached the shooting area began in that area; and just over 1/2 of all the attacks that began in the shooting area were from "regained possessions" (the defense failed to move the ball out of their end).

About 15% of all attacks that reached the shooting area resulted in a shot at goal and 22% of all attacks that started in the shooting area lead to a shot at goal. Intuitively, these proportions might have been deduced, but may not repeatedly fit any particular team. But as the number of games and teams increases, percentages come closer to these published figures. The age of the data may be in question, but only minor variations in the reported proportions occurred during the 14-year period, even when one considers the changes in tactics that occurred over the study's duration.

SUMMARY

These studies indicate two things. First, 20-30% of the game is spent moving at a fairly high speed, with frequent changes of direction. Training should be specific to meet these needs. Second, productive attacks occur quickly from regained possessions in the offensive quarter of the field, with 90% of all possessions being of three passes or less. These facts offer valuable insights into the type of training players need to perform to known or desired expectations.

REFERENCES

Reep, C. and B. Benjamin. "Skill and Chance in Association Football." J. Royal Stat. Society, Series A, 131:581-585,1968.

Reilly, T. and V. Thomas. "A motion analysis of work rate in different positional roles in professional football match play." J. Human Movement Studies, 2:87-97, 1976.

Withers, R. T., Z Maricis, S. Wasilewski, L. Kelly. "Match analysis of Australian soccer players." J. Human Movement Studies. 8:159-176,1982.

NUTRITION AND SOCCER PERFORMANCE
Donald T. Kirkendall

There is probably no area of health that is filled with more fadism, emotion and misinformation than nutrition. A look at the diet and nutrition section of a local bookstore is all the evidence one needs. Nutrition for sports is no different, as self proclaimed experts promote their latest gimmick. This installment will attempt to wade through the areas of nutrition and nutrition for performance.

GENERAL NUTRITION

Food, water and oxygen are basic requirements.

These foundations are the same whether one is an athlete or not. The basic nutritional building blocks are carbohydrates, fats, proteins, vitamins, minerals, and water. The major difference between athletes and non-athletes is not "what" should be eaten, but "how much".

Carbohydrates. These substances are the most readily available source of food energy. Carbohydrates (CHO) are stored as muscle and liver glycogen and circulate in the blood as glucose. The main food sources of CHO are the cereals and grains, starches, and the fruit and vegetable food groups. CHO should make up 60% of the caloric intake. The typical "American" diet typically consists of 40% CHO.

Fats. Fats are a vast storehouse of fuel, but the energy stored in fat is not as readily available as the energy stored in CHO. The body must go through a long series of events to obtain the energy stored in fat. Fat intake should be limited to less than 25% of the caloric intake. However, the "American" diet is typically 40% fat.

Proteins. Proteins form the structural foundations of the body. The most simple form is an amino acid. The energy contribution in exercise from protein is minimal, but increases as CHO stores become weight. The typical western diet will usually exceed the RDA suggestion. The remaining 15% of the caloric intake should be as protein. The "American" diet differs again from the recommended by being about 20% protein.

Vitamins. Vitamins are chemical regulators necessary for the metabolic pathways and are essential for good health. If a person has a well-rounded diet, vitamin supplementation is unnecessary, as excesses are eliminated.

Minerals. Sodium, potassium, chloride, calcium, phosphorous, magnesium and sulfur all have specific and varied roles. Once again, a well-balanced diet supplies all that is needed. The typical American diet tends to have an overabundance of salt. The usual worry is about excesses, not deficiencies. Requirements of trace minerals can also be met by a well-rounded diet.

Water. This is the most essential of all. Small deficits of water greatly reduce the capacity to do any activity. Between 60-70% of the body is water. The equivalent of eight glasses of water per day is generally recommended.

THE FOUR FOOD GROUPS

In order to attain this "well rounded diet", appropriate selection from the food pyramid are needed. The pyramid is based on 6-11 servings per day from the bread, cereal, rice and pasta group. Added to this are 3-5 servings per day from the vegetable group and 2-4 servings per day from the fruit group. From 2-3 daily servings from the milk, yogurt and cheese group as well as the fish, eggs, meat, poultry, nuts and dry beans group top out the pyramid. Fats, oils and sweets are to be used sparingly. The typical American diet is high in both the dairy products and meats food groups, and low in the vegetables and fruits food groups. Excess fat intake is the result and is a major health problem. Fried foods, whole milk and whole milk products, along with fatty meats all add excessive calories through undesirable fat.

Both coaches and players alike should be wary of excess fat intake. It is not beneficial for performance and is a main cause of the high cholesterol that leads to heart disease. One is never too young or too old to start watching fat intake.

NUTRITION FOR PERFORMANCE

In the late 60s, the Swedes proved that low glycogen in muscles limited performance and, with appropriate dietary manipulation, muscle glycogen could be raised above resting levels with improved endurance performance the result. They recommended a couple of days on a very low CHO diet while continuing training. Then, on the last few days before competition, eating most of the calories as CHO while reducing the training. A "super compensation" of muscle glycogen occurred. In practice, this original routine could only be tolerated a few times a year. There have also been some documented kidney problems resulting from over enthusiastic use of this practice. As a result, the original method has fallen out of favor. Only the latter half of the routine (reduced training volume and intensity with increased CHO intake in the few days before competition) is currently practiced.

In events where glycogen was a limiting factor (events 1-4 hours long), performance was improved. People who compete in half or full marathons, small triathlons, selected road cycling races, can all benefit. Ultra-marathons or events under 10,000 meters show little benefit from glycogen super compensation.

The demands of soccer allow it to be considered a glycogen depleting activity. There are only a few investigations into the use of fuels in soccer (all from Sweden). First, it has been shown that professional outdoor soccer matches depleted up to 85-90% of the available glycogen in thigh muscles of field players (1). Second, the dietary practices in the three days after a professional game only increased the glycogen levels by about 58%. Their total caloric intake was 15% protein (ok), 30% fat (too high) and just under 50% as CHO (too low) (2).

Finally, in two groups of players, one with half the muscle glycogen of the other, the low glycogen group had no glycogen at the end of the game (the high glycogen group had 10% remaining). More importantly, the low glycogen group covered less total distance and walked more than their high glycogen counterparts (3). The result of low muscle glycogen was a lower work volume at a lower intensity.

QUESTIONS WHICH MAY BE ASKED INCLUDE:

1. How long does it take to replenish muscle glycogen?

If endurance running depleted the glycogen, then up to 48 hours is needed (4). If intermittent exercise depleted the glycogen, then about 24 hours will suffice (5). These facts are made with the assumption that diet was appropriate.

2. What is the appropriate diet to refill glycogen overnight?

This is especially important when the team has less than two days between games. Two factors are to be considered, the timing of the meal and its contents. First, the muscles are the most "receptive" to storing glycogen in the six hours after activity. Have "locker room snacks" that are good sources of CHO like fresh or dried fruit and juices; pretzels are good also. Gatorade (Gatorload 2000) and Ross Labs (Excell 2) market drinks high in a CHO source that is rapidly emptied from the stomach and absorbed by the muscles (these would be consumed after a game and not on a regular basis as they are too high in calories). If you can find and afford these, use only when a quick glycogen replenishment is needed. (Mix Excell with orange juice to a 20%, not the suggested 25%, concentration. This tastes better and settles easier on the stomach.)

The meals between should supply a total of 500-600 grams of CHO (see Table 1 for examples). Given access to smorgasbords, a college team consumed only

TABLE 1-
FOODS HIGH IN CARBOHYDRATES*

MILK GROUP	gms. CHO	FRUIT-VEGETABLE GROUP	gms.	CHO
choc. milkshake, 10 oz.	63	raisins, 4 tbsp.		33
yogurt, fruit, 1 cup	42	french fries, 20 pieces		31
choc. pudding, ½ cup	30	baked potato		30
choc. milk, 1 cup	26	applesauce, ½ cup		30
cocoa, ¾ cup	19	banana, medium		26
vanilla ice cream, ½ cup	16	peaches, canned,½ cup		25
milk 2%, skim, 1 cup	12	pear, medium		25
milk, whole	11	fruit salad, ½ cup		25
		pineapple, large slice		24
GRAIN GROUP		grape juice, ½ cup		21
cornbread, 2 ½" x 3"	30	apple, medium		20
hard roll	30	boiled potato, 2 small		18
bagel	28	sweet potato, ½ md.		18
burger-hot dog roll	21	rice, ½ cup		25
egg noodles, ½ cup	19	lima beans, ½ cup		17
waffles, 2	17	orange, medium		16
cornflakes, ¾ cup	16	winter squash, ½ cup		14
grits, ½ cup	14	corn, ½ cup		16
corn tortilla, 6" diam.	14	mashed potato, ½ cup		13
white bread, 1 slice	12	pink grapefruit, ½ md.		13
oatmeal, ½ cup	12	orange juice, ½ cup		13
whole wheat bread, 1 slice	11	watermelon, 1 cup		13

MEAT GROUP

refried beans, ½ cup	26
blackeye peas, ½ cup	17

*from *Food Power,* National Dairy Council, pg. 17.

TABLE 2 -
SAMPLE PRE-GAME MEALS FOR VARIOUS TIMES OF DAY*

orange juice	1 cup	vegetable soup	1 cup
corn flakes	¾ cup	chicken	2 oz
banana	1 medium	white bread	2 slices
wheat toast	2 slices	applesauce	1 cup
jelly	1 tbsp	yogurt, low fat	1 cup
skim milk	1 cup		

TOTALS (gms.)		TOTALS (gms.)	
protein	17	protein	21
CHO	115	CHO	109
fat	2	fat	10

julienne salad	1 cup	pork and beans	1 cup
lettuce	1 oz	crackers	10
ham	1 oz.	carrot sticks	5" carrot
turkey	½ cup	fruit salad	½ cup
pudding	1 cup	skim milk	1 cup
grape juice	½ cup		

TOTALS (gms.)		TOTALS (gms.)	
protein	25	protein	29
CHO	76	CHO	110
fat	9	fat	11

*from *Food Power,* National Dairy Council, pg. 18.

300-400 grams of CHO in the 24 hours after a game. Their meal was heavy in fats and proteins (unpublished observations). Diets like this cannot refill muscle glycogen to the limit when time between games is limited. Also, stay away from "fast foods" as they are fried and add unnecessary calories as fat. The best part of those meals is the bread. In addition, realize that if the menu says "shakes" that the dairy content is so low that the use of the term "milk" is forbidden (their major constituent is cellulose – the prime ingredient in bulk laxatives).

If selections from above are eaten after the game and before bed along with some CHO at breakfast (remember, your goal is 500-600 grams of CHO), the refilling of the glycogen stores can be nearly completed in 24 hours. This might be done only at selected times when the schedule dictates.

3. Do pre-game meals affect muscle glycogen levels?

Food must empty from the stomach, pass through the intestines into the blood, and go to the muscles and liver for storage. The time for this process exceeds the typical two-four hours wait from meal to game. Amounts of complex protein and fat in the meal, as well as pre-game anxiety, all impair gastrointestinal function. Some examples of pre-game meals, low in fat and protein with a decent amount of CHO, are listed in Table 2.

There have been attempts at delaying glycogen depletion. If blood fuels are elevated (raised blood fats or blood sugar), then maybe the exercising muscle will use those fuels in preference to stored muscle fuels. Blood fats can be elevated by caffeine (an International Olympic Committee banned stimulant!), but are probably not useful in soccer. As stated, fat contains a lot of hard-to-obtain energy. The higher the intensity of exercise, the less fat is used as a fuel and the more the body uses CHO and other storage forms of energy. So high blood fats would probably not help in soccer. Elevated blood sugar has also been shown to improve endurance performance.

Drinking one of those two drinks mentioned (Gatorade and Excell) in the 10-15 minutes before a game can nearly double blood sugar and stored glycogen can be spared because the body uses the blood sugar. However, if one consumes any CHO 30-60 minutes before a game, an insulin reaction will lower blood sugar (the main fuel for the brain), resulting in a less alert player for the start of the game. However, if the CHO (and only certain types of CHO at that; a glucose polymer, not simple sugar as found in most beverages) is taken closer to game time, the insulin reaction is inhibited and the blood sugar remains elevated. One should be cautious in the use of this method. Remember, the drinks are extremely high in calories. Too much intake or intake too often could lead to weight gain as fat and a bit of a "sugar withdrawal" when consumption ceases. In addition, overconsumption and glycogen loading can upset the delicate diet-insulin-exercise balance of the diabetic.

4. What about food volume?

The typical teenager will consume somewhere between 1,500-1,300 calories (which varies with age, sex, height, weight and activity level). Athletes will typically eat more then their non-athletic peers due to their activity level. With training and once a week games, appropriate choices from the four food groups will probably satisfy the nutritional needs of the player (assuming that practice volume and severity decreases as game day approaches). Dietary changes may be necessary only when games are less than 48 hours apart or during particularly heavy training (i.e., late in the week two-a-days). The major difference between the athlete and non-athlete is in the volume of food eaten. Cyclists, distance runners and swimmers can eat 5-6000 + cal./day and not gain weight.

5. What will all this do for a team?

Remember the article by Saitin (3). The goal is to go into the game with a full tank of fuel. If the tank is less than full, then both the work volume and intensity of the players will be reduced. It makes no sense to go into the match with a team that is partly fuel depleted. This can be a major disadvantage and may affect the outcome of the game.

6. The league allows unlimited substitution, as a result the work done by a team is reduced by sheer numbers. Does this substitution policy affect these suggestions?

The suggestions presented have some limited application. The people who would benefit the most are those who undergo serious training and play the 90 minute game regularly. When the training and game work are diluted by either limited practices per week or numbers of players, then having the players follow a standard "well balanced diet" will usually suffice.

These selected practices are probably unnecessary for players whose games are of 60 minutes or less. In addition, the typical "city league" team (adult or youth) might only practice 1-2 times per week and play once per week. These special dietary changes would be unnecessary for these latter groups.

REFERENCES

1. Agnevik, G. "Football." Indrottsfysiologi: Rapport Nr7. Stockholm, Trugg-Hansa, 1970.

2. Jacobs, I., N. Westlin, J. Karisson, et al. "Muscle glycogen and diet in elite soccer players." Eur J Appi Physiot. 48:297-302,1982

3. Saitin, B. "Metabolic fundamentals of exercise." Med Sci Sports 5:137-146, 1973.

4. Piehl, K. "Time course for refilling of glycogen stores in human muscle fibers following exercise induced glycogen depletion." Acta Physiot Scan 90:297- 302, 1974.

5. MacDougall, J.D., G.R. Ward, D.G. Sale, J.R. Sutton. "Muscle glycogen repletion after high intensity intermittent exercise." J Appl Physiol 42:129-132, 1977.

SUGGESTED RESOURCE BOOKS

Better Homes and Gardens Books. *Eat and Stay Slim.* 1976. Meredith Corp., Des Moines, IA.

Smith, Nathan J. *Food for Sport.* 1976. Bull. Publ., Palo Alto, CA.

National Dairy Council. *Food Power.* National Dairy Council, 6300 North River Road, Rosemont, IL 60018 (312-699-1020).

A LOOK AT SPORT DRINKS
Dr. Donald T. Kirkendall

Doesn't the sports drink market drive you nuts? I mean it is a $1 billion industry. Gatorade, Exceed, Cytomax, Recharge, "Be like Mike" and it's enough to make you see double. Did you even know that there are three classes of drinks (fluid/electrolyte replacement, carbohydrate loading/replacement and nutritional supplements)? The research on the subject tells you that there are so many variables that have to be known that you throw up your hands and say "nothing can beat water."

At a recent American College of Sports Medicine (ACSM) meeting, Quaker Oats (makers of Gatorade, the official sports beverage of the USSF and sponsor of education programs for the NSCAA), sponsored a roundtable discussion on sports drinks in an attempt to summarize the topic. The following comments are directed at fluid/electrolyte replacement drinks and their use. I quote the consensus statement:

1. First, an oral-rehydration solution should provide water, carbohydrates, and electrolytes as quickly as possible. Sodium and small amounts of carbohydrates are essential in stimulating fluid uptake into the bloodstream.

2. Second, since optimizing performance is a critical objective of a sports drink, the carbohydrate concentration of the drink needs to be sufficient to

supply energy to working muscles without slowing intestinal absorption.

3. Third, the intestine has a large absorptive capacity and is capable of absorbing the volume of fluid required to replace sweat loss. Exercise itself does not compromise intestinal function. They actually had a fourth item related to more research, but roundtables always call for more research.

So what does this mean to you? You probably have been operating on the assumption that nothing is better than water for fluid replenishment during exercise. Well, you can do a bit better. Some hints based on the scientific literature:

• Never use sodas. The caffeine is a diuretic (makes you urinate - you are trying to retain water, not urinate it out) and the carbonation makes you feel full so you don't drink enough;

• Drinks flavored solely with fructose (read those labels!) frequently can cause stomach distress. However, because fructose is such a good sweetener, its presence in combination with other carbohydrates (like glucose polymers, sucrose, glucose) improves the taste of the drink. The better tasting the drink, the more that may be consumed. One of the drawbacks of water is its bland taste;

• Some carbohydrate is good, too much is not good. If the concentration of carbohydrate is too high, movement of the drink from the stomach to the intestine is slowed. A solution between 6 and 10 percent is suggested. Some examples:

Leons QEM	*4.9 percent*
Gatorade	*6.0 percent*
Exceed	*7.2 percent*
Cyto Max	*10 percent*
Orange juice	*11.8 percent*
Coca-Cola	*11 percent*

• Electrolytes are also good in helping get the drink across the cells of the intestine into the bloodstream. It also helps in retaining some of the fluids ingested. About 40 percent of water ingested during exercise shows up as urine in the first few hours while (around 30 percent of the water in an electrolyte drink shows up as urine in the same time period

• Cold drinks are absorbed faster (around 40 degrees fahrenheit, so keep it iced).

GUIDELINES

ACSM suggests the following:

1. Drink four to eight ounces of a drink 15-20 minutes before exercise, then four to eight ounces every 15-20 minutes during exercise (I know, soccer is two uninterrupted 45 minute periods, so there is no time for water. Nonsense. The ball is in play for only about 60 minutes of that time, so creative placement of drink bottles and use of injury time outs will almost always allow for drinks during the game).

2. The drink should be 5-10 percent carbohydrate.

3. The drink should contain electrolytes (sodium and potassium are the main ones) to help with intestinal absorption. Vitamins don't help, but they don't hurt either.

⚽

POWER DEVELOPMENT THROUGH PLYOMETRIC EXERCISE
Mike Worcik

When talking about the strength development of athletes, it is more appropriate to use the term POWER since strength is a component of POWER (Power = Force x Velocity). An athlete must not only be able to apply a great deal of force (which is strength) to the ground on each takeoff but he must also apply this force very quickly (velocity) since the duration of takeoff is a split second (11-13 seconds!) occurrence. In light of this important fact it is essential that the athlete have the ability to apply a large force in a very short time period. Pure strength is not enough, but rather the rate that this strength can be utilized. This is why the Soviets developed the plyometric concept in the late 1960's for their jumpers.

Plyometric exercises are those in which the exercised muscle is loaded in an eccentric (lengthening) contraction initially and followed immediately by a concentric (shortening) contraction. Numerous research studies have indicated that it is not the amount of dynamic exercise that is important but rather the rate at which the exercise is performed when attempting to develop one's power output. A concept that must be grasped at this point is that a muscle that is stretched prior to contraction will contract more forcefully. By loading a particular muscle in an eccentric fashion you are in effect stretching that muscle prior to its contraction which results in a more forceful contraction.

The plyometric concept was developed by the Soviets when they asked themselves the question: "Are slow strength exercises (the typical barbell ones) developing a strength that is transferable to high speed contractions by the same muscle?" After much research they concluded that the answer was NO.

In order for an athlete to be able to apply force rapidly they concluded that training should be conducted at speeds that simulate actual performance speeds. Not only must the muscular system (fast twitch fibers) be trained to react quickly but so must the neurological system as well. The Russians concluded that a type of exercise that placed the exercised muscle in an eccentric contraction that was immediately fol-

In order for an athlete to be able to apply force rapidly they concluded that training should be conducted at speeds that simulate actual performance speeds.

lowed by a concentric contraction would develop this ability to apply a great deal of force quickly. They felt that these exercises, called "plyometric exercises," would act as a "shock" to improve the reactive ability of the neuromuscular system of the athlete. Since such exercises are performed so explosively, they force the neuromuscular system to adapt and react more quickly. This is the specificity of training concept.

RUNNING IS PLYOMETRIC

Any activity in which a muscle is loaded eccentrically (lengthened) prior to contracting concentrically (shortened) is utilizing this plyometric principle. A simple example of this concept is the act of running. When the swing leg comes to contact the ground under the athlete it must support the body by contracting eccentrically from the hip, knee, and ankle joints. Failure to do so would result in the athlete collapsing downward and falling to the track surface. Immediately after this yielding (absorbing) contraction which stretches the extensor muscles, the athlete concentrically contracts the same muscles which results in driving the body in a forward/upward direction for the next running cycle.

OTHER PLYOMETRIC EXERCISES

1. **Double Leg Hops.** From a standing position the athlete hops out of both legs in a forward/upward direction for a distance of about 30 meters. (Upon landing after each hop the next hop must be done immediately.)
2. **Double Leg Jumps.** From a standing position the athlete jumps upward out of both legs in a continuous fashion for 15-30 seconds striving to achieve maximum height.
3. **Bounding (RLRLRLRLRL).** The athlete bounds from one leg to another over a distance of 30-50 meters. Emphasis should be on driving forward on each step and waiting for the ground to come up and meet the swing leg. Upon landing with this leg the athlete must explosively push the ground away from and behind him.

4. **Single Leg Hops (RRRRRRRRRR) (LLLLLLLLL).** The athlete hops continuously on one leg over a distance of 30-50 meters. Emphasis should be on driving the body forward/upward on each takeoff and attacking the ground with the hop leg upon landing to propel the body (pawing the surface).
5. **Alternate Hops (RRLLRRLLRR).** The athlete hops twice on one leg and then steps onto his left leg and hops twice. This sequence is repeated in a continuous fashion until the athlete has covered a distance of 30-50 meters. Emphasis is the same as with the single leg hops.
6. **Triple Jump Drill.** The athlete hops off of his takeoff leg and then (after landing on the same leg) steps onto his opposite leg and then steps back onto his original takeoff leg. Emphasis is upon driving the body forward on each takeoff and maintaining speed. The drill should be done with continuity over 30-50 meters.
7. **Speed Bounds/Hops.** Exercises 3-6 conducted as fast as possible over a distance of 30-50 meters. A six step run-up can be used and the athletes may race one another over the distance timed by the coach.
8. **Distance Bounds/Hops.** From a six step run-up the athlete performs numbers 3-6 for five successive jumps (RLRLR/RRRRR/LLLLL/RRLLR/RRLRR) with the final distance being measured. Emphasis is upon driving the body as far forward as possible on each takeoff.
9. **Sand Hops.** From a standing position the athlete executes three successive standing broad jumps into a long jump pit. He then performs two standing broad jumps trying to land in the same spot as in the previous jumps. After this he executes one standing broad jump with the intent of landing in his previous first jump spot. This 3-2-1 series is done for 10 repetitions for two or three sets. Emphasis is on a maximum distance.
10. **Hurdle Hops.** Five hurdles are placed approximately two feet apart and the athlete executes continuous double leg hops over them, landing between them. (Note: at first the athlete may have to stop between hurdles to prevent tripping over them.)
11. **Stair Hopping & Bounding.** Continuous hopping or bounding up and down stairs. Single, double, and alternate leg fashion.
12. **Depth Jumping.** From a box (approximately two feet high) the athlete jumps upward and upon landing immediately rebounds upward for maximum height out of both legs. This exercise should be done in sets of 10 repetitions.
13. **Rope Skipping.** Using double, single, and alternate leg fashion. Emphasis is on continuous rebounding off the ground (absorb & react).

14. **Box Drills.** The athlete executes a series of hop/bounds out of one or both legs onto and over several boxes.

PREPARATION WORK

Experience has indicated that a certain amount of general strength training should be done for 4-6 weeks prior to the conductance of these plyometric exercises. This is to allow the athlete time to develop resiliency in muscular and connective tissues. Failure to allow for this preparation period may result in injury to the athlete since plyometric exercises are very explosive and place traumatic stress on the knee, hip, and ankle joints of the athlete.

After this preparation period it is also advisable that plyometric exercises be conducted in conjunction with barbell exercises (isotonic) in order to maximize power development in the extensor muscles.

Remember, since strength is a component of power, it must still be improved to maximize power output. The key is for the athlete to increase his strength and develop the ability to use this strength quickly. Plyometric exercises help us to achieve this goal. It is important that the exercises be done with the proper form. The muscle will only gain through that part of the range of motion which is exercised. Make sure that the players flex at the knee and hip (to approximately 90°) on each bound or jump. They land in that flexed position and explode: hit and react! hit and react! hit and react! If the players understand why they are doing this, it will help.

⚽

FLEXIBILITY AND THE PREVENTION OF MUSCLE STRAINS
Dr. Donald T. Kirkendall

Stretching exercises have been suggested to both decrease injuries and also improve performance. (1) There is very little strong scientific data to directly show a decrease in injury due to improved flexibility, however, there appears to be good theoretical rationale for its application. Stretching exercises appear to be valuable in the treatment of various musculo-tendinous injuries such as strains and tendinitis.

An individual's flexibility can be influenced by a variety of factors: the joint capsule, ligaments, bony configuration, connective tissue and the muscle tendon unit itself.

Most individuals, due to the nature of our society, tend not to stretch on a regular basis. Most of our time is spent in a sitting position which tends to develop some generalized tightness of certain muscle groups. Major culprits are as the hamstrings, hip flexors, low back and the calf muscles. Participation in sports will also place increased demands on specific muscle groups (e.g. the calf muscles in running, shoulder muscles in racquet sports). Additional tightness may develop in these high demand muscular regions.

Several authors have indicated that the most effective stretch appears to be a moderate intensity for a long duration (7, 12). There is some variation in opinion on how long to hold a stretch. Some authors have suggested a 30 to 60 second hold period while others have noted (7, 12) a two to three minute hold is most effective. A quick, short duration stretch appears to have a limitation because it illicits the stretch reflex if the stretch is too intense or fast.

Tightness of the gastrocnemius/soleus (calf) group can cause increased pronation at the foot and lower leg stress. Hamstring tightness combined with calf tightness can lead to additional patello-femoral (knee joint) compression. Tightness of the hamstrings has also been noted to create potential negative effects on the back.

STRETCHING METHODS

Ballistic: This can be described as a bouncing or bobbing type of stretch that uses momentum of the body to force the muscle group into as much a stretch as can be tolerated. Ballistic stretching has the ability to increase range of motion but carries a high risk of injury. This stretch has the potential to cause a muscle spasm and may be associated with increased muscular soreness.

Static: This involves passively stretching a given muscle by placing it in a position of stretch and holding it there for an extended period of time. By stretching statically, the player is in less danger of exceeding the muscle's limits. The degree of stretch is controlled by the feel of the muscle. Relaxation during the stretch will help to achieve optimal results. Included with this article are basic methods of static stretching for problem areas in soccer.

Proprioceptive neuromuscular facilitation (PNF): PNF needs the assistance of a reliable partner. The partner gradually stretches the muscle group. Once the stretch is at its maximum, the one being worked on then performs a maximal isometric contraction against the partner for about a ten second push phase. This causes an increase in the tension on the tendons and will effect a reflex relaxation before the muscle is again placed on stretch by the partner. PNF has been shown to be quite effective in increasing range of motion.

FLEXIBILITY AND PLAYERS

As stated, there seems to be a consensus of opinion that a high degree of flexibility is desired to prevent or reduce the severity of muscular strains. Physical

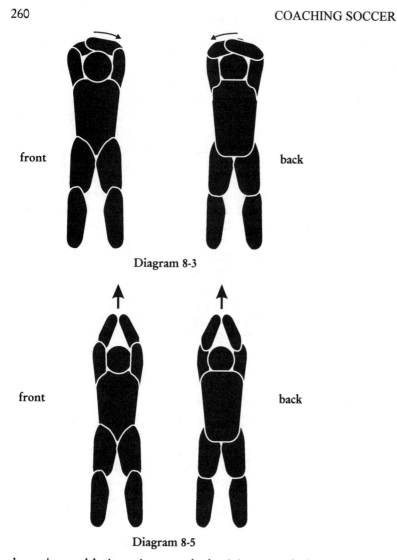

front   back

Diagram 8-3

front   back

Diagram 8-5

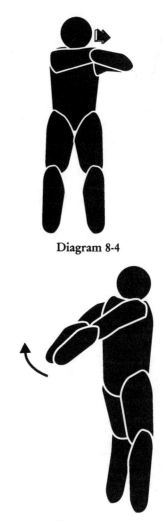

Diagram 8-4

Diagram 8-6

therapists, athletic trainers and physicians regularly stress the need for flexibility training.

The measurement of flexibility has typically been by one of two methods, either by measuring the range of motion of a joint or by using any one of a variety of screening tests that can be found in a good test and measurements book (for example, Chapter 6 of Johnson and Nelson (6)).

Muscle tightness of soccer players has been recently reported. Elkstrand and Guillquist (5) studied 86 Division IV men and Oberg *et al* (10) studied 186 Division IV Swedish men. They measured ranges of motion and reported normal levels and ranges of normal (plus or minus two standard deviations from the mean). Ciolek et al (3) looked at 55 college and professional (MISL) players and used a qualitative scale (0 = normal and 3 = very tight) based on degrees of motion. The table reports on the percentages of players who were listed as "tight" according to the author's definitions. According to the table, quadriceps and hip extensors were a problem for the Swedes, while groin, ankle and hamstrings were the problem for the American group. Using the standard sit and reach test (6),

soccer players averaged + 4 inches (seated straight legged - reached four inches beyond their toes) for collegiate players to 5.2 inches for U.S. National Team members. Ballet dancers and gymnasts will typically reach 10 inches or more.

ON THE PREVENTION OF SOFT TISSUE INJURIES

Muscular strains and ligamentous sprains are considered the most frequent of injuries in soccer (4). Muscular strains have been reported to account for 9.8% of all injuries in 9-19 year-old youth, between 4.4% in amateurs 10-35 years of age (2), and 13% in division IV Swedish professionals aged 17-38 (4). These types of strains have accounted for an average of 12 days off due to the injury (2).

Can a preventive program reduce the occurrence of these types of injuries? In an effort to answer this question, Ekstrand (4) put six Division IV Swedish teams on a supervised, supplemental program for the first six months of the playing season. Six other teams served as controls. The supervised teams averaged only one muscle strain per team over the six months while the control teams averaged four strains per team. Numerous other differences were mentioned, most no-

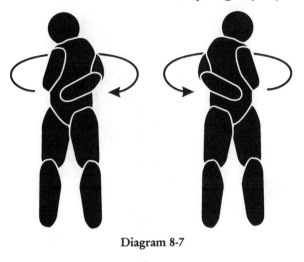

Diagram 8-7

Diagram 8-8

Diagram 8-9

Diagram 8-10

table, a 75-77% reduction in the overall injury rate plus a reduction in the number of practices and games missed.

SOCCER STRETCHING EXERCISES

1. Shoulders and Upper Arm

In a standing position with your arms overhead, hold the elbow of one arm with the hand of the other arm. Slowly pull the elbow behind your head. (Diagram 8-3)

2. Shoulder and Upper Arm

In a standing position, place your arms at shoulder level, grasp your right elbow with your left hand and stretch your arm across your chest. (Diagram 8-4)

3. Shoulders and Upper Arm

Extend your arms overhead with your palms together, stretch your arms upward and slightly backward. (Diagram 8-5)

4. Shoulder and Chest

Interlace your fingers behind your back. Slowly raise your arms up but do not bend forward at the waist. (Diagram 8-6)

5. Trunk Rotation

In a standing position, place your right arm behind and the left arm in front of your trunk. Rotate trunk to the right without moving your feet. Then, change the front of hand positions and slowly turn to your left. (Diagram 8-7)

6. Trunk-Sided Bend

Stand with feet shoulder width apart and left arm overhead. Bend to the side by sliding the right hand down the outside of your leg. Do not bend forward or rotate your body. (Diagram 8-8)

7. Quadriceps

Lying on your stomach, grasp your left ankle with your left hand. Slowly stretch your foot toward your buttock so that you feel the stretch on the front of your thigh. (Diagram 8-9)

8. Quadriceps

In a standing position, grasp your left ankle with your left hand. Slowly stretch your foot toward your buttock so that you feel the stretch on the front of your thigh. (Diagram 8-10)

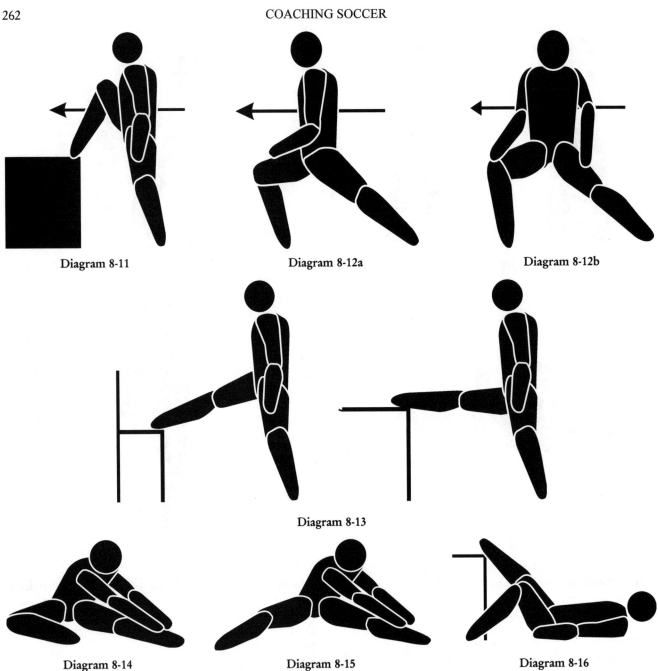

Diagram 8-11   Diagram 8-12a   Diagram 8-12b

Diagram 8-13

Diagram 8-14   Diagram 8-15   Diagram 8-16

9. Hip Flexor
Prop your right foot onto a high table or chair. Keep your left leg straight and body upright. This will stretch your left hip.(Diagram 8-11)

10a. Hip Flexor
In a forward stride position with both feet pointed forward, bend your right knee while keeping your left knee straight. Extend your back and stretch the front of your left hip or thigh. (Diagram 8-12a)

10b. Hip Flexor/Adductors
From the forward stride position deep your right foot planted and turn your body and back foot to the left. Slowly stretch your back leg down to the ground. Now the stretch will be felt at the inner thigh. (Diagram 8-12b)

11. Hamstring
In a standing position, place one leg on a chair or table. Choose a comfortable height that allows you to keep your knee straight. Keeping your back straight, lean toward the raised leg. (Diagram 8-13)

12. Hamstring
In a sitting position with you left leg straight, place the sole of your right foot against the inside of your left thigh. Bend your trunk toward your extended leg, keeping your knee straight and foot in a relaxed position. (Diagram 8-14)

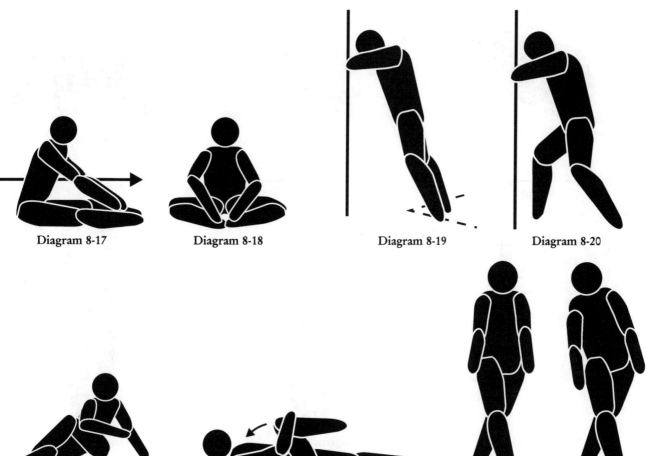

Diagram 8-17

Diagram 8-18

Diagram 8-19

Diagram 8-20

Diagram 8-21

Diagram 8-22

Diagram 8-23

13. Hamstring

In a sitting position with your legs spread apart and feet relaxed, reach your arms toward your left leg. Repeat and stretch toward your right leg. (Diagram 8-15)

14. Hamstring

Lie on your back on the floor. Prop your right leg onto the edge of a table or a wall, keeping your leg and knee straight. Maintain this position with a stretch on the back of your right leg. (Diagram 8-16)

15. Hamstring

In a sitting position, with legs straight and feet relaxed, bend your trunk forward, stretching your arms and head toward your legs. (Diagram 8-17)

16. Groin-Adductors

In a sitting position with your back straight, bend your knees and place the bottoms of your feet together. Pull your feet toward your groin. Place your elbows on your knees and gently push the knees toward the floor. (Diagram 8-18)

17. Gastrocnemius

Stand with feet shoulder width apart, knees straight and feet pointed slightly in. Keep your heels flat as you move your hips toward the wall. Stretch should be felt in the calf. (Diagram 8-19)

18. Soleus

Stand with feet shoulder width apart and pointed slightly in. Step forward with your right foot and bend both knees. Keep your heels flat as you move your hips toward the wall. Stretch should be felt in the lower calf of your right leg. Change leg positions and stretch the other leg. (Diagram 8-20)

19. Trunk-Hip Rotation

Sit with your right leg straight and left leg crossed over your right knee with your left foot flat on the ground. Place your right elbow against the outside of your left knee. Stabilize yourself with your left arm and slowly rotate your body to the far left. (Diagram 8-21)

20. Buttock-Low Back

In a lying position, pull your right leg toward your chest. Keep your head down and opposite leg straight. (Diagram 8-22)

21. Iliotibial Band

Stand with both knees straight and place your left leg behind your right knee. Slowly stretch to the right

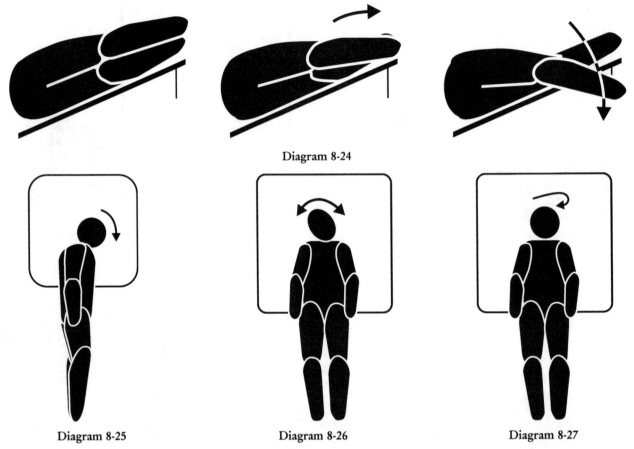

Diagram 8-24

Diagram 8-25　　　　**Diagram 8-26**　　　　**Diagram 8-27**

side by sliding your arm down the side of your leg. (Diagram 8-23)

22.Iliotibial Band

Lying on your left side on a table, slowly lift your right leg backward and stretch it down off the table. Do not allow your left leg to rotate backward. (Digram 7-24)

23.Neck-Flexion

Bend your head forward toward your chest, and slowly return to the upright position. (Diagram 8-25)

24.Neck-Side Bend

Bend your head sideways; first to the right, hold, and then to the left, directing your ear toward your shoulder. Keep your face straight ahead. (Diagram 8-26)

25.Neck-Rotation

Turn your head slowly; first to the right, hold, and then to the left, directing your chin toward your shoulder. (Diagram 8-27)

GENERAL GUIDELINES

• Emphasis should be placed on relaxation;

• Hold the stretch for 30-60 seconds. Repeat several times as necessary;

• Flexibility may be further increased with a slight increase in body temperature. It is advisable to warm-up prior to stretching (eg. brief calisthenics, light jogging);

• Post-exercise stretching is very important to help reduce muscle soreness and to maintain flexibility;

• Do not attempt to overstretch or create a painful response during the exercise.

The prudent soccer player will give strong emphasis to stretching the groin, calf, hamstrings, and quadriceps (thigh). The inclusion of a consistent and precise stretching program can be an effective asset to a soccer conditioning program. Teams should strive to perform regular flexibility exercises prior to and after practice sessions. Athletes who are tight may need to do additional stretching on those tight muscle groups.

PERCENT OF PLAYERS DEFINED AS "TIGHT"

	Ekstrand (1982)	Ciolek (1985)
Groin	17%	36%
Hip Flexion	4%	—
Hip Extension	31%	—
Hamstrings	—	22%
Quadriceps	36%	3%
Ankle	14%	56%

REFERENCES

1 . Arnheim, D.D., *Modern Principles of Athletic Training*. Times Mirror Mosby College Publishing, St. Louis, pp. 91-92, 1985.

2. Berger-Vachon, C., G. Babard, B. Moyer, "Soccer Accidents in the French Rhone-Alps Soccer Association", Sports Medicine 3:69-77, 1986.

3. Ciolek, J., D. T. Kirkendall, J. Grogan, "Relationship of Individual Muscle Group Flexibility Testing the Wells Sit & Reach Test", Presented National Athletic Trainers Assoc., San Antonio, Texas, June, 1985.

4. Ekstrand, J., "Soccer Injuries and Their Prevention", Linkoping University Medical Dissertations, No. 130, Linkoping, Sweden, 1982.

5. Ekstrand, J., J. Giliquist, "The Frequency of Muscle Tightness and Injuries in Soccer Players", Am J. Sports Med. 10:75-78,1982.

6. Johnson, B. L., and J. K. Nelson, *Practical Measurements for Evaluation in Physical Education*, Burgers Publishing Co., Minneapolis, MN, 1974.

7. Kirkendall, D. T., "The Applied Sport Science of Soccer", Physician and Sports Medicine 13 (4): 53-59, 1985.

8. Kisner, C., L.A. Colby, *Therapeutic Exercise Foundations and Techniques*. FA Davis, Philadelphia, pp. 122-126, 1985.

9. McCarroll, J., R. C. Meaney, J. M. Sieber, "Profile of Youth Soccer Injuries", Physician and Sports Medicine 12 (2):113-117, 1984.

10. Oberg, B., J. Ekstrand, M. Moller, J. Giliquist, "Muscle Strength and Flexibility in Different Positions of Soccer Players." Int. J. Sports Med. 5:213-216, 1984.

11. Schmidt-Olsen, S., L. K. H. Bunemann, V. Lade, J. 0. R. Brassoe, "Soccer Injuries of Youth", Brit. J. Sports Med. 19:161-164, 1985.

12. Wathan, D., "Roundtable: Flexibility", NSCA Journal Vol. 4 (Aug.-Sept.): pp. 10-22, 1984.

SCIENTIFIC BASIS OF INTERVAL TRAINING
Dr. Donald T. Kirkendall

In graduate school, I had a professor who liked what he called X:Y:Z questions. The instructions were to mark X if X was greater than Y, Y if Y was greater than X, and Z if X and Y were about the same. How would you answer the following:

X: Distance covered during an all out one minute run.

Y: Distance covered during six 10 second all out runs with 30 seconds rest between each run.

X: Perceptual fatigue after an all out one minute run.

Y: Perceptual fatigue after six 10 second all out runs with 30 second rest between each run.

ATP-PC STORES (-)

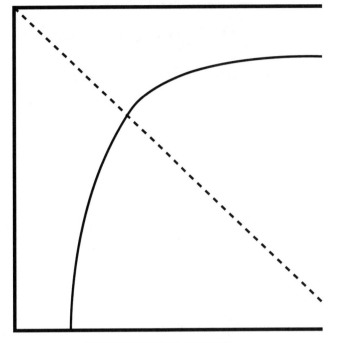

EXERCISE TIME
Diagram 8-28

The correct answer for each is Y. The reasons for which are the keys to interval training. The answers lie in the interaction of metabolic production of ATP from the ATP-PC system and glycolysis. This is especially important considering that soccer requires one sprint of about 20-30m every 60-90 seconds and a cruise or sprint once every 30 seconds. The recovery interval could be spent standing, walking, jogging or backing. The keys to interval exercise and training is the work intensity, recovery period and recovery period intensity in addition to the traditional sets and repetitions.

PHOSPHAGEN DEPLETION DURING CONTINUOUS AND INTERMITTENT EXERCISE

During our continuous, one-minute maximal exercise, there is a hyperbolic depletion of phosphagens (Diagram 8-28). This plateau can occur in a few seconds. This is evidenced by the accumulation of lactic acid after even five (5) seconds of maximal exercise (Jacobs, 1982). To continue the work requires ATP production from glycolysis with its subsequent production of lactic acid (Diagram 8-28). As a result, fatigue will reduce the exercise intensity.

Next, do the same run as six 10-second maximal bouts, each followed by 30 seconds of rest. Because of the length of the run, there is less of a depletion of ATP and PC stores. In addition, the recovery period allows for metabolism to replenish some of the phosphagens. The pattern that occurs is illustrated in

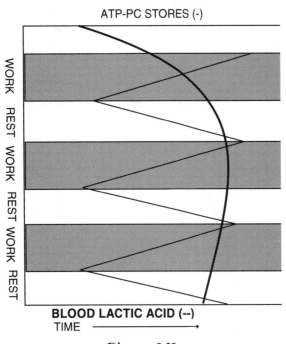

ATP-PC STORES (-)

WORK REST WORK REST WORK REST

BLOOD LACTIC ACID (--)
TIME ⟶

Diagram 8-29

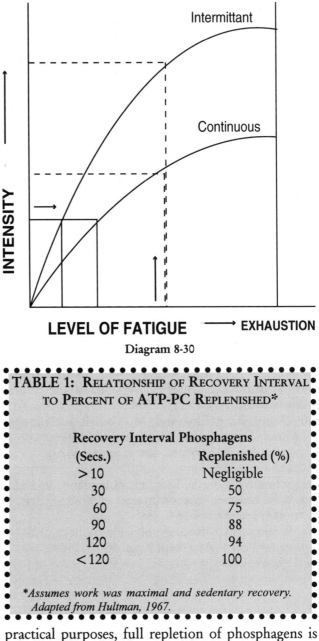

Intermittant

Continuous

INTENSITY

LEVEL OF FATIGUE ⟶ **EXHAUSTION**

Diagram 8-30

Diagram 8-29. In addition, because there is a replenishment of stored phosphagens there will be less of a need to supply ATP from glycolysis. Subsequent bouts will use these replenished phosphagens before glycolysis is greatly recruited. The result is a reduced production of lactic acid (Diagram 8-29).

Theoretical relationship of intensity and fatigue in continuous and intermittent exercise (modified from Fox and Matthews, 1974). What does this mean to training? It means that the intermittent work can be up to 2.5 times more intense than could be performed by continuous exercise. Diagram 8-30 shows three things. First, at any given intensity, the level of fatigue will be less than during continuous exercise (solid lines, Diagram 8-30). Second, at any given level of fatigue, the work intensity will be greater during intermittent exercise (dotted lines). This then leads to the final point. The intensity of intermittent work leading to exhaustion far exceeds that required from continuous exercise.

THE RECOVERY INTERVAL

Phosphagen replenishment is dependent on two things, the length of the recovery interval and the type of exercise performed during recovery. During recovery, oxygen is consumed and the aerobic processes produce ATP to replenish the phosphagens.

The rate of recovery is curvilinear. In the scientific literature, authors talk of half time (how long does it take for half of whatever to occur). Phosphagen recovery has a half time of 30 seconds. This means that 50% of the spent phosphagens are replaced in 30 seconds. Half again is replaced in the next 30 seconds, half again in the next 30 seconds, and so on. For all

TABLE 1: RELATIONSHIP OF RECOVERY INTERVAL TO PERCENT OF ATP-PC REPLENISHED*

Recovery Interval (Secs.)	Phosphagens Replenished (%)
>10	Negligible
30	50
60	75
90	88
120	94
<120	100

Assumes work was maximal and sedentary recovery. Adapted from Hultman, 1967.

practical purposes, full repletion of phosphagens is completed in two minutes (Table 1).

It should then be obvious that the shorter the recovery interval, the less restoration of phosphagens. The next bout of exercise will still need ATP, so glycolysis will become a greater supplier of ATP with its resulting production of lactic acid. The longer the recovery interval, the greater replenishment of ATP-PC. Subsequent exercises will not require glycolysis to play as great a role. Lactic acid will be less and fatigue should be less of a factor.

TYPE OF RECOVERY INTERVAL

There are two types of recovery intervals. Typically, people think of recovery as rest (eg., standing, sitting, slow walking). This is typically referred to as "rest-relief." The other type involves rapid walking or light jogging during recovery. This is referred to as "work-relief."

Rest-relief allows for complete restoration of phosphagens as has been discussed. Work-relief still requires some energy to fuel the recovery exercise. This will slow the replenishment of phosphagens and subsequent work will require a greater reliance on glycolysis. The choice of the type of recovery is dictated by the metabolic system to be stressed. If the desire is to improve the ability to use and replenish phosphagens, then rest-relief is the choice. If the desire to increase one's ability to tolerate lactic acid, then work-relief is the choice. Improvement of the aerobic system is related to use of a rest-relief during recovery.

In applying interval training principles, the work interval intensity must also be considered. If the work is all-out and maximal, the relief interval needs to be longer than if the work interval was lighter. Typically, a 1:2 or 1:3 work-relief ratio is applied; work 30 seconds, rest for 60-90 seconds. This assumes very high intensity work.

Should the work be lighter, the ratio can be reduced to 1:5 to 1:2; work 30 seconds, rest up to 15 seconds, work 30 seconds, rest for 60 seconds.

ADAPTATIONS OF INTERVAL TRAINING

Swimming and track and field coaches have been consistent practitioners of the interval method. A coach outlines a workout of sets, repetitions, intensity and recovery interval like: Three sets of five 400 meter runs at 70 seconds with 120 seconds of light jogging between runs and five minutes rest between sets. What are the results of interval training like this? Numerous adaptations occur. There appears to be a greater stroke volume (amount of blood pumped per beat of the heart) during early recovery. In continuous running, there is only one recovery period—at the end. Interval running has many recovery periods. As stroke volume is elevated in the early recovery period (therefore, more oxygen is pumped to the muscles), the heart learns to improve its pumping efficiency during the recovery intervals. Stroke volume is also improved by an expansion of the plasma volume. At the muscle level, elevated ATP and PC levels are seen. In addition, factors supporting the aerobic pathways (myoglobin, capillaries, enzymes of the oxygen pathways) are increased. Resting muscle glycogen levels are usually elevated (if the diet is appropriate) and the use of fat as a fuel source is also improved.

Enzymes of glycolysis itself probably don't change, but the muscle's ability to tolerate lactic acid is improved because the trained muscle is better at buffering ("neutralizing") the acidity that comes with lactic acid production (Sahlin, 1984). This is in contrast to training solely by submaximal continuous exercise (jogging laps) where the aerobic system improves, but the adaptations to the phosphagens and buffer capacity are negligible. It may well be that one of the most important aspects of interval training with work-relief is the improvement in buffer capacity. A player probably does not get much pure rest-relief during a game.

APPLYING INTERVAL TRAINING TECHNIQUES TO SOCCER

It is obvious that soccer is an intermittent game. In many ways, it is hard not to use interval training methods for soccer. Training is designed to improve a player's capacity so that sufficient reserves are available for use during a game. Some might interpret this to mean one 11 "plays their way into shape". However, when an opponent with greater fitness than yours is encountered, then your team is lacking the reserves to adequately compete.

Playing into shape only works if training equals the demands of the hardest game. The physical demands of the game need to be exceeded by the training. This can be done by increasing the intensity of the work interval, decreasing the relief interval, increasing the volume of work or various combinations.

Increasing the intensity of the work interval is done by applying some kind of pressure to the performance of the task. That can be related to time (cover more distance in X seconds, have more touches in X seconds) or opponent (add an opponent who works passively through maximally). Volume increase is simply doing more. Instead of doing three sets of five repetitions of some 1 v. 1 drill, gradually add repetitions and sets. Volume can also be increased by playing small-sided games in a larger area like controlled 7 v. 7 on a full field. Reduction of the relief interval can be a time constraint (reduction of the time between repetitions of that 1 v. 1 drill) or a reduction in the number of players during small group activities. This increases ball contacts (high intensity work) and reduces time between ball contacts (relief interval).

These types of manipulations require some creative organization of the practice in terms of personnel, equipment, and field use. In order to adequately satisfy the interval training criteria, you need to realize that you, as the coach, may not see everything done by every player. I saw a neat agility drill by an American football team. The offensive line coach faced a lineman, about five yards apart. He tossed a softball to the right or left of the player who sidestepped to it and tossed it right back. They went back and forth across the field. Then the next lineman stepped in. There were 11 linemen. Who got the best workout? The coach, of course.

When I took the USSF coaching course a 1 v. 1 in the penalty area was taught. As soon as a shot was taken another ball was tossed in—the first player to the ball became the attacker. One minute or more of this is quite demanding. But consider—two penalty areas and four players could leave 16 players standing during an extended relief interval. At best this would be a 1:4-5 ratio; not good enough. Don't just think about the demands of the work, but also about the relief interval. The coaching schools teach numerous activities, which, properly used, will satisfy the interval training criteria and adequately prepare players for the game.

CONCLUSION

One final word. Coaches are all continually manipulating practices to satisfy all corners of the fitness-technique-tactics triad. Emphasis is based on the needs of the team. Players with minimal skill and youth players (I define youth as under 10-12 years of age) probably need more emphasis on skill and less emphasis on fitness. Frequently, rules and numbers of players limit playing time, so training need not be so physically demanding that the players become so fatigued that their skills decline. Players who can run all day are of minimal impact if they cannot control the first touch.

P.S. I never liked X:Y:Z questions as a student because I had to reason during the test. But, as a teacher, I loved them for exactly the same reason.

REFERENCES

Fox, E.L. and D.K. Matthews, *Internal Training: Conditioning for Sports and General Fitness*, 1974, W.B. Saunders Co., Philadelphia, PA.

Fox, E.L. and D.K. Matthews, *Physiological Basis of Physical Education and Athletics*, 1981, W.B. Saunders Co., Philadelphia, PA.

Hultman, E., J. Bergstrom, N.A. McLennan, "Breakdown and Resynthesis of Phosphorylcreatine and Adenosine Triphosphate in Connection with Muscular Work in Man", Scand J Clin Invest 19:56-66, 1967.

Jacobs, I., P.A. Tesch, O. Bar-Or, et al, "Lactate in Human Skeletal Muscle After 10 and 30s of Supramaximal Exercise". J Appl Physiol 55:365-367, 1983.

Sahlin, K., J. Henriksson, "Buffer Capacity and Lactate Accumulation in Skeletal Muscle of Trained and Untrained Man". Acta Physiol Scand 122:331-339, 1984.

THE WARM-UP: GAME-RELATED
Dr. Chris Malone

After coaching soccer for several years, I became quite bored with the "traditional" warm-up performed by my soccer teams. Therefore, I began to watch other teams' warm-ups. Surprisingly, most teams' warm-ups were very similar to my team's warm-up. In fact, there was very little variation from one team to the next.

Most teams began their warm-up by getting into some formation and stretching - usually in the center circle. Next, they would do some light jogging which slowly built up to sprinting across the field. Finally, after passing and juggling the ball with two or more players, the warm-up ended with a shooting drill.

While the "traditional" warm-up may have some merit, the warm-up described in this article is more appropriate because all aspects are game-related (fitness, stretching, technique, and tactics). With the short practice time available in most coaching situations, practice time must be used wisely. Therefore, it makes sense that all aspects of practice be instructive and directed toward the overall game of soccer. I have found that by using the following warm-up at practice sessions as well as for pre-game, soccer players are better prepared physically and mentally to meet the demands of the games.

A warm-up should include the following aspects:
• Be game-related (tactically);
• Include stretching and flexibility;
• Demand fitness;
• Work on technique.

THE WARM-UP

Divide your players into groups of seven (five is an appropriate number also, but it is essential that there be an odd number - seven seems to work best). Assign each player a number from one to seven. This warm-up should take place in a confined or restricted space until the players understand how the warm-up is conducted, then any area of the field can be utilized. A grid, 20 x 20 yards is an excellent space for learning this warm-up. Using cones or any appropriate marking will work successfully if you cannot line a grid on your practice or game area.

The first part of this warm-up consists of players progressively passing the ball. The progression is numerical: player #1 passes to player #2, who passes to player #3, who passes to player #4, to #5, to #6, to #7, to #1, and continue. The player passing the ball should dribble to the outside of the restricted space while at the same time, the player who will receive the pass should run to the opposite side of the restricted space.

Both players turn back into the restricted space and approach each other in a direct line, the player with the ball passes (10 yards or longer) to the supporting player who asks for the ball by using such words as "yes" or "support", non-verbal signs, or whatever is appropriate for your team. At the same time, those players not directly involved at the moment should be running in any direction on the perimeter of the restricted space, thus allowing the two players involved

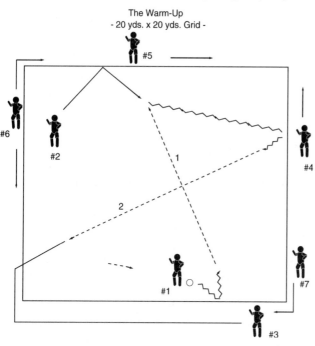

The Warm-Up
- 20 yds. x 20 yds. Grid -

Diagram 8-31

maximum use of the space within the restricted area. (Diagram 8-31)

This part of the warm-up is easily learned by the players and is the basis for all other variations of the drill.

As the coach, you must be sure that all players are correctly performing the soccer techniques and tactics demanded by the warm-up. For example, are the players using the correct technique in passing and collecting the ball? In other words, if your game philosophy is built around short passes on the ground, then the techniques for short passing and collecting should be stressed. Also, what type of runs are being made by the players receiving the ball? Are the runs direct, away from the ball, or some other type of run? Furthermore, are the players who are making the runs to receive the ball communicating to the players passing the ball? Some problems that you may notice when you first implement this drill are:

• Passes are too short, not accurate, or the wrong pace;
• Lack of communication - players are not demanding the ball;
• Players not involved in passing or receiving are not running on the perimeter;
• Poor technique (passing, dribbling, collecting, etc.);
• Poor tactics (timing runs to the ball, etc.);
• Failure to maintain possession of the ball or hold the ball long enough to make the drill occur in a game-related manner. Players must learn to be patient with the ball and allow the tactics to develop.

There are many variations of the initial warm-up drill that can be used by coaches. One variation might include asking players who receive the ball to turn

180 degrees and quickly dribble away (or other types of turns). Another variation might be playing "one-touch".

One of my favorites is practicing dummy runs to the ball by either shielding or allowing the ball to roll between your legs. A more difficult variation would be to use two balls in the same drill (#1 and #4 begin the numerical progression). These variations bring important parts of the real game into the warm-up and can be challenging and fun for the players. Most importantly, these variations allow players to be creative and develop "vision" (reading the game). Creativity and "vision" are weaknesses of too many players. This warm-up will allow coaches to develop creativity and vision in a way that is related to the players' learning ability.

It should be remembered, that you should consider the level of ability among the players you coach before implementing some of the different variations of the warm-up. Certainly, players with all levels of ability can benefit from several aspects of this warm-up, but some cannot be performed by players who do not have the necessary technique and ability to read the game (vision). However, be encouraged to teach the proper techniques during other practice time and develop drills to widen your players' vision.

STRETCHING AND FLEXIBILITY

As previously mentioned, this warm-up incorporates several aspects of the game of soccer into the drill. One of these aspects is stretching and flexibility. It has always been interesting to me that many athletic teams begin their warm-up by stretching cold muscles. Physiologically, it does not make sense to stretch cold muscles.

Furthermore, it is a waste of practice time to use 10 or 20 minutes for stretching. By using the warm-up described in this article, you can incorporate stretching and flexibility exercises into the drill. After the players have passed the ball progressively for several minutes, stop them and ask them to stretch whatever muscles you would like stretched. Once several muscles have been stretched, continue the warm-up. Stop the drill when appropriate and stretch a different set of muscles (and so on). By using this type of stretching format, you are physiologically stretching muscles that are warm and not cold, thereby getting a better stretch and building flexibility. Most importantly, you have been using your practice time wisely, in a way that is game-related.

In regards to fitness, this warm-up can be shaped to meet almost any of the game's demands. If the drill continues over a period of time (20 minutes or longer), you have gained endurance training due to the fact that all players have been running (jogging) for that period of time. You can add strength and flexibility training by having players perform certain exercises after passing the ball, such as five push-ups, sit-ups, squats, forward rolls, hopping, sprinting, etc. Coaches' imaginations are the only limitations in this warm-up!

Tactically speaking, when your team is capable of performing the game-related variations mentioned in this article, your team will have a greater chance of performing the same tactics in a game situation. Coaches who implement similar drills in practice that reinforce the combination plays used in the warm-up, may find that their team will begin to play a different style of soccer.

An added extra that comes from using this type of warm-up is the development of leadership and communication skills among players. Once your team has learned to do this warm-up, it makes sense that a player (captain of the group) in each group of seven should be assigned to determine which variation of the drill to use, when to stop and stretch, switch to a different sequence, and continue with other variations. This type of organization allows coaches the freedom to move from group to group and correct technique and tactical mistakes. Players all gain experience in communicating with each other, because the warm-up demands it, and this can only benefit your players in the game situation.

VARIATIONS OF THE WARM-UP

As your players learn and completely understand how to perform the initial sequence of this warm-up, you can move on to incorporate the following game-related tactics, including:

• Takeovers;
• Overlaps;
• Wall-pass;
• Double wall-pass;
• Short-short-long rhythm of passing or other tempos;
• Add goalkeepers.

Remember, each of these variations have different levels of difficulty and demand different technical skills and ability to read the game. As the coach, you must select the variations that are appropriate for your players.

1. **Take-overs.** Take-overs are one of soccer's most beautiful moments, and are a very effective tactical sequence in any match in any part of the field. A take-over is a crossing run made by two players. The player with the ball dribbles toward the player without the ball who takes-over the ball from the player with initial ball possession. (Diagram 8-32) You can implement take-overs into your warm-up by asking players to do take-overs instead of interchanging passes. Originally, two players were involved inside the restricted area, passing and receiving the ball. Now, the two players involved in the restricted space approach each other and complete a take-over. The other players continue to run in

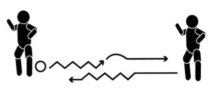

Diagram 8-32

any direction they choose on the perimeter of the restricted area waiting for their turn in the take-over sequence. The progression remains the same (1-2-3-4-5-6-7-1 ...).

The coaching points to be emphasized in regards to take-overs are proper technique and clear communication between players. The player dribbling the ball must "show" the oncoming player which side the take-over should occur. Since there are no defenders involved in this drill, the player with the ball should pretend that he is shielding the ball from the defender. Consequently he will have the ball on the opposite side from the imaginary defender for the oncoming player. The oncoming player communicates to the dribbling player to "leave" the ball. The dribbling player leaves the ball for the oncoming player. It is essential that this player does not pass the ball into the feet of the on-coming player. The proper technique is to bring his foot over the ball, leave it, and explode away. This technique will help freeze the defender for a brief moment. The oncoming player collects the ball and quickly dribbles away.

2. **Overlaps.** Overlaps occur during a soccer match in many ways and in any area of the soccer field. They are most effective when a player behind another player who has possession of the ball, accelerates past that player and runs into a space beyond the player with the ball. In order to simulate an overlap in the warm-up drill, use the same progression as previously explained. Player #2 overlaps player #1 and receives the pass from player 1, and so on. (Diagram 8-33)

The points that should be emphasized by the coach in regards to the overlap are proper technique, communication between players and how and when to make tactical runs employing the overlap. The run made by the overlapping player should bend away from the passing player. This type of run will allow the overlapping player to remain onsides, as appropriate in a game situation, and will always allow for better exploiting of available space. The pass can be made to the feet of the overlapping player or into the space being exploited by the overlapping player whenever possible. Both types of passes are appropriate in a soccer match depending on the situation. Be sure that your players understand this difference and its importance. This will help upgrade your players' mental reading of the

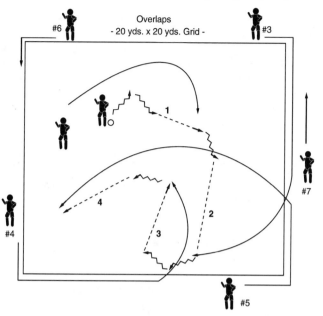

Overlaps
- 20 yds. x 20 yds. Grid -

Diagram 8-33

game.

3. **Wall-Passes.** The wall-pass is also known as the give-and-go and is an excellent way to beat defenders in tight spaces. In order to perform the wall-pass in this warm-up, each player must make six wall-passes and then perform a take-over. In other words, player #1 passes to player #2 who returns the pass to player #1 completing the first wall-pass. Then player #1 completes a wall-pass with players #3, #4, #5, #6 and #7. After completing six wall-passes, player #1 does a take-over with player #2 who then completes six wall-passes in progression and does a take-over with player #3. This progression continues until player #7 completes a take-over with player #1.

A coaching point that you may want to emphasize during this part of the warm-up is in regards to the supporting run and wall-pass completed by the player acting as the wall. This player's run should be directly to the ball and the return pass should be to the receiving player's feet, not into space where a defender could intercept.

Another coaching point to remember is that the player making the initial pass should concentrate on making the pass to either the right or left foot of the wall player and then making a bending run to the appropriate side. This process simulates what is most likely to be successful in the game situation. Just because there are no defenders involved in this drill, does not mean that players can be sloppy — they must simulate the game situation if they are to get maximum benefit from these warm-up conditions.

4. **Double Wall-Pass.** The double wall-pass is a sequence which rarely occurs in the game of soccer, but it is, without question, the most attractive combination play in the game. A double wall-pass occurs when two players initially perform a wall-pass and then the player who has received the wall-pass acts as a wall and returns a wall-pass to the original wall passer. (Diagram 8-34)

Unlike the wall-pass sequence which was previously explained, the double wall-pass progression is similar to take-overs and overlaps (1-2-3-4-5-6-7-1 ...). Coaching points to be emphasized in this part of the warm-up include proper wall-pass techniques and runs, as well as instructing the player who initially acted as the first wall to "spinaway" from his pass in order to receive the second wall-pass. In other words, the player acting as the first wall in a game situation may have a defender on his back and must "spin away" from his wall-pass around the backside of the defender. This type of run enables a player to stay on-sides as well as to exploit the space behind the defender in a way that is tactically effective.

With beginning players, this part of the warm-up may demand a larger restricted area. However, once players have learned how to complete a double wall-pass correctly, the sequence can be done in smaller spaces.

5. **Short-Short-Long.** The last tactical sequence to be explained in this article is the short-short-long pass drill.

This part of the warm-up represents the principle of tempo in soccer play. In this particular drill, there are two short passes completed and then one long pass to a player making a run into space. This type of progression demands four players reading the game simultaneously.

Diagram 8-34

Short-Short-Long
- 20 yds. x 20 yds. Grid -

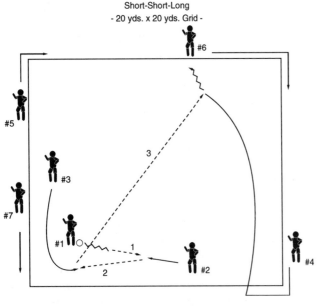

Diagram 8-35

For example, player #1 passes short to player #2, who passes short to player #3, who passes long to player #4 making a run into space, and then the progression continues, short-short-long. (Diagram 7-35) Without a doubt this variation is the most difficult, due to technical and tactical demands. Teams that can establish a rhythm to their style of play must have high level soccer players. Vision is of the utmost importance in developing a rhythmic tempo. This part of the warm-up will require additional space, depending upon the level of the players' ability.

6. **Goalkeepers.** Goalkeepers can be added to the warm-up. This addition provides players with the opportunity to practice the same tactical and combination plays with the chance to shoot. Again, a coach can instruct players to perform so many take-overs, wall-passes, overlaps, etc., and finish with a shot at the goalkeeper. This type of drill allows players to work on shooting technique and provides goalkeepers with a lot of work.

CONCLUSION

This article has described how to implement a warm-up session for your soccer team which is game-related.

The advantages of this type of warm-up are explained in regards to fitness, stretching and flexibility, technical and tactical training, and development of leadership and communication skills. Perhaps the greatest benefit your team will gain from incorporating this warm-up into their practice sessions and pre-game warm-ups is the improvement of their style of soccer. Through repetition of this warm-up in practice and implementation of similar drills that reinforce the warm-up's sequences, players may gain insight into

improving their tactical play (vision) and may become more creative in their combination play.

It is highly suggested that you implement only the variations of the warm-up that are appropriate for your players and that fit your game philosophy. Certainly, you are encouraged to improvise on the format described in this article. Remember, the only limitation to this warm-up is your imagination.

> *Author's Note: I want to express my thanks to Bob Scalise, Women's Soccer Coach at Harvard University, who in 1981 first exposed me to several ideas incorporated into this article. And, thank you to Carl-Heinz Heddergott who put my ideas all together at a clinic in 1983.*

⚽

BASIC OVERVIEW OF SPEED TRAINING
Bob Alejo

Without question, the number one hindrance to running fast in a non-track athlete is economy of movement. Track athletes run everyday and basically their technique is good. What separates them in competition are differences in strength, reaction time and strategy. However, for other athletes, running is not the only thing they have to do when they compete. They must also tackle, throw objects or kick objects. Running skills are secondary. Still, when economical running technique is learned, it will lead to economy which will result in a decrease of time over a distance.

Where does this process begin? Concentrating on running workouts consisting of hill training, intervals or distance work would be a waste of one's time. The first order of business is to choose a given distance, time the distance for speed and begin teaching the basics of running technique. The biggest flaw in the running technique of soccer athletes is in the effective use of their arms. Soccer athletes are lower body oriented and at times preoccupied with a ball, defender or both. It is during these times that there is little or no arm movement. It is also these skills that need the most attention.

Granted, working inside the 18 yard mark, turning a defender or marking tightly does not require great arm movement other than holding your position. Nevertheless, to get into great position on a run without the ball or getting back on defense quickly requires good speed where good technique is a must.

Other technical problems in running include poor body lean, a lack of stride length and other extraneous body movements which are not in the running plane (horizontal and directional).

Not only are the arms important to move straight ahead, but they should be the first active movement to change a direction. Aggressive turning of the arms in the chosen direction will initiate movement quicker and more efficiently. Once the importance and technique of arm carry is learned, it will also carry over in proper usage in changing direction.

Following are a few drills which can be used to help the soccer athlete become more economical in running.

Jog In Place

This light jog in place is to be done for 20-second work periods with a short rest period in between. Arm carry and tempo of arm movement is emphasized. The arm should be flexed at 90 degrees while hanging loosely at the sides. Hands should be open or loosely closed. While jogging in place the arm should move at the shoulder joint like a pendulum with the hand moving only slightly past the back "pocket" and not forward more than chest height. All this time the arm should remain flexed at 90 degrees. Critically evaluate all the athletes so that correct arm carry becomes natural. Repeat this drill 6-10 times.

100 Meter Jog

Incorporating arm carry and now taking into account body lean along with lower body movements, the 100M jog gives a low intensity look at running. Breaking light jogging into 100M segments allows the athlete short spans of concentration which are controlled by the coach, as well as the rest periods in between. Keep an eye out for arm carry, body lean (stiff, forward, backward, side-to-side) and fluidity. Repeating this drill 4-6 times adds up to about one mile of prescribed training. It is this kind of repetition and distance that will lay the foundation for speed.

Skip High Knees

This drill is only a modification of the kind of skipping most youngsters do. Hip flexor conditioning, body awareness and arm carry are introduced in this drill. The arms are flexed at 90 degrees as previously described with the right arm forward and left arm back. In this position the left knee is raised, but below belt level with the toe pointed upward. The right leg is straight and up on the toes. The straight leg will skip twice before it becomes the "up" leg. The coach should

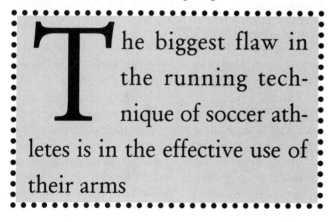

The biggest flaw in the running technique of soccer athletes is in the effective use of their arms

look for a relaxed upper body with a slight forward lean. The height of the knee should never be forced. High knees is a vertical movement and running is horizontal. During normal speed running the knee is lifted just high enough so the foot can come close to the buttocks and return to the ground. This should be kept in mind when evaluating this drill. To improve conditioning, this drill should start at 20M for 4-8 repetitions, progressing to 100M.

Walking Lunges

This drill will give us a chance to stretch and at the same time gain strength in the hamstrings and gluteals. Have the athlete step out as far as possible with three requirements: 1) the lower leg must be perpendicular to the ground; 2) the knee joint must be no greater than 90 degrees; 3) the upper body must be fairly upright, not bent over, to aid rising out of the lunge position. Earlier we talked about stride length being important in aquiring speed. This drill, as simple as it is, will stretch the stride out within the framework of good body position. Similar to the skip high knees, start with a short distance and progress up to 50M.

There are three types of running speeds you want to use during the teaching of speed improvements:

Strides

Technique: Exaggerated length of stride at 100 percent intensity, while maintaining framework of proper technique. Because the stride is longer, times will be higher.
Objective: To develop strength in hamstrings where speed is built. Also enables you to learn rhythm and tempo of the body at a submaximal speed.
This teaches the athlete not to abandon good running technique at full speed.

Accelerations

Technique: Divide a given distance into four segments, increasing speed until at top sprint speed for the final segment.
Objective: Proper progression before doing all-out sprint training.
It will ease the athlete into top speed technique. This also teaches the athlete change of speed on the run.

Sprints

Technique: All out sprint intensity, 100 percent effort.
Objective: To work the athlete at 100 percent effort over any distance, to maximize explosiveness. Usually not more than about 60M.

Generally speaking, these speeds graduate the training for the athlete so that he or she does not have to learn proper technique at 100 percent sprint intensity. As the speed quickens the distances begin to shorten, to bring out the quality of the run. Specifically working on running style would be a waste of time for the soccer athlete, so you should vary rest intervals, sets and repetitions to gain fitness at the same time. You can and should work both qualities at the same time. Strides, accelerations and sprints are no different than the previously mentioned drills. As a coach you should be constantly studying the athletes as they run and reinforcing or correcting any mechanics while they run. It is much better to coach during the run than to follow the run with praise or criticism. Some important points to remember while teaching speed:

1) When trying to teach all-out speed, make sure athletes get all the rest they can in between repetitions. It should be a non-fatigue state.

2) Because of the non-fatigue state, speed improvement should be done following the warm-up on practice days.

3) Be creative and work the ball into running drills so the speed can transfer into the game.

4) Interval training is a short effective way to teach technique and gain fitness.

5) Always pay attention to the arms in relationship to the speed of the run and length of the stride.

Player #4 of Central Florida's women's team has a lot at stake as she contemplates her injury. Coaches need to understand all of a soccer player's needs in these situations. (photo by Perry McIntyre, Jr.)

When an Athlete's World is Turned Upside Down
Dr. Alan Goldberg

A Player's Serious Injury Means Coping With Mental Pain, Too

You've been playing the game longer than you can remember. You've grown and so have your skills. You've worked your way into a starting position and you have been the one your team has been able to depend on to start that rally and shift the game's momentum.

Then the unthinkable happens! It's a crucial game late in the season and your team is in a must-win situation. The first half is a war on the pitch and ends in a scoreless tie. Late in the second half, your team slowly begins to dominate. You see a scoring opportunity developing if you can just win the ball.

You charge hard at it from one side as a defender simultaneously challenges you from the other side at full speed. You move the way you always do in those situations to control the ball and avoid full impact. But something goes dreadfully wrong. As you quickly try to change directions your ankle collapses, your right knee twists and you're temporarily knocked senseless by the collision.

When you come to your senses, every part of you hurts. But worse, your right knee and ankle have swelled to grotesque proportions. The trainer and team doctor are over you yelling for a stretcher and telling you to lie still. You want to get back in the game. As you try to stand, an electric bolt of pain shoots through your knee and ankle, bringing tears to your eyes. You suddenly realize that you're hurt, that you're out of the game, maybe even out for the rest of the season. Or maybe worse.

If you have ever had this kind of experience with injury as an athlete, then you know that the physical hurt is only one small part of the overall pain that you have to go through in the rehabilitation process. The psychological pain caused by your injury and the temporary or permanent loss of your sport hurts just as much as the physical pain.

Unless this psychological pain is directly addressed and "treated," your recovery will be slow and incomplete. Coaches who are sensitive to the issues of the injured athlete help speed up the recovery process and significantly lessen the mental pain suffered by the athlete. To better understand what happens psychologically when a soccer player is injured, it's important to examine the three major functions that sports play in an individual's life.

Sense of identity: If you are a serious athlete and have been playing the game long enough, you will soon come to see yourself in terms of the sport.

You are a soccer player. It's who you are and what you do. With your long term investment and commitment of time and energy over the years, soccer has become an integral part of you.

Just as Pele liked to feel the ball as an extension of his body, your sport has become an extension of your sense of self. In soccer this sense of identity further expands to include your position and role on the team.

Source of self-esteem: As a young tennis player growing up in a family with distant and uninvolved parents, tennis served as my sole source of self-esteem.

It was one of the only things that I did that brought me recognition. With each of my accomplishments, my ego was stroked by my friends, coaches, other players and the media. It was the one place in the world where I knew that I was OK. For most serious athletes, soccer provides this constant source of positive reinforcement and feedback. There is enjoyment and self-satisfaction in mastering new skills and overcoming ever more challenging obstacles. Further, the outside recognition of these accomplishments stokes the fires of self-esteem so they burn ever brighter. Having a great game feels fantastic and provides concrete evidence that your hard work is paying off and that you are "special."

A constructive way to cope with stress: There is absolutely no question that physical exercise helps you better handle stress of all kinds.

Individuals who have no physical outlets tend to internalize their stress. Since they have no way of getting it out of their bodies, it stays there and may emerge as stomach problems, headaches, etc. They may even turn to drugs, alcohol or some other addictive, self-destructive behavior to help them cope.

Many athletes discover that their involvement in sports is a constructive way to escape from the stress of a dysfunctional family or deprived environment. It offers them a safe way to channel their frustrations and aggression. Along these same lines, sports can provide an athlete with a vehicle to a better life. If you're good enough, your sport can get you a college scholarship and open up a door that might have been otherwise closed to you.

So what happens to all these psychological benefits when you're suddenly sidelined by injury? As the athlete struggles with the impact of many losses internally, all hell breaks loose.

If the injury is significant enough to knock you out of action for a lengthy period, the first thing that you lose is your identity as an athlete and team member. "Identity confusion" sets in. This means that you'll start to question who you are.

An Olympic gymnast permanently sidelined from her sport because of an injury put it quite clearly, "I've been doing gymnastics since I was six years old. It's all I know. If I'm not a gymnast then who am I?"

The individual's identity confusion is compounded by the fact that the injury has suddenly changed his or her identity on the team. You are no longer the leader, starter or clutch performer.

Hand in hand with this sense of identity confusion come other significant losses.

First, you lose your physical health and sense of invincibility. Many athletes are used to being dependent and relying upon their bodies to respond as trained and directed. With the injury, your body has somehow failed you. Injuries frequently make you dependent upon others such as doctors and trainers.

Second, you lose a major source of self-esteem. if you get your goodies from being on the field, you will get precious few from the sidelines. Suddenly you will have to struggle with questions of your own self-worth. If you are not toasting a defender, shutting your opponent down or scoring goals, then what value do you really have on the team?

COPING: WHAT YOU CAN DO AS A COACH

- Be empathic: Let your players know that you understand what they are feeling and having to go through. Understand where their anger, frustration and disappointment comes from and allow them time to mourn. Do not expect them to just "suck it up," "shake it off" and "be strong." Let them have their feelings without indulging them in self-pity.

- Work with their self-esteem: Understand that they have just suffered a major blow to their feelings of self-worth and therefore feeling quite vulnerable. Let them know in both your actions and words that you value them as a person, not just as an athlete.

- Give them a role on the team: Help them fight their feelings of worthlessness by giving them another role on the team. Assign them the role of "assistant coach," "scout" or "consultant."

- Do not allow the athlete to isolate themselves from the team: Insist on the athlete continuing to function as an important member/part of the team. Assign other players on the squad to monitor the player's involvement and to intervene whenever the athlete begins to isolate himself or herself.

- Let your athlete know that you care: Increase contact and communication with injured athletes. Call them if they are unable to show up at practice. If they are recovering from surgery, visit them in the hospital. A little of your time at this point will dramatically help ease the pain that the player feels.

- When appropriate, expect the athlete to "practice": Whether limited physical or purely mental, let your injured athlete know that you expect him/her to continue the training, however limited.

- Help them get in touch with other areas of personal strengths: Help injured athletes understand that excelling in sports demands a tremendous amount of success skills that they can transfer to other areas of life.

- If the athlete's depression does not lift or if there are warning signs, immediately refer him/her to a professional: If the athlete is seriously depressed refer the player for professional counseling.

COPING: WHAT YOU CAN DO AS AN ATHLETE

- Be sad: Allow yourself to mourn and feel whatever loss your are experiencing. Being "macho," "strong," "brave" by burying or hiding the feelings in this situation is not only a waste of energy, but will interfere with you effectively coping and recovering.

- Deal with "what is": Injured athletes have a tendency to focus on the "coulda beens," "shoulda beens," if only they hadn't been hurt. The fact of the matter is no amount of wishing will change the reality of the situation. Allow yourself to deal with where you are now.

- Set new, more realistic goals for yourself: As you begin the recovery process you may have to begin to measure success very differently than ever before, perhaps in millimeters instead of meters. It may mean that you have to relearn many things you've already mastered. Keep focused on your new goals and leave the old ones in the past for now, or at least until you have made a full recovery.

- Maintain a positive attitude no matter what: As difficult as this will be, try to stay as positive as possible. Understand that all healing is self-induced. Your attitude and outlook can speed your healing or retard it. It's up to you.

- Take an active part in your healing: Be conscientious about your physical therapy. Follow the doctor's advice closely. In addition, practice using healing imagery on a daily basis. It you're recovering from a broken bone, spend five to ten minutes imagining that bone beginning to fuse. See a healthy supply of red blood cells surrounding that area and facilitating the mending process.

  I can't scientifically guarantee that this will speed up your healing. However, I can promise you that will make you feel less helpless, more in control and more positive. These attitudinal changes in themselves will speed your healing.

- Continue to "practice" and "work out": If your injury allows you to continue any part of your training, do so. If not, "practice" mentally. Use mental rehearsal on a daily basis (five to ten minutes at a time) to see, hear and feel yourself practicing and performing your skills. You might even want to show up for regular practice and mentally rehearse while the team actually works out.

- Seek out the support of your teammates: Participate in team functions. Fight the urge to isolate yourself. You may feel worthless and suddenly different, but chances are good that you're probably the only one on the team who shares that opinion.

- Think about how to use your sports learning and experience in other areas of your life: If your injury forces you into permanent retirement you may feel that you have little or no skills or expertise that you can transfer from your sport to other endeavors. Nothing could be further from the truth. To excel in your sport you have to have dedication, commitment, persistence, motivation and the ability to manage time.

- If necessary, see a counselor: Seek professional help if you are depressed for an extended period of time. Other indicators of problems are loss of interest in favorite pastimes, a change in sleep and/or eating habits and even suicidal thoughts.

- Be patient: If your injury is temporary, allow yourself enough time to heal properly. If you're overanxious to get back out there and rush the healing process you may set yourself up for another injury which may cost you even more time. Sometimes the fastest way of coming back is the slowest.

For many athletes this is probably the hardest part of an injury. It's a huge blow to the ego. Suddenly less talented athletes are taking your place and doing what you should be doing but can no longer do.

The other significant feeling that accompanies these losses is a sense of alienation and isolation. Robbed of the limelight, unable to fulfill your old role on the team, it's common to struggle with feelings that now you are suddenly different or no longer fit in.

In H.G. Bissinger's *Friday Night Lights*, the author spends a year with the Odessa (Texas) Permian High School football team chronicling one of the most successful high school programs in the country. Bissinger singles out Booby Miles, the team's star running back. Suddenly sidelined by a career-ending injury, Miles is virtually forgotten on the bench. With his injury, his stock on the team and in the community plummets to zero. The media, coaches and fellow teammates contribute to his sense of isolation and alienation.

Third, there is the athlete's inability to constructively cope with stress. If being athletic is a way of taming chronic low self-esteem or managing psychic stress, an injury robs that athlete of this coping mechanism.

Consequently, as an athlete, you are in an even more vulnerable position and further susceptible to stress and depression.

For example, a distance runner was sidelined for four months for the very first time in his career because of broken ribs. After he was finally given the doctor's go-ahead to resume training, he was distressed to find that he was continually plagued by shortness of breath and anxiety. Despite the fact that the doctors had ruled out any medical reasons for his breathing problems, he continued to suffer.

After meeting with him I learned he had grown up in a very abusive home and from the time that he could remember, he dealt with his problems by literally running away from them. When his best and only way of psychologically coping had been temporarily taken away by the rib injury, a lot of problems he'd been avoiding caught up to him.

They were so anxiety provoking that they "took his breath away" and forced him to finally deal with them head-on.

So what does all this mean to you as an athlete or coach? If you want to speed up the rehab process you need to expect certain feelings and behaviors to emerge as a result of the injury. These feelings and behaviors are normal and a natural part of successfully coping.

As with any kind of loss, the athlete may go through a number of stages directly related to mourning. Some sport psychologists feel that these stages parallel Elisabeth Kubler-Ross's stages in her discussion of death and dying—denial, anger, bargaining, depression and acceptance.

Many athletes first meet their injury with outright denial. They may downplay or ignore the seriousness of the injury falsely believing that everything is OK.

The injury is often accompanied by intense anger. The athlete may adopt a "why me?" attitude and act hostile and resentful to coaches, teammates and friends.

Some athletes then get into bargaining with themselves in order to get back on the field quicker.

At some point in the process, depression finally sets in as the athlete comes to directly realize the nature of his/her injury. The depression may entail a loss of interest in or withdrawal from once-favored activities.

There may also be sleep and eating disturbances and possibly even suicidal thoughts and feelings. At the end of this process of loss, the athlete comes to an acceptance of the situation and makes the best of it.

Athletic injury, whether temporary or permanent, is and always will be a disruptive and painful interruption in an athlete's life. If you follow some of the guidelines put forth in this article you can speed up the rehab process and lessen the psychological pain that normally accompanies most athletic injuries. Keep in mind that the rehab process is usually very slow and painful.

When an athlete first gets back out on the field he or she is preoccupied with worries about reinjury. It's pretty normal to also find yourself mentally replaying the injury over and over. This focus on reinjury will distract the player from the task at hand and leave one physically tight.

In this condition you are actually more vulnerable to reinjury. Instead work on seeing what you want to have happen. Focus on what you need to do to perform well. This is easier said than done in the beginning because you'll probably be "gun shy."

Discipline yourself to maintain a focus on your performance, staying mentally in the "here and now."

Sports Psychology

· ·

Introduction
Dr. Mel Lorback

The contributions in this section reflect the diversity of theory and approaches so typical of the study of human behavior. They have been selected for several or all of the following reasons: presentation of basic concepts; treatment of specific problems, practicality of application, variety of issues and lastly, timeliness. While there is some chronology in the order of presentation, the more important guide was progression from general to specific. Therefore the articles range from psychological foundations and different theoretical applications to motivation, morale, stress, relaxation, mental imagery and perception.

Editors Note:

The school of thought in behavior analysis that seems to have dominated in recent years is "humanistic" psychology instead of the traditional behaviorism that has always been the bedrock of coaching. This rationale evolved from the existentialist philosophy of the late 60s and early 70s and considered the personality fragile and delicate and therefore needed to be handled with extreme care. It also produced the egocentric "I" and "Me" attitudes that have been so troublesome in all aspects of human interaction, especially sport.

Actually there is little or not scientific foundation for this approach and much of it is a prime example of pop psychology. The rise of the term "humanistic" is another example of the frequent appropriation of terms that seem invulnerable to objection or criticism. They are more a product of liberal political idealogy than scientific analysis of behavior, especially motivation. One of the consistent weaknesses in behavioral science is its gullibility to pressuring societal trends.

It is required of the performing athlete that he develop a psychological fitness or mental toughness in order to achieve success. The insistence from the "humanistic" school that we be ever vigilant to athletes' self-esteem and sensitivities is nonsense. The athlete must learn to take psychological as well as physical knocks and to inure themselves against stress.

In the final analysis, their leadership role requires coaches to be practicing applied psychologists. The accumulation of experience filtered through a decent intelligence results in their developing good judgement based on common sense. Sports psychology itself may provide principles and guides to action by the coach.

⚽

COACHING PSYCHOLOGY: A LOOK AT SPORTS PSYCHOLOGY
Mel Lorback

Sports psychology evolved, in the academic sense, as a sub-area of psychology about twenty-five years ago. It was about that time that the wave of existentialist philosophy with its emphasis on seeking the essence and meaning of existence brought challenges to established mores, values, and social institutions. From this developed the "humanistic" psychological interpretation of human behavior with its emphasis on the individual and "self." These circumstances had a dramatic effect on sports. Prior to this, sports organization, standards, and discipline had been congruent with the more hierarchal and authoritarian structure of society in general. The rapid and dramatic changes in the social matrix, especially among the young, put the expectancies of sports organizations, which had heretofore been considered a microcosm of society, into direct conflict with it. Hence the emergence of the "problem athlete".

People, including athletes, were nurtured in a milieu in which they developed attitudes which led to expectancies that standards and conditions should be adjusted to them rather than their being required to adapt. This situation, as those of us old enough so well remember, created some chaotic and disturbing conditions.

Up to that time coaches were generally considered the best applied psychologists, an impression that probably still exists. However many of them (especially those from the "old school") were perplexed and frustrated. Sport had almost always required the individual to conform to the standards and demands of the group. The reversal of this process, as interpreted by some athletes, created resentment and hostility. More athletes quit, and more coaches retired, resigned, or were fired than during any other time in our sport history.

The proponents of humanistic psychology brought a good deal of pressure on sport with accusations of barbarism, fascism, exploitation, and harsh, impersonal treatment. Competition as part of human endeavor was challenged. There were strong racial implications. Although this was all part of a general social neurosis, sport, because of its glamour and drama, was a favorite target. The proponents of the humanistic school insisted that it was the coaches' responsibility to guide, counsel, and adjust to the player—that tolerance should be the basic tool in attempting to "relate". There was a very penetrating introduction of social and psychological jargon that attempted to change fundamental relationships; to intimidate those who set standards into becoming super tolerant and flexible. Since excuses expand to fit the tolerance allowed them, these conditions only aggravated an already very unsound and unstable situation.

The radical left abused sport in every way possible including attacks on systems, structure, players, and coaches. They considered sport vulnerable because it was not democratic or egalitarian as indeed it is not. No system based on merit is. In isolated instances this intimidation caused upheaval. But for the most part the structure and systems remained intact. There were some attempts to be trendy and chic (primarily in California, where else?) by having the players involved in decisions such as those concerning systems of play, the rosters and lineups, and other options, for which they had no qualifications for making judgements. These experiments were, of course, destined to fail—and did. In all, theoretical left had very little impact.

However the general philosophical upheaval did. There was a lowering of standards, loss of discipline and much greater permissiveness. Coaches world-wide complained of personnel management problems. National team coaches of World Cup finalists, including the rigid, authoritarian, hierarchal Eastern Block countries and Russia complained of player attitude problems. They consistently ranked "lack of discipline" and "personal responsibility' as the most difficult and perplexing problem they faced. Throughout the world, and certainly we saw it in this country, there were players who exhibited prima donna, "spoiled-brat" behavior. There were defections and dislocations at all levels of sport. Players' egos, their concentration and dedication to narrow and selfish personal interests came into conflict with the very nature of sport which requires integration and cooperation. Conflict between players and their coaches and/or their organization gained international attention. Hence the genesis and development of the study of the "problem athlete".

The two prime movers in this area were Drs. Bruce Ogilive and Tom Tutko and San Jose State University in California. They have contributed the definitive work in identifying the characteristics and personality traits of "risk-takers" and successful athletes. There is no work in Sports Psychology that I would recommend more highly (much of the material

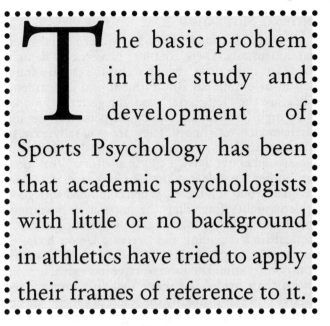

The basic problem in the study and development of Sports Psychology has been that academic psychologists with little or no background in athletics have tried to apply their frames of reference to it.

Dr.Ogilive furnished me is in unpublished monograph form; his Athletic Motivation Inventory, however was published. Dr.Tutko has published several books).

The basic problem in the study and development of Sports Psychology has been that academic psychologists with little or no background in athletics have tried to apply their frames of reference to it. This lack of experience, of "having been there", has left a gap interpretation of behavior under the severe demands of sport. It is difficult enough to analyze, interpret, and make recommendations concerning human behavior. But the complexity, number of variables, and unique stresses of sport make it even more difficult to transpose theoretical psychological constructs appropriate for normal human beings to special people like athletes. Coaches often gain the impression that psychologists expose naive and unrealistic concepts in an idiomatic jargon that reveals their lack of actual experience. This reaction reflects a principle with which psychologists themselves are familiar; that insight comes from actual experience and develops the empathy which is the basis of sound judgement. For example, psychologists have advised and taught that the coach must "handle" the athlete through counseling, persuasion, and tolerance, which is, of course, their method with the general population. This approach is more often not effective, except in the early stages of learning with athletes because they must learn to adapt and adjust to the many variables and stresses of sports performance. No coach can adjust to all of the individuals on the team. They must adjust to him, his discipline and organizational standards. This is not only a matter of common sense and practical efficiency but may very well be the most valuable lesson that the athlete learns.

Certainly people should have to operate in an environment in which they are not coddled and babied

because such treatment seriously impedes mature personality development and the mental toughness so critical in successful sports performance. The tolerant therapeutic approach is only effective in special circumstances and even then is only a stopgap measure. Permissiveness delays the onset of dealing with the reality of having to meet standards. What we need are more people with extensive athletic experience with training in psychology who will then be more definitively trained as sports psychologist!

MOTIVATION: ASPECTS OF THE PROBLEM
Mel Lorback

I have developed definite impressions, from my experience in teaching sports psychology to graduate students, to United States Soccer Federation National Coaching School candidates, and in coaching clinics, concerning the areas that the majority of the students consider to be of most interest and value. These are: motivation, discipline (including behavioral problems—handling the problem athlete, etc.), leadership, and teaching dynamics and coaching methods. Space does not permit the discussion of all these areas in this issue but hopefully we will be able to offer contributions in future editions.

The first question in the survey on sports psychology sent to some of the membership was:"What does motivation mean to you and how do you motivate your players?"

This, of course could be a very broad question but in space allotted I responded as follows: Stimulation to act; physical and psychic energy; drive and desire to succeed and accomplish goals. It is reflected in work, discipline, enthusiasm, aspiration and achievement, psychological perserverence and mental toughness. I try to motivate my players through emotional stimulation in portraying the rewards of winning such as the euphoria and feeling of well-being, the status and respect that goes with successful accomplishment, and the negative aspects and fear of failure. This is done in an atmosphere of discipline and demand for explicit standards of conduct and performance.

A BEHAVIORAL PHENOMENA

Motivation is an elusive and intriguing behavioral phenomena. Attempts to understand and manipulate this form of human behavior has generated more interest, speculation and frustration than any other dimension in psychology. It is of special interest to those involved in action and performance because it is so critical to achievement, In sport especially, its value is dramatically exposed. And while it commands almost universal respect in progressive societies, and indeed is probably the most essential and definitive characteristic of them, we simply do not have reliable way of developing it.

Motivation is observed and recognized far more than it is understood. Structures and tests to measure and evaluate it are not very reliable. Variability, of course, is the problem. It is manifested by energy and drive toward accomplishing a goal. It requires transposing aspiration into achievement through action and will. It varies, from time to time within an individual and certainly between people. This lack of consistency probably causes more frustration, concern, disappointment, resentment, hostility, and dislocation than any other aspect of sport. It is so often the most apparent factor between good, mediocre, and bad performance, winning and losing, and ultimately the feelings that emerge from these contrasting situations.

The nature of such stimulation is not well understood. Its manifestation in energy, drive, and accomplishment is usually apparent and not hard to recognize. The key question is "how is it produced?" And that, as we all well know, is a very perplexing one. It does not defy description. Indeed, untrained and uninvolved laymen recognize and evaluate it (i.e. fans and spectators). Reams of literature and millions of words are devoted to it, and have been throughout history. It is the most common and romanticized characteristic in heroic behavior, fundamental to leadership and influence, and critical in success and accomplishment. There are few traits that are more admired. It seems to have a mystique of its own.

The lack of objective, valid, and reliable analytical structures for evaluating it have for the most part left us with subjective and intuitive impressions. Editor Schum's effort to collect some of these from the accumulated experience of coaches within our sport is not only commendable but one of the few ways we have for gaining insight into why players behave as they do. It is a fundamental form of empiricism that is often our only avenue for investigation. Definition and delineation are often impossible because of the great number of variables in the complex problem. However, this lack of objectivity and consistency, and consequently, reliance on insight and intuition evolving from experience, produces disagreement. Nevertheless, I do not believe these factors leave us as weak in judgement as we may think.

In my opinion (as a result of my exposure and experience as a student, teacher, and often frustrated practitioner of psychology, especially as applied to sport) there are some principles that can be stated with relative confidence. Although some may not agree with the structure, order, or relationship with which they are presented, it simply represents my attempt to organize and clarify.

INTERNAL MOTIVATION

First, motivation seems to have internal and external dimensions. There are those players that demonstrate an "inner drive" which seems to rest on a foundation of emotional commitment and investment. They are the "self-starter" and "up-getter", the ones with high levels of psychological perseverance and often mental toughness. They are generally easy to coach because their psychic energy translates into consistent and above average physical effort. Work does not bother them. It may not be a high level in technical quality but "it is there". When combined with good athletic ability (including the imperative quickness, speed, and agility), fitness, technical development, and tactical understanding and execution, you have, of course, the magic potion. I am convinced that this consistently stimulated and reactive individual is more "born than made". I believe that this internalized motive power is primarily the result of genetic impact on the neurological system. Energy is often manifested in determination and will. Talent, both intellectual and physical, unfortunately, is too often not accompanied by this drive.

Although I believe genetic influences have been seriously underestimated by our environmentally biased social and behavioral scientists and the population in general, there are those who put forth strong arguments supporting the mental aspects as being the critical factor in performance. They point to direct evidence in the form of such athletes as Julius Erving and Bruce Jenner who, according to their own testimony say they were not naturally endowed, but achieved through intense aspiration, dedication, and long hours of hard work. These athletes and others, seem to credit mental toughness and psychological perseverance for their success. At any rate the argument, in the practical sense is academic, because we certainly cannot alter the genetic contribution. The mental aspects are the only factors that we can attempt to manipulate.

EXTERNAL MOTIVATION

External motivation is the product of environmental influences, such as the coach, peer pressure and acceptance, parental approval, community status, crowd stimulation and the like. Fun and enjoyment, role taking and modeling, personal satisfaction, the drive furnished from aspiration to achieve, are internalized. They are more powerful and dependable, but seem to be quite specific to the individual in contrast to the more generalized external influences. There are several theories of motivation, the most common of which seem to be:*

THEORIES OF MOTIVATION

Instinct and Reason. This is the consideration of behavior which is innate and not a product of experience. It is produced without conscious knowledge rather than conscious choice selected through reflection and rational analysis. Most proponents of this dichotomy believe both play a significant role and the distinction between them is not as firm as we once thought.

Imprinting. This is acquired or learned behavior. It is a result of imprints that have been formed by a process of filtering stimulus and experience through perceptual screening. Because they have been selected they are usually self-reinforcing.

Drive and Stimulus. This is a commonly held concept. Motive power or psychic energy continues in the direction in which it is rewarded. The goal may be stimulus reduction and/or reinforcement of the stimulus. Drives are separated into primary (innate) and secondary (learned and acquired).

Reward and Punishment. This is by far the best known and underlies most behavioristic approaches. It is the basis of associative conditioning (stimulus-response) psychology and the only scientifically verifiable method of behavior control and prediction. No other approach comes close to its efficiency or reliability in behavior modification, especially in physical performance.

Conflict, Dissonance and Displacement. A theory that says a person faced with two irreconcilable choices (i.e., whether to fight or flee) is in a conflict situation. This most often produces dissonance (dislocation or lack of internal harmony) which in turn often results in displacement (substitute activity), i.e., the batter does not know whether the pitch looks good enough to swing at, takes a called third strike, is angry and pounds the bat into the ground.

Pain, Fear and Anxiety. Those who hue to this line believe the primary drives are the most efficient motivators and indeed a good deal of evidence from laboratory experiments supports this contention. Used as techniques in reward/punishment they seem to be the most effective in conditioning responses through association.

Curiosity, Exploration, and Games. This theory holds that after primary drives are satisfied, which is easily accomplished in our society, then these activities and risk-taking are attractive and motivating.

Metamotivation. These are acts well beyond the norm — a super-motivation that Abraham Maslow considered to be the top level in the hierarchy of needs to self-actualization. This theory, not very reliable, says that as one level of need is fulfilled the individual naturally goes upward to fulfill the next level. The process demonstrates increasingly greater motivation to a point where some of the behavior may appear to be compulsive and obsessive.

These are very brief resumes of the most popular theories of motivation. Some of them are sometimes given different names. However they probably all contribute some valid knowledge to our understanding of motivation.

PRINCIPLES OF MOTIVATION

I think we can state the following with assurance that they are viable principles:

• Genetics probably plays a greater role in behavior, especially motivation, than is generally acknowledged;

• That mental stability is the ability to cope with reality. This in turn produces stimulation rather than depression;

• Both internal and external motivation are required for success. Success is the best motivator. Even though winning is the athletic equivalent of success, just satisfaction with personal performances can be very positively stimulating;

• Mental fitness, including mental toughness and psychological perseverance is developed, as is physical fitness, through overload. Therefore we should inure our athletes to stress through a system of gradually increasing pressure which produces adaptation and adjustment.

*   *We are indebted to a very nice monograph entitled "On Motivation" by Don Fabun, Director of Publications, Kaiser Aluminum and Chemical Corporation, published by Glencoe Press (A division of MacMillan Company), Beverly Hills, California.*

PSYCHOLOGY OF SOCCER: ANOTHER HAT FOR SOCCER COACHES TO WEAR!
Dr. Simon Davies, Ph.D.

Soccer coaches may frequently feel that they are losing their minds, and believe their players are lacking one! In examining the components of soccer performance, we should all be familiar with the four step pyramid: 1) attitude and psychology; 2) fitness; 3) technique and skill, and 4) tactical ability. Steps 2 through 4, although continually refined through innovative developments and interpretations, are based upon an established knowledge base, which is disseminated to coaches with varying degrees of efficiency. The psychological component of performance, while frequently alluded to, is both unused and abused. Good soccer coaches have to wear a number of hats; the soccer psychology hat often fits with the least degree of comfort! What does the progressive coach need to know about the psychological components of performance? Why should a coach be overly concerned with the psychological dimensions? How can a coach develop the necessary skills? What are the most important components of soccer psychology?

PSYCHOLOGICAL EDGE

Whether one accepts empirical research, or anecdotal snippets from sport celebrities, psychology is gaining wide acceptance as one of the most important keys to performance. Psychology impinges on all of the dynamics involved in coaching, ranging from individual attitudes to coach player communication. Especially at the more competitive/elite level, the difference between the good player and the excellent player appears to be their psychological preparation. Whenever a particular player can regularly execute a skill in practice, or perform at a prescribed level, and then fails to reproduce this in a game situation ("he just isn't playing up to his true potential"), we are probably dealing with a psychological limitation.

SOCCER PSYCHOLOGISTS ARE NOT SHRINKS!

Coaches sometimes react adversely to the notion of incorporating psychological dimensions into player preparation. This may stem from a misunderstanding of what is involved. In most instances, we are not talking about heavy duty analysis or assessment. Basic soccer psychology is easily incorporated into training programs, but requires a commitment and understanding on the part of the coach. The better prepared coaches are cognizant of basic psychological principles, and employ them to maximize team, individual player, and coaching effectiveness.

UNDERSTANDING YOUR OWN PSYCHOLOGICAL MAKE-UP

Coaches can have a tremendous impact on their players, both on and off the field. In accepting this responsibility, coaches must understand their own psychological makeup before involving other people. Coaches should understand why they react in a certain manner, so that their behavior is more predictable and controlled, especially in the coaching situation.

Coaches should identify:

- Their personal goals and objectives (what do they want to achieve from being involved in soccer coaching?)
- Their style of coaching (cooperative or commanding?)
- Their own level of self-esteem (how do they feel about themselves?)
- Areas/situations which they often find difficult to deal with.

> **B**asic soccer psychology is easily incorporated into training programs, but requires commitment and understanding on the part of the coach.

This information will provide coaches with a clearer understanding of their actions, identify possible areas of conflict, and help make adjustments which increase effectiveness.

SOME KEY AREAS OF SOCCER PSYCHOLOGY

Of paramount importance is the need to gear psychological techniques to the individual player. The coach must appreciate and understand the idiosyncrasies of the different players. This would involve all strengths and weaknesses, including, but not limited to, the following crucial areas.

Motivation. The coach should understand different factors affecting individual levels of motivation. This would include an appreciation of the needs and goals of the players. One must also have an understanding of the various types of motivation (e.g., intrinsic or extrinsic), and how this knowledge can be incorporated into effective motivational techniques. The concept of reinforcement is an integral part of motivation. Coaches must know the most effective reinforcement for their respective players. It should be established whether a player attributes outcomes to effort and ability or to luck and chance, as this has a major impact on motivational levels. Fluctuations in motivation must also be recognized.

Goal Setting. Individual goals should be identified and assessed. They must be appropriate, challenging, and realistic and should be constantly modified, depending upon individual outcome. The coach must understand the different types of goals, and reinforce the most effective. For example, the coach should understand the rationale for promoting performance (individual criteria) over outcome (win or lose).

Imagery/Visualization. The soccer coach should have knowledge of various techniques, and how they can be applied. This can range from assisting skill execution and overall game strategy, to relaxation skills and injury rehabilitation. Imagery training should be incorporated into regular training sessions, so that individual players can become competent in the techniques which they find most effective. The coach should be able to lead the players through a series of progressive exercises, explaining the rationale and justification.

Stress Management. The coach must be able to identify the debilitating consequences of stress, such as pre-competitive anxiety and overarousal, and develop appropriate coping techniques. This would include a diverse range of relaxation techniques, including: progressive muscle relaxation, breathing exercises, self-hypnosis, humor,and biofeedback.

Team Cohesion. Communication channels must be established which promote cooperation and support. A coach must be a good role model, and provide leadership, and encourage this throughout the team. Feedback and good listening skills are essential in conflict resolution, and establishing harmony. Coaches should avoid the development of cliques and avoid resentment at all costs. This comes from knowing your individual players, and understanding team dynamics.

HOW TO GAIN A WORKING KNOWLEDGE OF SPORT PSYCHOLOGY

Some coaches already employ basic psychological techniques in their programs, even though they might be unaware if it! The key is to gain an awareness of the fundamentals, so that their use becomes more deliberate and refined. As with other forms of knowledge, the coach should be discerning and selective, incorporating those psychological principles which complement their own style and particular needs (related to age range of players).

REFERENCES

Martens, R. (1987). *Coaches Guide to Sport Psychology*, Champaign, IL: Human Kinetics.

Orlick, T. (1986). *Psyching for Sport: Mental-Training for Athletes*, Champaign, IL: Human Kinetics.

Williams, J.M. (1986). *Applied Sports Psychology: Personal Growth to Peak Performance*, Palo Alto, CA: Mayfleld.

APPLIED SPORT PSYCHOLOGY ORGANIZATIONS

Association for the Advancement of Applied Sport Psychology. For information, contact Dr. Robin S.Vealey, Dept. of PHS, Miami University, Oxford, OH 45056.

The Sports Psychology Institute. For information contact Dr. John S. Sikes,109 58th Avenue, St. Petersburg, FL 33706.

TRAINING THE PSYCHOLOGICAL DIMENSION
Alan Goldberg

It's a crucial, must-win game for both teams. A conference championship and bragging rights rest on the outcome. The local media has fired up the community and fans resulting in a much larger than ex-

pected crowd turning out for the game. Right from the outset it's a war out on the pitch. Neither team is willing to give any ground to their opponents. Offensive probes by both teams have been consistently beaten back. There have only been a few shots on goal by both teams and none of them have been good scoring opportunities. The first half is hard fought and ends in a scoreless tie.The second half begins with the same kind of defensive intensity. Midway through this period, much to the home crowd's dismay, the visitors manage to score on a fluke goal. A ball is passed in front of the home goal and the keeper and a defender converge on it and collide. As they are falling to the ground the ball deflects off the keeper's foot and slowly rolls into the goal!

With just under a minute left in regulation time the score remains at 1-0 in favor of the visitors. The tension on and off the field has been steadily growing and reaches a crescendo when the home team's striker breaks free on a run but is fouled directly in front of the visiting team's net, just before he can get a shot off.

The crowd goes crazy and continues their screaming and yelling until the midfielder walks out onto the field to take the penalty kick. Suddenly an eerie silence seems to descend upon the entire field. The air is electric with the tension of the moment. The midfielder, a senior, has had a lot of experience in these kinds of situations and appears to be confident and in control. However, all is not right with him.

As he tries to get himself set, the importance of the kick seems to weigh him down. Time eerily slows down and as it does so, his mind starts to speed up. His thoughts race uncontrollably over what could go wrong. What if he blows it—it should be such an easy kick! But what if he misses the shot the way he did in that big game last year? What if he lets the team and his coach down? What if he kicks it straight to the keeper? He struggles desperately to rid his mind of these negatives, to regain his composure, but it's not working. He can feel his legs and arms tightening up and with that awareness he becomes even more nervous.

Despite the fact that he's only a few feet away, the goal seems to be off in the distance and has shrunk to the size of a hockey goal. Further, the keeper looks like an invincible giant. The midfielder stands there frozen in the silence of the moment, and then finally rushes the ball. Time stands still as his foot makes contact and the ball is shanked into the crowd!

If you have been coaching this sport for any length of time then you know that this is not an uncommon scenario. A sure goal missed for no apparent reason. Even during the last World Cup some of the best players in the world were guilty of the very same thing, missing shots that they routinely make.

The answer to this question is really not much of a mystery. There is much more to training for peak soccer play than just coaching the physical or technical aspects of the game. Conditioning, speed, good ball control skills and endurance are absolutely essential to success on the pitch. Furthermore, good game strategy is a must to produce a winner. However, if you as a coach stop there, and leave the psychological side of your players' games to chance, you will be short-changing yourself and your athletes, and leaving yourself open to much frustration and aggravation.

When an athlete or team does not come through under pressure, when they clutch in the clutch, when stupid little errors seem to snatch defeat from the jaws of victory, more often than not you can look to a lack of mental adjustment.

The mental part of the game comprises those intangibles that most coaches readily claim you need for success: mental toughness, concentrating and blocking out distractions, staying relaxed and composed, rebounding quickly from mistakes and bad breaks, maintaining a winning attitude, having self-confidence, emotional control, avoiding intimidation and playing together as a team.

You'd probably agree with me that these elements are absolutely critical to an athlete's and team's success. The big question is, if these mental elements are so important, how much actual practice time each week do you spend training this inner dimension? If you say almost none, don't feel too badly, because you're not alone. Very few coaches in the sport actually devote precious practice time to working on these mental intangibles.

However, if you want to be as successful as possible and maximize your team's chances of winning, if you truly want your team to consistently have that competitive advantage, then you need to begin to integrate this psychological dimension into your coaching. You have to develop a working awareness of the mental side of the game, i.e., what makes players shine and what makes them choke. If, for example, you have an understanding of where your athletes are mentally as they go into a big game, (i.e., their level of pregame nervousness), your pregame talk and coaching throughout the game will be much more accurate and effective than if you lack this psychological awareness.

To illustrate, last year a high school coach got his team ready for their biggest game of the season by pointing out to them in his pregame talk how this was "the most important game of your lives," that "a conference championship rests on your shoulders," that "the entire town is behind you and we don't want to let them down," and finally, to the seniors, "this is your last chance to finally prove to everyone in this town that our soccer program isn't a loser."

His team then went out in front of the biggest soccer crowd the town had ever assembled and, quite predictably, totally bombed. The coach's frantic yelling and screaming at his players during the game and at half-time further contributed to their tentative and tight play.

This may be an extreme example, but I wanted to point out that if this coach had had a better understanding of the relationship between pregame stress and performance and an awareness of the pressure that his players were undergoing into this game, he could have helped them refocus their concentration and relax for the game. Instead, he inadvertently distracted them with hype about the game's importance and drove their anxiety up to a performance-disrupting level.

The major mistake he committed was to be totally oblivious to the effects of the mind-body connection on performance, that the difference between good games and bad ones is predominantly mental and not physical!

What he failed to understand is that a player's pregame thoughts, feelings and self-talk goes directly into his or her body and changes its physiology. For example, self-talk can tighten muscles, speed up breathing and make it shallower, drain blood from the hands and feet leaving those areas cold and with no feeling. These physiological changes, in turn, dramatically affect the player's foot speed, coordination, reflexes, skill execution, endurance and feel for the ball. To put it simply, with tight muscles every area of a player's game will suffer. Furthermore, if your athlete's breathing rate has increased and gotten shallower because of anxiety, his or her endurance will suffer, regardless of his physical condition. Cold hands and feet leave a player without that all important touch necessary for peak performance.

The most successful coaches in every sport understand the critical importance of this mind-body connection on performance and actively train their players to be mentally tough. One of the reasons that Anson Dorrance has achieved the tremendous success that he has with his North Carolina team and the U.S. Women winning the World Cup is because he continually integrates the mental side of soccer into his coaching. In his words, he "trains the psychological dimension." John Wooden, the basketball coaching legend from UCLA and a holder of an unprecedented 10 NCAA National Championships was also a master of preparing his players mentally as well as physically.

Coaching the psychological dimension... So what does this really mean? Do you have to go back to school and become a sports psychologist in order to work with the mental games of your players? Far from it. Does it mean that you have to devote huge chunks of your already limited practice time to teaching mental skills? Absolutely not!

What it does mean is that you must first begin to appreciate the tremendous impact that the mental side of performance has on the way your players perform and the outcome of the game. I am not downplaying the importance of coaching skills and strategies. On the contrary, you can't produce a winning effort without the ability to teach your athletes how to play the game.

However, if you want to coach a consistent winner then you can't afford to stop there. If you are the head coach for your team then you have to learn to also be a "head" coach (pun intended).

What this entails, is integrating into your practice sessions opportunities for your players to learn to develop mental toughness. For example, the ability to handle competitive pressures is a cornerstone skill of mental toughness. There are ways that you can teach your athletes on a daily basis how to stay calm and composed under pressure. Preseason, you could spend two to three hours teaching specific relaxation techniques to your players so they would have some tools to use if they were under pressure.

In addition, integrating competitive elements into your practice sessions which simulate high pressure game situations is another way to prepare your players to perform at "crunch time." Anson Dorrance talks of creating a "competitive cauldron" in his practice sessions with his UNC women so that right from day one they get comfortable competing under pressure. Since a soccer game is really series of individual duels, Anson has his players aggressively compete against each other, one-on-one, while they go through their conditioning exercises and skill practice with the awareness that their effort are being closely evaluated. Practicing in this kind of aggressive competitive climate on a daily basis helps Anson's players make the easy transition into the high pressure "duels" of an actual game.

Mental toughness also entails numerous other skills that you can begin to integrate into your regular practice sessions, i.e., concentration, intensity, the ability to quickly bounce back from setbacks, winning thinking, etc. In this way you will help your players really maximize their physical potential.

JUGGLING STRESS
Marianne L. Oren

Did you ever feel, as a coach, that every call the official makes favors the other team? Or as a basketball player, every shot hits the rim and bounces out, or as a parent, your skillful child seems one step slower than the person that he/she is guarding?

Stress can be defined as an arousal of mind and body in response to demands made upon them. It is cumulative and unavoidable. We all feel stress at some point. Positive stress is arousal that contributes to health, satisfaction, and productivity. It helps us to prepare

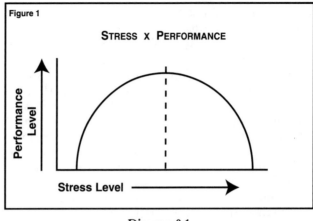

Diagram 9-1

for deadlines - a term paper due date, five o'clock deadline, or a filing date for tax returns. It also helps us realize potential over a period of years in athletics, academics and occupations and adds zest and variety to daily life. It calls attention to the need to resolve a situation of disharmony with others.

Distress, or negative stress, is too much or too little arousal resulting in harm to body or mind; a state of danger. The costs of distress to the mind and body may include the following: physical illness, lowered energy, lowered productivity, wasted potential, lack of career advancement, dissatisfaction with life, work and relationships, low self-esteem, non-involvement in public issues, joylessness and meaninglessness, absence of fun and play, and loss of interest in sex.

Although we often think of stress as a negative force that we should try to avoid, some level of stress is essential to perform optimally. Walt Schafer, author of *Stress Management for Wellness*, says that "...the goal, then, is to create optimal...stress — neither too much nor too little arousal. Most of the time, we want to stay within our zone of positive stress, while periodically pushing our limits in order to learn gradually to take on new responsibilities and challenges with minimum negative stress." Coaches, athletes and parents spend much of their time trying to reach this balance. (See Diagram 9-1, for one group's idea of a Stress vs. Performance curve.) The implication is to learn our personal "point of no return" and to make adjustments so that we stay within our positive stress zone.

Given Schafer's goal of determining this balance (something that will vary from person to person) our jobs as parents, coaches and administrators of youth involved in sport programs in sport programs can be one of solid influence. Our schools and athletic programs often teach young people to work for external rewards in life: the grade, the teacher's smile, a pat on the back, a blue ribbon. Eventually, as adults, success can sometime become closely tied with money, and we find ourselves trying to obtain more—whether that results in material possessions, a large saving account or luxurious vacations.

Stress management involves learning to listen to ourselves and our own internal measure of when we are successful and within our zone of positive stress. Most children will not learn this skill through the educational process. As adults we can serve as guides to help them begin to learn their own internal limits, while encouraging growth through helping them look toward higher goals. By educating them about some of the symptoms of stress, sharing our techniques for coping, facilitating their our self-education process in identifying their personal "point of no return," and helping them to use positive self-talk we can help them achieve this very important knowledge.

In educating our athletes about stress, the best place to start is with our own understanding of the issue. The following information can be adapted to meet the needs of various ages and population.

SYMPTOMS OF STRESS

The symptoms of stress fall into two general categories. One category includes the physical symptoms that we have experience. Hyperventilation and shortness of breath are indications of the respiratory system's involvement in the process. The gastrointestinal system can be affected resulting in symptoms of indigestion, stomach cramps and diarrhea. Low back pain or neck pain are common results from distress to the musculoskeletal system. Some individuals experience an increase or decrease in appetite with distress. The heart rate and blood pressure increase as a result of arousal to the cardiovascular system. Insomnia is another common symptom,. The immune system is also affected and our body's ability to prevent illness is weakened. For this reason, we may find ourselves more susceptible to viral infections and colds. Research has shown that there may be a connection between the development of many illness and prolonged exposure to stress. The amount of stress in our lives can be a major factor in our physical well-being.

The second category of stress symptoms involves the mind. However, this category can be just as destructive as the physical effects. As we experience increased amounts of stress our thought process changes, often resulting in loss of concentration, worrying, negative thoughts, and daydreams. Increases in complaining, criticizing, emotional temper outbursts and depression are not uncommon. Our behavior also changes and there can be excessive smoking, procrastinating, spending, excessive or decreased eating or quit-

ting projects that we have he ability to complete. Stress us our relationships can result in attempts to get attention, and rejecting or avoiding people alltogher. Leisure time can no longer be enjoyed and nervous habits are sometimes acquired.

Being aware of some of the symptoms and how we react to stress is the first step in achieving stress management.

COPING WITH STRESS

Coping with stress involves constantly changing our efforts to manage the external and/or internal demands that we feel are causing the intense anxiety. To manage stress we must take an active part in dealing with the problems, issues and dilemmas that contribute to our distress. Below are some healthy ways to deal with stress.

- Utilize aerobic exercise to deal with the tension you are feeling.
- Be assertive. Learn to prioritize the demands you have in your life. Learn to set limits, speak up, and say "no" to people.
- Play time, such as going to a movie, reading a good book, going window shopping, etc. can provide a wonderful break (use whatever you define as "play").
- Talk with a trusted friend about the difficulties you're experiencing; (this combats the myth about the effectiveness of "holding it in": if we don't talk about what's bothering us, it will go away.) The reality is that identification and acknowledgement of the stress or unknown fear can reduce anxiety.
- Utilize time management techniques; schedule activities on your calendar so that practices and upcoming events don't surprise you.
- Build in balance in your life: include rewards for dealing with tension-causing events; as you approach difficult periods of stress for you, build in some "me" time.
- See it through – use visualization techniques to see yourself successfully "walking through" a difficult drill, play, interaction, etc. that you are anxious about.
- Laugh – read a joke or humor book to allow yourself to take a break from your stressors and create some distance between yourself and what you are doing - this can be helpful when you are feeling overwhelmed.
- Stretch – use relaxation techniques such as deep breathing and tension reducing body focus exercise (tensing and releasing various large muscle groups

Being aware of some of the symptoms and how we react to stress is the first step in achieving stress management.

in your body).

- Risk – try something that you've never done before; this involves taking a risk, and going outside your "comfort zone" to try a fresh technique to a problem that you are facing; risk-taking can be an energizing experience!
- Finally, change takes time. Recognize that initial failure or setbacks are part of the trial and error process that will help you learn to be a successful manager of stress. Be gentle with yourself in learning this process.

There are many other ways to deal with stress. The important point is to develop a list of coping tactics that work for you. When you feel overwhelmed, pull out your list of techniques and put them to work. Do what is right for you, and remember, what is healthy coping for you may not be appropriate for someone else.

A coach can help younger athletes tremendously just by talking about the pregame jitters. As coaches, parents and administrators, we all have unique opportunities to work with young people in the self-education process of stress management, not only as facilitators, but as role models as well.

Resources

Kroll, Walter (1982). "Competitive Athletic Stress Factors in Athletes and Coaches" in Zaichkowsky, Leonard D. and Sime, Wesley E. (Eds.) (1982). *Stress Management for Sport*. Published by the American Alliance for Health, Physical Education, Recreation and Dance. 1900 Association Drive, Reston, VA 22091.

Shafer, Walt (1978). *Stress Management for Wellness.* Published by Holt, Rinehart and Winston, p. 311.

Psychological Skills for a Championship Season
Colleen M. Hacker, Ph.D.

Why is it that some athletes can always be counted on to make the big play while others, with the same physical skill, wilt under pressure and habitually underperform? Your answer is probably like most coaches: you'd chalk it up to "mental problems" or to "head games." In fact, many of the greatest barriers to athletic excellence are not due to technical or tactical deficiencies, but rather, to self-imposed psychological barriers. Just as athletes differ in physical performance factors (some are faster, stronger or more technically proficient) they also differ in psychological characteristics as well.

If one of your athletes lacked strength you should develop a specific strength training program to improve the musculoskeletal deficiency in order to help the athlete reach optimal level of performance. Like physical skills, athletes' mental skills can also be improved with practice and systematic training. We should address the psychological dimension of soccer with the same systematic attention that is afforded the physical aspects of the sport. As a soccer coach, you not only have the responsibility of teaching the physical, technical and tactical aspects of the sport, but also for illuminating a myriad of factors that influence athletes' thoughts, emotions and expectations. The two roles are inseparable. Rather than hoping these psychological skill are inherent in players, it would be prudent to design and implement a psychological skill training (PST) program as part of the your regular soccer practice. In fact, it's never too late to begin PST and the sooner you start training to better.

Mental skills, like physical skills can be learned, developed and improved with practice. Just as one strength training program doesn't fit every athlete, one mental skills program won't fit every person either. You must carefully assess the needs and strengths of each athlete and structure the program to meet their unique characteristics. Almost all athletes can benefit from psychological skills training and almost all coaches recommend its use, but unfortunately, PST is not usually done in a scientific, systematic way.

Frequently, athletes practice these skills several times a year and then, when they don't see immediate and dramatic improvements, claim that it's all a sham. Can you imagine only practicing penalty kicks or defending skills once or twice and expecting those techniques to be perfectly executed under the strain of competition? Like most aspects of sport, if you want a successful result you must plan for it, teach it and then continually implement it, learning from your successes and failures.

PST. Some Common Mistakes

Paradoxically, the small percentage of coaches who implement psychological skills training utilize methods that simply will not work. A few of the most common and least effective methods include:

1. Only conducting PST sessions away from the practice field (in a classroom, meeting room etc.). While initial orientation sessions can benefit from the quiet space, PST should optimally occur on the field and locker room, since it's in those environments where the mental skills are most frequently needed.

2. Conducting a two or three day seminar-type introduction to PST, or asking a "guest expert" to address the team without consistent follow up and practice. Psychological skills must be practiced to work. There is a significant difference between

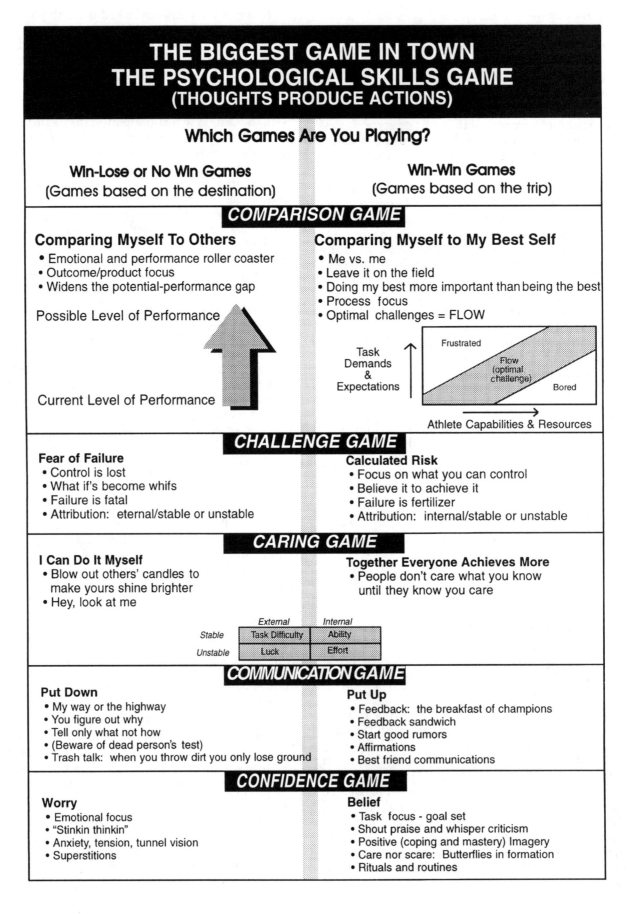

THE BIGGEST GAME IN TOWN
THE PSYCHOLOGICAL SKILLS GAME
(THOUGHTS PRODUCE ACTIONS)

Which Games Are You Playing?

Win-Lose or No Win Games	Win-Win Games
(Games based on the destination)	(Games based on the trip)

COMPARISON GAME

Comparing Myself To Others
- Emotional and performance roller coaster
- Outcome/product focus
- Widens the potential-performance gap

Possible Level of Performance

Current Level of Performance

Comparing Myself to My Best Self
- Me vs. me
- Leave it on the field
- Doing my best more important than being the best
- Process focus
- Optimal challenges = FLOW

Task Demands & Expectations

Frustrated

Flow (optimal challenge)

Bored

Athlete Capabilities & Resources

CHALLENGE GAME

Fear of Failure
- Control is lost
- What if's become whifs
- Failure is fatal
- Attribution: eternal/stable or unstable

Calculated Risk
- Focus on what you can control
- Believe it to achieve it
- Failure is fertilizer
- Attribution: internal/stable or unstable

CARING GAME

I Can Do It Myself
- Blow out others' candles to make yours shine brighter
- Hey, look at me

Together Everyone Achieves More
- People don't care what you know until they know you care

	External	Internal
Stable	Task Difficulty	Ability
Unstable	Luck	Effort

COMMUNICATION GAME

Put Down
- My way or the highway
- You figure out why
- Tell only what not how
- (Beware of dead person's test)
- Trash talk: when you throw dirt you only lose ground

Put Up
- Feedback: the breakfast of champions
- Feedback sandwich
- Start good rumors
- Affirmations
- Best friend communications

CONFIDENCE GAME

Worry
- Emotional focus
- "Stinkin thinkin"
- Anxiety, tension, tunnel vision
- Superstitions

Belief
- Task focus - goal set
- Shout praise and whisper criticism
- Positive (coping and mastery) Imagery
- Care nor scare: Butterflies in formation
- Rituals and routines

knowledge of and implementation of PST. As with physical skills, coaches need players who can actually execute with technical precision rather than players who "know how to but can't."

3. Practicing psychological skills before games or before the big games. Psychological skills are an adjunct to training just like proper nutrition, fitness and strength. It must be a lifestyle habit that is part of the everyday training routine. PST should be woven into every aspect of pre-, in- and post-season contact with athletes.

Certainly, psychological skills will not take the place of physical talent or technical capability. Nor will mental training overcome the pitfalls of an ill-conceived game plan or a tactically immature decision. Rather, the goal of PST is to help each athlete reach an optimal level of performance. Its aim is to narrow the gap between how the athlete (or team) could possibly perform. As importantly, coaches need to practice and become proficient in these same skills. When coaches learn by habit, demonstrate, utilize and model these psychological skills on a consistent basis, then athlete adherence and success will also improve.

The most common PST program includes a triad of techniques that include imagery, affirmations and goalsetting. What follows, however, is an attempt to incorporate that triad into a larger framework. PST is more than positive thinking. The entire perspective is based on the fact that thoughts produce actions. In many respects, humans cannot tell the difference between vivid thoughts and physical reality.

THE FIVE PSYCHOLOGICAL GAMES

A graphic presentation of the PST framework outlines five psychological "games" that are always being played by soccer athletes and coaches in addition to the observable, physical game of soccer. The issue isn't whether or not you are play these games but rather which games are you playing? The five include: The Comparison, Challenge, Caring, Communication and Confidence Games. Each game is based in two divergent perspectives of competitive sport.

The first of these perspectives is called the Win-Lose or No Win perspective. It is a game based primarily upon measurable outcome of performance such as the scoreboard, season record, a starting position or a championship result. In that game there is one winner and at least one loser. The measure of success is how well you played relative to how well someone else played. Frequently people playing the Win-Lose game are focused only on the final destination. If the goal is achieved then you've reached your destination and are considered successful. If the goal is not achieved, you're viewed as a failure. In that game only one "winner" emerges along with a plethora of "losers."

The second game is called the Win-Win game. From this perspective, the focus is on the journey itself, not simply the destination. It is a game that utilizes process measure of success such as improving the number of times that possession is regained in the offensive third or out-performing a previous best performance. Most often than not, successful outcomes will result from controlling actions that lead to success rather than focusing on success itself. The opponent becomes yourself and the measure of success is an internal one. This is the preferred perspective underlying the PST framework.

THE COMPARISON GAME

Athletes can play a Win-Lose, or a Win-Win comparison game. Athletes playing the former measure their success and their talent by comparing themselves to others. If my team beats your team then I win. If I start and you don't, then I win. Of course with every "winner" there is also a "loser." It's an emotional and performance roller coaster. When the focus is on the who is better, you or me, then I'm confident and successful when I'm the winner. Conversely, I'm depressed and a failure when I'm not. Sadly, the athlete has relinquished control of success and put someone else in charge. The focus is on the outcome, the scoreboard, the final destination. Athletes and coaches fail to realize that almost without exception, it's as easy to find someone worse. Winning in this game tells you much more about who you've scheduled or who is in your league than it does about your team's actual ability.

Focusing on a comparison between yourself and others rarely closes the potential-performance gap. That gap is represented by who you are now as a player (or team) and who you could be. Here, the comparison is an internal one. It is a comparison between you and your best self. Hopefully the goal for all coaches and players is to narrow the gap between what is and what could be. By playing the me vs. me game, your opponent becomes your previous best performance. The pressure is internal and under your control. Athletes strive to maximize their effort on the soccer field. No regrets. Nothing held back. What isn't given is lost forever. Athletes realize that doing their best is more important than being the best. The challenge is to narrow their own personal performance gap with the journey itself as the prize.

One of the best avenues for narrowing the potential performance gap is to achieve what psychologist Csikszentmihalyi (1990) termed a FLOW experience. An athlete experiences FLOW when the demands of the sport are congruent with his/her personal capabilities and talents. Thus, the goal for coaches is to plan training sessions that optimally challenge their particular athletes, to schedule competitive games that optimally challenge their teams, and to play a style of soccer that fits the unique talents of their team. It takes time, analytical ability and preparation, but it can be done.

When teams are not experiencing FLOW the consequences generally fall into two broad categories. One response is frustration. Athletes are frustrated when they have lower ability and talent than the competition and the coach places unreasonably high demands on them, individually and collectively. The second response is boredom. Boredom occurs when athletes have greater ability and resources than their competitors but the coach expects too little and fails to adequately challenge the athletes. Similar to their frustrated counterparts, bored athletes do not train well in practice, appear unmotivated, do not respond positively to constructive criticism and fail to reach their full soccer potential.

The Challenge Game

Athletes can play the fear of Failure or the Calculated Risk challenge game. Fear of failure athletes worry about what may happen if they make a mistake or fail to please their teammates, coaches and fans. They dwell on negative possibilities and the consequences associated with those images. "What if we don't win this game?" "What if I miss the PK?" "What if the coach doesn't start me?" These are the athletes most likely to choke or underperform in competition. In fact, what coach hasn't seen a player shoot the ball high over the crossbar at point-blank range, shank the critical penalty kick or demonstrate, through body language, that they don't deserve a starting spot.

Fear of failure athletes view setbacks as both fatal and final. When these athletes are asked to give reasons (termed attributions) for their lack of success, the reasons typically include variables outside the athlete's control. Athletes may say that they lost the game because the other team's defense was too strong, or that the penalty was missed because of a lucky keeper save, or that they didn't start because the coach has no clue about good talent selection. In each instance, the reasons are viewed as outside the athletes' direct control and are neither their fault nor their responsibility. These athletes can be expected to exhibit lower future expectations for success, a lack of persistence in the face of adversity and lower self-confidence.

Athletes who play the Calculated Risk challenge game focus instead on what they can control. They focus on the processes that lead to success rather than on the outcome itself. For instance, athletes and coaches shift the focus to immediately regaining possession of the ball, forcing more offensive corners, or taking more shots on goal because each of these actions dramatically increase the chances of scoring. The focus is shifted to factors that lead to success and are under players' direct control. Each of these scenarios involves a calculated risk rather than a guarantee. Not every team that regains possession early will score, every cross will not always produce a goal and the keeper may still make a brilliant save on a well-struck penalty kick. Athletes feel successful, however, knowing that they did all that could be done to control the inherently unpredictable arena of sport.

Calculated risk athletes view failure as fertilizer. They realize that they lift weights against resistance to make the body stronger just like they must play through adversity to become mentally tough. They see themselves like bread in the oven, always preparing to rise. Setbacks are opportunities for growth, fruitful assessment and challenges to overcome.

Unlike athletes who have to experience success to believe that it's possible, calculated risk athletes realize that belief precedes achievement. They understand that thoughts produce actions. When calculated risk athletes are asked to give reasons for a particular outcome, they attribute results to factors under their control. With diligence, perseverance, and effort, internal attributions almost always can be changed. For example, athletes might respond to another team's smothering defense by assuming personal responsibility for inadequate preparation and vowing that next time they will be tactically prepared to exploit potential weakness. The calculated risk athlete who doesn't get a starting spot would focus on what physiological, technical, tactical or psychological deficits could be improved by the next game or line-up change so that they might earn a higher spot. The responsibility and the control is personal and internal.

The Caring Game

Athletes can play the I Can Do It Myself or the TEAM caring game. TEAM is an acronym that stands for "Together Everyone Achieves More." People playing the Win-Lose game exhibit a "what's in it for me" attitude. Much like youngsters five or six years of age, the prevailing sentiment is "Hey look at me. Look what I can do." They believe that the way to make themselves more successful or more recognized is to intimidate or over-shadow other team members. Unfortunately, they often believe that they need to blow out others' candles to make their own shine brighter. They crave the spotlight. They fail to realize that the brightest soccer field is one lit by many candles, not just one.

People wrapped up in themselves frequently make very small packages. They don't realize that even in the competitive world of soccer, cooperative interplay is essential to both personal and team success. Teammates and opponents alike cooperate to play by the letter and spirit of the rules to insure a fair and equitable outcome. When teammates strive together to bring out the best in themselves, the best in their teammates and perhaps most surprisingly, the best in their opponents, the game of soccer offers its greatest reward. To be the type of player (or team) that brings out the best in their competitors is the player who ultimately commands the highest respect.

When you bring out the best in teammates you do two things well. You show off your talents and knowledge of the game and you encourage others so that the likelihood of team success is enhanced. Players should strive to make a teammate look good. When the focus shifts from getting the credit to getting the job done, good things happen for everyone.

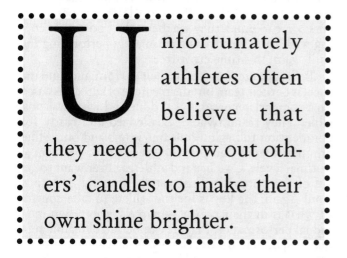

Unfortunately athletes often believe that they need to blow out others' candles to make their own shine brighter.

Often coaches and veteran players believe that they should be automatically respected for their status, knowledge and expertise. More often than not, respect is something you give before you get any back. It's common knowledge in the education profession that people don't care what you know until they know you care. The same holds true in sport. Players will go the extra mile for a coach they respect, value and appreciate. Coaches who can turn the demands of soccer into a "want to" rather than a "have to" will reap the highest rewards. When athletes want to follow sound training policies you'll have conscientious, self-motivated individuals. Athletes are eager to please. They are inherently high-achieving, goal-directed individuals. If coaches can challenge athletes to work cooperatively for everyone's benefit, it's amazing how much actually gets accomplished. An additional benefit is that the entire team monitors and encourages one another rather than relying on coaches and other external sanctions to enforce adherence.

THE COMMUNICATION GAME

Ben Franklin was quoted as saying "Any fool can criticize, any fool can condemn, any fool can complain and most fools do." Perhaps that old adage tells us everything we need to know about individuals playing the Put Down Game. Our number one tool as coaches is our ability to communicate. Technical details must be conveyed. Game plans must be transmitted. Pre- and post-game analyses must be offered. In each arena, players and coaches are constantly engaged in both verbal and non-verbal dialogues.

It is crucial for players to be explicitly told the reasons for drill selection, tactical decisions, line-up preferences, training regimes and any other salient infor-

mation affecting the team. The autocratic coach who believes that it's up to the players to figure it out for themselves or worse yet, that it's none of the players' business, fail to see the long term consequences of their actions. Frequently players learn drills without ever understanding the relevance or relationship to the larger game. Because players may not know the reasons for various actions taken by coaches, they'll provide their own, frequently self-serving explanations. Team cohesion, player satisfaction and team success will ultimately be sacrificed.

When players are given technical, tactical or psychological corrections, it is imperative that they be told how to accomplish the desired goal. On most soccer fields it's more common to hear pointed remarks about mistakes made rather than helpful corrective comments being offered. The most useful feedback needed by athletes is information on the correct execution of skills. This is especially true in psychological advice. Coaches frequently fail the "dead person's test." Briefly, if you tell a player to do something that a dead person could also accomplish then crucial information is missing. Examples of these expressions are "relax," "don't worry," "don't be distracted," "don't let them get to you," etc. The athlete is told what to do or what not to do—but not how to do it. Athletes should be taught how to relax, what cues to focus on and how to concentrate in the face of competitive pressure.

Feedback given to athletes should also utilize the K.I.S.S. principle: keep it short and simple. How often they receive the opposite! Athletes crave positive feedback. Rarely do players complain about getting too much feedback. They want to know where they stand with you, with their teammates and with their soccer ability. Feedback is the breakfast of champions.

Individuals playing the Put Up game utilize a four-step approach in delivering feedback, called the feedback sandwich. The two outer pieces of bread in the sandwich are positive first and last statements. The meat of the sandwich is a triad of information that includes what the athlete did, what the athlete should do, and how the athlete can accomplish it. An example might be "Good hustle after the ball, but you closed down too much space too fast on the offensive player. Next time allow another yard or two for someone that fast and then they can't beat you goalside. I know you can do it." All of that information should be conveyed in a few seconds. Give athletes something tangible to do, not simply a concept to consider. Remember to keep it short and simple.

It is not only communication between players or between coaches and players that influences a team's success. The internal dialogue within players also impacts performance. Trash talk, as it's come to be known, disrupts the focus of the giver and the receiver.

When you throw dirt with your language or thoughts, you only lose ground.

Put up athletes affirm the strengths both in themselves and in others. They find the good and praise it. Have athletes monitor their internal communication patterns and determine whether they would use that same language with their best friend. Athletes intuitively know that when a teammate makes an error, immediate support and positive reassurance is needed. Yet, that same athlete, upon missing a clear goal-scoring opportunity, thinks nothing of accompanying the negative internal talk with physical, quasi-violent gestures. Now imagine responding to a teammate in a similar fashion? No one would expect good results. Challenge athletes to give themselves positive feedback just like that which they give to teammates.

THE CONFIDENCE GAME

The final game to be played is the Confidence game. Win-Lose athletes exhibit an emotional focus that frequently centers around worry. Like the "what if" athlete, individuals playing a worry game think in terms of the worse-case scenario. Not only do they worry about the awful things they know might happen, these athletes also fear the unknown. Heightened anxiety sets off a chain reaction of thoughts and behaviors that usually inhibits performance. Because breathing is more rapid and shallow in highly anxious athletes, they tend to tire quickly and physically fade in critical parts of the game. Frequently their attention narrows and their thinking becomes rigid. This tunnel vision prevents them from seeing open teammates, covering important marking assignments and recognizing scoring opportunities.

Because of the heightened anxiety and perceived loss of control that accompanies those feelings, athletes begin to rely on superstitions to help "control" the uncertainty. Superstitions are an individual's attempt to bring order and control to what appears random and chaotic. Rituals and routines, however, are characteristic of Win-Win athletes and need to be distinguished from superstitions. Routines are consistent behavioral patterns or coping responses that are directly under the athlete's control and serve as realistic aides to performance.

Thus, the key factor that separates superstitions from rituals or routines is the amount of direct control that the athlete has. A superstition might be "I have a good game only when we win the coin toss" while a ritual might be "I have a good game when I warm up with the same teammate and follow the same order of activities." In the first example,control is lost to the chance flip of a coin while in the second instance, the athlete can follow the same pre-game routine in every match.

Athletes who play the Belief-oriented confidence game are focused on the task at hand and on factors under their direct control. Confident performers think they can and they do. Their images are successful ones. They vividly imagine themselves mastering a particular skill or strategy and use every sensory modality to do so. They smell the grass on the field, taste the sweat on their upper lip, hear the voices of teammates, and feel the touch of the ball on soft leather shoes. If errors come to mind, they see themselves positively coping with the adversity and ultimately performing the skill again, this time error-free.

Belief athletes care about their performance and the success of their team but the measure of success is based on a comparison of what was done and what was possible. They're motivated, challenged and ready for competition to begin. Pre-game jitters and butterflies are the athlete's sign that they're ready to perform at optimal levels. Coaches and athletes never want to get rid of the butterflies, just get them to fly in formation! Again, the key is for the athlete to take control of what is in their power — namely, their own individual performance. Players can't control teammates, coaches, opponents or referees. What can be mastered are the comparisons used to measure success, the challenges established for optimal performance, the care that's offered to others, the intent and style of communication and the confidence players have in their own success. Believe it and you can achieve it.

REFERENCE:

Csikszentmihali, M. (1990). *FLOW:The Psychology of Optimal Experience*. Harper Perennial, New York: New York.

⚽

PSYCHOLOGICAL CONSIDERATIONS IN COACHING SOCCER

Frank Olszewski

The utilization of psychology by coaches in sports is not a recent phenomenon. Formal psychology, however, has been applied to athletics on a greater scale within the past two decades. This article will discuss the role psychology plays in the coaching of soccer. More specifically, it will deal with the psychological issues encountered by coaches and their players.

A fundamental task of the coach is to modify behavior. The primary change of behavior is related to motor habits. These habits are formed early in one's soccer career. The ability to alter this behavior becomes more difficult as the player matures and habits harden. For example, behavior is more easily changed in the high school athlete than in their college counterpart (whose habits have been firmly established). Coaches must be particularly sensitive to the experience level of their players as they attempt to modify their technique in skills such as passing, dribbling, trapping, and shooting. The younger the player, the less there is unlearn. Therefore, it is imperative that players receive proper training in the early stages of their soccer careers.

As a modifier of behavior the coach must also be concerned with several other psychological issues that affect players. The aspects that we will view involve how players learn, the factors that affect this learning process, how players react to the stress of competition, and methods to enhance the players' effectiveness in dealing with this stress.

Soccer players tend to learn through various processes. The most effective procedures that can be utilized by coaches are through verbal instruction, physical demonstration, and by encouraging the player to learn via self discovery. It should be noted that the degree of effectiveness is dependent upon the personal desire of the players, which can be bolstered by the enthusiasm of the coach. In addition to this, coaches must give special attention to the experience level of the group they are teaching to assure that information is not passed on to players either too rapidly or too slowly. This would also apply to the dissemination of information that is too elementary or too sophisticated for the group of players a coach is instructing. Both of these instances could hinder the learning process.

The predominant advantage for a coach to utilize verbal instruction in the learning process is that he can convey information to a relatively large group. A major disadvantage for this type of learning procedure is that some of the information doesn't get processed at the same rate by everyone; it is impersonal. Therefore, it is helpful if coaches use examples in verbal instructions. This adds a personal touch. This is important because learning to play soccer is essentially a personal process.

It is also easier for a player to understand a particular skill or tactic when the coach can divide the skill or tactic into several explicit components (A,B,C, and D). This is where demonstration plays a vital role in learning. Along with these detailed explanations, the coach can be a more valuable resource when he/she can convert these particularized instructions into ac-

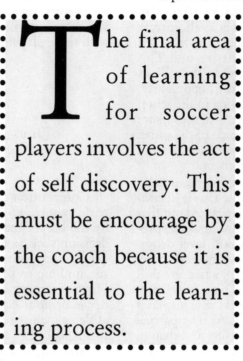

The final area of learning for soccer players involves the act of self discovery. This must be encourage by the coach because it is essential to the learning process.

tion. This is especially true when the coach adds enthusiasm to the visual presentation.

Let's take a look at how this would work in actuality. If a coach was going to teach the instep trap (mainly utilized for settling a ball out of the air) this skill could be divided into the following areas: A) weight is kept on the non-trapping foot; B) the trapping foot is relaxed, which can be accomplished by keeping the foot loose (as well as inhaling as the ball arrives and exhaling right before it is collected); C) the trapping foot is positioned close to the ground for balance; and D) eyes are kept on the ball as it is literally pulled out of the air. This procedure can also be effective in teaching tactics.

While teaching, the coach must pay particular attention to a factor known as retroactive inhibition. This refers to a circumstance that may hamper the learning process. Retroactive inhibition occurs when similar skills, tactics, or their components are taught in succession. Confusion arises and interference to the learning process transpires because the player encounters difficulty distinguishing one skill, tactic, or its component from the other. Coaches increase the players' opportunity to learn effectively when they make sure that tasks taught in succession are dissimilar. An example of retroactive inhibition can be seen when similar variations to restarts are taught. Should the variations not be explicit enough, confusion results and the players cannot effectively carry out the tasks of these preplanned dead ball situations.

The final area of learning for soccer players involves the act of self discovery. This must been encouraged by the coach because it is essential to the learning process. It also helps to enhance the imagination of the players, which is a significant element in the development of the game. A coach can foster self discovery by urging his/her players to improvise and experiment in games of keepaway, small-sided contests, and full-sided scrimmages. Furthermore, the coach should affirm the incorporation of a new skill the players utilizes during the course of a scrimmage or match. This can be accomplished by verbally recounting the details of the skill to the players. This allows the coach to present the players with positive reinforcement and immediate validation for the completion of a skill the players may or may not be aware they performed. Once skills are learned, the players gets the opportunity to test them out in competition. In itself, competition produces stress. The stress that the players encounters in competition and the methods a coach can employ to enhance the players' performance despite this pressure, demands discussion.

Stress is defined as the subjecting of a person to pressure or strain. Athletic competition and the atmosphere that surrounds it creates stress on the athlete. A soccer player's stress may come from internal sources, the game itself, and/or external sources. The internal sources of stress are related to the player's personality and perception of performance. This has to do with the player's physical and mental health which greatly influence reactions to stress. The stress of the game itself comes from the pressure to perform definitive skills. The burden increases as the player must integrate these skills in conjunction with ten other team members to form a cohesive unit.This could occur as the player makes a mistake that allows the other team to score, misses a scoring opportunity, or simply becomes frustrated by trailing in the score. External sources of stress take place when pressure imposed on the player originates outside of the game. This may be seen as a result of present strains from the home, work, school, or social domain.

When a person is under pressure he/she usually reverts back to an earlier level of skill. This is known as regression under stress. It has been pointed out that athletic competition (a soccer match for instance) produces stress, and as a consequence skill level drops. Under the stress of competition, players tend to become stronger than they would be in practice, yet skill level is reduced to an earlier level. This can be illustrated by the team or individual players who display a high level of skill in practice sessions. As they participate in the match they become more physical than in practice (due to the stress of competition) and invariably revert to an earlier level of skill. With this knowledge in hand, the coach must focus on goals that help prepare the player for this situation.

This may be accomplished by having the players continually practice specific skills that occur often in competition. This is known as over learning. The aim of the coach must be to develop the player's backup form (those skills that are visible under the stress of competition) to such a level that when the athlete is challenged, a new and much more refined response is elicited. An example of this may be the player who collects the ball via the chest trap in drills that are utilized in practice. Yet when the situation arises in the match, the player, full of excitement and flowing adrenalin, meets the ball with added force. This causes the ball to bounce away, uncontrolled. The response of the coach should be to have that particular player continually practice the skill of the chest trap. Initially, this should be without the presence of opposing players and then eventually introducing them as additional forms of pressure. The psychological tactic of over-learning can also be utilized in teaching team strategies such as restarts, offensive build-ups, and defensive tactics.

The intention of this article has been to acquaint soccer coaches with some of the psychological issues that affect their players. The subject of sports psychology, although relatively new, must not be overlooked. It is an area that coaches must take the effort to become familiar with in order to serve the needs of their players more effectively. The coach can make his/her job much easier and more enjoyable by understanding the role of psychology in athletics such as soccer. More important than that, however, they can improve the performances of the athletes they are coaching, as well as enrich the relationships they currently enjoy with these players.

⚽

DEVELOPING CONSISTENCY
by Dr. Steve Boutcher

Competition can devastate even the best athlete's performance. The missed open net,, the fumbled ball by the keeper that leads to a goal, the wrong tactical decision such as whether to dive in on the tackle or delay an opponent are soccer examples of athletes, succumbing to the demands of intense competition. However, many athletes do compete successfully under enormous competitive demands. How do these athletes maintain consistently high standards of performance? How do they regulate their emotions and avoid thoughts of failure? How do they maintain their focus of attention?

Athletes who consistently deliver in clutch situations tend to rely upon performance routines. For example, basketball players and archers may have a performance routine for establishing their stance and shooting position, whereas golfers may waggle the club a set number of times before executing a shot. Soccer keepers go through set warmup routines to prepare them to meet the demands of the game (see Barbour article in this issue of *Soccer Journal*). These athletes may also go through a preplanned sequence of imagery, relaxation, and other mental strategies as part of their performance routine. These routines could be used before or after skill performance, or while waiting on the sidelines.

Research evidence for the existence of performance routines has come from a number of different sports including golf, archery, riflery, basketball, baseball, and weightlifting. Our own research has demonstrated that professional golfers' preshot behaviors are remarkably consistent over many hours of play. Professional golfers repeatedly take the same amount of time and the

Coach Bruce Arena (far right) observes as team member is interviewed by Seamus Malin following Virginia's capture of its third NCAA Division I championship. Obviously the Cavalier team has learned how to develop both individual and collective patterns of behavior that lead to a consistent level of play. (photo by Perry McIntyre, Jr.)

same number of practices swings and glances at the target before playing each shot. Furthermore, the overall results of these studies suggests that these routines can enhance performance.

How Routines Develop Consistency

The effectiveness of performance routines has been demonstrated in at least three areas: First, routines may enable athletes to concentrate more efficiently. By focusing on certain cues it is possible that distractions (e.g., crowd noise) are less likely to influence performance; Second, routines may help prevent "warmup decrement. " Research has shown that there is often a drop in performance after a brief rest until one can get warmed up, or back in the groove. Routines can serve the purpose of "keeping you warm" during these periods of down time; Third, routines may also prevent athletes from thinking about the details or mechanics of well learned skills that are better performed automatically.

Recent investigations in sport have attempted to explore the mechanisms underlying the performance routine. A number of studies have examined cardiovascular and brain wave patterns. For example, cardiac deceleration has been found with shooters. Researchers have demonstrated that elite rifle shooters reduce their heart rate just prior to the trigger pull. Similar effects have been found with archers and golfers. Attentional states during the pre-performance routine have also been assessed through monitoring left-

and right-brain wave activity of elite shooters while shooting. Results indicated that seconds before pulling the trigger, shooters exhibited more activity in their right hemisphere compared to their left. This suggests that elite marksmen many possess such a high degree of attentional focus that they can effectively reduce conscious mental activities of the left hemisphere, thus reducing thoughts unnecessary to performance of the task.

Terry Orlick maintains that routine or psychological plans hold one's focus away from negative self-talk. An effective routine can therefore "make the body respond just as you would like it to respond, and much more consistently."

Ritual versus Routine

There is an important difference between a routine and a ritual. Rituals include wearing certain clothes, using lucky symbols, or repeating the same behaviors or thoughts solely because of superstition. This is compared to the well-developed performance routine that can be adapted to varying conditions and different situations. Rituals tend to control the athlete, whereas a well-developed performance routine is controlled by the athlete.

Laying the Foundation

The development of effective performance routines is based on previously acquired psychological skills. Psychological skills such as imagery, relaxation, attentional control and coping strategies all serve to create a foundation from which to build a routine that serves its purpose. The development of such skills will not be described here but it is emphasized that the athlete must progress through a series of stages in order to acquire the mental skills necessary to develop an effective individualized routine.

Individualized performance routines focus specifically on establishing optimal psychological and physiological states immediately before, during, and after skill performance. The following section offer suggestion for developing consistency through the use of performance routine at various stages.

PRE-PERFORMANCE ROUTINES

The main components of pre-performance routines are attentional control, physical and mental control, and behavioral consistency. Thus, athletes need to have the ability to focus their thoughts on task relevant cues, they need to be able to acquire an appropriate routinized set of behavioral actions. Consequently, the challenge for the athlete is to find the most efficient routine and to repeat this routine before every performance.

Pre-performance routines will vary in content for athletes in the same sport. For instance, in golf there are clear differences regarding the speed of pre-performance routines of the faster, more spontaneous golfers compared to their more methodical, slower counterparts. Similarly, pre-performance routines will vary between sports. Thus, a pitcher's routine when standing on the mound preparing to pitch will have different attentional and behavioral components than those of a springboard diver preparing to dive. Skill level will also influence the type and nature of the routine, If the skill is still being acquired, and not performed automatically, then a less complex, abbreviated routine may be more appropriate.

Pre-performance routine can be divided into either self-paced or reactive categories. During self-paced routines the athlete will initiate movement, whereas in reactive routines, the athlete is waiting to react to an environmental cue (i.e.,the goalkeeper will react to the cues of the coach warming him up). An example of a self-paced routine would be a penalty shot in soccer or serving in tennis.

SELF-PACED ROUTINES

Self-paced pre-performance routines consist of a series of both mental and physical steps, as indicated by the soccer and golf examples below. Each component of the routine is also enhanced by general mental skills previously acquired by the athlete. Relaxation, imagery, and breathing techniques could be used to develop the "setting" response and then specific relaxation cues could be transferred to the routine. For example, a setting response in a routine could be achieved through the use of a combination of techniques such as a cue word like "cool" coupled with breathing technique.

The imagery component of the routine would be developed in a similar manner. Initially, the effectiveness of imagery for each individual needs to be assessed. Soccer players before taking a penalty shot can use imagery and see the ball hitting in upper 90 before making their attempt. Imagery may help to avoid focusing on irrelevant task information and provide a way to activate the appropriate set. For instance, in golf there are clear differences to activate the appropriate set. Research examining the influence of imagery on gymnastics, tennis, and badminton performance routines has suggested that imagery immediately before execution may enhance skill performance.

The kinesthetic coupling component is concerned with establishing the feel of the upcoming shot. This component seems to be especially relevant during chipping and putting as elite golfers tend to rehearse far more when performing these kinds of shots. Thus, this component will entail rehearsing the correct action and attempting to establish the correct "feel" of the actual performance behavioral actions.

The next stage is the set-up. In most accuracy sports the alignment of the body to the target is of crucial importance. Thus, a routine which directs attention to the stance, grip, posture, alignment, ball position, and so forth, is a vital component. A quick mental checklist, supplemented by kinesthetic cues, could be performed as part of the routine.

The golfer is now ready to swing the club. Initiation of the swing is often preceded by a "waggle" which comprises small movements of the hands and club. Waggles usually consist of a forward press of the hands in the address position preceded by a number of small movements of the club away from the ball.

During the swing, which should be automatic and reflexive, a common technique used by golfers is to focus attention on a swing thought such as "tempo." Thus, timing the backswing to "tem" and the downswing to "po" focuses attention on the overall rhythm and timing of the shot rather than on specifics of the swing.

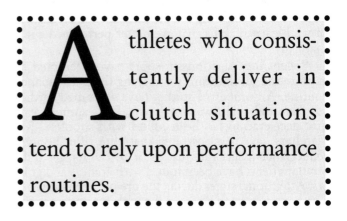

Athletes who consistently deliver in clutch situations tend to rely upon performance routines.

Clearly, athletes in other sports will require different components in comparison to golfers. The basic principle that applies, however, is that the pre-performance routine establishes a rhythm and a focus of attention that simultaneously prepares the body and mind for the ensuing skill. It should be emphasized that although the routine is aimed at establishing consistency the routine itself should be flexible. Thus, athletes who have an imagery component in their routine may have three or four different images that could be used if the one they are using does not appear to be effective for that particular situation.

In attempting to develop an effective pre-performance routine for your sport you must first establish a sequence of mental steps and behavioral actions similar to those outlined in the golf example. The content and structure will be highly individual and will vary for different sports. The refining and fine-tuning of each component will be a continuous process. Once a routine has been developed, its effectiveness can be assessed through videotaping and time analysis. For most sports the preliminary work should occur in practice settings (on the practice range, at the swimming pool), but will eventually be monitored and observed during competition.

Once a routine has been established, distraction can be used to test the consistency and attention efficiency of the routine. For instance, loud music could be played during the routine and its resulting effect assessed on video and through discussion with the athlete after performance. Eventually, other irrelevant competition cues such as camera clicks, crowd noises, crowd movement, and so forth, can be simulated. Vicarious experiential techniques can also be used to create competition-like environments. For example, a competitive situation in the Olympics could be created through imagery, by structuring the environment to simulate the competitive setting, and by playing video tapes of world class athletes who will be competing in actual competition. The challenge for athletes will be to focus attention away from distractive thoughts and concentrate on their own individualized pre-performance routine.

REACTIVE ROUTINES

The major difference between self-paced and reactive routines is that in their active situation environmental cues will play a more important role. Thus, the separate components may be similar to the self-paced routine but there will be a greater emphasis on responding to vital environmental cues. Vision training for athletes in sports such as baseball and tennis is a vital component of the reactive routine. For example, for the hitter in baseball, focusing on the placement of the ball in the pitchers' hand before the pitch could be an early cue in the reactive situation.

POST-PERFORMANCE ROUTINES

How the athlete reacts, thinks, and feels after executing a skill (the post-performance routine) is another area where routines can be utilized. There is a tendency for athletes to focus on negative aspects immediately after unsuccessful performances. Thus, a poor golf shot or a bad pitch can carry over and affect subsequent performance. The post-performance routine attempts to stop this negative transfer. Components of this routine may include emotional release, post-performance analysis, kinesthetic rehearsal of the correct skill, coping strategies, and mind clearing techniques. Emotional release refers to an emotional catharsis immediately following performance. Some athletes may need to release emotions through verbal or behavioral responses; however, other athletes may not feel the need to vent emotions. The analysis component might include a review of the performed skill to monitor any form or technique flaws. Kinesthetic rehearsal might involve performing the correct action to reinforce the feel of the skill. Coping strategies might include a relaxation technique such as the setting cues used at the start of the pre-performance routine. Thus, if the athlete perceived he/she is over-aroused, a quick, efficient coping strategy can be employed to re-establish optimal physiological arousal levels. Finally, mind clearing techniques to eradicate all thoughts about performance of the last skill can be employed. The athlete may use a technique such as centering to clear the mind and prepare the body for the next skill. Centering involves focusing thoughts on cues such as breathing to clear the mind in preparation for the next performance.

The following is an example of a post-performance routine for a missed penalty shot in soccer:

- Emotional release: exhale a long breath and remind self the last shot is history and now the important thing is the next shot;
- Analysis: "I missed the foul shot because I did not extend fingers through the ball to the basket";
- Physically rehearse the free throw minus the ball – extend fingers through imaginary ball to the basket;
- Mind clearing: take a long breath and use a quick centering or relaxation technique;
- Use a pre-performance routine for the next shot.

EVALUATING AND EXTENDING ROUTINES

Evaluating Performance Routines

There are a number of ways that athletes and coaches can assess the effectiveness of their performance routines. For instance, the routine can be videotaped and examined for consistency over repeated performances in different situations (e.g., practice, matches). The athlete can also monitor his/her own routine to assess how useful it was in avoiding distractions and keeping attention focused on the task at hand.

For example, the athlete could rate the overall effectiveness of the routine on a 1 to 10 scale for distraction, mind-clearing, and emotional control. With further development of the routines, each component can be evaluated, modified, and/or fine-tuned. Ultimately, the routine would allow for flexibility in each of the components.

Before the Competition

Pre-competition routines have two aspects: the first deals with preparation leading up to an athletic event (e.g., activity, sleeping, and nutritional patterns), whereas the second is concerned with preparation immediately before performing (e.g., warm-up, controlling arousal, and pre-performance thoughts). Many athletes have reported experiencing a variety of problems during the days prior to an important athletic event: For example, disruption in eating and sleeping habits, excessive worrying, and increased muscular tension levels have all been associated with the buildup to competition. Thus, it is important that the athlete be able to prepare adequately before competition. As each athlete may have different preparation strategies the challenge is to select the most efficient for that particular athlete given the unique characteristics of the athlete's sport. Thus, a preparation routine could be developed that guides the athlete through a series of steps during the days before competitions. The routine could consist of certain exercise activities, particularly nutrition habits, and previously developed stress management techniques.

The period right before performance can be crucial for athletes. It is here that athletes may experience the pre-match nerves often associated with performing in competitive situations. Thus, a routine could be developed to handle the minutes leading up to the match or game. Much has been written regarding self-regulation during these important minutes before the match. For instance, strategies used in this period by athletes included relaxation, breathing, coping, and positive affirmations. Athletes typically will find some of the techniques more useful than others. Again the challenge for athletes and coaches is to develop a routine before competition that uses the most suitable techniques and strategies for the athletes' particular sport. One interesting technique suggested by David Kauss is the "readying spot." This should be a place where you can be totally alone for at least 20 minutes so that you can give 100 percent attention to your performance. It is a place and time that you can use to get yourself into a specific frame of mind.

Interruptions and Stoppages in Play

The between-performance routine is pertinent for athletes engaged in sports that take many hours to complete and are characterized by periods of inactivity. Thus, football players and basketball players sitting on the bench, golfers waiting for their next shot, and weather delays in tennis will challenge the athlete's ability to maintain optimal psychological and physiological readiness. This waiting during performance many induce a warmup decrement and may also give the athlete additional time to worry about losing or performing badly. The between-play routine then is a strategy to use the time between performing effectively. Components of the between-play routine may take the form of distraction techniques could include imaging personal scenes or successful past performances. For example, the golfer waiting for an upcoming shot could image a private scene such as walking through an alpine meadow or along a sandy beach. Other distraction strategies could be talking to fellow competitors and spectators, observing the scenery, and listening to music. Preparation may include a physical warmup, stretching, and use of setting cues as discussed earlier.

MEDIA

Interacting with the media can be more stressful for many athletes than actually competing. However, handling interviews can follow the same principles already discussed. Athletes should be well prepared before the interview. Terry Orlick maintains that dealing with the media can be positive if the athlete develops a media plan. One of the most important components of this plan is to understand the agenda before you do the interview. To assist in determining this, part of the routine may be interacting with the reporter before the interview to find out what type of questions they will be asking. You could suggest topics or areas for the reporter to consider. Armed with this information, you can organize your thoughts so that you know what you want to say. You may also develop a plan for listening to questions offered by the interviewer as well as a plan for responding to particularly probing questions. Finally, you may want to role play the interview with a teammate, coach or sport psychologist to simulate the actual interview session. The key point is to have a plan that you have practiced so that when you are in front of the camera or microphone you can give an effective interview.

Performance routines can be great allies. David Kauss maintains that they build the foundation of discipline and self-control. Moreover, having a routine that "readies" you for the challenges of competition can generalize to other areas of your life. Remember, routines are not rituals, they are systematic patterns of thinking, feeling and behavior that you control. In building your routines start simply. Focus on building consistency in your actions. Once this consistency is established add cognitive and emotional components. Begin using your routines in low stress, practice situations. As their effectiveness increases, you will find that the use of the routine becomes automatic, a part of your game. As is the case with any mental skill, regular practice is essential. The more you employ routines, the more automatic and effective they will become. Be patient and above all, find what works for you so that you can let go and trust yourself.

⚽

COMMUNICATION: A TWO-WAY PROCESS
Cal Botterill (with Joe Taylor)

Most coaches do more talking than listening. They're better at supplying information than receiving it. After all, as a coach your job is to transmit the benefits of your vast knowledge, insights and motivation skill. Right?

The best answer is, "Yes, but..."

How do you motivate if you don't know much about the people you're trying to influence? How can you use your knowledge and insights to solve problems if you don't know what the problems are? How can you coach effectively if you don't have enough self-confidence to accept ideas from others without feeling threatened by them?

As an autocratic, dictatorial coach, you may be able to order your players to do what you want. But if your goals and objectives do not happen to coincide with theirs, you face a frustrating season, particularly if you're coaching young players.

SCENARIO

Consider this scenario. You have your heart set on the not-unreasonable goal of winning a league championship. But many of your players just want to have some fun, go on trips and be with the gang. If you can't get this out in the open and reach a mutually-acceptable compromise, you're probably headed for trouble.

Fortunately, most coaches are aware that communication is a two-way street. They establish good relationships and athletes frequently come to them with their problems and ideas.

But others simply do not have the type of personality that invites this sort of sharing of opinions and feelings. For them, it is difficult to establish easy connections. Problem athletes remain problem athletes, and certain team weakness in morale, concentration or learning potential may never be brought out in the open so that a mutual solution can be found.

If you feel there's room for personal improvement in this area of coaching, what can you do, short of remaking your entire personality? A good place to start is with goals and objectives. These are fundamental to having both a strong development program and easy communication with your athletes.

GETTING IT TOGETHER

While goal-setting – and we're talking about more than such performance goals as winning a championship or a certain number of games – is best done at the beginning of the season. It's never too late to make a start.

I believe strongly in holding an open meeting at which you outline the major things on which you and the team, as partners, are going to work. Such a meeting will help you to create a solid framework for training, and for solving difficulties that come up along the way.

Here are the five areas I consider essential, not necessarily in this order (some coaches have even more): Skills, Tactics, Conditioning, Mental/psychological (e.g., concentration, positive attitude), and Communication.

By including communication here, you send your players a signal that talking to you is one of their goals. As a result, if problems arise – either on the field or off, they will be more likely to come to you for help.

IMPORTANT

One of the things I always encourage coaches to do is set up a cyclical interview process with each of their athletes individually. Whether there are problems are not, sooner or later the coach will sit down with each one and share information on how we think it's going, what we've go to do better, what we feel. It is important to reinforce players in such areas, especially those who are starting to struggle, and it gives them a chance to share their concerns.

Some coaches try to do it all in one day, perhaps once a month or so. But that can get to be a huge task and it might be better to try scheduling a few meetings every week and keeping it an ongoing thing so that you're touching bases at regular intervals.

If you do a good job of goal-setting, your coaching style can change. You don't have to be so dictatorial. Instead of telling your athletes what they have to do, very often you just have to remind them that these things are part of their plans – they agreed on where they wanted to go, and so now it's up to them to go after what they want and not mess around.

POSSIBILITIES

If you have a weak team, it is critical that you reassess goals from time to time, because they may be unrealistic. The championship may be out of reach, but other goals skills — positional play, conditioning, good effort throughout the contest — are not, and by achieving these you can have a motivated team and a good season even without winning many games.

As I suggested earlier, start the season with a group meeting or meetings at which you outline your program and its objective and then have a good discus-

> ## You can admit mistakes and still be tough.

sion about what it means and how you plan to operate. Lay down the ground rules, but ask for input.

How do you get such a discussion going? Sometimes the best way to start the process is to ask your athletes to write down a few of their goals before they come to that initial meeting.

Have them rate themselves on their abilities in each of the five basic areas I mentioned earlier - skills, tactics, mental attributes, etc. — or perhaps just list some of their objectives in those areas. Ask them to articulate the biggest concerns they have had with programs in the past.

Question

A great question is; "Describe your idea of the ideal coach." This will help them tell you what they want from you and the problems they have had with past coaches. You can find out a lot that will help you communicate.

Their answers usually will supply the basis for some good solid dialogue on what they need and also will enable you to put forward your thoughts on what you expect from them, as a team and as individuals.

Clare Drake, the winningest coach in Canadian college history while at the University of Alberta and now assistant coach with the Winnipeg Jets, used to start with two simple questions: "Why did you come out this year?"(motives in general); and "What's your idea of an ideal coach?" (specific ideas).

This gave him a lot of information to discuss with his players, either as a group or individually. From there, he would go into goal-setting. If specific problems emerged, he would explore them with each athlete in one-on-one sessions.

I think you should have at least quarterly meetings over the season during which you sit down with the whole group and reassess what you've done so far: your progress, your failures. Get their ideas - don't simply impose your own. If it becomes one-sided, two-way communication stops.

I recently had such a meeting with the Chicago Black Hawks, and I asked four basic questions: What have we handled really well, on-ice and off-ice? What do you as players need to do to make it better? What does the staff (coaches, trainers, etc.) have to do better? We got some very straightforward and useful suggestions.

Reinforcement

The most important thing for players to realize is that you're open to such information. A good coach will integrate some of their concerns into the discussion, even if he/she don't always take the advice. You have to reinforce the athlete for providing it. It is important that they know that you appreciate them putting forward their ideas, and that these ideas will contribute to what all of you are trying to do.

One of the things you can say is, "I'm not sure if we can do all of that, but we can do this part of it." Almost always you can find something that you know will fit in with your plans.

If you are using written questionnaires, and I recommend this, they occasionally should be the anonymous type. The players may want to say certain things, but they may not want you to know the source.

For example, you want to track down special fears or anxieties that are spoiling concentration and motivation, or you want to find out if there are problem cliques or personality clashes within your team. You may need to ask such personal questions as: Who do you like or dislike? Who do you want to play with and who don't you want to play with? and so on.

If you've got a really good trust relationship going, an anonymous questionnaire may not be necessary. But it could be useful for sensitive issues of a personal nature,especially with athletes who are very reserved.

Sometimes you may feel you need specific feedback on an upcoming game or tournament. With the Olympic hockey team, I sometimes ask a very pointed question to find out what they're thinking or feeling: "What did you visualize an effective response to today?"

The replies - covering perhaps defensive play shooting, passing, etc. - were made anonymously rather than publicly I would add them all up and share them, again anonymously. It made a nice composite of good things to think about.

A second question was, "What was difficult for you to park today?" (referring to an anxiety or other distractions that they had to put out of their mind). This provided a picture of their worries about the nature of opposition—did they think it was too strong, too physical, were they having trouble getting 'up,' was something interfering with their concentration, and so on.

It doesn't hurt, if the season is not going well, for you as coach to take some of the heat. It will help to clear the air and set the stage for mutual reassessment of needs and objectives.

For example, I've heard coaches such as Jack Donohue, the former national basketball coach, come into the dressing room and take a piece of the responsibility for things: "You guys did a great job out there today and if I'd only coached you a little better we might have won."

It's amazing the response he got from his players by doing that, and how they opened up to him because of it. In that way he found out what he wanted to know about their attitudes and reactions to what had happened. Then they would work really hard on solutions the following week.

As a coach who wants the trust and admiration of your athletes, you shouldn't have to worry about your image, about seeming soft. You can admit mistakes and still be tough.

After the Chicago Bears had lost four in a row to drop-out of contention for the NFL playoffs, Mike Ditka went on national television to take the blame for a poor coaching job. Nobody can accuse Mike of being a wimp.

Finally remember that these principles apply to all levels of sport, not just to elite and Olympic level teams. The younger the age group, the more important it is to do a good job of goal-setting and establishing communication.

It's easy to forget when coaching seven year-olds that they have goals too, but that they may be timid about speaking up. For these youngsters, you're something of a father-figure. Before you start dictating what they're going to do, consider that you and your team may want to go in different directions.

UNITY

Their goals and objective will be all over the map—some are there for the fun, some for the road trips, some simply because their peers expect it of them. It's up to you to develop some kind of unity so that everyone is working in more or less the same direction.

In conclusion, remember this: Whether they're highly motivated or not, whether they're nine-year olds or 90-year olds, almost everyone wants to get better at what they're doing. Physical and mental improvement, even winning championships, are not incompatible with fun.

TEAM BUILDING

By Edward Etzal, ED.D., and Chris Lantz, M.A.

"Coming together is a beginning; Keeping together is progress; Working together is success"
— Henry Ford

How often have you heard a fan lament, "They've done so little with so much..." Indeed, many teams that have very skilled members and have all the "right stuff" to succeed often fail to live up to their potential and the expectations of others. In contrast, how is it that teams who seem to be less talented and have fewer resources develop into success stories?

The highly successful but out-manned 1980 U.S.A. Olympic Hockey Team provides a good example of how much can be done with relatively little. Although there are unique reasons underlying the achievements amid disappointments of particular sport teams, one factor that is instrumental to success is team building (TB).

Well-functioning teams are comprised of people (athletes, coaches, managers) who intentionally work together on shared goals. Unfortunately, many coaches and athletes mistakenly assume that just because their team wears the same uniform it somehow is an effectively functioning unit. Despite all of the talk about teamwork, the slogans on the locker room wall, and the endless pep talks, often little is done to systematically promote and maintain an effective functioning of sport teams. Just like well-functioning families, well-functioning sport teams are built, not made. "Healthy," families are the product of years of skillful nurturing.

Similarly sport teams do not become effective organizations overnight. It takes considerable knowledge, sensitivity, time and effort devoted to the process of shaping the values, attitudes and behaviors of team members to mold and preserve a team. Like families, sport teams are systems of people. Teams are made up of individuals who regularly interact with each other in the locker room, on the field or court, on a road trip, or socially .

Team members are connected to each other through a complex, yet understandable, network of relationships, roles and interactions—some stable. most constantly in flux. So, to understand a team and its needs at any one time, one must understand the current team system that exists. For example, if a soccer team is not as productive as it once was, the coach should not merely focus on the performances of certain players on the field. Rather, a broader perspective takes into consideration how individuals are getting along, what goals members have or have not achieved, and what other things may be occurring in members' lives that could contribute to their underachieving.

THE TEAM BUILDING PROCESS

Although TB means different things to different people, it can be thought of as the process of unifying individuals that make up sports teams. While it may take many forms, TB involves the development of cohesion and commitment in meeting the teams' challenges.

BUILDING A TEAM

Albert Carron has suggested that the following factors are most important when attempting to a build a team.

- Proximity: locker rooms, residences, training tables, and travel all work toward increasing the physical and social proximity of teams.
- Distinctiveness: the more distinct from others a team becomes, the more feelings of unity increase.
- Similarity: similarity in attitude about the team's objectives and modes of conduct all have a bonding influence on the team.
- Establishment of group goals and rewards: to ensure unity, individual goals must be consistent with team goals.
- Personal sacrifices by team members: sacrifices by team members who have high status produces a sense of commitment and involvement in individual members a well as demonstrates the importance that high status members give to the welfare of the team.

CHARACTERISTICS OF EFFECTIVE TEAMS

The following is a list of critical characteristics of effective teams as suggested by Phillip Hanson and Bernard Lubin in the Organization Development Journal (1986).

- A shared purpose
- A commitment to team building
- Knowledge of the team's resources
- A commitment to effective communication
- Sensitive to individual differences
- Conflict resolution
- Task focused
- Role clarity and balance
- Views mistakes as opportunity
- Sensitive to needs
- Intra-member attraction
- Intra-member trust

According to Donald Fuoss and Robert Troppman, the goal of TB is synergy. Synergy is a unified effect in which the whole becomes greater than the sum of its parts. That is, the overall productivity of a team becomes greater than the sum of each individual's ability. TB is not a new phenomenon. In fact, numerous successful organizations in business and industry have been involved in the process for years.

In a sense, effective parenting is also a form of team building. Much can be learned from unsuccessful and successful efforts applied to the building of sports team. TB is an ongoing process. It is not a one-shot intervention that can be done by coach, guest speaker, or sport psychologist in a one hour meeting or presentation. There is no "quick fix" that can create an instant, effective functioning team.

Indeed, TB is an ongoing process because teams are always in flux. Teams change over time as people age, are injured, move away, lose interest, are traded or as the tasks to be met by the team also change. These changes may be minor and barely noticeable or major causing significant upheaval. They may occur suddenly or at a slow pace. A team may be a team one day or when involved in one activity or not another. Invariably, as people and their challenges change, so does the team. Therefore regular "navigational" adjustments need to be made to keep the team's ship on course.

STAGES OF TEAM BUILDING

Keith Henschen and Jane Miner have observed that teams go through four identifiable stages of performance development: forming, storming, norming and performing. During the forming state, the team spends most of its time getting to know each other and the system. This is often an anxious period, with team members assessing or testing the situation. Actions that facilitate teammate familiarity and interaction are most effective in this early stage of team development. Although this is a rather short stage, the direction of the team efforts are initiated and it is, therefore, fundamental to TB.

During the storming stage, conflict and infighting often emerge. The anxieties regarding determining roles and how members "fit" into the team underlie this stage. To assist in moving through this stage, the coach should attempt to reduce some of the uncertainty in the environment by clearly communicating each member's strengths and weaknesses, and their role and potential contribution to the team.

The quiet following the storm is the norming stage. This stage is characterized by the team coming together, organizing itself into an effective unit. The notion of "there is no I in Team" becomes very prominent and team cohesion becomes defined. Instead of competing against one another, teammates desire to work together to achieve higher levels of performance and satisfaction. The focus is on encouraging members to provide mutual support for each other.

Last is the performing stage. Members have a close rapport with each other, roles are clearly delineated, teammate support is genuine and abundant, and according to Francis and Young, the team evidences a mature closeness. Activities that facilitate team harmony, delivery of positive reinforcement, and recognition of the special role of each member will help maintain this level. While these stages do not always occur automatically, nor do all teams move through them in strictly sequential manner, knowledge of where a team is in the process can assist in the development of cohesion.

THE BENEFITS OF TEAM BUILDING

Team building can be beneficial because it facilitates "team chemistry" and cooperative goal-directed action. Regular, open communication between team members and the coaching staff helps build understanding and trust in each other. People learn to feel valued by their peers and coaches. Given regular opportunities to express themselves and listen to others, team members can acquire a sense that they belong on the team, a feeling that reduces uncertainties and anxiety.

Everyone is seen as a valuable contributor to the team's success. Most players can assist the team in reaching its goals, given the opportunity.

Team building can be thought of as a form of psychological enhancement and have major positive effect on the overall performance of a team.

Accordingly, the team is seen as an interdependent system, not merely a collection of independent parts. Further, it is assumed that acquiring and demonstrating empathy will foster cooperative effort both on and off the field. In general, team members are quite interested in helping others. TB efforts both encourage and reinforce cooperative behavior.

RECOMMENDATIONS

The construction process clarifies the specific purposes of TB. Team building can become a valuable part of the team's culture in the following ways:

• "Enculturating" new team members. Becoming a member of a team is often a stressful experience. TB activities can facilitate learning about the team's culture (i.e., values, roles, cooperating procedures and personalities), reduce the amount of time it takes to be accepted as a team member, as well as reduce the anxiety felt by newcomers as well as veteran team members;

• Disseminating information. From an administrative standpoint, coaches can use TB meeting times to inform members about upcoming activities. Team members can ask questions about procedures, policy and upcoming activities;

• Teaching new skills. TB gatherings can be used to teach new skills. It is an excellent time to introduce or practice psychological performance enhancing skills;

• Goal-setting. Sessions can be used throughout the season to discuss, set and evaluate team goals. TB may also be involved in individual goal setting. However, it has been our experience that this is perhaps not the best forum to discuss individual goals;

• Problem-solving/conflict resolution. Personal conflicts can be devastating to the success of teams. TB time can serve as a special opportunity to inquire about concerns and solve problems. Exploration of the relationships between team members can increase understanding;

• Providing support for injured team members. A common consequence of the injury is isolation. TB meeting time can be used to support those who cannot participate and help keep them involved in team activities.

Whatever the focus of, the coach must be a strong proponent of TB. Enthusiasm for the process comes from the "top down." Regular support for TB activities provided by team leaders communicates that the coach is interested in each team member, not just the team's win and loss record. Allotting time for TB can be more conducive to the success of individual athletes and the team than many hours of physical practice. This is often the case with highly trained and experienced athletes who require little coaching and training to maintain their skill level, as well as at the end of a season when more practice leads to burnout.

SCHEDULING TB SESSIONS

How does one "go about" TB?

The most common way is to conduct team meetings. TB meetings should be gatherings involving all team members and staff and should start at the beginning of the team's training season. A regular time and day convenient for everyone should be set aside to conduct the meeting. Before establishing a specific time for TB sessions, members will gradually make the practice a habit for everyone. TB meetings are quite flexible and portable. They can be called as needed (e.g., when a crisis develops), when traveling "on the road," as well as pre- and post-competition, to discuss what is expected and what has occurred.

Intervals for TB meeting can vary. For example, an intercollegiate team with the luxury of daily contact can schedule a session. Other groups may not have the opportunity to meet so frequently. Teams with members who live a great distance from each other (e.g., regional or national teams) may only be able to meet every month or at training sessions or competitions.

Establish ground rules for TB sessions. Four simple "ground rules" are important when conducting TB sessions:

• Confidentiality is essential. Confidentiality is a foundation of trust. What occurs in TB sessions is exclusively for team members' ears. To ensure that team members feel comfortable enough to explore important, personal issues, all information about the content of TB sessions must stay within the team;

• No team member should be required to participate. Each person is encouraged to listen to what occurs and to be an active contributor to the team. While attendance may be mandatory, no one should be required to participate unless they want to. Members should also be able to remain silent;

• TB meetings are not a place to gripe or attack others. While it can be a proper time to raise issues of concern, discussion should move in a purposeful and problem-solving direction;

• The leader (in the case of an outside facilitator) is not a member of the group. The primary role is to facilitate interaction between team members and insure that the ground rules are adhered to.

Let go of your role. Sport teams encounter problems just as other organizations do. As mentioned above, TB meetings can be useful for the solving of difficulties. Meetings of this nature can become quite energized and uncomfortable for members—especially those who are involved in conflicts. Therefore, coaches and athletes should avoid personally conducting these types of TB sessions to avoid conflicts.

This type of TB activity (if not all TB meetings) is best undertaken with the assistance of an objective professional trained in team building skills. This person can act more effectively as a traffic cop who helps with the conduct and control of the meetings. Such an arrangement frees coaches and athletes of the problem of dual relationships. Team building efforts will be more effective when they relinquish their roles, especially leadership, during these meetings. Coaches and athletes who let go of their roles will learn a great deal about their teams, but often not without some discomfort.

Go beyond your comfort zone. The training of most coaches and athletes typically focuses on learning and teaching skills, rules, conditioning and training methods. If you want to enhance your personal effectiveness and the success of your team, consider implementing team-building activities. Although TB may not be part of your repertoire, learn more about the process and its potential benefits. If you are willing to take some risks (e.g., listen to some criticism), consider ways that you might go about implementing TB activities. If there is a psychological or management consultant with interest and experience available to you, seek him out for information, training, or professional assistance. Given the opportunity, obtain TB training at coaching seminars in your area. If such programming is not included in seminars, request some in the future. Talk with other coaches and athletes who may have been involved or utilized a psychological consultant. Learn about their experiences with TB activities and see how you might apply what they have learned to your team. Consider stretching your team's style a little.

Clear Blockages. According to Mark Anshel, TB is facilitated by "clearing blockages" if and when they exist. To assist in this process, Mark suggests that athletes and coaches should seek answers to the following seven questions posed by David Francis and Donald Young:

• What are our objectives?
• How will we handle the organizational aspects of our team?
• Who is in charge?
• Who, outside the team, is concerned about our success?

• What is our method of handling problems?
• How do we relate to other teams or organizations?
• What are the costs and benefits of being a member of this team?

Establish a good climate. David Yukelson suggested that the coach-athlete communication system and team harmony can be enhanced in the following ways:

• Establish open communication channels. The foundation of effective communication between coaches and athletes is mutual trust and respect for each other. This is a two-way venture; both the coach and athlete are responsible for making it work. Listening is just as important a form of communication as talking;
• Develop pride. Feelings of pride and satisfaction develop when teams attain challenging but realistic goals;
• Establish common expectations of appropriate behavior. Teams unite behind common goals;
• Value unique personal contributions. Each member of the team should have their role clearly defined as well as understand their potential contribution to the team;
• Recognize those who excel individually and who contribute to accomplishing team goals;
• Attain consensus and commitment to team goals;
• Hold periodic team meetings to resolve conflicts;
• Stay in touch with interpersonal grapevines;
• Seek grails rather than slay dragons. Focus first on achievement, then move to how mistakes can be corrected to facilitate future performance. Look for opportunities before the obstacles.

Become a responsible model. If you have never been involved in a team whose culture emphasizes team building, participation in TB activities may require expanding your perspective. It may also necessitate some changes in your behavior. To contribute in your own way you probably will need to assume greater personal responsibility. This may take various forms.

You should become more sensitive to the needs of others who make up your team.

Seek out opportunities to show interest in others and in their concerns. Take time to ask team members "How things are going." Give them the opportunity to be heard. Learn some of the practical skills associated with being a better listener. When doing so, communicate acceptance, positive feelings, support and encouragement to others, especially in situations during which a teammate has experienced frustration or is under stress. By doing so, you'll encourage your teammates to do the same for you and others. As the saying goes, you can never listen yourself into trouble.

Furthermore, take advantage of opportunities to express your own thoughts and feelings to teammates and coaches. Of course, you'll need to carefully determine when it is appropriate to do so (e.g., in team meetings or when meeting with your coach) and when not to do so (e.g.,in public). Nevertheless, when it is OK to do so, take the risk of being a more assertive contributor to the team. Regular communication between team members facilitates team unity and successful performance.

Knowing that everyone has an impact on the behavior of each team member, start to monitor your own behavior a bit more closely when you are around your team or coaches. Whenever possible, refrain from critical, angry, or aggressive comments and behavior. Others will observe what you do and can be affected by it. Be a responsible model who is respectful of the needs of others.

Finally, respect the confidentiality of what people share with you personally or in team meetings. Avoid gossiping and complaining behind others' backs.

For example, if you have a concern that involves another teammate or coach, talk directly to them about your concern. Avoid communicating through a third party and don't wait hoping that the problem will take care of itself. Such behavior can be detrimental to the success of the team. To a great extent, the success of TB efforts is dependent on the cooperation of each team member.

Coach Randy Johnson attempts to clarify things for his Vanderbilt women's team at halftime of its match. Clarity of goals is an issue that all coaches need to articulate.

(photo by Perry McIntyre, Jr.)

COACHES, PLAYERS AND FAMILIES: BUILDING FOR SUCCESS
Dr. Gary M. Miller

INTRODUCTION

There has been a tendency for coaches and players to describe their teams as a family and that all involved are one big family. In examining this analogy, coaches must sometimes wonder as they read about dysfunctional families in the media if the dilemmas of these families may someday impact their teams. This paper will examine characteristics of winning teams, sound leadership, dysfunctional roles and the relationship to successful teams as families.

THE WINNERS

Recently there have been a number of books and training programs designed to help individuals come together and function as a team. Works by Martin (1993), Riley (1993), and Larson and LaFasto (1989) examine what can be done to develop excellence.

Larson and LaFasto (1989) broadly define the concept of a team as: A team has two or more people; it has a specific performance objective or recognizable

goal to be attained; and coordination of activity among the members of the team is required for the attainment of the team goal of objective (p. 19).

Larson and LaFasto (1989) examined a number of effective teams including corporate groups, governmental agencies and athletics. Through their research they were able to identify specific traits necessary for a successful team. The first trait was that effective teams had a clear, elevating goal. The goal for the team needed to be clear and concrete so that the members were able to recognize when they had met their goals.

To foster success, coaches need to establish goals for their team and individual goals for each player on their team. It is important for coaches to meet with their players and develop individual and team goals that are clearly understood by all team members. Martens (1987) suggests that goal-setting follow these principles:

• Setting performance goals over which the athlete has control;

- Setting challenging goals which promote striving on the part of the athlete;
- Setting realistic goals which help the athlete to gain knowledge about one's self;
- Setting specific goals so that behavior may be channeled toward a specific success criterion;
- Setting short-term goals which will lead eventually to achieving longer-term goals;
- Setting individual goals to motivate each athlete on the team.

For goals to be elevating, the team members must believe that the goals they have established can really make a difference in terms of the team's performance. This helps promote the sense of commitment necessary to attain success. Periodic seasonal reviews of these goals will help the team stay focused and renew the players' individual commitments to both the team and personal goals.

Structure that is results-driven is the second trait Larson and LaFasto (1989) identified. Soccer teams resemble the tactical teams they researched in that there is a clear definition of who is responsible for specific performances at specific times during the game. Team structure is enhanced when the team members have clear roles, responsibilities and are accountable for their actions. Clear communication can foster team structure. Therefore, coaches and players need to have access to information that can help them improve. The more credible the source of this information, the greater the likelihood that individuals will use it. It is also important that team personnel have their individual performances monitored and be given feedback on their efforts. When a coach must make a decision, using facts is the soundest way to present information to the team, as it helps to promote the structure of the team. Emotionally-based decisions may be tempting to make, but in the long run it is better to be objective when making a decision about the team and its players. Even though the final decision a coach has to make may not be the most popular one, if facts are used, players realize that the coach is being consistent in the decision-making process.

Competence is another trait found in the study by Larson and LaFasto (1989). Coaches are very skilled at identifying the competencies needed by their players. The technical competencies of being able to execute specific soccer skills are essential for a player to succeed. Practice sessions are designed to refine the skills of players and enhance their confidence. The personal competencies of the players are essential for the team to function. Sometimes called "team chemistry" these skills are ones that allow personnel to identify problems the team faces and develop ways to resolve issues that may lead to a lack of team cohesion. Competent team members must also want to contribute to the team and be willing to work with others to achieve the goals of the team.

Strong commitment and dedication are other traits Larson and LaFasto (1989) identified. Team personnel must have the physical and psychological energy to invest in the team. From commitment comes the team unity. When unity exists the team members are more likely to be open and honest with each other as they believe such communication enhances the team's effort at achieving its goals. Sometimes individuals may need to revise their personal goals in order to help the team achieve its goals. Such behavior exemplifies a committed team member.

The ability to collaborate with each other represents another essential trait of a successful team (Larson & LaFasto, 1989). In order to collaborate, team personnel must collectively trust each other and demonstrate honesty, openness, consistency and respect. These concepts were cited many years ago by Carl R. Rogers (1942) when he wrote of the characteristics of a helping relationship in counseling. When a trusting environment exists there is greater probability of clearer communication amongst the group. Trust also comes into play when one player is able to compensate and help another during practice or in a game. How many times have you seen a player taking another aside and demonstrate something or try to cheer a teammate up after a particularly tough play?

Excellence in performance is something winning teams strive for and can be assessed in a variety of ways (Larson & LaFasto, (1989). Coaches and team members need to determine what the rewards for success and what the consequences of failure should be for all concerned. Each member must strive to meet the joint goals once they are established. The pressure of the team to encourage individuals to meet individual goals can not be underestimated. When team pressure involves the striving for excellence, everyone is a winner. However, when team pressure focuses on low standards of achievement, mediocrity follows. We must remember, individuals and teams do not set out to fail and team confidence thrives on successes. Coaches represent one source of pressure as they attempt to inspire the team to reach the demanding and achievable goals. As the coach focuses on excellence, the pressure exerted on the team will raise standards and expectations of all involved. Coaches must remember that such standards of excellence need to be performance-based and understood by all team members. The standards will require hard work, dedication and discipline in order for success to be achieved.

Coaches recognize that external support and recognition are important factors in promoting team success (Larson & LaFasto, 1989). A study by Coleman cited by Larson and LaFasto indicates that when teams experience success, they credit themselves with the successes, however, when the tide turns, they tend to look to situations outside of themselves to blame for their lack of success. How often have you seen a player credit the team with having achieved success on the field? Have you ever watched a coach take the responsibility for a team's loss? This latter often happens to deflect the responsibility and protect the team members from blaming themselves for their failure.

The final component of effective teams cited by Larson and LaFasto (1989) is that of principled leadership. They believe that effective leaders help a group stay focused on the agreed goals. Sometimes, the coach may have to make changes on a team in order to achieve a new vision. Nanus (1992) has presented some suggestions that indicate when there is need to change the direction of an organization. Several of these apply to soccer teams. When players complain that they do not feel challenged or that the fun of playing soccer is declining it is time to take a look at what the coach and team are trying to accomplish. When players appear to have lost pride in their team and question their efforts, or appear to not want to take responsibility for team improvement, they are sending a signal that a change is needed. Another signal involves players who do not feel they are progressing enough on the team and begin to question their commitment to the team. Lastly, rumors about the team and personnel on the team are another warning that the time has come to reevaluate the team's goals.

THE EFFECTIVE COACH

In examining the literature on effective coaching there a several schools of thought presented. In the book *Successful Coaching* (Martens, 1990), presents a systematic way to train coaches for working with their athletes. He describes a variety of coaching styles in the program, emphasizing the need for coaches to develop a cooperative leadership style which promotes goal-setting and seeks development of responsible athletes. Lombardo (1987) suggests that coaches be flexible and adjust their style to meet the individual needs of the players on their teams and at same time present challenges that stretch players to the limits of their abilities. Bell (1989) sees one role of the coach as that of a resource person and as a teacher of various lessons. However, Bell still places the responsibility for learning in the hands of the athlete.

Larson and LaFasto (1989) have indicated that effective leaders curtail their own egos to promote those of team members. This type of behavior results in team members developing leadership skills. Empowerment is a term often used in the 1990's and coaches can effectively promote this goal within their teams. Such leadership creates self-confidence in people, thereby encouraging them to take risks, make decisions, and act - in short, to be leaders themselves (Larson & Lafasto, 1989, p. 129). When team members feel empowered Bennis (1989) notes that they feel significant, realize that learning and competence do matter on the team, sense they are part of the team and find their efforts exciting. What more could a coach ask for?

> Team structure is enhanced when the team members have clear roles, responsibilities and are accountable for their actions. Clear communication can foster team structure.

TEAMS AND FAMILIES

As cited earlier, often coaches and players speak of their team as a family. In examining the mental health of families, Sedgwick (1981) noted that:

> The family is made up of people who have a shared sense of history, experience and some degree of emotional bonding, engage in directionality and goal setting for the future and whose activities involve group issues as well as individual concerns (p.5).

Considering the earlier definition of a team, one can see some similarities between teams and families. Coaches know that their teams share a history together. These shared experiences expose the coaches and players to the highs and lows of athletic competition. Over time, the roles of the coaches and players change and shift as the team experiences such successes and failures.

Emotional bonding occurs between coaches and players. Coaches strive to bond their team together as a functional unit and realize that the emotional bonding will be critical as a team progresses through an entire season together. The emotional bonding combined with the goal-setting noted earlier help promote a sense of teamwork among your players.

FAMILY FEUDING

There are times when coaches sense that things are not going well with their teams. Slumps, players not reaching their potential, lack of motivation and team bickering are troublesome signs.

The system of a team is very similar to that of a family. In dysfunctional families, chaos and uncertainty reign. People in these situations use inappropriate ways of dealing with the issues facing them.

Consequently they engage in behavioral patterns that are unauthentic and highly manipulative. In these situations individuals try to control others, working to get the upper hand.

In dysfunctional families, communication is unclear and the members lack the skills necessary to seek clarification and often get involved in playing games that promote miscommunication. Communication becomes a means to conceal and protect a person as the individual tries to put on a "good front" to others. On teams, such communication can be seen when unclear messages are given to players and they are unable to execute a specific skill needed in a game.

DYSFUNCTIONAL TEAM ROLES

The noted family therapist, Virginia Satir (1972) examined some of the roles individuals in dysfunctional families play. Some of these same roles can be seen on teams and often create frustration for the coach. Placaters are individuals who try to keep the peace and work at keeping others from getting angry. They are the "yes sir" and "yes ma'am" types. These individuals will take the blame for many miscues, hoping to keep the coach from criticizing their efforts and at the same time trying to shelter themselves from resentment of their teammates for not doing well. How often have you heard players say "My fault coach, I blew it!" One may wonder if this is a pattern of a player and if the player is not really trying to avoid criticism. If the coach accepts such statements, the player may miss the opportunity to learn from the coach's critique and may continue to execute skills improperly.

Another dysfunctional role is that of the blamer. These players find fault with others, be they teammates, opponents, officials, or their coach. Rather than take responsibility for their play, they quickly find fault and shift the focus from themselves to others with the hope of deflecting criticism of their own efforts. Blamers can cause disruption on a team and place themselves as the judge of others, while at the same time presenting themselves as above criticism. Such behavior can have a negative impact on team morale and motivation.

The last type of player that represents dysfunctional behavior is the computer. These players have learned not to show their feelings to their coach, thus controlling the relationship. This type of behavior distances the player from the coach and inhibits good communication. Some of these types of players are often very scared and fear letting their coach know their true feelings. It is not only players who exhibit this behavior, but some coaches take on this role and severely diminish the opportunity to clearly communicate with their players. Players may have difficulty relating to such a person.

SUGGESTIONS

Coaches can do much to increase their effectiveness with their players. The skills of active listening, demonstrating support and effective verbal communication are three that can be of significant help to the coach.

Active listening has been cited as a method for coaches to enhance their communication with their

It is suggested that a coach have a planned format in mind prior to criticizing a player. Here a coach addresses a problem with one of his players at halftime of an ODP match. (photo by Perry McIntyre, Jr.)

players (Rosenfield & Wilder, 1990). They suggest that coaches develop their own mental plan prior to discussing things with a player. These authors encourage coaches to use supportive statements that are descriptive, rather than blaming ones, when attempting to critique the play of an athlete. Rather than screaming, "Why did you miss that pass?" they suggest the coach (1) describe the situation, (2) describe their observation of what the player was doing, (3) clarify the consequences of the player's behavior, and (4) finish with a description of what behavior is expected in the future. It is the wise coach who not only verbally corrects a player, but takes the time to demonstrate the skill several times, from several angles, to the player has a clearer understanding of what is expected. Using this sequence provides a chance for the player to learn and know what to correct for in the future. This method eliminates ridicule, which often results in the player getting angry, possibly committing an infraction and maybe costing the team a chance to win. If taken to extreme, angry players may undermine your efforts and interfere with the sense of teamwork a coach tries to build with a team.

Parents can also use active listening. When a player complains to her parents by saying "That Coach Johnson is a fool. She never puts me in. I am the best goalie she has. I should quit the team, I'll show her." Some parents may reply with "You're right, she can't coach. The school should fire her." or "I don't know how anyone can play for that jerk. What does she know about soccer? Your middle school coach could coach rings around her". A sounder reply would be one that indicates the parent understands what the daughter has said and would be "You're disappointed with your coach and right now you would even quit the team to show her how upset you are." This statement lets the player know that her parent has heard her and that the parent is concerned about what the player is experiencing. A parent can not make decisions for coaches, but they can take responsibility for listening and responding to the child in a nonjudgmental, caring manner.

Positive non-verbal behaviors can let players know that you are interested in them an want to assist them. Making eye contact that is comfortable, standing at a distance that does not invade the player's

ATHLETES' VIEWS ON TEAM BUILDING

Suggestions for Athletes

· Bring the problem out in the open so that the whole team can be made aware of it and then collectively seek a solution. This can be done through an athletes-only brainstorming session.

· Organize regular, at least once a month, social gatherings.

· Discuss team goals with coaches. Make sure everyone agree on the team goals. Also, have team sessions that monitor and evaluate the effectiveness of achievement of the team goals. Don't be hesitant to modify the goals where necessary.

· Take some time off to clear the head and think through some options.

· Commit to only positive verbal and non-verbal communication. Always encourage other members to perform well and remember to sympathize with injury or illness.

· Develop a tangible team identity through appearance, behavior or labels.

· Value and respect individual differences.

· Try to accomplish skills in a team environment. All members perform in repetition after each other until the particular skill is accomplished satisfactorily by everyone.

· Don't forget about having fun. Laugh at yourself and with your teammates. Humor can play a major role in easing team tensions.

Suggestions for Coaches

· Give constructive positive and negative feedback to all athletes.

· Hold individual meetings with players in an attempt to isolate the problems. Follow these with a team meeting to discuss the problems and identify solutions.

· Provide and opportunity for an athletes-only meeting.

· Change the training stimulus. Provide a day off or put some variety and fun in practices.

· Meet with the other members of the coaching staff to discuss their perceptions of the problem and potential solutions.

· Have more team building activities during each training session.

· Make a better effort to know the players on a personal level.

· Don't be afraid to seek outside professional expertise to assist with team building.

· Make sure roles are clarified and give positive feedback about each athlete's responsibilities to the team.

· Evaluate your coaching behavior. Enlist a peer to critique your coaching behavior during practice and competitions.

Suggestions for Parents

· Make sure you let your athletes know that you are there for them. Combine your efforts with other parents so that athletes feel supported by a group of parents.

· Suggest that your athletes participate in other activities to help give them a new perspective on the problems related to the team.

· Ask members of the coaching staff how you can help the situation.

· Attend practices and competitions; find something positive and share it with the team.

· Sponsor a team social event.

· Model effective cohesion within your own "family team."

· Discourage negative criticism of teammates and coaches.

with players and should be used in both practice and in games. Players will begin to model similar communication efforts when they are able to observe their coach applying this strategy. In fact, some players may be able to help each other using this approach, resulting in more positive relationships among team members and promoting a greater sense of belonging to the team.

Paraphrasing and reflecting can also be powerful skills to use with players and parents off the field as well. When discussing concerns, the coach can actively listen to the player and parents and paraphrase what has been said to be sure everyone is clear on what is being discussed. When emotions emerge in discussions the coach can move into the reflection of feeling mode, letting the player and the parents know that their feelings are heard and respected. Then, all involved can begin developing ways to deal with the issue at hand. When players and parents sense that the coach is hearing them, there is a good probability of them hearing the coach's point of view as well. Coaches know that some parents see their children as the professionals of tomorrow and some even live out their own dreams of athletic stardom in their children. When the dreams do not materialize, it helps when coaches are able to use paraphrasing and reflection to assist the player and parents discuss their views of the situation.

COACH'S CHECKLIST

The concept of dysfunctional families was used as a way to look at some faulty behaviors that may disrupt a team. There are positive traits of healthy families that coaches can also examine. In her research about healthy families, Curran (1982) discovered several traits that healthy families have. It is suggested that coaches use this check list for comparison of what they see on their teams.

√ Having communication and listening abilities
√ Affirming and supporting members
√ Teaching respect for others
√ Developing a sense of trust
√ Having a sense of play and humor
√ Having shared responsibilities
√ Having rituals and traditions
√ Seeking help with problems

Teams can be like families. Coaches who behave positively and communicate effectively can make the athletic experience a positive one for their players, parents and themselves. Perhaps, with some work and effort the theme song adopted by the Pittsburgh Pirates several years ago, "WE ARE FAMILY", will also become yours.

References

Bell, K. (1989). *Coaching excellence*. Austin: Keel Publications.

Bennis, W. (1989). *Why leaders can't lead*. San Francisco: Jossey Bass.

Curran, D. (1983). *Traits of a healthy family*. San Francisco: Harper and Row.

Ivey, A.E. (1994). *Intentional interviewing and counseling*. (3rd ed.) Pacific Grove: Brooks/Cole.

Larson, C.E. & LaFasto, F.M.J. (1989). *Teamwork*. Newbury Park: Sage.

Lombardo, B.J. (1987). *The humanistic coach*. Springfield: Thomas.

Martens, R. (1987). *Coaches guide to sport psychology*. Champaign: Human Kinetics.

Martens, R. (1990). *Successful coaching*. (2nd ed.) Champaign: Leisure Press.

Martin, D. (1993). *Teamthink*. New York: Dutton.

Nanus, B. (1992). *Visionary leadership*. San Francisco: Jossey Bass.

Riley, P. (1993). *The winner within*. New York: Putman.

Rosenfield, L. & Wilder, L. (1990). *Active listening*. Sport Psychology Training Bulletin,1,(5), 1-7.

Satir, V. (1972). *Peoplemaking*. Palo Alto: Science and Behavior Books.

Sedgwick, R. (1981). *Family mental health theory and practice*. St. Louis: Mosby.

COACHING WOMEN'S SOCCER

● ●

While the "basics" of coaching technique and tactics are essentially similar for both women and men, there appear to be subtle physical and psychological dimensions of coaching women players that need to be taken into consideration as one prepares to coach women.

Of interest is the fact that the U.S. women's teams captured both the aforementioned competitions and so our nation's coaches of womens' teams have reached the pinnacle of world competition.

Coach Anson Dorrance directed the U.S. challenge in 1991 and this chapter will find him offering two articles for consumption. One will detail how to successfully build a competitive attitude in female players while the second contains his ideas on how to successfully lead (coach) female athletes. Coach Jan Smisek adds to the Dorrance articles from the perspective of a woman coach of women players.

Coach Tony DiCicco directed the U.S. Olympic team to the 1996 title and also was Anson's goalkeeper coach in 1991. In addition, coach DiCicco's background includes extensive work with our national men's teams. Thus readers will find his comparisons in terms of coaching male and female goalkeepers of value.

He also evaluated goalkeeper play in the inaugural 1991 World Championship and shares that information on these pages.

Dr. Jack Levine affirms the important roles coaches of young women play in the lives of those individuals in another related story. Ruth Callard also offers a piece centered on how social factors affect the way girls/women make decisions.

The physical aspect of coaching women is addressed by two writers. Author Pat Croce talks about the physiological responses to exercise between the sexes and his thoughts are abetted by Donald Kirkendall as he outlines some ideas relative to the physical preparation of women players — particularly addressing areas of concern relating to the female population in general. Coaches cannot divorce these troublesome questions from their preparation.

Perhaps no area of U.S. soccer has grown faster than the women's game.

The explosion began in the late 70s and has continued unabated until it is estimated today that females comprise more than 40% of the game's participants.

The surge of soccer interest is not centered just in the U.S. but has extended itself to countries throughout the world with the result that the first FIFA-sponsored World Championship was contested in China in 1991 and the first women's Olympic Championship was staged in Atlanta in 1996.

LEADING WOMEN ATHLETES*
Anson Dorrance

*"A man's style of leadership is a very top-to-bottom structure.
A woman's style is more like a network."*

When we do coaching clinics and talk to people who have coached only men, we talk about the differences in coaching men and women. There is a cliché we use: "You basically have to drive men, but you can lead women." You have to drive a men's team to get them to conform to your position, but a women's team is more easily coached to that position. And, in my opinion, the way you coach women is a more civilized mode of leadership. If you read any books about leadership styles of men and women, you learn that the men's style is a hierarchical style. It is a very top-to-bottom structure. A woman's style is more like a network.

There is a great book about this called "The Female Advantage." The author, Sally Helgesen, talked about how she looked at great women leaders in the business world and philanthropy, and she took you through a typical day. The way these women led is by connecting with everyone they conceivably could within their organization. It was not by a hierarchy. A great female leader's secretary would almost be like a partner in the leadership process, and she would have a direct connection to her and almost everyone around her. No matter how far down in the organization they were, they all got the impression that they were personally connected to the leader. That is critical in coaching a women's team. All the players on the team have to feel like they have a personal connection with the coach, and it has to be unique. It seems like a male leadership style is done through status, memorandum and intimidation. The great leaders of men, the outstanding and consistently successful coaches of men, are strong personalities who lead with a powerful presence and will. Their effectiveness comes through their resolve. Yet with women, your effectiveness is through your ability to relate. They have to feel that you care about them personally or have some kind of connection with them beyond the game. Women want to experience a coach's humanity.

A coach's approach to men and women is definitely different. This, however, does not apply to young boys because I think you can coach young boys and girls the same way. I don't know if it is a hormonal thing. I don't know if when testosterone starts to kick in it makes these young boys more rebellious,

but they begin to resist any sort of authority. So to lead them, you almost have to dominate them. And there are different ways to dominate them. One way is with intimidation, through the power and force of your own personality. Another one is with some sort of aggression or superior strength of ego. That is one of the things that was tiring about coaching men. This was not the case with all the men that I coached—I coached men for thirteen years. But to get them to conform to your vision of the game, there does seem to be a constant warfare between you and different personalities on your team. They all have their own opinions. You might suggest something to them, and they think, "This is not what made me an All-American in high school." Then they go off in their own direction and you have to convince them that your vision is the correct one. The difference between convincing men and women that your vision is correct is that women are willing to at least look at your system and try it. The men generally don't want to do anything that they are not accustomed to doing. Usually, the way you get them to try is by demanding it. To be an effective leader of a men's team you don't need a personal rapport as long as there is respect. That's the extent of the relationship. That's all that's really required. But in a women's team, respect is only part of it, and it is derived from a personal relation-

Coaches of womens' teams such as Bill Hempen of Duke (here shown addressing his team at halftime) have to use a slightly different approach. (photo by Perry McIntyre, Jr.)

ship. Women have to have a sense that you care for them above and beyond their soccer capabilities. If they feel their relationship with you is dependent on their soccer success, it will not be a very close and effective leadership relationship. So it's critical that women do not get a sense that there is some sort of distance personally due to some athletic failure. The personal relationship with them has to be preserved at all costs. In fact, you can destroy your leadership of a great women's team if the players feel your respect for them is based purely on athleticism or their effectiveness on the field. Women have an understanding beyond the superficiality of athletics. And what is critical to them is the way people are treated and the reasons for which you choose to respect them. Athletic prowess does not rank at the top of their list of things for which they want to gain respect. In their minds, it should be other human qualities that are above and beyond athleticism. And in reality, athleticism and soccer are not that deep and quite superficial. We all make a coaching mistake if we try to make that the priority in their lives. Your players will see through you and view you as one-dimensional.

Also, much of your coaching has to be done through a positive tone and supportive body language, even when you are upset with them and much of what you are saying is critical. Through trial and error, I have learned that the women I have coached listen less to what I say than to how I say it. In other words, they listen less to the language and more to the tone. If my tone is negative, it doesn't matter how positive the words are. They are going to hear negative. If your body language is negative, it doesn't matter how careful you are in constructing your sentences to create a positive impression. It still comes out negative. Women listen to your tone and watch your body language, regardless of what comes out of your mouth.

In Deborah Tannen's introduction to her book "You Just Don't Understand" a husband and wife are going down the highway, and the husband is driving. The wife turns to him and says, "Honey, are you thirsty? Do you want to pull over and get a drink?" And he says no and keeps driving. Well, the wife gets upset. She could care less whether he was thirsty. But it was a test of his sensitivity. He was supposed to say, "No honey, I'm not thirsty. Are you thirsty? Would you like me to pull over so you can get a drink?" And since he was just answering her question, he failed miserably. Of course, the joke is that men speak English and women speak Hidden Agenda. So the whole idea in talking to women is to understand there is a completely different conversation going on that is above and beyond the English language. And for men coaching women for the first time, the coaching vocabulary, tone and body language they brought with them from the men's game will not have the same effect. The way men communicate is by listening to

> **I**t's crucial when you are coaching women to use the correct tone and body language to communicate, or at least have some sort of positive approach even if you are being critical.

what someone says and interpreting it. They are discovering in research that a woman has so many other faculties in her brain that she draws on in a conversation, and these faculties are above and beyond her intellectual interpretation of the words you are using to communicate. She is looking at your body language, and she is listening to your tone. Through a combination of all these factors, she is deciphering exactly what you are thinking about her regardless of what you are saying. It's crucial when you are coaching women to use the correct tone and body language to communicate, or at least have some sort of positive approach even if you are being critical. If you are criticizing a woman in training—and obviously sometimes you are going to—they have to get a sense that it's nothing personal. But it is hard for a male who has coached only men to do this. This is one of the challenges in the clinics I give—teaching male coaches to have a positive rapport so their relationship with the female athlete is never in jeopardy. It's difficult for men to have positive body language and use a positive tone, especially in an athletic coaching arena that is filled with frustration and correction. Invariably, what ends up being communicated is disgust. That's the nature of athletics. But when a man is criticized in this fashion, he understands it's just someone taking his game apart, not taking his life apart. A woman does not separate the two.

In clinics, we also talk about the use of videotape. You don't need to show a videotape to a women's team to critique them. If you are in front of a bunch of men giving them general criticisms of a game, a videotape is crucial. If you are saying there was not enough defensive pressure in the game, every male in the room is thinking, "Yeah you jackasses, I was the only one working out there. The rest of you were useless." In his mind, he immediately blames everyone else for the lack of defensive pressure. If you made that general criticism to a women's team, and said,

"This is garbage. Our defensive pressure was terrible." Every woman in the room would think, "He's talking about me." So it's critical with a men's team to coach with videotape. That way, when you make a general statement, you can look at the tape and say, "See Billy. Look, there is no pressure from your position. They are coming up their right side. You are my left midfielder, and the amount of distance you are giving that guy is about seven or eight yards." Billy will say something like, "Yeah, but he's not penetrating." And you say, "There's more to defense than stopping penetration. So what if he is not dribbling around you? You are giving him so much bloody room he can serve the ball anywhere he wants." There's a constant argument about who is failing, and you have to actually show it on tape before they guy ever has an idea that he's to blame. And even then, he'll have some kind of excuse.

So when criticizing men, it is almost essential to use videotape because they are not going to believe you. They're not going to believe they have ever made a mistake, and obviously, to a degree I'm exaggerating. But with women, a video is actually more effectively used to show that they can play well and to show the positive aspects of the performance. I think a lot of women do not have the confidence to feel they are as good as they actually are. So videotape for the sexes should be used in completely contrasting modes. Not that you can never show negative aspects of a performance to a women's team, but seeing their mistake on tape does not really help them. If you tell them they made a mistake, they'll believe you. A video almost makes it worse because they see how bad they actually were. If self-confidence is a problem to begin with, the video does nothing but magnify the mistake. Now they can see how poorly they have performed. I find it interesting that a male will look at the video and see everyone making mistakes, including himself, and start to blame everyone else for his inability. But a woman will see herself and take full responsibility for that problem emotionally. That, of course, does not build her self-confidence at all. You have to balance that with something good that she did. I do not want to pretend that men do not respond to positive things, but you have to have a balance of showing the positive and the negative. Coaches have a tendency to only stop practice during an entirely negative environment to point out and correct mistakes. Yet one of the best times to stop a training session is during or right after a brilliant series of performances to confirm exactly what you want.

* *Published with permission of author from his book* Training Soccer Champions, *JTC Sports, Raleigh, NC, 1996. 159 pp.*

*It's Okay To Compete
Anson Dorrance

"Women have a superior understanding that their relationships are more important than the game itself."

One of the major factors in the development of our players over the course of time is that we create a wonderful training intensity. And the toughest challenge in developing female players is getting them to compete against their friends in practice. They don't struggle competing against other teams. But when they compete against their friends in practice, there's usually a lessening of intensity.

Women have a superior understanding that their relationships are more important than the game itself. Men, obviously, never struggle with that. Men never take competing with best friends personally, but women do. I think the way in which girls are socialized exaggerates the difference between males and females. When they are growing up, girls are not encouraged to compete as much as boys. But I also think head-to-head physical confrontation with friends and teammates is not where girls are naturally comfortable. I think if you socialized a boy against competing, he would not be socialized easily, and if you socialized a girl toward competing, it would also not be easy. That is basically what we try to do here at UNC. We take young women who do not feel comfortable in those directly competitive arenas and throw them into a fierce competitive pool, and they sort of beat it into each other that it's okay to compete.

There was an interview done by one of our alumni magazines about the program, and the reporter really did a good job. This idea of competing intrigued her, and she really got to the core of this issue. She interviewed a lot of the girls on the team, and the girls told her that the difficulty they had coming in here as freshmen was that they all wanted to be a part of this great program, but they also wanted to be accepted personally. So they come into our pre-season with incredibly mixed emotions — they want to be the best they can be on the field, but they don't want to alienate anyone. They have this internal war going on between wanting to prove they are great soccer players and the social agenda of wanting to be accepted by the group they are joining. So when they go into direct confrontation with a veteran, it's almost like they feel they have to acquiesce — no matter how good they are — just because they want to be accepted by the veteran. Of course, I am standing next to them saying, "I saw you play in high school and this is not

The US's Julie Foudy (11) competes with Japan's Afako Takakura for a head ball in a women's international match. Teaching women to be competitive is a key coaching component according to coach Dorrance. (photo by Brett Whitesell)

what I saw." Now, they are getting mixed messages. The freshman is getting the message from her socialization and her gender about trying to bond with everyone, and she is getting a message from me and the girls who are beating her to death that it's okay to pound your teammates. That's the way it's done here. It's a very difficult period for them. In fact, almost every player's freshman year here is very difficult. Not just from a soccer perspective, but from a social perspective. Things they have been taught all their lives are brought into question, and it's a very difficult adjustment period. The greatest example of this in terms of teaching young women to win is Carla Overbeck. We do a lot of one v. ones here. It's a direct one-on-one competition and over the course of the season each girl plays against everyone else on the team. It's like an ongoing one v. one tournament among all the members on the team. In Carla's freshman year, she didn't win a game. Not one game. Her freshman year was an emotional catharsis for her because we really needed her to play, really needed her to win for us because she was our starting sweeperback. She was under a lot of pressure. It was a very difficult transformation for Carla to go from where she was a freshman to what finally happened as a senior. Her senior year, she did not lose a single one v. one game. By then you would not recognize her. In fact, Carla's

competitive fury was so developed by the time she was a senior, she would tell me from the field, "Anson, you gotta sub So-and-So. She's killing us." She would not tolerate any lack of effort from anyone in front of her. She would scream at me to substitute any player on the field who did not give everything she had. Now for the United States National Team, she is one of the most competitive people and one of their greatest leaders. But if you saw her as a freshman, she was a really nice girl, wanting to be a part of everything. And now, if you watch her in a national team training session, she is aggressively encouraging, directing and leading every session in which she's involved. There is a competitive anger in her, and she developed it here. I know she did because I watched it happen.

If we are playing a four v. four tournament in practice at UNC, and two veterans are on a team with two younger kids, there's going to be times when the younger kids are going to feel like easing off a bit, like it's not important. When this happens, the veterans will get on them immediately. All of a sudden, the freshmen understand that if they are not pushing at one-hundred percent, they are letting the veterans down. The veteran's body language and tone will tell them "If you give up and we lose, I lose. That's unacceptable." Then eventually — or right away with some — intensity comes to be taken as the norm. We try to create training environments that are incredibly intense. And by recording everything, it gives the players permission to compete. It tells these women it's okay to be the best. It's okay to win. And we think this competition has a hardening effect on the women on our team. A mistake many male coaches make when they are trying to make the transition from coaching men to coaching women is they try to motivate with the intensity of their own personality. In my experience, aggressive, loud, in-your-face fury does not motivate women. I know because I tried it my first few years with the team. So we substituted this "Competitive Cauldron," this "Keeping Score" to create the intense environment we knew was critical for top player development. In fact, we named one of our early clinics after it — "Keeping Score:" "Training the Female Psychological Dimension." That clinic is still one of the more popular we do.

I had a long meeting with Tracy Noonan after the 1994 season. We were talking about how beneficial the season was for the goalkeepers. Rarely have we created a competitive atmosphere in goal, but we've always succeeded in creating it for field players. In 1994, for the first time in our history, we had two goalkeepers—Tracy Noonan and Shelly Finger—who we allowed to compete on the same level, even in games. During the season, we rotated who started and who played in the second half. It was all a competition to see who would play in the NCAA Tourna-

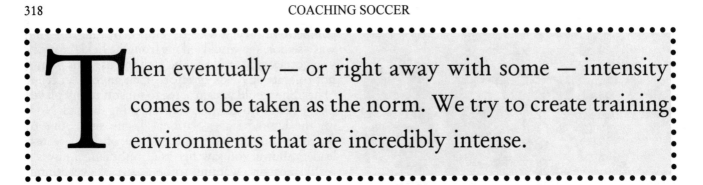

T hen eventually — or right away with some — intensity comes to be taken as the norm. We try to create training environments that are incredibly intense.

ment. So there was a competitive cauldron in goal. Tracy and I were talking about how we thought it was similar to the way Briana Scurry and Skye Eddy were developed. In 1993, Skye Eddy transferred from UMass to George Mason and took them to the national championship final, and Briana Scurry might be the best goalkeeper in the world today. How were those two wonderful keepers developed? It happened at UMass in a competitive cauldron where every practice was critical to see who would play that weekend. We discovered that the competition made Noonan and Shelly Finger each so much better. We rotated them every game. Not alternating games but basically every half. I'm convinced that's the way to develop high-caliber keepers. But it's better to have the starting job up for grabs every day. I'm convinced of that now. But I'm not convinced that you should let that keeper play the whole game. For years, I've been trying to figure out a way to develop my goalkeepers the same way my field players are developed. I know how my field players develop—there is no mercy paid on them in practice. Everything is win-lose all the time. Playing time is based on objective evaluations, and so there is a competitive fury in practice. That has never existed in goal before. What was lacking in goal? We'd go with one keeper for the majority of the season, and that would shatter the confidence of the other one. It also would not give the reserve a chance to play in games, which is critical for growth. More importantly, it would give the starter a kind of complacency, but also a kind of fear—the fear that if she ever made any mistakes, the roles would be reversed. Obviously, if the roles were reversed, the starter would become the reserve, and now her confidence is totally shattered. The reserve is now thrust into the starting position without much playing experience. Her confidence is probably not built to the extent that she really feels she can do the job. The ideal way to develop them, in my opinion, is to do exactly what we did with Noonan and Finger—split games in half but alternate who starts. Now, both goalkeepers are getting up for every game. They're competing with each other in practices. The regular season just develops them for the NCAA Tournament, but each keeper still has to compete to preserve their status. We're convinced that having a competitive cauldron

in goal is the way to go. Noonan, when called upon against Notre Dame in the 1994 finals, was absolutely brilliant.

I've seen goalkeepers come to college as tremendous keepers, but end up very average. Why? They have no competition in practice. They have a complacency that stunts their growth. Coaches will try to shake things up by benching the starter after a poor performance. But the starter knows she's better than the other goalkeeper. If she didn't, she wouldn't be complacent. So good teams at the collegiate level, or at any competitive level, will benefit from having two comparable keepers, two very good keepers. And every game should be split in half. One goalkeeper doesn't win the starting job for good, which permits them to genuinely compete in practice because they know they are going to play. Save the one keeper for the do-or-die post-season tournament. Your goalkeeping will certainly benefit, as will your chemistry in goal, if handled properly. With Noonan and Finger, we told them, "We think you're very close. Both of you have earned the opportunity to play." In 1993, I made a mistake in goal. In the preseason, I thought Shelly Finger was playing better than Tracy Noonan, and I rewarded Shelly by starting her two out of every three games. Noonan was an excellent goalkeeper, but playing only one out of every three games did not permit her to feel like she was effective. The luck of the draw also gave Noonan many of the tough games, ballooning her goals-against average. When that was added to her relative lack of playing time, it did little for her confidence. In the off-season, she did a lot of work on her own, and she absolutely killed herself in the weight room, unlike any player we've ever had. Before the 1994 season, I thought Noonan was better. But Shelly was close enough to compete. I didn't want to make the same mistake again, so they split games in half. They didn't have to win the position for each game. That would be unbelievable pressure. Now you've created that competitive cauldron in practice for everyone, goalkeepers and field players.

* published with permission of the author from the book Coaching Soccer Champions. JTC Sports Inc., Raleigh, NC. 1996. 159 pp.

COACH THE ATHLETE, NOT THE GENDER
Jan Smisek

"If my father hadn't treated me just like my brother — always telling me I was capable of the best in whatever I did — I would never have made it to the Olympic victory stand."
—Donna De Verona, Olympic Swimming Gold Medalist

With the increased participation of girls and women in soccer, there have been an increased number of males coaching females and, more recently, females coaching males at all levels of the game. For those coaches who have not coached the opposite sex before, questions and concerns about boys or girls because they are "different" are being raised. According to the Women's Sports Foundation's *Parent's Guide to Girls Sports*, these worries are unnecessary, but the fact that questions continue to be raised about difference between coaching boys and girls suggests that it is important to address this issue.

It is vital to realize how the game of soccer is the same for all players. The laws of the game make no special exceptions or distinctions with regard to gender. Any modifications of the rules of soccer are age appropriate changes made to create the best environment for player development. The qualitities of players and their roles within the team are not gender specific. All players, male or female, must possess some combination of knowledge of the game, skill, mental ability, fitness and impact.

The principles of play are constant within the game. The principles of defense will always include delay depth, balance, compactness, concentration, control/restraint, and defensive shape. Attacking principles will always consist of support, creation and utilization of space, balance, penetration, improvisation, and attacking shape.

Team management guidelines make no distinction between how to manage male or female players, they simply tell us that all athletes respond best in terms of their character, skill development and performance to such environmental factors as positive feedback, constructive criticism, the right number and type of attributions to build self-confidence and finally, well-organized, fun and challenging practice sessions.

When addressing differences, keep in mind that all individuals playing or coaching the game are not the same. Any differences in coaching players have nothing to do with the game of soccer itself and they are not specific to either gender. The differences between how players are coached or managed lie within

COMMENTS FROM THE NATIONAL WOMEN'S SOCCER COACHING SYMPOSIUM, MUHLENBURG COLLEGE, SUMMER, 1993

Tony DiCicco

"There's a definite need to coach girls and women toward their strengths and it's not necessarily the same way as coaching men...Women are competitive against other teams, but are not naturally as competitive among themselves...In some ways, women are superior human beings. They know that relationships are more important than competition.

"There are ways of creating competitive practices. Girls are not wimps, but you can't just go into their face and blow them away like you do with guys or they won't respond."

Jeff Tipping

"The speed of the game is different and the physical aspect is different...and coaching women tends to be more relationship oriented than coaching men. Anson has said that coaching males is ego management and coaching women is emotion management.

"I'm not sure I agree with everything these guys are saying, but many of Anson's ideas are brilliant and obviously they work. I think the same kind of thinking can be applied to males with just as much success. The concept of building relationships with players, which Anson preaches, certainly applies to men and has worked for me."

the personalities, abilities, perceptions, socialization and life experiences of the persons involved.

Within any social group or team there will be persons who exhibit personality traits that are considered to be stereotypically male or female. The composition of each team is unique and it is the coach's responsibility to evaluate the needs of the players and the team and then coach and manage them accordingly.

Expectations that are formed based on gender bias can perpetuate sex-role stereotypes that may affect the standard of play that the athlete aspires to or that the coach expects them to achieve. The impact of a coach's expectations can lead to a self-fulfilling prophecy which either retards the player's development or enhances it. The self-fulfilling prophecy is a cycle which begins when a coach forms expectations of an athlete or group of athletes. The assumption that a coach forms at the beginning of the season concerning each athlete's potential can affect the way the coach behaves toward each athlete. The coach's behavior, in turn, affects the athlete's performance and behavior. The athlete's performance conforms to the coach's expectations, completing the cycle.

In order to achieve exellence in all levels of the game, coaches need to operate under the premise that the demands of the game are dictated by the game, not by the sex of the athlete. Limiting or elevating your expectations of players simply because they are male or female can retard their development. Coaches should get to know each individual and what makes them tick, know their team and the character of it as a unit, and know themselves and coach within their own personality.

Each individual within a team posseses different physical, technical, tactical and psychological qualities. Coaching is all about recognizing these qualities and creating a learning environment where all players are encouraged to polish their strengths, improve their weaknesses, try everything and are expected to give their best at all times.

⚽

ADOLESCENCE, SELF-ESTEEM AND GIRLS SOCCER: DO GIRLS JUST WANT TO HAVE FUN?
by Dr. Jack Levine

Coaches of girls soccer teams face a very disturbing problem that goes far beyond youth sports. Many young girls are losing their enthusiasm, confidence and self-esteem by the time they reach high school. The 1990 study by the American Association of University Women, "Shortchanging Girls, Shortchanging America," shows that while 60 percent of elementary school girls say they are "happy the way I am", only 29 percent of high school girls feel the same way. This striking drop in self-esteem and confidence, along with increasing conflict and negative body image, begins in junior high school at about 11 or 12 years of age.

The causes of this tragic drop in self-esteem are complicated. Girls change dramatically during adolescence both in body and mind. It is usually a time of turmoil and conflict. In school, where there is often a male-oriented curriculum, unequal treatment still exists, as in scholastic sports. Adolescent girls begin to feel the conflicts and contradictions that surround a woman's role in our society. Today, more than ever, women (and men) tend to be judged by their appearance. The media defines "attractiveness" in way that

very few girls can attain. Some positive inner qualities, such as compassion and gentleness, are often considered stumbling blocks to success. The feelings of rejection from friends and conflicts with parents can be very stressful.

Self-esteem is how we think of ourselves as an individual and in comparison to others. High self-esteem means we think that we are a "good" person. It reflects the self-confidence to take a chance and try something new, the ability to risk failure and be able to bounce back. Positive self-esteem lets a person share themselves with others and develop cooperative relationships. Low self-esteem leaves one vulnerable to the negative influences of others. It becomes difficult to connect with other people. There is doubt when trying to accomplish new tasks. It may even cause sadness or depression.

The family is the strongest force in shaping self-esteem. But youth sports and girls soccer, in particular, can help to develop positive self-esteem.

When girls play soccer, they are judged by their performance on the field, not by their looks. Soccer encourages taking risks and independent thinking. The girls must make hundreds of decisions during each game. Some are right and others are wrong. Learning from mistakes helps to build character. Creative problem-solving, in games and practices, help to build confident minds. Learning skills in practice and applying them successfully on the field also builds confidence. Gaining strength, endurance and athletic ability improve self concept and body image. Soccer also requires cooperation teamwork. When the girls develop trust in each other, they feel good about themselves.

As coaches, how can we help?

DO: Be committed to your vision and goals for the team. Communicate this with the players and parents. Provide leadership and guidance. Make being on your team a special experience.

DO: Teach and stress basic skills. With solid fundamental skills, the girls will develop competency. They can feel confident in their soccer playing ability.

DO: Treat everyone with the respect that they deserve. Admit when you make mistakes. Learn from the girls.

DO NOT: Embarrass any players. Use a gentle approach without singling out anyone. Adolescents are very sensitive.

DO: Communicate openly and honestly with your team. Explain your decisions and give reasons. Most people can accept an honest explanation. Otherwise, some girls may misunderstand you, take things too personally or incorrectly blame themselves.

DO: Teach and stress sportsmanship, clean play, teamwork and cooperation. By appreciating team-

Leadership development such as this keeper directing teammates starts at the youth level with sensitive coaching according to author Levine. (photo by Perry McIntrye, Jr.)

mates, opponents and referees, the girls will better understand themselves.

DO: Stress the idea of playing hard to win rather than as an end in itself. Reward girls who take risks and try new things regardless of the outcome.

DO NOT: Yell instructions from the sidelines. The players need to be able to make their own decisions comfortably. Yelling may be misinterpreted as anger.

DO: Maximize positive and successful experiences. Always play at an appropriate level of competition. Losing badly becomes frustrating and winning easily is no challenge.

DO NOT: Set up players for failure. Maximize the player's success by carefully matching their position and role on the team with their skills and attitude.

DO: Compliment the girls frequently about their play, appearance and attitude. Treat them with kindness and concern. Show them that they are appreciated.

DO NOT: Tease or criticize the girls about their physical appearance—ever.

DO NOT: Talk about or encourage weight loss. The incidence of eating disorders in female athletes is extraordinarily high. Teenage girls are the most at risk.

DO: Encourage all family members, female and male to come to games. Stress the importance of family support. It is particularly important at this age when many adolescent girls drop out of sports.

DO: Read and learn about the psychological development of adolescent girls.(see references)

DO: Become an advocate for girls and women's sports.

DO NOT: Tolerate sexists remarks from parents, coaches, referees, spectators, or friends. Speak up for what you know is right.

DO: Be a good role model. A female coach can be an excellent example for young girls to aspire to. A male coach should exemplify the type of non-aggressive, non-threatening behavior that we would like girls to experience as they grow up.

As the coaches of adolescent girls, we have a great responsibility, beyond teaching soccer and winning games. We need to work hard to increase self-confidence and improve self-esteem. Their participation in youth soccer should be a stepping-stone to becoming self-assured, confident women.

REFERENCES:

Clark, Michael, A. "Diplomacy in Coaching: Make Tough Decisions Without Hurting Anyone." *Soccer Journal*, 39:6, 1994, p. 53.

Ersing, Walter F. "Process or Product: A Challenging and Provocative Choice for the Coach." *Soccer Journal*, 39:3, 1994, p. 41.

How Schools Shortchange Girls. American Association of University Women. Washington, D.C. 1992.

Marone, Nicky. *How to Father a Successful Daughter.* McGraw Hill, New York, NY 1988.

Martinez, John. "Coaching with Self Esteem: Belief in Ourself Helps Others." *Soccer Journal.* 39:3, 1994, p. 17.

Pipher, Mary. *Reviving Ophelia: Saving the Selves of Adolescent Girls.* Ballantine. New York, NY 1994

⚽

Social Factors Determine Interest*
By Ruth Callard, Women's Soccer Foundation, Seattle

The NCAA Gender-Equity Task Force recommends in its preliminary report that the goal of each institution should be to provide intercollegiate athletics participation opportunities for women and men in the same proportion as the numbers of men and women in the undergraduate student population.

Some have suggested that this is unfair because men are more interested than women in sports.

It is difficult to read the arguments about whether women are as interested in sports as men. Girls may be more interested than boys in sports. We don't know. We have no data to indicate how interested in sports girls are. Why? We live in a society in which girls and boys have been, and still are, more socialized toward some activities and away from others. Let me share an example.

One of the young women on the high-school team I coached approached me before practice. She very excitedly told me that she had been selected to the homecoming court. She stated that she would not be coming to soccer practice because she had to be fitted for a gown.

The next morning, I asked the football coach whether any of his players had made the homecoming court. He said yes, but that none of them had missed practice. They had found a tux shop that was open in the evening. He added, "They know they can't miss practice."

Are the boys inherently more interested? Or have they been encouraged for generations that sports are important and that a commitment to a varsity athletics team implies they will not miss practice? Their "interest" was so ingrained that the coach never even had to state the rule of no missed practice.

On the other hand, was the girl less interested? Or had she also been told, like other generations of girls, that the homecoming court activities should take precedence over a commitment to a varsity athletics team?

Parents and teachers made up the homecoming court advisory group. Adults told her that she wasn't as interested in sports. We all send subtle messages often that serve to restrict or channel the interests of young people. Ideally, some adult would have taken the time at least to point out to her the set of expectations that had been set up by the advisory group. This

at least would have given her more opportunity to make her own decision as to how interested she was in sports.

We can look at this "interest" issue in another setting. Take parenting. In the past 10 years, there has been a far greater recognition in the courts that men are capable of parenting. In the state of Washington, courts are obligated to the concept of being sex blind. This means that, all other things being equal, parenting should not be awarded to the mother just because she is a woman.

Not very long ago, however, there were presumptions in favor of moms. Does this mean that only recently men have been "interested" in parenting? Or does it mean that perhaps men always were interested but only recently have been given the opportunity to be active in parenting?

Does it make sense to limit men's future opportunities at parenting based on what we deem is their level of interest today?

Young men and women deserve to have the doors open to whatever interests them. If educational opportunities are going to be restricted for women, hopefully someone will come up with a stronger reason than lack of interest. We tend to be interested in what society allows us to be interested in.

* *This piece originally appeared in* NCAA News, *June 23, 1993.*

⚽

How Different are the Sexes?
Pat Croce

"Whether women are better than men I cannot say," Golda Meir once said. "But I can say they are certainly no worse."

Better or worse may be a point of debate in some quarters, but the two sexes are created equal when it come to exercise—that is, the cellular mechanisms controlling most of the bodily responses to exercise are similar for both sexes.

But if that's the case, why are men and women generally separated during athletic competitions? Basically, because the magnitude of the physiological response in men and women is quite different.

Here are some of the distinctions:
• Hemoglobin. Women have a 30 percent lower concentration of hemoglobin in their blood than men. Because hemoglobin plays a key role in transporting oxygen within our system, a woman's cardiovascular endurance is 30 percent less than a man's.
• Muscles. Muscular growth is regulated mainly by

the hormone testosterone, which is about 10 times more prevalent in men's blood than in women's. Women have about one third less muscle strength than men, but when this strength is measured in terms of lean body weight, this difference is reduced.

• Fat. Although women have about 20 percent less muscle mass than men, they have more adipose or fatty tissue, especially around the breast and hips. The amount of fat differs with each person and is related to the amount of exercise he or she gets. For example, women generally have 20 to 26 percent fat tissue, but active women may have only 18 to 22 percent fat. Men generally have 15 to 20 percent fat, but less-sedentary men may have 12 to 15 percent fat.

• Hormones. In men, the hormone testosterone causes the development of wide shoulders and increased muscle mass. In women, the hormone estrogen leads to wide hips, increased fatty tissue — and here's the good news — a decreased chance of heart disease.

• Sweat. You may have heard the old saying, "Horses sweat, men perspire, and women glow." Well, humans do sweat, especially during intense exercise. Men, however, produce more sweat in response to heat and begin sweating sooner than women. Although sweating is healthy and may prove advantageous for men when exercising in a hot, dry environment, it also subjects men to a greater rate of dehydration.

• "Cold hands, warm heart." Men actually are less susceptible to the cold than women. Women have a tendency to feel chilly because their smaller muscle mass burns fewer calories and therefore generates less heat. Smaller blood vessels in women slow the circulation of blood throughout the system, thus creating a cold feeling. Women's fat distribution heats primarily the areas around the breasts and buttocks, leaving other areas of the body feeling cold. Finally, women's body temperature fluctuates over the course of a month.

• Growing up. By age 21, most males attain their adult height. Women reach their maximum height by age 17, but begin growing two years earlier than men, due to production of the female hormones.

• Bones. Women have smaller, less dense bones. When estrogen production stops during middle age or a woman goes through menopause, the retention of calcium in the bones lessens. This causes the bones to lose strength and become more brittle, often leading to osteoporosis.

• Iron. Because of blood loss during their menstrual cycles, about 25 percent of all women are iron-deficient.

Weighing the differences between men and women on an athletic level, men have an advantage because of greater muscle mass, heart and lung size, and aerobic capacity. These abilities generally give the average man more strength, power and speed than the average woman. Women, however, are superior in flexibility and buoyancy.

Obviously, athletic ability differs greatly among individuals, male or female, but preliminary studies of trained women athletes indicate that, with proper training, women can approach the aerobic capacity of trained men.

Because of the physiological differences between men and women—especially during puberty, when the bodies of both sexes are undergoing enormous change—separate athletic competitions are the norm. Unisex athletic events do not allow for these differences and often discourage those who are not on the same level as their competitors.

Finally, although physiology dictates that the male is stronger and faster and has greater endurance than the female, those who have seen a woman experience natural childbirth know that the myth of women as the weaker sex is simply that—a myth.

⚽

ISSUES IN TRAINING THE FEMALE ATHLETE
Donald T. Kirkendall

I do not think that most people severely objected to the expanding sporting opportunities for women. It was fair and proper. Expanded opportunities meant enhanced exposure to coaching, practice, competition, and visibility. Added sports, practice time, seasons and season lengths all place stresses on the athletic female. While many people advocate this opportunity, there does appear to be a price to be paid above and beyond the potential for the injuries typical to a particular sport. There exists the potential for selected problems, unique for the most part, to female athletes. These problems are, to use a term coined by a study group of the American College of Sports Medicine, The Female Athlete Triad: amennorhea, osteoporosis, and disordered eating. As you will see, there appears to be a common denominator (solution?) to these problems in adequate nutrition.

AMENNORHEA

The effects of training on menstrual function should be of critical interest to everyone involved in sports and medicine. I will not address what (if any) influences training may have on the onset of menstruation (menarche). According to Dr. John Lombardo, chair of Family Medicine at Ohio State University, disruption of normal menstrual function should be viewed medically first and not assumed to be linked to training. The public thinks delays or cessation of menstruation due to training are to be expected. Dr. Rosemary Agostini, one of the chairs of

The physical training for a women's soccer team has to take into considerations several important issues. Here the US Women's National Team stretches and rejuvenates itself prior to an overtime match. (photo by Perry McIntyre, Jr.)

the ACSM study group, points out that roughly 5 percent of the general population, 20 percent of the exercising population and as high as 50 percent of the "elite athlete" population may experience disruption of menstrual function. No survey of a wide cross-section of female athletes suggests that delays or cessation of menstruation affects all women. In addition, Dr. Agostini is quick to point out that there are no good data on women in team sports with respect to this problem.

A discussion of the hormonal cycling is beyond the scope of this article. Training does appear to alter normal function in subtle as well as very obvious ways. When a woman increases her training load, slight, but measurable and physiologically significant alterations in the hormonal pattern occurs. This typically occurs within the first few months of training. Should the training continue with increases in volume and intensity, the changes may be significant enough to cause obvious changes in menstrual patterns. The most significant hormonal change is the reduction in estrogen secreted. While this is a reproductive hormone, it also influences bone health (see osteoporosis below).

The mechanism of this disruption is unknown. Physical and emotional stress play a role. Professional dancers develop what they call performance amennorhea, when their periods are delayed or cease during stage performances. Another thought is called the "energy drain theory." Female athletes will increase their training without increasing their dietary intake hoping to minimize competitive weight. Menstruation (among many other things) requires energy as does their extra training. The caloric intake may

be insufficient to support both so the body "chooses" to support the training and normal menstrual function becomes disrupted. A reduction in training (or an increase in caloric intake?) should bring back normal menstrual function. But keep Dr. Lombardo's comments in mind; never assume anything about this delicate problem.

OSTEOPOROSIS

The progressive demineralization of bone is termed osteoporosis (ost-bone, porosis-porous). Bones no longer support the stresses they used to and are then prone to fracture. This generally begins to occur after menopause in females due to the loss of circulating estrogen. Three things are necessary for adequate bone health.

Stress

Two stresses are needed to maintain adequate bone health. First is gravity. While you may think this is a constant for all, consider the bedridden patient or the astronaut, both of whom lose bone density. The second is functional stress; things like supplemental exercise. The more a person is active, the stronger (and denser) are their bones.

Nutrition

Vitamins A, C, and D are needed for the maintenance of bone density. In addition, calcium and phosphorous are also required. A well rounded diet will easily supply all these nutrients.

Hormones

A variety of hormones are needed for bone health notably calcitonin and parathyroid hormones which control the deposition and release of calcium and phosphorous from their storage sites in the bones. While other hormones assist, the other main hormone is estrogen.

All three properties are needed for bone health. Remove or reduce one, and bone density declines. In the training female, as previously mentioned, the potential exists for a temporary change in normal menstrual function resulting in a decline in circulating estrogen. This loss of estrogen accelerates the expected age related decline in bone density of females. The bone age of an athletic women is usually "older" than her chronological age. This puts her at a greater risk of fractures in those bones being stressed by the exercise. Ask any trainer and they will tell you that stress fractures are more common in women than in men. Dr. Agostini says that the training female may have a "bone age" that is far older than her chronological age. There are reports of female runners whose bone density has declined so much that one would expect to find such "porous" bones in a women in her 50s. Add an eating disorder to that and the bone age may be even older.

EATING DISORDERS

The primary eating disorders in females are bulimia and anorexia nervosa. The person with bulimia follows periods of the binge-purge cycle (eating followed by self-induced vomiting) while the latter has a distorted view of her body image and relentlessly attempts to lose weight through a variety of methods. The two disorders are on the minds of many people and care must be taken before one of these diagnoses is carelessly applied. The diagnosis of either is a complex psychiatric process.

The incidence of eating disorders in the general population is difficult to document considering the shroud of secrecy that surrounds individuals in their attempt to conceal their problem. In athletes, the incidence of eating disorders is no doubt more common in "aesthetic" sports (e.g. dance, gymnastics, figure skating, diving) but occurrences in other sports is also possible. While eating disorders are a serious clinical problem, it only serves to exaggerate the previously discussed problems.

The interaction of these three problems only makes things worse. If the woman is restricting her diet to achieve some weight, she will be limiting her dietary intake of essential nutrients. This restriction will have two effects. First, inadequate intake of nutrients for bone density will hasten the removal of minerals from the bones. Second, the reduced caloric intake may hasten menstrual dysfunction according to the "energy drain" hypothesis. The loss of circulating estrogen from the effects of increased training and restricted diet will further decrease bone density.

CONCLUSION

The conclusion one might reach is that maybe intense exercise training in females may not be advisable. However, there may be an alternative. The above scenarios all revolve around restricted caloric intake. It is quite likely, although unproved at this time, that during intense training women should not be attempting to make some competitive weight. The combination of intense training and dietary restriction is counterproductive to bone health. Weight reduction to achieve some competitive weight should be attempted during the off season (this also supports the argument that a competing female should maintain her competitive weight year round) which would allow for adequate caloric intake during competition to minimize the risk of the Female Athlete Triad.

* * *

THE DIFFERENCES IN GOALCOACHING MALES AND FEMALES
Tony DiCicco

I've now had the privilege of coaching goalkeepers in two FIFA world championships: The First Women's World Championship, held in China in 1991, and the Youth (U-20) Men's World Championship in Australia this year.

Having coached both males and females in international championships gives one a unique perspective. Bob Gansler, former U.S. national team coach, recognized that too on a bus ride back from a training session Down Under when he asked me, "What are the differences between coaching men and women goalkeepers?"

I said, "Bob, I'm still learning, but from what I've seen so far, there are far more similarities in goalcoaching men and women than there are differences."

Technically, in fact, I have found virtually no difference. The techniques I teach and use in training our national women goalkeepers are the same I use with our men. If there is any difference, it is that I may spend more time on technique with the women, because a male keeper can more easily make up for a technical mistake with athleticism and size. Most female keepers cannot match up, athletically or in terms of stature, with most male keepers (though I am finding more and more superbly athletic female keepers).

I have also noticed that, while a woman's hand is generally smaller than a man's, the ball size is constant. Therefore, female keepers must be more exact with their hand placement when catching shots or crosses.

Having said all that, however, it would be a mistake to think I omit technical training with our male keepers. Technical training is vitally important for all goalkeepers!

Physically, I have already alluded to some of the big differences between male and female keepers. The goal is the same for all keepers, yet most women are smaller than their male counterparts. The U.S. national team female keepers average 5'6" tall, while the U-20 men's national team keepers average 6'. Consequently, the goal the women play in seems larger.

In addition, the average vertical jump for the female keepers I work with is 21 inches—four inches less than for the U-20 male keepers. Again, the effect is to make the goal bigger for women than for men.

What does this mean for our training? Almost every exercise I do with the U.S. women involves an athletic maneuver. For example, I may do an exercise where the keeper covers the near post, and a ball is played to the center of the goal where a striker takes a shot. I may start the women at the near post, but on the ground, so they have to athletically "re-stand" and then get into position to make the save.

But athleticism knows no gender bounds; it saves goals. I recall a stop that Rick Koczak made during a final tune-up match prior to the World Championships, against the University of South Florida. One of their players broke through one-on-one. Rick made the initial save but the ball bounced back to the striker, who received it with his chest and was ready to carry it past Rick toward goal.

Rick's re-stand was so fast and dynamic that he dove and took the ball right off the striker's chest, before he could move past him. That sort of save is special, and is the type of athletic save more possible from a male than a female keeper.

Tactically, there is only one difference. It has to do with positioning. The only instance in which goalkeeper positioning is different for males and females is when the ball is entering the keeper's defensive third of the field, in a central spot. The high level male keeper can be positioned three to six yards from the goal line (younger or less experienced keepers must be closer to their line; they need time and training to extend their range).

The female keeper should be one to two yards off her line—no more. This puts the female keeper at a disadvantage, because she has to be responsible for more space than the male.

We keep the female goalkeeper closer to the line because most females have some difficulty playing balls over the top of the goal, especially if they are moving back or diving back toward their goal line. In an international game last summer against Norway, U.S.

keeper Saskia Webber faced a long shot struck from just inside her defensive third. Well positioned, she used her agility and footwork to get to the left corner, where she touched the ball over the goal. Had she been four or five yards off her goal line, that ball would have scored.

There are some psychological differences between male and female keepers, too. I have learned that when coaching females, my body language and tone of voice can create a negative or positive response. For example, if a shot goes in and I slump my shoulders and stare at the ground, male and female keepers receive two very different signals.

The male's response is something like, "Does Coach think I could have saved that? No way!" Or, "Coach thinks I can save that. I'll be ready for it next time."

A female's response to my body language is something like, "Coach is disappointed in me because I didn't make that save." Or, "I've let Coach down because he's been working on that save and I didn't make it." Females are more concerned than males with relationships between teammates and coaches. Sometimes fear about damaged relationships can get in the way of training and performance.

If my tone of voice is stern, it more likely will have a negative impact on a female than a male. The tone of voice must be uplifting and optimistic: "Okay Susan, forget that play. I've seen you make it consistently; you'll get it next time."

Interestingly, I've found that the coaching delivery I learned to be effective with women is also effective for men.

As I said to Bob Gansler, there are far more similarities than differences between men and women goalkeepers.

⚽

GOALKEEPING AT THE FIRST FIFA WOMEN'S WORLD CHAMPIONSHIP
Tony DiCicco

There were some spectacular goals scored in China, some from long range and many were "highlight film" quality. Credit most of these with excellent players making outstanding plays. There was also some exciting goalkeeper saves and of course, some goals were the result of goalkeeper misplays.

The two biggest blunders that I witnessed were both in the same game by the same goalkeeper. The game was the quarterfinal, Norway vs. Italy. Norway was missing their star striker, Medalsen and if I was told that they would give up two weak goals, I would have guessed that Italy would have been in the semifinals. In this game, Norway scored first, but within a minute of halftime, an Italian player lofted from her own half a long kick into the Norwegian penalty area. The keeper (Seth) misplayed the bounce and the ball scored over her head. Norway again took the lead in the second half and within one minute of the end a soft shot from an Italian midfielder was misplayed by the Norway keeper and the rebound was converted. Fortunately for Norway, they earned a penalty kick in overtime and the final was 3-2. Even though the Norwegian keeper had a nightmare in this game, she did make strong plays in other games throughout the championship. Give her credit for being able to rebound.

Obviously, there were many strong goalkeeper saves. Some of the best, however, took place in the same game. U.S.A. vs Sweden with the U.S. keeper Mary Harvey making key saves at pivotal times to help earn the victory.

Overall, the goalkeeping was strong in the following areas:
1. Shot stopping of low and medium height balls;
2. Catching of crossed balls in space #1 (see Diagram 10-1);
3. Courage of attacking through balls;
4. Punt or drop kick foot clearances;
5. Defensive organization;
6. Poise and control of emotions.
The goalkeeping was weak in the following areas:
1. Saving high shots;
2. Catching; too many rebounds were given up and many resulted in goals;
3. Deflecting or redirecting of shots;
4. Handling of crossed balls in spaces #2 & #3 (see Diagram 10-1);
5. Boxing crossed balls;
6. Throw distributions;
7. Decision-making, reading the attack;
8. Positioning;
9. Athleticism.

The best goalkeeping in this tournament was provided by Harvey of the U.S. and Elizabeth Leidinge from Sweden. Zhong Honglian from China I also rated high, but China was eliminated in the quarter finals when Sweden beat them 1-0. The styles, however, that made each successful differed. Harvey was the most athletic and the best shot saver of the three. Mary also dominated the goal area on high balls utilizing her quickness and a good read of flight to get to balls.

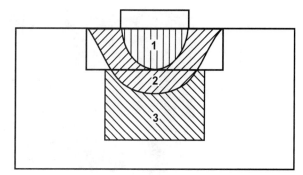

Diagram 10-1

In contrast, Elizabeth Leidinge of Sweden, at 34 years of age, was the oldest player in the Championship. Her strength was her positioning and reading of the game. Without the quickness of Harvey, she also dominated crossed balls because of her experience. Leidinge finished the tournament with four shutouts in six games. Harvey finished with three shutouts and the least amount of goals given up in six games (five). Zhong Honglian (China) gave up four goals in four games and saved two penalties before elimination. Her athleticism and overall strength and size added to her effectiveness. Her one shortcoming compared to Harvey and Leidinge was her psychological dimension.

So how do we need to improve girls' and women's goalkeeping? And how must we accomplish this?

First, athleticism. Of the twelve teams and the sixteen goalkeepers that I studied (some were back-ups), only four showed excellent athleticism. The remainder were good athletes, but this still leaves an area of concentration and improvement.

How to improve overall athleticism? The U.S. keepers, Harvey, Kammerdeiner and Allman were put on a footwork and vertical jump program once I joined the team. When the team was not together, they worked the program on their own. This phase required self-training discipline and no ball. When we were together as a team, another phase of the program was implemented under my direction with much more emphasis with the ball. We continued on the program throughout the championship. The program included:
1. Plyometrics training, no ball;
2. Agility training with and without a ball;
3. Vertical jump testing and agility/fitness testing;
4. Keeper training exercises utilizing an overload on athletic requirements, (drills requiring athletic moves prior to and after save).
The results of the training were:
1. Ability to cover higher areas of the goal frame and more success for touching balls over the top;
2. Quicker and more positive first step and ability to initiate movement;

Tony DiCicco in China at First FIFA Women's World Championship with goalkeepers (left to right) Mary Harvey, Kim Maslin-Kammerdeiner, and Amy Allman.

3. More horizontal range (form post to post) and more vertical range (from the goal line out towards the eighteen).

4. Quickness to dive laterally (Harvey demonstrated this when she made a big second half save against Sweden);

5. Quickness from the ground to get back into position and quickness to the ground to make a save.

The following are a few exercises that I used to accomplish the desired level of athleticism:

• Footwork training with and without the ball: lots of jumping;

• No diving allowed: that is, with the keeper in goal have ball hit from just outside the penalty area. The goalkeeper cannot dive, but must move and utilize footwork to make every save. Don't be concerned when some goals are scored. Concentrate on quickness of movement and ground covered;

• Prone position save at opposite post: i.e., six balls at the corner of the six. The keeper is one yard off the line, parallel to the line on their stomach, head in front of the post. On command, the keeper gets up as the striker inswings the ball to the opposite post;

• Start at six, save over the cross bar: have the keeper stand at the six, while you stand at the goal. Allow the keeper's stance to open just slightly in your direction. On command, toss the ball straight up, the keeper must utilize footwork to get back to the bar and power to reach the ball over the crossbar to touch clear.

GOALKEEPING POSITIONING
Tony DiCicco

Don't be mislead. My studies of the women goalkeepers in China are lessons that all goalkeepers male or female, regardless of playing level can learn from.

I have found that the differences between male and female keepers are far fewer that the similarities and most of the differences are involved with the positioning of the goalkeeper.

First, however, allow me to say that proper positioning for the female keeper is even more critical for success when compared to a male keeper playing at a comparable level. The reasons are:

1. Most female keepers are smaller in stature. To be out of position provides an even bigger opening for the striker to take advantage of.

2. Most female keepers do not have the athletic dimension of a comparable male keeper. Thus, it is more difficult for them to make up for a positional mistake with pure athleticism.

Many women keepers do have an advantage in one area, they are more cerebral. They are great students of goalkeeping. They constantly evaluate and question aspects such as technique and positioning.

However, this is not an article about the similarities and differences of men and women keepers. It is, in fact, an article to help male and female keepers be

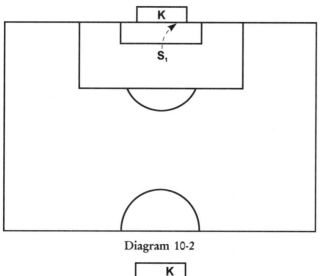

Diagram 10-2

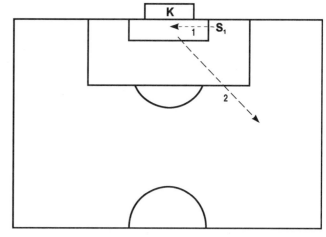

Diagram 10-4

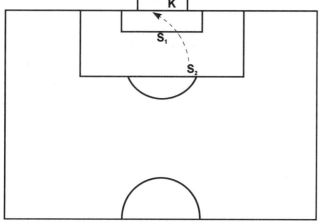

Diagram 10-3

more effective keepers and for all coaches to become more effective goalcoaches.

Just to set the record straight, there are countless similarities between men and women keepers. Everything from defensive organization to decisions on when to go to win a ball are exactly the same. The key component here is that each goalkeeper knows his or her strengths and limitations. Through practice both male and female keepers can learn which balls they can get consistently and which are just out of their comfort zone. How to handle the breakaway and when, how and why to control game tempo.

For his article, we will concentrate on positioning concepts and they are the same for boys, men, girls, and women keepers. Each must find the most effective positioning strategy that makes him or her a sound goalkeeper.

CENTERING BODY WEIGHT

Very often, goalkeepers are caught moving as the ball is hit by the striker. If they are moving in the correct direction then they have a chance to make the save; however, if the ball is played at their exact position at the time of contact or behind them, they

very often are left "groping in the dark." This is incorrect positioning.

Because of the nature of goalkeeping, very often a keeper may find themselves out of position. Rebounds from hard to control shots is one scenario. The keeper's instant thought process identifies the exposed portion of the goal and they immediately move to cover it. Now we must teach the keepers to gather or "center" their body weight just as the ball is struck. Remember: It is better to be slightly out of positioning but centered (set) than to be in position, but possessing a lot of motion in one direction.

There are a couple of exercises to practice this. Adjust the exercise to suit your playing or coaching level.

1. Put the keeper in goal with a hand server standing at the six. Serve the ball towards the post, but reachable for the keeper to make a save (it should be some level of diving save, collapse or extension dive, see Diagram 10-2). As soon as the save is made and the ball returned to the server, a striker (between the 12 and the 18) touches a ball to prepare for a shot. (Diagram 10-3) The shooter goes for goal, either hitting the open side or if the keeper is carrying too much speed towards the open side, the striker slots it behind. The keeper must learn to center, just as the striker is hitting the ball. Repeat to both sides. Determine your own level of intensity.

Important point. As the keeper "re-stands" to save the striker's shot, any movement should be slightly out away from the goal line, not close to and parallel to the goal line.

Second important point. There is one exception to this rule and that's when the goalkeeper is caught away from his or her goal line and is in a position to have the ball chipped over him or her. Here the keeper should continue moving back to the line as fast as possible to diminish the chip potential. It's always easier to come forward if the ball is played short.

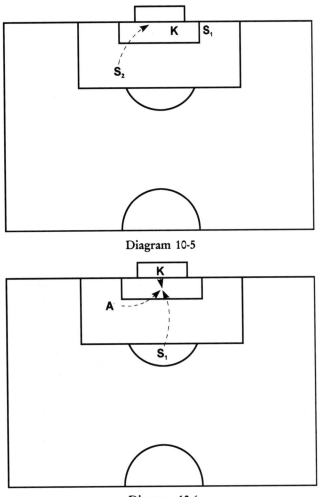

Diagram 10-5

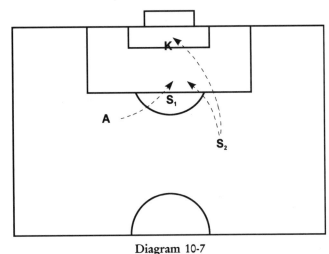

Diagram 10-7

Diagram 10-6

3. Have a hand server with a number of balls at the 18. The server will toss balls high to be caught or boxed (challenge players trying to win head balls and finish can be used). (Diagram 10-6) Once the ball is caught or boxed away a second server located approximately 35 yards from goal tries to chip or drive the ball and score on the keeper. The obvious demand on the keeper is great and depending on when the long server strikes the ball can be adjusted.

   a. Now, complicate the environment for the keeper. After catching or boxing the first serve, the keeper knows to cover for the ball over the head. Add for the long server another option, a through ball pass into the penalty area with an attacking player running onto it. The positioning decisions for the keeper become much more acute. Each time there is an obvious mistake in judgement and positioning, take the time to coach or make sure the keeper has analyzed and has initiated self coaching. (Diagram 10-7)

   Obviously, this is just one aspect of positioning. There are countless little lessons to be learned. The reason why most of the best goalkeepers are in their 30's is because it takes a long time to learn and perfect positioning. Don't get frustrated, just train and get better.

2. The second exercise sets up a server (hand) wide of the goal just outside the side of the six. Toss a ball high and make the keeper come slightly beyond his or her front post to box it high, long, wide and accurate. (Diagram 10-4) As soon as the keeper lands, a striker hitting balls with the inswinger tries to score. (Diagram 10-5) Because the keeper is outside the goal frame, the positioning read of the shot will have to be even more exact. This exercise should create some exciting diving saves toward the far post and some quick change of direction saves at the near post.

GETTING ORGANIZED TO COACH YOUTH SOCCER

The following series of articles are offered to aid the youth soccer coach in the various roles they must assume in taking on this important function.

The initial articles seek to furnish information in terms of providing perspective for the type of philosophy that might be adopted by a youth soccer coach. Once coaches form a basis for the "why" and "how" of their coaching involvement, two experienced youth soccer coaches shed light on their own personal growth while engaged in this "part-time job."

The second series offers some practical organization/ coaching information that is better stated early than later in one's coaching career. From dealing with parents to instilling discipline to understanding the substitution rules — it's all there for the taking by the youth soccer coach.

The third segment of the chapter outlines various aspects of organizing youth practice sessions. From content of the session to when and how to implement it, youth coaches will find plenty of worthy ideas on the construction of a practice and its implementation.

Finally a series of technical and tactical ideas are presented in the last segment of the chapter. From the use of small-sided games to submissions relative to such topics as goalkeeping and teaching heading, the youth coach will find plenty of information to digest — and hopefully implement into their practices.

Coaching during a game is but part of a youth coach's responsibilities. Adopting a philosophy that is based on the welfare of their young charges is one of the first steps a youth coach should formulate. (photo by Brett Whitesell)

DEVELOPING A YOUTH SOCCER COACHING PHILOSOPHY

A BEGINNING PHILOSOPHY
Ron Quinn

Organized youth sports programs are a phenomenon of the post-World War II era.[1] At no other time in history are we able to find so many happy boys and girls on the playing fields. In fact, millions of young people are involved in organized play, which is largely developed and run by parents whose intentions are to give their child an experience that they may have had as children. The desire on the part of the parents to provide a better experience for their children has helped create a new category in the coaching profession — the youth coach.

The youth sports explosion offers as many benefits to parents as to children. Much research has been done concerning the outcomes of physical activity and sports on children, such as improved health, motor, social and emotional development. Some research sug-

gests that sports deter general delinquency, drug use, and truancy. Additionally, the parent who undertakes the role of coach can also improve his or her own health, physical development and can contribute to the community as a whole. The coach also receives the special bonus of being able to return something to the sport that earlier rewarded him or her with personal accolades, trophies, championships - and happy memories. As for the parent who perhaps was not a star athlete or did not participate in sport, there now exists a new opportunity to succeed in the role of the youth coach. However, the new parent/coach soon discovers that the demands placed on the coach are very different from those on the player.

In the past, if you were fortunate enough to be termed a "natural athlete," you may now find it very frustrating to try to teach a child a specific skill or concept that you did not have to learn because it was inherited. If you were not a natural athlete, you will need to learn the skills at least well enough to teach the children on your team. Thus, in both cases, the key words here are "to teach," which is the primary objective in all youth sports programs. It is necessary, then, for anyone who accepts the position of youth coach to develop a philosophical framework from which to grow in this vital new area of physical education.

YOUTH COACHES AS PROFESSIONALS

Currently, youth sports programs are growing faster than the available number of coaches. Therefore, it is not a difficult profession to enter. In most cases, willingness alone is enough to get you the job. Youth coaching is a professional field and parents who volunteer must realize that youth coaching, like any other profession, is challenging, and can be frustrating. Realistically, the term profession is applied in this instance because youth coaching requires true dedication in the field and some preparation and training. Thus, people who spend a great deal of time teaching children should consider themselves to be professionals and behave accordingly.

As Dr. Rainer Martens stated in his article, "The Uniqueness of Young Athletes", "Volunteer coaches teach leadership, sharing, and healthy competition and deserve most of the credit for the success of the programs and the effect that participation in them has on a person's future sports career and general outlook on life."[2] Thus, parents of youth athletes cannot afford to have their children taught by someone who does not possess a professional attitude.

The remainder of this article will focus on a starting point for a beginning youth coach. As in any field, youth coaching should have clearly defined goals and objectives. You should begin by asking yourself why you are drawn to this area of sport. Basically the reason should be that it is a priority in your life (i.e., your child is involved). Next on your agenda is establishing a philosophy of coaching.

Developing a philosophy of coaching is not an easy task. It involves considerable thought, self-examination, and soul-searching. However, one thing is certain, the philosophy should have a framework that you are comfortable with. It can later serve as a sounding board for those stressful and frustrating moments in coaching. It will also act as a reassuring friend when you know you are correct in your methods — but are challenged.

At this point, getting started is probably the most difficult task. Below are a few questions which may provide the initial structure. For each of the questions, form a list of at least five statements or comments that answer that particular question for you.

• Why do you want to be a youth coach?
• What do you expect out of coaching?
• What do you believe are your roles and responsibilities?
• How do you view winning? Losing?
• What rights belong to the player?
• How would you define a successful season?

Once you complete this list, reread the questions and your responses. Ask yourself if this is how you view coaching. If you are satisfied with your comments, continue to read them throughout the season, especially after a tough loss. Developing a philosophy of coaching is an ongoing process and may change as you develop or as your goals and objectives change. There are, however, a few concepts which should never change:

• You should continue to enjoy what you are doing;
• Treat the whole child as a child and not as a miniature adult, and
• Try to help each child develop his or her potential.

The youth coach must accept individual differences in physical size, strength, and skill, as well as different abilities in learning concepts and differences in emotional maturity. Not everyone's biological clock ticks at the same pace.

Thus, the framework provided here is just that — a place to begin as a person enters the profession of coaching youth sports. Your participation can have a major effect on a child's self-concept, confidence, and general outlook on life.

Alongside the demand that each youth coach develop a workable philosophy of coaching is one that places special responsibility on the coach to learn how to teach and coach the particular sport. In short, a philosophy must be combined with understanding the principles of the game he has opted to teach. The coach must try to quickly master pedagogical techniques that many teachers successfully conquer only after years in education. The youth coach must also hasten to learn techniques of teaching fundamentals of the sport, means of attaining physical fitness to meet the demands of the sport and finally to apply the various levels of tactics that are appropriate for his youth team. Finally, the psychology of handling players is an area of coaching that demands a quick study and mastery.

Ideally, as you begin this new professional hobby, please keep an open mind toward various methods of coaching. Always try to improve your skills by attending clinics and coaching schools. No one system is perfect or has all the answers. There may be more than just one way to accomplish a goal and nothing ever comes in nice little packages which are totally self-contained. Learn to seek alternative methods. Ultimately develop the affection and respect of your players and reflect that there is more to sports than winning and losing. These skills will pay big dividends. Teaching players how to play the game well and to do their best will allow your team to become successful, win or lose.

Finally, the rewards can be great for both athlete and coach, child and parent. You will have a profound impact on your own child and his friends. You will improve your own health, render a service to your entire community, and perhaps, relive your days of athletic glory. These benefits are worthwhile in themselves. However, perhaps the greatest reward will occur many times over when your players say, "Hey Coach ... thanks."

[1]Sports in Childhood", The Physician and Sports Medicine, August, 1982, p. 52.

[2]R. Martens, "The Uniqueness of the Young Athlete: Psychologic Considerations," Am. J. Sports Med., 8, Sept-Oct. 1980, pp. 382-385.

[3]Youth Sports Guide, For Coaches and Parents, Washington, D.C.: The Manufacturers Life Insurance Co. and the National Association for Sport and Physical Education, 1977.

The Philosophy and Practical Implications of Coaching Youth
Ron Quinn

The youth coaching profession is one of the fastest growing professions in the United States. People enter for a variety of reasons, but generally because their child is participating. We must treat this group of practitioners as educational professionals in that they are responsible for the growth and development of young children. That these young people have a right to proper guidance and the opportunity to develop their potential is an absolute.

A study on early childhood education reported in the American Educator, titled "Changed Lives - A Twenty Year Perspective on Early Education", stated that:

Several stages of development converge to make the pre-school age an opportune time for intervention. Physically, the young child has matured to the point where he or she has achieved both fine and gross motor coordination and is able to move about easily and freely. Mentally, the child has developed basic language capabilities and can use objects for self-chosen purposes. In terms of Jean Piaget, the child has shifted from sensory motor functioning to pre-operational capacity. Socially, the child is able to move away from familiar adults and social contexts into new settings. The fear of new strangers, so common earlier, is gone, and the youngster welcomes relations with new peers and adults.

When we look at the basic accomplishments of early education, what stands out is that the child develops new competencies related to emerging social and physical skills and intellectual thought. Armed with these new competencies, the child learns to relate to new adults who respond to his/her performance very differently from the family. In short, the child learns to demonstrate new abilities in new settings and to trust new adults and peers enough to display these skills willingly. The child's willingness to try new things and develop new competencies is the seed that is transformed into later life success. Early success is linked grade by grade, year by year, into young adulthood; each stage leads to a better performance at the next. These steps are documented by research. It is as the old adage has it 'As the twig is bent, so the tree grows.

I believe this is also most appropriate at the youth level. Young athletes are at a period of rapid growth, they enjoy demonstrating new skills, and they want to learn and have fun. High school and college coaches often state, if a player does not have the basic skills when they reach this level, they never will. Unfortunately, this is generally true. Therefore, the youth soccer experience is the area of greatest importance and area of concern. The youth coach's role and impact cannot be underestimated.

Where to start?

Where do we start or, more appropriately, how do we start? The NSCAA Coaching Academy is an excellent place to begin, and the how is answered by developing and operating within a philosophical framework. This framework is an on-going working agreement with yourself. The combination of beliefs, motivations, experiences and methods provide the basis of your philosophy, which provides the foundation for a decision which is then followed by the appropriate action. Within each of the areas of beliefs, motivations, experiences and methods you may ask yourself the following questions:

Beliefs:
• Why do you want to be a youth coach?
• Why do we have youth soccer?
• What are my responsibilities?
  1. to each player;
  2. to the team;
  3. to myself;
  4. to the community.
• Define a successful season.

Motivation:
• I am interested in coaching because...
• What do you enjoy most about coaching?
• What do you enjoy least about coaching?

Experiences:
• Past — your early athletic experience — was it enriching or inhibiting?
• Present — self evaluation — what am I doing now?
• Future — an ongoing process — what experiences

will I seek to improve my coaching?

Methods:

• What is my coaching style? Walt Chyzowych in the *Official Soccer Book* cites five styles:

1. the hard nose;
2. the nice guy;
3. the intense coach;
4. the easy-going coach;
5. the business-like coach.

• What is my teaching method?

1. What decisions must I make in the pre-impact, impact, and post-impact phases of a session?
2. To what degree do I involve the players in the decision-making process at each level?

At the conclusion, try to see it all together and ask yourself, is this what I truly believe? Will this philosophy lead me in a direction which will enrich the lives of children? Following these questions, check your philosophy with these additional questions:

• Will it provide the players with a desire to improve?
• Will they gain a sense of security?
• Will they gain a sense of responsibility?
• Will they have the ability to make decisions?
• Will they gain satisfaction in doing their best while accepting differences in others?
• Will they have FUN?

The youth sports debate is a controversial one. Proponents for youth sports see them as miniature life situations which provide experiences to better cope with the stresses of later life. Opponents question the excessive physical and/or psychological stress placed on children. As reported by the Youth Sports Institute at Michigan State University, "Neither advocates nor opponents of youth sports have much scientific evidence to support their position." They believe that organized sports are neither universally good nor bad for children, but they are convinced of the tremendous positive potential that exists in sports. Therefore, our challenge as youth coaches is to maximize this potential. Coaches must realize the influence they have on players. How you treat each player may affect his/her own self-perception. Some coaches may even fill the parental needs of a player, whose parents are missing (physically or psychologically). Thus when planning practices, selecting activities, or competing, following an appropriate coaching model should keep you on task and consistent with your philosophy. Here is a suggested coaching model, which is also consistent with the Coaching Academy.

A YOUTH COACHING MODEL

• It should be fun for everyone involved – players, coaches, and parents.
• The youth coach is the facilitator of the environment.

• Activities are presented where children can buy in at their own level.
• Children learn best when everyone is involved rather than waiting to take a turn.
• Success is measured from the game process rather than the game outcome.
• Not every child will become highly proficient, however it is every child's right to have the opportunity.
• The coach's role is not only coaching his/her team, but that of also nurturing each team member.

In addition to a coaching model, the rights of the athlete must also be recognized. The National Association for Sport and Physical Education has developed a Bill of Rights for Young Athletes which states that children have a:

• Right to participate in sports;
• Right to participate at a level commensurate with each child's maturity and ability;
• Right to have qualified adult leadership;
• Right to play as a child and not an adult;
• Right of children to share in the leadership and decision-making within their participation in a sport;
• Right to participate in safe and healthy environments;
• Right to proper preparation for participation in sports;
• Right to be treated with dignity;
• Right to have fun in sports.

It is easy to agree with these concepts and say this is the way it should be. It is much more difficult, however, to maintain in practice. But it is worth the effort and your duty as a coach is to work within this framework.

The next step is developing a positive relationship with each player and team as a unit. The quality is most important and is similar to quality time with your own children. The effects will go far beyond the length of the season. Establishing guidelines is an important part in developing player relationships. Guidelines need to be fair, realistic, and age appropriate. The players need to know what you expect from them, such as attendance at practice, good behavior at practice and matches, and support of each other. They should also know what they can expect from you; your availability, that you will not criticize players in a negative fashion, that you hold each player in a position of trust, and that you expect that they will make mistakes.

Players can also and perhaps should also be involved with establishing team policies. This will show them that they are an important part of the team.

Knowing your players as individuals can also help develop a positive player/coach relationship. Completing a demographic card, followed by a personal interview with each player, is one method of getting to know players. The demographic card is an index card on which players write down the following information: name, address, telephone number, birth date, family structure, hobbies, other sports played, soccer experience and position. On the back, ask them to write about what they plan to contribute to the team, and what goals they have for the season. Always leave a space on the back of the card for any notes you may want to make. It is also important to let the players know that no one else but you will read the card. With this information you will have a place to begin when you talk with each player. If the player's perception of his/her role on the team is similar to yours, great! However, if there is a difference, you know about it from the beginning and can begin to work on it before it develops into something that will not benefit anyone. Taking steps to reduce failure and acknowledging effort are two additional methods to assist in developing the player/coach relationship. To reduce the fear of failure, you should be sensitive to group selections, provide appropriate tasks, and as stated earlier, let them know mistakes are OK.

In the Sept./Oct. 1984 issue of the *Soccer Journal*, Dr. John Charles presented an opinion concerning taking a humanistic approach to coaching. I believe it was most appropriate and on target. He identified four areas in need of attention:

- A dynamic philosophy for effective coaching;
- An understanding of the psychological aspects of coaching;
- Verbal and non-verbal communication; and
- Counseling theories and styles.

PRACTICAL APPLICATION TO APPLY THIS PHILOSOPHY

It is my belief that a games/activities approach to teaching technique, and stressing learning to enjoy playing are very valid methods in youth coaching. An activities approach will allow for success, provide maximum participation and maximum ball contacts, will reinforce skills and encourage good technique. Activity selection is based upon what you wish to accomplish. Some objectives may be specific technique, physical needs, tactics, social growth, and listening skills.

I have been collecting and developing a variety of activities for youth training. Below is a description and brief analysis of each activity. It should be also noted that games belong to no one and that all games can be changed or modified to meet your particular needs. You could also ask your players how might we make this game better, more challenging and fun?

GAMES AND ACTIVITIES

1. **Body Part Dribble.** Each player has a ball and begins dribbling in a confined area. They attempt to keep control without touching anyone else. While they are dribbling, you call out a body part and they must stop the ball with that part. You can call "elbow", "knee", "chin", etc.

Analysis:

Technique — dribbling in a confined area, close control.

Listening Skills — tuning in to exactly what you are saying.

Physical Needs — reaction time, learning body parts.

Social Growth — working within a group.

Tactics — looking and moving into spaces.

2. **Math Dribble.** Same formation as above. While the players dribble, the coach or player leader calls out a math problem. The players immediately solve the problem by forming the appropriately sized group. This activity is a good way to organize groups without players choosing a partner or counting off. For example, if your next activity requires partners, call out 1+1.

Analysis:

Technique — dribbling in confined area, change direction, change speed.

Listening Skills — paying attention to the problem stated.

Physical Needs — reaction time, coordination, balance.

Social Growth — forming groups with many different players, not just a best friend.

Tactics — looking for players, moving quickly.

3. **Shadow Dribbling.** Partners (perhaps formed from math dribbling) play with one ball. The player without the ball jogs; the player with the ball follows behind. Go for one minute and switch. The player with the ball should try to look at his/her partner's back while still seeing the ball.

Analysis:

Technique — dribbling while changing direction and changing speed.

Physical Needs — balance, coordination, fitness.

Social Growth — working with a partner.

4. **Hospital Tag.** In this dribbling game each player has a ball. The object of the game is to dribble your ball within the designated area and tag other players without letting them tag you. However, unlike most games, when you are tagged you are not out. The first time someone tags you, that spot is injured and you must hold it with one hand. The second time, whenever you are tagged, you must hold that place with the other hand. Remember, during this you are still dribbling the best you can. The third time, you go to the hospital (just a designated area where you juggle the ball a number of times) until you are healed and continue playing.

Analysis:

Technique — dribbling while compensating for usual

body positioning.

Physical Needs — adjusting to different body positions; balance, agility, strength.

Social Growth — having fun, assuming challenges, working within a group.

5. **Bulldog.** Played in a designated area (center circle, penalty box). Provide enough balls for each player. The game starts with one player dribbling, trying to pass his/her ball to hit the other players below the waist. All other players are running without the ball trying not to get hit. Once a player is hit by the bulldog, that player gets another ball and becomes a second bulldog. Game progresses until all players have a ball. Thus, who wins the game? (Everybody.)

Analysis:

Technique — dribbling and passing; trying to hit a moving target.

Physical Needs — jumping, agility, fitness.

Social Growth — allows all ability levels to play equally. Allows each player to be successful. If players are hit early they will dribble longer. If they manage to avoid getting hit until the end, at that point they become very challenged.

Tactics — looking for players, chasing, tracking, playing to a target.

6. **Knockout.** This game is often played when teaching shielding. Each player has a ball and while keeping control of the ball, they attempt to kick away someone else's ball. Generally, when their ball is kicked out, they are out of the game until one player is left. But who gets the most practice? The best dribbler does. To modify the game, when the ball is kicked away the player who can get to it before it stops rolling is let back in. If the ball has stopped, have him/her do five ball juggles ar anything along that line, then rejoin the game. After a few minutes, state that there are 30 seconds left and now if their ball is kicked out they must stay out. In this manner the most anyone would be out is 30 seconds. Would this approach help team unity?

Analysis:

Techniques — dribbling, shielding, tackling.

Physical Needs — balance, agility, fitness.

Social Growth — determination, success, acceptance by the group.

Tactics — one v. one.

7. **Team Knockout:** Similar to knockout but is played on a half field with two teams. Team "A" is on the field, each player with a ball. Team "B" is outside of the field without balls. On the signal, team "B" runs in and is timed in how long it takes them to knock all the balls off the field. The clock does not stop until the last ball is off the field. When team "A" members have their balls kicked out they

can have someone on their team pass them his/her ball to keep it away from team "B".

What is actually happening is one team is trying to keep possession on half a field.

Analysis:

Techniques — dribbling, passing, receiving, heading, tackling.

Physical Needs — fitness, balance, agility, coordination.

Social Growth — teamwork, helping each other, working toward a common goal, success, patience, composure.

Tactics — 1 v. 1, 2 v. 1, 3 v. 1, 2 v. 2, to 8 v. 8 or whatever the size of the group; possession.

CONCLUSION

Coaching youth can be a lot of fun and a very valuable learning and growing experience. Creativity can abound in youth coaching. If children are starting to play organized soccer by age six, then we should make every effort to see that at age 15 they still possess the same enthusiasm. We not only need to teach the skills of the game, but also and maybe more importantly, teach an appreciation and love of the sport. While all this takes place we need to encourage the development of friendships, emphasizing working together and playing with a spirit that celebrates the joy of movement.

REFERENCES

Charles, J., "Humanistic Soccer Coaching", *Soccer Journal*, Sept/Oct. 1984.

Chyzowych, W., *The Official Soccer Book*, The United States Soccer Federation, McGraw Hill, New York, NY, 1979.

DuBois, N., "The Role of the High School or Collegiate Coach in the Development and/or Operation of a Youth Soccer Program", *Soccer Journal*, July/August 1984.

Gould, D., *Motivating Young Athletes*, Youth Sports Institute, Michigan State University, 1980.

Gould, Seefeldt, Smoll, Smith, *A Winning Philosophy for Youth Sports Programs*, Youth Sports Institute, Michigan State University, 1981.

Lammich & Kadow, *Warm Up for Soccer*, Sterling Pub. Co., New York, 1976.

Marten, R., Seefeldt, V., *Guidelines for Children's Sports*, National Association for Sport and Physical Education, 1979.

More New Games, *The New Games Foundation*, Headlands Press, San Francisco, 1981.

Quinn, R., "First Parent/Coach Certificate", *Academy Update, Soccer Journal*, Sept/Oct. 1984.

Quinn, R., "The Youth Coach: A Beginning Philosophy", *Soccer Journal*, May/June 1984.

Smith, R., Smoll, F., *Improving Relationship Skills in Youth Sport Coaches*, Youth Sports Institute, Michigan State University, 1979.

The New Games Book, *The New Games Foundation*, Headlands Press, San Francisco, 1976.

Torbert, M., *Follow Me: A Handbook of Movement Activities for Children*, Prentice-Hall, 1980.

Weikart, D., "Changed Lives: A Twenty Year Perspective in Early Education", *American Educator*, A.F.T., Winter 1984.

"Why Do Coaches Fail?", *Soccer Journal*, Sept/Oct. 1984.

THE VALUE OF USING AN INVITATIONAL APPROACH IN COACHING YOUTH SOCCER
Peter S. Broadley

While taking a class in the School of Education of the University of North Carolina at Greensboro, I was introduced to a theory and a model that was developed by Dr. William Purkey and a number of associates over the past ten years. The model has been used primarily in counseling and teaching and was centered around what Dr. Purkey called "the Inviting Relationship" (Purkey and Schmidt, 1987).

The theory is being expanded slowly to incorporate many of what are referred to as the helping professions. As a soccer coach I felt it may be worthwhile to explore how the invitational approach may be used to good effect in coaching youth soccer. Coaching soccer, of course, does not require us to be expert counselors but it is important, I feel, to be aware of the effect your behavior may have on the lives of young players. The following quotes were taken from "Youth Sports Guide for Coaches and Parents" (J.R. Thomas, Ed;, 1978, p. 10).

...."My Coach was the one person that I could talk to. Even though I couldn't really discuss the trouble I was having with my folks, my coach was one person who made me feel that someone cared..."

..."I was a punky kid without much talent. But my coach made me feel as if I was better than I thought I could be..."

..."When I was a kid, I had a great coach. He taught me how to bounce back when things were tough. I wish I could thank him now — but I don't even remember his name..."

So you see, whether we like it or not we can certainly have a major influence on the future of the young people that we coach. I do not mean to infer that we should involve ourselves with learning counseling skills but there are almost certainly times when we need to be a good listener or a "group therapist"

and I think with this in mind an invitational approach to coaching can be useful.

DEVELOPING THE INVITATIONAL APPROACH

We are reminded continually how quickly soccer is growing as a participant sport in this country; however, we hear very little about those boys and girls who could have been participating had they been given the opportunity to do so. Now you may say that of course children have plenty of opportunities these days, with recreational teams, traveling classic and select teams, and many well organized recreation programs, but it is the children who are already in these programs who may be put off playing soccer for good by coaches who are creating a "lethal presence" to young players and in turn damaging the future of the game.

In many cases coaches are failing to provide or to highlight opportunities during practice and match situations for young players and also failing to invite them to take advantage of opportunities when they arise. The most effective coaches at the youth level are those who can help each player to recognize opportunities and in turn to use them to achieve full potential. The hallmark of such coaches is an awareness of the makeup of each player and the ability to be flexible in approaching each individual. This allows them to do the most effective thing at the most appropriate time.

Coaching is without doubt a "helping profession" and although there are many coaches who in literal terms do not coach professionally, especially at youth level, as members of a coaching association such as the NSCAA we would like to think that coaches recognize the responsibility they have to their players themselves, and to other coaches. With this in mind it is important that we should take a strong, pro-player initiative. There has to be some substance behind what we, as coaches, say and do. We have to operate with structure and direction.

THE INVITATIONAL APPROACH

The invitational approach offers four elements that we can use in taking a positive stance.

1. Optimism

We have to believe that the young people we are coaching are valuable, capable, and able, and should be treated accordingly.

2. Respect

We should be aware of appropriate behavior in relation to when to invite and when not to invite and when to accept and not accept. Although soccer is a team game, we are dealing with individual personalities, and this should be reflected in caring for an individual's needs. For example, a young boy returning to practice after a two week layoff due to an acute flu virus might not survive the rigorous session that you had planned for the rest of the team. Making him

Children's involvement in youth soccer should be predicated on enjoyment and fun — as these young players seem to depict.
(photo courtesy of the Joe Morrone Soccer Camp)

do it in order to be considered for selection next Saturday is not appropriate behavior and certainly shows little respect for the boy's current condition.

It is important to remember that each individual is ultimately responsible for his or her own actions. If both coach and players have respect for each other, then there is a certain sense of "being together" which helps to promote the team concept. We have all seen the results of a team where both coach and players have little respect for each other. Disharmony and lack of effort are usually very evident.

3. Trust

Many of us have observed the situation where the smallest member of a team may have been put in goal nearly all season until the time comes to play the strong cross-town rivals. Suddenly there is a goalkeeper change for that match!

Dr. Purkey tells us that "A basic premise of the invitational model is that everything counts. Human potential, though not always apparent, is always there, waiting to be discovered and invited forth." Lack of trust in an individual can have long-lasting effects on the personality and development of that person as a soccer player.

4. Intentionality

As mentioned earlier, effective coaches help players to realize their potential. This may be done through effective use of the following:

● **Places**

The environment, practice fields, game fields, gymnasium are extremely important. The coach should do everything possible to provide an inviting environment. For example, the best possible playing surface (practice and match field), adequate number of balls, cones, bibs or vests, and goals, if possible. In many parts of the United States soccer fields are very poorly maintained by local councils but this will not change as long as coaches accept the situation and do nothing to put pressure on those who should be providing our young players with safe and well-maintained fields.

● **Policies**

The polices that coaches create, add to or subtract from the overall effectiveness or ineffectiveness of their team and individual players. For example, a coach may initiate a policy that requires any player who is late for practice to run five laps of the field. This does not take into account how far individuals travel, by what mode they travel, or whether Mom or Dad who drive them to practice have any regard for punctuality.

● **Programs**

I think we would all agree that coaches need to develop a style to suit their personality but many youth coaches also feel that they have to develop their own unique program to suit their team. There is a vast body of knowledge pertaining to youth coaching available in this country with programs that have survived the test of time.

There are a number of development programs for youth coaches aimed at helping parent/coaches and youth coaches to improve their coaching techniques. However, a coach must take the opportunity to "get in the game" and not sit back and expect the experts to send them handouts in the mail. Coaches should be intentionally inviting with themselves and others, personally and professionally. The more intentional a coach is, the more accurate his or her judgments and appraisals are likely to be.

The inviting relationship encourages coaches to be consistent in their approach to their players. Once a coach has developed a stance from which he may effectively operate, again using the Invitational Model we can identify four levels of functioning.

FOUR LEVELS OF COACHING

Intentional Disinviting

Fortunately the coaches who are intentionally disinviting are the least in number. These are the people who deliberately design practice sessions that dissuade or discourage certain behaviors by being insulting or discriminatory. For example, players whose skills do not quite match up to the rest of the team may be left out of certain practice drills because they "always mess them up." Or young players may be deliberately left on the bench for long periods of time in the hope that they will not turn up the following week. If they do, the coach may "have" to play them!

This type of behavior towards young players should never be tolerated by the coaching profession regardless of "win/loss" record. I recently overhead a coach tell his players (10-year old boys) playing on a dry hard field, on a windy day "If you guys don't get control of this ball I'm going to bench ya!" Another parent/coach was overheard saying to his son, the goalkeeper of the team, "If you try to save another ball like that again you won't get any dinner tonight. Now get back in there and don't be hesitant." Does this type of coaching promote long-term involvement in the sport? No. These coaches are being "intentionally disinviting" towards their young players.

Unintentionally Disinviting

Coaches who operate at this level are normally well meaning people who can be characterized by "thoughtless" behavior. A typical situation may be a coach who always wonders why his or her players don't come to practice, why they are always late, or why the referees are always against them.

Unintentionally Inviting

Coaches who are unintentionally inviting find that coaching comes fairly naturally to them and they are generally well-liked and reasonably effective with their players. However, generally they are unaware as to why they are successful and when difficulties occur during practice sessions or match situations they have a hard time figuring out why things are going wrong and what to do to put them right. For example, a coach who produces an inviting environment for his or her players and is genuinely concerned about their development may have a very narrow knowledge base and, therefore is inconsistent when it comes to answering questions or correcting faults in techniques.

Intentionally Inviting

Coaches who are able to operate and maintain this level are those who believe that everybody and everything adds to or subtracts from the quality of their coaching and their players' potential. Coaches who are intentionally inviting to their players will generally take time to prepare practice sessions well, ensure that the environment is as realistic as possible, and that the players are given plenty of opportunities to "play" and "get in the game."

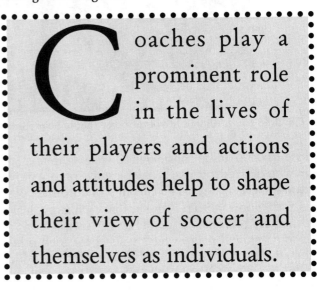

Coaches play a prominent role in the lives of their players and actions and attitudes help to shape their view of soccer and themselves as individuals.

Practices are generally varied, interesting, informative and above all — fun. Players will generally want to play anytime and anywhere for this type of coach and are eager to practice.

There are two basic approaches to influencing people: The positive approach is designed to strengthen desirable behaviors by motivating people to perform in a desirable way. The second approach, the negative approach, involves attempts to eliminate negative behaviors through punishment and criticism. The motivating factor in the second approach is fear. Both approaches are used by coaches but the positive approach fits in very well with the invitational model which I believe to be more desirable to the profession. The negative approach creates a lethal presence and can be very damaging to the development of young soccer players.

Invitational Functioning

Four areas of functioning are available to coaches who may choose an invitational approach to coaching soccer. First they should always bear in mind that they need to be personally inviting with themselves. For example, they should take time away from soccer and coaching to do something different that may be extremely satisfying, such as reading, listening to music, or running to keep in shape. If a coach is seeking to influence young people's lives in relation to soccer, it is important that his own personal lifestyle is in good order. Coaches play a prominent role in the lives of their players and actions and attitudes help to shape their view of soccer and themselves as individuals. All of us, especially children, learn as much from what coaches do as from what they say. In fact they will remember what a coach did long after they have forgotten what a coach said.

This brings me to the second area of functioning which is being personally inviting to others. Purkey & Novak, (1984) state that "Professional success, no matter how great, cannot make up for the lack of success in personal relationships". Self disclosure of your feelings should not be seen as a weakness, as it often helps to share feelings with others including your players. This may help to let them know that even though you are a coach you are first of all a human being!

Ridiculing players about their physical appearance or behavior, background or misfortune can often be very disinviting. Saying "I was only kidding," with some children may not be sufficient to repair the damage of a cruel jest.

Professional Development

The third area of functioning is being professionally inviting to oneself. A coach who does not invite himself or herself to grow and develop new and improved programs and policies, runs the risk of becoming stale and complacent. I am sure that we all know youth coaches who have been practicing and coaching in the same manner for years with the philosophy that "what was good for us when we played is certainly good enough for these kids now".

There are many ways for a coach to grow professionally. Being in a rut, even a successful one, tends to narrow a coach's perspective and reduces enthusiasm and vitality. For example, it is essential that a coach participate in courses and programs that are designed to sharpen skills and develop new techniques and methods. Attending such courses is a very beneficial experience and will help to upgrade skills, techniques, and knowledge of coaching soccer. There are a number of excellent courses offered at national, regional, and local levels. Parent/coaches who are new to the game should be encouraged to attend basic level courses and not assume that because they have coached football, baseball, or basketball that coaching soccer will be easy.

It helps for coaches to spend some time reading. There are many good sources of information on soccer or coaching in general. A coach who is aware of some of the physical, psychological, social, and emotional needs of his players will be capable of recognizing potential problems before they arise or find recognition and correction of faults an easier process.

Being a member of a professional group such as the National Soccer Coaches Association of America (NSCAA), and being active in local coaching or club administration helps to maintain a high level of professionalism. Finally, to be professionally inviting with oneself it is important to ask for feedback and constructive criticism from players, parents, or colleagues which may help coaches to evaluate where they can improve their coaching. This helps also to show respect for the opinions of others while improving your own performance as a coach.

The fourth area of functioning is being professionally inviting to others. This may well be the primary purpose of coaching and can be achieved in a number of ways. For example:

• Be positive and point out things that are right, and you will find that players generally will respond better to success; However, if something is unacceptable then say so and try to improve it. For example, in a practice session where a coach may be working on one-on-one defensive principles where a ball is played into an attacker by a defender and he or she must then defend a goal, do not accept a poorly-weighted, inaccurate pass to start the practice. Point out or demonstrate how you want the ball passed in and then invite the defender to play the same type of pass;

• Invite action during practice and match situations. Coaches should try to emphasize what players can do rather than what they can't do. Players who are inactive during practice sessions are not being provided with opportunities to improve. Players waiting in line to shoot on goal or for their turn to make a pass are wasting valuable time and missing out on a tremendous learning experience. Young players need to be invited to experience maximum touches of the ball during practice and match situations. They cannot achieve this by being inactive;

• Coaches should recognize their responsibility to be trustworthy, obey rules, support the club or organization that pays their salary and be punctual to practices and matches.

• Finally, it is vital for a professionally inviting coach not to give up when things go wrong. If invitations are given to players as often as possible then they may or may not be accepted. However, if players are not sent an invitation they may never accept. Being criticized or rejected may be difficult to accept sometimes but in "The Youth Sports Guide" John Wooden is reported to have once told a group of coaches:

> ..."You must know quite well that you are not perfect, that you are going to make mis-

takes. But you must not be afraid to act because you're afraid of making mistakes or you won't do anything, and that's the greatest mistake of all. We must have initiative and act and know that we're going to fail at times, for failure will only make us stronger if we accept it properly." (p. 17)

CONCLUSION

A coach who chooses to use the invitational approach will, I feel, see a different side of himself or herself, the players, and the game in general, that he or she never thought existed. Opportunities will arise for both coach and players to develop together and achieve goals that they may have always thought were far out of reach.

Don Gregory, the coach of Strake Jesuit College Preparatory School in Houston, Texas, in an article in *Soccer America* (February 19, 1987) said that his program should assure that each player:

"Develops a love for the world's most popular sport."

"Develops a strong sense of self-worth."

"And learns that perfection isn't paramount, but rather the striving for perfection is." He added "Self-discipline and strong commitment to a common task will being success and winning." (p. 14)

The invitational approach points to a number of positive and negative traits in our personalities to which we can all relate. The question is, do we wish to be a lethal or beneficial presence in the future development of youth soccer in the United States? Being intentionally disinviting with young players does absolutely nothing to promote the future of soccer and the hard work and dedication that professionals in coaching are striving to maintain will be wasted unless coaches who choose this approach are removed from the sport.

The invitational approach offers a much brighter future for soccer in that each coach who is intentionally inviting with regard to the people, places, policies, and programs that he or she may contact, design, or initiate will be a beneficial presence in the coaching profession and perpetrate a much stronger stance from which each new participant can operate. Each of us as coaches has responsibility to ourselves, our players, and our profession to maintain and demonstrate respect. Realizing these responsibilities becomes easier when we adopt an invitational approach in our coaching.

REFERENCES

Gregory, D. (1987) Editorial—Prep Touchline, Dave Payne, "Coach preaches education on and off the field." *Soccer America*, February 19, 1987, p. 1

Purkey, W. W. & Novak, J. M . (1984) *Inviting School Success: A Self-Concept Approach to Teaching and Learning.* Belmont California: Wadsworth Publishing Co.

Purkey, W, W. & Schmidt, J. J. (1987) *The Inviting Relationship: An Expanded Perspective for Professional Counseling.* Englewood Cliffs, New Jersey: Prentice-Hall, Inc.

Wooden, J. In J. R. Thomas (Ed.) (1978) *Youth Sports Guide for Coaches and Parents.* Washington, D.C.: AAHPER Publications.

A COACH'S REWARD COMES FROM PLAYERS
Dan Woog

When I do it in the fall, for the high school, my salary works out to about minimum wage. When I did it this spring, for the local soccer association, I got paid for the first time in 13 years, though far less than I could have earned at my real job as a writer.

I'm a soccer coach. I conduct practices in searing heat and raw wind. I stand on the sidelines in pouring rain. I field phone calls at all hours from parents who excoriate my judgement, players who seek reassurance, even townspeople who just want to chat about games.

Why do I do it? Obviously, not only for the money, the working conditions or the hours. Nor do I coach for positive emotional strokes. Occasionally, a parent calls to congratulate me after a particularly big win, or to thank me for a special act of kindness, but by and large, the psychic awards are nil.

I've grown to expect that, and, besides, pats on the back shouldn't be the reason anyone does anything.

No, the reasons I coach are far less tangible, far less definable. I coach because:

• I love the sport. Soccer is a game of creativity and intelligence, of grace and power. It's a simple game, one that youngsters pick up easily, but it's a game that must constantly be worked at. Happily, practices can be fun and games are even more fun because the action is virtually non-stop.

• I love to teach. The work of a soccer coach takes place during practice sessions, when he instructs skills, explains strategies and molds a team out of disparate individuals. But come game time, soccer players are on their own. There are no timeouts as in other sports. My team wins or loses on its own, based upon what we've worked on all week, month and year. I'm reminded of the saying: If you give a man a fish, you feed him for a day. If you teach a man to fish, you feed him for a lifetime.

• I love to travel. Soccer is an international game, and

American youth teams take full advantage of travel opportunities. I've visited Europe and South America five times. This summer, I'm taking a team to Australia and New Zealand. On each trip, we live in homes of host players and discover more about foreign lands, cultures and people than could ever be possible staying in hotels and taking packaged tours.

• I love to stay young. Coaching provides me with an outlet during the day when I can step outside the adult world, when I can connect with youngsters who have an enthusiasm, a sense of humor and a view of life that we former adolescents must shed as we grow older. I feel energized by the questioning, the posturing, the testing I hear these young soccer players express at every practice session and game.

• I love to help youngsters grow up. It's wonderful to conduct an invigorating practice and to share in victory celebrations. But the deepest satisfaction I get from coaching is longer range. I'm proud when former players write college application essays describing what soccer has meant to them. I'm even prouder when those essays help them to get into their first-choice schools where, intrigued by political science, cellular biology or art history, they plunge into previously unexplored worlds.

They may or may not continue to play soccer, but they carry the lessons they've learned about accepting challenges, making their own decisions and putting forth their best efforts into these new areas of their lives.

And I'm particularly proud when, as I see happening more, former players become involved in their communities as youth coaches. I see them bringing the same enthusiasm:

• For soccer, for teaching, and for life;

• To their young players that I have tried to bring to them, and I can only hope that they receive as much satisfaction from their coaching as I have received from mine.

⚽

COACHING AND ORGANIZATIONAL ISSUES IN YOUTH SOCCER

ORIENTING PARENTS TO YOUR YOUTH SPORTS PROGRAM
Dr. Deborah Feltz

As youth sport coaches, you have numerous responsibilities, including organizing for their season, planning practices, scheduling games, and providing qualitative instruction. Another important responsibility that should not be overlooked, however, is dealing with parents. The support and aid from parents can be very helpful, although some parents, out of lack of awareness, can undermine the basic goals of your program, thereby detracting from the benefits a program can provide. For this reason, parents should be informed of your coaching philosophy, the league's objectives, and their children's and their own responsibilities.

The most effective way of providing parents with this information is through a parent orientation program. Not only will a parent orientation meeting inform parents of the league's objectives, your coaching philosophy, and parent and child responsibilities, it will also serve to improve parents' understanding of the rules and regulations of the sport. This will allow them to be more knowledgeable spectators. A meeting for parents is also a way for them to become acquainted with you. Meeting you in person may increase the possibility that clear lines of communication between you and the parents will be established.

THE CONTENT OF A PARENT ORIENTATION MEETING

Parents will probably have a number of questions concerning their child's program. With proper preparation and an outlined agenda, you should be able to answer most of them. The following agenda is based on some of the questions that parents frequently ask:

1. Introductions
2. Understanding the sport
3. Dangers and risk of injury
4. Equipment needs
5. Coaching philosophy
6. Emergency procedures
7. The child's responsibilities
8. The parents' responsibilities
9. The season schedule

Each agenda item and its relationship to the sports program is explained in the following paragraphs.

Introductions. Parents should be acquainted with three individuals in their child's youth sport program: the administrator, the coach, and the team sponsor. You may wish to begin the meeting by informing parents who sponsors the program, whether it is a national group, community agency, school, religious organization or a community parks and recreation department. They should know your telephone number and that of the sponsor. Next, you should briefly describe your background, coaching experience, and your reasons for coaching. The parents should also introduce themselves to each other during this period. By getting to know other parents they may be able to establish working relationships for specific committees and share transportation responsibilities. Finally, the purpose of the meeting should be described and if handouts are available, they should be distributed at this time.

Understanding the sport. After introductions, information about basic rules, skills, and strategies may be beneficial to parents who have little knowledge about the sport. Many times spectators are critical of officials because they do not know the rules. Informing parents of the rules may alleviate some of this criticism. Information concerning the sport may be presented in the form of a film (if monies and equipment are available), a demonstration of techniques and rule interpretation, or both. A handout could also be provided containing basic rules of the game. If you prefer not to use this time to cover this information, you could invite parents to attend one of the early practice sessions where a demonstration of playing positions, rules and strategies could be presented.

Dangers and risk of injury. The parents should be told what they can expect in terms of possible injuries for a particular sport. Are bruises and contusions mainly involved or is there a possibility for broken bones and torn ligaments? Let them know if a medical examination is required prior to their child's participation; and if so, who will conduct the exam, and whether the parents or program sponsors pay for it. Safety rules for games and practices should be outlined and parents should be assured that the playing/practice area will be kept safe and free of hazards. Lastly, the program's policy of accident insurance should be described. Inform parents if the sponsoring program has athletic accident coverage or whether the parents' insurance company will be responsible for injuries incurred during athletic competition.

Equipment needs. Some program sponsors provide the equipment needed to participate in the sport, while others do not. If the sponsors do not provide the equipment, you should explain what equipment the children need and where it can be purchased. You may also wish to offer advice on the quality of particular brands and how much parents can expect to pay for specific items.

Coaching philosophy. Whatever your goals and those of the program, they should be presented to the parents. Parents will then be able to judge whether the goals are compatible with their own and those of their child. Some goals that have been identified by young athletes as most important are: (a) to have fun, (b) to improve skills and learn new skills, (c) to make new friends, (d) to succeed or win, and (e) to become physically fit. Most educators, physicians, coaches and parents consider these to be healthy goals for which coaches and children should strive. Parents should be informed of the amount of emphasis that will be placed on these goals.

Other concerns that should be addressed are your policies on eliminating players after tryouts, missing practices (including vacations), and recognizing players through awards. Will players be allowed to compete if they missed the last practice before a game? Will the player be excluded from contests or eliminated from the team if she or he goes on a two-week vacation? Will players receive trophies or other tangible rewards? How much emphasis is placed upon these rewards? Are the rewards contingent upon performance or are they given to all participants regardless of achievements?

Emergency procedures. You should obtain a list of the parents' names, addresses, telephone numbers and names and telephone numbers of their family physicians. This list should be typed and distributed to all parents of your team so that parents will be able to contact each other. You should also outline the procedures that will be followed in case of an emergency.

The child's responsibilities. Adults need to be reminded that the child's welfare is primary above all other objectives. Children and their parents must realize, however, that along with rights, children have certain responsibilities if they wish to participate on a sports team. Young athletes must be responsible for (a) reporting promptly to practice and games, (b) cooperating with coaches and teammates, (c) putting forth the effort to condition their bodies and learn the basic skills, and (d) their own conduct and its consequences. These responsibilities should be discussed so that parents may help reinforce them at home.

The parents' responsibilities. Parents of young athletes have a number of responsibilities that should be discussed at the parents' orientation meeting. Martens (1978) has identified a number of these responsibilities. You may wish to cover all or a portion of the following responsibilities in the parent orientation meeting.

1. The parents should learn what their children want from the sport.
2. Parents should determine if their children are ready to compete and at what level they want to compete.
3. Parents must have realistic expectations and must help their children develop their own realistic expectations of their capabilities in the sport.
4. Parents should help their children interpret the experiences associated with competitive sports, such as helping their children understand the meaning of winning and losing.
5. Parents are responsible for disciplining their children and ensuring that their children meet specific responsibilities for participating in their sport.
6. Parents have the responsibility not to interfere with their children's coach and to conduct themselves in a proper manner at games.

The season schedule. The more organized you can be with regard to the schedule for the season, the less time you will have to spend in making telephone calls and sending memos later on. The most efficient way

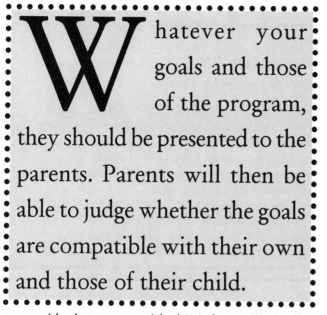

Whatever your goals and those of the program, they should be presented to the parents. Parents will then be able to judge whether the goals are compatible with their own and those of their child.

to provide the parents with this information is via a handout containing the schedule for the entire season. This schedule should inform the parents about the length of the season, practice and game dates, sites, lengths of practices and games, number of games, number of practices, and mid- and post-season events.

ORGANIZING A PARENT ORIENTATION MEETING

Conducting a parent orientation meeting is not as overwhelming as it may seem if you are well prepared and organized. Prior to setting a meeting time and contacting parents, you should outline an agenda. In addition to this, you should outline your philosophy. If you have never formulated a coaching philosophy, a book you may wish to review as an aid in developing one is entitled: *A Winning Philosophy for Youth Sport Programs* by Seefeldt, Smoll, Smith and Gould, which is available from The Youth Sports Institute (IM Sports Circle; Michigan State University; East Lansing, MI 48824). Also examine the league's philosophy to ensure that your philosophy is not in conflict. Next, develop any handouts that will be distributed at the meeting. These may include an outline of the agenda for parents to follow, a list of basic rules for that particular sport, and a seasonal schedule. If the parents' addresses and telephone numbers are known, this list could be prepared and distributed at the meeting.

When all the preparations have been made, the coach should select a date, time and place for the meeting. Parents may be notified about the meeting by telephone or with a letter. Additionally, it is probably a good idea to call parents the night before the meeting to remind them about it. After the meeting, mail a list of the parents' names, addresses and telephone numbers, if this information was not available prior to the meeting. Handouts should be mailed to parents who could not attend the meeting.

FOLLOW-UPS ON THE PARENT ORIENTATION MEETING

Although you may try to answer all of the questions parents may have about their child's participation through a parent orientation meeting, problems will also arise during the season. Thus, it is important to keep the lines of communication open. You should indicate your willingness to discuss any problems that were not discussed at the original meeting. This might be accomplished with a telephone conversation or a coach-parent/coach-parent-athlete conference. You may even wish to have another general meeting midway through the season to provide the parents with an update on the team's progress and/or any problems that are occurring, and to receive input from parents. By keeping the lines of communication open with parents within the appropriate guidelines, coaches will be able to make the best use of parental involvement.

REFERENCE

Martens, R. *Joy and Sadness In Children's Sports*. Champaign, IL: Human Kinetics, 1978.

HOW DO I MAINTAIN DISCIPLINE?
Dr. Deborah Feltz

Coaches often react to their athletes' misbehavior by yelling, lecturing, or using threats. These verbal techniques are used because we often do not know what else to do to regain control of the situation. Many of the problems associated with discipline could be avoided if coaches anticipated the occurrence of misbehavior and developed policies to deal with it.

Although threats and lectures may prevent misbehavior in the short term, they create a hostile and negative atmosphere and, typically, their effectiveness is short-lived. Moreover, this type of relationship between a coach and team members does not promote the learning of the sport nor does it motivate the players to accept the coach's instructions.

Sound discipline involves a two-step plan that must be in place before the misbehavior occurs. The steps are:

• Defining how players are to behave and identifying behaviors that will not be tolerated, and;

• Identifying the consequences for individuals who do not behave according to the rules.

Children want clearly defined limits and structure for how they should behave. This can be accomplished without showing anger, lecturing the players, or threatening them. As the coach, it is your responsibility to have a systematic plan for maintaining discipline before your season gets underway. Coaches who have

Table 1:

Items to Consider when Making Team Rules
Examples of Desirable and Undesirable Conduct in Sports

Desirable Conduct:	Undesirable Conduct:
Attending to your instructions	Talking while you are trying to give instructions
Full concentration on drills	Inattentive behavior during drills
Treating opponents with respect	Fighting with opponents or using abusive language
Giving positive encouragement	Making negative comments to teammates about teammates
Avoiding penalties	Intentionally fouling during the game
Being prompt to practices and games	Being late or absent from practices or games
Helping to pick up equipment after practices	Leaving equipment out for others to pick up
Bringing all your equipment to practices	Forgetting to bring a part of your equipment or uniform to games and practices

Table 2:

Code of Sportsmanship*

Sportsmanlike Behavior:	Unsportsmanlike Behavior:
Behavior toward officials —	
when questioning officials do so in an appropriate manner (e.g., lodge an official protest, have only designated individuals, such as a captain, address officials)	arguing with or swearing at officials
Behavior toward opponents —	
treating all opponents with respect and dignity at all times	arguing with the opposition; making sarcastic remarks about the opponents; making aggressive actions towards opponents or swearing at opponents
Behavior toward teammates —	
giving only constructive criticism and positive encouragement	making negative or sarcastic remarks; swearing at or arguing with teammates
Behavior towards spectators —	
making only positive comments	arguing with spectators; making negative remarks/ swearing at spectators
Rules acceptance and infraction —	
obeying all league rules	intentially violating league rules; taking advantage of loopholes in rules (e.g., every child must play, so the coach tells unskilled players to be ill on important games days)
Spectator behavior —	
making only positive comments to players, coaches, or officials	making negative or sarcastic comments

* Reprinted from Seefeldt et al. (1981) *A Winning Philosophy of Youth Sports*. East Lansing, MI: Youth Sports Institute.

Table 3:

Examples of Rewards and Penalties

Rewards	Penalties
Being a starter	Being taken out of the game
Playing a desired position	Not being allowed to start
Leading an exercise or activity	Sitting out for part of practice
Praise from you	Dismissed
Decals	1) next practice
Medals	2) next week
	3) rest of season

taken the time to establish rules of conduct will be in a position to react in a reasonable manner when children misbehave.

MAINTAINING DISCIPLINE

Defining Team Rules

The first step in developing a plan to maintain discipline is to identify what you consider to be desirable and undesirable conduct by your players. This list can then be used to establish relevant team rules. A list of potential items to consider when identifying team rules is included in Table 1.

Your players (especially if you are coaching at the older levels) should be involved in establishing the rules for the team. Research has shown that players are more willing to live by rules when they have had a voice in formulating them. Smoll and Smith (1979) suggest the use of the following introduction to establish rules with players:

> *I think rules and regulations are an important part of the game because the game happens to be rules and regulations. Our team rules ought to be something we can agree upon. I have a set of rules that I feel are important. But we all have to follow them, so you ought to think about what you want. They should be your rules, too.*

Rules of conduct must be defined in clear and specific terms. For instance, a team rule that players must "show good sportsmanship" in their games is not a very clear and specific rule. What, exactly, is showing good sportsmanship? Does it mean obeying all the rules, calling one's own fouls, or respecting officials' decisions? The Youth Sports Institute has adopted a code of sportsmanship which defines sportsmanship in more specific terms. This code has been reprinted in Table 2. You may wish to use some of the items listed as you formulate your team rules.

Enforcement of Rules

Not only are rules needed to maintain discipline, but enforcement of those rules must be carried out so that reoccurrences are prevented. Rules are enforced through rewards and penalties. Players are rewarded when they abide by the rules and penalized when they

break the rules. The next step, therefore, in developing a plan to maintain discipline is to determine the rewards and penalties for each rule. Your players should be asked for suggestions at this point because they will receive the benefits or consequences of the decisions. When determining rewards and penalties for rules, the most effective approach is to use rewards that are meaningful to your players and appropriate to the situation. Withdrawal of rewards should be used for misconduct. A list of potential rewards and penalties that can be used in sport is in Table 3.

The best way to motivate players to behave in an acceptable manner is to reward them for good behavior. When things are done well, comment accordingly or be ready to use nonverbal interactions such as smiling or applauding. Penalties are only effective when they are meaningful to the players. Typically, the types of penalties that are used for rule violations are ineffective because they are not important to the players. Generally, they leave no room for positive interactions between you and your players. Examples of ineffective penalties include showing anger, embarrassing the player by lecturing the player, shouting at the player or assigning a physical activity (skating laps, extra push-ups). Assigning a physical activity for certain misbehavior may develop a negative attitude in the player toward the activity. Avoid using physical activity as a form of punishment; the benefits of youth sports, such as learning skills and gaining cardiovascular fitness, are gained through activity. Children should not associate activity with punishment.

Sometimes it is more effective to ignore inappropriate behavior if the infractions are relatively minor. Continually scolding players for pranks or "horseplay" can become counterproductive. If team deportment is a constant problem, the coach must ask, Why? Misbehavior may be the players' way of telling the coach they need attention or they do not have enough to do. Coaches should check to see if the players are spending a lot of time standing in lines while waiting a turn to practice. This lack of activity could lead to counter-productive or disruptive behavior.

When the rules for proper conduct have been outlined and the rewards and penalties have been determined, they must then be stated clearly so the players will understand them. Your players must know exactly the consequences for breaking the rules and their rewards for abiding by the rules. You must also follow through, consistently and impartially, with your application of rewards for desirable conduct and penalties for misconduct. Nothing destroys a plan for discipline more quickly than its inconsistent application. Rules must apply to all players equally and in all situations, equally. Thus, if your team is in a championship game and your star player violates a rule which requires that he or she not be allowed to start, the rule must still be enforced. If not, you are communicating

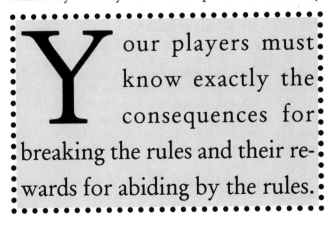

Your players must know exactly the consequences for breaking the rules and their rewards for abiding by the rules.

to your players that the rules are not to be taken seriously, especially when the game is at stake.

Summary

Although threats, lectures and/or yelling may deter misbehavior in the short term, the negative atmosphere that results reduces long-term coaching effectiveness. A more positive approach to handling misbehavior is to prevent it by establishing, with player input, clear team rules and enforcement policies. Use fair and consistent enforcement of the rules, primarily through rewarding correct behavior, rather than penalizing wrong behavior.

References

Smoll, R.L. and Smith, R.E. (1978). *Improving relationship skills in youth sport coaches.* East Lansing, MI: Institute for the Study of Youth Sports.

⚽

Substitutions: Playing with players
Jim Prunier

The age old question of how many players should play in the game returns again and again somewhat akin to a ping pong ball coming back again with fresh vigor and undiminished spunk, notwithstanding its having been so skillfully rebuked before. Oh, if only there were a definitive work on substitution so that we may direct yet another dissatisfied person to these scriptures and no longer be anguished by the waste of publishing space taken up by rationalizations of what ought to be.

To the parent of the woefully unskilled player, there's no harm in giving all the players a time of glory in the game. To the parent of the almost first-stringer, equal playing time among the more equal players is appropriate. To the players in the best season of their lives, only the starters should play. Of course, in the lopsided games, all the subs should play. Equal playing time is proper for eight-year-olds first entering the sport. In the competitive games for the older teams, certain key players seem to get the most playing time. Where the coach is paid or otherwise expected to produce winning teams, substitution is a tactic to be judiciously used. The rationale of substitution is inconsistent from game to game.

The teams that want to train players and have fun may reserve the learning of how to play in critical games to those players expected to perform best and be more generous when sharing the fun time in those games where the outcome is predictable. In fewer words, the mission of the team shifts as the coach responds to both natural and applied pressure.

Ideal of Soccer

Substituting players, and the problems it brings to the game, is contrary to the ideal of the sport. From its earliest origins, soccer was intended to be played by the participants who started the match. The expectation was that the contestants undergo the arduous demands of the game and endure. This reasoning incepts from the time when teams were drawn from a limited population (school or town), where competition would go on for decades. Mostly, time would even things out but when it didn't, there would be a rivalry built. An invincible team might have challenged the mettle of the surrounding teams, giving them a hopeful anticipation before the encounter. This atmosphere would only have meaning where the best eleven represented the home teams. It was likened to a prize fight where the idea of a sub taking part in the battle goes against the intent of the sport.

Substitutes change the makeup of the contest by sending in surges of strength and thereby negate the need for player endurance. To persevere against one's own physical limits and prosecute the game against an opponent is the defined objective of soccer. When players are changed during a game, it becomes a trial between groups and their leaders; not teams, not an identifiable unit.

It was apropos for soccer in its origins to field only eleven players because all the players came from the locality of the club and it was all amateur. Players won bragging rights and nothing more. In time some well-to-doers found ways to relocate players from afar and to slip a little something into the boots of those players who did well in a match. This charade of amateurism was dropped and the game became professional. But even with this transition from pauper level to plenty the use of subs held to the original spirit of the game. Until the 1950s substitution was not permitted in the games. Even injured players started in matches. However, the paying public's right to see proper teams at play and the increasing brutality of some players forced the game open to subs. It remains so today in FIFA soccer: two players may enter the game, no one may re-enter. Of course, this has become more than a way to replace an injured player.

When is Subbing Appropriate?

Coaches routinely replace excellent by less skillful subs in order to achieve some result. Where a goal is needed or in need of holding onto, an appropriate substitution may be made. Or, a fast runner may be instructed to exhaust an opponent and then be replaced by fresh legs to capitalize on the situation thus created. Or, ...well, the list is too long. Suffice it to say that substitution is a way for coaches to influence the course of the game.

Not all games are played at a professional level or with puristic concern over historical images of the sport, so adaptations to the FIFA laws are permitted.

*WHAT KIND OF COACH ARE YOU?

The National Institute for Child Centered Coaching prepared this quiz for coaches to evaluate themselves. Circle the response that best reflects your thoughts about each statement.

1. The major reasons children should be involved in sports is for fun, not winning.
    A. No. Winning is important to young children and older children.
    B. Sort of. Winning is important, but not necessary.
    C. Yes. Enjoyment is the key, winning is only secondary.

2. It is important for children to learn how to compete at an early age.
    A. Yes. They stand a better chance of being successful later in life.
    B. Sort of. Competition is important, but it shouldn't be the basis for playing sports for young children.
    C. No. The earlier young children learn to be competitive, the less enjoyment they have in playing.

3. A good, strong self-image can be developed in young children with a no-nonsense approach to coaching.
    A. Yes. They need to be told "who is boss" and to follow the rules.
    B. Sort of. Children need to be managed with a firm yet manageable approach.
    C. No. Children need to be encouraged to do their best.

4. Praising a child's ability is OK, but a coach shouldn't overdo it.
    A. Yes. If praised too often, they'll develop a false sense of their abilities.
    B. Sort of. Children need to be told accurately and honestly about their weaknesses.
    C. No. If it is honest praise, there is no such thing as "overdoing it."

5. Children who develop too high a sense of self-esteem grow up to be spoiled.
    A. Take any of these high-priced superstars in today's sports, and you'll see what a spoiled child is like.
    B. A child must be taught humility; a child with high self-esteem often acts conceited.
    C. Children with high self-esteem often make the best players.

6. Most parents want their young children to win — not necessarily to have fun.
    A. Agree.
    B. Some do, but not all.
    C. Parents need to be educated.

7. Disciplining a child in front of the team sets an example to others.
    A. Other children learn to do the right thing really fast.
    B. Peer pressure is the most effective form of team discipline.
    C. Disciplining a child is a private issue between coach and child.

8. Team rules should be set by the coach and given to the players.
    A. A coach needs to show who is in charge; children must respect authority.
    B. A coach needs to demonstrate leadership; children need to comply.
    C. A coach needs to provide guidance, children should be empowered.

9. The coach sometimes acts like a teacher, sometimes like a parent.
    A. A coach should not be confused with a parent or a teacher; a coach is a coach.
    B. A coach might sometimes take on the role of a teacher or a parent but should remain first a coach.
    C. A coach is at times a parent and a teacher.

10. A parent's role in children's sport should be:
    A. To be mildly involved.
    B. To be moderately involved.
    C. To be involved to the maximum limit.

To score your responses, give each "A" response 1 point, each "B" response 2 points, each "C" response 3 points. If you totaled:

10-16 POINTS: Attitudes of traditional coaching. Believes winning is the primary reason for playing sports, takes a hard line in discipline uses an autocratic approach to coaching, finds too little value for parental involvement. Needs a lot more instruction in child-centered philosophy and techniques.

17-23 POINTS: Tendency toward leadership, not autocratic rule; problem- solving, not ruling; motivating, not commanding; needs continued study and practice in child-centered coaching philosophy.

24-30 POINTS: Believes in making the game fun; is willing to be both a parent figure and teacher; offers guidance, encouragement and support and maximizes parental involvement; needs to continue practicing skills.

(*Reprinted with the permission of USA Today from a series entitled "Coaching Children Responsibly.")

At the recreation level, where parent-coaches who don't have a soccer background are the norm, subbing rules almost don't exist. After all, the spirit of game is hardly broken when two seven year-old goalies are both defending the same goal while the coach frantically calls to one of them to come off. At a notch above, at the local league level, we find substitute rules which are guidelines only to keep the worst of the mayhem in check. Naturally, there will be parents and coaches who will try to have the letter of the rule applied to certain favorable circumstances; to the detriment of the playing atmosphere. When the competition level clicks up another notch, to an area league involving travel teams, the need for substitution rules requires the work of a rules committee; and likely the discipline committee.

At the top of things, the FIFA laws allow subbing at any stoppage where the referee believes it will not impede the flow of the game. The idea of using up the clock by excessive subbing, in free sub games, is left to the referee to deny or add time onto the match. This basic is circumvented in America by allowing teams to sub at specific stoppages. Who hasn't heard the objection: "You're letting them sub on MY throw-in!," as though it was a RIGHT? The very notion that the referee may refuse to accept a sub stirs up emotions of indignation. Never mind that the call to sub cuts the rise in player excitement as they get on a roll, or stops an incisive quick restart.

With all the emphasis placed on winning games, too much attention is paid to how the other teams operate administratively. Indeed, it is often considered a real impediment to go to a match without subs on hand. This ultimately leads to players reaching maturity who believe that they should be taken out of the game periodically for a rest. If leagues limit rosters, to say 13 players, then the players would max out in playing time, contests would be more meaningful, subbing would be a small matter. Where there is not real limit on rosters, as in some schools, we sometimes see a virtual whole team substitution. This scoffs at the principle of there being a contest of teams. The same result can be effected by continually subbing one player at a time.

The arguments most often heard in favor of carrying an excess number of players are the assurances that at least the right number of players will appear at the games and that the job of soccer will be spread over a larger number of players. No experienced soccer coach would be very troubled over having 10 players for a match, especially when it's equally likely to happen to all teams during the season. The point about spreading joy is doubtful. Less time for more players of a non-endurance game is what is being dished out.

Other Subbing

Substituting players at games is the situation under examination here, but recognition of the ultra subbing problem should not go unnoticed. It occurs on advanced teams which are engaged in an important schedule of tough games where player redundancies exist. It's most pronounced where two almost equal goalkeepers are involved, but it also affects men-markers, ball-getters, maestros and other specialists. World class players have dried up on benches waiting for the starter to falter or become injured. The "board of directors" of such teams may be correct in hoarding such players, but no true coach would ever sign up a player for bench duty or keep any player forever on the bench.

An understanding of the substitution question has to recognize its uses in the game. These track the responsibilities of the coach at the game:
- welfare of players; mostly treating injury but also caring for mental upset and the avoidance of exposure to hazards;
- team performance; correction of assignments, revising tactics;
- time sharing, dispensing game time equitably or inequitably among the players;
- teaching and training; explaining, educating, elucidating and giving players exposure to match play;
- rest and recuperation, stimulating morale, enervating players, resetting the response to game demands upwards, cooling hotheads.

To this list is added another cause for subbing players, not in the realm of coaching responsibilities: meddling. Every coach has guilty marks under this heading. It's probably due to a desire to become more helpfully involved, an unwillingness to say NO to players on the sideline and a bending to pressure from fans.

How many players should be put into the game? How often? For how long? For how many times each? It's a problem related to the number of players put on a roster in the first place. The plan for the team and the resoluteness of the coach in holding to the plan will be vital in solving this meandering question. It should not be some individual's thinking of what is appropriate for his or her child.

⚽

ORGANIZING YOUR YOUTH PRACTICE SESSIONS

More Challenges, a Better Practice
Ron Quinn

Before a coach gets into "the meat" of any practice session for youngsters ages 5, 6, and 7, he or she should understand that perhaps the single most important habit that they can inculcate in young charges is the desire to play without adult leadership present.

When presenting clinics, I suggest to coaches that they establish a practice protocol in which the first two children to arrive at practice put down cones or shirts and begin playing 1 v. 1. When the next person arrives, the game now becomes 2 v. 1, then 2 v. 2 and so on until the entire team arrives at which time the coach has adjusted the field and goals to meet the needs of the group.

The final result is a child-organized, child-directed, small-sided match. At this point the coach should sit down and observe the game for 10 minutes or so.

YOUTH COACHING PHILOSOPHY

As I state in my book *The Peak Performance: Soccer Games for Player Development*, each youth coach should develop a coaching philosophy that underpins his or her approach to coaching younger players.

Two essential concepts that are discussed in the book are Muska Mosston's "slanty line" approach to teaching and Dr. Marianne Torbert's "expansion, equalization and interactive challenge" theory of child education.

The slanty line concept takes the traditional method of the straight-line concept as typified in the old rope game of high-water, low-water, where the rope starts on the ground and everyone jumps over it. Then two children raise the rope to a new level. As children are unable to jump over the rope they are eliminated until only one person is left. Again, this approach is highly counterproductive in the development of young people, because you first eliminate those individuals who are most in need practice in order to improve their jumping ability.

Mosston's approach is to use the rope—but slant it. Now those children who want to run and jump and feel successful can do so. When the players feel comfortable and secure, they seek out new challenges. In this approach everyone participates at his or her own ability level. Mosston's slanty line concept is centered on the belief that all children have a right to participate in activities at their own ability level. Children will not continue activities in which they are continually eliminated or are forced to wait to take turns in order to participate. Given opportunities, children will seek to meet challenges and will take risks.

The activities to follow apply the slanty line concept so that soccer players can participate at their own ability level and do not stand in lines waiting for their turn to succeed — or fail.

Dr. Torbert has identified three interrelated concepts that when applied to play activities increase the growth and development of children.

- Expansion is thought to be anything that increases the number of potential growth experiences. In youth soccer it could include such things as allow-ing more turns, more ball contacts, increased equipment (i.e., a ball for every player). Reducing the down time between activities and selecting activities that allow everyone to play are further refinements of this principle of learning.

- Equalization is that which equalizes the opportunity for each participant to be challenged and grow at his or her ability level. This closely relates to the slanty line concept and when applied to youth training means that the coach must make a conscious effort to select, design and provide training sessions that motivate each player. Peak Performance contains exercises that can aid the fledgling youth coach in terms of selection of such activities.

- Interactive challenges are the final piece of the Torbert triad and states that activity should allow players participating at personal ability level to contribute to the growth of other players who may be a level below them. The achievement of this objective is critical for one to be successful at the youth coaching level. All teams have players with a wide range of ability. It is the responsibility of the coach to stimulate the growth of each player. Providing activities that pose interactive challenges enables each player to participate at his or her own level while also inspiring others with whom they interact. The game of PAC Man in my book demonstrates this concept. As the game progresses, players of lesser ability become the additional PAC men. As more and more players become PAC men, they get more dribbling practice. Near the end of the game, the faster, more agile players become more challenged since the environment is now more complex.

The following games/exercise build upon the two tenets I have discussed. If challenged at their level, you will find your players begin to develop various game strategies, will reflect a higher degree of motivation and enthusiasm for practice and begin to make better decisions during matches.

MUSICAL BALLS

Organization: Start with one ball per player.

Structure: General area, defined space not necessary.

Procedures: Play like musical chairs, could use a music box, your own melodic voice or a whistle. Everyone begins dribbling within an area (the center circle would work). When the music stops or you blow the whistle, all players must leave their ball and run to another. During the change take one ball away. Player without a ball continues to run in area until the next change, then attempts to take a ball. Continue this until you have eliminated four or five balls. Then begin adding them back. You would not want to play until the last ball because too many players would be without a ball to dribble. (Diagram 11-1)

Diagram 11-1

Diagram 11-2

Diagram 11-3

Diagram 11-4

Other variations

1. After each switch, players sprint outside circle and run around circle and then back to a ball;

2. Players who find themselves without a ball move outside circle and the objective for the players with balls is to dribble outside the circle and then back in as many times as they can. Players on the outside attempt to dispossess and then move back into the circle themselves;

3. Place four goals 10 yards distance from the circle; players must dribble from circle, evade opponent and shoot ball for a score. Whoever retrieves the shot gets to dribble back into the circle and resume the activity.

Analysis

Technical: Dribbling.

Physical: Agility, quick reactions.

Tactical: Quick decisions to challenge for a loose ball.

Social/Psychological: High group interaction. Develops assertive play within an appropriate setting.

TRIANGLE TAG

Organization: Groups of four without a ball.

Structure: Three players form a triangle by placing arms on each others' shoulders. One of the players wears a scrimmage vest and is the "target." The fourth player is on the outside.

Procedures: The group designates one player to be the target. The outside player tries to tag the target. The other two players move the triangle to protect and prevent the target from being tagged. The triangle moves within a limited space, they do not run. This continues until all players have had an opportunity to be the target and the outside player. (Diagram 11-2)

Analysis

Technical: No soccer ball techniques are used; however it is a great warmup activity.

Physical: Agility, quickness, and balance are the key physical components. Develops ability to change direction quickly.

Tactical: Using deceptive movements to fool the triangle.

Social/Psychological: Players protecting teammates. What a nice trait for your players to transfer onto the field. Small group cooperation.

KEEPER'S NEST

Organization: Groups of four with one ball per group.

Diagram 11-5

Structure: Small area with ball in the middle.

Procedures: One player (keeper) guards, but cannot touch the ball. The keeper may stand over the ball. The objective is for the other three players to get the ball away from the keeper without being tagged and frozen by the keeper. The keeper's goal is to freeze the other three players. Once a player is frozen, he can either remain frozen until all players are frozen or until the ball is snatched away. You can also allow a frozen player to count to 10 by thousands and then return. Players try to steal the ball away by pulling or tapping it to another player with their hands or feet. Continue until all players have an opportunity to be the keeper. Caution players that they are not to swing their arms wildly in an attempt to tag players. (Diagram 11-3)

Analysis.

Technical: No direct soccer ball techniques are being performed.

Physical: Development of leg strength results from bent leg position all players naturally assume. Agility and balance.

Tactical: Timing of when to initiate movement. Creates an awareness of reacting when the opportunity arises.

Social/Psychological: Development and awareness of three players and cooperating to achieve a group goal.

KEEPER'S NEST 3 V. 1

Organization: Groups of four with one ball per group.

Structure: Three cones to make a triangle. The three players on the outside possess the ball. The triangle creates three goals.

Procedures: One player (keeper) is in the middle and tries to prevent the ball from penetrating the triangle from a pass. The objective is for the three players to pass the ball between them and move the keeper out of position so that the ball may be played through two sides. If the keeper intercepts the ball,

the player who last played the ball becomes the new keeper. (Diagram 11-4)

Analysis.

Technical: Short passing to a teammate's feet.

Physical: Development of leg strength results from the bent leg position all players naturally assume. Defensive posture for the player in the keeper position. Agility and balance.

Tactical: Passing the ball to create a penetrating pass behind an opponent. Develops an awareness of reacting when the opportunity arises.

Social/Psychological: Development and awareness by three players of cooperative movement to achieve a group goal.

SIAMESE SOCCER

Organization: Similar to PAC man, except there is one ball for two players. These players are partners who can only pass to each other. All other players are paired and must hold hands.

Structure: Random in a confined area.

Procedure: Players with ball dribble and pass while attempting to hit the other paired players, who are trying to avoid getting hit. To hit a player, the pass must be one touch. If one of the pairs gets hit, they break apart, get a ball and attempt to dribble and pass to hit other pairs. Game continues until all paired players have a ball. (Diagram 11-5)

Analysis.

Technical: Dribbling at an opponent, change direction, change speed. Passing to targets and one-touch passing.

Physical: Fitness, agility, balance.

Tactical: Two players combinations, wall passing.

Social/Psychological: Cooperation with two players working toward the same objective.

SUMMARY

As one can sense from the organization of these exercises, each incorporates several objectives, not all strictly soccer related. It should also be evident that the game's approach to coaching challenges the players to improve their skills while having fun.

I might add that by no means are these games finalized in their structure. Coaches (perhaps even your players) can modify them as their imaginations allow.

In conclusion, the best youth practices for the very beginning players are those in which the soccer lessons are subtle in their execution and are based on a solid underlying philosophy of coaching.

⚽

Make Good Use of Time and Equipment
David Carr

Youth soccer programs dominate the park and school fields of America during both spring and fall seasons. Any day of the week, all across the country, children of various ages, shapes, and sizes are playing soccer under the direction of adult volunteers. Most youth teams only practice once or twice a week for 60 to 90 minutes and play a game on weekends.

The goal of this article is to help coaches use these few minutes of practice as effectively as possible. How do you conduct your soccer practice? Do you have a plan? What do you do when you get to practice? I will propose a number of strategies that hopefully will help make your practice with your team both more enjoyable and more effective. We will take a look at the youth soccer practice and the establishment of "protocols" that will allow you, the youth soccer coach, to conduct more successful practices. Before protocols can be established for your practices, there are four areas that need to be addressed as you begin your first day of practice. These areas are the practice setting, planning for practice, "enough" appropriate equipment, and waiting time.

The Practice Setting

Most youth soccer teams are assigned or claim a practice site in the community where they live. This site might be a soccer field with fixed goal posts or it may be a field with no dimensions or goals. Many coaches find themselves sharing a field with one or more different teams. You will need to work with these other coaches so that it is clear who practices where. Once you have established your practice space, it is important to get the maximum use out of it.

Planning for Practice

Coaches need to be ready to meet the challenges of practice from the very first day. Successful coaches design and implement effective learning environments. These provide an atmosphere that is pleasant and conducive to learning. Children can learn to adjust to the environment you create. There is no magic formula or single definition for creating a pleasant atmosphere at practice. The decisions that are made, however, are made by the coach and he/she must determine how the practice will be conducted, what behavior is acceptable, and what is unacceptable.

Your plan should include an overall emphasis for practice (objectives), on what skill work players will concentrate and how the sessions will be structured, what small-sided games will take place and what the emphasis of those games will be, and if you scrimmage, how long will it take.

The process of teaching and learning what behavior is appropriate takes time but will lead to a much more enjoyable and effective practice session. Establish rules for what is expected of the players when you are talking and conducting practice. Plan for what happens when players break the rules. Fairness is very important.

Appropriate Equipment

Part of this effective environment includes having enough appropriate equipment. Every player should have a ball. Most experienced coaches support the use of hand-stitched balls of appropriate size (3, 4, or 5) for the age of their players. Many of the synthetic panel balls don't "give" much when kicked. Often, kids say it is like kicking a rock. Stitched balls lose air faster but your players will have an easier time practicing skills, especially when it is time for heading practice. Have each player bring his or her own ball to practice or carry a bag or two of balls in the trunk of your car so that you always have enough. Put a bicycle tire pump in the trunk also so the balls that have lost air can be quickly reinflated. Your players can be taught to inflate their own balls.

Other equipment also can enhance a practice. Cones help delineate space, can be used as targets, and can serve as goals. Disc cones are inexpensive and are easy to carry and store. Colored vests allow for multiple small-sized games and allow for exercises that feature offensive players v. defensive players run much more smoothly. Many coaches suggest a dozen vests of one color and half dozen of two other colors. Vests and cones can be obtained from most soccer specialty stores or sporting goods stores and are relatively inexpensive.

If goals are available, nets that are put up in advance of practice will enhance the practice experience for your players. Kids get a thrill out of seeing the ball "hit the back of the net". Nets are often available from youth league directors. If there are not, a pair of nets can be purchased for less than $100. If goals are not part of the practice site, portable goals certainly can help. These are somewhat expensive (over $500) and although there are a number of companies that make them, they require a pickup truck or station wagon to get them to and from practice. Some coaches have developed their own portable goals by using PVC pipe. You can run a very effective practice without goal posts, but to enhance instruction in scoring, defensive tactics and goalkeeping, some of your practices should be conducted with goal posts of some type.

A good practice session includes a variety of elements blended together. One fundemental
is to have everyone playing and learning with the ball. (photo by Tony Quinn)

WAITING TIME

Now that you have a defined practice space and
you have planned how you will conduct your practice, it is important to make effective use of the time
you have for practice. Structure your practice so that
children are actively engaged in appropriate soccer activity for as much of the practice time as possible. A
number of research studies in physical education state
that the amount of time students spend practicing (either measured by time or the number of skills trials)
at an appropriate or successful level is positively related to student achievement (Silverman, 1991). Your
players need multiple quality touches of the ball (the
skill should be performed correctly and often) in all
of soccer's techniques in order to become skillful.

There are too many instances in which children
stand around waiting to touch the one or two balls
the coach has brought to practice. An extraordinarily
large amount of time is wasted when after every kick
the goalkeeper or other field player has to chase the
ball into the parking lot. Time is also wasted putting
children in lines waiting for their "turn". If all of your
players can be working with a ball (dribbling in defined space, passing with a partner, ball juggling, shooting at multiple goals, etc.), waiting time can be greatly
reduced and active involvement in practicing soccer
techniques is increased.

By developing content that can be made easier or
harder, skills can be acquired more quickly and efficiently. Utilize small-sided games to engage more players with a ball. Four groups of four will involve more
children in positions of play than two groups of eight.
Organize drills that involve all of your players and
put them in areas that will minimize balls being out
of your practice space.

ESTABLISHING PROTOCOLS

With the space for practice identified and the equipment readily available, you are now responsible for
the soccer education of over a dozen young athletes.
The first thing that the coach needs to know is that
children can learn to understand and follow directions.
The coach needs to be able to expect that children
will listen, follow directions and basic rules, not push
and shove, and understand within a framework of
instruction what you players are to do. This framework is referred to as establishing "protocols" for your
practice (Graham, 1992).

The word protocol refers to established norms or
courtesies that have been predetermined and put into
action as an accepted method of operation. They are
routines and courtesies that are practiced (Graham,
1992). By teaching and practicing protocols, you can
develop a more effective contest that will foster learning and enjoyment for you and your players. Establishment of protocols in the following areas will be

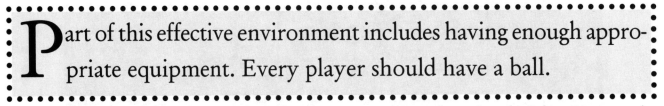

Part of this effective environment includes having enough appropriate equipment. Every player should have a ball.

discussed: players arriving to practice, starting and stopping activity, the use of equipment, and selecting partners, groups and teams.

ARRIVING TO PRACTICE

As I travel around the country and observe children and coaches in youth soccer settings, I have been able to paint an internal picture of how these coaches conduct their practices. Children under the age of 16 rely on someone to bring them to practice. Parents usually fulfill this responsibility but sometimes brothers, sisters, grandparents, or neighbors drop off and pick up these players. Some kids live close enough to the practice site to walk or ride their bicycles. The point here is kids arrive at practice by different means and at different times.

What do these kids do once they arrive at practice? In many cases, the coach waits until he/she has enough players to begin the practice. While waiting to begin, some players sit and talk, some kick balls as hard as they can into the goal, and others sometimes choose to participate in non-soccer related activity (i.e. wrestling, throwing soccer balls at each other). What can you as a youth soccer coach do to create a more effective atmosphere for teaching the game of soccer to your players?

The beginning of practice gives you a perfect opportunity to work one-on-one or in small groups with the players who arrive first. There is an endless supply of individual ball skills that players can work on, under your direction, when they get to practice. Dribbling skills, juggling, feints and fakes, receiving and controlling air balls are just the beginning. This "instant activity" also serves as an effective warmup, clearly more effective than running laps around a field.

Once a second player arrives, he/she can be challenged by individual skill work or can work with the first player on attacking and defending skills. Passing and receiving and 1 v. 1 keepaway are examples. Coaches have an opportunity here to work directly with their players. As more players arrive, they will be responsible for knowing and understanding what the protocol is. They can get a ball and begin ball skill work, play 1 v. 1, 2 v. 1 keepaway or possession games. These activities can continue until all your players arrive and you determine the point that formal practice will begin.

STARTING AND STOPPING

You must develop a signal for starting and stopping that your players will hear or see. The context

you are in may determine what is best. Many practice sites may not be that quiet. If there is a busy road nearby or other teams practicing on the same field, you need to establish a personal signal that your players will recognize immediately.

A starting signal can simply be the word "go" or "begin." Stop signals that I prefer are the words "freeze" or "stop." Whatever you choose to use, make sure your players clearly understand what you want them to do. Players should stop within one or two seconds of the signal, the first time they hear it. They should also prepare to listen for directions from you as to what to do next.

This needs to be practiced until learned. Practice starting and stopping in a dribbling drill where all players are working with a ball in a defined space. Use the word "freeze" or "stop" and insist that they stop their activity immediately (within one or two steps or have them put their foot on the ball). The ball should also remain on the ground, as many young players develop the habit of picking it up in their hands.

Players also should practice staying on their feet when they hear the stop signal. There always seem to be a few who fall and roll on the ground. These protocols will save time and allow for more practice opportunities which in turn will help each player improve.

The use of a whistle by a coach should only be used when players are participating in actual game conditions that need to be controlled by a referee. Teach your players to respond to a normal, controlled tone of voice.

USE OF EQUIPMENT

As I mentioned, every player needs to have a ball. Players should each have their own balls and bring them to practice. Players need to be taught to keep track of all equipment and help collect it at the end of practice. If a player strikes a ball out of the practice area, he/she should retrieve it immediately. Care must be exercised if a ball goes in to the road, parking lot or other potentially dangerous area.

A pet peeve of mine is seeing players carrying soccer balls during practice. Players should use their feet to move the ball from one place to another—always. When you have a signal to stop activity, players should stop with the ball between their feet or with one foot on top of it. Again, this protocol needs to be taught. Have your players move the ball from one practice area to another by dribbling, not carrying their ball. Have a specific area where equipment is stored during practice (i.e. behind a goal, at midfield on the sideline). Equipment not being used should be placed in that area and your players must practice retrieving and returning equipment from that area. This will help keep you from misplacing one or two balls at the end of practice.

Selecting Partners, Groups and Teams

A well-structured practice will involve players with partners or in a small group, playing in small-sided games, and performing skills in a team environment. The days of selecting two captains to "pick" teams is over. Too many children have suffered blows to their self-esteem to allow this process to continue. It is embarrassing and emotionally damaging to be chosen last.

Kids can be given the task of quickly getting a partner or getting in groups of three or four. Care must be taken to have a strategy to deal with odd numbers of players. If you want your players to get into groups of three, what happens if you have 14 players at practice? You need to have a plan readied in advance to deal with situations like this. Design your drills so that four groups of three and one pair of two can participate or two groups of three and two groups of four.

Often coaches will have groups of players pre-selected for play in certain structured sessions. Small group activities give everyone a chance to continuously practice in game-like conditions. Forwards can play with other forwards in attack, defenders can play with other defenders or midfielders on both offensive and defensive tactics, etc. One key is to teach all of your players basic offensive and defensive concepts. Avoid situations where some players are always defenders and some are always forwards.

The protocol that you need to practice with your players is teaching them to form pairs or groups quickly and without excluding anyone. Any player who wants to be part of a group is to be welcomed not rejected. An important point to remember is to take care of children's feelings and still remain fair to everyone involved. One way to accomplish this is by having players change partners often and foster an attitude that every player on your team needs help to become a better player.

Conclusion

Protocols will help you have a more enjoyable time at practice. Your players will learn what is required of them and will benefit by having to spend less time getting organized or having your requests repeated. Less management time means more time to be actively engaged in learning how to play soccer. By providing more engagement time, your players will spend more time "playing" soccer.

References

Graham, G. (1992). *Teaching Children Physical Education: Becoming a Master Teacher*. Champaign, Ill.: Human Kinetics.

Silverman, S. (1991). "Research on Teaching in Physical Education." *Research Quarterly for Exercise and Sport*, 62 (4), pp. 352-364.

Challenge the Advanced Player
Dr. Tom Fleck

Many articles that I write deal with the very young recreational, or developmental level player. In this article, I would like to discuss the advanced or higher level player and the kinds of things we can do to further his or her development.

Advanced is a relative term and for the purposes of this discussion, let's consider advanced players as those who can do things more efficiently in confined spaces and can function with confidence and success while at speed, under the pressure of an opponent. This may sound a bit long winded, but it beats the heck out of somebody identifying the advanced player as "he can really play." Let's break it down and take a look.

Space

Does the player get to the right spaces at the right times? Does she know what to do when she gets there? Can she understand the concept of selling an opponent on a bad space as a decoy? Can she create space to allow one of her teammates to play more effectively? Does she know how to handle herself when her space is confined or shut down?

Technique

Can the player execute with mechanical speed? Does he have a crispness in execution? Is he efficient (two juggles rather than ten to accomplish a particular move)?

Tactical

Does the player make correct, quick decisions? Does he know when to take on another player; and when to pass off? Does he know when to shut down an opponent and when to buy time by giving space? Does he know when to go forward with speed and when to slow the attack to build it?

The above are just some of the considerations we must observe in players and be able to rate them highly on 95 percent of the items in order to consider the player as advanced.

Incidentally, I did not include physical characteristics since that aspect of a player is quite readily observable to even the more casual observer. Quite simply: Does the player have or not have physical speed? If she has it, how does she use it? If she does not have it, how does she compensate for the lack of it?

Now that we have the above established, let's look at some imperatives for the training of the advanced player.

- Training session should be mentally and physically stimulating;
- Even warmups must be technically challenging (some type of pressure or conditions);
- Place technical conditions on small-sided games;
- Training session should be challenging, not frustrating.

The difference here is that if the demands placed on the player are too advanced, he will lose interest and intensity. Incidentally, it is the main responsibility of a coach of advanced players to design training sessions that will be in accord with the players' ability levels and stimulate them to raise those levels.

Often easier said than done. However, through observation of their individual performances in games and training, you should have a good fix on their levels of play. Of course, we can always just throw out the ball and tell them to scrimmage.

But wait a minute, didn't we gear this article toward the advanced with scrimmage as a daily training diet? Nothing beats playing the game to get better at it, but how much better or faster could the players develop if these same scrimmage periods were used with more mental, technical and tactical objectives in mind?

In conclusion, let me leave you with some notions for training the advanced player. These notions were recorded by Dean Conway while attending a clinic by John Cossoboon and myself in Washington, D.C. last year:

- Challenge the advanced player to make technical decisions faster;
- Practices should call for her to take responsibility for leadership role-playing;
- The coach should build new problems into practices, but allow the players to work out solutions;
- If playing problems remain unsolved in one practice, bring the problem back for re-examination in the next session;
- Physical aspects of the game should be turned over to the player to troubleshoot on his own;
- Have the expectation that practices can move along at a more accelerated pace;
- Tactical aspects of the practice may occupy a greater percentage of practice time, but will result in the slowest progress of players.

If your training sessions are too intense over extended periods of time, your players will suffer from psychological burnout. If the session is too loose, the players will lose interest and become "soccer lazy." Somewhere in between these two approaches is what is right for your team. Finding exactly where is your job as a coach of the advanced level player.

FORCING SOCCER PLAYERS TO EXERCISE OPTIONS
Alan Maher

In the course of any soccer season, all players are taught and given practice in wall passing. In the process of learning how to wall pass, players are also taught the option of holding the ball and not passing if the defender drops to the ball side to block the wall pass.

The player with the ball must then take on the defender in a one-on-one situation and try to get behind him with the ball.

In Diagram 11-6 the wall pass is "on," and in Diagram 11-7 the wall pass is "off," because the defender (D) has blocked the passing of the ball from A1, to A2.

Players are taught these and other options in the course of training. Yet in game situations, when players are given the option of passing the ball or possessing the ball, a vast majority of players will opt to pass.

Why is this so?

The obvious answer to this question is that most players lack the confidence to hold the ball. The easy option is to pass the ball. The harder option is to hold the ball with some assurance that the defender can be beaten. As only one option is practiced and reenforced, the second option ceases to exist through lack of use. Thus, where the player appears to have two options, in reality, he/she has only one choice.

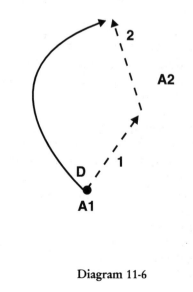

Diagram 11-6

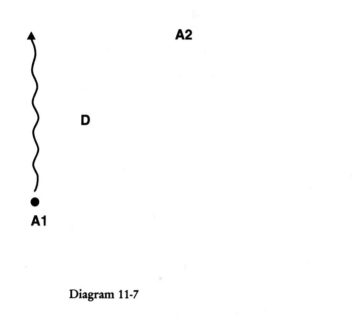

A2

A1

Diagram 11-7

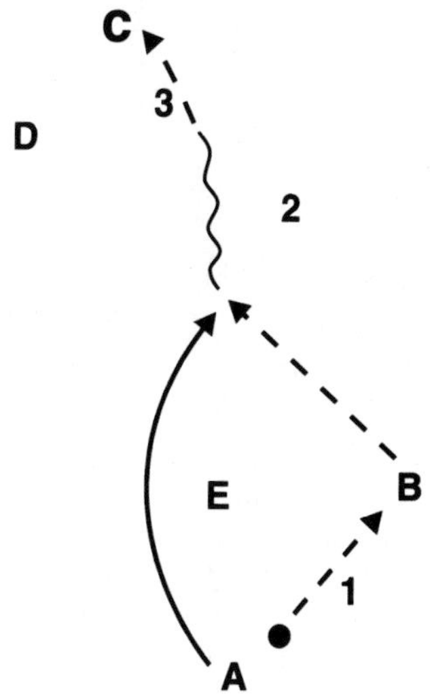

C

D

3

2

E

B

1

A

Diagram 11-8

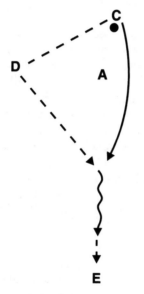

C

D

A

E

Diagram 11-9

E

B

Diagram 11-8 area labels

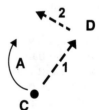

2

D

A

1

C

Diagram 11-10

What can be done about this situation?

Training activities must be designed to force the players to exercise the less popular option. In fact, the less popular option must be practiced so often that the player had complete confidence in successfully executing that option. Only then does a soccer player truly have options in the execution of plays.

The following drill and its modification illustrate how players can be forced to exercise options.

Player A has the ball. He wall passes to B and runs beyond defender E, collects the ball, dribbles briefly and passes to the end man C. Now the drill is re-organized and run in the opposite direction. Thus, C has the ball and wall passes to D and runs beyond the new defender A, collects the ball from D, dribbles briefly

and passes to the new end man E. The drill can be run back and forth to give practice in wall passing.

But the player with the ball must become aware of the fact that the wall pass cannot be executed every time he is approached by a defender. There are times when the player with the ball must attack the defender.

Therefore, the drill must be modified to show both options. (Diagrams 11-8 & 11-9)

In Diagram 11-10, defender A has dropped to one side to force player C to wall pass. After this option has been run a few times to give the ball player success and confidence, the defender can be instructed to drop to the other side to prevent the successful execution of the wall pass.

The player with the ball, C, will have no choice but to try to dribble beyond defender A. (Diagram

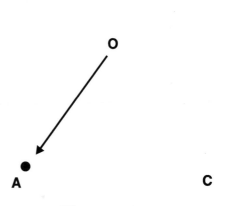

Diagram 11-11

Diagram 11-13

11-11) This option may have to be run many times before the player with the ball attains success and confidence. When this point is reached, the defender can approach the player with the ball in a straight move. The offensive player is faced with two true options - pass or dribble! Now the drill can be run as explained in Diagram 11-8.

Other drills can be modified in the same way.

Karl-Heinz Heddergott has mentioned that one-touch passing is most useful in a game, but that on occasion a player must be able to hold the ball. We will show how a popular drill can be modified to teach this.

In Diagram 11-12, a 3 v. 1 drill is seen in two steps. First, player A has the ball with players C and B supporting him to the right and left. Player O is the opponent. Next, player A passes to player B. Player C moves to the empty corner to allow B to have support to the right and left. Finally, player B passes on to C and A must run to the vacant corner to support C. When this drill runs well, it is an easy one-touch

drill. In fact, the players can be instructed to one-touch the ball.

But suppose the player with the ball cannot one-touch pass to his left or right. Suppose that there is no teammate to whom he can pass? What does he do?

He learns to hold the ball!

In order to learn to hold the ball, the above drill is slightly modified. The same organization is used with new rules.

Players are told to three-touch the ball. Thus, player A is told:

• Touch and move to shield from defender O.
• Touch again and hold from the defender O.
• Touch a third time, hold briefly, and pass to teammate B or C.

The new player with the ball has the same three-touch restriction. That is, he must touch the ball at least three separate times. (Diagram 11-13)

The single opponent now has time to apply pressure on the ball. The two support players may be told

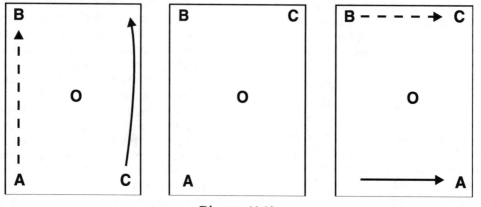

Diagram 11-12

to move from their corners to be more available for a pass when it is finally delivered.

These are but two examples of how drills can be modified to force players to learn to execute options that are available.

The more versatile a coach is in offering options, the more versatile his players will be. Finally, an option not taken is no option at all. Force the options!

NECESSITIES TO RUN A SUCCESSFUL YOUTH PRACTICE
Karl Dewazien

The tension developed before a dentist appointment or job interview seem mild when compared to the stress formed by many coaches before a practice session. Coaches can avoid this dramatic emotional crisis and ease their teaching task considerably by addressing the following:

Your Players Are Children. The dictionary says, "Children are young persons of either sex and at any age less than maturity; persons in the process of developing both physically and mentally."

Your Players Are Learners. They must be allowed to develop at their own pace. Remember, they had to crawl, walk, run, jump, hop, in that order so also will they develop their soccer skills.

Consider The Present Skill Level Of Each Player... then gear exercises and games so that each player is challenged. If conditions are too simple they will get bored. If conditions are too complex they'll be confused. Therefore, create an environment which forces the players to make decisions and learn on their own.

If they are technically weak... they should always work with a ball, in a large area and against fewer opponents (opponents who are either walking or jogging).

If they are technically strong... they should work with and without the ball, in confined areas and against more opponents (opponents who are playing at game speed).

Duplicate The Excitement Of The League Game... by minimizing listening and lecture time... and maximizing touches with the ball and playing time.

This is accomplished by playing small-sided games such as 1 v. 0; 1 v. 1; 2 vs 2, etc...

The coach's duties during these games is to observe and help but only when necessary... and only one individual at a time if possible (just like coaching a substitute during the league game).

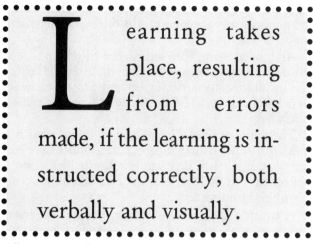

Learning takes place, resulting from errors made, if the learning is instructed correctly, both verbally and visually.

All Games And Exercises Must Include Two Goals...
One to attack, one to defend
Players must learn to instinctively respond to ball possession. This means:
Our ball - respond by attacking
Their ball - respond by defending
All Games And Exercise Must Include Shots On Goal..
The habit of shooting... at every opportunity is created in good practice sessions... and besides it's a lot of FUN.
Children Learn From Their Mistakes...
Learning takes place, resulting from errors made, if the learning is instructed correctly, both verbally and visually. It is crucial that coaches turn player error into a positive learning situation. The player self-confidence should not be affected by mistakes that are made when playing soccer.

Note this comment about professional soccer: "it is a game played by 22 error-prone, overpaid juveniles... who are surrounded by 80,000 mistake-free, perfect expert spectators."

YOUTH COACHING: REMINDERS

DID YOU KNOW THEY TAUGHT YOU HOW TO COACH IN KINDERGARTEN?
Karl Dewazien

For many years I have set myself to the task of writing a "short" article on developing a personal coaching statement: a philosophy. In the past, such attempts ran for many pages and resulted in the *FUNdamental SOCCER* book series. I tried to cover every base, with no loose ends. I thought that words and pictures could resolve all the dilemmas that arise in youth coaching.

And, once again, I am setting out to get a philosophy down to less than a book's length, in simple terms. The inspiration for working on this project came to me while reading *All I Really Need to Know I Learned in Kindergarten*.

The author stated, "I managed to fill an old car's tank with super-deluxe high octane go-juice. My old hoopy couldn't handle it and got the willies — kept sputtering out at intersections and belching going downhill. I understood."

A coach's mind and spirit can get like that from time to time. In some cases, it is perceived to be because the coach has too much soccer knowledge; in other cases, because he or she does not have enough. In either case, you must realize that you already know most of what's necessary to be a successful youth soccer coach — that it isn't that complicated. Coaching knowledge is not found in any special book, video or coaching class.

You know it. And you have known it for a long, long time. However, no one may have pointed this out to you...

All you really need to know about how to deal with your players; what to do in practices or at a game and how to do it... you learned in kindergarten. These are the things you already know:

- Share everything;
- Play fair;
- Don't hit people;
- Clean up your own mess;
- Say you're sorry when you hurt somebody;
- Learning the fundamentals is good for you;
- Shake hands with opponents;
- Coach a balanced practice — learn some and teach some and demonstrate and explain some and correct and compliment some and experiment and play every day some;
- Be aware of progression. Everything is learned in stages;
- During the game... apply the first word you learned in the Dick and Jane books... the biggest word of all... LOOK... (Observe).

Everything you need to know is in there somewhere. The Laws of the Game, sportsmanship and gamesmanship. Take any of the items and change them into sophisticated coaching terms. Apply them to your team or the opponent and they will hold true and clear and firm every time. It is just a matter of attitude and application.

You Are Not Alone as a Coach, Just Remember the Three R's
Karl Dewazien

"Nothing splendid has ever been achieved by those who dared believe that something inside of them was superior to circumstance" — Bruce Barton

A caller stated that he had just returned from signing up his child to play soccer next year... and baseball season had not even started. The caller seemed rather anxious and frustrated. Reading between the lines one could hear the burning questions, "Why am I still coaching youth soccer? Should I coach again next year?" Many of you are currently asking yourselves these or similar questions.

Yearly the turnover in youth soccer coaches is phenomenal. We don't want you to quit and simply join the echelon of couch potatoes. It is our hope that the following will stimulate some logical thinking and then keep you in our youth coaching ranks!

Even the most enthusiastic coach cannot escape some negativity while coaching youth soccer. Negativity from parents' attitudes, referee's judgments, win/loss records and players' performances can lead to frustration. These frustrations can produce feelings of incompetence and expectations of future failure. Such feelings are infectious and may nullify the positive attitudes your coaching/teaching may have generated. Naturally these factors can cause you to lose your confidence and enthusiasm.

Many coaches suffering from these symptoms merely try to endure the problems and wait for them to go away. When the problems don't go away, these coaches just quit!

If you feel that you may not want to coach soccer next year, please apply the three "R's" and stay in a program where the children need your help!

RECOGNIZE

Decide what made you so angry, frustrated, resentful or apathetic. Ask yourself, "What is the source of the problem? Can it be resolved? Am I hurting the children using the current process?" Only after you recognize the problem can you deal effectively with the solution.

REALIZE

Realize that you need time for yourself — time away from soccer. Take time off. Avoid coaching any other youth team sport. Find other interests you can enjoy with your family friends. Put your priorities in order and realize that coaching soccer is only one part of your life.

REVITALIZE

Here are some positive steps that will make you feel good about yourself and the job you have done:

- Focus on the present. Remember that the past has passed. Focus on your strengths and the enjoyment you gave the players. Be aware that this year will not repeat itself and that next year will be totally different;
- Concentrate on the reasons you entered coaching in the first place — time spent with your child, the competitive element of the game and the friendships you have formed;
- Look for enthusiasm among your players and fellow coaches;
- Read literature designed for youth coaches, which may expose you to exciting new methods of coaching and teaching the game. Readers are leaders!
- Attend coaching course. You can be fired up instead of burned out. Put youth coaching in perspective. Take time to do thing for yourself. Learn new methods. Then go and enjoy coaching youth soccer to the fullest and move from game to game and season to season with renewed energy. You must remember, this is a game for the children, and they need our support so they can play!

On behalf of the children you coached/taught/influenced this last season, we thank you!

⚽

COACHES: USE BUZZ WORDS, KEEP IT SHORT
Karl Dewazien

Their livelihood depends on gaining and keeping our attention. In order for them to be successful they continuously research human behavior. Since we are willing to give them billions of dollars each year we can assume that they are competent in their jobs. Who are these experts? They are advertisers and here is what they have found. We retain:

- 10 percent of what we read;
- 20 percent of what we hear;
- 30 percent of what we see;
- 50 percent of what we see and hear;
- 70 percent of what we say (teach);
- 90 percent of what we say and do.

Let's learn from the experience of successful advertisers and try to apply some of their proven methods.

Their initial promotions in the black and white TV days were considered inadequate. Commercials then were 60 seconds in length with announcers giving detailed praises of the product. Marketing researchers found that the commercials did not meet with total success and they modified their approach.

Today, during the week, commercials are less than 30 seconds long. Our initial attention is gained through music designed to appeal to a specific target audience. Attention is maintained through attractive models demonstrating the product. Catchy buzz words or phrases ("Coke is it"; "I love what you do for me") are spoken, sung or flashed on the screen — and we are ready to buy the products.

On Saturdays the commercials are designed to reach a different target audience, the younger generation. Here commercials are even shorter, usually, less than 15 seconds. The music is intolerable to adults and colorful action characters scream out the buzz words and phrases — and the younger generation is ready to buy the products.

Since we are working with the younger generation our approach in coaching should follow this hugely successful example. When doing the demonstration/explanation portion of practice, the coach should wear a bright colored outfit, play rap music in the background and scream buzz words applicable to the theme. But anticipating possible arrest for indecent dressing or disturbing the peace, he may want to make a slight modification of this approach.

The demonstration/explanation must take place at the beginning of practice while the players are alert.

- The players must pay attention and the coach must be aware of the sun's location and other background distractions;
- They must listen while the coach uses buzz words to be repeated —while practicing the theme;
- They must be observant and the coach should make sure everyone can see the highlighted points;
- They should touch so the coach should have them tap the part of the body or foot to be used (muscle memory).

If you are unable to demonstrate the theme, have one of your players or a guest instructor do the honors. The demonstration must be given slowly and be technically correct!

The explanation, as in the commercials, must be brief and if buzz words work for successful advertising, why not create some of your own. Buzz words are words that trigger the mind to highlighted points of emphasis. They shorten a long-winded speech into several key words.

If your theme is shooting, here are some ideas for buzz words — push, peek, place:

- Push the ball slightly ahead of yourself, to give you time to peek to see the space where you intend to

place the ball. Remember it is accuracy over power. If your theme is controlling, here are some ideas for buzz words — behind, relax, go;
• Get your body behind the ball in line with the ball's sight;
• Relax and release tension in that part of the body that will cushion the ball;
• Go take the ball in the opposite direction of the opponent.

Each coach needs to make up his or her own buzz words. Take the approach that if the buzz words work for your players, then they are the right buzz words.

As a reminder, successful youth coaches combine explanation with demonstration. They are as brief as possible. In other words, if it can't be said in 30 seconds or less, then maybe it should not be said. The best youth coaches take this approach a step further. They use the 30-second limit every time they talk to their players at practice or games.

To paraphrase the most successful biblical coach, Moses, "Stop with the talking and let my children play."

A List for Interactive Relationships
Cor Van Der Meer

In one of the classes I teach at, we spend some time discussing parent/child relationships. While doing research for the class, I ran across a piece that was called "Memo from a Child to his Parents." After reading it, I felt that the memo could just as well have been directed from player to coach. I'd like to share the memo with you. I can't give credit to the author, because he or she is unknown. Here goes:
• Don't spoil me. I know quite well that I ought not to have all I ask for — I'm only testing you.
• Don't be afraid to be firm with me. I prefer it. It makes me feel secure.
• Don't let me form bad habits. I have to rely on you to detect them in the early stages.
• Don't make me feel smaller than I am. It only makes me behave idly "big."
• Don't correct me in front of people if you can help it.
• Don't make me feel that my mistakes are sins. It upsets my sense of values.
• Don't protect me from consequences. I need to learn the painful way sometimes.
• Don't be too upset when I say, "I hate you." It isn't you I hate but your power to thwart me.

• Don't take too much notice of my small ailments. Sometimes they get me the attention I need.
• Don't forget that I cannot explain myself as well as I'd like. That is why I'm not always accurate.
• Don't nag. If you do, I'll have to protect myself by appearing deaf.
• Don't put me off when I ask questions. If you do, you will find that I stop asking and start seeking information elsewhere.
• Don't be inconsistent. That confuses me and makes me lose faith in you.
• Don't tell me my fears are silly. They are real to me and you can do much to reassure me if you try to understand.
• Don't ever suggest that you are perfect or infallible. It hurts and disappoints me when I learn that you are neither.
• Don't ever think that it is beneath your dignity to apologize to me. An honest apology makes me feel surprisingly warm to you.
• Don't forget, I love experimenting. I couldn't get along without it, so please put up with it, within limits.
• Don't forget how quickly I'm growing up. It must be very difficult for you to keep pace with me, but please try.
• Don't forget that I don't thrive without lots of love and understanding.
• Please keep yourself fit and healthy. I need you and I love you.

COACHING THE PRACTICE: TECHNICAL AND TACTICAL IDEAS FOR YOUTH PLAYERS

Let the Game Teach: The 4 v. 4 is a Practical Way for Young Players to Learn
Dave Simeone

The 4 v. 4 game is a wonderfully economic way to approach teaching the game of soccer to young players. In addition to educating players to playing on both sides of the ball, i.e., learning how to react both defensively and while on attack, the coach can manipulate the 4 v. 4 game to achieve different objectives.

The variables that can be manipulated by the coach include:

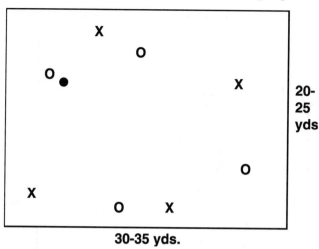

Diagram 11-14

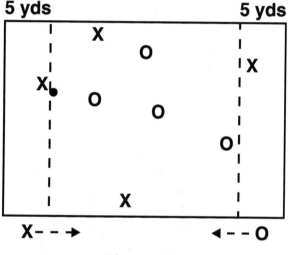

Diagram 11-15

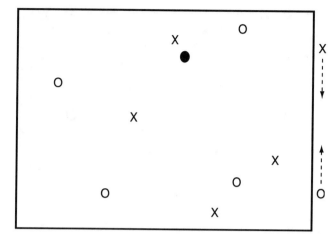

Diagram 11-16

- The use of small or large goals;
- The shape and size of the playing area;
- Creating direction or destinations, by introducing lines;
- Restricting the number of touches a player has with the ball;
- Moving the goals closer or farther apart.

Begin with the playing area marked 30-35 yards in length by 20-25 yards in width. The size of the playing area is influenced by the age and maturity of the participants. Most importantly, the playing field must always be rectangular. Start with one group of four blue players with one ball. Allow them to pass and move throughout the entire area freely. Observe if they are too close to one another and if they recognize how to utilize the available space. This type of behavior, especially for younger children, is natural. It also illustrates the lower level of "organization" with which youngsters view the game when compared to the adult version of soccer.

The 4 v. 4 game permits some semblance of "spacing" to begin to develop naturally between players. It simplifies identifying and solving problems for the youth soccer coach. One of the superb features of the 4 v. 4 game is that "spacing," the angle and distance players need to be in relationship to one another, is easily identified. The "shape" of the four players is that of a diamond (Diagram 11-14). Add a second group of four players, in a contrasting color, and allow them also to pass and move freely throughout the entire playing area.

Next, play 4 v. 4 in the same size area but create defined zones on each end of the area. You can do this with discs. The zone on each end can be five yards in depth. Each team has one end to attack and one end to defend. The object of the game is to stop the ball in the zone you are attacking.

The method used to get the ball into the zone on the end of the playing area can vary between dribbling or passing. If attacking players are put under pressure and feel they cannot accomplish stopping the ball once it is in the zone, they may keep possession of the ball by passing or dribbling it out of the zone and try again. (Diagram 11-15)

Vary the shape of the playing area by creating destinations and direction of play with lines as goals. Set up the game so that the playing area is wider than it is long. The same size area is appropriate—only the shape and direction of play change. The object of the game is to attack one line and defend one line. To score, stop the ball on any part of the line your team is attacking. In order to get the ball to the line utilize dribbling and passing. (Diagram 11-16)

Modify the game shown in Diagram 11-16 to incorporate small, multiple goals. This change emphasizes changing the direction of play, since there is more than one goal to attack. In order to score, the attacking team can stop the ball in either of the two small goals. When a team is without the ball, two goals must now

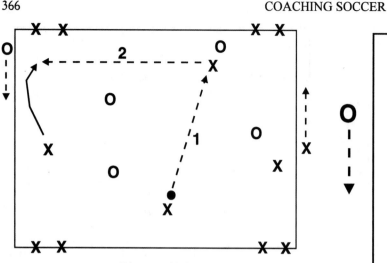

Diagram 11-17

be defended. (Diagram 11-17) This game allows for players to learn change of direction by dribbling and passing.

Change the shape of the playing area so that it is long and narrow. Alter the width of the field so that making it narrower will create a channel. This highlights the need for length, or depth, in the game. Narrowing the field takes some of the width out of the game and renders ineffective the side-to-side, square-type passing. This game requires players to look forward, find a target, and penetrate by passing.

Establish lines as destinations on the ends of the channel with each team attacking one line and defending one line. The object of the game is to stop the ball on the line. (Diagram 11-18a) Change the destinations: attack two small goals and defend two small goals. Thus lines and small goals are combined to establish destinations and direction of play.

By adding larger goals with flags, cones or portable goals, you begin to incorporate "finishing." (Diagram 11-18b) To generate even more opportunities to score, move the large goals closer to each other—the distance will depend on the age and maturity of the players. A good point of reference is the depth of the penalty area. A regulation size goal, on an 11-a-side field, is 18 yards from the top of the penalty area when placed on the goal line. Bring the goals close enough together so that the midfield line would be the meeting of the two penalty areas (each 18 x 22 yards.). For younger players, adjust this distance accordingly. Ideally, the two goals would be close enough to each other to maximize opportunities to shoot and score goals. (Diagram 11-19)

While this exercise provides many opportunities to shoot, it also provides an excellent environment for goalkeepers. The pressure of tight space with field players shooting and taking "half chances" challenges the goalkeeper to catch balls rather than allow for rebounds. This type of activity produces a good example

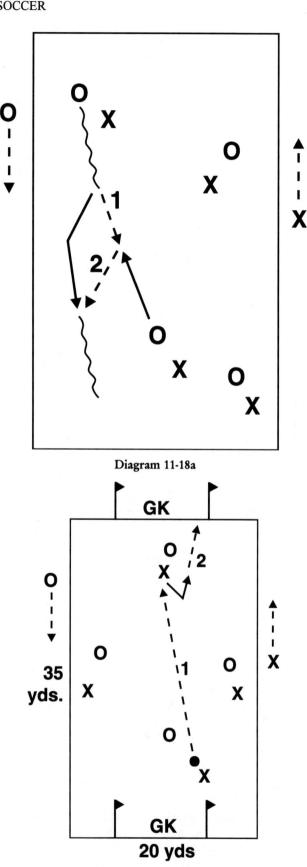

Diagram 11-18a

Diagram 11-18b

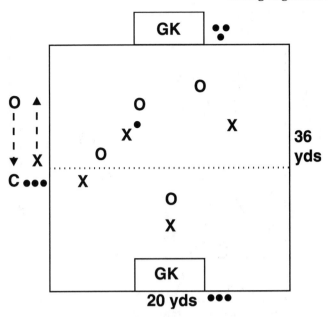

Diagram 11-19

of economical training where goalkeepers and field players alike are learning from the game.

If the space is appropriately sized (20-25 x 35-45 yards), encourage the goalkeeper to play as a field player and to move away from the goal. The goalkeeper plays as the deep player in the group of four. While their team is in possession of the ball and attacking, the player serving as the goalkeeper must move away from the goal and support the attack. While defending, they must situate themselves at the appropriate distance and angle to deter goal scoring chances by the opponent. In this activity, goalkeeping can be accomplished with either hands, feet or a combination of both.

These ideas for modifying the 4 v. 4 games are simple, but effective. They reflect what national associations in other countries with advanced soccer environments are passing on as information to their youth coaches.

The Netherlands has had a good deal of success in implementing the 4 v. 4 game. That country has experienced a declining "street soccer" environment. Some of the main reasons this is occurring is the increased population in the cities which has contributed to less open spaces for children to freely play the game. Also European children now have broader choices in terms of leisure and recreational activities. This underscores the significance of compensating for cultural changes by offering more structured youth practice sessions.

The 4 v. 4 game obviously encourages youth coaches to set up the conditions for learning and allow the game to "be the teacher." It reflects the prevailing philosophy in this country today to move away from the "drill approach" to a "PLAY AND LEARN"

philosophy. More importantly, it supports the idea of player development taking place in a setting that truly represents and reflects what is germane in long-term player development, and that is to play.

SMALL-SIDED GAMES: TACTICS FOR THE YOUTH PLAYER
Dave Simeone

The overall emphasis for the under twelve year-old youth player is the development of individual skill. As we use games to teach and develop skill, it is also necessary to include simple tactical principles in order to develop a youngster's "soccer brain."

Tactics can be defined simply as "a way to play." This means that our overall concerns shift from skill to decision-making. For the player with the ball, this becomes the choice of whether to pass, dribble, shoot, cross and so on. For the player without the ball, but whose teammates have possession of the ball, the choice is how best to support the player with the ball: whether to come closer or go further away. Defensively, the problem is to regain possession in order to attack. This can be accomplished in a variety of ways ranging from tackling to intercepting a pass cleanly.

Eventually we anticipate that players can make decisions within the context of the eleven-a-side game. But youth players, particularly those under the age of twelve, will respond in small-sided games that demand specific behavior and decision-making. Remember, the game demands and the player responds. The following games begin with 1 v. 1 and graduate to 3 v. 3.

1 v. 1

Players are exposed to very fundamental tactics in 1 v. 1. For the attacker the problem is possession and, ultimately, dribbling and eliminating the defender to score. For the defender the principle goal is getting between the goal and the player with the ball with the intention of getting the ball back and to become the attacker. (Diagram 11-20)

Diagram 11-20

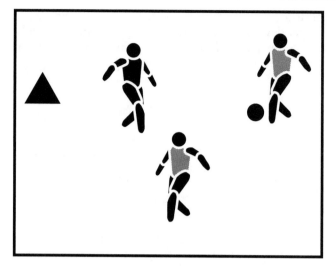

Diagram 11-21

Diagram 11-23

The cone serves as the goal with the two players being able to attack and defend the cone from any direction. It is possible to incorporate some guidelines for the game such as the defender must only touch the ball in order to reacquire possession and become the attacker.

2 v. 1 (1 v. 1)

This game proceeds with the two playing against the one trying to score a goal at one cone to start. The problem for the one is to reattain possession of the ball.

The addition of the second attacker creates "numbers up". The player with the ball can keep it or give it to the supporting attacker. The supporting attacker's role is to create a good angle of support for the player with the ball—try not to get out of sight behind the defender so that passing the ball becomes impossible. The one player who is against the two can reattain possession by just touching the ball. Upon possessing the ball, the task for the one is simple: dribble, keep it as long as you can (possession). Add another method of scoring for the one by dribbling for "nutmegs". The two must get the ball

back, organize, possess and score goals by striking the cone with the ball. (Diagram 11-21)

Change the game by adding a second cone as a second goal. The two playing together can score at either cone. The one playing alone scores by dribbling between the two cones and crossing the imaginary line. Play in any direction around the cones. (Diagram 11-22)

As we develop these small-sided games, the emphasis leans toward decision-making. In developing games with greater numbers of players, it is necessary to educate players as to the possibilities of solving problems within the context of the game.

The player with the ball has one of two fundamental decisions to make: to dribble or pass. Many times we over-emphasize passing v. dribbling resulting in a loss of possession. In 2 v. 1, the single defender playing alone will eventually figure out that committing him- or herself unnecessarily leads to being beaten, so the alternative is to give the two attackers more space and to keep them and the ball in front of the defender. This creates a problem for the attackers: without the

Diagram 11-22

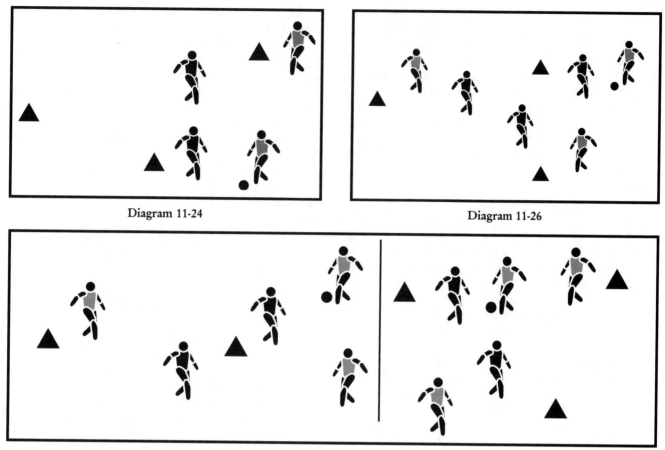

Diagram 11-24

Diagram 11-26

Diagram 11-25

defender committing and coming forth to play, the attackers pass the ball, but all of the passes are in front of the defender. It is imperative to educate these youngsters that to commit the defender it is necessary to dribble at them. This makes practical the decision of whether to keep or pass the ball. In this game of 2 v. 1 the attackers are "numbers up" which means they need to take the initiative to eliminate the defender. As we progress to 2 v. 2 the numbers are even, so the player with the ball must attempt to eliminate a defender by dribbling as to create "numbers up" for the attackers.

Play in any direction around the cones. The distance between the cones can vary depending on the level of your players. To begin with 2 v. 2, both teams score at either cone. (Diagram 11-23)

Create a different game by establishing that while the light team scores at either cone, the dark team scores by passing the ball low and on the ground between the two cones to the teammate. Change each team's method of scoring after they have played for some time. Add a third cone. (Diagram 11-24)

The next step is to add a third player to one team to create 3 v. 2 (2 v. 3). (Diagram 11-25)

The three with the ball score at either cone. The two without the ball attempt to regain possession. Adding the third attacker changes everything because not only is it necessary for the player with the ball to

have close support, but also the support much farther away in order to "stretch" the two defenders. When the two regain possession of the ball, they score by completing three of five passes consecutively as they are numbers down.

The final stage is 3 v. 3 involving three cones. The addition of the third player creates even numbers. (Diagram 11-26)

These small-sided games give coaches the "tools" to teach and evaluate decision-making by players. Remember, "play" is the key word in developing youth soccer players!

⚽

DEFINING INDIVIDUAL POSITION EXPECTATIONS TO LMPROVE TEAM PLAY
Ric Granryd

OUR PROBLEM

We faced a situation in which players were performing functions outside of those expected from their position. This does not refer to place-changing (switching positions, which occurs frequently in high level soccer), but to the execution of the responsibilities of a particular position. Our players were attempting to do their teammates' jobs in addition to their own. The result, of course, was confusion, including a duplication of runs, unnecessary double-teaming (in defense), and finally, dissension, frustration and distrust. We were not a team of players, but a group of individuals with various "agendas." All athletic teams have experienced this situation to a degree. This is how we handled it.

OUR SOLUTION

The root of the problem is non-soccer related: players' personal insecurity, the need to prove "I'm better, more important to the team than he/she is," the need for peer/girlfriend approval in the stands, etc. These factors were acknowledged. However, we deemed it necessary to devise some system of responsible adherence to function. Performance evaluation, and therefore playing time and first team designation, would be dictated by the extent of satisfactory completion of position roles.

The intent of this method is for each player to understand explicitly what is expected of each position. So, when a midfielder drops to cover for the overlapping outside fullback (the midfielder is now a defender, the fullback an attacker), both players know their responsibilities until they switch back. Ideally then, you have eleven positions performing specific functions in attack and defense, and each player knows his or her teammates' responsibilities.

POSITION ROLES AND EXPECTATIONS

The examples following illustrate our expectations of positions within a 3-5-2 system, in attack and defense. (3-5-2: sweeper, two central defenders, five midfielders, two forwards).

RESULTS

Team members responded well. Players felt they understood what was expected of them. More importantly it became clear to them that the quality of performance would be dependent on team play, not solely the plan of our three or four "star" players. The "rest of team" became more involved and responsible, and enhanced the stars' abilities being "allowed" to do their jobs. The team went from two straight losses to twelve straight wins.

One paramount difficulty arose despite the organization. Unsatisfactory role performance permeated the entire team and we reverted back to earlier individualistic patterns. A-hhh, the joys of coaching!

We managed to get back in sync after a horrible four-game stretch, to win the last four in convincing, cooperate, and team-oriented fashion.

The lesson learned through all of this: a full team of players, respecting each others' talents and responsibilities, is far more effective than individual players

trying to do it all themselves. Team sports require collective action and group responsibility.

Certainly, all situations may not require such a rigid, defined approach. However, for our particular collection of talents, personalities, and idiosyncracies, the specific role designations proved an effective means to achieve successful team play. It should be noted that any strategy, tactic, or coaching method should be specific to your team, your situation. That's one of the great things about coaching — each player, each team, each season is different, and we must adjust constantly to changing needs.

ATTACKING ROLES

Forwards:

Immediate transition to attack - recognize attack is on: Build Up (series of passes to commit defenders); or Immediate Penetration required.

A. Build Up:
- create space for build up, make runs to unbalance defense;
- support ball at end of build up - check runs/width maintenance/filling space;
- improvisation in attacking goal.

B. Immediate Penetration:
- immediate support of ball - check runs, create angle to receive pass, cross over runs/penetrating runs behind defenders/look what cooperating players are doing, 3 roles: (1) attack defender with ball (2); support first attacker; (3) unbalance - width;
- in attacking 1/3 - dribble to shoot or pass to shoot are first objectives. If not on, then wide ball is first priority;
- in attacking 1/3 - when ball is in wide position, runs to near and far posts are "on."
- second wave play - lay balls down for supporting players;
- improvisation.

Inside Midfielders

Recognize: build up v. immediate penetration

A. Build Up:
1. Settle ball and lay off to open player and start principles of build up:
   - stay wide to create space;
   - make runs to unbalance markers;
   - check back to receive balls;
   - support check runs;
   - see what cooperating players are doing:
     √ check;
     √ support;
     √ depth.
2. Improvisation.
3. One-touch balls to face-up players — create numbers up situation.
4. Switch fields.

B. Immediate Penetration:
  1. Finding supporting positions
     • checking to ball;
     • support position;
     • depth and width;
  2. Look for creative, early runs to corner flags — get ball or not (usually the wide/depth player).
  3. Improvisation .
  4. In attacking 1/3: second wave support.
  5. Center half: place changing with attacking stopper or sweeper.

DEFENSIVE ROLES

Forwards

A. Immediate Chase: sprint goal side/shut down space/ pressure ball/keep ball in front/push to touch line. "Marine Trenching" while teammates retreat. Drop to middle or mid 1/3 of field.
B. Mark outside backs making overlaps.
C. Pressure from behind — chase in back 1/3.

Inside Midfielders

A. Immediate transition (goal side) - sprint back.
B. First 2 back - find marking responsibility - man-to-man coverage, third man recovers to support ball or cover attack from middle.

Outside Midfielders

A. Immediate transition (goal side) - sprint back.
B. Man-to-man coverage.
C. Tight coverage on ball side.
D. Falling off man on weak side.

Stoppers

A. Immediate Transition (goal side) - sprint back.
B. Man-to-man coverage.
C. Tight marking goal side.
D. No diving in .
E. Falling off man on weak side.
F. Keep man and ball in view.

COACHING THE DEFENDERS
Rodney Spears

Good defense only comes from a team effort; however, in most cases it is the back defenders who have to make the key plays when the pressure is really on. No matter what system of play your team uses to organize the defense, your players must play as a unit. For the purposes of this article I will be referring to a 4-3-3 system of play with the back four playing a diamond formation. The sweeper is the last man, with a stopper playing in front of him and two outside backs. (Diagram 11-27)

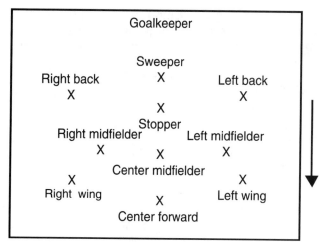

Diagram 11-27

PERSONNEL

It is important to find players on your team who can handle these positions. If you cannot do so then you should possibly use a different system.

1. Sweeper — This player should possibly be your smartest defender. In many cases he/she is the best athlete on the team. He does not have to be your fastest player because by intelligent play if he is smart he will not require great speed. ANTICIPATION is very important because this player should be able to read opponents in order to anticipate their next move. The sweeper must also be highly verbal because of the location in the back where he/she can see which opposing players need marking, etc. The sweeper should be free from marking responsibilities himself because the main role is as the final supporting player on defense. The sweeper must be skillful in the air and on the ground and be able to start a counter-attack after winning the ball. He/she should also possess attacking skill when it is necessary to go forward in attack.

2. Stopper — This is usually your best 1 v. 1 defender. This position requires great concentration because the stopper usually has to mark the opposing team's center forward. CONCENTRATION is so important because usually the stopper is marking a player who only needs one opportunity to score. This opportunity may come because the stopper loses concentration which results in an opportunity for the center forward. The ability to tackle hard and win the ball are the most important skills. The stopper is usually not expected to attack but I like for my stopper to be able to when called upon. Since the stopper is usually playing in the middle it is also important to be good in the air being able to play balls accurately from all angles.

3. Outside backs — The first thing I look for is running speed. They are usually marking the opposing winger who has great speed. These players also require concentration and the ability to mark an opponent well. Also of importance is their ability to overlap and involve themselves in the attack. They must also be in great physical condition because they must return to their defensive positions quickly after perhaps a 50-60 yard run.

After you have chosen your personnel it is then important to organize these players into an effective unit. In this article I will concentrate on defense, assuming that these players are also important in the transition game from defense to offense. They should not be stereotyped as destroyers with no skill to attack. Most of my team defensive sessions end with the defenders attacking a goal.

ORGANIZATION OF THE DEFENSE

Our goal is put constant pressure on the man with the ball close to the ball and mark our opponents so that passes can be intercepted. Then we begin our counterattack. Our players are instructed to win the ball whenever possible and then not just clear it downfield or kick it out of play. Whenever we lose the ball, the man closest to the ball will apply immediate pressure. He should only tackle if he is sure that he can win the ball. It is important to keep his/her balance and stay on one's feet. He can use several techniques to control his opponent. He can JOCKEY, which is a method of delaying his opponent or he can force his opponent to play the ball on his weak foot or to push him to the touchline. His primary objective is to keep his opponent from getting behind him with the ball.

1.   Defensive positioning — Players off the ball must take marking positions in relation both to the location of the ball and to the goal they are defending. The general rule here is to be GOAL SIDE and BALL SIDE. This means that your man should be marked by positioning yourself on the same side of your opponent as the goal you are defending and on the same side of your opponent as the ball. Your distance depends upon your distance from the ball. When close to the ball you should mark tightly and when away from the ball you should be further away from your opponent. We constantly emphasize proper positioning throughout the season. This is accomplished through training sessions conducted under game conditions. (Diagram 11-28)

- D3 is applying pressure to the player with the ball.
- D1 is marking his man at a distance because the ball is on the other side of the field. He/she is also no deeper than the sweeper (D4) because we are in a position to trap a player offside if they run behind our defenders. Our goalkeeper should be able to pick up a through pass when it is this close to our goal. If the player D1 is marking makes a diagonal run, then D1 must maintain the goalside ball position but close down the distance as he/she runs closer to the ball.
- D2 is marking his man tightly because they are close to the ball. In this position the player is in a position to intercept or tackle if the opponent tries to

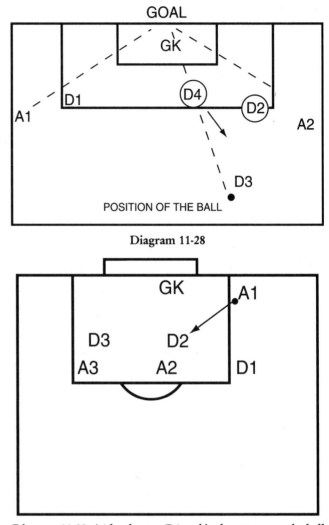

Diagram 11-28

Diagram 11-29: A1 has beaten D1 and is about to cross the ball to either A2 or A3. D2 must mark his/her man in this position in order to cut off the cross to A2. If A2 was standing behind all the defenders he/she would not be offside because A1 has penetrated the defense to the goalline. That is why D2 must be sure to take up a goalside position.

receive a pass running toward the goal or the opponent can also be forced to receive the pass going away from the goal.

- D4 is playing the sweeper position providing support for marking teammates by covering the space behind D3. If there were an extra attacker then the sweeper would mark that player.

All players mark close to an imaginary diagonal drawn from their opponent to the goal (dotted lines in diagram). This diagonal line represents the opponents' quickest path to the goal (a straight line). A good defender must know at all times where the goal is because their back is usually towards the goal. This can only come from experience.

The sweeper supports close to this diagonal also. He/she is prepared to help teammates if they get beat.

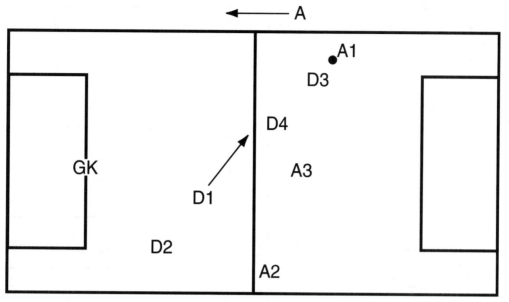

Diagram 11-30

The sweeper also picks up any extra attackers in the area.

Players adjust along this diagonal according to their opponents' speed, skill, etc. In the diagram, D1 is not along the diagonal because he does not want to drop behind his sweeper or other defender in the middle of the field in order to make the defense square (even across the back) to trap opposing players offside if they try to make penetrating runs. In this case players must remember that if the player with the ball penetrates this line that the attacking players will not be called offside if they are not ahead of the ball. This is illustrated in Diagram 11-29.

In Diagram 11-30 we look at the positioning of defenders when the ball is near midfield. In this case D1 is the sweeper but he is not the deepest player. D2 is now the deepest player because we do not want our defense to be square in the back when the ball is near midfield. A through pass in this position could kill us because the goalkeeper is too far away to pick it up as in Diagram 11-28. He/she is also in a position to provide support in the middle in case our defense is beat in the middle. He/she can afford to do this because of his distance from the ball. He would have time to adjust to a long cross to his man. The goalkeeper is playing at the top of the penalty area because, with the ball in this position, he/she doesn't have to worry about a goal being scored. The keeper can offer some support to his defense on long through balls but must retreat as the opponents move toward the goal. In the event that either player is beaten, the sweeper picks up their man and the defender that is beaten should then recover to the middle of the field and become the sweeper.

COMMUNICATION

Communication begins with the goalkeeper and the sweeper. It can be coached during all defensive sessions. These two players must be in charge of the defense because of their position to see the field. The sweeper directs things in the midfield area but as the ball gets closer to the penalty area, the goalkeeper takes charge. Other players must be trained to give directions in proper manner in order to earn the respect of their teammates.

SWEEPER: THE "FREE MAN" ON THE FIELD
Bobby Howe

Most youth and senior teams throughout the world play with a free player behind their defense. This very important and exciting position is called sweeper in the United States or libero in Europe.

While the priority for this "free man" is defense, the sweeper may be equally effective on offense.

Defense: midfield area — When a team is on defense and the ball is in the midfield area, the sweeper plays freely behind his teammates who are marking their opponents on a man-to-man basis. While he/she does not have a man-marking responsibility, the sweeper does have the responsibility to support on the ball side of the field. Not only must he/she be in a position to assist a teammate who is challenging an opponent, but must also be in a position to deal with any potentially dangerous balls played over the top of the defense (through passes).

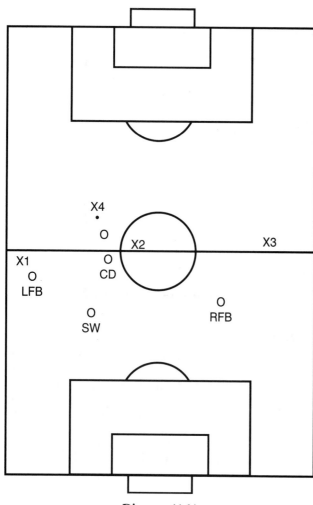

Diagram 11-31

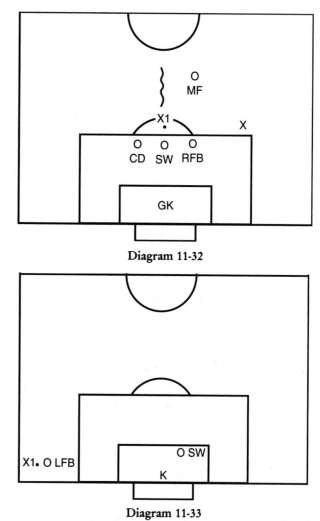

Diagram 11-32

Diagram 11-33

In Diagram 11-31, X4 is in possession of the ball. The sweeper (SW) does not have the marking responsibilities of his/her other defenders. LFB, CD and RFB are marking X1, X2 and X3 respectively. However, SW is poised to assist any of his/her defenders should their opponents receive the ball. He/she is in a good position to deal with any balls that are played over the top of the defense.

Note the positions of LFB and RFB. While they are marking X1 and X3 on a man-to-man basis, they are not standing next to their opponents. Their positions, as shown, not only allow them to reach their opponents at the same time as the ball, but allow them to be first to any balls played over their heads into the space behind them. Specifically, the RFB plays more "off his/her man" and incorporates a more zonal concept (marking both man and space) with his/her positioning.

In dealing with through passes, the sweeper (or his/her defenders) must get the ball quickly to take advantage of room and time possession.

Defense: defensive third — The sweeper's greatest responsibilities in the defensive third of the field are those of communication and organization. The nearer the ball is to his/her own goal, the less he/she is required to have a free role. Within opposing shooting range of his/her goal, he/she must communicate with his/her defenders as to who will pressure the opponent in possession of the ball. In many cases, it is the sweeper who will apply pressure either to make a tackle or, at least, to affect the quality of the shot by perhaps double-teaming the shooter of the ball.

In Diagram 11-32, X1 has dribbled around the opponent's midfielder, MF, and is moving into a dangerous shooting position. SW must move forward to apply pressure, as shown, to try to prevent a shot at goal. While many sweepers can provide support when play is through the middle of the field, they are more reluctant to support when the play is wide.

In Diagram 11-33, the attacker, X1, is given a lot of room to take on his/her opponent, LFB. SW is waiting in the penalty area to deal with the potential cross. At this point the danger is with the player of the ball and it should be the goalkeeper's job to clean up crossed balls.

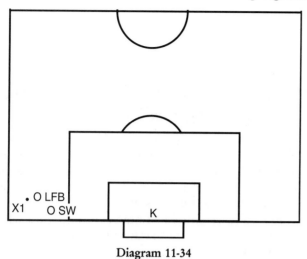

Diagram 11-34

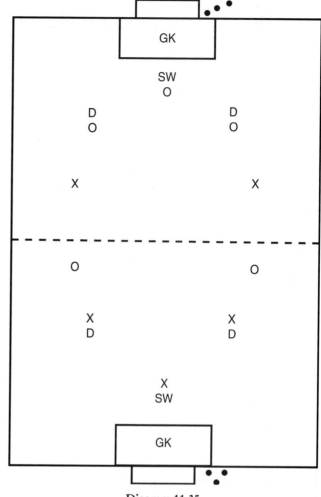

Diagram 11-35

In Diagram 11-34, SW has moved to help LFB, therefore, giving the defensive team a much better chance to prevent the cross in the first place.

It is always better to prevent the cross than to deal with a cross in the penalty area.

Offense — When experienced soccer people discuss the offensive qualities of a sweeper, they invariably talk about Franz Beckenbauer, the innovator of this role. Not only did Beckenbauer possess outstanding vision, awareness and passing ability, but also, the timing of his forward runs to support play was such that opponents found it extremely difficult to mark him or track him down. On many occasions, he was able to complete a move originating in his own third of the field by having a shot at goal in and around his opponents' penalty area.

The beauty of the sweeper position on offense is that, with good timing and correct support, he/she is difficult to mark and he/she is able to produce an element of surprise. However, it is important to understand that the forward movement of the sweeper at most times is in support of the play. Unless his/her timing is perfect, he/she should rarely make runs in advance of the ball. If play breaks down on offense, he/she should always be in a position to recover quickly to a free defensive role.

Qualities — The qualities required to play this very important role are many and varied. On defense, the sweeper must have outstanding positional sense, he/she must know how to perceive changes and react quickly to deal with the problem. He/she must be able to organize and communicate. He/she is very often the last line of defense and from this position, he/she is able to "see what is on" and read the game for his/her teammates: he/she should have vision and awareness.

On offense, he/she should be an outstanding passer of the ball; very often he/she is the initiator of an at-

tack. He/she very often has time in possession of the ball and should make the best use of the options that present themselves. The ability to support and timing of forward runs are also crucial to success.

The position of sweeper is exciting and important. The player selected for this role should have leadership qualities. Very often he/she is the captain.

PUTTING THE SWEEPER UNDER PRESSURE

I have described the functions of the sweeper and indicated some of the qualities required to play this very exciting and important role. Following is a training game that forces the sweeper to exhibit command of the position while under pressure. (Diagram 11-35)

Game Rules

• Set up the game in an area approximately 50 x 35 yards;

• Use 10 field players and two goalkeepers;

• Define the halfway line by using markers or a cone on each touchline at the midfield mark;

• Three defenders start against two forwards in each half of the field;

- Have a supply of balls behind the goal;
- One of the goalkeepers starts play by throwing the ball to his team;
- The forwards on both teams may not play in their defensive half of the field;
- One of the defenders may cross the halfway line only when the ball has been passed over the halfway line accurately to a teammate (forward) in the attacking half either by himself or another teammate. Any of the defenders may cross the line but only one at a time;
- Players may not dribble the ball across the line;
- Players may not pass the ball back from the attacking half to the defending half;
- Violation of the above will result in an indirect free kick to the opposing team;
- The release of one defender across the line produces 3 v. 3 in half of the field;
- Immediately upon loss of possession by the attacking team, the defender must retreat to his/her own half; he/she may not help to win the ball back in the attacking half;
- Throw-ins may be thrown in either direction across the halfway line;
- There are goalkicks but no corners;
- The objective of the game is to score goals;
- Duration of the game: 20-25 minutes.

COACHING POINTS
Observe the functions of the sweeper(s).

Defense
- Communication;
- Covering position; how he/she supports teammates;
- How quickly he/she steps up to deal with third opponent in his/her half;
- How he/she defends in 1 v. 1 situations;
- How he/she adjusts to a marking position when a fellow defender crosses the half-way line to join his/her attack;
- How he/she adjusts when the defender returns;
- How quickly he/she gets back from the attacking half when he/she has joined in the attack; assess the path he/she takes to reestablish his line of defense.

Offense
- Supporting positions when teammates are in possession;
- Decisions — when and where to pass;
- Accuracy of passing;
- When, where, and how to join the attack;
- Combination play with teammates;

Note: This game may also be used to work other functional facets of play, i.e. forwards, midfielders, defenders.

GOALKEEPING TIPS FOR YOUTH COACHES
Dan Gaspar and Tony DiCicco

Through our work with goalkeepers we have stressed the importance, as well as the complexity, of playing soccer's most demanding position. We hope we have delivered this message.

However, we still encounter youth coaches who have the misconception that goal is the place to stick the poorest player.

Not only is this attitude wrong, it's counter-productive. First of all, Under-12 teams should not even have a full-time keeper. All players should develop all their skills. To do this, coaches should rotate their players through all the different positions. A good time to do this is during training sessions. If no one has volunteered to be a keeper, then one may emerge during this experimental stage. Also, if personal attention is being given to the position of goaltender during training sessions, or if the coach personally explains how important this position is, very often a youngster's interest will be excited.

At the other end of the spectrum, what if everyone wants to play goal? This is great under the age of 12. Beyond that age, the team concept should be paramount and the position should be reserved for the two or three best.

Here are some other suggestions for coaching youth goalkeepers:
- Allow young players time to develop their field skills, as well as the opportunity to experiment in goal;
- The coach must take the time to teach proper goalkeeping skills. If no assistant is available, or time is a problem, incorporate goalkeeper training into team training. Instruction at the young level should emphasize technique through a progressive method;
- Stress proper positioning. Without question, technique and positioning are the key to success. Good technique reduces the chance of injury, while positioning prevents unnecessary, desperate saves;
- Develop a library on goalkeeping;
- Seek out goalkeeper clinicians;
- Talk to high school or college keepers. They can give you ideas to add variety to your training sessions;
- Make sure there are plenty of the proper size balls available;
- Make sure keepers are properly dressed for practices as well as games. This includes such items as a

long sleeved keeper's shirt, elbow and knee pads, shin guards and long pants. Seek out soft landing areas, especially during players' early development. Sand pits are excellent;

• Always warm the keeper up with stretching activities and ball gymnastics. Incorporate the ball as much as possible. Avoid demanding drills, unless the keeper is properly prepared — mentally as well as physically;

• In drills involving field players, always instruct field players to avoid contact. In training sessions, the keeper always has the right of way;

• Games, games and more games are a keeper's best teacher;

• It's a good idea to review a goaltender's performance with him.

We hope these ideas are helpful. If you highlight the position of goalkeeper, you'll attract more young athletes to it. As you know, a good team with an average keeper is average — but an average team with an excellent keeper is good.

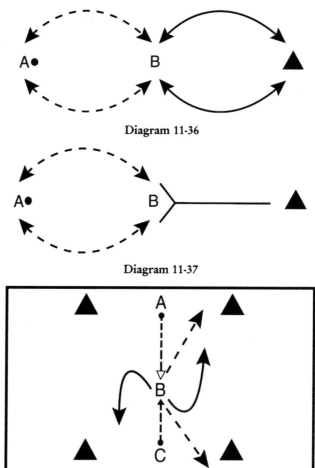

Diagram 11-36

Diagram 11-37

Diagram 11-38

WINNING IN THE AIR: COACHING TIPS FOR IMPROVED HEADING
Timo Liekoski

Once again I am starting to get the feeling that winter is almost behind us. In our area we are already ending the second indoor session; therefore, it may be the proper time to start turning our thoughts towards outdoor soccer once again.

The one skill that is almost totally neglected during indoor play is heading. The following are examples of exercises to improve heading; exercises which can be done indoors or outdoors involving small groups of players.

EXERCISE 1

Player A has the ball. Player B turns, goes to the marker as quickly as possible, turns and sprints towards A who throws the ball to B to head back to A. B does 10 repetitions after which the roles are reversed. Concentrate on accuracy and correct technique. Make sure that you attack the ball. As you approach the ball, get your shoulders back, spring forward to the ball and follow through. (Diagram 11-36)

EXERCISE 2

Same as 1, but the players must jump and head the ball while hanging in the air. The technique is the same as when heading the ball with the feet on the ground. Again, 10 repetitions and change roles.

EXERCISE 3

The same exercise as 1, except that B is now asked to run to the left or to the right of the player. The players must now head the ball back at an angle. Concentrate on aiming your face and shoulders towards the receiver when heading the ball. This exercise will help you to get more accuracy and power. (Diagram 11-37)

EXERCISE 4

Same as exercise 3, but the player heads the ball back to his partner while he is hanging in the air. Again the technique is the same as before, but it is important to note that you must always take off with your inside foot, i.e., when heading left, take off with your left foot.

EXERCISE 5

In this exercise we add goals. Player B starts in the middle. Players A and C act both as servers and goalkeepers. A serves B who tries to score on A by heading, B now turns around and receives service from C. Make sure the players do proper heading both with their feet on the ground and while hanging in the air, Create a game, keep score and rotate the players fre-

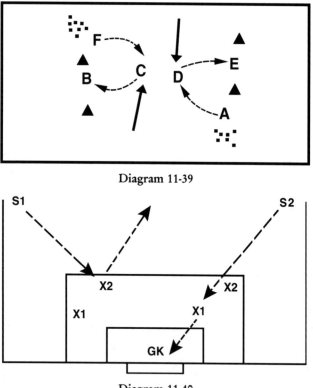

Diagram 11-39

Diagram 11-40

quently . This exercise uses the techniques from exercises 1 and 2. (Diagram 11-38)

EXERCISE 6

In this exercise we use only one goal, while one player acts as a server. B must approach the ball from a side and must now turn his or her head and shoulders towards the goal in order to get power and accuracy. Heading should be executed while moving. Again keep score and change roles frequently. This exercise uses the techniques from exercises 3 and 4, heading with feet on the ground and while hanging in the air. Please note: If the players are good enough, they should use a volley kick in order to serve to their partners. If not, then they must throw the ball. Always insist that the services be accurate so the technique can be executed properly.

EXERCISE 7

The following exercise involves six players, two as servers, two as goalkeepers and two as headers.

A serves a ball to D who tries to score on E by heading, as soon as D has headed the ball, F serves to C who heads against B. The players in the middle must do everything possible to head the ball, i.e., power heading, jumping, diving headers, etc. Again change roles and make it a competition. (Diagram 11-39)

EXERCISE 8

Same organization as in #7, but in this case the ball is now served from a flank position to the players in the middle.

EXERCISE 9

Practice the exercises 7 and 8 but now the two players in the middle must compete for the ball, i.e., 1 v. 1 in the middle. Initially keep the goalkeepers on the line, later allow them to come out to compete for the ball as well. Although the above exercises can be done indoors as well as outdoors, the last exercise is best suited for outdoor training.

EXERCISE 10

The players work in pairs. Server, S1 lobs a high ball for the two X's to fight for. One is a defender trying to clear the ball. As soon as they have dealt with the ball from S1, S2 serves a ball into the penalty area and X2 tries to score while X1 defends. The partners must change roles in attacking and defending. (Diagram 11-40)

Heading is one of the most neglected techniques, particularly in areas where much of the play is indoors. It is important that our players not only learn the proper techniques for heading, but they also develop an aggressive attitude toward balls that must be dealt with the head.

As is the case with all the training ideas, the coaches should sense what's good and insert their own ideas and improvisations into the exercises. This will not only improve the quality of training but the performance as well.

HEADING
Dr. Tom Fleck

Heading, or using the head to direct the ball, is unique to soccer. It is an essential technique to learn, but can be difficult to teach to young players. Many young players become fearful headers, developing habits such as blinking and ducking as the ball approaches. Through proper teaching methods and activities, these habits can be corrected.

As the ball approaches, the player must keep his eyes open and trained on the ball. His back should be arched, knees bent, and heels raised from the ground as he makes contact with the ball and heads through it in the desired direction.

Heading should be taught with activities and not with drills. Standing in drill lines and heading the ball is boring and does not allow for creativity. Players need to be given a problem and the opportunity to solve the problem through activities. If the activity is challenging, keeps players moving, and is game-related, essential techniques will be developed.

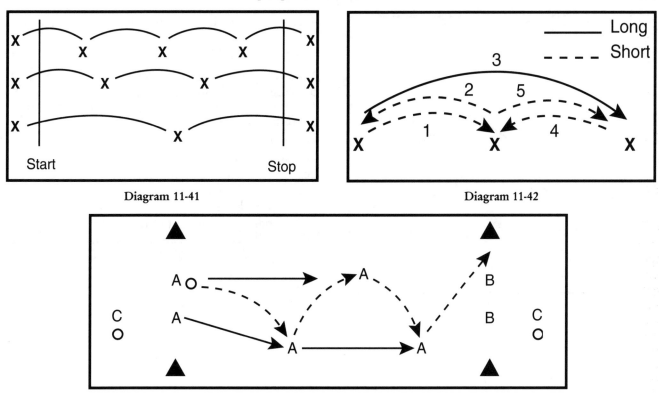

Diagram 11-41

Diagram 11-42

Diagram 11-43

WARMUP EXERCISES

Start with cautious and confidence-building activities.
1a. Walking in any direction, throw ball into air, head then catch.
1b. Jogging in any direction, throw ball into air, head, then catch.
1c. Head ball twice consecutively; after second head, touch ground with hands before ball touches ground and catch it
1d. Walk in any direction bent over with ball resting on bridge of neck.
1e. Repeat 1d and stop and go down on all fours without losing control of ball.
1f. Head ball three times consecutively and settle ball on ground.
1g. Head ball twice and turn without letting ball touch the ground then head ball twice in the other direction.

PARTNER WARMUP EXERCISES

Players want to have fun and fun is touching the ball.
2a. Sitting position: A performs sit-ups while B serves ball to head.
2b. Standing position: A and B hand ball to each other as they stand with backs to each other: hand to each other through each other's legs and collect over each other's head; hand ball to each other at hip height and collect on other side of body at hip height; roll ball around feet and roll to partner who rolls ball around feet and exchanges with partner on the ground.

COMPETITION ACTIVITIES

If the players are not finding success, stop the activity to help and coach.
3a. Groups of four continuously head ball while counting number of volleys within one minute.
3b. Players are given a starting and stopping point and are told how many volleys of the ball are allowed to get to stopping point. (Diagram 11-41)
3c. Groups of three players volley short, short, long and compete against number of consecutive volleys by other groups. Always start the ball with a hand serve from the middle player. (Diagram 11-42)

POWER HEADING ACTIVITIES

Never serve ball to head, but to space ahead of player to allow whip into the ball.
4a. Players A head toward goal to score. Goal must be scored below the waist. Players B stand in goal and play defense to block any shot. After shot, team A sprints back to goal to defend. Players C have extra ball and will chase passed balls to keep activity moving. (Diagram 11-43)
4b. Team A starts activity by throwing and catching the ball to keep it away from team B. If team B intercepts ball or tags player A who is holding the ball, the ball then becomes team B's ball. Each player is only allowed four steps with the ball and the ball must be headed into the goal to score.

Variations:

4c. A team must have two bounces to score.

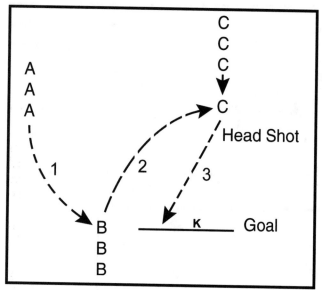

Diagram 11-44

4d. B team must have the ball driven by a head to score.

CLOSING ACTIVITIES

Always finish with successful activities around the goal.

5a. A serves ball (underhand serve) to B beside goal who heads ball to C for a power head on goal. (Diagram 11-44)

Variations:

5b. Add defender to create vision problems.

5c. Add defender to shoulder defend player C.

5d. Add goalkeeper — ball must be scored below keeper's knees.

Defenders are instructed to get possession of the ball or balls and kick them out-of-bounds. Play continues with the balls that remain in the game.

INDOOR SOCCER

• •

Indoor soccer was a segment of the sport that grew as teams and coaches in the more severe climate areas of the U.S. sought a means of continuing their involvement with the sport during the winter months.

In this chapter we will examine the tactics of indoor play including an analysis of defense. Defending one's goal is an act of courage but also demands some understanding and that subject is dealt with here with two articles by noted U.S. coaches.

⚽

INDOOR SOCCER TACTICS
Klaas de Boer

DEFENSIVE PRINCIPLES

The primary objective of defense is to prevent opponents from scoring. The secondary objective is to regain possession of the ball and initiate an attack+.

Preventing opponents from scoring is best accomplished by denying opponents time and space in which to work. Discipline is at the heart of a good defense. Every player must know his role and the responsibilities which come with that role. An effective defense is no more or less than a united effort by a group of well-disciplined players willing and able to work hard for each other. When a team loses possession of the ball, all five players must make an immediate transition from attack to defense.

Since the position of "sweeper" is foreign to indoor soccer, it is essential for each player to contain his/her immediate opponent. Defenders do not have the luxury of a free defender behind them covering up for their mistakes. More so than in outdoor soccer, players have two basic responsibilities when defending. First, each player must mark his immediate opponent. Second, cover must be provided for a teammate challenging for the ball.

Although some teams play strictly man-to-man defense, where each player is responsible for a specific opponent, others play a zone defense where each player covers a roughly defined zone. Generally the best method is a combination of the two. For example, most teams will play a zone defense in the middle and attacking third of the field but within their own defensive zone play strictly man-to-man.

There are two basic methods of defending after a team loses possession of the ball. One is called HIGH PRESSURE, the other one is called LOW PRESSURE. Which of these two methods a team uses is dictated, first of all, by its personnel and secondly, may depend upon the playing style of the opponent.

HIGH PRESSURE

In hockey, high pressure is the equivalent of forechecking. In basketball it is called a full court press. The aim of high pressure is to lock the opponent in his/her own half and make it difficult for them to get out. This is accomplished by attempting to regain possession of the ball at the place and moment possession is lost. The basic principles of high pressure are:

• Getting goalside of opponents the moment ball possession is lost;

• Immediate chase by the player who lost the ball to the opponent;

• Closing the opponents down by placing them under immediate pressure, thus delaying the opponent from attacking and giving time for teammates to get goalside of the opponents and organize the defense. The player closest to the opponent with the ball must close that player down;

• When closing an opponent down never face him head on. Always approach at an angle so the opponent is forced to pass inside or outside. It is preferable to force the play inside so the ball can be intercepted by another teammate.

The two forwards should not be caught square when closing opponents down. Instead they should be forcing the opposing defender to make a square pass. When one forward is challenging, the other forward must position himself/herself whereby they can provide cover for his teammate and at the same time be able to close the opponent down should the ball be played square. (Diagram 12-1)

Defender X1, by positioning at an angle, is forcing O1 to pass inside. X2 is covering for X1. If the ball is passed square to O2, X2 will immediately close him down and X1 will cover for X2.

• If beaten, players must recover goalside of the ball and then look to pick up an opponent.

• Control and Restraint — Players must exercise good judgment and discipline during transition from attack to defense. Players must know when to win the ball (risky) or when to simply delay and contain. Jockeying is a skill all players must master. Over-committing is a cardinal sin. Because there is no free defender every time a player overcommits, the opponent has a numerical superiority. It is good advice therefore to: a) stay on your feet; b) don't dive in; c) keep your opponent in front of you. Remember, "Fools rush in". Nowhere is this more true than in indoor soccer.

In order to high pressure effectively it is important that the opposition be coaxed into bringing the ball up out of the defense. How can this be accomplished when the goalkeeper is in possession of the ball? First of all, the two forwards must drop back to the opponent's red line. Except for the two opposing defenders, all other opponents must be marked man-to-man. The only outlet the goalkeeper has, therefore, are his two defenders. The moment the ball is played to one of the two defenders, the two forwards immediately close them down. (Diagram 12-2.)

If the defender in possession passes the ball back to the goalkeeper, the forward must chase the ball to the keeper, making sure he stays between the defender and the keeper. (Remember, the keeper cannot handle the ball in this situation.)

Obviously it is somewhat risky to chase the ball back to the keeper since one field player is now unmarked. To make it less risky, a midfield player can be instructed to position himself between the opponent he is marking and the opposing defender in such a way that if the ball is played to either one he can immediately close him down.

An alternative is to mark one defender when the keeper has the ball and leave the other defender open. For example, if one defender has good skill and is good

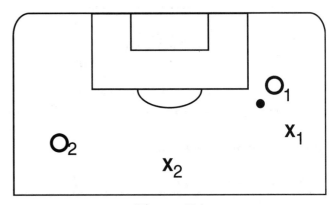

Diagram 12-1

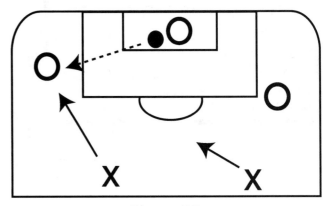

Diagram 12-2

at building out of the defense, one forward should mark that defender, encouraging the goalkeeper to give the ball to the less skilled defender. Once he has the ball, the other forward immediately closes him down. (Diagram 12-3)

The effectiveness of high pressure depends upon mobile and aggressive forwards. If one player does not do the job, high pressure falls apart. Generally high pressure suits players who are very fit, have a high work rate and possess a high degree of intensity and concentration.

LOW PRESSURE

Low pressure in indoor soccer is similar to a half court press in basketball. Instead of attempting to regain possession of the ball in the opponent's half, the team which has lost possession withdraws into its own half before challenging for the ball. The basic principles of low pressure are:

• All five players must get behind the ball upon losing possession;

• Three players drop back immediately to their own red line. Two forwards must attempt to delay opponents from attacking by containing players with the ball. When ball possession is lost, the player closest to the opponent who has won the ball must immediately close him/her down and delay the attack. (Diagram 12-4);

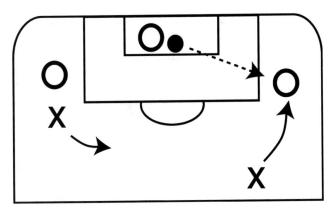

Diagram 12-3

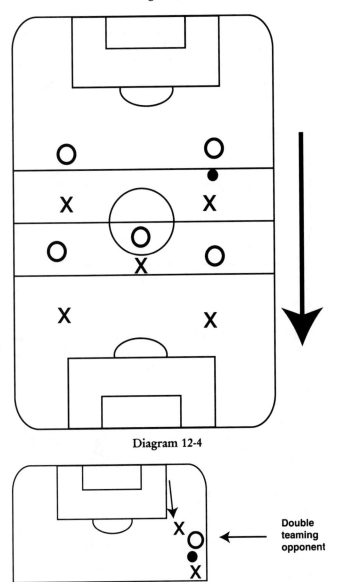

Diagram 12-4

Diagram 12-5

Double
teaming
opponent

• Once all five players have withdrawn well into their own half, all opponents must be marked man-to-man within the defensive third of the field. In other words, low pressure is high pressure within the defensive zone. Opponents should be allowed to play outside the defensive red line. It is essential the two forwards keep the two opposing defenders in front of them;

• Compactness is the key. With all five players withdrawing into their defensive zone, the opponent is denied time and space;

• Control and Restraint - As with high pressure, players must exercise good judgment and discipline. Keeping the opponent in front of you, not overcommitting and knowing when to tackle and when to retreat are only some of the decisions players have to make;

• A very effective tactic is to double team opponents when they are in possession of the ball near the boards. While the opponent is being challenged in front by a defender, one of the forwards drops back and challenges the player from behind or from the side. (Diagram 12-5)

This tactic is equally effective if a team plays high pressure.

• Upon winning possession, the team must counterattack quickly and attempt to get behind opposing defenders. A low pressure defense is particularly suitable for a team with an effective counterattack. By withdrawing into its own half a team encourages the opposition to push their defenders up to the halfway line or beyond leaving vital space behind them which can be exploited with a quick counterattack.

If a team does not possess forwards capable of winning the ball in the opponents' half, a low pressure defense may be more suitable. Of course it is always possible to play high pressure with one line and low pressure with another line. The ultimate consideration is that the system must suit the players.

ATTACKING PRINCIPLES

There are two basic forms of attack in indoor soccer. One is a counterattack or breakaway. The other is a planned attack based upon a deliberate build-up out of defense with the emphasis on possession. Which system a team elects to use is dictated by two factors:

• Playing ability and tactical awareness of your own players;

• Playing style of your opponent.

COUNTERATTACK

A quick counterattack may be likened to the "fast break" in basketball. When a team has gained possession of the ball there must be an immediate transition to attack. The primary aim of the counterattack is to get behind opponents with one or two passes and finish with a shot on goal. A team is most vulnerable to a counterattack when its attack breaks down in the attacking third of the field and it has committed many players into the attack. By a quick counterattack the opposition seeks to establish a numerical superiority (2 v. 1; 3 v. 2; 4 v. 3) which hopefully will result in a shot on goal.

The key ingredients for a successful counterattack are:
- If a team plays with a target player up front, that player must provide a target by showing for the ball (running into open space) at the right time. The right time is when the player in possession is ready to pass the ball. (Diagram 12-6) If a team plays with two forwards, they must break out quickly by running into open space and providing targets for the player with the ball;
- The first or second pass upon gaining possession should be played to the target player(s). Obviously dribbling the ball out of the defense will only give the opposition time to organize its defense.
- The player (including the goalkeeper) who has gained possession of the ball in the defensive zone should always look for a long target first. Generally when a player is in possession of the ball he needs players near him for short support but also one or two players farther away from him for long support.

Looking up for a long target first accomplishes two things:

√ If the target player is open, the ball can be played to him/her directly;

√ By looking up the player uses his peripheral vision so he can immediately see what is to the side of him and directly in front of him. If the long pass is not "on", he can pass the ball short to another teammate.

- The target player must have the ability to hold the ball under pressure. If he finds himself 1 v. 1 with an opponent he/she can either turn and take the opponent on, or hold the ball and wait for support and perhaps create a 2 v. 1 situation. Of course any time he/she is confronted with two opponents he has no choice but to hold the ball until support arrives;
- Once the ball has been played to a forward player he needs immediate support by teammates. If support is not forthcoming any numerical advantage the attacking team had will be immediately lost. Remember, time is always in favor of the defense.

A counterattack is effective against teams who are slow getting behind the ball to mark opponents. It is also effective against teams which commit too many players into the attack and thus leave themselves short-handed in the back. A team which relies on high pressure also may be susceptible to counterattacks, particularly if they are somewhat slow in closing down the player with the ball. By committing players in the opponents' half to win the ball, obviously fewer play-

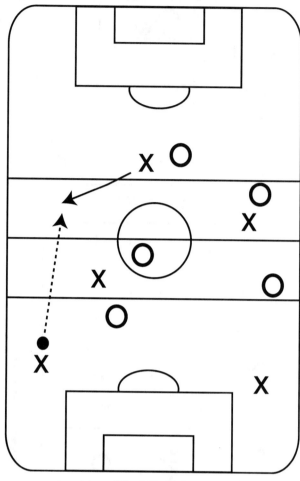

Diagram 12-6

ers are back in defense covering the vital spaces into which balls can be played.

The most difficult teams to counterattack against are teams which play a very conservative low pressure defense where all five players retreat quickly into their defensive zone denying the opposition any space behind defenders into which balls can be played.

DELIBERATE BUILD-UP

The only effective form of attack against an opponent where all five players retreat into their defensive zone is a deliberate build-up out of the defense with the emphasis on keeping possession. The key factors in an effective buildup are:

- **Patience** — In order to draw opponents out of their defensive zone it is essential a team is patient in its attack. It must attempt to draw opponents out of their defensive posture by keeping possession in the neutral zone.
- **Position Changes** — Interchanging of positions between teammates is essential in order to get free from tight marking and create space.
  √ For every position change at least two new paths are quickly opened up into which a pass can be made;

√ The aim of position changes is always for one player to occupy the space opened up for him by another player;

√ The ultimate success of a position change depends upon a correctly timed pass into the open area.

• **Mobility** — In order to get free from man-to-man marking it is essential that players learn to become mobile. Players must learn to show for the ball at the right time.

√ When — A player must show for the ball when the player with the ball is ready to give it. If a player gets away from his opponent too early the opponent has a chance to catch up with him. If he shows for the ball too late the element of surprise has been lost. Smart players always show late.

√ How — A quick increase in pace or using some sort of disguise or sharp nudge with the shoulder. For example, a player may use checking runs — feinting by taking a few quick steps in one direction before turning and sprinting in another. If a player wants the ball at his feet he can make space for himself by first running away from the ball, checking his run and then running back into the same space to receive the ball. Conversely if he wants the ball played over the top, he can first run to the ball taking his opponent with him and then turning and sprinting after the ball which has been played behind the defender.

• **Penetration** — Once one or more opponents have been drawn out of the defensive zone and players are moving into open spaces, the emphasis must be on penetration and finishing with a shot on goal.

• **Improvisation** — Players who have the ability to take opponents on 1 v. 1 should be encouraged to do so in the attacking third of the field. Beating an opponent may result in a numerical superiority for the attacking team.

• **Combination Play** — One-two passes and takeovers are very effective ways of beating a packed defense.

OTHER INDIVIDUAL AND TEAM TACTICS

• Learn to play quickly. Playing one-, two-, or three-touch soccer in practice will teach players to think more quickly. Playing quickly means less running, therefore conserving players' energy. Remember, in indoor soccer there is less time and space, therefore players must learn to make decisions quickly;

• Don't dribble out of the defense under pressure;

• Create "width" and "depth" - In order to create space the attacking team must strive to make the field wide and long. Width is obtained by having players going wide to the boards. By going wide, defenders are forced to follow their opponents, thereby creating space between them which can be exploited by the attacking team. Space can be created also in the length of the field. Forwards should strive to go deep into the opponents' half, forcing the opposing de-

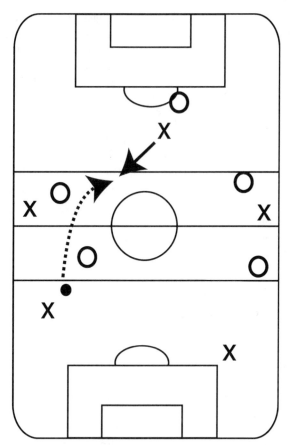

Example of creating width and depth in attack.

Diagram 12-7

fenders back. Space is hereby created in front of them into which balls can be played. When a team is bringing the ball out of its defensive zone, one or two forwards should push up to the opponents' red line and show for the ball from there; (Diagram 12-7)

• Play balls to the player's feet or slightly in front of him so he can take the ball into his stride without slowing down;

• In your own half of the field, always run toward the boards. Avoid making square passes in your own half of the field;

• If defenders make a run forward with the ball they must not lose possession. An attacking defender must keep in mind the following:

√ He/she must either get a shot off or make a good pass;

√ After passing or shooting he/she must come straight back to his/her own position;

√ Before making a forward run he/she must make certain there is a teammate in position to cover for him/her. If there is no one to provide cover, the defender should stay back.

• **Far Post Passes and Runs** — The importance of far post shots and passes and having a teammate run on to the pass cannot be overemphasized. Because of the reduced playing area and small size of the goal it is virtually impossible to beat goalkeepers with a near post shot. However, by covering the near post, the far post is left open. Every time a player is ready to shoot (unless the shot is taken from straight on) a teammate must make a well-timed far post run.

The timing must be set so that the run is made at the moment the player with the ball is about to pass the ball. If the run is made too soon, the player will end up waiting for the ball and will undoubtedly attract a defender. It is good advice to shoot balls across the goalmouth to a teammate ready to tap it in at the far post. (Diagram 12-8)

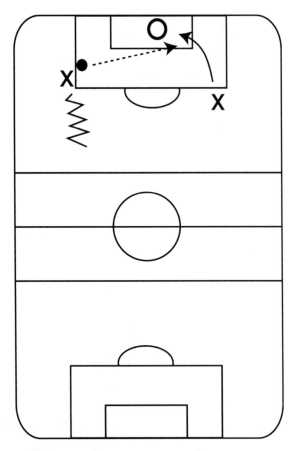

Far post passes and runs

Diagram 12-8

Defending Tactics - Indoor Soccer
Gordon Jago

Introduction

Indoor soccer differs from outdoor soccer in many ways, but the major factor is that indoor soccer does not require the various specialists of the outdoor game. For example: the tall commanding central defender good in the air — the quick dribbling wing forward able to beat a defender and deliver accurate crossing passes — are not necessary in the indoor game. Nor is the tall, tough, all-action center forward/striker nor the midfield playmaker type with top flight distribution skills needed in the indoor game. What is needed for good team play in the indoor game are players with a good, basic all-around game. The more well-rounded players are those that survive in today's indoor play.

To be successful, indoor players must be all-around players, able to attack and defend. Forwards have to chase back, mark and be able to defend in 1 v. 1 situations. Defenders must be able to move forward in control of the ball and be able to shoot accurately or to create a scoring opportunity for a team member. The forward who wishes to remain upfield can become a liability as the opposition sends forward a player from the back unmarked. The defender who cannot move forward with confidence and the midfield player who cannot mark and tackle will soon be exposed. Training as defenders, therefore, becomes a top priority for all indoor soccer players.

I. Individual Defensive Requirements

Objectives: to get forwards and midfielders to play defense, fitness.

Exercise: 1 v. 1 in fours using resting players in goals, 45-second periods, building to 12 periods.

II. Basic Defensive Understanding

Objectives: To get first defender to pressure the ball, the second defender to provide cover, depth and communication. Add proper positioning, angle of approach, speed of approach, etc. Exercises: 2 v. 2 in eights, 90 second periods. 3 v. 3 - emphasize taking the scoring opportunity when it is presented.

III. Game Situations - 1 v. 1

A. Objective: Do not allow the player receiving the ball to turn. Watch distance from the player (at one yard), see the ball, ignore feints.

Exercise: 1 v. 1 tightly marked from a service using a keeper and a full-sized indoor goal; increase the pressure on the offensive player.

B. Objective: Do not permit the player with the ball facing the defender to beat the defender.

Exercise: 1 v. 1 with the player having the ball facing the defender after receiving the service, use goalkeeper. Add the use of the boards as an option for the player with the ball.

IV. Game Situations - 2 v. 2

Objective: To get the two defenders to work as partners.

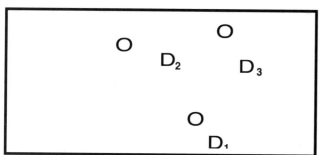

Diagram 12-9

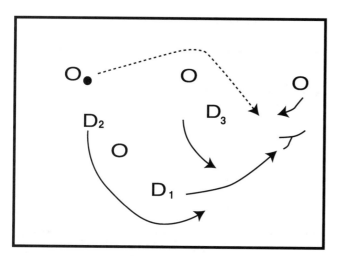

Diagram 12-10

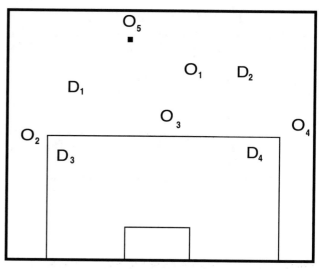

Diagram 12-11

Exercise: 2 v. 2 to goals; coaching emphasis - in addition to the points in II above, add distance from the ball and by positioning, close off penetration to one side by the first defender.

Note: The secret to indoor attacking play is to get an overload or numbers up situation taking place in the attacking zone. Thus there are a good many 2 v. 1 and 3 v. 2 attacking situations that take place in the indoor game. The boards act as a "player available for a pass" in the indoor game. It is a much easier situation when all five players get back, hence the need for defensive tactical training.

V. Defending Against Counter Attacks - 3 v. 4

Objective: Offense tries to keep the ball on one side, draw the defense, and play the ball to the other side. So the objective for the three defenders is to maintain balance and delay until the other two players get back.

Exercise: 3 v. 4 with coaching points emphasizing that the balancing defender D1, does not go out right away but moves out a bit to deny the through ball as D2 becomes the "new" balancing defender. (Diagrams 12-9 and 12-10)

VI. Team Defending

A. In the Attacking Zone

Objective: Immediate and full pressure to hold the ball in the attacking zone.

Exercise: 5 v. 5 plus keepers, ball begins with opposing goalkeeper back in his goal.

Coaching Points: Mark man-to-man, three line passes are illegal, so the last defender moves in front of the most forward opposing player; cut-off the goalkeeper after the ball is played out from the goalkeeper, very much akin to a basketball full-court press.

B. In the Mid-Zone

Objective: Be goal-side of the ball to deny space and prevent 1 v. 1 situations (very dangerous situation with the boards).

Exercise: 5 v. 5 plus two keepers, opposing keeper has the ball.

Coaching Points: Drop back, half-pressure in the midzone.

C. In the Defensive Zone

Objective: Deny scoring opportunities.

Exercise: 5 v. 5 plus goalkeepers, begin with the ball on the defensive zone line.

Coaching Point: Full pressure!

VII. Defending Power Plays

Objective: Deny scoring opportunities while wasting time.

A. Box Formation (Diagram 12-11)

Coaching Points: The front two players vary the pressure on the ball; there should not be too much space between the defensive lines — D1, D2, D3, and D4; players move out just enough to prevent the shot; D1 and D2 also try to deny the ball to the outside Os (O2 and O4).

B. Box Formation (Diagram 12-12)

Coaching Points: If the ball does get outside, defensive movement is pictured here; if the ball goes to the center player (O3) then D3 or D4 closes them down.

C. Diamond Formation (Diagram 12-13)
Coaching Points: D1 closes off frontal pass as the offense is usually trying to play the ball behind the diamond to the player near the goal.
D. 1 - 3 Formation (Diagram 12-14)
Exercise: Play 4 v. 5.
VIII. Corner Kick Defense (Diagram 12-15)
Objectives: D1 - deny the direct shot; D2 - watches for post runs; D3 - prevent the square ball off the wall; D5 - watches for square cross and players from behind; D5 - watches players from the point penetrating.

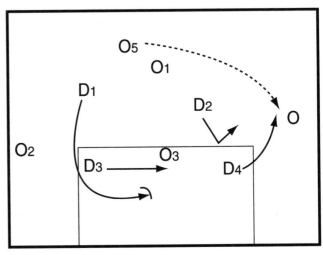

Diagram 12-12

THE SCIENCE OF INDOOR GOALKEEPING
Joe Machnik

INTRODUCTION

Indoor soccer has grown rapidly in recent years. Many players have switched from the outdoor game without adapting their style of play to the demands of the smaller surface and dasher boards which give new meaning to the phrase "wall pass".

This article is designed to help ease the transition to indoor soccer for the many goalkeepers and coaches who are more familiar with goalkeeping techniques for the outdoor game.

PHYSICAL REQUIREMENTS

First, for indoor goalkeepers, as in outdoor soccer, size, speed (reflex action), flexibility, and agility play important roles. The indoor game also requires strength to withstand collisions in front of the goal. Strong hands are needed to catch and box shots out or deflect them without suffering hand injuries.

Indoor gloves, long pants and padding for hips and elbows are necessary equipment. Fast feet and some ability as a field player are also helpful, because the goalkeeper in an indoor soccer match may need to come off the line and contribute to the attack.

It's a tremendous tactical advantage to have a goalkeeper who can join the attack and create a numbers-up situation. This is especially vital on power play opportunities or when trailing by a goal near the end of the game and a sixth attacker is needed to press for the tying goal.

If the goalkeeper does not have field-playing skills, he will have to be substituted for in those situations, weakening the team's defenses in case the opponent gains possession and makes a counterattack.

MECHANICS...

are also important. Successful indoor professionals have Machnik-modified the accepted techniques of

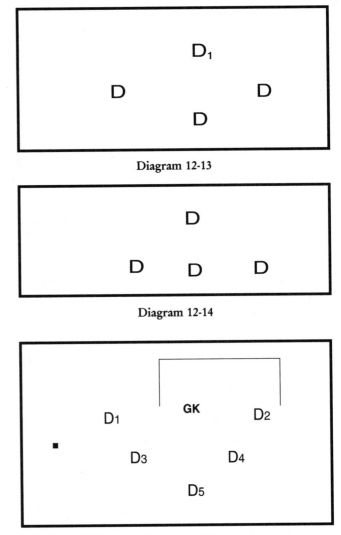

Diagram 12-13

Diagram 12-14

Diagram 12-15

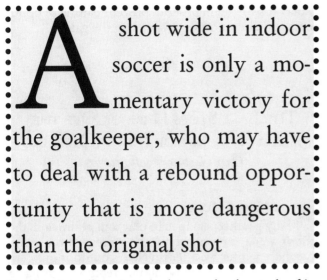

A shot wide in indoor soccer is only a momentary victory for the goalkeeper, who may have to deal with a rebound opportunity that is more dangerous than the original shot

(outdoor) goalkeeping to adapt to the demands of indoor soccer. Zoltan Toth, now with San Diego, and Mike Mahoney of Los Angeles are two leading indoor goalkeepers who have learned to stay on the line and stay on their feet.

They assume a posture which covers as much of the goal as possible and try to avoid leaving their feet. They almost never dive, and they certainly never dive to save a "wide" shot, which could embarrass them by rebounding off the dasher board, hitting the goalkeeper in the back, and ricocheting into the goal.

Tim Harris of Minnesota has also adopted this style, as has Tino Lettieri of the Minnesota Strikers, who is not big for a goalkeeper. At the near post, these goalkeepers hold the line and lean with their bodies against the post, allowing any ball driven around the wall or directly at them to bounce off their body back into the corner.

While coaching the New York Arrows several years ago, I trained goalkeepers in this technique by using a Jugs Shooting Machine to fire the ball along the near boards and around the corners. I used the machine because very few field players have the patience to do this in practice and it doesn't make much sense to them. But the indoor game has countless occasions where this technique at the near post is essential for the goalkeeper's survival.

Even when an opposing forward is attacking straight down the middle, this new technique calls for the indoor keeper to take a posture of standing up and bending one knee with arms spread high and low, rather than throwing himself at the feet of an opponent. This guards against the possibility that the forward may intentionally shoot the ball wide of the diving keeper, step around him and get the rebound off the boards to score a goal on an easy tap-in.

A shot wide in indoor soccer is only a momentary victory for the goalkeeper, who may have to deal with a rebound opportunity that is more dangerous than

the original shot. Stay in the goal. Make yourself "BIG." Force the forward to pick the corner and score a great goal rather than giving him a "freebie."

KICK SAVES

Outdoors, they are taboo, but indoors, a save is a save, and the goalkeeper had better be prepared to have forwards shoot the ball at the goalkeeper's legs, or between the legs. After all, if the forward catches the goalkeeper with his weight on the wrong foot and unable to make a kick-save effort, he can score the goal right past the goalkeeper's leg. Kick saves are an important technique for the indoor goalkeeper. He must remain standing up, ready to save reflexively (and intentionally) with his feet.

DISTRIBUTION

Throwing the ball back into play is even more important indoors than in outdoor soccer. There are many opportunities in the indoor game for goalkeepers to contribute to the attack with accurate, well-timed throws.

From nowhere, a goalkeeper with a good arm can put the ball at the feet of a teammate in the scoring area in less than three seconds. The throw must be low because the rules say the opponents get a free kick unless the throw-from-goalkeeper ball is played in the neutral zone or hits the carpet or side boards. It must be thrown hard to reduce the possibility of being intercepted by an opponent who can turn it into a scoring attempt against you.

And it must be accurate, thrown to the feet of your teammate or into the space ahead of him, so he doesn't have to break stride or stop and wait for the ball, allowing a beaten defender to recover. Sometimes it must be thrown off the boards, away from both your teammate and his marker, to a spot where your teammate can shield the opponent off, then pick up the ball on the run. It is not unusual for the goalkeeper to be credited with a direct assist on an indoor goal, sometimes with two in the same game. And there have been several "thrown goals" in the MISL, scored against a team which has pulled its keeper and put in a sixth attacking player, leaving an empty net as it presses for the tying goal.

TACTICS

Strong throwing ability, footwork and field playing skills are important techniques. If a goalkeeper has them, they allow his coach to develop team tactics that would not otherwise be possible. The Pittsburgh Spirit, under coach John Kowalski, were devastating in the 1983-84 season once they had a lead because they were able to use goalkeepers Joe Papaleo and Peter Mowik as releases. Pittsburgh would play the ball back to the keeper and force the opponent to chase it down because they needed the ball to get the tying goal. This drew the opponents out and spread their defenders, opening up space in Pittsburgh's attacking third and in the neutral zone.

Papaleo or Mowik would hold the ball at their feet just outside the penalty area and then make "killer passes" to unmarked teammates to launch them into good scoring chances at the other end. No MISL team did this better than Pittsburgh which went 32-16 that season.

Sooner or later, coaches and goalkeepers will come to grips with the reality that indoor soccer is not a one goalkeeper game. There is too much action, too much mental anguish, too many collisions, too many goals. Many games are lost by failing to substitute a goalkeeper at the start of the fourth quarter or even at halftime, regardless of how well the starting goalkeeper has played the first half.

This is, of course, a generalization, and there are special circumstances which would make a change of goalkeepers inappropriate. But by the start of the third quarter, the goalkeeper is often fatigued and weakened by suffering various indignities in the first two periods. A change is warranted, but the coach must handle this carefully.

The incoming goalkeeper should have prior knowledge that he will be going into the game in the second half to secure the victory, and the outgoing goalkeeper must know that he is not being substituted for due to poor performance. He must know that this substitution is part of the overall game plan and is in the best interests of the team. There must be no hard feelings between the goalkeepers, or toward the coaches. Each goalkeeper must be prepared to start the next game and to relieve when called upon. Indoor soccer presents a direct contradiction to the outdoor game. Even if you are playing only once a week, the second goalkeeper, coming off the bench late in the game, may be the difference between winning and losing, assuming that the two keepers are nearly equal in overall ability.

As in the outdoor game, the indoor goalkeeper sets the pace, speed and rhythm of the contest. Although there is no four step rule indoors, the goalkeeper may take no more than five seconds to get the ball out of the penalty area after gaining possession.

Under those circumstances and the small size of the penalty area, five seconds can be a long time. If the goalkeeper gains possession 30 times in a 60-minute game, he could consume 2:30 minutes by holding the ball. Depending on the opponents' tactics, the goalkeeper may, on occasion, be able to hold the ball at his feet just outside the penalty area for an additional ten seconds without advancing it, and, if he does it six times in a game, it could eat up another minute. (A rule change instituted two years ago prevents the goalkeeper, once having played the ball outside the penalty area from bringing it back into the penalty area, to play it by hand in order to prevent baiting of opponents and also in order to speed up the game.)

THE BALL STOPS HERE OR OFF THE WALL: THE ART OF INDOOR KEEPING
Dan Gaspar & Jeff Sturges

INDOOR MEANS MORE

Many goalkeepers love to play and perform in the indoor arena, particularly in those areas of the country where winter weather precludes outdoor play. Indoor soccer is fast, intense and incredibly exciting to watch and to play. Although there are fewer players and the playing area is much smaller, many more goals are scored! Does this mean that indoor keepers aren't as good or don't play with the same intensity? Hardly. The combination of small field size and player positioning create a great deal of congestion in front of the goal. Because of the player density, the goalkeeper often has a difficult time seeing the ball and many goals are scored off deflections. Many goals are also scored from intentional and unintentional rebounds off the wall. Because the ball is so frequently caromed off a player or a wall many soccer purists discount this so-called "billiards soccer" or "pinball soccer" as a poor imitation of the traditional full field 11 v. 11 game. Well if they do, they don't know what they're missing!

We guarantee that the indoor game is here to stay. For the American fan it provides a much more exciting form of play. There is more shooting and more scoring. The spectators are closer to the players. There is more body contact. The pace of play is faster and the shifts from offense to defense and back are much more frequent. For the indoor soccer player there is more opportunity for individual participation. Field players get more chances to dribble. Defenders get more opportunities to tackle. Attackers get more opportunities to shoot. Keepers get more opportunities to make saves. Everyone gets more ball touches. The close proximity of the defenders puts a premium on ball control skills. Finally, for those players who live in the cold weather climes, there is no viable outdoor alternative during the winter months. Most importantly, it's fun for everyone involved!

GOALKEEPING DIFFERENCES BETWEEN "BILLIARDS SOCCER" AND THE TRADITIONAL GAME

Psychological Differences

Particular considerations of indoor soccer include: confined space, congested goal area, frequent quick changes between attacking and defending, rapid hard shots with multiple deflections off players, and rebounds off the boards. These conditions put a premium on three key psychological considerations for the keeper. They are courage, concentration, and coping skills.

Courage: From the goalkeeper's perspective the increased concentration of players, the rapid pace of the ball, the short distances over which shots are taken, and the hardness of the playing area all create an environment that is very unfriendly to the goalkeeper. Any keeper who willingly accepts the role of target in this rapid fire shooting gallery must possess tremendous courage. Effective indoor keeping is definitely not for the faint of heart!

Concentration: Shots can be taken from anywhere at anytime. There is simply no opportunity to relax once the whistle blows. Not all goals that are scored will be the result of goalkeeper mistakes, but most goalkeeper mistakes are a result of a lapse in concentration. These concentration lapses will likely result in goals scored against. The indoor keeper must be 100% focused on the "here and now" at all times. In addition to concentrating on the various attacking threats from the opposition the keeper must mentally look ahead to envision options for distribution that'll initiate the attack for his/her own team.

Coping Skills: Many more goals are going to be scored indoors even with the best defenses and the best of goal-keeping. The keeper needs to emotionally accept that conceding four to six goals is not unusual and is, indeed common. The indoor keeper must, as always, accept the responsibility for giving up goals. At the same time the keeper must have the resilience to rebound from each disappointment and let the negative emotions pass in order to be able to refocus on the task at hand. This is perhaps the most difficult difference for the indoor player and requires a great deal of maturity.

These psychological differences combined create a lot of physical and mental stress on indoor keepers. Therefore, it is usually advisable to divide this among at least two keepers. This is often done with hockey goalkeepers as well as with baseball pitchers. From a coaching standpoint, it often makes sense to announce the rotation ahead of time so that when a keeper is removed, the substitution is regarded as part of a well-developed plan rather than a personal punishment for poor performance. It is important to allow the keeper to maintain as much self-confidence as possible or the coach may have a difficult time filling the nets at all.

The best way for the keeper to deal with the stressful aspects of indoor play is for the indoor keeper to recognize and accept these stress factors and make sure to set goals that are realistic in light of the environment. Setting a goal of achieving a shutout is simply not realistic. A more reasonable goal would be to personally improve some specific aspect of the game that is within the keeper's span of control. For example, I will distribute the ball more rapidly and more effectively after each save. I will effectively communicate with and direct my defenders. I will make sure that I will always know exactly where I am and I will effectively position myself for the best angle play.

Technical Considerations

Just as the differences between the indoor and the outdoor game create the need for different psychological considerations, these factors also create the need

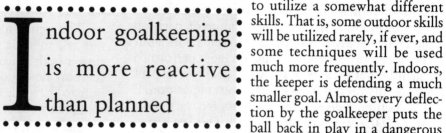

Indoor goalkeeping is more reactive than planned

to utilize a somewhat different skills. That is, some outdoor skills will be utilized rarely, if ever, and some techniques will be used much more frequently. Indoors, the keeper is defending a much smaller goal. Almost every deflection by the goalkeeper puts the ball back in play in a dangerous area. Rapid fire, high speed, close proximity, deflected shots are the norm. Offensive use of the boards is typical. Immediate attacking opportunities can be created by quick distribution from the keeper. Finally, communication with, and control of, all of the defenders remains very important.

Catching/Deflecting: Because a deflection past the post rarely gets the ball out of immediate danger, indoor play puts a premium on the caught ball. Whenever possible, terminate the save! By this we mean that the ball is brought under the complete control of the goalkeeper. Now instead of worrying about further attacking threats, the keeper himself becomes the attacking threat against the other team.

Many keepers are shot blockers not shot stoppers. Terminating the indoor save is not easy. Ricochets, deflections and rebounds all provide difficulties in capturing the ball, but that is the challenge. Fast, soft hands are the key. Hard, slow hands create rebounds, if they touch the ball at all. Try to use the base of the hand as much as possible as that is where the maximum strength of the hand is concentrated.

Effective indoor catches are best made with the body in front of the ball. The blazing pace of the typical shot means that many shots may get through the hands. Therefore, getting the body behind the ball provides an extra measure of insurance. The basket catch is generally preferred. As soon the ball contacts the hands, bring the low ball into the stomach area. Similarly, bring high balls into the chest area.

If the save cannot be made with the hands, any other part of the body may be used to make the save. Most commonly, this will be the foot or the leg. Typically these reaction saves result in a rebound. Hard shots just have too much pace to allow the ball to be safely trapped. In these cases the objectives of the deflection is similar to the objectives of boxing in the outdoor game. These include: width, depth, height, and accuracy. Width obviously becomes much less important indoors than outdoors, but the other three factors remain important. Depth provides the safety of distance, height provides time to regroup, and accuracy in directing a ball to a teammate not only eliminates the threat but initiates the attack for your own team. The base of the hand can help facilitate the deflection by guiding the ball wide, but you must remain prepared for the follow-up shot.

Indoor goalkeeping is more reactive than planned. That is, indoor keeping puts a greater premium on lightning reactions and less of a premium on decision making. Generally it is important to remain on your feet as much as possible. Collapse diving is performed frequently, but because of the small goal size full out flying is only needed if the keeper is out of position. If the keeper must dive, a lightning fast recovery must be made if the save is not terminated. This fast recovery skill after the dive should be practiced. With fairly little practice, this recovery speed can be greatly improved. Remember though, positioning, fast footwork and agility are better techniques than the ability to recover quickly.

Angle Awareness: As previously stated, positioning is key to indoor keeping because there is insufficient time to get into position after the shot has been taken. By then the ball is already in the back of the net. Proper positioning is dictated by angle awareness and the best estimate of the location of the primary threat. The primary threat is usually the attacker with the ball, but an unmarked attacker in position to receive a pass and shoot may also be a major threat especially if the attacker with the ball is well marked.

One of the unique aspects of indoor play are the walls. The ball remains in play after wall contact so the keeper seemingly never has time to relax. Balls sent into the typical indoor rounded corners tend to hug the walls and end up coming out of the corner just in front of the goal line by the near post. Whereas in outdoor play the keeper would typically go to the far post to handle crosses that originate deep from the corner, the opposite is true indoors. The keeper must advance to the near post and protect it with the body tight against that post so that no corner wall balls squeeze through.

Another popular tactic by indoor attackers who are effectively denied a direct shot is to pass the ball to themselves by shooting the ball at the back wall, contacting the boards just outside the goal and then shooting a follow-up shot. How the keeper reacts to this situation depends upon the pace of the ball. If the shot is soft the keeper may be able to turn and face the wall and capture the ball before the attacker gets another shooting opportunity. If the ball is kicked with pace the keeper must continue to face the field of play as that is where the threat will be the greatest. These are the situations where the keeper may feel like they are in a human pinball machine.

Distribution: Rapid distribution is very important in the indoor game. If done well, it can even result in assists for the goalkeeper. Most distribution will be by the overhand or windmill throw. Advance as far forward in the penalty area as possible. This forward movement slightly reduces the throws distance, improves accuracy, and helps generate momentum that will add power to the throw.

The second method of hand distribution is to roll the ball to your teammate. Because this method is slower both in execution and in ball pace, insure that there are no opponents nearby to pick off this pass so near to the goal. Get low and deliver the ball low to minimize bounce.

Although, you can't generally punt effectively indoors (in small arenas it is not allowed) foot distribution can be very effective especially if the keeper possesses good ball control skills and can make an accurate pass. An indoor keeper who has these skills can also advance out of the penalty area and function as an additional attacker, especially in man-up power play situations. As the last supporting player, the goalkeeper is in a unique position to quickly change the point of the attack especially if he/she is skilled in one touch passing.

Direction/Communication: Whether indoors or outdoors, the goalkeeper must assume a leadership role and function as the field general. The keeper has the best view of the entire field of action and has the ultimate responsibility for the defense. Because the indoor acoustics are often poor and fans typically make a lot of noise it is important that the keeper's commands be brief, clear and forceful. Identify the defender, the action, the threat and the location. "John, mark number ten, top of the penalty area."

Physical Considerations

Protective Gear: The indoor goalkeeper's body takes extreme abuse. The playing surfaces are not forgiving, nor is the opposition. The volume and intensity of shots is incredible. Double up on your protective gear to protect yourself from hard playing surfaces and hard contact. We suggest a long sleeve T-shirt and elbow pads under a padded goalkeeper jersey. On the bottom we recommend an athletic cup (if appropriate), padded underwear, padded long goalkeeper pants and heavy duty shinguards. Most indoor keepers wear the harder, more durable training glove for all occasions. An outdoor match glove may not even make it through warmups. Some keepers also wear elastic ankle and wrist supports. We also know of at least one top level indoor keeper who wears a full foam helmet. He swears by it and never plays without it. You only have one body, respect it and protect it.

Adequate Warmup: Indoor venues are typically booked to stay as busy as possible. This often means little or no warmup on the game playing surface prior to the match. Be smart. Arrive early. Go through your basic stretching routine and gradually warm up your body so that you are match ready when play begins. Even if there is no alternate playing area, be creative. Get with the other keeper along the sidelines. Dropkick the ball to each other. Gradually increase difficulty by increasing kick frequency and ball pace. Gradually make shot placement farther away from the body. If a partner isn't available use a wall. Remember you're certainly going to see plenty of shots off the wall during the game.

Conclusion

Indoor "Off the Wall" goalkeeping is a great deal of fun. The keeper will touch the ball more frequently and will have opportunities to assist on goal scoring opportunities. Good keepers will be aggressive, will be fully focused on the task at hand, and will have the resilience to bounce back after having been scored upon. Indoor keepers will always want to be in position to react quickly and "terminate the save" with a caught ball. If the save is not terminated, they must leave their feet and recover immediately. Once the save is terminated they will distribute the ball in a manner that will effectively result in goal scoring opportunities for their team. The smart goalkeeper will effectively prepare for the match by wearing the necessary protective equipment and allowing sufficient time prior to the match for stretching and proper warmup. Have a great season and make sure that when you're in goal, "The Ball Stops Here!

TEAM MANAGEMENT

• •

Coaching a soccer team on the field resembles the proverbial "tip of the iceberg." Considerable time and effort must be expended behind the scenes for the eventual field work to have its maximal inmpact. From the onset of the season until its conclusion the coach is responsible for organizing the team. That phase of coaching we label "Team Management." This chapter will outline how to motivate players and the team unit through the process called "motivation by objective."

Once the playing unit has established its goals for the season, a coach must, in today's litigious society, be concerned with issues of safety and liability and these important aspects are discussed in this segment. There are common coaching problems that beg for solutions and whether at the youth or professional level, they raise their head every season. A preview of what to expect and ideas to combat these issues is offered here as well as ideas about practice organization and coaching methodology.

How to resolve ineffective play is always an issue for coaches. One technological advance is the use of video tape analysis in dissecting play. How to blend this into your coaching methodology is advanced by one of our authors. While soccer budgets are among the most reasonable in sports today, nevertheless finances always need boosting and fundraising ideas for the coach are given a thorough airing.

Whether professional coach or directing a youth team, dealing with the media is vital for the coach, and globally for the sport of soccer. Some tips in this aspect of one's coaching will be found in this section. Finally, common sense approaches are put forth on such basic questions dealing with team morale, team discipline, motivation and dealing with defeat by some of our best soccer minds.

OFF-THE-FIELD ORGANIZATION

MOTIVATION BY OBJECTIVES
Dr. Jay Martin

Motivation by objectives (MBO) is a method of continuously motivating athletes on your team. The following steps outline the process:

1. A player self-evaluation (see page 400);

2. A written statement of goals;

3. An interview with the coach;

4. A performance appraisal by the coach;

5. An appraisal interview with player by coach;

6. A player self-evaluation starts the chain of events.

As you can see, the process is cyclical and ongoing. This process helps the player get the most out of himself. He does not rely on the coach to motivate him.

MOTIVATION BY OBJECTIVES (MBO)

WHY MBO?

There are a number of reasons we use MBO at Ohio Wesleyan University. MBO is a means of developing internal motivation without emotion which is critical in play of soccer at the advanced level. The player input allows the coach and player an opportunity to measure player achievement and allows the player the chance to increase his self-esteem. MBO is challenging. By setting goals and working toward these goals over a period of time, the player is constantly challenged in games and practice. Finally, with expanded game schedules at every level of play, it is impossible for coaches to appeal to players' emotions with a "win one for the Gipper" speech each game.

Before we discuss a program that revolves around goal-setting, we must first define goals. A goal is the aim or object of a player's efforts. There are basically three types of goals. The first type is a numbers goal. This type of goal measures the increased production during the season (or game, or practice). A player, for example, may target as his/her seasonal objective as scoring twenty goals. The second type of goal is a behavioral goal. This goal reflects a change of behavior that may be needed in order to improve one's level of play. The last type of goal is the numbers/behavioral goal. This type of goal causes players to change behavior to help them improve their output.

Some coaches feel that a quantitative type goal is a bit self-centered. This is not true. If a player sets a goal to score twenty goals and does it, it will only help the team. A key here is the constant emphasis on how may your goals and the team goals mesh to be successful. There will be more on this later.

A goal must be meaningful before there will be motivation to achieve it. The four criteria that make a goal meaningful are:

• The goal must be realistic: not too tough, not too easy;

• The goal must be specific: the player must know exactly what the goal is;

• The goal must be comprehensive: all conditions for meeting the goal must be detailed;

• The goal must be understood by the coach and the player;

• The coach must realize that a goal(s) is a means of satisfying a need of the player.

The key to goal-setting is recognizing the needs of your players and using that as a motivator. A single goal may satisfy many needs (i.e., achievement, recognition, status, etc.) or several goals may satisfy the same need (i.e., All-America, All-Ohio or NCAA champ may satisfy the need for recognition). The key here is to identify the behavior that must change in order for the player to achieve his goals and thereby satisfy his desires. For example, to satisfy the need for recognition, the player may want to earn All-America honors. The coach then must identify the behavior that needs to be changed to reach that goal. For example, the behavior to change may include improving skills, understanding team concept, increasing fitness and learning the strengths and weaknesses of teammates. The coach and player now know what exactly must be accomplished to reach the goal.

TEACHING GOAL-SETTING

Players do not just set goals, they must be taught to set goals. The steps for goal-setting should start the first day of practice. The first step is an indepth and realistic self-evaluation by the player of his/her soccer ability. This may be hard to achieve. Freshmen must learn this technique. Upperclassmen will have a better grasp through their years of practice. It is important that you ask the player about both his perceived strengths and weaknesses. After the player has completed the self-evaluation, the player must then list his personal and team goals. The next step (and, perhaps, the most important) is describing the target performance or behavior necessary to reach the aforementioned goals. This step is critical. The player must use the input from his self-evaluation and look at stated goals and then decide what steps must be taken to reach the goals.

This information should be obtained through a very specific questionnaire that each coach should develop. In the questionnaire form the coach must ask for specific information or he will never get the answers that are necessary to formulate the actions or behavior to improve the player's performance. A sample questionnaire used by OWU is shown on the following page.

ATTACHMENT I
INDIVIDUAL PERFORMANCE AND ANALYSIS SHEET

Name:_____ Date:_____ Conditions:_____

Technique —Dribbling_____

_____

— Heading_____

_____

—Passing: Long Dist._____

Middle Dist._____

Short Dist._____

—Escorting Ball: 1st Touch_____

(+) & (-) Bodypart_____

—Vision & Creativity: Ability to See Field_____

Opponents_____

Teammates_____

Ability to Use Tech w/Flair_____

Tactics — Understands Role - Accepts & Performs_____

_____

_____

Fitness — Acceleration_____

Speed Over 20 Yds._____

Aerobic_____

Anaerobic_____

% Body Fat_____

Strength_____

Attitude —Desire to Improve_____

Discipline_____

Achiever_____

Risk Taker_____

Leadership_____

Other_____

continued on the following page

ATTACHMENT I
INDIVIDUAL PERFORMANCE AND ANALYSIS SHEET (CONT.)

Player's Evaluation:_____

_____

_____

_____

_____

_____

_____

What Does the Team Need to Work On:_____

_____

_____

_____

What Kind of Policy Changes:_____

_____

_____

How Can We Improve the Program:_____

_____

_____

As a Coaching Staff:_____

  How to get the team to win:_____

  How to make the team better:_____

  How to make the practices more enjoyable:_____

  How to get the players to train harder:_____

  Other Ideas:_____

_____

_____

_____

_____

_____

_____

_____

ATTACHMENT II
OHIO WESLEYAN UNIVERSITY
COACH'S SEASONAL GOALS

Season Breakdown: Four Parts

Part One: Fred Myers Tournament to Denison

a. preparation
b. fitness
c. regional games of concern
d. solidifying team concept

Part Two: Oberlin to Wilmington

a. improve tactical considerations
b. develop substitution pattern
c. identify top 18 players
d. improve mental concentration and motivation

Part Three: CWRU to Kenyon

a. NCAC games
b. gear up for playoffs

c. finalize and polish restarts
d. improve fitness level

Part Four: NCAA Championship season

Preseason Objectives

a. improve technique
b. improve fitness
c. improve match experience
d. understanding the OWU team concept

Seasonal Objectives

a. NCAC Champs
b. NCAA Champs
c.
d.
e.

The following outline will give you an idea of the types of questions to ask and types of goals to be set:
• Seasonal goals: for the player and for the team;
• Daily goals: for the player's improvement;
• Game goals: for the team and for the player;
• Practice goals: how will you improve today?;
• Player goals: strengths, weaknesses, etc.

After the information is obtained through the questionnaire, the coach and player should have a conference or what we term a review session. This gives the coach the opportunity to have input into the goal-setting procedure. At that time, the coach can discuss changes in behavior that must occur for the goal to be realized, discuss some obstacles that may impact on the achievement of the goals, or modify the goal to make it attainable. Remember, the purpose of goal-setting is to increase motivation. If the goals are too high, too low or otherwise unattainable, then motivation is lost. The most important part of this meeting will be a discussion of a plan of action by the player to obtain the goals. This plan must be specific in order for the player to follow the plan and achieve the goals. For example, if a player wants "to get fit", he should tell the coach exactly how he intends to proceed. Will he run three times a week? How far? In what time? The following outline will give you an idea of what is done at Ohio Wesleyan up to this point.

I. Coaching goals: these will set the tone for the season.
  A. Seasonal goals:
    • recruiting players;
    • break season down into parts and goals for each part of the season (see above);
    • team playing system to be employed;
    • skills to teach/progression of teaching;
    • right player positions for each team member; fun!
  B. Daily goals: practice
    • where are we?;
    • where are we going?;
    • what must we do to get there?;
    • who will we play?;
    • improvement for individuals.
  C. Daily goals: games
    • opponent's strengths;
    • opponent's weaknesses;
    • weather conditions;
    • injuries.
II. Players' goals: from questionnaire (see Attachment III on following page).
  A. what position?;
  B. what are your strengths?;
  C. what are your weaknesses?;
  D. how will you improve?;
  E. mental attributes/physical attributes.
III. Team goals: from questionnaire.
  A. seasonal goals: win NCAA bid, win NCAAs, have fun, etc.;
  B. game goals for players: use 3 x 5 card on locker before game;
  C. game goals for team:
    • win 50-50 balls;
    • 2-1 ratio in our favor on corner kicks;
    • score three goals;
    • hold opponent to fewer than 10 shots.

ATTACHMENT III
OHIO WESLEYAN UNIVERSITY SOCCER
PLAYER SELF-EVALUATION & QUESTIONNAIRE

Name_____

What position do you want to play on this team?_____

What are your *personal* goals for this season?_____
_____

What are your goals for the *team* for this season?
_____
_____
_____
_____

Using a scale of 1-10, rank the following physical capabilities in the following areas:

speed _____
endurance _____
strength _____
quickness _____

What are your strengths as a soccer player?_____
_____

What are your weaknesses as a soccer player?_____
_____

What is (are) your main reason(s) for playing soccer at OWU? (i,e., competition, recognition, challenge of the game, etc.)_____
_____

On a scale of 1-10, rank the following mental attributes:

desire _____
assertiveness _____
sensitivity _____
endurance _____
tension control _____
confidence _____
personal accountability _____
self-discipline _____

We use these goals to motivate both the team and individual players. For the players, we help with practice preparation, help the player through a slump, discuss goals in a conference at mid-season and help the player work on SPECIFIC areas in the off-season. For the team, we emphasize the importance of a single game, help the team through a slump and help motivate in practice. We simply re-emphasize the goals the PLAYER has made.

PROBLEMS

As a coach, you must be aware of the problems that may arise with goal-setting. These can cause problems in the area of motivation if not identified and dealt with early in the season. The areas of concern would include:

• Pushing too hard: A goal that is unrealistic runs a high risk of failure. The coach meeting with the player will help reduce this risk;

• Turning goals into ceilings on performance: If a goal is too low, there will be a drop off in performance once these goals are met;

• Ignoring areas in which goals have not been set: Goals focus attention on activities that bring spe-

cific results. Do not let players forget the less visible aspects of the game;

• Using goals as a tool for punishment: Players should be motivated to achieve goals for positive outcomes. Failure to meet goals is a problem to be solved, not a sign of personal failure or reason for punishment. At this time, go back to the original cycle and try to discover why the player did not reach the goal;

• Encouraging dishonesty: Players may find ways to appear as if they are making progress toward the goal at the expense of changing behavior. The coach must be supportive, provide feedback and show a willingness to modify goals;

• Failure to explain how individual goals mesh with team goals: Focus the player's attention on the tasks around which the player's goals are entered, but only in the context of the TEAM and TEAM GOAL'S.

The majority of these problems can be avoided through the meetings between the coach and the player. These meetings are VERY important and can create a good line of communication between player and coach.

Appraisal of Player Performance

How many times have you been faced with the player who asks, "Coach, can you tell me why I'm not playing?" Goal-setting is a means by which the coach can focus attention on progress toward goals and not the player's personality. We call this the appraisal of player performance. The following steps will help the coach incorporate MBO and player appraisal:

- Maintain a record of the player's progress each week, each game;
- Recognize achievements and point out progress toward goals;
- Encourage self-development based on practice work. The purpose of MBO is self-motivation;
- Be honest. Let the player know where he stands;
- Identify potential. Give opportunity to move up the team ladder;
- Record the results of this conversation and put in a folder.

It is important to set standards that you as a coach want for your team. Evaluate your goals and your team and set realistic expectations against which individual performance can be measured. These standards should not reflect what the players feel they ought to do, but what you expect them to do.

The player questionnaire(s) should be kept in a folder for the four years the player is on your team. The results of the appraisal meetings should also be maintained. The appraisal form can be used to record these meetings. This form is a formal written rating for each player and shows the player and coach exactly where he stands. Each coach can design his/her own form.

However, it is important to include the following on the form to help each party understand exactly what the outcome of the appraisal might be:

- List the categories of major focus: These may include work rate, quality of play, technical level, attitude, etc;
- Develop a rating system for each category: It can be a code or a more complex system of comments;
- Comments' section: Have space for additional items that may be important, i.e., injury, fitness problems, etc;
- Coach report: Fill it out after the meeting and record all feelings and comments you may have.

Appraisal Interview

The aforementioned appraisal interview may be the most critical part of the performance evaluation. It is critical for positive communication between player and coach. You have evaluated the player, but now you must communicate the results. This interview serves two very important purposes. First, it will provide feedback to the player and help assess progress toward the written goals. Second, it provides the coach the opportunity to counsel the player on how to improve performance. There are certain steps that may be helpful in making an uncomfortable situation very positive:

- Indicate to the player what you hope to accomplish in the interview – why are you doing this? What impact will this have on the player? The intent of the interview is to improve performance;
- Present the results of your ongoing evaluation to the player. Emphasize his/her strong points and his/her weak points;
- Ask the player for his/her comments. Record them;
- Close by discussing what will be accomplished by following your suggestions. What will their impact be on the player? Try to end on a positive note by discussing how such progress will help improve the player's role on the team.

This appraisal can motivate the player in a number of ways. If handled properly, it can create an awareness of the player's potential and help improve consistency. From the appraisal, you can map out a strategy to change behavior to reach goals. The appraisal also offers the opportunity to expose the player to some new experiences by urging work on a new move or promoting leadership and responsibility. The most important use of the appraisal at OWU, however, has been in the development of off-season programs for individuals. The appraisal interview at OWU is a very positive experience and the players are constantly asking for a new appraisal or evaluation.

Conclusion

In conclusion, goal-setting/MBO is hard work and may seem time-consuming, but the benefits far outweigh the investment. If you follow the cycle and get yourself and your team into a routine, the process is easy and ongoing. At OWU we have found that:

- Goal-setting helps players and coaches share responsibility;
- Goal-setting helps increase work rate/work quality;
- Goal-setting clarifies the expectations of the coach;
- Goal-setting makes for more meaningful practice work;
- Goal-setting keeps internal competition at a healthy level; the players compete with themselves and not with team members;
- Goal-setting WILL improve internal motivation.

Legal Liabilities
Vern Seefeldt

Lawsuits are an undesirable part of athletics. Unfortunately, coaches who ignore the possibility of a lawsuit may also be avoiding the procedures that decrease the likelihood of being sued. The thought of a lawsuit is so distasteful that most individuals dismiss the possibility as an event that could never happen to them. Unfortunately, such an attitude is naive and shortsighted. The best way for sports coaches to avoid lawsuits is for them to know their responsibilities and rights in their specific roles as teachers or supervisors. This article underscores what is meant by "being a reasonable, prudent person" during the conduct of one's duties as a sports coach.

Do not assume you are immune from lawsuits because you participate in an agency-sponsored, nonprofit program of athletic competition for children. Whether you are paid for your coaching services or volunteer your time, you are responsible for the welfare of your team. Recent lawsuits have defined more clearly what is expected of individuals in their roles as coaches and supervisors of young athletes. Experience has also provided us with methods of reducing the potential of liability in ways that will lead to greater safety for the children under your supervision. By following the procedures that are suggested in this article, you will also aid your defense if a lawsuit is filed against you.

RESPONSIBILITIES OF THE COACH

Parents enroll their children in youth sports because they expect them to receive certain benefits as a result of time spent in the program. The most modest of these expectations is that their children will emerge from the experience as healthy individuals. When this premise is violated, that is, when children suffer psychological and/or physical injury as a result of participation in sports programs, lawsuits are a distinct possibility. The reasonable expectations of parents for the welfare of their children are, therefore, translated into obligations of the youth sports coach. These obligations have been classified in five categories and are discussed in the following sections.

The following discussion concerning the legal responsibilities of a coach is limited to techniques and procedures associated with the prevention, care and rehabilitation of physical injuries. Obviously, the psychological development of young players is equally as important and probably more vulnerable to injury. Omission in this article of the implications for litigation because of psychological injury to young players stems from our inability to locate information about lawsuits in which claims of psychological injury precipitated the legal action.

PROPER INSTRUCTION

A coach is responsible for the players' safety during practices and games. Responsibility for the players' safety may be shared between coaches, officials, administrators, and other players; but specific portions of the players' involvement in practices and games are the direct responsibility of the coach.

The coach is responsible for teaching the physical skills of the sport in a manner that will reduce the likelihood of injury while those skills are performed. This implies that a coach must first know the progressions in skill development and conditioning, and then know how to implement them, based on the readiness of athletes to coordinate the new levels of proficiency. Coaches, generally with the eager compliance of athletes, have a common tendency to exceed the body's readiness to accept new levels of stress. Athletes are particularly vulnerable to over-exertion early in the season, when their state of fitness lags behind the aspirations of achievement held by both the athletes and the coach. The chance of injuries are also increased when players of various sizes and ability levels compete against each other.

The coach is often the final authority during practices or contests where the safety of athletes is concerned. Exceptions occur when physicians or officials exercise their right of authority in specific situations. The burden of directing proper training and conditioning, proper rehabilitation of injuries not treated by a physician, appropriate skills progressions, proper matching of opponents by size strength, and experience, and maintaining proper nutrition and hydration during practices and contests all rest with the coach. When conditions exist that are likely to cause physical or psychological injury to players, the coach is obligated to change the situation in order to alleviate the risk, even to the point of removing the team from the contest.

Coaches should have a written record of the skills that have been taught and the competence achieved by each player. This record may be the most important source of evidence against claims that an athlete was injured because of inadequate preparation for a specific situation that may have led to an injury.

Coaches are considered to be in a supervisory role during any duly scheduled practice or contest, unless this responsibility has been assumed by another adult. This means that coaches must arrive before the scheduled time of practices or games so that they will be able to inspect the facilities and monitor the arrival of

Parents expect their children to receive physical and psychological benefits from their participation in youth sports.

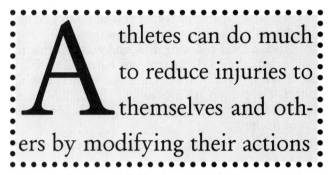

Athletes can do much to reduce injuries to themselves and others by modifying their actions players. Coaches who have irregular schedules which cause frequent tardiness should arrange to have another take charge until they or another coach arrives. Coaches who cannot find adult supervisors to replace them in event of late arrivals should terminate their coaching responsibilities rather than promote scheduled, but unsupervised activities.

FAILURE TO WARN

Injuries are an inherent part of sports and are generally accepted as such by athletes and their parents, unless a serious, catastrophic, or fatal injury occurs. Injuries which are caused by someone's negligence increase the accusations of blame and the chances of a lawsuit.

Warning players of their potential for injury is an essential, yet often neglected, part of any sport program. Coaches may fail to warn their players of possible injuries for various reasons: "The injury couldn't happen on my team"; "These players are too young for that kind of injury"; "We don't play that kind of game in our league"; and/or "Mentioning injuries will only frighten the players." Whatever their aversion to a discussion of injury may be, coaches must inform the players and their parents about the risks involved in the sport, and preferably give them some written information about the frequency and the severity of injuries sustained in that sport by their specific age group. The material should also contain information about how players can avoid injuries.

ASSUMPTION OF RISK

Athletes and their parents must understand that no matter what precautions are taken, injuries in sport cannot be completely avoided. All athletes must compete under the assumption of risk, but they can do much to control their own destiny by the way they conduct themselves during practices and contests. Coaches must stress daily that the rules of safety are in place to protect everyone. However, if the emphasis on safety is to have any impact, athletes must conduct themselves within the letter and the spirit of the rules. Specific actions by players that will reduce the risk of injury include:
- Participating fully in conditioning drills which are designed to strengthen muscles, tendons, and ligaments which are vulnerable to the stress of physical contact;
- Wearing required, properly fitted, protective equipment and replacing those articles that are worn or inadequate;
- Obeying the rules and specifically refraining from infractions which may cause injury to oneself or others;
- Partaking of proper nutrition, sleep, and a healthy lifestyle so that they are more likely to remain attentive and alert during practices and games;
- Reporting all injuries to the coach or trainer and seeking medical advice when the injury requires professional attention;
- Returning to action after an injury only when the full function of the injured part has been restored.

Coaches should promote safety by teaching their athletes personal responsibility for injury prevention by behaving in the manner stated in the six points mentioned above.

FAILURE TO PROVIDE PROPER EQUIPMENT AND FACILITIES

Coaches' responsibility for the safety of their players extends to the facilities they use and the equipment they wear. Even though the maintenance of facilities may be beyond the coaches' control, they must judge whether the standard of safety is sufficient to permit their teams' participation in the facility. Equipment and clothing, whether personal or agency-owned, requires the same kind of periodic, supervisory inspection by the coach.

The concept of individual and team safety must be stressed daily. Only when players respond by thinking "safety first" should coaches be content that they have fulfilled their responsibility in preventing injuries. The supervision of personal equipment is difficult because players may not always cooperate when changes are required. For example, an old and inadequate piece of equipment may be more comfortable than a new article, or the cost of replacing an old item may be prohibitive. Some agency-sponsored programs may actually encourage the use of ill-fitting, worn equipment by sending hand-me-downs to the younger age groups. Despite these obstacles, the coach must educate players to the important contribution made by good equipment.

CAUSATION

Injuries generally prompt athletes, coaches, and parents to ask, "What occurred?", "Why did the injury occur?", and "Who caused the injury?" The answers to these questions have eluded us for many years, despite the changes that have been made in rules and equipment to promote safer games. In situations involving legal liability, lawyers will attempt to establish cause, and judges or juries will be asked to assess the degree of causation by certain individuals. The coach's role in such circumstances is difficult to determine because the many conditions that may have contributed to the cause of the injury are quite likely not under anyone's direct control.

For example, fatigue that was exaggerated by a long trip and cold temperatures may have been a contributing factor; the size and physical condition of the opposing team may have influenced the style of play; incompetent officials may have encouraged more contact than has normally been permitted. Yet, when injuries occur, many of these variables are subsumed under the category of "responsibilities of the coach."

The best defense against the threat of litigation is to have competent coaches in charge of all teams. Through appropriate teaching, planning, and supervision, competent coaches reduce the chances of injury. Competent coaches are prepared to respond in a prudent manner when injuries occur. After the injury and during the rehabilitation period, they initiate the kind of public relations that will discourage many lawsuits. Parents who are convinced that their child's coach acted in a responsible manner are less likely to initiate litigation than those who suspect or know that the coach was incompetent. The best way to deal with the question, "Who caused the injury?" is to be sure that you, as the coach, fulfill all of your responsibilities.

Some Thoughts on Effective Organization of Practices
Dan Woog

We often assume every coach knows how to structure a practice, when in fact there are very few books, articles or publications that address the issue. We are eager to help new coaches with strategy tactics and game-related mumbo jumbo, but we often forget that most coaches spend most of their time in practice sessions, not games.

We've compiled the following list of suggestions for coaches who aren't quite certain they're doing the right things in training. It might even prove helpful for veterans coaches too!

Plan practice sessions in advance.

Sound simple?

You'd be surprised how many coaches walk out on the field without any idea of what they'll be covering in the next hour or 90 minutes. Not only does this make for plenty of wasted time — time that's precious to you and your players — but it also sends a message to the team: the coach doesn't know the game, doesn't know what he's doing, doesn't have his heart or head with us here today.

Of course, that's not saying you shouldn't be flexible. If you've planned to spend 30 minutes on a 2 v. 1 drill, then a 2 v. 2 shooting drill, and you find that the players love the 2 v. 1, are working hard and are learning from it, by all means continue with it a while longer. The point is, it's a lot easier to be flexible within a pre-set framework than it is to improvise something out of nothing.

How far in advance you plan your practice sessions is up to you.

Some coaches – the well-organized types who run off schedules on their PCs and provide weekly updates of how every other team in the league is doing — like to plan out their entire year prior to their first practice. Week one, they say, we'll work on dribbling; then we'll advance to passing; by mid-season we should be far enough along to work on overlapping, or overloading one side. That's fine – provided a coach realizes there may be reasons to alter, or even scrap, this "schedule" if the season doesn't go according to plan.

Other coaches – the types who have cryptic, handwritten directions to each away field, like "turn left at the second shopping center after the apple orchard" – prefer to make their plans while driving to work the morning of the practice. Today we'll work on keeping the ball in bounds along the sideline, they say, and they'll design a practice around that concept. That's fine too – as long as there is a coherent plan somewhere.

It's not a bad idea, if you plan to scrimmage, to have pre-selected the teams. That eliminates the few minutes you'd otherwise spend dividing up the sides; it allows you to group players together the way you want, rather than having to make decisions on the spur of the moment while they're all staring you in the face. It also eliminates the temptation to have two players pick sides, which always results in the same couple of youngsters standing around unpicked at the end.

Bring everything you'll possibly need to every practice. A coach should have a checklist. It should include balls, cones (the small. easily transportable kind, rather than the heavy-duty highway monsters), pinnies for identifying teams, an up-to-date first-aid kit (including tape, bandages and ice packs), water (and cups!), and any written information relative to upcoming games and practices. Tote everything with you to the field. That's a lot easier than having to send someone to your car in the middle of practice.

Drills should progress through three levels.

First is stationary, or walk-through: next is moderately paced; finally, add pressure to the situation (in other words, make it "match-related"). How much time you spend at each level depends, of course upon such factors as the level of your players, the stage of the season, and whether they're attempting the drill for the first time or the 50th.

**Don't fail to organize things for the goalkeepers to do each practice.
Here keepers help each other with catching exercises.** (photo by Brett Whitesell)

Similarly, a practice session should proceed through three levels. First comes the purely technical phase, during which players work on such skills as passing, controlling and heading. Next comes the technical/tactical phase. Here, the technical skills can be combined with match situations, such as receiving a ball and deciding whether to lay it back to the original passer, pass it off to a teammate on the side, or turn and dribble upfield with it.

The final phase should be primarily tactical, in other words, a game-related, scrimmage-type situation. This level does not have to be practiced full-field. It can be 4 v. 4, 5 v. 4, 4 v. 5 or whatever. It can build upon a skill introduced earlier; say, short passing. If you've already drilled the skill, and added some pressure to it (i.e., put a defender on the receiver's back and given him the option of passing to either of two teammates), then in this final phase you can play a large game of keepaway, with no goals. A team "scores" by completing five short passes without the other team touching the ball. It's tactical, it's match-related, but it's not necessarily a full-field scrimmage.

Demonstrate each skill or drill, or have players demonstrate, before having the group attempt it.

No matter how good you are at explaining things, no matter how strong a communicator you are, it doesn't hurt to remember the old adage: a picture is worth a thousand words. Youngsters learn by watching, then imitating, not by listening. Don't feel bashful about not being able to demonstrate perfectly. Pick one player (not always the same one!) and let him/her show it. The players will understand. The point is, an active demonstration is much more effective – and often less time-consuming – than a lecture.

Small-sided games (3 v. 3, 5 v. 5) are better learning situations than larger-sided affairs.

There is far more ball contact – better for the youngsters, and better for you if you're trying to figure out what someone is doing wrong. Small-number situations are really what the game is about. Soccer is not truly a game of 11 v. 11; it's a microcosm: two attackers isolating one defender, or a group of three trying to work against a trio of opponents.

Alternate high-intensity drills with low- and medium-intensity ones.

If you've just had them working hard for 10 minutes, make the next drill a bit easier. The purpose of practice isn't to kill children; it's to teach them. They want to work hard, and they will, but they won't learn effectively if they're exhausted.

Don't make children run laps as punishment, or as "conditioning."

There are several reasons for this.

One: by associating running with something bad, children are taught to dislike it. Since soccer is a running game, that's obviously disadvantageous.

Two: soccer is not a game of long-distance laps; it's a game of short stop-and-go bursts of speed, punctuated by a few longer sprints. If you can tailor your running to that concept – stop-and-gos and sprints – you'll be developing a much better soccer player.

Three: soccer players need touches with the ball. The sooner they learn to run with a ball at their feet, the quicker they'll develop those elusive "ball skills."

Four: American football coaches like to assign laps as punishment. Soccer coaches shouldn't bring that mind-set to this game.

Don't neglect your goalkeepers.

They deserve specialized training for their position. If you can't give it to them, try to find a parent or older player who can. Even if you don't know as much about goalkeeping as you do about field playing, you can still give your goalies some drills of their own. Of course, it's difficult to send one or two players off to a corner to work on their own. That's why it always helps to have an assistant. Even a parent who knows nothing about the game, but can toss and fetch balls and provide a certain amount of structure, is O.K. But don't always isolate your keepers. They need field skills and they need interaction with their teammates. Include them in some of the drills you do – they're not that special. You never know when a goalie might be needed in the field. Talk often to your keepers to make certain they're getting the right training. It's an area many of us ignore.

Always include some form of shooting in a practice.

After all, the object of the game is to put the ball in the net. International observers agree that Americans are most deficient in that area. The shooting need not– indeed, should not – be the straight head-on, shooter v. goalie variety day after day. You can vary the angle, the number of defenders, the type of pass. The point is every player on the field must know how to get the ball in the back of the net. (A shooting drill can contain other elements. If you're working on, say, give-and-gos, it's just as easy to do them in the penalty area as it is at midfield.)

Be sensitive to your players' stages of development.

Select drills that are appropriate to their ages and talk to them in language they can understand. A six year-old has little sense of team play. He's got a limited attention span and needs constant movement. A 12 year-old has a great sense of team play and is eager for skill development. However, if he's suddenly started to grow, he might not be able to kick a ball as well as before. A good coach can empathize with that and design an appropriate practice around it.

Keep your teaching and coaching simple.

Don't worry about sophisticated concepts or formations. Don't try to cover everything you know in one practice, or in every practice. Introduce and reinforce only one or two key ideas per session. Even when a player makes several horrendous mistakes all at once, resist the temptation to solve every problem in one fell swoop.

Have players stretch out both before and after practice.

It's not as important with pre-pubescent children, who are active all the time and don't tighten up, but the older they get, the more important it becomes. A coach who encourages stretching prevents injuries, introduces good health and safety habits, and helps promote a sense of team unity.

Finally, a few more coaching "odds and ends".

Every player should bring a ball to every practice. That way you're always sure there are enough to go around. Players tend to chase after them a little more carefully when they go in the woods, plus you know they've got one at home for practice. (Practice at home is an idea you should encourage as much as possible.)

Let players experiment with different positions, especially during practice sessions. You never know when your reserve attacker might suddenly blossom into a first-rate defender, or your back-up goalie might show signs of becoming a great striker.

Make practices fun. Soccer is a fun game; training for it shouldn't be drudgery. If you keep your training sessions interesting, and fun, it's almost guaranteed your season will be a success.

Trust your instincts. They're usually right.

⚽

COMMON COACHING PROBLEMS: COURSES OF ACTION*
Dan Woog

Although every coaching problem is unique - different characters, different situations, different circumstances – there are often similarities. In other words, the same types of problems occur season after season, year after year, from one end of the country to the other. Although the following problems and courses of action are by no means all-inclusive, we're presenting them with the idea that they will provide a start toward understanding the problems and the search for solutions all youth coaches struggle with. There's a universality to these situations and to their solutions as well.

• The player who wants to play only one position. "I'm a left winger." "I can't play defense." "I've never played halfback before." This is a problem best nipped in the bud because the sooner a youngster learns that a soccer player is a soccer player, period – that a soccer player plays offense and defense always, that a team needs change and that different coaches see players' abilities and roles in different ways – the better off that player will be.

There are two good ways to deal with this problem. One is through communication - explaining to the team as a whole, and to the player individually, how fluid 11 positions must be (especially compared to such specialized sports as baseball and football). This verbal communication works only if the player is old enough to reason, and mature enough to have a dialogue with his coach.

The second method is to ease the player into a new role during practice. Let them get the feel for a new spot during non-threatening, non-pressure situations. Spend time teaching them new responsibilities; don't simply announce before the game, "Claudia, you're our new stopper." Follow this up with concerned questioning: "How do you like playing in the back? What's better about it, compared with striker? What's worse?" You may be surprised how many times the answer is, "It's fun!"

• The player who thinks the coach's (pick one) lineup, strategy, substitution policy, etc. is wrong. This is more insidious than the previous problem. Usually the player is older, more independent. Often, in fact, it's the better player, the one with excellent skills or a solid game sense, who is apt to challenge the coach's way of coaching.

Certainly coaches can learn from their players. Someone out on the field has a different perspective than someone on the sidelines - not always better, or worse, or righter, or wronger; just different - and the player's insights or suggestions can often be valuable. But it's the coach's job to see that those suggestions are offered at the appropriate times; that is, times designated by the coach himself. Time can be allocated during certain practice sessions for questions about strategy; that's when a rational, team-wide discussion can be held. Possibly the halftime remark, "Anyone have any comments about the first half" can elicit some responses. But no coach can allow killer statements about other players, or negative comments about coaching policy, to disrupt team unity. Criticism by players must be restricted to private conversations with the coach; breaches should result in loss of playing time.

There is a time for open discussion and a time for coach's authority; any coach who does not recognize the difference, or who abrogates his responsibility, is doing his team and his young athletes a grave disservice.

• Parental interference. This can get pretty hairy indeed. Dealing with peers, friends and colleagues is a lot different than dealing with children. Coaches need the wisdom of Solomon, the patience of Job and the diplomacy of Kissinger when interacting with the numerous and varied adults who make up the so-called "cheering section."

One clever way of dealing with parental pressure is to suggest that the parent come help you coach.

Often the loudest mouths are those who know the least. "You know, I really appreciate your interest. Could you help me run practices and take over next week when I'm away?" This will usually produce the response, "Oh, I couldn't, I don't know enough about the game." Use that line as a wedge to open a discussion about the need to let the coach operate without outside interference, unless the parent wishes to "put his money where his mouth is."

When the critics do know what they're talking about — say, your assistant, or a particularly knowledgeable parent – and they're vocal enough to be undermining your authority, organize a meeting of all the adults. Calmly confront the issue head-on, ask for criticism, answer it as rationally and articulately as you can, then stress the need for a united front. The next time the critics carp, they'll be facing pressure themselves from other parents – the middle-of-the-roaders – who will pay them less mind. To switch the maxim around, the best defense is a good offense.

• Coaching a "superstar." This is a problem? You bet! And it can take several forms. One form is the player who clearly knows more than the coach, especially when everyone else knows it too. (This is almost always an adolescent problem.) The coach must be smart enough to recognize the situation, and to admit it to himself. He must learn from the player, while not turning the team over to him. Here again, good one-to-one communication skills are a must. The coach has to impress upon the player the need for cooperation and patience, with his team and his coach, while at the same time letting the player know that he is not special, that rules or expectations will not be bent or twisted just for him.

A superstar can also present a problem if he feels he is too good for his teammates. If a coach expects his team to always feed the ball to the star, if he singles him out for constant praise and uses him for every good example, yet is loath to ever criticize him, this reinforces the player's feeling of uniqueness. Good young players should be used as examples for oth-

> **N**o coach can allow killer statements about other players, or negative comments about coaching policy, to disrupt team unity.

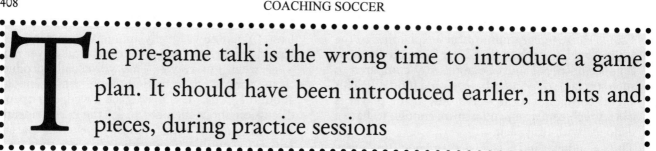

The pre-game talk is the wrong time to introduce a game plan. It should have been introduced earlier, in bits and pieces, during practice sessions

ers – but they also need to be criticized (constructively!), prodded, shown the necessity for working selflessly with others. Too many great athletes have stagnated as youngsters because they haven't been pushed: pushed to improve even more, pushed to develop team concepts and skills they'll need once they advance to a higher level of play. And a coach can't be afraid to sit a superstar down. If he misses too many practices, he should sit; if he breaks a rule, he should sit; even if he's having an off-day – and everyone does – the coach should resist the temptation to think that the star must be on the field at all times or the team will fall apart. As far as can be determined, no youth soccer player in the U.S. is God – and the sooner our youth soccer players learn this, the better.

• Disruptive players. Often players disrupt practices, or cause problems on the bench, because they're bored. And usually they're bored because they're inactive. The cures for inactivity are simple. During practices, less talking by the coach, more movement by the players, smaller groups so each youngster touches the ball more will help. During games, don't just keep your eyes glued to the field. Ask the players on the bench questions, tell them how soon you'll be substituting them in, remind them to keep cheering for their teammates. Most children are disruptive only because they want attention.

• Information overload. Youngsters' attention spans are short. They cannot handle as much information at one time as adults. Yet there are many coaches who insist upon forcing every scrap of detail they know on their players, often at the most inappropriate times.

The pre-game talk is the wrong time to introduce a game plan. It should have been introduced earlier, in bits and pieces, during practice sessions, so that players could have had time to assimilate the information and understand it thoroughly. New concepts should be introduced singly, and completely. Similarly, when reinforcing old (previously explained) ideas before a game, concentrate on one or two key ones. If you use the scattershot approach – throwing out eight or ten different thoughts, in random order, as they occur to you – you'll lose your audience entirely. (Older youngsters, in particular, are masters at looking straight at you, as if enraptured,

while their minds are a zillion miles away.)

This has the added advantage of refining your own coaching skills. It's easy to attack every problem in sight every single day, hoping something, sometime, will sink in. It's more difficult to pick out one or two ideas and reinforce them systematically; that requires foresight, planning and patience. It's like the introduction to a letter Abraham Lincoln is purported to have sent to a friend: "I would have written you a shorter note, but I didn't have time."

• Improper warm-ups before a match. Too many coaches are content to let their players kick aimlessly before a game. As much as possible, warm-ups should be match-related: goalkeepers should be working on their diving, jumping, catching, throwing and punting skills; field players should be working on controlling the ball, passing it on the ground, and working it around as much as possible. 5 v. 2 and keepaway are two good ways to include these concepts in a warm-up.

When it comes time to practice shooting, make it also match-related. Don't always use the same angle, or distance, for the drill; include defenders as defenders, too. Be certain that your corner kickers practice these prior to game time as well, especially if you're playing away. Every corner of every field is different and it doesn't hurt to test them all.

Many coaches sit their youngsters down for 15 or 20 minutes prior to a game and start telling them everything they need to know about soccer. Before a match, children are restless. They want to be active and do things, not sit and listen. Keep your comments to a minimum, especially with young children. Your coaching should really be done in practice sessions, not just prior to kick-off. On the other hand, don't let your players tire themselves out. Half an hour of warm-up is plenty. Any longer and they become tired and bored. If they run the risk of warming up too long, sit them down – but don't feel you have to bore them with soccer talk!

• Helter-skelter comments at halftime. Here again, the need for carefully-thought-out, well-organized, judicious comments is crucial. Spend the few minutes prior to halftime thinking to yourself what you want to say. That way, you won't ramble, or hem and haw, in the few minutes allotted to you.

Again, don't overburden your players. If things are

going poorly, twelve different ideas won't change things. Concentrate on one or two. If things are going OK, you probably only need to mention one or two things they can work on in the second half. If things are going well, as an old Yankee once said, "If it ain't broke, don't fix it."

Of course, half-time comments should nearly always be positive. Very little is to be gained from negative criticism, unless the players are old enough to handle it, and you use it so seldom it makes them sit up and take notice. Whenever you offer criticism, be sure to couch it in non-threatening terms: "Susie, you're heading the ball well, I know, but really, we need to keep the ball on the ground, away from their big backs."

• Failure to communicate. There are two times communication is especially important: when a player comes out of a game and when the match is over. No child likes to be substituted for. Worse, though, is coming out, walking over to the sidelines and being ignored by the coach. Every child who comes out of a game should be greeted personally by the coach. A pat on the head, shoulder or rump is good. Better is some verbal comment, such as, "Good work out there, I just needed to get Darin in." Or, "Wow, you really worked hard. Take a rest, and I'll get you back in in the second half." Even if a player was removed because he was playing poorly or couldn't handle his position, use the substitution situation to teach: "Megan, listen, next time you're in there and you're playing against someone as fast as she is, this is what you do ..." (It goes without saying, of course, that you should never, ever, remove a player immediately after he commits a mistake, no matter how grievous the error. To do so can only demoralize an already desolate youngster. Whatever you want to say to him can wait a few minutes.)

After the game is a fair time to talk a bit. You don't have to deliver an oratorical masterpiece, or go over every player's performance minute by minute, but you can wrap up the game briefly. This is what we did well, this is what we did poorly, this is what we'll work on next week, practice is at the usual time. Any questions or problems or injuries? Thank you, goodbye. Resist the temptation (and the parents who are hanging around like vultures, waiting to drive their children to their next engagement) to let everyone leave immediately after the match.

• Too many substitutions, too often. This is a mistake made most often by coaches who have never played soccer. Soccer is not football, where subs run in and out on every play bringing in secret messages from the coach. Nor is it hockey, where line shifts every 90 seconds are *de rigueur*.

In soccer, it takes at least 10 or 15 minutes for a player to get into the flow of the game, to under-

stand the rhythm of that particular match, as well as to figure out the capabilities of his particular opponent, the idiosyncracies of the field, the weather and whatever else makes every game different. It also takes that long for his legs to feel comfortable, his nervousness to disappear, his second wind to arrive. To substitute for him without giving him a chance to play at least 10 or 15 minutes (except in emergencies) is doing him a disservice. It's also unwise to send in subs in "waves," or "lines." Some coaches do it, some with notable success – the University of Connecticut's Joe Morrone comes to mind but the feeling here is that it's bad for two reasons. One is that it disrupts the flow of the game – it takes your own players on the field longer to adjust to three or six new players than it does to adjust to one or two – plus it runs counter to the international concept of the game.

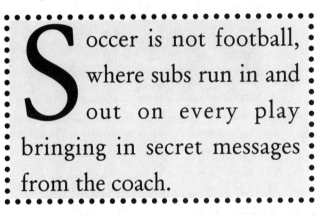

Soccer is not football, where subs run in and out on every play bringing in secret messages from the coach.

All over the world, soccer is a game of fluidity and fitness, played from start to finish with no more than two reserves. Of course, in American youth sports we want to give as many youngsters as possible a chance to participate — that's good, and every child should play in every single match — but it's not soccer when children start thinking of themselves as "the second forward line" or "the third wave of midfielders." If they see themselves in this image, they're not thinking of themselves as "soccer players" — players who can play anywhere, who are creative, intelligent athletes able to think and adapt under ever-changing, pressure-filled situations. This leads to another coaching problem.

• Stereotyping youngsters by position. It's unfair for a coach to say, "No, you can't play striker, you're a fullback." Or, "Why do you want to switch? You're doing fine at right midfield." Children are constantly changing, each at different rates. Some are growing into their bodies, while others are getting more awkward by the minute. Some suddenly become more aggressive, while others begin to lag in the capability to visualize the entire field at once. For a coach to label his players as capable of playing only one position harms them developmentally, and harms

Once the match begins the soccer coach must adopt a contemplative posture—the better to evaluate the play. Here coach Karen Richter of the University of Central Florida calmly assesses play. (photo by Perry McIntyre, Jr.)

the team tactically.

A coach must be willing to take risks with their players. If he is having problems keeping his midfield together during a game, he must be able to look down his bench and give anyone else a try - or switch in someone who's at another position on the field. And, certainly, in a runaway game, he must be willing to move players around with abandon. If you're up by several goals, it may help keep the score down – and if you're down by a few, what's the harm in trying something different?

• Failure to plan for emergencies. Every coach should know ahead of time what he will do if the unthinkable happens. Who is the third goaltender – the backup behind the backup? What formation will you use if (heaven forbid) one of your players gets red carded? If you're down by one goal in a must-win situation, and your sweeper is your best athlete, do you ever plan to move him up on attack? How about your goalie. Would you move him up, as the final "roving back"? At what point in the game would you do this?

These are the kinds of questions that a coach must think about before the game. If the coach has to spend time answering them during the match – or if he/she has never even thought of them before they arise – then they haven't done their homework.

• Too much yelling from the sideline. One of the most appealing aspects of soccer is that once the whistle blows, the players are on their own. There are no time-outs, no huddles, no strategy sessions - in other words, once the game begins, the coach has very little input into the final outcome. For those of us with big egos, that's a sobering thought. For the youngsters, that's great. They're their own coaches during a game. More than most team sports, the contest is theirs to win or lose.

"Go to the ball!" "Be aggressive!" "Mark your man!" All these are advice a coach can call out during a game. They offer good advice. But they lose their effectiveness when shouted over and over and over again. They tend not to get heard when several different people – the coach, his assistant, the parents and all the youngsters on the sidelines – are yelling them at the same time. And they are not really that revolutionary. After all, soccer players know they should win loose balls, be aggressive and mark their men. Why not try spending one or two games quietly on the sidelines. Do your teaching during practice sessions. Then let the players play during the match. Limit your advice to one or two key moments each half. You may surprise yourself at how well your players do without hearing your dulcet tones.

• Focusing on the score, rather than the play. There are 1-0 games, and then there are 1-0 games. By this we mean, consider the 1-0 match you've won against a team you usually beat 7-0. Then consider the 1-0 match you've lost against a team you've never held below five goals. Too many coaches look only at the final score. They tell their team in the first instance, "Great game!" without realizing the opposition is getting a lot better, or without warning their team that they might be getting complacent. They also tell their team in the second instance, "Well, you lost again," without congratulating them for how close this game was, or giving them encouragement that perhaps the next time the score will finally be different.

We hate to use cliches, but this one happens to be true. "It's not whether you win or lose, it's how you play the game." You can play well and lose, just as you can play poorly and win. Your team knows after a match whether it won or lost. It's your job, as coach, to tell them how they played the game.

* Ed. Note: While author Woog's article was written with the youth coach in mind, its principles are applicable at every level of coaching. That's its reason for inclusion in this chapter of the book.

THE EFFECTIVE USE OF
VIDEOTAPE ANALYSIS
Jape Shattack

INTRODUCTION

Every good training scheme sets goals and guides players toward those goals. There are many ways to do this but they all share two components:

1. The training program must communicate its goals clearly, convincingly and inspirationally to all of the players.
2. The training program must feed information back to the players as to their progress in attaining these goals.

The simplest way to meet these needs is for the coach to communicate personally, either through an accurate demonstration, or by speaking clearly and persuasively. Masterful coaches meet these communication needs economically, using the bare minimum of training time.

The master coach can convincingly paint an accurate picture for a group, detailing exactly what is his expectation of them. Videotape is one means of supplementing the coach's personal expressions. Therefore, coaches need to be as disciplined and as thoughtful with their use of videotape as they are with their use of demonstration or their use of their own voice.

While the master coach can give feedback in succinct fashion, videotape helps the educational process by minutely pinpointing and elaborating a coach's points.

OVERVIEW OF VIDEOTAPE

Videotape analysis can be used as an valuative tool for both individuals and the collective group including: 1) technique breakdown; 2) tactical analysis; 3) psychological implications.

The positive points favoring its usage are that it is 1) very specific; 2) very clear; 3) very accurate. The negative factors influencing the incorporation of vid-

EQUIPMENT

Coach Shattuck shared with the audience a handout which listed his recommendations were a coach to purchase videotape equipment. He noted that computer-driven editing systems are a coach's savior.

THE EQUIPMENT LIST:

The recommended format is S-VHS. It has High 8 quality but is interchangeable with VHS decks.

Source Deck
KVC BRS 525U DNR
    Dynamic tracking, super still,
    super slow motion......................$7,000-$9,000
JVC BRS 622....................................$3,500-$4,700

Recording Deck
JVC BRS 822U.................................$5,000-$6,400
JVC, SONY, Hitachi 4-head VCR's
    with "Jog/Shuttle" switch.................$400-$500

Controller
JVC RMG 810U parallel
    "cuts only" controller..........................$1,920
SMIA 4 Special Effects
    Keyboard Switcher..........................$300-$400

Camera
JVC GY X2 UL-13 full-sized,
    2-chip camcorder, 13:1 lens...................$8,000
Panasonic AG 455U Industrial,
    1 chip.........................$2,000-$3,000
Panasonic PVS 372 or PVS 63 #l chip,
    consumer S-VHS camcorder.....$1,300-$1,900

Monitors
TM 1400-SU 7 pin, S-VHS input...............$785
JVC TM-13U 14" basic unit......................$355

Time Code Generator/Reader
JVC SAR-22U
    (One unit per VTR)......................$500-$670
Cables..$200

Tape Stock
VHS 120 minute cassettes....................$4 each
S-VHS 120 minute cassettes.................$13 each

eotape in the coaching scheme include: 1) the expense; 2) the time consumption factor; 3) it is not immediate as previewing is needed; 4) it demands technical expertise that takes time to learn; 5) it is not always convenient.

Some feel that videotape is too exhaustive and breaks down the spontaneity of the sport. Soccer tends to become too scientific when dissected under the glare of videotape analysis!

Coaches must not become too negative to individuals/teams when dissecting soccer play. A suggestion is to alternate positive and negative comments. Further, if there are to be negative comments about a player, that he or she might be consulted in advance to request permission to use a sequence which might place him/her in a negative light.

USES OF VIDEOTAPE

Confirmation of problem

Following his freshman year, the Duke coaching staff was concerned with the behavior of Bobby Hurley. There was a perception within the team that he was showing too much disgust with referee's decisions and as a result was losing focus on the subsequent game activity; he was losing his concentration. With the objective of improved leadership training, the coaching staff had Bobby select game scenes that clearly showed his facial contortions following referee's calls. By seeing himself in action, the problem had real clarity. He now could begin to work on the problem, and his leadership ability during his last years at Duke was at a higher level.

Coach Bob Bradley (formerly at Princeton) watches every game tape two times before he lets his team view it. In that way he makes certain to be objective in his analysis.

Recruiting

A highlight tape with music is a great sales tool!

Scouting

Soccer teams should begin to share tapes with opponents as do other sports. It saves money.

Setting practice objectives

Sometimes by using videos before a practice session to demonstrate the theme of a practice session, a lackluster team attitude can be changed. Sigi Schmid of UCLA subscribes to using tape in this manner.

WHERE/WHEN ARE PLAYERS SHOWN VIDEOTAPES

A survey of college coaches found videos most commonly viewed in the following settings: 1) the locker-room; 2) team meeting rooms; 3) on buses; 4) the coach's office; 5) at home; 6) before training; 7) in place of training; 8) after a light training session; 9) during team travel; 10) apart from training.

VIDEO AS AN INSTRUCTOR OF VALUES

By selecting segments of matches of the team, the coach can use video to demonstrate: 1) individual and collective intensity; 2) perseverance; 3) love of the game; 4) honesty; 5) excellence — here the use of Italian League tapes, etc., is the best teacher; 6) humor/perspective — here the viewing of a *Fish Called Wanda* can do wonders for a team that is wound a little too tight.

Where in the season to insert video into the coaching scheme is important. Pre-season, early season, regular season and post-season all place emphases on individuals and the team that a coach must recognize in making selection of video material for consumption.

SURVEY OF CURRENT USES OF VIDEOTAPE

Coach Shattuck shared with the audience the current uses of videotape in a cross section of collegiate soccer programs.

Purpose	Content	Methods
Goal setting	1. Motivational tapes	Commercial highlights
	2. Team tactics	TV games
	3. Team intangibles	Custom highlight tapes
		Commercial movies
Feedback	Team tactics	Custom highlight/lowlights
	Restarts	Custom highlight/lowlights
	Individual performance	Selected match portions
	Phase of play	Selected match periods
Practice planning	Previous match	Review by coach
	Previous several games	Review by coach
Archive/Recruiting	Full season	Edited highlight tape
Scouting	Tapes of opponents	Selected portions
Team selection	Tapes of practice games	Selected portions

SOLUTIONS TO VIDEOTAPE PROBLEMS

Expense

Share costs with another team. Or fundraise (Bob Warming at Creighton fundraised $14,000 for equipment!). Use of institution's equipment.

Camerawork

Use the same person throughout the season. Pay them out of your budget. High school/youth coaches can use booster club members or parents. Use students from college cinema departments. Give academic credit to cinema students to develop a highlight video.

Time

Delegate your assistant coach or grad coach to oversee the operation. Purchase computer-aided editing system ($14K!) to cut down on time commitment. Such equipment can break down game s into two—five themes (passing, shooting, defensive repossessions, restarts, saves, etc.). The coach must first go through the entire game tape and pick out scenes that he or she believes fit into categories that have been chosen to analyze. He then notes the location of those scenes electronically and then the machine will automatically sort those choices onto assigned tapes.

Viewing Time

Use bus travel time or the occasion of a pre-game meal. Many coaches use motel "down time" as video time. Incidently, camera angles are very important. In viewing the Portugal-Ireland match, one can see from shots taken at three different angles that the information perceived was different from one camera shot to the next.

It just points out that while video is a great learning tool — it is not foolproof.

⚽

PROMOTION, MARKETING AND PUBLIC RELATIONS ISSUES IN COACHING

SOCCER MARKETING: SOME TIPS ON ATTRACTING SOCCER SPONSORSHIP
Lynn Berling-Manuel

Have you ever had your landlord skip your rent because he loved soccer so much?

Has your grocer ever accepted your soccer registration card in lieu of payment?

Has your local soccer store ever given you all the free uniforms you want for the "love of the game"?

It's doubtful that you've experienced any of these occurrences, yet that is exactly how many organizations approach potential sponsors and even potential fans.

When you want to attract a sponsor or a fan to your program or project it takes a combination of an attractive "product", an attention to detail and the clear realization that neither the sponsor nor the fan owe you, your program or soccer anything. In fact, when you approach a sponsor or a fan, your job is to put yourself in THEIR shoes and determine what you can do for THEM. Coming up with money for a program, a team or an event is no easy trick and usually the only two sources of revenue are fans and sponsors. One way or the other you're asking for money and support, so your job is to make sure they get what they want.

What is a sponsor? What makes a company, large or small, want to give money to your team program or project? What does it take to convince them your particular project is worthy of their support and what do they expect in return?

A sponsor, simply defined, is any organization or company that gives a project funds or merchandise in exchange for exposure. And when a company or organization donates money, it isn't going to be because of its love of soccer – at least not strictly speaking – because it also must make good sense from a business point of view. And that's the point of view you, as the group or individual looking for sponsors, must also adopt.

There will be the occasional individual "sponsor" who simply acts as a patron to a program and donates money with no desire for recognition. But this is a very rare breed. For most programs, it will be the business sponsor that you'll be approaching.

Even though giant corporations may seem like an endless source of money, they, just like the landlord, grocer or soccer store owner, must be able to justify each expenditure by how it will contribute to their bottom line. For a smaller company, which will be the most likely target of your sponsorship solicitation, making its involvement attractive from a business point of view is even more critical because it has fewer dollars to spend.

Why should a company, any company, give your program money? Sure, you'll get better uniforms or you'll be able to put on a luncheon at the tournament or pay for something else you'd like to add to the event. But again, what does the sponsor get?

Determining what the sponsor wants to get, and making sure that he can get it, is what selling sponsorships is all about. It may sound crass and commercial, but you're asking someone to give you money and if you were in his shoes, wouldn't you want the same?

The key to selling a sponsor on your program, trip or tournament is to put yourself in his shoes. That's

No matter how attractive your program seems to you, don't tell a sponsor it can do more than it really can.

the simplest, and often most difficult, advice you'll ever receive, but it is the only way to attract a sponsor to your program. Most companies, both large and small, use three primary means of getting new customers and therefore increasing business. The first is advertising, the second is promotion and the third is word of mouth. With a sports sponsorship, a company hopes to combine all three and it is this need that you must fill.

Sponsorships are essentially promotions. In other words they are promoting the product or company, but not selling directly as an advertisement does. Yet via the promotion, a company will want to obtain new customers. If you can add in an advertising element and plenty of word of mouth, you probably have a sale on your hands. You are selling when you go out and pursue sponsors, yet that shouldn't intimidate you. Selling is really only the process of matching up products or services with a customer who will find them useful and making sure that the consumer gets the information. In this case the consumer is your potential sponsor and your job is to pick a sponsor who will get good mileage from your program by making sure that you present the information in a concise, interesting and honest fashion.

Let's take an example:

Your high school team would like to host a tournament. You would like to invite the five key schools in your area and pick up the tab for a banquet, awards, minor travel expenses, tickets, etc. In your case a local sponsor would probably be your best bet, or a national sponsor that has targeted your area as one of its key markets.

Let's say you select a local pizza chain as your prospect. You know that this is a type of restaurant that's always looking for teen business and you'll have at least the teams as a beginning group to offer the business. But what if you advertised in the local high school papers and used the sponsor's name? Perhaps you advertise that everyone at the game will receive a discount pizza coupon for after the game. If you print the ticket with the pizza restaurant's logo, you could have the ticket serve as the "discount coupon". That's double exposure for your sponsor. Could his logo go on anything else? Can you insure that he gets more than one exposure? (Perhaps besides the ticket coupon good for after the game, you also distribute a coupon good for a future use.) Can you hang a banner with the restaurant's name? If you're asking for big bucks, perhaps you can make it the "XYZ Pizza

Tournament" which would mean a much greater likelihood that the sponsor's name would appear in the newspaper coverage of the tournament.

Speaking of coverage, that's the key element that every sponsor is looking for. Handling press and public relations may end up being your most significant organizational task. Send out a press release, including a personal invitation with tickets, to the local sportswriters and editors (and don't forget local dignitaries such as the mayor, city council, school superintendent, etc.).

One juice company spokesman still talks about putting up several thousands of dollars to help out a team that had qualified for the regional level of a national tournament. The coach was interviewed several times, but never once mentioned the sponsor's helpful involvement. That juice company will probably be leery of sponsoring a soccer project again. It is remembering all these little things that makes a sponsor happy. Here are some more tips on working with a sponsor:

- Put your proposal in writing. Make it easy to read, concise and short on fluff.
- Make your proposal specific. Tell the potential sponsor exactly what this program will do for him. Exposure is terrific, but what does it really mean in terms of sales?
- Price it in a realistic way. Be able to justify the price, both in terms of what you want and what the sponsor receives in return.
- Don't change the price because someone has more money. Even large companies get annoyed when the same proposal crosses their desk asking twice the price of what you would have charged a smaller company. Don't assume that word doesn't travel because you'll be amazed at how often it does.
- Start small. If this is your first experience at selling a program to a sponsor, don't start with a tournament for 90 teams. Start with local sponsors for one game (maybe homecoming or your most arch rival), one clinic or one award. Develop a successful track record of not just selling to a sponsor, but also fulfilling your obligation in a successful fashion. Nothing is easier to sell than a track record.
- Find a need and fill it. This is the legendary advice of all great salespeople. If you can find a need that your program will fill, you've probably got a sale.

For example, if a local company needs more foot traffic, a sponsor program that includes a coupon that must be redeemed in the store will be very attractive.

- Know your consumer. Whether it's a fan or a sponsor, here is where your homework will pay off. For sponsors, do some research and find out what market they're going after: kids, teenagers, parents, male, female? The big names like Coke or Met Life are always attractive, but thousands of groups are approaching them and you may find there's a store or company right in your neighborhood that needs the kind of exposure you have to offer. If you've got a children's tournament, but your sponsor prospect is seeking a teenage audience, you'll probably hit a dead end.

- Realize your program's limitations. No matter how attractive your program seems to you, don't tell a sponsor it can do more than it really can. You may be able to have a sponsor's name on your team's jerseys or use their balls, shoes or whatever, but you can't usually guarantee press coverage to anybody but a titled sponsor; and you can't usually guarantee increased sales. You can only lay out a good case with plenty of information and substantiation. If you've chosen the right potential sponsor and you've matched up your project well, that will be your best shot.

- Don't forget aftermarketing. Can you send all the participants a letter thanking them in the sponsor's name? Can you supply a mailing list of all the audience for the sponsor to do a follow-up mailing? Or could your team follow-up with a clinic at the sponsor's place of business?

- Always go the extra mile. Always give more than expected. Keep the sponsor informed as the project progresses. Send them a thank-you note. Put the sponsor's logo or slogan on more than was agreed. Take every opportunity to tell the press about the sponsor's involvement. Don't skimp on your time or your resources. The sponsors are the funding backbone of your program and you want them to have had a very happy experience when the program is complete. They'll be back and they'll advise their associates of the quality of your program.

- Don't forget your fans. That's the consumer that the sponsor is trying to reach. Be sure your fans are well taken care of and again, put yourself in their shoes. What would they find fun? A band show at halftime? A preliminary game of six-year-olds? A clinic? Turn every event into a good time and you can't go wrong. A great game is a good beginning, but what can you add to give your audience even a better time? It will keep them coming back for more.

COACHES: MAKE IT EASIER FOR THE SPORTS REPORTER
Matt Robinson

One of my experiences was as a sports reporter covering high school and college athletics, including soccer. In the position I interviewed coaches and players and fielded phone calls. After playing experiences at the high school and college levels I appreciate the views of both sides. As a player I often was disturbed about the lack of coverage about my team and more than once I did not receive credit for a goal or an outstanding play. I realize now that in some cases a reporter is to blame, but in many cases the blame is the coach's. As a reporter I have dealt with uncooperative coaches who have been responsible for the reporter receiving incomplete or incorrect information.

In order for a reporter to do his job effectively, the coach must act as the public relations arm of the team. Even though many colleges have sports information departments that know what a reporter is looking for, the coach is still the main source of information. He knows the most about his team and what happened in a game. Developing a rapport with reporters, participating in postgame interviews, providing preseason information and offering ideas for feature stories are ways a coach can succeed in that capacity. These suggestions will not only allow the reporter to write more detailed and better developed stories, but it will also help give a team or team members and the sport proper recognition.

DEVELOPING A RAPPORT WITH SPORTS WRITERS

A successful coach takes pride in his work, and a successful sports reporter is no different. Although some coaches have an unfavorable view of the press, it must be remembered the sports reporters are just trying to do their job. People want to know what happened and the writer provides that service. A coach who is reluctant to talk, and who is not cooperative in providing information is creating a bad rapport with the reporter. If the reporter does not have the information or quotes to write a good story, it is the readers and the deserving players that suffer. If a reporter continues to remain on bad terms with the coach, he will not make an effort to cover a game or do a story on one of the players. Develop a working relationship with the reporters. Make an effort to be available after games, even if your team loses, and to answer or return phone calls, especially if the reporter has made the effort to come to the game or to phone you.

How To Talk With The Media

Frank Marra

If the opportunity arises when you get to talk to the media, you'll want to make the most of it.

- There is no such thing as an off-the-record comment. If you don't want to be quoted - mum's the word.

- Never "wing" interviews. Take the time to collect your thoughts and look up appropriate information. It's more important to be accurate than be quick.

- Don't ramble. Offer brief, to-the-point answers to reporters' questions.

- Don't let reporters put words in your mouth. Just because a reporter uses in a question a particular word or phrase doesn't mean you have to use the same phrase in your answer. Example: "Is player Smith a problem to handle? Your answer: "Jim Smith does have a problem keeping training rules." Your answers will be remembered more than the reporters' questions. Beware!

- Tell the truth, even if it hurts. In other words, you coached poorly, the team was ill-prepared, etc. Credibility is critical. You won't have any if you distort the truth.

- Before the interview, select one or two positive points you want to make and weave them into your answers. If you are trying to build up a player or if there is a particular phase of the game that you gave attention to in practice and then incorporated in the match itself, explain these facts to the reporter. In this way you publicly reward your players and team for their work.

- Never guess or speculate – never second-guess things. While it may rid you of frustrations, remember to never second-guess your players in public. They do hang on your comments – be they in private or in public. Never speak for the other coach.

- Don't bluff. If you don't know the answer to a question, say so. Have as much material ready, record books, schedules, statistics, etc., as possible. But if for some reason there is a question you can't answer – get back to the reporter – but don't bluff.

- Practice out loud. Set up mock interviews so that you can anticipate questions a reporter might ask. Listen to yourself on tape and correct those things that, if you were the reporter, you would find aggravating.

One helpful hint in developing this rapport is to develop your own predetermined guidelines. Some reporters may be pushy in trying to obtain information. If you make your guidelines known (i.e., when you are available to talk, if you want your players to be interviewed, etc.) a responsible reporter will adhere to them. If these guidelines are broken then you can turn the matter over to the reporter's editor. Both parties can benefit from this understanding. The reporter satisfies his readers with a interesting story.

The Post-Game Interview

Although the reporter watches a game for the details of who scored the goal and at what time, the reader wants to hear from the coach about what really happened. That is where the post-game interview becomes important. A coach's quotes give the reporter's story credibility. A reader will appreciate a coach's explanation of a certain play or his evaluation of a star player. In fact, the reporter sometimes bases his entire story on a post-game remark. Who knows more about what happened on the field than the person who was responsible for planning it?

I have seen many coaches lose their communicative powers, so evident while on the sidelines, when a reporter is standing in front of him with a notepad and pen after the game. The best advice is to forget he is a reporter and pretend you're talking with a friend or spouse about the game. A yes-no answer really does not help a reporter. If the reporter asks you about a certain play, go into detail about it. Did you work on it in practice? Was it luck? When he asks about a player explain the type of player he is. Do you expect that from him every game? Was it his first game as a starter? Was he sick with the flu all week? The more you elaborate the more informative the story will be.

Providing Preseason Information

A good way to make sure none of your players has his name misspelled or class year reported incorrectly is to provide preseason information. On the college level the sports information department usually compiles a brochure, but on the high school or small college level all it takes is a typed information sheet. The information sheet should include players' names, uniform numbers, (both home and away if they are different) class, position, and if he has earned any notable honors: all-league honors, starter, letterwinner. Career goals, career saves, etc., is another statistic worth inclusion. A newspaper's sports department will keep this on file and refer to it if there is a question on the spelling of a name or the class of a player that comes up. The players' numbers can be used for identifying players in a photo.

The Post-Game Phone Call

A sports department does not have the luxury of sending a reporter to every soccer game nor the space to have a detailed story on every one. Although a reporter is not at the game, it still may turn out to be an exciting game that warrants a detailed story. It is an unwritten rule among coaches that the home coach calls in the results. It is up to him to provide the game information, even if he is on the losing end.

The coach should call in the results. Although a scorekeeper may be competent in keeping the score, he may not realize the significance of particular goals or plays. When the coach calls in the game he can relay the keys in the outcome of the game. Was it the other team's defensive strategy that stopped the star midfielder? A coach should know the most significant factors of a victory or defeat, a scorekeeper may not. The reporter may also be able to use a coach's quote in the story.

It is also important to have first names of the members of the opposing team. A newspaper can't print a last name without a first name. Although the reporter fielding the call in some cases can take the time to get the information by calling the other coach, it is just time better spent in writing the story. In the case of a college game he may not be able to gain that information if the opponent is from out-of-town. An easy way to avoid this problem is for the coach to have the scorekeeper record both first and last names of all opponents in the scorebook before the game starts.

To add to the story, have statistics available. Was it the fifth win in a row? Did a player tie the school record for goals in a season? Did the coach earn his 200th career victory? Once again it is news and the person deserves the recognition. It may be a bother for a tired coach to make the call after going through a long, arduous game, but in the long run it is helping the newspaper develop a more detailed story while giving recognition to some players or a team, even if they are not yours, who are deserving of it. In this way, the cooperative coach is doing his bit for the sport of soccer.

SUGGESTING A FEATURE STORY

A feature story gives the reader a chance to acquaint himself with a player or coach whose name appears in game stories. The reader meets the league's leading goal scorer whose hobby is sky diving, or the player who only played the game for one year before being named all-league, or the team that has an unusual pregame ritual.

In many cases a good feature story jumps right in the face of a reporter or sometimes he stumbles upon one. I have had both occur. Another way that does not depend so much on luck is a call from a coach. In most cases a sports writer only gets to know the player on the field. He doesn't get to see him in the other aspects of life. A coach does. He knows his players' personalities and characteristics. A call to a reporter about a player can't hurt. The reporter may be searching for a story idea at the time and your player might be the answer. The readers are interested in getting to know the players they read about in game stories. Why not make it one of yours?

SUMMARY

The suggestions I have offered might add a few more minutes to a coach's long day, but in the long run it is the sport, players and the newspaper reader that benefit. You can be an important factor in giving both deserving players and the sport recognition they deserve while helping the sports reporter do his job. So do yourself a favor and make things easier for the sports writer. A little forethought and planning will

start to bridge some gaps in your soccer team's ability to attract better media coverage.

⚽

THE CARE AND FEEDING OF THE NEWS: A COACH'S GUIDE TO PUBLIC RELATIONS
Lynn Berling-Manuel

I. Good public relations is not strictly based on winning games.
II. Sports newspeople are there to report news, not give publicity.
III. Be prepared to sell your story to the media:
 • Explain why the story is worth printing.
 • Editors always have more material than they can print.
IV. Begin by defining your goals for your public relations program.
 • Be realistic.
 • Be specific.
 • Put them in writing.
 • Copies of your plans and objectives should be held by everyone in your program.
 • P.R. won't work miracles if there is no substance to your program.
V. Getting Organized
 • Establish two card files:
  1. Resource people to draw upon.
  2. Outlet file - every place you can gain publicity – include notes on peculiarities of dealing with specific outlets.
 • Media Kits: Remember, if you don't do it, it most likely won't get done. It is your team's profile:
  1. Always type releases.
  2. Use good action photos.
  3. Fact sheet on team.
  4. Biographies on players and coaches.
  5. Photos of individual players and coaches and other key personnel.
  6. Include black and white copy of team logo.
VI. Dealing with Editors:
 • Put yourself in the editor's shoes for a change.
 • Try to determine what the editor is looking for in an article so that its form and content fit the publication.
 • Write a short note to an editor; phone calls are not that good a basis for beginning a relationship.
 • Never put editors on a spot with "...why didn't you print my story?" You probably made errors in writing or content that make it too hard to print.
 • Meet deadlines – if you are late, turn it into a feature article.

- Be courteous – send editors press passes, tickets, etc. They make life easier for an editor.
- Always have one person only contact the press. Send in that person's name and day/night phone numbers to the editor.
- Thank-you notes are always appreciated by editors.

VII. What makes a story special:
- Read the publication you are sending to – understand the perspective of the publication. Make sure the nature of your article is compatible with the nature of publisher.
- Get names and facts correct. It is very embarrassing to the editor if you are wrong in what you supply.
- Make articles short, concise and accurate.
- Always type and double space your copy.
- Never be vague.

VIII. Good P.R. can get you a sponsor:
- Develop a written proposal emphasizing what the sponsor will get from his support dollars or services.
- Show a budget.
- Involve your sponsor as much as possible.
- Maintain a continuous flow of information to the sponsor of what you are doing and your accomplishments.
- Send thank-you notes, send tickets, plaques, etc., to let sponsor know you are appreciative.
- Be sure to keep a file of clippings, later present to sponsor.

IX. Don't get confused—major news outlets are not the only outlets:
- Shoppers guides.
- Foreign language papers.
- Newsletters—from various organizations.
- Radio and TV may just need a news short.
- Provide data for reporter prior to match, tournament, etc.

X. Newsletters:
- Give quick, concise news.
- Tips, calendars are useful in newsletters.

XI. Budget your money effectively: Never force your P.R. people to spend their personal money to give your operation P.R.

SOLUTIONS TO COMMON SEASONAL ISSUES

COMING TO GRIPS WITH DEFEAT
Compiled by Chris Malone

The following attempts to delve into one more aspect of the psychology of coaching: "How do you come to terms with defeat?" and "How do you handle the locker room after a loss?" No matter what one believes about winning, losing can definitely be psychologically painful. Soccer players and coaches are individualistic in the way they express their emotions and behaviors after suffering defeat. A combination of disappointment, anger, depression, and other emotional reactions are normal behaviors and to be expected from both coaches and players. Unfortunately, sometimes our emotions cause our behaviors to be inappropriate after a losing experience.

The following comments by selected coaches are offered to the membership as suggestions for handling defeat in a positive and meaningful way. Some experiences of these coaches are appropriate for us as coaches, while others may not necessarily relate to our own coaching situations.

COACHES' COMMENTS

Mike Berticelli (then UNC-Greensboro) views defeat as a learning experience. He suggests that, "We must look at defeat as an unpleasant learning experience. Every student-athlete has studied at one time or another very hard for an exam, felt well prepared and then somehow failed the test. He then must stop and look for a reason. It usually is his preparation for the exam. What makes the low test score so difficult to accept is that the student prepared long and hard for the exam, but the study plan was incorrect." Berticelli believes that coming to terms with defeat in soccer is not different. As in most test situations, the soccer game is won or lost during the preparation.

Therefore, as coaches and players, we must evaluate how and why the game was lost. There are many methods for evaluating a defeat, but the most important consideration is to be realistic in our evaluation and in our approach to explaining these reasons to our players.

Billy Charlton (U.S. Army) provides coaches with a realistic approach to dealing with defeat. He suggests that, "The defeat at the hands (or feet) of an opponent who outclassed and outplayed my team is easy to handle. I give the opponent appropriate recognition and my own team appropriate praise. However, the defeat at the hands (or feet) of an opponent of lesser caliber than my own team is a different situation. In the locker room after the game, I have each player give an analysis of the game and an analysis of his own performance. After identifying faulty play, the player must then give recommendations as to how to correct the problem areas. At the end of the session, I summarize and try to get the players to think positively about themselves and about the team."

While many coaches will attempt to deal with defeat immediately after a game, other coaches suggest that more positive things will occur by waiting until the next day or practice session. Tom Griffith (then at Dartmouth) feels that, "After a loss, we will usually

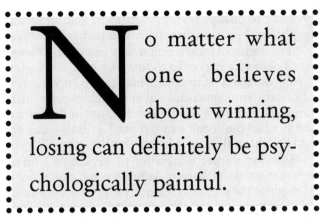

No matter what one believes about winning, losing can definitely be psychologically painful.

not go into the locker room and have match analysis. The players are too upset, and they don't want to hear anything right then, in my opinion. We usually make a brief general comment, then stay around to talk briefly with each player and make sure no arguments, bickering, etc. break out which could affect overall team spirit and morale. If we lose, the next day we analyze the match, give the other team credit if they deserve it, and then go over what we did incorrectly to lose the match, what we can do better to prevent the same errors, etc." Gordon Jago agrees with the concept of waiting until tomorrow after his team is defeated, but suggests that coaches immediately offer a few brief words, such as, "We have some problems" — "it was a poor performance" — "You go away and think about your performance and we shall discuss it tomorrow."

John Cossaboon (then North Texas Youth State Soccer Association) attempts to consider the psychological dimensions of defeat for his players when setting up a future match analysis session. Cossaboon believes that defeat is never accepted by those involved in a given contest immediately after competition. Therefore, "It is too much to ask of a young player to come off of a losing effort and immediately look for those things that could improve the next effort. For this reason, I tend to simply go over the upcoming plans from an organizational and administrative standpoint. They don't want to be told that they played well or poorly. Players simply need some time to deal with the loss in their own way. If I feel my players need to be thinking about some general aspect of their team play, I might suggest something just to set up the general concepts to be covered in the following training sessions, but I don't advise pointing out individual weaknesses at this emotional time. Finally, there will be those players who need some feedback from the coach immediately following a loss. This must be read by the coach and dealt with on an individual basis."

Whether a coach provides immediate feedback after a game or avoids discussing the game until future training sessions is a decision that each coach must make. This decision may be based upon a coach's philo-

sophical approach to coaching. For example, Hank Steinbrecher (Boston University at the time) believes that how a coach deals with defeat is a matter of priorities. Steinbrecher does not emphasize winning, but rather individual and team goals for each match. Therefore, "If we lose and still play to our potential then everyone should be happy. It is only when we do not cooperate and meet our goals that defeat enters into the picture. Our priorities are brotherhood, playing good soccer, winning. Winning without the first two is shallow. We never talk of defeat or corrections after a game until the next practice."

John Eden (then North Babylon H.S., NY) has a similar approach to defeat as Steinbrecher. He suggest that, a coach's comments, whether immediately after the game or at the next practice, should not be influenced by the outcome of the game. "They should be influenced by what can be improved. Normally more mistakes are made in defeats but many mistakes are also made in victories. The first hour of the next practice following a match, and later sessions if necessary, should be designed to correct the mistakes, whether they are technical, tactical or both."

Jeff Vennell (then Kenyon College, OH) also agrees with a philosophical approach to handling defeat. He believes that, "Defeat or victory are not proper terms for performance, they simply define the outcome of competition. Teaching goals, determination and desire to succeed are more important measures. Defeat or victory should be dealt with in these terms. A measure of where the team and individuals are, and where the team and individuals have to go is what a contest is all about."

CONCLUSION

As coaches we all have our own distinct coaching style, and how we deal with defeat is an integral part of our coaching style. Whether we immediately address defeat in the locker room, or wait until a future training session, is our choice. However, there are several psychological dimensions of our players and ourselves which must be considered.

Emotions and consequently behaviors of both players and coaches can be severely influenced by winning or losing. Perceptions of game situations may be distorted by these intense emotions. Therefore, coaches and players are both capable of making inaccurate evaluations of a loss. Even after a "cooling off" period, inaccurate judgments made immediately after a contest may not be eradicated, and can possibly affect future team and individual performance.

Perhaps coaches should use the time immediately after a loss to attend to players' individual needs, whether they be psychological or medical needs. Furthermore, coaches may create a future reference point by placing general aspects of past performance in their players' minds. Remember, some players and coaches want to be left alone after losing. Evaluations of individual and team performances should be done in a constructive match analysis situation. Coaches and players must both realistically assess their performances and not offer excuses.

Coaches may be concerned more with evaluating how they prepared their team, while players can concentrate on their mistakes, correct them and move forward. The overall philosophical approach of the coach to winning plays an important role in how a team reacts to defeat. An overemphasis on winning can lead to an overreaction to losing. Coaches and players lose together, and therefore must deal with losing together.

⚽

MOTIVATION OF SOCCER PLAYERS - A SURVEY
Compiled by Tim Schum

Coaching as defined by most experts in the field consists of four major areas of consideration: 1.) Technical training; 2.) Tactical training; 3.) Fitness training and 4.) Mental preparation.

The fourth dimension of coaching, the mental-psychological aspect, is something which intrigues many soccer coaches. Each coach has a certain mode of dealing with the psychological dimension of their team.

In the spring of the year the author mailed 200 questionnaires to selected NSCAA members to solicit their thoughts on several questions pertaining to the area labeled "Psychology of Coaching." The questions delved into the areas of motivation, team morale, cooperation vs. competition, discipline, role of substitutes, and dealing with defeat.

As coach Mel Lorback states in his overview on motivation, empirical studies on motivation and concrete definitions on the subject of motivation are few. "What works for you" may be the right answer. Nevertheless, following are some thoughts sent along by NSCAA coaching members which seek to shed light on this mystical portion of coaching.

The question directed to the group of coaches was: What does motivation mean to you and how do you motivate your players?

"Motivation is having the players mentally in a state where they perform best and they WANT to perform. Motivation is influenced by all the environment surrounding a player including press, fans, wife, girl friend, habits, basic personality, money, home crowd (and away), club atmosphere, excitement of opponent, anger, fear, ego, team attitude towards game, youth, professionalism, coach's personality and handling abil-

ity. I like to change (vary) practices to help motivate the players." — Al Miller, then Tampa Bay Rowdies.

"The degree of motivation is very important. Never try to deceive a player in motivating him, Don't try to impress them with something that is not significant. Vary your motivational approach in each situation and knowing what approach to use in each situation is what can make a difference." — Bob Guelker, then Southern Illinois at Edwardsville

"Motivation means inspiring players to play up to their potential. You must determine the psychological needs of the players. Generally all players need recognition, approval and self-esteem. Meeting these needs is best accomplished through praise and constructive criticism and being sensitive to the individual athlete's needs. Motivation also implies setting attainable goals and convincing players to believe they can reach these goals. Personality of the coach dictates what kind of motivator he is. Fear can be turned into a constructive force by instilling in players what is expected of them, what the goals are and what they must do to reach the goals." — Klaas deBoer, former NASL Los Angeles Aztecs coach.

"We look for players who are already motivated and try to create an environment in which they can fulfill their potential." — Richard Broad, former George Mason University (VA).

"Hopefully, the players motivate themselves and maintain a constant level of desire to play well each time out. This is preferable to peaks and valleys. Some matches need no priming or pushing from the coach; others "less important" have to be brought to their notice. Logic and consistency rather than hype have more lasting effects in motivation." — Howard Goldman, former Marist College (NY) .

"Make each game special unless it is special and then the coach may need to downplay the game to ease tension." — Ron Newman, then San Diego Sockers.

"I do not believe in 'pep talks'! I try to save any inspirational talks for the few most critical games or parts of a game. To me motivation means one thing: you, the player, and the team must have one thought CONSTANTLY in mind during practice sessions: improvement! This requires concentration, 100% of the time. It is very difficult to achieve, but there isn't any substitute for it." — These were the comments of NSCAA Secondary Coach of the Year John Eden of then North Babylon High School (NY).

"There are two primary aspects of motivation, individual and group. Motivation is the process of arousing an individual or group to achieve greater heights than they believe possible. Individually this is only done by building an intimate relationship with the player. Collectively this is done by fostering a sense of esprit de corps." — Hank Steinbrecher, then Boston University

"By motivation we mean to assure ourselves that our players' goal is to excel and when this is true, more often than not, they will be successful." — Ibrahim M. Ibrahim, then Clemson University.

"Motivation is very much an individual, inner drive that causes the player to perform well. The coach must understand and appreciate each player's motives. He must then identify the common denominator acceptable to all his players before he can provide the outer stimulus, or inducement, which encourages and inspires the team to perform as a unit." — Billy Charlton, U.S. Army Soccer Coach

"Motivation is the incentive or desire that causes or influences an athlete to do something. Incentive or desire is related to expectancy—anticipation that a particular result is the outcome of a particular behavior. I attempt to get the athletes to realize that self-motivation is the most important part of motivation; things such as working when they don't want to, budgeting of time for studies, sleep, etc, and setting priorities. Practices should be interesting and rewarding and variety is a help here. Positive reinforcement should be used, not harping on what went wrong. Players should understand what the practices are meant to accomplish and goals should be set for each practice." — Jeff Vennell, then Kenyon College

"Motivation to me is the ability to continually rise to the excitement and challenge of a new goal, regardless of how immediately attainable that goal may seem to be. We motivate by constantly challenging them with both short and long range goals. A short range goal may be as minimal as the successful completion of a drill with various restrictions imposed. Or it may be a long range goal such as making the "Final Four" at season's end. The player's experience in attaining both short and long range goals, along with variety and creativity provided by the coach, is the true key to motivation." — Mike Berticelli, then North Carolina University, Greensboro

"I am fortunate to have a winning tradition; more than enough talented players; several assistants; and there is pressure on the players due to strong community and peer group support for soccer. Motivating our players and creating the proper attitude is our biggest challenge. Motivating means assisting people to bring an increased percentage of their potential to bear on a mutually-shared goal. We have found that the

forming of mutual seasonal and short range (match) goals has enabled us to work toward success against a statistical model. If you start with realistic goals relative to the team's technical and tactical abilities—then it is amazing what statistical records can be amassed. All too frequently, highly motivated teams are as much a product of the chemistry of the mix of personalities and identifying the long-term goal they all share and that is a topic all its own." — Gary Avedikian, then Centerville High School (OH).

"Having compiled a record of 118-4-2 (four years), having won our Berks Conference title in each of the last seven years, we have a "built-in" stimulus which motivates our current squad each year. They attempt to emulate older brothers, friends or classmates who have contributed to the program in previous years." — Ray Buss, then Fleetwood High School (PA).

"Motivation is an attitude of the mind that brings about a controlled, but very determined performance. I draw on a player's pride of performance to motivate him and also use the club's reputation of success and future rewards in terms of status and finance," — Gordan Jago, former Tampa Bay Rowdie coach

"Stressing the importance of being physically and mentally fit will help enhance the motivation factor among your players. Motivation is also helped by reminding the players that what they do will reflect on something much larger than themselves, their institution!" — Bill Hughes, then Roberts Wesleyan College (NY).

"Motivation refers to the level of desire of an individual to attain his/her full potential. The level of motivation dictates the degree of sacrifice and effort put towards a given goal. Motivation techniques are nearly as numerous as individuals. Some players are affected more by an outside motivational force (i.e., coach, parent, peers, honors) while others draw effort from deep within. I personally try to get my players to look within themselves regarding effort, training habits and general habits. By attempting to make them look at themselves and feel accountable for their actions, I feel they will establish longer lasting and far more important values, in relation to the game and life in general." — John Coosaboon, then North Texas State Youth Soccer Association.

"We motivate our players from day one of their soccer careers by trying to get them to have a disciplined approach to things — doing things correctly all the time — on and off the field. Generally speaking our players are motivated from within to do well and

> Empirical studies on motivation and concrete definitions on the subject of motivation are few. "What works for you."

because our schedule is so competitive and the league so balanced, it is not too tough to get them up. We have a saying that helps everything -'Respect all; fear none'." — Tom Griffith, then Dartmouth College.

"A soccer player is motivated when he is prepared physically and mentally for the match. He knows his training should carry him successfully through match play. Genuine motivation does not occur in a speech given before a game. It is developed concomitantly in a systematic, progressive, rigorous training program. Win or lose, the potential to play your best depends on how prepared you are and feel for a specific task." — Jim McGettigan, then Penn State Ongontz

"Each athlete is unique and must be treated individually. Some need individual attention and some find just being a member of the team is enough to motivate them. I try to gain their respect by assisting the player to build a strong character, a better self-image, and stress integrity and loyalty to the team, These are qualities they will carry with them throughout their lives." —Eugene Chyzowych, Columbia High School (NJ)

And then there is the humorous side of the problem as expounded by one Cliff McCrath of Seattle Pacific University (WA): "Motivation is taking a grain of mustard seed and parlaying it (with a few, smooth stones) into the Mojave desert. It's getting human beings with eleven different ideas to blend their life dreams into one, all-encompassing thought/notion/goal! I do this by telling them that either they use their native intelligence to arrive at this predetermined station in life or they will soon join the Minnesota Kicks - Hartford Bicentennials - Los Angeles Aztecs - Colorado Caribou - Calgary Boomers - Dallas Tornado - Memphis Rogues - Philadelphia Fury/Fire/Atoms/Who Cares - California Surf - Oakland Stompers - Detroit HubCaps - San Antonio Thunderballs - Team Hawaii - Washington Bullrushes Hall of Fame Club! If this fails, I stick my nub in their eye!"

"I expect players to be motivated or otherwise they would not be out for the team" was Penn State coach Walter Bahr's response to the question on motivation.

DEVELOPMENT OF TEAM MORALE
Compiled by Tim Schum

The second question directed to selected coaches of the NSCAA membership was: "How do you develop the proper morale and spirit of cooperation among your players?"

Our starting off point this month is with our resident sports psychologist, Mel Lorback of West Chester

State (PA). Mel's synopsis of the development of proper morale and spirit of cooperation among the players is that morale is the transfer of ego identification from the individual to a group which in turn manifests itself as mass emotional commitment. The essential ingredients of morale are a unity of purpose and spiritual cohesion. Group motivation and like motivation on an individual level includes at least the following:

A. Identification - the athlete must identify with the sport and the group;
B. Incorporation - the player must add admired aspects of others to his own behavior;
C. Emotional Commitment - the person actually becomes the model he hopes to be; he finds attractive the adoption of a role or roles within the group.

The survey of respondent coaches to our NSCAA survey on the area of the psychology of coaching reveals many of them targeting the three aspects of the problem emphasized by Coach Lorback.

Coach Jerry Yeagley's overall approach is to work on attitude with certain rules underlying its development on his Indiana University team. The end result of such an approach would be a team with a united approach to its objectives. Jerry comments:

We strive to have each player develop a positive attitude toward his teammates and coaches, the opponents, the laws of the game and the officials who enforce these laws and most important, toward himself as a worthy member of a worthy team. Only positive constructive comments are allowed between players. Negative comments and gestures quickly destroy player relationships and tear down team morale. Likewise, only positive comments may be directed toward an official by the players.

Giving the proper respect to the laws of the game and the officials will pay dividends in the long run. If a team cannot win within the framework of the rules, then victory is worthless. Opponents are to be respected and any intentional physical or verbal abuse is not allowed. There is no need for a 'kill your enemy' approach because a player needs to address his full attention to his role as a player on his own team. If a player allows himself to become intimidated by the opposition, he loses concentration and becomes a much less effective team member.

Each player must feel good about himself and see himself as a worthy team member. He must be willing to work in order to achieve as an individual and a team.

Following are some questions each player is asked when he tries out for the team: What is your objective in soccer? Are you willing to pay the price to find out how good you can be? If you are not willing to follow good personal health habits, such as not smoking, and if you are not willing to train and keep fit during the off-season, then don't plan to be a great soccer player. However, if you desire to be the best and you are willing to work for excellence, then you have the right attitude to become a great player. If every player trains and performs to the best of his ability then the team will be at its best and this is the ultimate anyone could hope for regardless of the record. Be proud, don't settle for less. Here lies the challenge, are you willing to accept it now?

Tom Griffith, of then Dartmouth emphasized the same points as Coach Yeagley with the reminder that... "if one (player) messes up, regardless of who it is, we all suffer. We all win or we all lose."

Mike Berticelli, then North Carolina-Greensboro, emphasizes the word "respect": "Morale and spirit of cooperation come from one area — respect. Respect for the coach and for each other as players. The respect of a coach only comes from the players' awareness of the coach's sincere dedication to the team, its success, and the honest development of players as people. Players' respect of each other is also earned by performance and dedication. We as coaches set the team's guidelines for practice, performance, and dedication. Dedication and performance result in success and success breeds morale and spirit."

Al Miller of the then Tampa Bay Rowdies also dealt with the question by listing mutual respect as the first element in good team spirit. He then zeroes in on things a coach must be sensitive to during the season, including the need to:
• Control all elements that impinge on the team, i.e. fans, booster clubs, administration of school or club;
• Be prepared to deal with a crisis or problem, but best of all to be very observant in order to act and react to potential problems or head them off.
• The coach must be in control of himself at all times including such elements as speech, behavior, decision-making, and even in such things as his dress.

The late Bill Hughes, of Roberts Wesleyan (NY), lays everything at the foot of the coach: "The 'nuts and bolts' of any sports program begins with the coach. The effort that he or she puts into the program will be reflected in both the attitude and spirit of their players."

Walter Bahr of then Penn State emphasizes the role of the coach and continuity: "Morale, spirit are expected and are passed on from player to player and from year to year. Tradition and reputation of the school and coach are also a factor."

John McGettigam (then Penn State-Ongontz) has leaned heavily on captains to carry on in terms of creating the right atmosphere on the team. He notes: "It is the major job of the captains of the team to develop morale and spirit. If possible, I select individuals to be captains who have experienced success with my team the previous soccer season. (I would like to clarify the word 'success.' Success does not necessarily mean 'winning.' To me, it means getting the most out of the talent you have on hand.) These individuals, the captains, have seen the worthwhile value of the preparation procedures, and therefore can visualize what you, the coach, are trying to accomplish. They have experienced where you, the coach, is going and how you prepare the team to get there. If the leaders of your group accept and have developed a respect for you and your program it will become contagious to the rest of your team and morale and spirit will not be a problem."

> Sport is a cooperative venture not a competitive venture. The ultimate contest is between groups to demonstrate cooperation. Those teams that cooperate the most will win.
>
> — *Hank Steinbrecher*

Joe Bean of Wheaton College also feels the captains are important: "I give responsibility to the captains to serve as 'sounding boards' and develop a real open line of communication from players to the coach. It has worked well for us."

Ron Newman, of the then San Diego Sockers, talks about pride in his game, his team, his school and professionally, his city, as important ingredients in good team morale as does North Babylon's John Eden. John emphasizes pride and responsibility: "The team is told before the season, constantly during the season, and after the season that they represent the school, the community and their parents. If they, the players, cannot do this properly then they will not play for this team. They are told that winning IS important, but winning is only important if it is accomplished within

BACKING UP OFFICIALS

"I would like to suggest that every institution that is a member of this association take definite affirmative steps to let it be generally and unmistakably understood that the institution stands squarely behind, and will support to the limit, every fearless, competent official and his or her decisions and that no such official shall ever suffer from having done his or her duty on the field, whether from unfavorable comment or criticism or the withholding of future patronage." — E.K. Hall

GAITHER ON DISCIPLINE

Jake Gaither, Florida A&M University's famous former football coach, said, "Kindness is the universal language that all people understand. I made it a habit to never leave the field with a boy feeling that I was mad at him. Before I left the field, I'd pat him on the shoulder and say, 'don't think I got anything against you. I'm chewing you out for your own good. You're still my boy.' That means a lot to a kid."

As quoted in the 1977 book, *Jake Gaither:America's Most Famous Black Coach* by George Curry, Jake continued, "If you don't do something like that to the boy, when he comes to practice the next day, he's got a chip on his shoulder-he figures coach is mad at him and he's still in the doghouse. He'll sulk and you won't get the best work out of him. But if you let him know that you'll forgive him — just don't make that mistake again — the guy will come back with plenty of enthusiasm, believing, 'I'm still want to be the coach's boy.' They want to be in the good graces of the coach; they don't want to be in the doghouse."

The above comments from E.K. Hall of Dartmouth College are excerpted from his presentation on learning sportsmanship first and then the rules. He was speaking as chair of the NCAA Football Rules Committee to the 1921 NCAA Convention. Both the quote from Mr. Hall and Jake Gaither's comments are courtesy of the Michigan Soccer Officials Association newsletter, Chapter Leaders, *August, 1994.*

the proper spirit of the game. The proper spirit of the game includes sportsmanship and cooperation among the entire team. We do not make ANY exceptions here regardless of the ability of the player."

Ray Buss of then Fleetwood High School (PA) feels that guidelines must be established to provide for a common ground that everyone must follow for the well-being of all concerned. Also he states that "Our fundamental drills and practice sessions are mostly competitive in nature – yet enjoyable and fun – which perhaps leads to good team morale and working towards a goal of cooperation on the field of play."

Billy Charlton of the U.S. Army takes the approach (as with Buss) that practice sessions play a role in the morale of a team, emphasizing: "Morale is a mental condition within an individual player and within an entire team. Since morale involves individual and team confidence, enthusiasm and willingness to endure hardship, the development of it can easily be integrated into the types of drills and practice sessions directed by the coach. Good morale is usually accompanied by a good spirit of cooperation among players."

Klaas deBoer, formerly of the Los Angeles Aztecs, differs somewhat with Charlton. He emphasizes the role of communication in establishing good team morale: "Presumption that proper morale and spirit of cooperation are prerequisites for success is not necessarily true, although it is a big help. The 1981 Aztecs were very successful on the field (19-13), despite internal conflicts and tension, brought on primarily by communication and cultural differences. When the team was winning there were no problems but after a loss some of the conflicts would surface. Teams with a variety of nationalities or particularly teams with two distinct groups almost invariably incur these problems. The key to developing morale and cooperation is communication. The coach and team must have commonly agreed upon goals. This is best accomplished through team and individual meetings with players. A coach must appeal to the player's pride and sense of responsibility and instill in the players a sense of mutual respect and cooperation."

Gary Avedekian of then Centerville (OH) High School feels the coach must strive to be logical and progressive with individuals in terms of teaching, in order to move players and the team forward. He replied: "We maintain morale and cooperation by trying not to lose our sense of humor. We try to stay analytical, not angry. We assign individual tasks, such as vacuuming the locker room, and we always get at least one meal together a week. We try to help individuals identify their deficiencies, and we give analysis and develop corrective training programs. As the individual gets better, he is rewarded and the team benefits. The total benefit is victory and that's always good for morale. Hard work for the sake of hard work will not be beneficial. Unless the players see its relevance and it brings obvious results, hard work is meaningless. Appropriate hard work stiffens their resolve to win."

Jeff Vennell of then Kenyon College also likes the role of correction of performance, stating: "Try to build confidence from doing things correctly and avoid labels, using performance-criteria instead."

Gordon Jago, long-time professional coach, picked up on Avedekian's "victory" comment, with some cautions: "Success is the easiest way to obtain a good spirit but it is important to see that players accept a team concept, for individuals cannot be totally responsible for success. Bring all problems out into the open and attempt to get players to accept constructive criticism."

Howard Goldman of then Marist College (NY) picked up on the themes of other coaches but added his own emphases. He encourages his team to do things other than soccer off the field, i.e., play intramural softball together, hold team parties, etc. He also continually reminds the team of how the group must function, including the need for the team to have fun and enjoy its soccer. Lastly he feels that certain team traditions unique to the soccer team need to be maintained each year as a means of uniting the group (hosting indoor tournaments, annual team dinner, etc.).

"Favoritism" is something the coach tries to avoid if he expects to develop good morale among his players, states John Cossaboon of the North Texas Youth State Soccer Association. His thoughts: "Proper morale and spirit of cooperation can only exist if all players feel they are being dealt with in a fair and equal manner. Players can handle their playing and non-playing roles much more easily if they feel that there is a genuine concern for their development by the coach. Players can accept their deficiencies if the coach presents them in a proper way. They can't accept inconsistent treatment based on current ability level. I can't think of a single greater contributor to team friction than 'favorite' type treatment."

The late Bob Guelker of SIU (Edwardsville) felt that equality of treatment of players is important, that the coach must treat everyone with dignity and not have double standards – and finally the coach must show that he cares for his players.

Richard Broad's, then George Mason, DC, short comment pertained to role-playing. He feels that it is important for every player to have a role defined for him in order for good team morale to be present. Unstated is the fact that the player must accept the role!

Hank Steinbrecher's analysis of the match itself is interesting and involves the question (morale) under discussion: "Sport is a cooperative venture not a competitive venture. The ultimate contest is between groups to demonstrate cooperation. Those teams that cooperate the most will win. The competitive essence in soccer is which team demonstrates the highest degree of cooperative spirit. Thus team play is the ultimate goal. This cannot be done without a bond between players, a sense of brotherhood."

DEVELOPMENT OF TEAM DISCIPLINE
Compiled by Chris Malone

INTRODUCTION

This article explores another question related to the psychology of coaching: "How hard a disciplinarian does a coach have to be?"

As expected, coaches' responses varied considerably. However, most coaches' responses addressed several common themes. Many coaches suggested that before team discipline could be established, it was necessary for individual players to develop self-discipline. Another area of common interest reflected in the coaches' responses dealt with the coaching situation which was unique to each coach.

In other words, the coaching environment has unique factors which determine how coaches develop discipline. Selected coaches also suggested that coaches develop their own style of discipline based upon previous experiences, either successful or not successful. What works best for one coach may not work for another!

Joe Cummings, then Algonquin Regional H.S., MA, attempts to define discipline in the following manner and provides keen insight about how important discipline is for team success. "Discipline is a derivative of the word 'disciple', which by definition means: one who adheres to the doctrines of another. In other words, as a disciplinarian, coaches must demand from their players no more than they demand of themselves. The hours of preparation for practice and/or games, scouting, attending clinics, working camps or reading articles are all part of a coach's discipline. This is imparted to their players. In the end, the discipline that coaches exhibit will foster self-discipline in our athletes."

Without a doubt, all coaches believe that developing team and individual player discipline is important. But many coaches do not know how to begin to establish discipline. Howard Goldman, then Marist College, NY, feels that coaches can build team and individual player discipline by doing the following:

• Demand excellence in performance on the field and off (academics);

• Set an example;

• Encourage self-discipline;

• Not be a "buddy" with players. Create a difference between coach and player that can be recognized by players.

Klaas de Boer agrees with many of the above points and stresses the point that coaches must be themselves when developing their teams' discipline. If coaches are to be taken seriously, they must earn the respect of their players. There are many ways for coaches to earn the respect of their players and de Boer provides an interesting example of how two coaches used completely different methods in developing respect. "Rinus Michels demanded instant respect based on past reputation and by demeanor. Known as a disciplinarian, he communicated very little with players, but everyone knew where he stood. His personality and demeanor was such that players did not question him. On the other hand, Claudio Coutinho was a firm believer in talking to players in order to win them over.

He continually stressed the need for self-discipline. Two different approaches, yet both men were successful and were respected by their players."

Joe Cossaboon, then North Texas Youth State Soccer Association also believes that coaches must use their own individual strengths and apply them to their own particular situation. "Some coaches can control their teams with a minimum of outright discipline by earning their players' respect. Respect can be achieved by demonstrating their knowledge of the game, providing fair and equitable treatment of players, and through their own playing ability. Other coaches believe that only through a set of rigid rules and regulations can discipline be maintained. Perhaps by integrating these two methods of attaining team discipline, coaches will be able to find a balance in maintaining discipline and not stifling a teams' individuality."

Coaches develop their own coaching style through their experiences and by adjusting their coaching style to the environment in which they work. Tom Griffith (then Dartmouth) points out that when players are highly motivated there may not be much need for a system of rigid discipline. However, if players' actions are detrimental to the team, then disciplinary actions must be taken. At Dartmouth, the team has a saying, "No one is above the team."

Ron Newman (then San Diego Sockers) agrees with Griffith. He suggests that coaches approach discipline in a limited way depending on the situation. Coaches should approach discipline only in the way that a team requires. In other words, the more rules coaches make, the more rules there are to break. And, the more rules players break the more discontent coaches and players become. Therefore, Newman stresses, "Be strong and firm, but considerate."

Al Miller (then Tampa Bay Rowdies) addresses another aspect of the coaching situation and how it may affect discipline. He believes that discipline depends upon the level of players on a team. A professional team might have completely different needs than collegiate players. Therefore, discipline will be different for various teams. Yet, coaches must still control individual players, and consequently the team will have good discipline.

In regards to enforcing rules, the coaching sample offered several ideas. Gordon Jago agrees with many coaches that discipline is dependent on the group of players involved. There must be discipline on and off the field. If rules are broken, action must be taken, but these actions must be consistent.

Ray Buss (then Fleetwood H.S., PA) also feels that disciplinary action must be taken when necessary. There are occasions when an issue must be faced and no player is above the rules. On such occasions, there is no "turning the cheek" by coaches. A decision must be made and the "chips fall where they may. " Eventually players will realize that discipline is essential to team success when the rules are enforced.

According to the late Bob Guelker (S.I.U. - Edwardsville IL), coaches "must be strict and firm, but fair" when enforcing rules. Guelker emphasizes that "Discipline can be attained by minimizing rules. The only good rules are rules that can be and should be enforced by coaches."

Jeff Vennell (then Kenyon College, OH) feels that coaches' methods of disciplinary action should reflect their principles. Soccer players should have the opportunity to help develop rules for teams based on coaches' principles. Coaches should then be firm in implementing and applying these rules. "Discipline is a key ingredient to success but must be applied fairly and be understood by athletes."

Jim McGettigan (then Penn State - Ongontz, PA) suggests that "Rules should be realistic, flexible and apply to all involved in an impartial manner. Discipline rarely becomes a problem when team members know why discipline is exercised. By establishing rules which are realistic and agreeable to all players early in the season, discipline is exercised. Coaches who allow their players to develop their own rules create a feeling among players that they must discipline themselves. When players sanction and create their own rules they are more likely to abide by these rules. Furthermore, when players make their own rules they

SOME THOUGHTS FROM STAGG

Amos Alonzo Stagg was one of the early football coaching giants and his philosophy on life and sport was chronicled by *Sports Illustrated* in a classic 1962 article by John Underwood. Among Stagg's thoughts were:

... The only tangible rewards Stagg gave his players were sweaters and letters. Stagg abhorred recruiting of any sort and was never told-or perhaps did not want to be told-that there were players on scholarship at COP (College of the Pacific). He said that recruiting breeds dishonesty and was not right for a coach whose profession should be one of the noblest and far-reaching in building manhood. "No man is too good to be the athletic coach for youth."

Until he went to the rest home six months ago, where he will live out his days, Stagg mowed his lawn with a hand mower. "He mowed that lawn to death," said Stella Stagg. One day a neighbor advised him that kids had been playing on it daily, ripping up the turf. "You'll never raise grass that way," he said. "Sir," answered Stagg, "I'm not raising grass. I'm raising boys."

tend to reflect the same rules that coaches would establish."

An interesting analogy by Billy Charlton (U.S. Army) provides keen insight for coaches about the importance in developing realistic and flexible rules. "The setting up of a system of rules for a team is similar to setting up a system of play. Both systems should be dictated by the type and caliber of players on the team. To be a hardnosed disciplinarian as a coach is the same as being hardnosed about playing a 4-4-2 or 4-3-3 without considering the players who will work within the system."

Perhaps the philosophical approach of Mike Berticelli (then UNC-Greensboro, NC) and Hank Steinbrecher (then Boston University) in regards to developing discipline should be considered by all coaches. These coaches both agree that discipline is essential to success, but they go a step further. They believe that discipline is established through the learning process to experience not through punishment. In this way, players develop self-discipline which in turn promotes team discipline. Berticelli emphasizes that "Soccer players must be disciplined by being educated. To discipline a player to one touch a ball or not to go charging out as a wing defender, can be accomplished by punishment. But, the growth of the players and the team is dependent on that individual's understanding and learning why they must do certain things." Steinbrecher maintains that "The good coach demonstrates that discipline is an internal quality. Self-discipline is the goal to be achieved. External discipline or forced discipline rarely works. Our only rule is 'Never do anything on or off the field that will embarrass your brothers or yourselves.'"

CONCLUSION

No matter what coaches' beliefs and attitudes are concerning team and individual player discipline, they have the responsibility to determine which behaviors from their athletes will or will not be acceptable. The method by which coaches develop rules varies from coach to coach. The environment in which coaches work must be considered when developing these rules. Such things as the level and age of players, cultural background of players, area of country, community size, etc., are just a few of the variables which are different for all coaches. Players' behaviors are different due to such factors.

We have all observed soccer teams which have no discipline due to the lack of control of the team's coach. This situation is a tragedy for soccer. Often times these coaches have failed to recognize the importance of team and individual player discipline for success, or more likely, these coaches do not understand how to develop team and player discipline. Eventually these coaches may learn how to establish discipline through their coaching experiences. Perhaps the key for good team and individual discipline is for coaches to learn how to earn the respect of their players and in return give their respect to their players by being open, honest, realistic and flexible.